Computing Essentials

2017

Timothy J. O'Leary
Professor Emeritus
Arizona State University

Linda I. O'Leary

Daniel A. O'Leary
PhD
University of California at Santa Cruz

COMPUTING ESSENTIALS 2017 COMPLETE EDITION
Published by McGraw-Hill Education, 2 Penn Plaza, New York, NY 10121.

Some ancillaries, including electronic and print components, may not be available to customers outside the United States.

This book is printed on acid-free paper.

1 2 3 4 5 6 7 8 9 RMN 21 20 19 18 17 16

ISBN 978-1-259-92127-8
MHID 1-259-92127-1

www.mhhe.com

Co ntials

2017

work for you

The O'Leary Series

Computing Concepts

- *Computing Essentials 2014* Introductory & Complete Editions
- *Computing Essentials 2015* Introductory & Complete Editions
- *Computing Essentials 2017* (Complete Edition)

Microsoft Office Applications

- *Microsoft® Windows 7: A Case Approach*
- *Microsoft® Office 2013: A Case Approach*
- *Microsoft® Office Word 2013: A Case Approach* Introductory Edition
- *Microsoft® Office Excel 2013: A Case Approach* Introductory Edition
- *Microsoft® Office Access 2013: A Case Approach* Introductory Edition
- *Microsoft® Office PowerPoint 2013: A Case Approach* Introductory Edition

Dedication

We dedicate this edition to Nicole and Katie—our inspiration.

Brief Contents

Contents

SYSTEM SOFTWARE *88*

THE SYSTEM UNIT *114*

INPUT AND OUTPUT *140*

New to Computing Essentials 2017

Every chapter's Making IT Work for You, Privacy, Ethics, and Environment features have been carefully revaluated, enhanced, and/or replaced. Additionally, every chapter's Look to the Future has been revised to show that the expected breakthroughs of tomorrow are rooted in today's advances. More specific new coverage includes the following.

Chapter 1	Revised Figure 1-1 Parts of an Information System to include mobile devices (tablets and smartphones), Windows 10 operating system, and Office 10
Chapter 2	Added coverage of Microsoft's new Edge browser, *https* and MMS (Multimedia Messaging Service)
	Expanded coverage of Facebook Messenger, Google Hangouts
	Added coverage Instagram, Pinterest, Tumblr, and Vine
	Added a major new section on the Internet of Things (IoT)
Chapter 3	Added coverage of video editors and video game design software
	Added discussion of game apps including role playing games (RPG)
	Expanded Cloud Computing to include Microsoft Office 365 for Office and iPad.
Chapter 4	Expanded coverage of voice recognition and real time operating systems (RTOS)
	Undated operating systems to include coverage of Windows 10 and Cortana
	Expanded coverage of Mac OS including Yosemite and related system software
	Expanded coverage of Chrome OS
Chapter 5	Expanded coverage of laptops to include two-in-one, gaming, and ultrabooks
	Expanded coverage of tablets to include keyboard attachments, digital pens, and speech recognition
	Added a new major section on Wearable Computers
	Expanded and updated ports and cables
Chapter 6	Added coverage of gaming mice, 3D scanners, and smart cards
	Expanded coverage of voice recognition systems to include digital assistants (Siri, Cortana, and Google Now)
	Updated resolution standards to include UHD 4K and UHD 5K
	Added coverage of UHDTV, 3D UHDTV, digital projectors headsets and headphones
	Expanded coverage of drones, robots, and virtual reality
Chapter 7	Reorganized chapter to give more prominence to solid-state storage
	Expanded solid-storage, flash memory coverage, and NAS
Chapter 8	Updated Wi-Fi standards to include 802.11ac and 802.11ax
	Added cellular as a wireless connection technology including discussion of cells and cell towers
	Expanded coverage of LTE as a fourth-generation mobile telecommunication technology
Chapter 9	Added Privacy relating to drones and the Dark Web
	Added Ethics boxes relating to the right to be forgotten and net neutrality
	Added a Tip on creating strong passwords
	Added a new section on security tools including password managers
Chapters 10, 11, 12, and 13	New end of chapter case

Preface

The 20th century brought us the dawn of the digital information age and unprecedented changes in information technology. In fact, the rate of change is clearly increasing. As we begin the 21st century, computer literacy is undoubtedly becoming a prerequisite in whatever career you choose.

The goal of *Computing Essentials* is to provide you with the basis for understanding the concepts necessary for success. *Computing Essentials* also endeavors to instill an appreciation for the effect of information technology on people, privacy, ethics, and our environment and to give you a basis for building the necessary skill set to succeed in the 21st century.

Times are changing, technology is changing, and this text is changing too. As students of today, you are different from those of yesterday. You put much effort toward the things that interest you and the things that are relevant to you. Your efforts directed at learning application programs and exploring the web seem, at times, limitless. On the other hand, it is sometimes difficult to engage in other equally important topics such as personal privacy and technological advances.

At the beginning of each chapter, we carefully layout why and how the chapter's content is relevant to your life today and critical to your future. Within each chapter, we present practical tips related to key concepts through the demonstration of interesting applications that are relevant to your lives. Topics presented focus first on outputs rather than processes. Then, we discuss the concepts and processes.

Motivation and relevance are the keys. This text has several features specifically designed to engage and demonstrate the relevance of technology in your lives. These elements are combined with a thorough coverage of the concepts and sound pedagogical devices.

VISUAL CHAPTER OPENERS

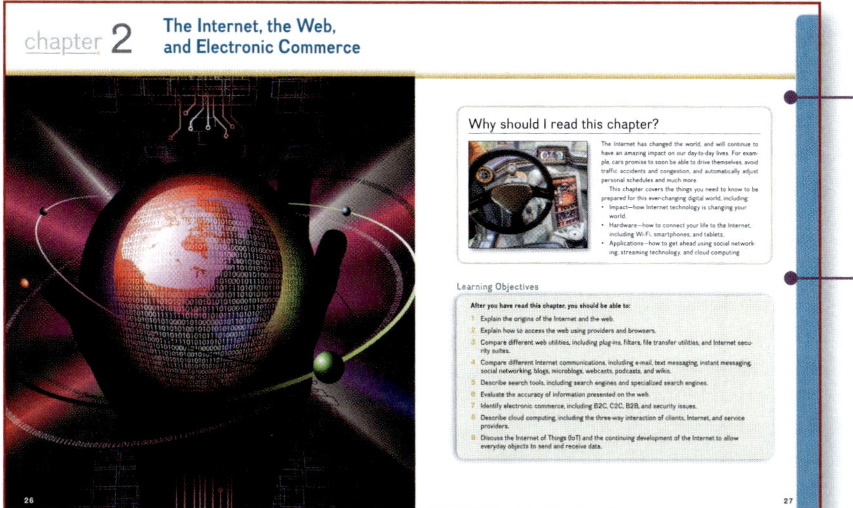

chapter 2
The Internet, the Web, and Electronic Commerce
Why should I read this chapter?
Learning Objectives
26
27

Each chapter begins with a Why Should I Read This? feature that presents a visually engaging and concise presentation of the chapter's relevance to the reader's current and future life in the digital world. Then a list of chapter learning objectives is presented providing a brief introduction to what will be covered in the chapter.

VISUAL SUMMARIES

Visual summaries appear at the end of every chapter and summarize major concepts covered throughout the chapter. Like the chapter openers, these summaries use graphics to reinforce key concepts in an engaging and meaningful way.

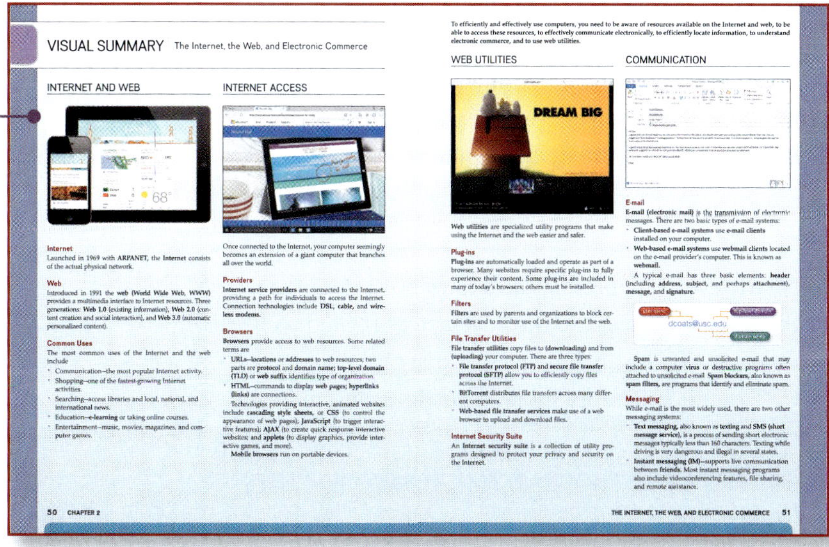

VISUAL SUMMARY The Internet, the Web, and Electronic Commerce
INTERNET AND WEB
INTERNET ACCESS
WEB UTILITIES
COMMUNICATION
DREAM BIG
50 CHAPTER 2
THE INTERNET, THE WEB, AND ELECTRONIC COMMERCE 51

Unique Content

MAKING IT WORK FOR YOU

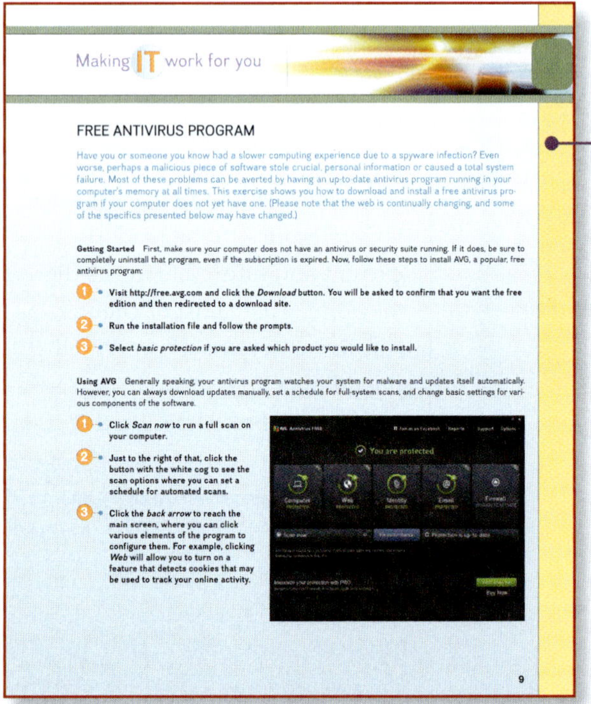

Making IT work for you

FREE ANTIVIRUS PROGRAM

Have you or someone you know had a slower computing experience due to a spyware infection? Even worse, perhaps a malicious piece of software stole crucial, personal information or caused a total system failure. Most of these problems can be averted by having an up-to-date antivirus program running in your computer's memory at all times. This exercise shows you how to download and install a free antivirus program if your computer does not yet have one. (Please note that the web is continually changing, and some of the specifics presented below may have changed.)

Getting Started First, make sure your computer does not have an antivirus or security suite running. If it does, be sure to completely uninstall that program, even if the subscription is expired. Now, follow these steps to install AVG, a popular, free antivirus program:

1. **Visit http://free.avg.com and click the *Download* button. You will be asked to confirm that you want the free edition and then redirected to a download site.**
2. **Run the installation file and follow the prompts.**
3. **Select *basic protection* if you are asked which product you would like to install.**

Using AVG Generally speaking, your antivirus program watches your system for malware and updates itself automatically. However, you can always download updates manually, set a schedule for full-system scans, and change basic settings for various components of the software.

1. **Click *Scan now* to run a full scan on your computer.**
2. **Just to the right of that, click the button with the white cog to see the scan options where you can set a schedule for automated scans.**
3. **Click the *back arrow* to reach the main screen, where you can click various elements of the program to configure them. For example, clicking *Web* will allow you to turn on a feature that detects cookies that may be used to track your online activity.**

9

Special-interest topics are presented in the Making IT Work for You section found within nearly every chapter. These topics include Installing a Free Antivirus Program, Online Entertainment, Google Docs, Skype, and Cloud Storage.

PRIVACY, ETHICS, AND ENVIRONMENT

Nearly every chapter has a Privacy box located in the margin adjacent to the coverage of related technologies. Topics include protecting personal information when using a free Wi-Fi network or when disposing of an outdated computer.

Nearly every chapter has an Ethics box located in the margin adjacent to the coverage of related technologies. Topics include proper disposal of older CRT monitors, empty inkjet cartridges, and old computers.

Nearly every chapter has an Environment box located in the margin adjacent to the coverage of related technologies. Topics include plagiarism of online materials, editing images to promote a particular message, and the use of monitoring software.

privacy

Did you know that one type of specialty processor is devoted exclusively to protecting your privacy? Called cryptoprocessors, these microchips perform encoding and decoding of data faster and more securely than a CPU. These specialized chips exist in ATMs, TV set-top boxes, and smartcards.

Figure 5-10 **Chip mounted onto a chip carrier**

ethics

Because labor costs are much lower in China, many computers and peripherals are manufactured there. While this has resulted in the loss of jobs elsewhere, it has improved the standard of living for millions of Chinese. Unfortunately, their working conditions are considered to be very poor. Do you think consumers have an ethical responsibility regarding where and/or how products are manufactured?

networking card plugs into a slot on the system board to provide a connection to a local area network.

- Connecting lines called **bus lines** provide pathways that support communication among the various electronic components that are either located on the system board or attached to the system board.

Generally, the system board found on a desktop is larger than that found on a laptop, and much larger than one found on a tablet, smartphone, or wearable computer. Although these system boards vary in size, they nevertheless all perform the same function of communicating between the components of the personal computer.

concept check

- What is the system board, and what does it do?
- Define and describe sockets, slots, and bus lines.
- What are chips? How are chips attached to the system board?

Microprocessor

In most personal computer systems, the **central processing unit (CPU)** or **processor** is contained on a single chip called the **microprocessor.** The microprocessor is the "brains" of the computer system. It has two basic components: the control unit and the arithmetic-logic unit.

- **Control unit:** The **control unit** tells the rest of the computer system how to carry out a program's instructions. It directs the movement of electronic signals between memory, which temporarily holds data, instructions, and processed information, and the arithmetic-logic unit. It also directs these control signals between the CPU and input and output devices.
- **Arithmetic-logic unit:** The **arithmetic-logic unit,** usually called the **ALU,** performs two types of operations: arithmetic and logical. **Arithmetic operations** are the fundamental math operations: addition, subtraction, multiplication, and division. **Logical operations** consist of comparisons such as whether one item is equal to (=), less than (<), or greater than (>) the other.

environment

Have you ever wondered what you should do with your old computers equipment? Consider donating them to charitable organizations that work with local schools and low-income families. Or, recycle them. Many computer retailers and local government agencies accept recycled equipment.

Unique End-of-Chapter Discussion Materials

MAKING IT WORK FOR YOU

Making IT Work for You discussion questions are carefully integrated with the chapter's Making IT Work for You topics. The questions facilitate in-class discussion or written assignments focusing on applying specific technologies into a student's day-to-day life. They are designed to expand a student's awareness of technology applications.

PRIVACY

Privacy discussion questions are carefully integrated with the chapter's marginal Privacy box. The questions facilitate in-class discussion or written assignments focusing on critical privacy issues. They are designed to develop a student's ability to think critically and communicate effectively.

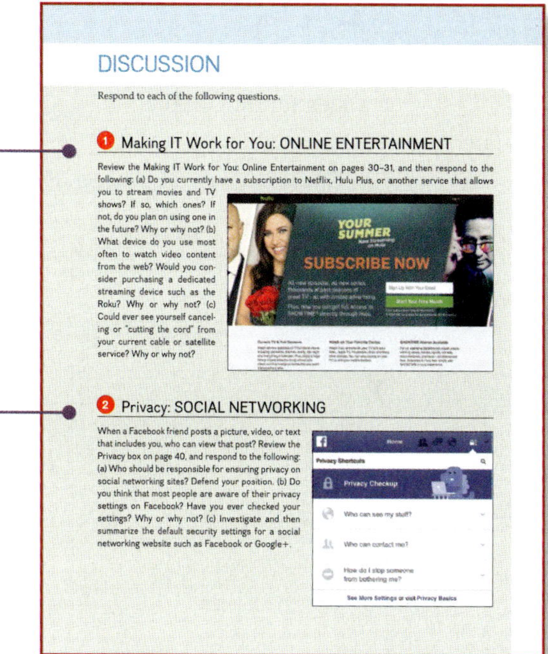

DISCUSSION

Respond to each of the following questions.

1 Making IT Work for You: ONLINE ENTERTAINMENT

Review the Making IT Work for You: Online Entertainment on pages 30–31, and then respond to the following: (a) Do you currently have a subscription to Netflix, Hulu Plus, or another service that allows you to stream movies and TV shows? If so, which ones? If not, do you plan on using one in the future? Why or why not? (b) What device do you use most often to watch video content from the web? Would you consider purchasing a dedicated streaming device such as the Roku? Why or why not? (c) Could ever see yourself canceling or "cutting the cord" from your current cable or satellite service? Why or why not?

2 Privacy: SOCIAL NETWORKING

When a Facebook friend posts a picture, video, or text that includes you, who can view that post? Review the Privacy box on page 40, and respond to the following: (a) Who should be responsible for ensuring privacy on social networking sites? Defend your position. (b) Do you think that most people are aware of their privacy settings on Facebook? Have you ever checked your settings? Why or why not? (c) Investigate and then summarize the default security settings for a social networking website such as Facebook or Google+.

3 Ethics: FILTERING AND MONITORING

Parents can use content filters and monitoring software to restrict or monitor their child's Internet behavior. Review the Ethics box on page 35, and respond to the following: (a) Is it ethical for parents to filter or monitor Internet content for their children? Does your answer depend on the age of the child? Defend your position. (b) Should parents inform their children that Internet activity is being filtered or monitored? Why or why not? (c) Do you feel that filtering or monitoring software is the best way to protect children? Defend your position.

Norton Family

Help your kids enjoy the Internet safely.

4 Environment: E-MAIL

Review the Environment box on page 37, and then respond to the following: (a) When it comes to sending letters, holiday cards, and invitations to friends and family, do you mostly use e-mail or postal mail? What are your reasons for choosing one over the other? (b) Are there any situations where you feel that using e-mail would be inappropriate? (c) Have you signed up for paperless billing from your financial institutions and utility companies? Why or why not? (d) Go through all the paper mail you have received in the last week or two. Is there anything there that you could receive via e-mail or view on the web? If so, list a few examples.

green

A better web.
Better for the environment.

ETHICS

Ethics discussion questions are carefully integrated with the chapter's marginal Ethics boxes. The questions facilitate in-class discussion or written assignments focusing on ethical issues relating to technology. They are designed to develop a student's ability to think critically and communicate effectively.

ENVIRONMENT

Environment discussion questions are carefully integrated with the chapter's marginal Environment boxes. The questions facilitate in-class discussion or written assignments focusing on environmental issues relating to technology. They are designed to develop a student's ability to think critically and communicate effectively.

Reinforcing Key Concepts

CONCEPT CHECKS

Located at points throughout each chapter, the Concept Check cues you to note which topics have been covered and to self-test your understanding of the material presented.

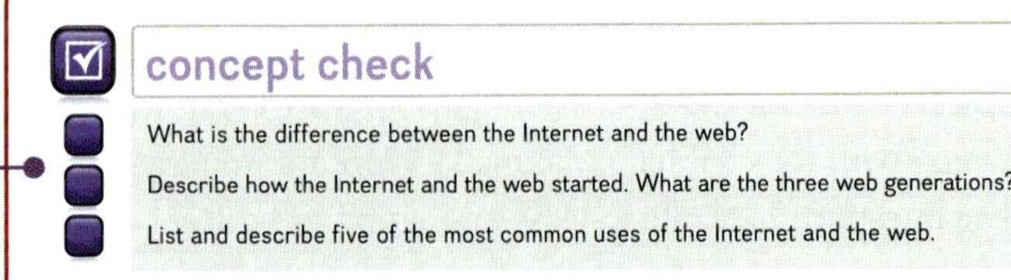

concept check

What is the difference between the Internet and the web?

Describe how the Internet and the web started. What are the three web generations?

List and describe five of the most common uses of the Internet and the web.

KEY TERMS

Throughout the text, the most important terms are presented in bold and are defined within the text. You will also find a list of key terms at the end of each chapter and in the glossary at the end of the book.

KEY TERMS

address (33, 37)
Advanced Research Project Agency Network (ARPANET) (28)
AJAX (33)
applets (33)
attachment (37)
BitTorrent (35)
blog (41)
browser (32)
business-to-business (B2B) (45)
business-to-consumer (B2C) (44)
cable (32)
cascading style sheets (CSS) (33)
Circles (40)
client-based e-mail system (38)
cloud computing (46)
consumer-to-consumer (C2C) (44)
digital cash (45)
domain name (33)
downloading (35)
DSL (32)
e-commerce (44)
e-learning (29)
electronic commerce (44)
electronic mail (37)
e-mail (37)
e-mail client (38)
Facebook (39)
Facebook groups (40)
Facebook Pages (40)
Facebook Profile (40)
file transfer protocol (FTP) (35)
filter (34)
friend (39)
Google+ (40)
Google Plus (40)
Hangouts (40)
header (37)
hit (43)
hyperlink (33)
Hypertext Markup Language (HTML) (33)
instant messaging (IM) (39)
Internet (28)
Internet of Things (IoT) (47)
Internet security suite (36)
Internet service provider (ISP) (32)
JavaScript (33)
link (33)
LinkedIn (40)
location (33)
message (37)
microblog (41)
MMS (multimedia messaging service) (38)
mobile browser (33)
online (28)
plug-in (34)
podcast (42)
protocol (33)
search engine (43)
search service (43)
secure file transfer protocol (SFTP) (35)
signature (37)
SMS (short messaging service) (38)
social networking (39)
spam (38)
spam blocker (38)
spam filter (38)
specialized search engine (43)
spider (43)
streaming (41)
subject (37)
texting (38)
text messaging (38)
top-level domain (TLD) (33)
tweet (41)
Twitter (41)
uniform resource locator (URL) (33)
uploading (35)
virus (38)
web (28)
Web 1.0 (28)
Web 2.0 (28)
Web 3.0 (28)
web auction (44)
web-based e-mail system (38)
web-based file transfer services (35)
webcasts (41)
web log (41)
webmail (38)
webmail client (38)
webmaster (48)
web page (33)
web suffix (33)
web utility (34)
wiki (42)
Wikipedia (42)
wireless modem (32)
World Wide Web (28)
WWW (28)

CHAPTER REVIEW

Following the Visual Summary, the chapter review includes material designed to review and reinforce chapter content. It includes a key terms list that reiterates the terms presented in the chapter, multiple-choice questions to help test your understanding of information presented in the chapter, matching exercises to test your recall of terminology presented in the chapter, and open-ended questions or statements to help review your understanding of the key concepts presented in the chapter.

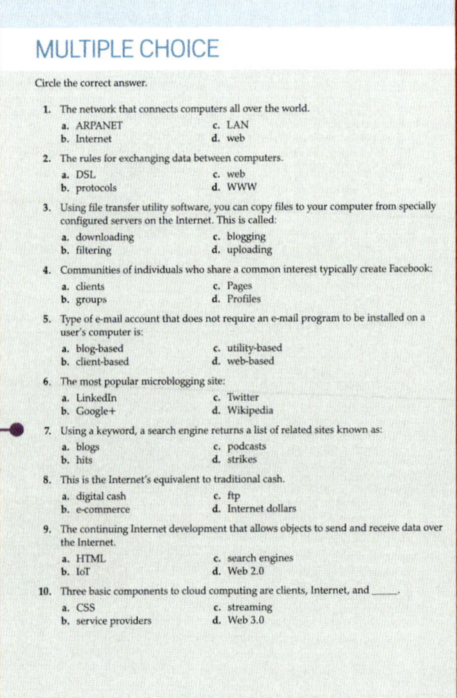

MULTIPLE CHOICE

Circle the correct answer.

1. The network that connects computers all over the world.
   a. ARPANET c. LAN
   b. Internet d. web
2. The rules for exchanging data between computers.
   a. DSL c. web
   b. protocols d. WWW
3. Using file transfer utility software, you can copy files to your computer from specially configured servers on the Internet. This is called:
   a. downloading c. blogging
   b. filtering d. uploading
4. Communities of individuals who share a common interest typically create Facebook:
   a. clients c. Pages
   b. groups d. Profiles
5. Type of e-mail account that does not require an e-mail program to be installed on a user's computer is:
   a. blog-based c. utility-based
   b. client-based d. web-based
6. The most popular microblogging site:
   a. LinkedIn c. Twitter
   b. Google+ d. Wikipedia
7. Using a keyword, a search engine returns a list of related sites known as:
   a. blogs c. podcasts
   b. hits d. strikes
8. This is the Internet's equivalent to traditional cash.
   a. digital cash c. ftp
   b. e-commerce d. Internet dollars
9. The continuing Internet development that allows objects to send and receive data over the Internet.
   a. HTML c. search engines
   b. IoT d. Web 2.0
10. Three basic components to cloud computing are clients, Internet, and _____.
   a. CSS c. streaming
   b. service providers d. Web 3.0

The Future of Information Technology

CAREERS IN IT

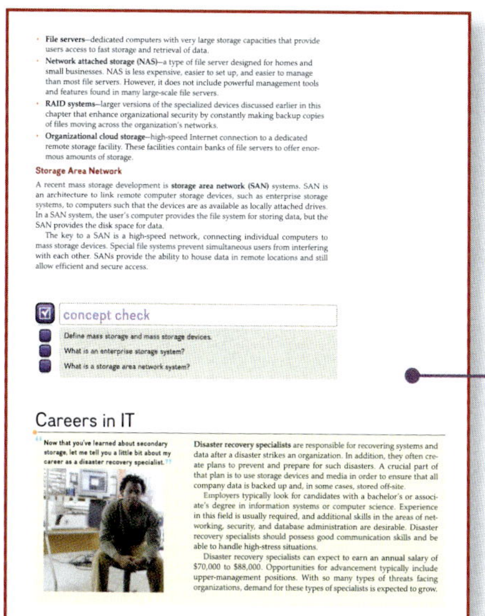

- **File servers**—dedicated computers with very large storage capacities that provide users access to fast storage and retrieval of data.
- **Network attached storage (NAS)**—a type of file server designed for homes and small businesses. NAS is less expensive, easier to set up, and easier to manage than most file servers. However, it does not include powerful management tools and features found in many large-scale file servers.
- **RAID systems**—larger versions of the specialized devices discussed earlier in this chapter that enhance organizational security by constantly making backup copies of files moving across the organization's networks.
- **Organizational cloud storage**—high-speed Internet connection to a dedicated remote storage facility. These facilities contain banks of file servers to offer enormous amounts of storage.

Storage Area Network

A recent mass storage development is **storage area network (SAN)** systems. SAN is an architecture to link remote computer storage devices, such as enterprise storage systems, to computers such that the devices are as available as locally attached drives. In a SAN system, the user's computer provides the file system for storing data, but the SAN provides the disk space for data.

The key to a SAN is a high-speed network, connecting individual computers to mass storage devices. Special file systems prevent simultaneous users from interfering with each other. SANs provide the ability to house data in remote locations and still allow efficient and secure access.

concept check

- Define mass storage and mass storage devices.
- What is an enterprise storage system?
- What is a storage area network system?

Careers in IT

"Now that you've learned about secondary storage, let me tell you a little bit about my career as a disaster recovery specialist."

Disaster recovery specialists are responsible for recovering systems and data after a disaster strikes an organization. In addition, they often create plans to prevent and prepare for such disasters. A crucial part of that plan is to use storage devices and media in order to ensure that all company data is backed up and, in some cases, stored off-site.

Employers typically look for candidates with a bachelor's or associate's degree in information systems or computer science. Experience in this field is usually required, and additional skills in the areas of networking, security, and database administration are desirable. Disaster recovery specialists should possess good communication skills and be able to handle high-stress situations.

Disaster recovery specialists can expect to earn an annual salary of $70,000 to $88,000. Opportunities for advancement typically include upper-management positions. With so many types of threats facing organizations, demand for these types of specialists is expected to grow.

Some of the fastest-growing career opportunities are in information technology. Each chapter highlights one of the most promising careers in IT by presenting job titles, responsibilities, educational requirements, and salary ranges. Among the careers covered are webmaster, software engineer, and database administrator. You will learn how the material you are studying relates directly to a potential career path.

A LOOK TO THE FUTURE

Each chapter concludes with a brief discussion of a recent technological advancement related to the chapter material, reinforcing the importance of staying informed.

A LOOK TO THE FUTURE

Your Car's Dashboard as a Powerful, Internet-Connected Computing Device

Do you often wish that you could shop online or make dinner plans while your car drove itself? Would you like your car to use the Internet to suggest a better route, or stream a music list tailored to your likes? A computer located within the vehicle already governs many of your car's functions. That computer is responsible for various safety and diagnostic features. Recently, cars have begun offering Internet access for driving directions, streaming audio, and cell phone connectivity. In the future, cars will drive themselves and seamlessly integrate into our digital lives. Technology has been making better cars, and will continue to evolve to improve our lives as we look to the future.

Apple and Google have created partnerships with automobile manufacturers to place iPad or Android devices into the center of a vehicle's main console. Cars can connect to Wi-Fi access points or 4G networks to reach the Internet as the modern smartphone does. These developments allow your vehicle to provide many services that normally require a smartphone but in a safer and more integrated manner.

One of the immediate benefits involves quick access to information. Drivers get real-time traffic data, weather, store hours, and much more. Also available is access to all the apps that you expect to have. One example is the Pandora service, which allows you to stream free, ad-supported music from stations you create yourself. Why pay for satellite radio or listen to stations that you don't enjoy when you can access your favorite online music services right from your dashboard? Another benefit is the entertainment of your passengers or children. Some vehicles include screens that face the back seats, allowing parents to play DVDs for their children. Internet-connected vehicles allow individuals already paying for an online streaming video service to give their children access to this enormous library of cartoons and movies right in the vehicle. In fact, with a tabletlike interface, your child can choose from a preset selection of movies or educational games, depending on his or her mood.

Now, such a tool at your fingertips has the risk of becoming a distraction while you're driving. There is no question that safety features must be built in to prevent accidents from occurring. Luckily, there is already a piece of technology that prevents the driver from ever having to touch the dashboard: voice recognition.

In the same way that Apple's "Siri" has revolutionized the way individuals interact with their iPhones, similar systems are installed in the new dashboards. Drivers simply speak their commands to get the information they need and to use the vehicle's controls. Furthermore, this computer system uses existing technologies that recognize and speak English to the user. This will allow the driver to hear e-mail messages, social network updates, and today's news and weather while driving to work.

Some companies have already taken steps in implementing this technology. Ford uses voice recognition in some of its vehicles with a feature called Sync with MyFord Touch. Audi has added 3G connectivity in its new A7 model. However, the real breakthroughs will come when you can drive in safety while being as productive as when you are on your laptop. Advances in dictation software will one day allow users to easily dictate e-mail responses. Changes in sensors and automated driving will allow users to devote less attention to driving and more to getting things done. Google and Mercedes are currently testing self-driving cars, and they may be available in the next ten years. When it does, do you see yourself paying for this upgrade in your next car? Would you be comfortable allowing a car to drive itself while you worked on your laptop or tablet?

49

MoviesOnline: Information Systems

Alice's First Assignment

***Bob:** Oh, hi Alice . . . come on in! I know that we were scheduled for an orientation meeting this morning. But I'm afraid that will have to wait. There is an important fire to put out today. Let me introduce you to one of your coworkers. This is Jamal.*

Alice and Jamal exchange hellos and Bob motions Alice to take one of the chairs across from his desk as he speaks.

"She said she was concerned about how our members were connecting to our Web site."

***Bob:** I just came back from a meeting with Carol, our CEO. While we were discussing the Monthly Membership Report, she said she was concerned about how our members were connecting to our Web site. This really caught me off guard! Our membership growth has exceeded projections and I had assumed that our meeting was to discuss how to handle all the new members. She requested that her Morning Report be modified to include the percentage of our customers who use mobile devices, and she wants us to analyze the changes in laptop and desktop customers versus mobile device customers over the past year.*

***Bob:** Jamal, here is the Monthly Membership Report. I'd like you to review it and then create two profiles. One profile will describe our members who use computers, such as laptops and desktops. The other profile will be for our members who use mobile devices, such as cell phones and tablets.. I'm interested in any differences or unique characteristics you can uncover.*

Bob removes the cover page, hands the rest of the report to Jamal, and hands the cover page to Alice.

Found in Connect for Computing Essentials 2017, Using IT at MoviesOnline—A Case Study of a fictitious organization provides an up-close look at what you might expect to find on the job in the real world. You will follow Alice, a recent college graduate hired as a marketing analyst, as she navigates her way through accounting, marketing, production, human resources, and research, gathering and processing data to help manage and accelerate the growth of the three-year-old company.

Required=Results

McGraw-Hill Connect®

Learn Without Limits

Connect is a teaching and learning platform that is proven to deliver better results for students and instructors.

Connect empowers students by continually adapting to deliver precisely what they need, when they need it, and how they need it, so your class time is more engaging and effective.

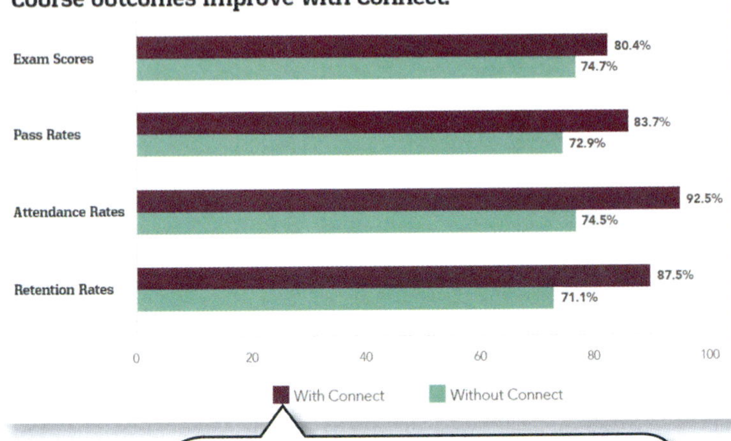

Using **Connect** improves passing rates by **10.8%** and retention by **16.4%.**

88% of instructors who use **Connect** require it; instructor satisfaction **increases** by 38% when **Connect** is required.

Analytics

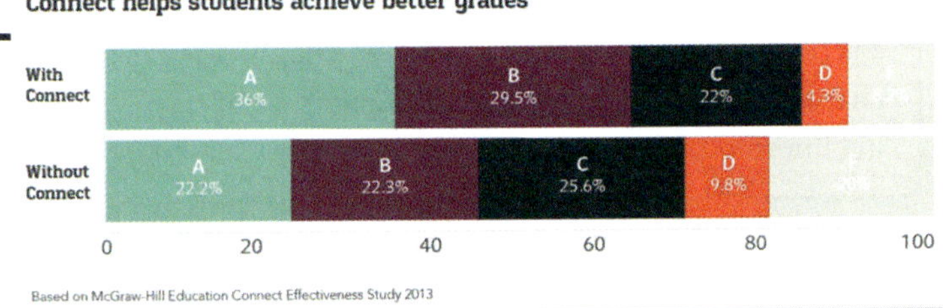

Connect Insight®

Connect Insight is Connect's new one-of-a-kind visual analytics dashboard—now available for both instructors and students—that provides at-a-glance information regarding student performance, which is immediately actionable. By presenting assignment, assessment, and topical performance results together with a time metric that is easily visible for aggregate or individual results, Connect Insight gives the user the ability to take a just-in-time approach to teaching and learning, which was never before available. Connect Insight presents data that empowers students and helps instructors improve class performance in a way that is efficient and effective.

Students can view their results for any **Connect** course.

Mobile

Connect's new, intuitive mobile interface gives students and instructors flexible and convenient, anytime–anywhere access to all components of the Connect platform.

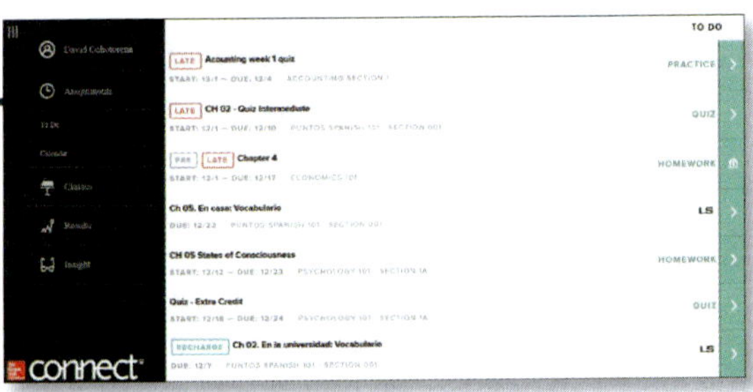

Adaptive

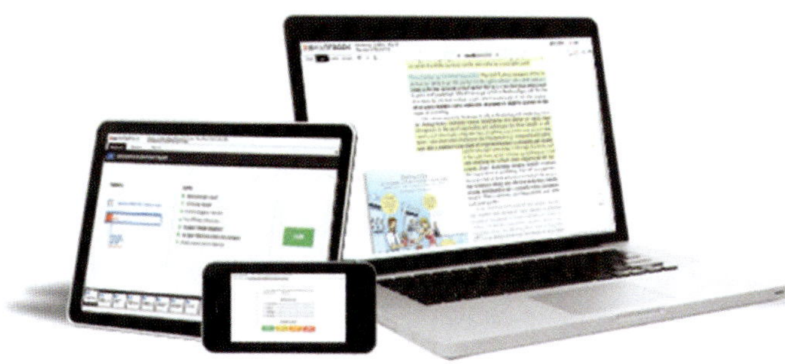

THE FIRST AND ONLY **ADAPTIVE READING EXPERIENCE** DESIGNED TO TRANSFORM THE WAY STUDENTS READ

More students earn **A's** and **B's** when they use McGraw-Hill Education **Adaptive** products.

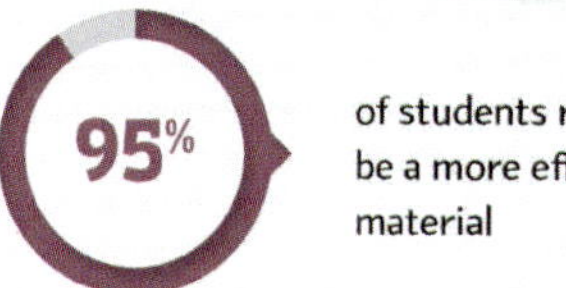

of students reported **SmartBook** to be a more effective way of reading material

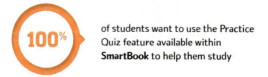

of students want to use the Practice Quiz feature available within **SmartBook** to help them study

of students reported having reliable access to off-campus wifi

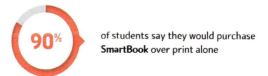

of students say they would purchase **SmartBook** over print alone

reported that **SmartBook** would impact their study skills in a positive way

*Findings based on a 2015 focus group survey at Pellissippi State Community College administered by McGraw-Hill Education

SmartBook®

Proven to help students improve grades and study more efficiently, SmartBook contains the same content within the print book, but actively tailors that content to the needs of the individual. SmartBook's adaptive technology provides precise, personalized instruction on what the student should do next, guiding the student to master and remember key concepts, targeting gaps in knowledge and offering customized feedback, and driving the student toward comprehension and retention of the subject matter. Available on smartphones and tablets, SmartBook puts learning at the student's fingertips—anywhere, anytime.

Over **4 billion questions** have been answered, making McGraw-Hill Education products more intelligent, reliable, and precise.

Support Materials in Connect

The Instructor's Manual offers lecture outlines with teaching notes and figure references. It provides definitions of key terms and solutions to the end-of-chapter material, including multiple-choice, matching, and open-ended questions.

The PowerPoint slides are designed to provide instructors with a comprehensive resource for lecture use. The slides include a review of key terms and topics, as well as artwork taken from the text to further explain concepts covered in each chapter.

The testbank contains over 2,200 questions categorized by level of learning (definition, concept, and application). This is the same learning scheme that is introduced in the text to provide a valuable testing and reinforcement tool. Text page references have been provided for all questions, including a level-of-difficulty rating.

SIMNET ONLINE TRAINING AND ASSESSMENT FOR OFFICE APPLICATIONS

SIMnet™ Online provides a way for you to test students' software skills in a simulated environment. SIMnet provides flexibility for you in your applications course by offering:

- Pretesting options
- Posttesting options
- Course placement testing
- Diagnostic capabilities to reinforce skills
- Web delivery of tests
- Learning verification reports

For more information on skills assessment software, please contact your local sales representative, or visit us at www.simnetkeepitsimple.com.

Acknowledgments

A special thank-you goes to the professors who took time out of their busy schedules to provide us with the feedback necessary to develop the 2017 edition of this text. The following professors offered valuable suggestions on revising the text:

Brenda Nickel
Moraine Park Technical College

Pamela Silvers
Asheville-Buncombe Technical Community College

Natalie Cooper
Madisonville Community College

Melissa Nemeth
IU Kelley School of Business Indianapolis

Kate LeGrand
Broward College

Tiffany Ford
Ozarks Technical Community College

Laurence Hitterdale
Glendale Community College

Paulette Comet
Community College of Baltimore County

Lacey Lormand
University of Louisiana at Lafayette

Kathleen Morris
University of Alabama

Katherine Oser
Central Texas College

Debra Luna
El Paso Community College

Brenda McFarland
Asheville-Buncombe Technical Community College

Jennifer Krou
Texas State University

Mark Jackson
Columbus State Community College

Kamal Kakish
Georgia Gwinnett College

Joshua Cuneo
Georgia Gwinnett College

Our sincere thanks also go to Laurie Zouharis at Suffolk College for revising probes for LearnSmart; to Brenda Nielsen at Mesa Community College for revising the Instructor's Manual, and online quizzes; to Rose Marie Kuebbing for revising the testbank; and to Rachelle Hall at Glendale Community College for revising the PowerPoint presentations to accompany this text.

About the Authors

Tim and Linda O'Leary live in the American Southwest and spend much of their time engaging instructors and students in conversation about learning. In fact, they have been talking about learning for over 25 years. Something in those early conversations convinced them to write a book, to bring their interest in the learning process to the printed page. Now, they are joined by their son Dan O'Leary as a coauthor. Dan has recently completed his PhD in Electrical Engineering with significant experience in teaching and consulting in information technology.

The O'Leary's form a unique team blending experience and youth. Tim has taught courses at Stark Technical College in Canton, Ohio, and at Rochester Institute of Technology in upstate New York, and is currently a professor emeritus at Arizona State University. Linda offered her expertise at ASU for several years as an academic advisor. She also presented and developed materials for major corporations such as Motorola, Intel, Honeywell, and AT&T, as well as various community colleges in the Phoenix area. Dan has taught at the University of California at Santa Cruz, developed energy-related labs at NASA, and worked as a database administrator and as a consultant in information systems.

Tim, Linda, and Dan have talked to and taught numerous students, all of them with a desire to learn something about computers and applications that make their lives easier, more interesting, and more productive.

Each new edition of an O'Leary text, supplement, or learning aid has benefited from these students and their instructors who daily stand in front of them (or over their shoulders).

chapter 1 Information Technology, the Internet, and You

Why should I read this chapter?

The future of computers and digital technology promises exciting challenges and opportunities. Powerful software and hardware systems are changing the way people and organizations interact in their daily life and on the Internet.

This chapter introduces you to the skills and concepts you need to be prepared for this ever-changing digital world, including:

- Information systems—how the critical parts of technology interact.
- Efficiency and effectiveness—how to maximize the use of technology.
- Privacy, ethics, and environment—how to integrate technology with people.
- Connectivity and cloud computing—how the Internet, web, and the wireless revolution are changing how we communicate and interact.

Learning Objectives

After you have read this chapter, you should be able to:

1. Explain the parts of an information system: people, procedures, software, hardware, data, and the Internet.
2. Distinguish between system software and application software.
3. Differentiate between the three kinds of system software programs.
4. Define and compare general-purpose, specialized, and mobile applications.
5. Identify the four types of computers and the five types of personal computers.
6. Describe the different types of computer hardware, including the system unit, input, output, storage, and communication devices.
7. Define data and describe document, worksheet, database, and presentation files.
8. Explain computer connectivity, the wireless revolution, the Internet, cloud computing, and IoT.

Introduction

"Welcome to *Computing Essentials*. I'm Alan and I work in information technology. On the following pages, we'll be discussing some of the most exciting new developments in computer technology including smartphones, tablet computers, and cloud computing. Let me begin in this chapter by giving you an overview of the book and showing you some of its special features."

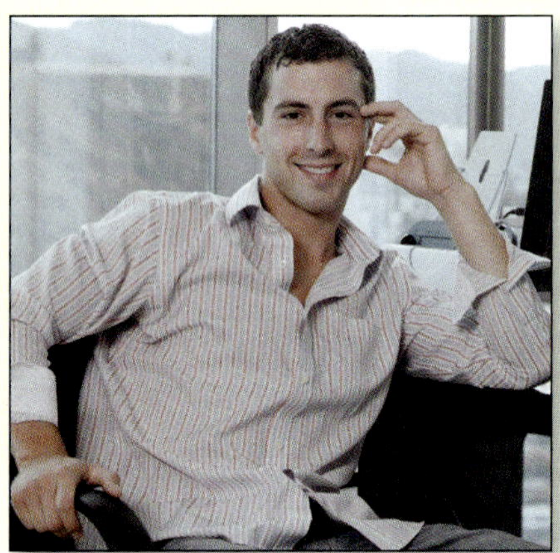

The purpose of this book is to help you become a highly efficient and effective computer user. This includes how to use (1) apps and application software; (2) all types of computer hardware including mobile devices like smartphones, tablets, and laptops; and (3) the Internet. Becoming a highly efficient and effective computer user also requires a full understanding of the potential impact of technology on privacy and the environment as well as the role of personal and organizational ethics.

To effectively and efficiently use computers, you need to know the parts of an information system: people, procedures, software, hardware, data, and the Internet. You also need to understand the wireless revolution, the mobile Internet, and the web and to recognize the role of information technology in your personal and professional life.

Information Systems

When you think of a personal computer, perhaps you think of just the equipment itself. That is, you think of the screen or the keyboard. Yet, there is more to it than that. The way to think about a personal computer is as part of an information system. An **information system** has several parts: *people, procedures, software, hardware, data,* and *the Internet.* (See Figure 1-1.)

- **People:** It is easy to overlook people as one of the parts of an information system. Yet this is what personal computers are all about–making **people, end users** like you, more productive.
- **Procedures:** The rules or guidelines for people to follow when using software, hardware, and data are **procedures.** These procedures are typically documented in manuals written by computer specialists. Software and hardware manufacturers provide manuals with their products. These manuals are provided in either printed or electronic form.
- **Software:** A **program** consists of the step-by-step instructions that tell the computer how to do its work. **Software** is another name for a program or programs. The purpose of software is to convert **data** (unprocessed facts) into **information** (processed facts). For example, a payroll program would instruct the computer to take the number of hours you worked in a week (data) and multiply it by your pay rate (data) to determine how much you are paid for the week (information).
- **Hardware:** The equipment that processes the data to create information is called **hardware.** It includes smartphones, tablets, keyboards, mice, displays, system units, and other devices. Hardware is controlled by software.
- **Data:** The raw, unprocessed facts, including text, numbers, images, and sounds, are called data. Processed data yields information. Using the previous example of a payroll program, the data (number of hours worked and pay rate) is processed (multiplied) to yield information (weekly pay).
- **Internet:** Almost all information systems provide a way to connect to other people and computers, typically using the Internet. This **connectivity** greatly expands the capability and usefulness of information systems.

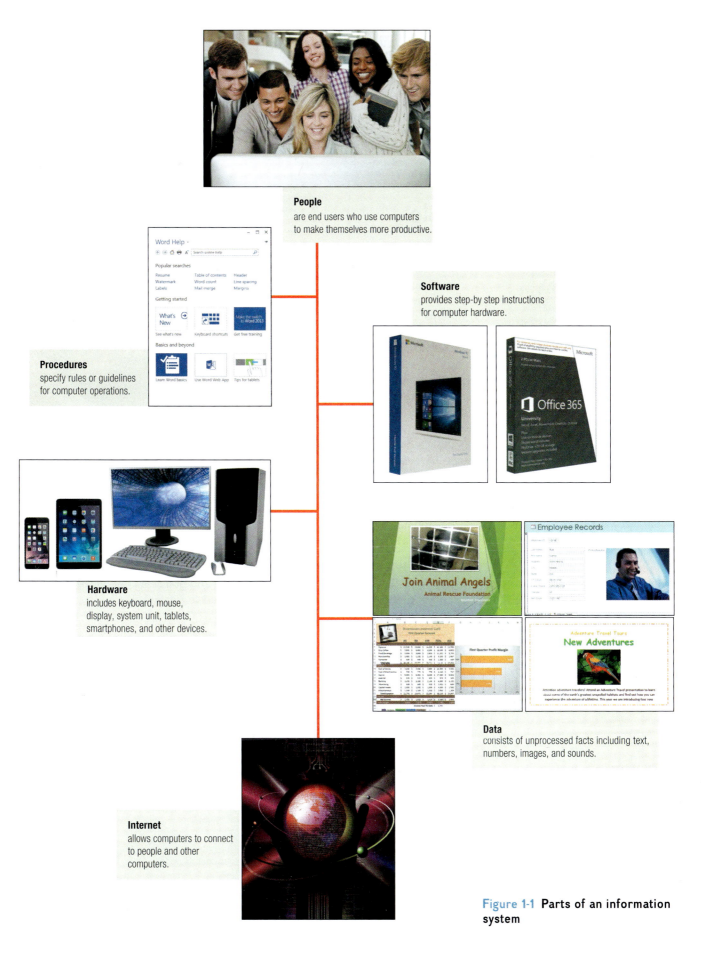

Figure 1-1 Parts of an information system

concept check

What are the parts of an information system?

What is a program?

What is the difference between data and information?

environment

Did you know that over 10 million tons of material was diverted from landfills last year alone as a result of recycling efforts? This success is largely due to voluntary participation of people across the country, who have made "reduce, reuse, and recycle" a personal commitment. This includes recycling old computers, cell phones, printers, and displays. Your participation in recycling means fewer one-use products, cleaner water, and cleaner air. But recycling may someday pay off financially too. Many now see waste as a resource, and one that we shouldn't squander by filling up the garbage can instead of the recycling bin. Imagine a future where the garbage collector drops off a check for your contributions to going green.

People

People are surely the most important part of any information system. Our lives are touched every day by computers and information systems. Many times the contact is direct and obvious, such as when we create documents using a word processing program or when we connect to the Internet. (See Figure 1-2.) Other times, the contact is not as obvious.

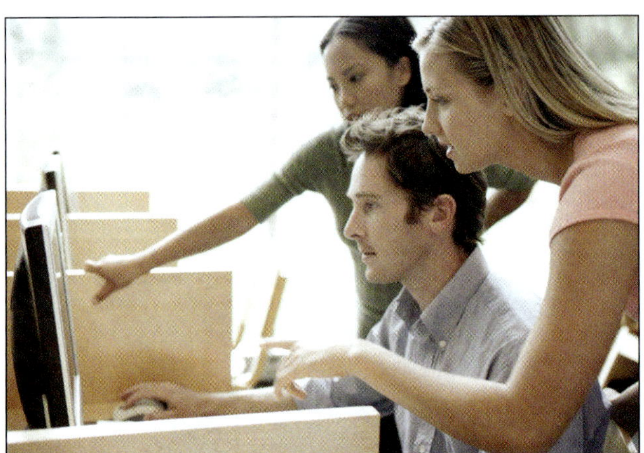

Figure 1-2 **People and computers**

Throughout this book you will find a variety of features designed to help you become an efficient and effective end user. These features include Making IT Work for You, Tips, Privacy, Environment, Ethics, and Careers in IT.

- **Making IT Work for You.** Throughout this book you will find Making IT Work for You features that present numerous interesting and practical IT applications. For just a few of the Making IT Work for You topics, see Figure 1-3.
- **Tips.** We all can benefit from a few tips or suggestions. Throughout this book you will find numerous tips to make your computing safer, more efficient, and more effective. These tips range from the basics of keeping your computer system

Application	Description
Free Antivirus Program	Protect your computer by installing and using a free antivirus program. See page 9.
Online Entertainment	Use your computer to watch your favorite television programs, movies, and other video content. See page 30.
Google Docs	Create, collaborate, and access documents from almost anywhere with a free online office suite. See page 78.
Skype	Visit face to face with friends and family located almost anywhere at little or no cost. See page 157.
Cloud Storage	Send large files using a free tool and the cloud. See page 182.

Figure 1-3 **Making IT Work for You applications**

running smoothly to how to protect your privacy while surfing the web. For a partial list of the tips presented in the following chapters, see Figure 1-4.

- **Privacy.** One of the most critical issues today is how to protect the privacy of our personal information. Throughout this book you will find Privacy boxes in the margin that present information about protecting our privacy.
- **Environment.** Today it is more important than ever that we be aware of our impact on the environment. In this chapter and the following ones, you will find Environment boxes in the margin that present important relevant environmental information.
- **Ethics.** Most people agree that we should behave ethically. That is, we should follow a system of moral principles that direct our everyday lives. However, for any given circumstance, people often do not agree on the ethics of the situation. Throughout this book you will find numerous Ethics boxes posing a variety of different ethical/unethical situations for your consideration.
- **Careers in IT.** One of the most important decisions of your life is to decide upon your life's work or career. Perhaps you are planning to be a writer, an artist, or an engineer. Or you might become a professional in **information technology (IT).** Each of the following chapters highlights a specific career in information technology. This feature provides job descriptions, projected employment demands, educational requirements, current salary ranges, and advancement opportunities.

Are you getting the most out of your computer? Here are just a few of the tips to make your computing safer, more efficient, and more effective.

1. **Low battery.** Do you find that your laptop's battery keeps its charge for less time than it used to? Here are some ways to make your battery last longer. See page 128.
2. **Language translation.** Have you had trouble communicating with someone who does not speak English? If so, Google Translate may be just what you need. See page 148.
3. **Lost files.** Have you ever accidentally deleted or lost important files from your flash drive? Here are a few suggestions that might help. See page 178.
4. **Protecting your identity.** Identity theft is a growing problem and can be financially devastating if you are a victim. Some steps to protect your identity are on page 233.
5. **Wireless networks.** Do you use your laptop to connect to wireless networks at school, coffee shops, airports, or hotels? If so, it is important to use caution to protect your computer and your privacy. A few suggestions are on page 208.

Figure 1-4 **Selected tips**

concept check

Which part of an information system is the most important?

Describe the Making IT Work for You, Tips, and Privacy features.

Describe the Environment, Ethics, and Careers in IT features.

Software

Software, as we mentioned, is another name for programs. Programs are the instructions that tell the computer how to process data into the form you want. In most cases, the words *software* and *programs* are interchangeable. There are two major kinds of software: *system software* and *application software.* You can think of application software as the kind you use. Think of system software as the kind the computer uses.

System Software

The user interacts primarily with application software. **System software** enables the application software to interact with the computer hardware. System software is "background" software that helps the computer manage its own internal resources.

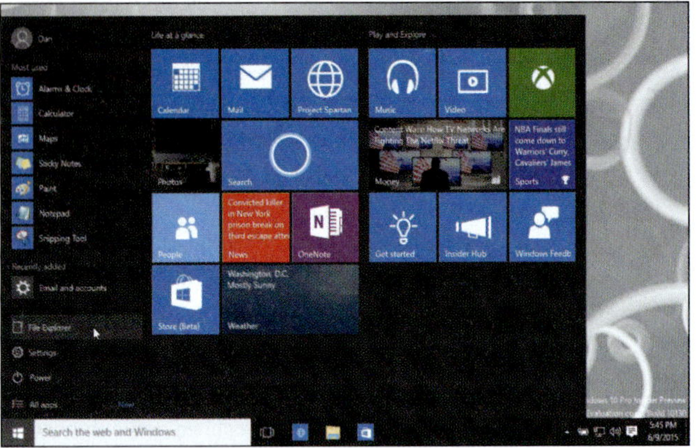

Figure 1-5 **Windows 10**

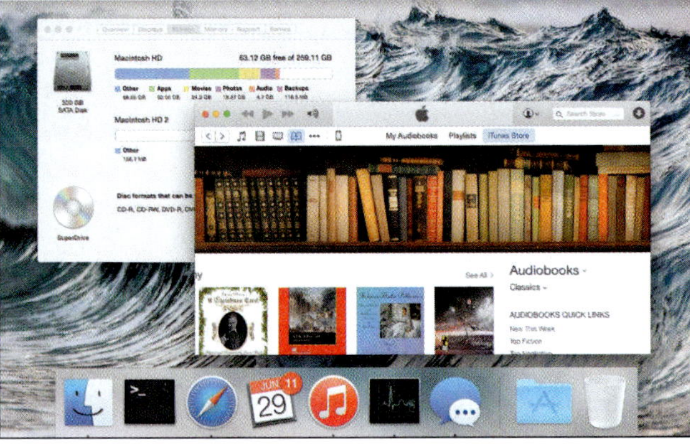

Figure 1-6 **Mac OS X**

System software is not a single program. Rather, it is a collection of programs, including the following:

- **Operating systems** are programs that coordinate computer resources, provide an interface between users and the computer, and run applications. Smartphones, tablets, and many other mobile devices use **embedded operating systems,** also known as **real-time operating systems (RTOS).** Desktop computers use **stand-alone operating systems** like Windows 10 or Mac OS. (See Figures 1-5 and 1-6.) Networks use **network operating systems (NOS).**
- **Utilities** perform specific tasks related to managing computer resources. One of the most essential utility programs that every computer system should have is an antivirus program. These programs protect your computer system from **viruses** or malicious programs that are all too often deposited onto your computer from the Internet. These programs can damage software and hardware, as well as compromise the security and privacy of your personal data. If your computer does not have an antivirus program installed on it, you need to get one. To see how you can install a free antivirus program on your computer, see Making IT Work for You: Free Antivirus Program on page 9.

Application Software

Application software might be described as end user software. Three types of application software are *general-purpose, specialized,* and *apps.*

General-purpose applications are widely used in nearly all career areas. They are the kinds of programs you have to know to be considered an efficient and effective end user. Some of the best known are presented in Figure 1-7.

Specialized applications include thousands of other programs that are more narrowly focused on specific disciplines and occupations. Two of the best known are graphics and web authoring programs.

Mobile apps, also known as **mobile applications** or simply **apps,** are small programs primarily designed for mobile devices such as smartphones and for tablet computers. There are over half a million apps. The most popular mobile apps are for social networking, playing games, and downloading music and videos.

Type	Description
Browsers	Connect to websites and display web pages
Word processors	Prepare written documents
Spreadsheets	Analyze and summarize numerical data
Database management systems	Organize and manage data and information
Presentation graphics	Communicate a message or persuade other people

Figure 1-7 **General-purpose applications**

FREE ANTIVIRUS PROGRAM

Have you or someone you know had a slower computing experience due to a spyware infection? Even worse, perhaps a malicious piece of software stole crucial, personal information or caused a total system failure. Most of these problems can be averted by having an up-to-date antivirus program running in your computer's memory at all times. This exercise shows you how to download and install a free antivirus program if your computer does not yet have one. (Please note that the web is continually changing, and some of the specifics presented below may have changed.)

Getting Started First, make sure your computer does not have an antivirus or security suite running. If it does, be sure to completely uninstall that program, even if the subscription is expired. Now, follow these steps to install AVG, a popular, free antivirus program:

1. **Visit http://free.avg.com and click the *Download* button. You will be asked to confirm that you want the free edition and then redirected to a download site.**
2. **Run the installation file and follow the prompts.**
3. **Select *basic protection* if you are asked which product you would like to install.**

Using AVG Generally speaking, your antivirus program watches your system for malware and updates itself automatically. However, you can always download updates manually, set a schedule for full-system scans, and change basic settings for various components of the software.

1. **Click *Scan now* to run a full scan on your computer.**
2. **Just to the right of that, click the button with the white cog to see the scan options where you can set a schedule for automated scans.**
3. **Click the *back arrow* to reach the main screen, where you can click various elements of the program to configure them. For example, clicking *Web* will allow you to turn on a feature that detects cookies that may be used to track your online activity.**

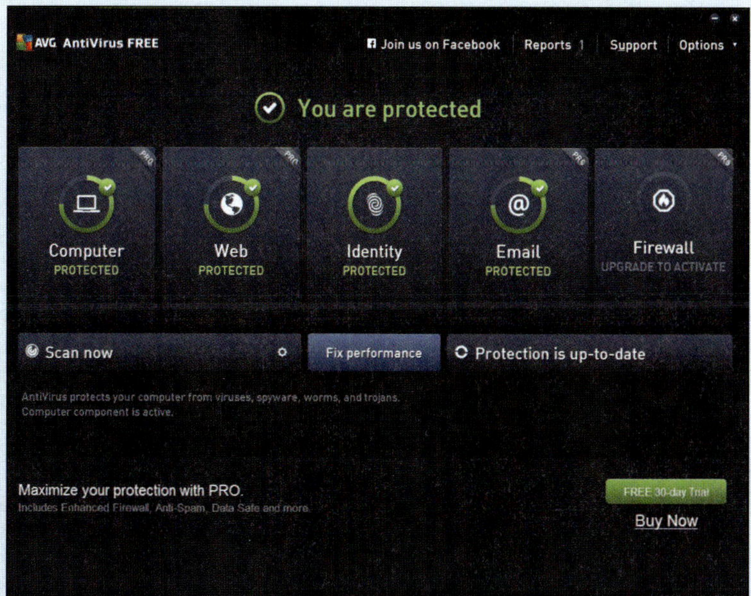

concept check

Describe the two major kinds of software.

Describe two types of system software programs.

Define and compare general-purpose applications, specialized applications, and mobile apps.

Hardware

Computers are electronic devices that can follow instructions to accept input, process that input, and produce information. This book focuses principally on personal computers. However, it is almost certain that you will come in contact, at least indirectly, with other types of computers.

Types of Computers

There are four types of computers: supercomputers, mainframe computers, midrange computers, and personal computers.

- **Supercomputers** are the most powerful type of computer. These machines are special, high-capacity computers used by very large organizations. Supercomputers are typically used to process massive amounts of data. For example, they are used to analyze and predict worldwide weather patterns. IBM's Blue Gene supercomputer is one of the fastest computers in the world. (See Figure 1-8.)
- **Mainframe computers** occupy specially wired, air-conditioned rooms. Although not nearly as powerful as supercomputers, mainframe computers are capable of great processing speeds and data storage. For example, insurance companies use mainframes to process information about millions of policyholders.
- **Midrange computers,** also referred to as **servers,** are computers with processing capabilities less powerful than a mainframe computer yet more powerful than a

Figure 1-8 Supercomputer

Figure 1-9 **Desktop**

Figure 1-10 **Laptop**

personal computer. Originally used by medium-size companies or departments of large companies to support their processing needs, today midrange computers are most widely used to support or serve end users for such specific needs as retrieving data from a database or supplying access to application software.

- **Personal computers,** also known as **PCs,** are the least powerful, yet the most widely used and fastest-growing type of computer. There are five types of personal computers: *desktops, laptops, tablets, smartphones,* and *wearables.* **Desktop computers** are small enough to fit on top of or alongside a desk yet are too big to carry around. (See Figure 1-9.) **Laptop computers,** also known as **notebook computers,** are portable and lightweight and fit into most briefcases. (See Figure 1-10.) **Tablets,** also known as **tablet computers,** are smaller, lighter, and generally less powerful than laptops. Like a laptop, tablets have a flat screen but typically do not have a standard keyboard. (See Figure 1-11.) Instead, tablets typically use a virtual keyboard that appears on the screen and is touch-sensitive.

  Smartphones are the most widely used handheld computers. Smartphones are cell phones with wireless connections to the Internet and processing capabilities. (See Figure 1-12.) Other mobile computers include **wearable devices** like Apple's watch. (See Figure 1-13.)

Figure 1-11 **Tablet**

Personal Computer Hardware

Hardware for a personal computer system consists of a variety of different devices. This physical equipment falls into four basic categories: system unit, input/output, secondary storage, and communication. Because we discuss hardware in detail later in this book, here we will present just a quick overview of the four basic categories.

- **System unit:** The **system unit** is a container that houses most of the electronic components that make up a computer system. Two important components of the system unit are *microprocessors* and *memory.* (See Figure 1-14.) The **microprocessor** controls and manipulates data to produce information. **Memory** is a holding area for data, instructions, and information. One type, **random-access memory (RAM),** holds the program and data that is currently being processed. This type of memory is sometimes referred to as *temporary storage* because its contents will typically be lost if the electric power to the computer is disrupted.
- **Input/output: Input devices** translate data and programs that humans can understand into a form that the computer can process. The most common input devices are the **keyboard** and the **mouse. Output devices** translate the processed information from the computer into a form that humans can understand. The most common output device is the **display,** also known as a **monitor.**

Figure 1-12 **Smartphone**

Figure 1-13 **Wearable**

Figure 1-14 **System unit**

Figure 1-15 **Solid-state storage**

- **Secondary storage:** Unlike memory, **secondary storage** holds data and programs even after electric power to the computer system has been turned off. The most important kinds of secondary media are *hard disks, solid-state storage,* and *optical discs.*
  Hard disks are typically used to store programs and very large data files. Using rigid metallic platters and read/write heads that move across the platters, data and information are stored using magnetic charges on the disk's surface. In contrast, **solid-state storage** does not have any moving parts, is more reliable, and requires less power. It saves data and information electronically similar to RAM except that it is not volatile. (See Figure 1-15.) **Optical discs** use laser technology to store data and programs. Three types of optical discs are **compact discs (CDs), digital versatile** (or **video**) **discs (DVDs),** and **Blu-ray discs (BD).**
- **Communication:** At one time, it was uncommon for a personal computer system to communicate with other computer systems. Now, using **communication devices,** a personal computer routinely communicates with other computer systems located as near as the next office or as far away as halfway around the world, using the Internet. A **modem** is a widely used communication device that modifies audio, video, and other types of data into a form that can be transmitted across the Internet.

concept check

 What are the four types of computers?

 Describe the five types of personal computers.

 Describe the four basic categories of personal computer hardware.

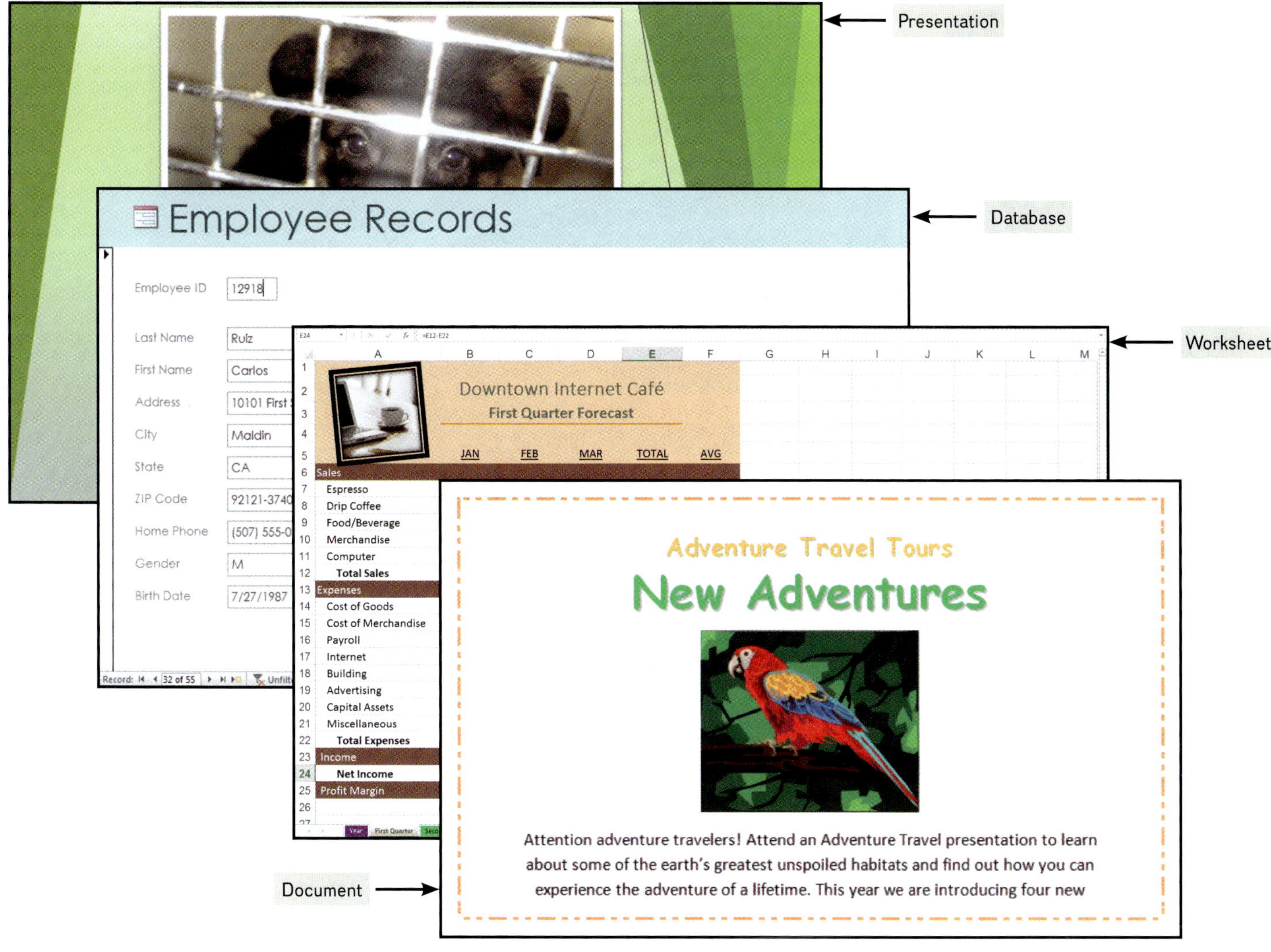

Figure 1-16 **Four types of files: document, worksheet, database, and presentation**

Data

Data is raw, unprocessed facts, including text, numbers, images, and sounds. As we mentioned earlier, processed data becomes information. When stored electronically in files, data can be used directly as input for the system unit.

Four common types of files (see Figure 1-16) are

- **Document files,** created by word processors to save documents such as memos, term papers, and letters.
- **Worksheet files,** created by electronic spreadsheets to analyze things like budgets and to predict sales.
- **Database files,** typically created by database management programs to contain highly structured and organized data. For example, an employee database file might contain all the workers' names, Social Security numbers, job titles, and other related pieces of information.
- **Presentation files,** created by presentation graphics programs to save presentation materials. For example, a file might contain audience handouts, speaker notes, and electronic slides.

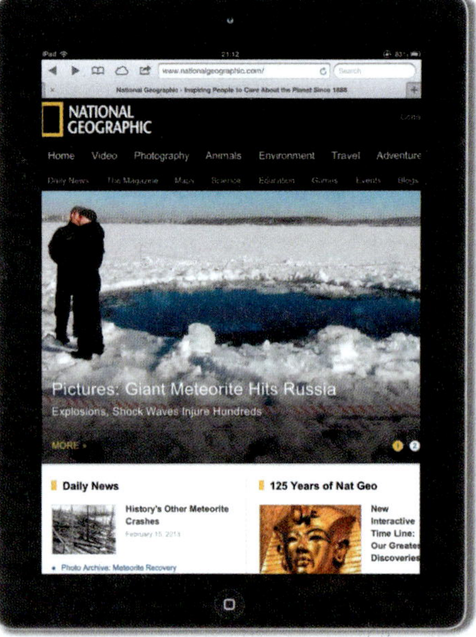

Figure 1-17 Wireless communication devices

Connectivity and the Mobile Internet

Connectivity is the capability of your personal computer to share information with other computers. Central to the concept of connectivity is the **network.** A network is a communications system connecting two or more computers. The largest network in the world is the **Internet.** It is like a giant highway that connects you to millions of other people and organizations located throughout the world. The **web** provides a multimedia interface to the numerous resources available on the Internet.

The Internet has driven the evolution of computers and their impact on our daily lives. In fact, the rate of technological change is accelerating at an ever faster pace. Along with the Internet, three things that are driving the impact of technology on our lives are cloud computing, wireless communication, and the Internet of Things.

- **Cloud computing** uses the Internet and the web to shift many computer activities from a user's computer to computers on the Internet. Rather than relying solely on their computer, users can now use the Internet to connect to the cloud and access more powerful computers, software, and storage.
- **Wireless communication** has changed the way we communicate with one another. The rapid development and widespread use of wireless communication devices like tablets, smartphones, and wearable devices has led many experts to predict that wireless applications are just the beginning of the **wireless revolution,** a revolution that will dramatically affect the way we communicate and use computer technology.
- The **Internet of Things (IoT)** is the continuing development of the Internet that allows everyday objects embedded with electronic devices to send and receive data over the Internet. It promises to connect all types of devices from computers to smartphones to watches to any number of everyday devices.

Wireless communication, cloud computing, and IoT are driving the mobile Internet. They promise to continue to dramatically affect the entire computer industry and how you and I will interact with computers and other devices. Each will be discussed in detail in the following chapters. For just a few of these mobile devices, see Figure 1-17.

concept check

 Define data. List four common types of files.

 Define connectivity and networks.

 What is cloud computing? Wireless revolution? IoT?

Careers in IT

"Now that you know the basic outline and important features of this book, I'd like to talk about some of the most exciting and well-paid careers in information technology."

As mentioned previously, each of the following chapters highlights a specific career in information technology. Each provides specific job descriptions, salary ranges, advancement opportunities, and more. For a partial list of these careers, see Figure 1-18.

Career	Description
Webmaster	Develops and maintains websites and web resources. See page 48.
Software engineer	Analyzes users' needs and creates application software. See page 77.
Computer support specialist	Provides technical support to customers and other users. See page 104.
Computer technician	Repairs and installs computer components and systems. See page 130.
Technical writer	Prepares instruction manuals, technical reports, and other scientific or technical documents. See page 161.
Network administrator	Creates and maintains computer networks. See page 212.

Figure 1-18 **Careers in information technology**

A LOOK TO THE FUTURE

Using and Understanding Information Technology

The purpose of this book is to help you use and understand information technology. We want to help you become proficient and to provide you with a foundation of knowledge so that you can understand how technology is being used today and anticipate how technology will be used in the future. This will enable you to benefit from six important information technology developments.

The Internet and the Web

The Internet and the web are considered to be the two most important technologies for the 21st century. Understanding how to efficiently and effectively use the Internet to browse, communicate, and locate information is an essential skill. These issues are presented in Chapter 2, The Internet, the Web, and Electronic Commerce.

Powerful Software

The software that is now available can do an extraordinary number of tasks and help you in an endless number of ways. You can create professional-looking documents, analyze massive amounts of data, create dynamic multimedia web pages, and much more. Today's employers are expecting the people they hire to be able to effectively and efficiently use a variety of different types of software. General-purpose, specialized, and mobile applications are presented in Chapter 3. System software is presented in Chapter 4.

Powerful Hardware

Personal computers are now much more powerful than they used to be. Smartphones, tablets, and communication technologies such as wireless networks are dramatically changing the ways to connect to other computers, networks, and the Internet. However, despite the rapid change of specific equipment, their essential features remain unchanged. To become an efficient and effective end user, you should focus on these features. Chapters 5 through 8 explain what you need to know about hardware. For those considering the purchase of a computer, an appendix—The Computer Buyer's Guide—is provided at the end of this book. This guide provides a very concise comparison of desktops, laptops, tablets, and smartphones.

Privacy, Security, and Ethics

What about people? Experts agree that we as a society must be careful about the potential of technology to negatively affect our lives. Specifically, we need to be aware of how technology can impact our personal privacy and our environment. Also, we need to understand the role and the importance of organizational and personal ethics. These critical issues are integrated in every chapter of this book as well as extensively covered in Chapter 9.

Organizations

Almost all organizations rely on the quality and flexibility of their information systems to stay competitive. As a member or employee of an organization, you will undoubtedly be involved in these information systems. In order to use, develop, modify, and maintain these systems, you need to understand the basic concepts of information systems and know how to safely, efficiently, and effectively use computers. These concepts are covered throughout this book.

Changing Times

Are the times changing any faster now than they ever have? Almost everyone thinks so. Whatever the answer, it is clear we live in a fast-paced age. The Evolution of the Computer Age section presented at the end of this book tracks the major developments since computers were first introduced.

After reading this book, you will be in a very favorable position compared with many other people in industry today. You will learn not only the basics of hardware, software, connectivity, the Internet, and the web but also the most current technology. You will be able to use these tools to your advantage.

VISUAL SUMMARY Information Technology, the Internet, and You

INFORMATION SYSTEMS

The way to think about a personal computer is to realize that it is one part of an **information system.** There are several parts of an information system:

- **People** are an essential part of the system. The purpose of information systems is to make people, or **end users** like you, more productive.
- **Procedures** are rules or guidelines to follow when using software, hardware, and data. They are typically documented in manuals written by computer professionals.
- **Software (programs)** provides step-by-step instructions to control the computer to convert **data** into **information.**
- **Hardware** consists of the physical equipment. It is controlled by software and processes data to create information.
- **Data** consists of unprocessed facts including text, numbers, images, and sound. **Information** is data that has been processed by the computer.
- The **Internet** allows computers to connect and share information.

To efficiently and effectively use the computer, you need to understand **information technology (IT),** including software, hardware, data, and connectivity.

PEOPLE

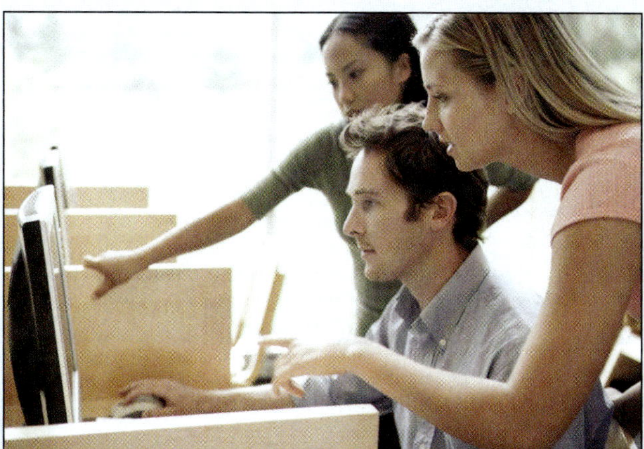

People are the most important part of an information system. This book contains several features to demonstrate how people just like you use computers. These features include the following:

- **Making IT Work for You** presents several interesting and practical applications. Topics include using digital video editing and locating job opportunities.
- **Tips** offer a variety of suggestions on such practical matters as how to improve slow computer performance and how to protect your privacy while on the web.
- **Privacy** marginal boxes discuss threats to your personal privacy and suggest ways to protect yourself.
- **Environment** boxes discuss important and relevant environmental issues. The impact of computers and other technologies is more critical today than ever before.
- **Ethics** boxes pose a variety of different ethical/unethical situations for your consideration.
- **Careers in IT** presents job descriptions, employment demands, educational requirements, salary ranges, and advancement opportunities.

To efficiently and effectively use computers, you need to understand the basic parts of an information system: people, procedures, software, hardware, data, and connectivity. You also need to understand the Internet and the web and to recognize the role of technology in your professional and personal life.

SOFTWARE

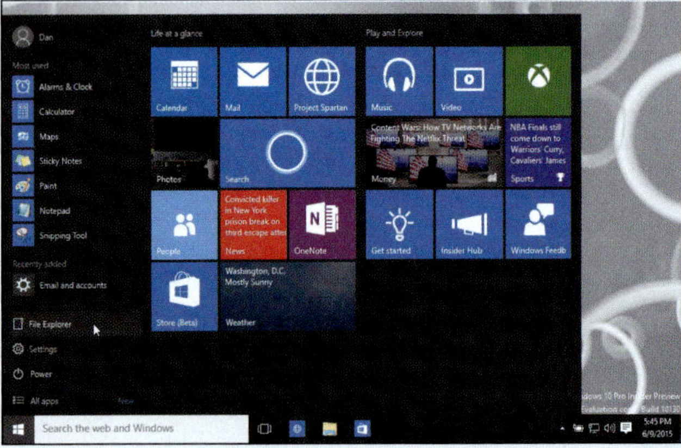

Software, or **programs,** consists of system and application software.

System Software

System software enables application software to interact with computer hardware.

- **Operating systems** coordinate resources, provide an interface, and run applications. Three types are **embedded (real-time, RTOS), stand-alone,** and **network (NOS).**
- **Utilities** perform specific tasks to manage computer resources.

Application Software

Application software includes general-purpose, specialized, and mobile applications.

- **General purpose**—widely used in nearly all career areas; programs include browsers, word processors, spreadsheets, database management systems, and presentation graphics.
- **Specialized**—focus more on specific disciplines and occupations; programs include graphics and web authoring.
- **Apps (mobile apps, mobile applications)**—designed for mobile devices; most popular are for text messaging, Internet browsing, and connecting to social networks.

HARDWARE

Hardware consists of electronic devices that can follow instructions to accept input, process the input, and produce information.

Types of Computers

Supercomputer, mainframe, midrange (server), and **personal computers (PCs)** are four types of computers. Personal computers can be **desktop, laptop (notebook computer), tablet, smartphone,** and **wearable.**

Personal Computer Hardware

There are four basic categories of hardware devices.

- **System unit** contains electronic circuitry, including **microprocessors** and **memory. Random-access memory (RAM)** holds the program and data currently being processed.
- **Input/output devices** are translators between humans and computers. **Input devices** include the **keyboard** and **mouse.** The most common output device is the computer **display (monitor).**
- **Secondary storage** holds data and programs. Typical media include **hard disks, solid-state storage,** and **optical discs (CD, DVD,** and **Blu-ray).**
- **Communication devices** allow personal computers to communicate with other computer systems. **Modems** modify audio, video, and other types of data for transmission across the Internet.

DATA

Data is the raw unprocessed facts about something. Common file types include

- **Document files** created by word processors.

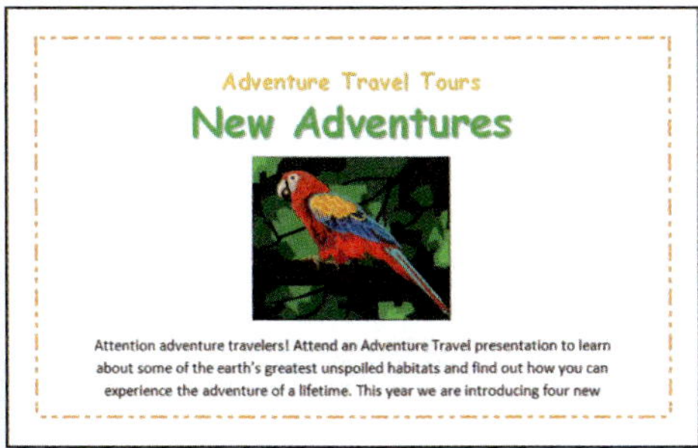
Adventure Travel Tours
New Adventures
Attention adventure travelers! Attend an Adventure Travel presentation to learn about some of the earth's greatest unspoiled habitats and find out how you can experience the adventure of a lifetime. This year we are introducing four new

- **Worksheet files** created by spreadsheet programs.

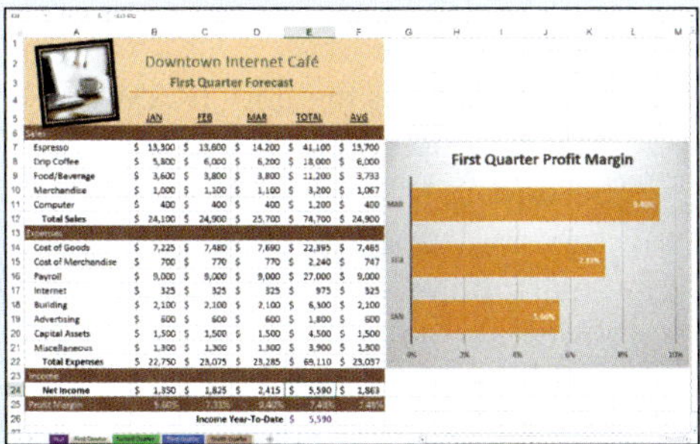
Downtown Internet Café
First Quarter Forecast
First Quarter Profit Margin

- **Database files** created by database management programs.

Employee Records

- **Presentation files** created by presentation graphics programs.

Join Animal Angels

CONNECTIVITY AND MOBILE INTERNET

Connectivity describes the ability of end users to use resources well beyond their desktops. Central to the concept of connectivity is the **network** or communication system connecting two or more computers. The **Internet** is the world's largest computer **network.** The **web** provides a multimedia interface to resources available on the Internet.

Along with the Internet, three other things are driving the impact of technology:

- **Cloud computing** uses the Internet and the web to shift many computer activities from a user's computer to computers on the Internet.
- **Wireless revolution** has changed the way we communicate and use computer technology. Wireless devices include tablets, smartphones, and watches.
- The **Internet of Things (IoT)** is the continuing development of the Internet that allows everyday objects embedded with electronic devices to send and receive data over the Internet.

CAREERS in IT

Career	Description
Webmaster	Develops and maintains websites and web resources. See page 48.
Software engineer	Analyzes users' needs and creates application software. See page 77.
Computer support specialist	Provides technical support to customers and other users. See page 104.
Computer technician	Repairs and installs computer components and systems. See page 130.
Technical writer	Prepares instruction manuals, technical reports, and other scientific or technical documents. See page 161.
Network administrator	Creates and maintains computer networks. See page 212.

KEY TERMS

application software (8)
apps (8)
Blu-ray disc (BD) (12)
cloud computing (15)
communication device (12)
compact disc (CD) (12)
connectivity (4, 14)
data (4)
database file (13)
desktop computer (11)
digital versatile disc (DVD) (12)
digital video disc (DVD) (12)
display (12)
document file (13)
embedded operating systems (RTOS) (8)
end user (4)
general-purpose application (8)
hard disk (12)
hardware (4)
information (4)
information system (4)
information technology (IT) (7)
input device (11)
Internet (14)
IoT (Internet of Things) (15)
keyboard (11)
laptop computer (11)
mainframe computer (10)
memory (11)
microprocessor (11)
midrange computer (10)
mobile app (application) (8)
modem (12)
monitor (11)
mouse (11)
network (14)
network operating systems (NOS) (8)
notebook computer (11)
operating system (8)
optical disc (12)
output device (11)
PC (11)
people (4)
personal computer (11)
presentation file (13)
procedures (4)
program (4)
random-access memory (RAM) (11)
real-time operating system (RTOS) (8)
secondary storage (12)
server (10)
smartphone (11)
software (4)
solid-state storage (12)
specialized application (8)
stand-alone operating system (8)
supercomputer (10)
system software (7)
system unit (11)
tablet (11)
tablet computer (11)
utility (8)
virus (8)
wearable device (11)
web (14)
wireless communication (15)
wireless revolution (15)
worksheet file (13)

MULTIPLE CHOICE

Circle the letter of the correct answer.

1. The keyboard, mouse, display, and system unit are:
   - **a.** hardware
   - **b.** output devices
   - **c.** storage devices
   - **d.** software
2. Programs that coordinate computer resources, provide an interface, and run applications are known as:
   - **a.** application programs
   - **b.** operating systems
   - **c.** storage systems
   - **d.** utility programs
3. A browser is an example of a:
   - **a.** general-purpose application
   - **b.** specialized program
   - **c.** system application
   - **d.** utility program
4. Although not as powerful as a supercomputer, this type of computer is capable of great processing speeds and data storage.
   - **a.** mainframe
   - **b.** midrange
   - **c.** laptop
   - **d.** tablet
5. Apple's Watch is what type of computer?
   - **a.** laptop
   - **b.** smartphone
   - **c.** tablet
   - **d.** wearable
6. RAM is a type of:
   - **a.** computer
   - **b.** memory
   - **c.** network
   - **d.** secondary storage
7. Unlike memory, this type of storage holds data and programs even after electric power to the computer system has been turned off.
   - **a.** primary
   - **b.** RAM
   - **c.** ROM
   - **d.** secondary
8. The type of file created by word processors, for example, memos, term papers, and letters.
   - **a.** database
   - **b.** document
   - **c.** presentation
   - **d.** worksheet
9. Uses the Internet and the web to shift many computer activities from a user's computer to computers on the Internet.
   - **a.** cloud computing
   - **b.** high definition
   - **c.** network
   - **d.** solid-state storage
10. The largest network in the world is [the]:
    - **a.** Facebook
    - **b.** Internet
    - **c.** supercomputer
    - **d.** web

MATCHING

Match each numbered item with the most closely related lettered item. Write your answers in the spaces provided.

a. desktop
b. modem
c. network
d. output
e. presentation
f. program
g. software
h. solid-state
i. system software
j. system unit

___ **1.** Consists of the step-by-step instructions that tell the computer how to do its work.
___ **2.** Another name for a program.
___ **3.** Enables the application software to interact with the computer hardware.
___ **4.** Type of computer that is small enough to fit on top of or alongside a desk yet is too big to carry around.
___ **5.** A container that houses most of the electronic components that make up a computer system.
___ **6.** Devices that translate the processed information from the computer into a form that humans can understand.
___ **7.** Unlike hard disks, this type of storage does not have any moving parts, is more reliable, and requires less power.
___ **8.** The most widely used communication device.
___ **9.** A type of a file that might contain, for example, audience handouts, speaker notes, and electronic slides.
___ **10.** A communications system connecting two or more computers.

OPEN-ENDED

On a separate sheet of paper, respond to each question or statement.

1. Explain the parts of an information system. What part do people play in this system?
2. What is system software? What kinds of programs are included in system software?
3. Define and compare general-purpose applications, specialized applications, and apps. Describe some different types of general-purpose applications. Describe some types of specialized applications.
4. Describe the different types of computers. What is the most common type? What are the types of personal computers?
5. What is connectivity? What is a computer network? What are the Internet and the web? What are cloud computing, the wireless revolution, and IoT?

DISCUSSION

Respond to each of the following questions.

1 Making IT Work for You

Making it a habit of keeping current with technology applications can be a key to your success. Numerous full-page spreads identified as *Making IT Work for You* are presented in the following chapters. These sections address some of today's most interesting and useful applications. They include online entertainment in Chapter 2, Skype in Chapter 6, and cloud storage in Chapter 7. Select one that you find the most interesting, and then respond to the following: (a) Why did you select this application? (b) Have you used this application? If so, when and how? If not, do you plan to in the near future? (c) Go to the chapter containing your selected application, and locate the application's Making IT Work for You coverage. Review and briefly describe its contents. (d) Did you find the coverage useful? Why or why not?

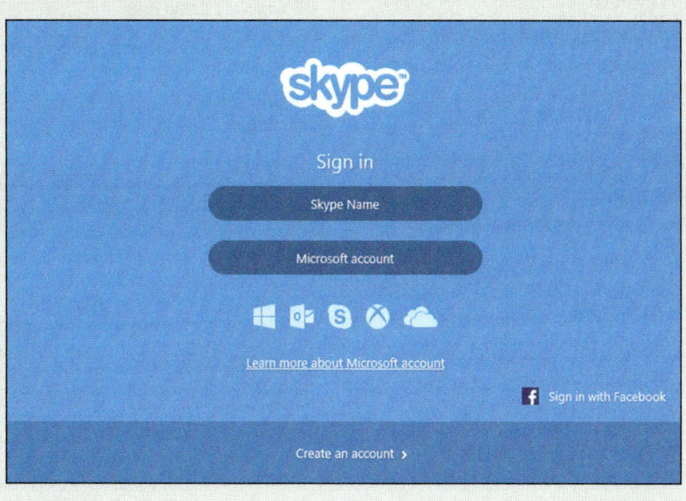

2 Privacy

Privacy is one of the most critical issues facing society today. Numerous Privacy boxes appear in the margins of the upcoming chapters presenting a variety of privacy issues. These issues include apps that track smartphone and tablet user locations without their knowledge or consent in Chapter 3, access by government and organization networks to obtain unauthorized detailed personal information in Chapter 8, and protection of personal privacy while using social networking sites such as Facebook in Chapter 9. Select one that you find the most interesting, and then respond to the following: (a) Why did you select this issue? (b) Do you have knowledge of or experience with the issue? If so, describe your knowledge or experience. If not, do you consider the issue to be important for protecting your privacy? (c) Go to the chapter containing your selected issue, locate the Privacy box, read it, and describe its contents. (d) Did you find the coverage thought-provoking? Why or why not?

3 Environment

Almost everyone agrees that protecting our environment today is more important than ever before. Numerous Environment boxes appear in the margins of the upcoming chapters. These boxes present a variety of environmental topics including e-mail benefits in Chapter 2, operating systems reducing energy consumption in Chapter 4, and recycling old inkjet cartridges in Chapter 6. Select one that you find the most interesting, and then respond to the following: (a) Why did you select this topic? (b) Do you have knowledge of or experience with the topic? If so, describe your knowledge or experience. If not, do you consider the topic to be important for protecting the environment? (c) Go to the chapter containing your selected topic, locate the Environment box, read it, and describe its contents. (d) Did you find the coverage thought-provoking? Why or why not?

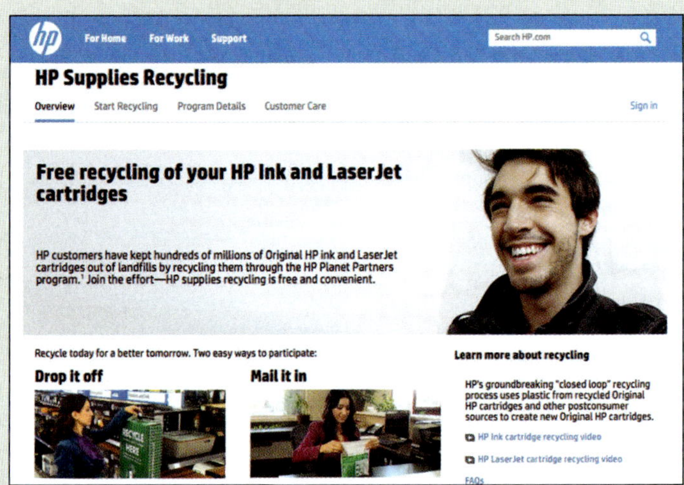

4 Ethics

Computer ethics are guidelines for the morally acceptable use of computers in our society. Numerous Ethics boxes appear in the margins of the upcoming chapters presenting a variety of ethical issues. These issues include image editing in Chapter 3, unauthorized use of webcams in Chapter 6, and unauthorized monitoring or eavesdropping of Internet activity in Chapter 8. Select one issue that you find the most interesting, and then respond to the following: (a) Why did you select this issue? (b) Do you have knowledge of or experience with the issue? If so, describe your knowledge or experience. If not, do you consider the issue critical for individuals or organizations? (c) Go to the chapter containing your selected issue, locate the Ethics box, read it, and describe its contents. (d) Did you find the coverage thought-provoking? Why or why not?

PHOTO CREDITS

CHAPTER 1

Opener: © Carol and Mike Werner/Alamy; p. 3, 16: © Simone Brandt/Alamy RF; p. 4, 15, 17 (left): © Inti St. Clair/Taxi/Getty Images; 1-1 (people), p. 17 (left): © Image Source, all rights reserved, RF; 1-1 (procedures), (data), 1-5, 1-16, p. 18 (left), 19: Microsoft product/screen shot(s) reprinted with permission from Microsoft Corporation; 1-1 (Office): Used with permission from Microsoft; 1-1 (Windows): © McGraw-Hill Education/Aaron Roeth, photographer; 1-1 (phone and tablet), 1-11, 1-12, p. 18 (right): © Stanca Sanda/Alamy; 1-1 (desktop), 1-9: © Maxim Kazmin/Getty Images RF; 1-1 (internet): © liangpv/iStock Vectors/Getty Images RF; 1-2, p. 17 (right): © Fancy Photography/Veer RF; 1-6: Djaypro screen shot copyright © Algoriddim.com. Used with permission; p. 9: Copyright © AVG Technologies, used with permission; 1-8: © Everett Collection Historical/Alamy; 1-10: © David Vernon/Getty Images RF; 1-13: © PG Pictures/Alamy; 1-14: © Willis Technology; 1-15: © Bob Dormon/theregister.co.uk; 1-17 (top-left): BlackBerry®, RIM®, Research In Motion® and related trademarks, names and logos are the property of Research In Motion Limited and are registered and/or used in the U.S. and countries around the world. Used under license from Research In Motion Limited; 1-17 (top-right): © Lenovo, used with permission; 1-17 (bottom-left): Source: Duncan Hull/Flickr/CC; 1-17 (bottom-middle): © IanDagnall Computing/Alamy; 1-17 (bottom-right): © T3 Magazine/Contributor via Getty Images; p. 23 (top): The Skype name, associated trade marks and logos and the "S" logo are trade marks of Skype or related entities, © 2015 Skype and/or Microsoft; p. 23 (bottom): Brenden Smialowski/AFP/Getty Images; p. 24 (top): © 2015 Hewlett Packard; p. 24 (bottom): © 2015 Electronic Frontier Foundation.

chapter 2 The Internet, the Web, and Electronic Commerce

Why should I read this chapter?

The Internet has changed the world, and will continue to have an amazing impact on our day-to-day lives. For example, cars promise to soon be able to drive themselves, avoid traffic accidents and congestion, and automatically adjust personal schedules and much more.

This chapter covers the things you need to know to be prepared for this ever-changing digital world, including:

- Impact—how Internet technology is changing your world.
- Hardware—how to connect your life to the Internet, including Wi-Fi, smartphones, and tablets.
- Applications—how to get ahead using social networking, streaming technology, and cloud computing.

Learning Objectives

After you have read this chapter, you should be able to:

1 Explain the origins of the Internet and the web.

2 Explain how to access the web using providers and browsers.

3 Compare different web utilities, including plug-ins, filters, file transfer utilities, and Internet security suites.

4 Compare different Internet communications, including e-mail, text messaging, instant messaging, social networking, blogs, microblogs, webcasts, podcasts, and wikis.

5 Describe search tools, including search engines and specialized search engines.

6 Evaluate the accuracy of information presented on the web.

7 Identify electronic commerce, including B2C, C2C, B2B, and security issues.

8 Describe cloud computing, including the three-way interaction of clients, Internet, and service providers.

9 Discuss the Internet of Things (IoT) and the continuing development of the Internet to allow everyday objects to send and receive data.

Introduction

"Hi, I'm Sue, and I'm a webmaster. I'd like to talk with you about the Internet, the web, and electronic commerce, things that touch our lives every day. I'd also like to talk with you about the role the Internet plays with Facebook, Google+, LinkedIn, Twitter, and cloud computing."

Want to communicate with a friend across town, in another state, or even in another country? Searching for a long-lost friend? Looking for travel or entertainment information? Perhaps you're researching a term paper or exploring different career paths. Where do you start? For these and other information-related activities, most people use the Internet and the web.

The Internet is an interconnected mesh of computers and data lines that connects millions of people and organizations. It is the foundation of the digital revolution and allows people around the world to share words, images, and any digital file almost instantaneously. The web provides an easy-to-use interface to Internet resources. It has become an everyday tool for all of us to use.

To efficiently and effectively use computers, you need to be aware of the resources available on the Internet and the web. Additionally, you need to know how to access these resources, to effectively communicate electronically, to efficiently locate information, to understand electronic commerce, and to use web utilities.

The Internet and the Web

The **Internet** was launched in 1969 when the United States funded a project that developed a national computer network called **Advanced Research Project Agency Network (ARPANET).** The Internet is a large network that connects together smaller networks all over the globe. The **web,** also known as the **World Wide Web** or **WWW,** was introduced in 1991. Prior to the web, the Internet was all text–no graphics, animations, sound, or video. The web made it possible to include these elements. It provided a multimedia interface to resources available on the Internet.

The first generation of the web, known as **Web 1.0,** focused on linking existing information. In this generation search programs, like Google Search, were created to provide links to websites containing specific words or phrases. In 2001, the second generation, **Web 2.0,** evolved to support more dynamic content creation and social interaction. Facebook is one of the best-known Web 2.0 applications. **Web 3.0** is the current generation. It focuses on applications that automatically prepare personalized content for users. For example, Google Now uses data from the web (e.g., an individual's calendar of planned activities, weather reports, traffic reports, etc.), searches for interrelationships among the data (e.g., the effect of weather and traffic on an individual's planned daily commute to work), and automatically presents relevant information to the user (e.g., sends an early morning message to the individual's smartphone regarding expected bad weather and/or traffic delays). See Figure 2-1.

It is easy to get the Internet and the web confused, but they are not the same thing. The Internet is the physical network. It is made up of wires, cables, satellites, and rules for exchanging information between computers connected to the network. Being connected to this network is often described as being **online.** The Internet connects millions of computers and resources throughout the world. The web is a multimedia interface to the resources available on the Internet. Every day over a billion users from

Figure 2-1 **Web 3.0 application**

nearly every country in the world use the Internet and the web. What are they doing? The most common uses are the following:

- **Communicating** is by far the most popular Internet activity. You can exchange e-mail, photos, and videos with your family and friends from almost anywhere in the world. You can locate old friends and make new friends. You can join and listen to discussions and debates on a wide variety of special-interest topics.
- **Shopping** is one of the fastest-growing Internet applications. You can window shop, look for the latest fashions, search for bargains, and make purchases.
- **Searching** for information has never been more convenient. You can access some of the world's largest libraries directly from your home computer. You can find the latest local, national, and international news.
- **Education** or **e-learning** is another rapidly emerging web application. You can take classes on almost any subject. There are courses just for fun, and there are courses for high school, college, and graduate school credit. Some cost nothing to take and others cost a lot.
- **Entertainment** options are nearly endless. You can find music, movies, magazines, and computer games. You will find live concerts, movie previews, book clubs, and interactive live games. To learn more about online entertainment, see Making IT Work for You: Online Entertainment on pages 30–31.

The first step to using the Internet and the web is to get connected, or to gain access to the Internet.

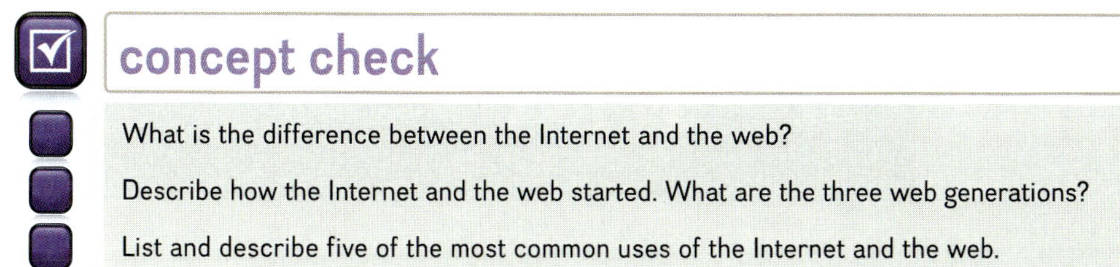

concept check

- What is the difference between the Internet and the web?
- Describe how the Internet and the web started. What are the three web generations?
- List and describe five of the most common uses of the Internet and the web.

ONLINE ENTERTAINMENT

Are you one of the millions of people who regularly use their computers to watch their favorite television programs, movies, and other video content? Many have "cut the cord" from their cable or satellite TV providers and have turned to online content. It's easy and convenient. Typically, the content is provided by a subscription or a pay-as-you-go service. Users watch the content on their TVs or their computers (including tablets and smartphones).

Subscription Services These services provide access to their library of videos for a fee. You can select and view as many of these videos as you want. Three of the most popular subscription services are Netflix, Hulu Plus, and Amazon Prime.

1 Hulu and Amazon Prime offer streaming access to their online movie and TV video libraries. Hulu is the only subscription streaming service that offers current season programming. Netflix offers the largest library of movies and TV programs for a low monthly fee. Amazon Prime, a newer service, provides similar content for an annual fee.

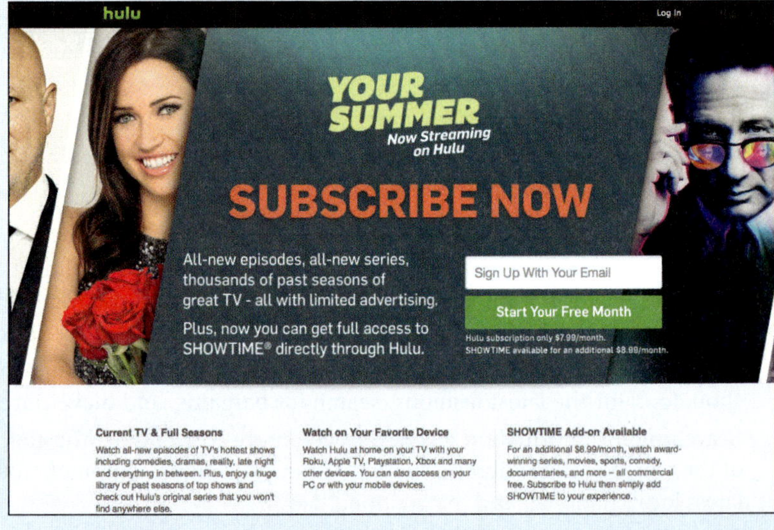

2 CNN, CBS News, and NBC offer live television content streamed directly to your computer for free.

3 Spotify and Pandora offer online access to large music libraries. These services offer free versions for desktop and laptop computers that include advertisements. For a small monthly fee, other versions are available that eliminate advertisements and provide additional access to smartphones and tablets.

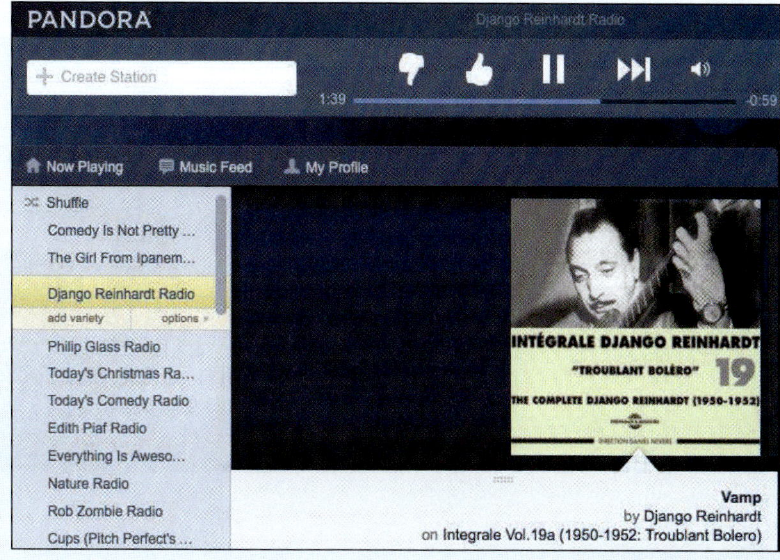

Pay-As-You-Go Services These services provide online access to specific titles in their libraries for a charge. Amazon, iTunes, and Vudu are just a few of the companies that let you rent or purchase movies and TV programs. Movie rentals cost only a few dollars and can be viewed several times over a 24-hour period. The price can increase by one or two dollars for HD quality.

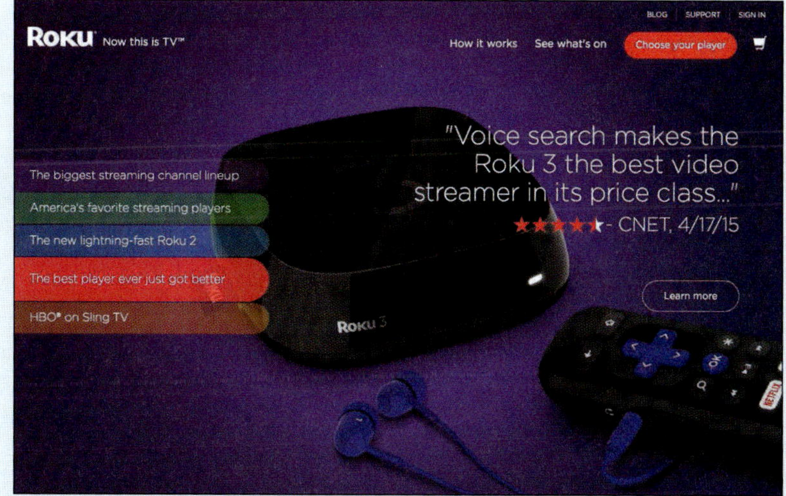

Viewing Video Content Many people own Internet-ready TVs that will directly accept content from the Internet. Most Blu-ray disc players and many gaming consoles also provide this access. You can also purchase specialized devices like Roku, which will connect TVs to many of the services listed above.

Many viewers use their computer and a browser to display the video content. Also, many services provide apps for tablet and smartphone viewing.

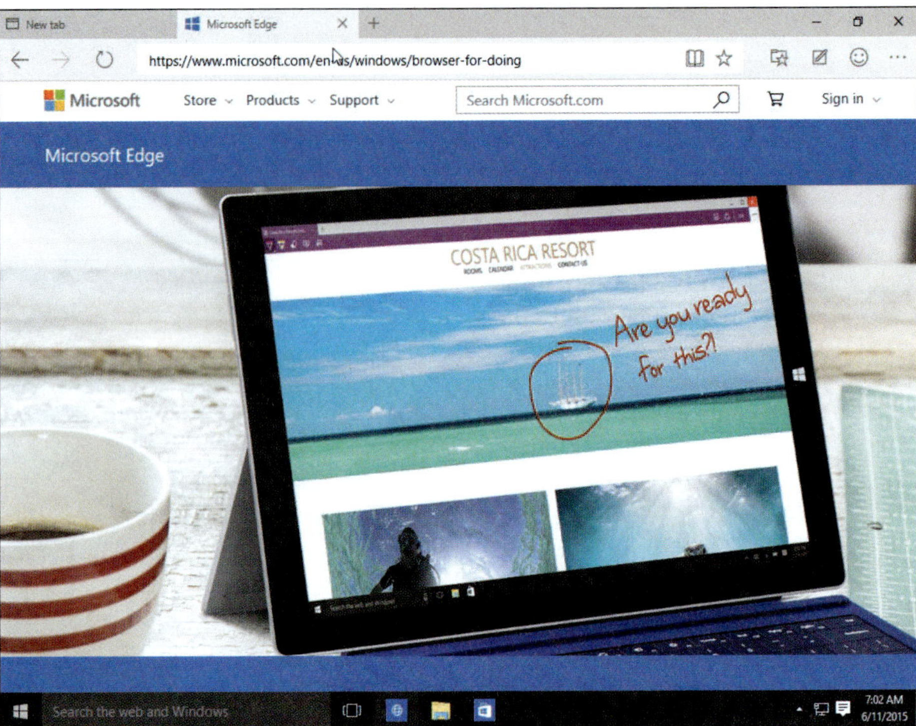

Figure 2-2 **Browser**

Internet Access

tips

Are you getting the most out of your web browser? Here are a few suggestions to make you faster and more efficient.

1. **Bookmarks/Favorites Bar:** Most browsers have a bookmarks or favorites bar just below the address bar. Add your top 5 or 10 most-often-visited websites here. The next time you want to visit one of these sites, select it from the bookmarks/favorites list rather than entering the site's URL.
2. **Shortcuts:** Keyboard shortcuts are often faster than using a mouse. Use the following: F5 (refresh); Alt + left arrow (back); Ctrl + T (new tab); Ctrl + W (close tab); Ctrl + Enter (adds "www" and ".com" to any domain name you type in the address bar).
3. **Extensions/Add-Ons:** Many browsers, such as Chrome and Firefox, allow users to install small, third-party programs that extend, or add to, the capabilities of the browser. These programs can perform a variety of tasks, from providing easy access to your cloud services to making it easier to capture information on a web page.
4. **Configure Settings:** All browsers have a settings or options page that provides many time-saving options. For example, you can set all the web pages that should open when you start your browser, or you can configure autocomplete options that help you to quickly fill out web forms.

The Internet and the telephone system are similar—you can connect a computer to the Internet much like you connect a phone to the telephone system. Once you are on the Internet, your computer becomes an extension of what seems like a giant computer—a computer that branches all over the world. When provided with a connection to the Internet, you can use a browser program to search the web.

Providers

The most common way to access the Internet is through an **Internet service provider (ISP).** The providers are already connected to the Internet and provide a path or connection for individuals to access the Internet.

The most widely used commercial Internet service providers use telephone lines, cable, and/or wireless connections. Some of the best-known providers in the United States are AT&T, Comcast, Sprint, T-Mobile, and Verizon.

As we will discuss in Chapter 8, users connect to ISPs using one of a variety of connection technologies including **DSL, cable,** and **wireless modems.**

Browsers

Browsers are programs that provide access to web resources. This software connects you to remote computers; opens and transfers files; displays text, images, and multimedia; and provides in one tool an uncomplicated interface to the Internet and web documents. Four well-known browsers are Apple Safari, Google Chrome, Microsoft Edge, and Mozilla Firefox. (See Figure 2-2.)

For browsers to connect to resources, the **location** or **address** of the resources must be specified. These addresses are called **uniform resource locators (URLs).** All URLs have at least two basic parts.

Figure 2-3 **Basic parts of a URL**

- The first part presents the protocol used to connect to the resource. As we will discuss in Chapter 8, **protocols** are rules for exchanging data between computers. The protocol *https* is used for web traffic and is one of the most widely used Internet protocols.
- The second part presents the **domain name.** It indicates the specific address where the resource is located. In Figure 2-3 the domain is identified as www.mtv.com. The last part of the domain name following the dot (.) is the **top-level domain (TLD).** Also known as the **web suffix,** it typically identifies the type of organization. For example, *.com* indicates a commercial site. (See Figure 2-4.)

Domain	Type
.com	Commercial
.edu	Educational
.gov	Government
.mil	U.S. military
.net	Network
.org	Organization

Figure 2-4 **Traditional top-level domains**

Once the browser has connected to the website, a document file is sent back to your computer. This document typically contains **Hypertext Markup Language (HTML),** a markup language for displaying web pages. The browser interprets the HTML formatting instructions and displays the document as a **web page.** For example, when your browser first connects to the Internet, it opens up to a web page specified in the browser settings. Web pages present information about the site along with references and **hyperlinks** or **links** that connect to other documents containing related information—text files, graphic images, audio, and video clips.

There are various technologies used to provide highly interactive and animated websites. These technologies include

- **Cascading style sheets (CSS)** are separate files referenced by or lines inserted into an HTML document that control the appearance of a web page. CSS help ensure that related web pages have a consistent presentation or look. Netflix uses CSS to visually connect all its web pages.
- **JavaScript** is a language often used within HTML documents to trigger interactive features, such as opening new browser windows and checking information entered in online forms. The Microsoft search engine Bing.com uses JavaScript to make its website more interactive and to assist its users by auto-filling search requests as they type content into the search box.
- **AJAX,** an advanced use of JavaScript, is used to create interactive websites that respond quickly. Google Maps uses AJAX to make the maps fast loading, dynamic, and interactive.
- **Applets** are programs that can be downloaded quickly and run by most browsers. They are used to display graphics, provide interactive games, and much more. For example, many of the online games at Yahoo! Games are JAVA applets.

Today it is common to access the Internet from a variety of mobile devices like smartphones and tablets. Special browsers called **mobile browsers** are designed to run on these portable devices. Unlike a traditional web browser that is typically displayed on a large screen, a mobile browser is displayed on a very small screen, and special navigational tools are required to conveniently view web content. The Apple iPhone, for example, enables you to "pinch" or "stretch" the screen with two fingers to zoom web content in and out. (See Figure 2-5.)

Figure 2-5 **Zoom web content**

concept check

What is the function of an ISP, a browser, and a mobile browser?

What are URLs, HTML, web pages, hyperlinks, CSS, JavaScript, AJAX, and applets?

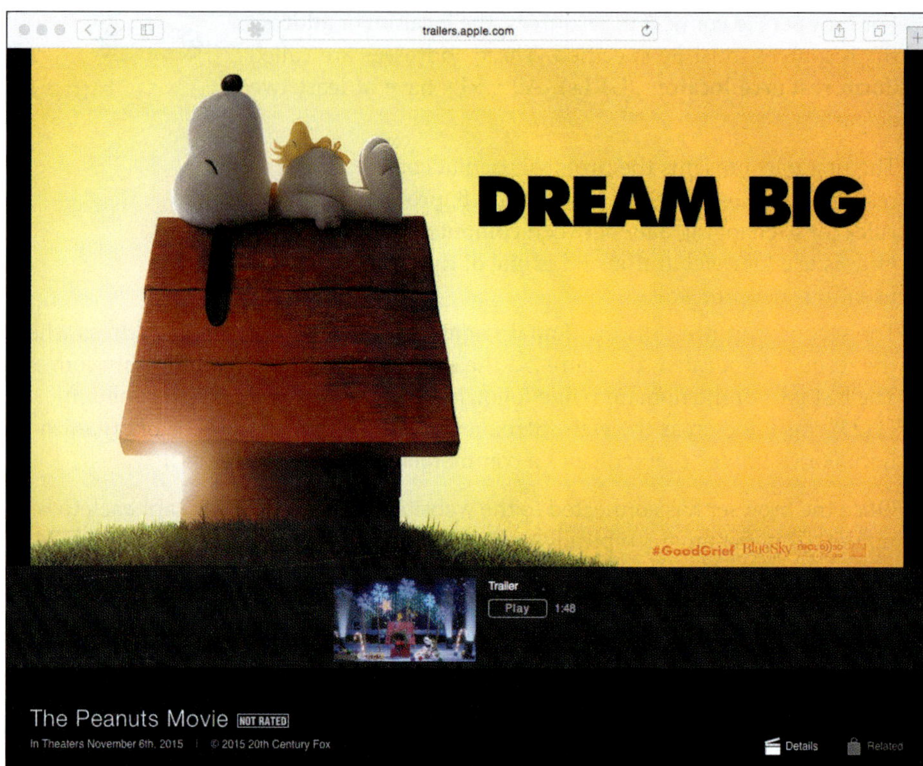

Figure 2-6 QuickTime movie at Apple.com

Web Utilities

Utilities are programs that make computing easier. **Web utilities** are specialized utility programs that make using the Internet and the web easier and safer. Some of these utilities are browser-related programs that either become part of your browser or are executed from your browser. Others are designed to protect children from dangerous and inappropriate website material. File transfer utilities allow you to efficiently copy files to and from your computer across the Internet. Internet security suites enhance security and privacy.

Plug-ins

Plug-ins are programs that are automatically started and operate as a part of your browser. Many websites require you to have one or more plug-ins to fully experience their content. Some widely used plug-ins include

- Acrobat Reader from Adobe—for viewing and printing a variety of standard forms and other documents saved in a special format called PDF.
- Flash Player from Adobe—for viewing videos, animations, and other media.
- QuickTime from Apple—for playing audio and video files. (See Figure 2-6.)
- Windows Media Player from Microsoft—for playing audio files, video files, and much more.

Some of these utilities are included in many of today's browsers and operating systems. Others must be installed before they can be used by your browser. To learn more about plug-ins and how to download them, visit some of the sites listed in Figure 2-7.

Plug-in	Source
Reader	get.adobe.com/reader
Flash Player	get.adobe.com/flashplayer
QuickTime	www.apple.com/quicktime
Silverlight	www.microsoft.com/silverlight

Figure 2-7 Plug-in sites

Filters

Filters block access to selected sites. The Internet is an interesting and multifaceted arena. But not all aspects of the Internet are appropriate for all audiences. Parents, in

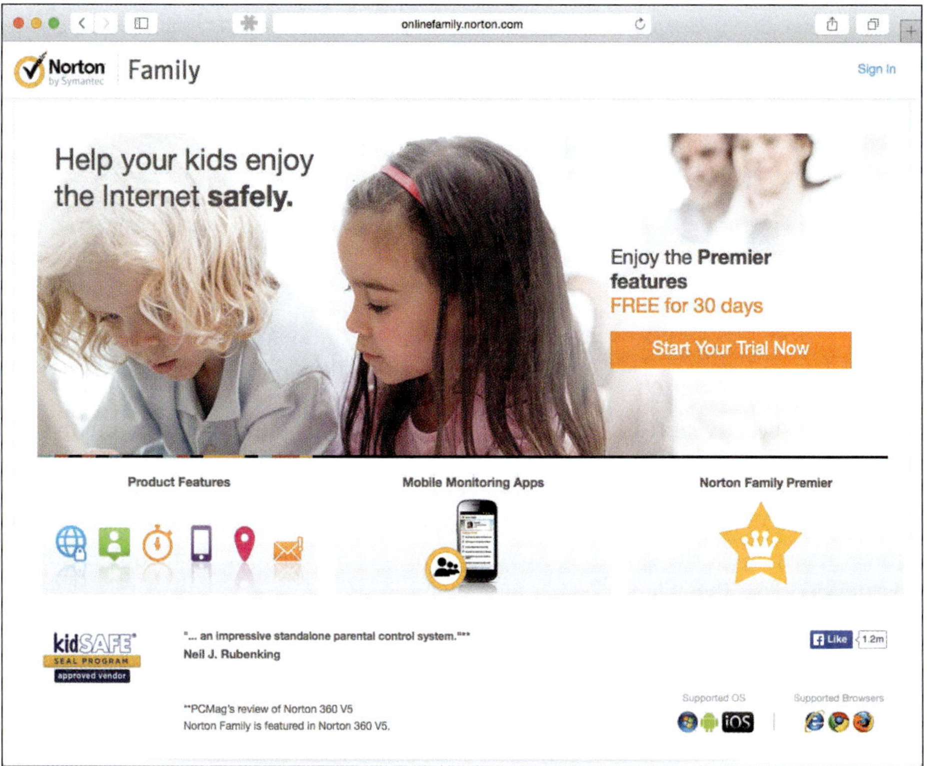

Figure 2-8 **Norton Online Family is a web filter**

particular, are concerned about children roaming unrestricted across the Internet. Filter programs allow parents as well as organizations to block out selected sites and set time limits. (See Figure 2-8.) Additionally, these programs can monitor use and generate reports detailing the total time spent on the Internet and the time spent at individual websites. For a list of some of the best-known filters, see Figure 2-9.

Filter	Site
Net Nanny	www.netnanny.com
Qustodio Parental Control	www.qustodio.com
AVG Family Safety	familysafety.avg.com
Norton Online Family	onlinefamily.norton.com
McAfee Family Protection	www.mcafeefamilyprotection.com

Figure 2-9 **Filters**

File Transfer Utilities

Using file transfer utility software, you can copy files to your computer from specially configured servers. This is called **downloading.** You also can use file transfer utility software to copy files from your computer to another computer on the Internet. This is called **uploading.** Three popular types of file transfer are FTP, web-based, and BitTorrent.

- **File transfer protocol (FTP)** and **secure file transfer protocol (SFTP)** allow you to efficiently copy files to and from your computer across the Internet, and are frequently used for uploading changes to a website hosted by an Internet service provider. FTP has been used for decades and still remains one of the most popular methods of file transfer.
- **Web-based file transfer services** make use of a web browser to upload and download files. This eliminates the need for any custom software to be installed. A popular web-based file transfer service is Dropbox.com.
- **BitTorrent** distributes file transfers across many different computers for more efficient downloads, unlike other transfer technologies whereby a file is copied from one computer on the Internet to another. A single file might be located on dozens of individual computers. When you download the file, each computer sends you a tiny piece of the larger file, making BitTorrent well suited for transferring very large files. Unfortunately, BitTorrent technology often has been used for distributing unauthorized copies of copyrighted music and video. For a summary of web utilities, see Figure 2-10.

ethics

Most agree that it is ethical and prudent to shield young children from violent or sexual Internet content by using software that filters such content. Some parents of older children have installed computer monitoring software that records all their children's Internet activity. They believe this is warranted because they need to know what their kids are doing online. Do you believe it is ethical of parents to do this?

Web Utility	Description
Plug-ins	Automatically start and operate as part of browser
Filters	Block access to selected sites and set time limits
File transfer	Upload and download files from servers
Internet security suite	Collection of utility programs for security and privacy

Figure 2-10 **Web utilities**

Internet Security Suites

An **Internet security suite** is a collection of utility programs designed to maintain your security and privacy while you are on the web. These programs control spam, protect against computer viruses, provide filters, and much more. You could buy each program separately; however, the cost of the suite is typically much less. Two of the best-known Internet security suites are McAfee's Internet Security and Symantec's Norton Internet Security. (See Figure 2-11.)

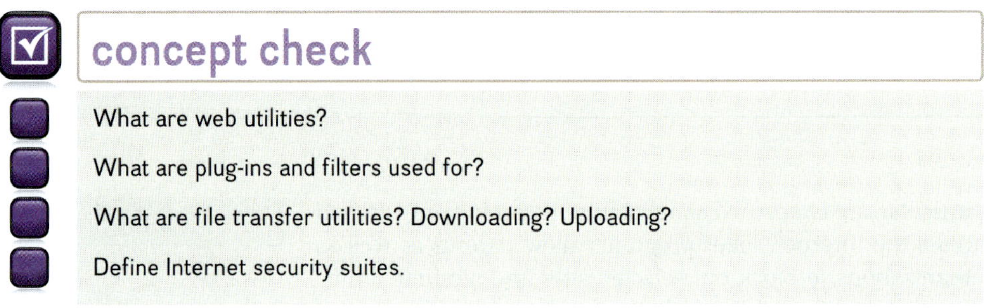

concept check

- What are web utilities?
- What are plug-ins and filters used for?
- What are file transfer utilities? Downloading? Uploading?
- Define Internet security suites.

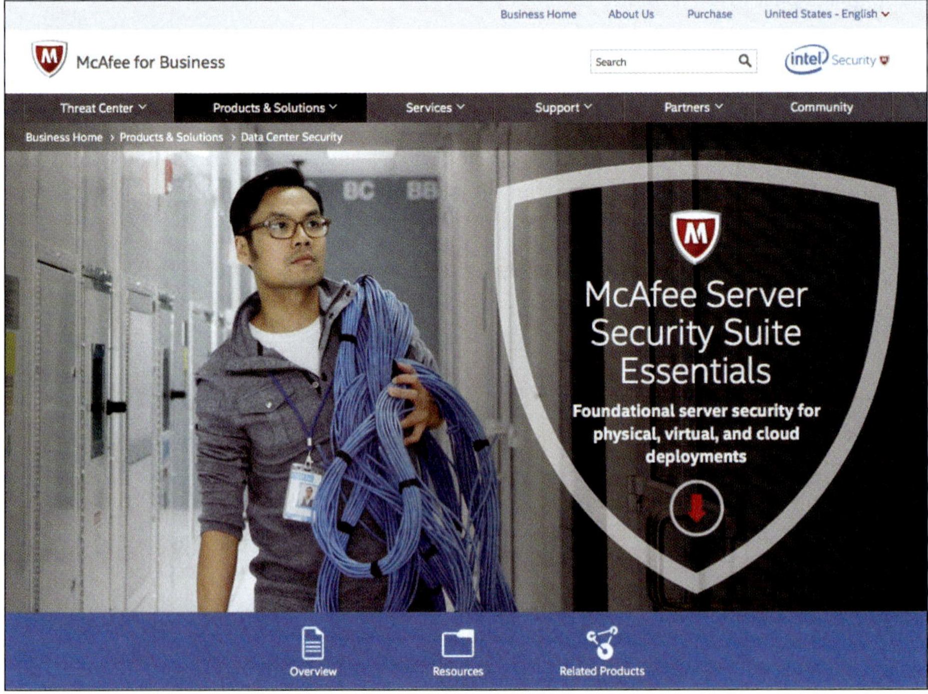

Figure 2-11 **Security suite**

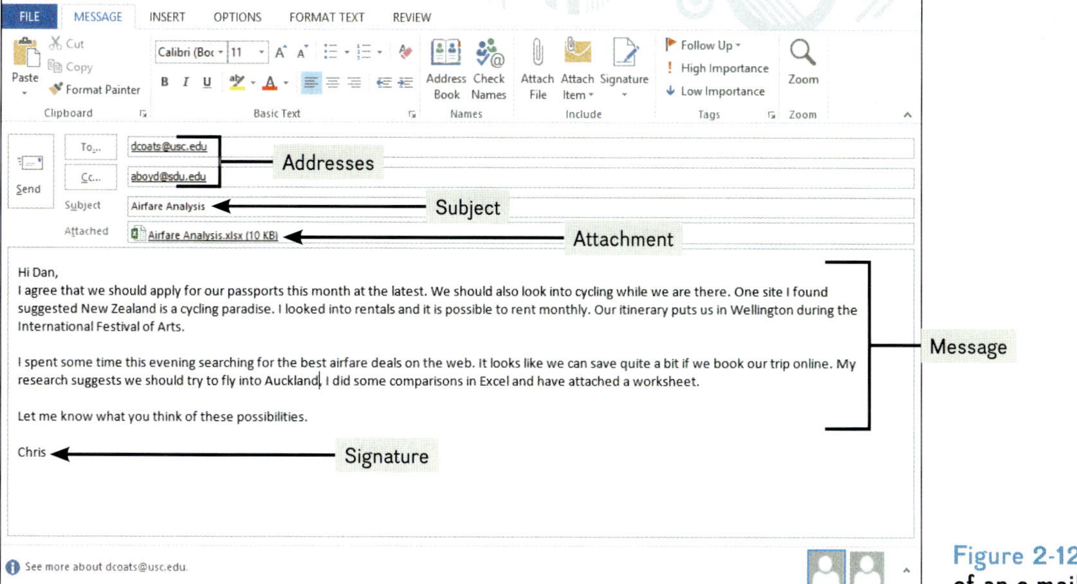

Figure 2-12 Basic elements of an e-mail message

Communication

As previously mentioned, communication is the most popular Internet activity, and its impact cannot be overestimated. At a personal level, friends and family can stay in contact with one another even when separated by thousands of miles. At a business level, electronic communication has become a standard way to stay in touch with suppliers, employees, and customers. Some popular types of Internet communication are e-mail, messaging, social networking, blogs, microblogs, webcasts, podcasts, and wikis.

> **environment**
>
> Did you know that using e-mail is good for the environment? Writing letters and attaching files using e-mail reduce the amount of paper sent via postal mail. In addition, managing your financial and utilities accounts on the web is also healthy for the environment as it reduces the amount of paper bills you receive at home.

E-mail

E-mail or **electronic mail** is the transmission of electronic messages over the Internet. A typical e-mail message has three basic elements: header, message, and signature. (See Figure 2-12.) The **header** appears first and typically includes the following information:

- **Addresses:** E-mail messages typically display the addresses of the person or persons to whom the e-mail is sent. The e-mail message in Figure 2-12 is to dcoats@usc.edu, with a copy sent to aboyd@sdu.edu. E-mail addresses have two basic parts. (See Figure 2-13.) The first part is the user's name and the second part is the domain name, which includes the top-level domain. In our example e-mail, *dcoats* is Dan's user name. The server providing e-mail service for Dan is *usc.edu*. The top-level domain indicates that the provider is an educational institution.
- **Subject:** A one-line description, used to present the topic of the message. Subject lines typically are displayed when a person checks his or her mailbox.
- **Attachments:** Many e-mail programs allow you to attach files such as documents and images. If a message has an attachment, the file name typically appears on the attachment line.

Figure 2-13 Two parts of an e-mail address

The letter or **message** comes next. Finally, the **signature** identifies the sender. This information may include the sender's name, address, and telephone number. For many business communications, the signature also includes the sender's company name, address, and telephone number.

There are two basic types of e-mail systems: client-based and web-based.

- **Client-based e-mail systems** require a special program known as an **e-mail client** to be installed on your computer. Before you can begin e-mailing, you need to run the e-mail client from your computer, which communicates with the e-mail service provider. Two of the most widely used e-mail clients are Apple's Mail and Microsoft's Outlook.
- **Web-based e-mail systems** do not require an e-mail program to be installed on your computer. Once your computer's browser connects to an e-mail service provider, a special program called a **webmail client** is run on the e-mail provider's computer and then you can begin e-mailing. This is known as **webmail.** Most Internet service providers offer webmail services. Three free webmail service providers are Google's Gmail, Microsoft's Hotmail, and Yahoo!'s Yahoo!Mail.

For individual use, webmail is more widely used because it frees the user from installing and maintaining an e-mail client on every computer used to access e-mail. With webmail, you can access your e-mail from any computer anywhere that has Internet access.

E-mail can be a valuable asset in your personal and professional life. However, like many other valuable technologies, there are drawbacks too. Americans receive billions of unwanted and unsolicited e-mails every year. This unwelcome mail is called **spam.** While spam is indeed a distraction and nuisance, it also can be dangerous. For example, computer **viruses** or destructive programs are often attached to unsolicited e-mail. Computer viruses and ways to protect against them will be discussed in Chapter 4.

In an attempt to control spam, antispam laws have been added to our legal system. For example, CAN-SPAM requires that every marketing-related e-mail provide an opt-out option. When the option is selected, the recipient's e-mail address is to be removed from future mailing lists. Failure to do so results in heavy fines. This approach, however, has had minimal impact since over 50 percent of all spam originates from servers outside the United States. A more effective approach to controlling spam has been the development and use of **spam blockers,** also known as **spam filters.** Most e-mail programs provide limited spam-blocking capabilities. Additionally, powerful specialized spam-blocking programs are available. Many of these programs are free, including SPAMfighter and Intego Personal Antispam for Mac.

tips **Are you tired of sorting through an inbox full of spam? Here are a few spam-reducing suggestions:**

1. **Keep a low profile.** Many spammers collect e-mail addresses from personal web pages, social networking sites, and message boards. Be cautious when posting your address.
2. **Use caution when giving out your address.** Many companies collect and sell e-mail addresses to spammers. Be sure to read the privacy policy of a site before providing your address.
3. **Don't ever respond to spam.** Many are a trick to validate active e-mail addresses. These addresses are worth more to spammers, who then sell the addresses to other spammers.
4. **Use antispam and filter options.** Most e-mail programs and web-based e-mail services have antispam and filter options that can be configured. Use them.

Messaging

While e-mail was one of the first and is one of the most popular electronic messaging systems, other messaging systems have followed. Two of the best known are text messaging and instant messaging.

- **Text messaging,** also known as **texting** or **SMS (short message service),** is the process of sending a short electronic message, typically less than 160 characters, using a wireless network to another person, who views the message on a mobile device such as a smartphone. Today, billions of people send text messages every day. It has become one of the most widely used ways to send very short messages from one individual to another. While text messaging was originally limited to characters, you can now send images, video, and sound using a variation of SMS known as **MMS (Multimedia Messaging Service).** Although popular and convenient, there are downsides to using this technology in the wrong context. A great

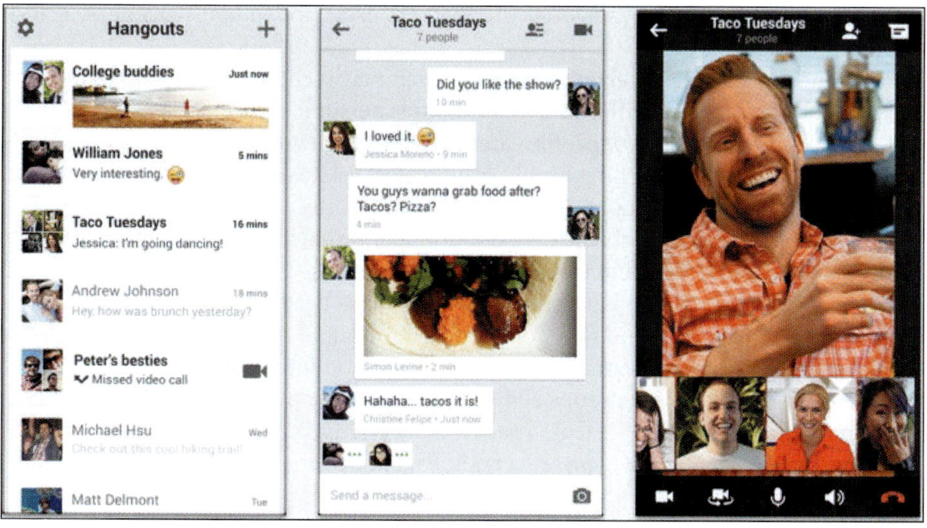

Figure 2-14 **Instant messaging**

deal of attention has been directed toward texting while driving. A study by *Car and Driver* concluded that texting while driving had a greater negative impact on driver safety than being drunk. Several states have passed laws prohibiting texting while driving.

- **Instant messaging (IM)** allows two or more people to contact each other via direct, live communication. (See Figure 2-14.) To use instant messaging, you register with an instant messaging service, such as Facebook or Google+, and then specify a list of **friends.** Whenever you connect to the Internet, your IM service is notified. It then notifies you of all your friends who are available to chat and notifies your friends who are online that you are available. You can then send messages directly back and forth to one another. Most instant messaging programs also include video conferencing features, file sharing, and remote assistance. Many businesses routinely use these instant messaging features. Two of the most popular instant messaging services are Facebook Messenger and Google Hangouts.

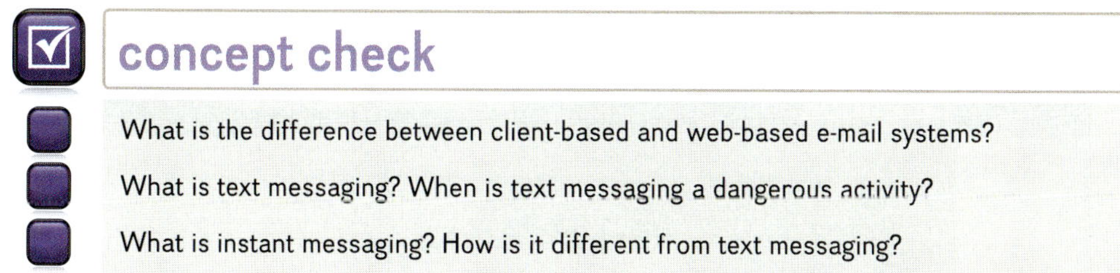

concept check

- What is the difference between client-based and web-based e-mail systems?
- What is text messaging? When is text messaging a dangerous activity?
- What is instant messaging? How is it different from text messaging?

Social Networking

Social networking is one of the fastest-growing and most significant Web 2.0 applications. Social networking sites focus on connecting people and organizations that share a common interest or activity. These sites typically provide a wide array of tools that facilitate meeting, communicating, and sharing. There are hundreds of social networking sites. Three of the best known are Facebook, Google+, and LinkedIn.

- **Facebook** was initially launched by a student at Harvard University for college students in 2004. By 2008 it was the most widely used social networking site. It now has a billion users worldwide. Facebook provides a wide array of features and applications including instant messaging, photo and video sharing, games, and much more.

privacy

Have you ever seen one of those funny or not-so-funny embarrassing personal videos on the Internet? Unless you are careful, you could be starring in one of those videos. Without privacy settings, images and videos posted to these sites can be viewed and potentially reposted for all to see. If a social networking friend were to post an embarrassing video of you to Facebook, would all your friends be able to see it? What about parents, teachers, or potential employers? To check your Facebook privacy settings, go to Facebook and click on the security lock icon.

There are three basic categories of Facebook users: individuals, businesses, and communities.

Individuals create **Facebook Profiles,** which may include photos, lists of personal interests, contact information, and other personal information. (See Figure 2-15.) In general, these profiles are available to friends, family members, and others who may be searching for old friends, lost relatives, or people who share a common interest. Facebook profiles are easy to create and to update.

Businesses create **Facebook Pages** to promote products and services. Public figures such as politicians and entertainers frequently use Facebook Pages to connect to their constituents and fans. Facebook Pages have become a standard way for promoters, musicians, and other celebrities to promote themselves.

Communities of individuals who share a common interest often create **Facebook groups.** These groups allow a number of people to come together online to share information and discuss specific subjects. Typically, groups are organized around topics, events, or ideas. Facebook Pages are widely used by clubs and political organizations to coordinate activities and share information.

- **Google+** also known as **Google Plus,** was launched in 2011. It is a combination of some of Google Inc.'s previously existing services with some new services. These new services include **Circles** for grouping individuals according to common interests or other criteria and **Hangouts** for communicating with up to 10 people at a time.

  Facebook and Google+ offer similar services. Facebook has been around longer and has many more users. Google+, however, offers integration with other Google services including Google Docs, Chat, and Calendar.
- **LinkedIn** started in 2003 and has become the premier business-oriented social networking site. Although not nearly as large as Facebook or Google+, it is the largest social networking site focusing on business professionals. It has well over 100 million users. LinkedIn provides tools to maintain business contacts, develop extended business networks, research individual businesses, search for job opportunities, and more.

There are many social networking sites, each with its own unique features and interactions. For a list of some of the most popular sites, see Figure 2-16.

Figure 2-15 **Facebook Profile**

Blogs, Microblogs, Webcasts, Podcasts, and Wikis

In addition to social networking sites, there are other Web 2.0 applications that help ordinary people communicate across the web including blogs, microblogs, webcasts, podcasts, and wikis. These communication alternatives offer greater flexibility and security; however, they are often more complex to set up and maintain.

Many individuals create personal websites, called **blogs** or **web logs,** to keep in touch with friends and family. Blog postings are time-stamped and arranged with the newest item first. Often, readers of these sites are allowed to comment. Some blogs are like online diaries with personal information; others focus on information about a hobby or theme, such as knitting, electronic devices, or good books. Although most are written by individual bloggers, there are also group blogs with multiple contributors. Some businesses and newspapers also have started blogging as a quick publishing method. Several sites provide tools to create blogs. Two of the most widely used are Blogger and WordPress. (See Figure 2-17.)

Organization	Site
Facebook	www.facebook.com
Google+	plus.google.com
LinkedIn	www.linkedin.com
Instagram	www.instagram.com
Pinterest	www.pinterest.com
Tumblr	www.tumblr.com
Vine	www.vine.com

Figure 2-16 **Social networking sites**

A **microblog** publishes short sentences that take only a few seconds to write, rather than long stories or posts like a traditional blog. Microblogs are designed to keep friends and other contacts up to date on your interests and activities. The most popular microblogging site, **Twitter,** enables you to add new content from your browser, instant messaging application, or even a mobile phone. Over 250 active users send over 500 million Twitter messages, also known as **tweets,** each day.

Both webcasts and podcasts deliver media content such as music and movies over the Internet to your computer. **Webcasts** use **streaming** technology in which audio and video files are continuously downloaded to your computer while you are listening to and/or viewing the file content. After a webcast has been completed, there are no files remaining on your computer. Webcasts typically broadcast live events. For

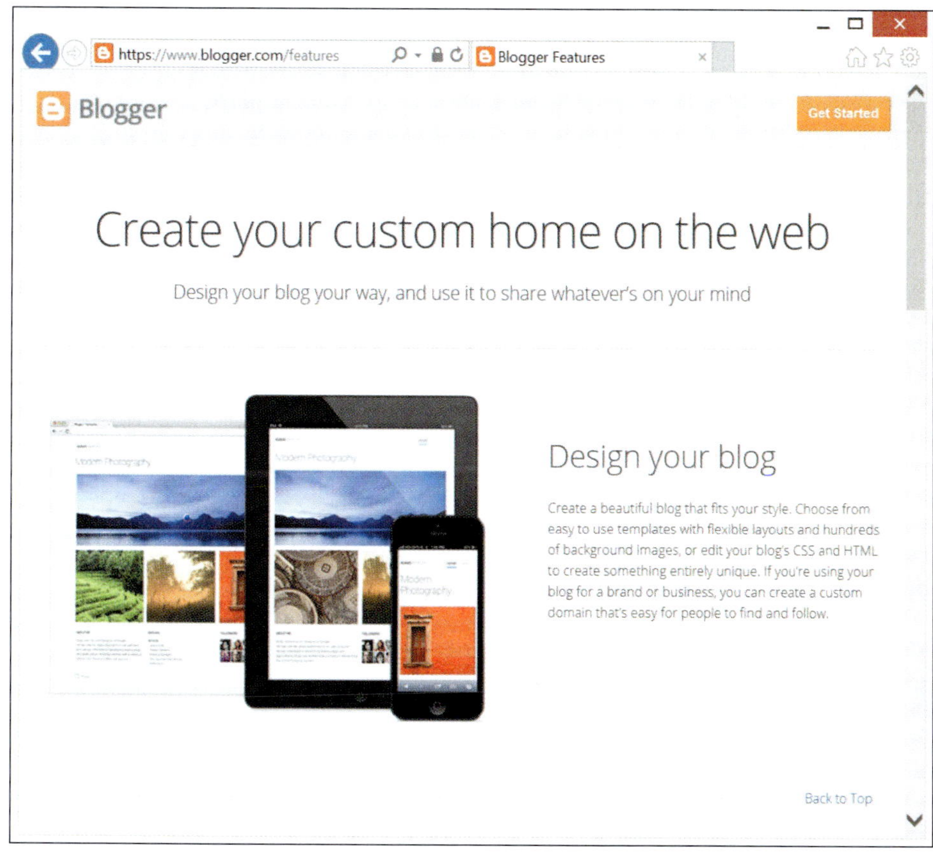

Figure 2-17 **Blog creation site**

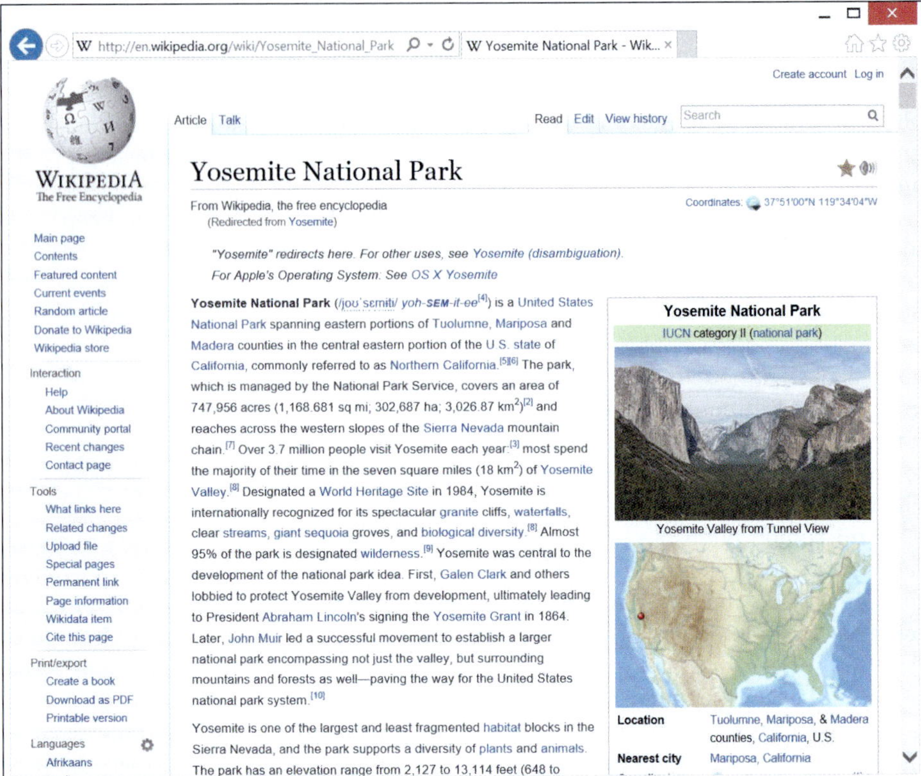

Figure 2-18 **Wikipedia**

example, the popular website YouTube.com as well as other sites routinely webcast live movie premiers and sporting events.

Podcasts do not use streaming technology. Before a podcast can be run, the media files have to be downloaded and saved to your computer. Once downloaded, the files can be run to listen to music or watch a movie as often as you would like. The media files can also be transferred from your computer to a media player such as an iPod. Podcasts are widely used to download music, tutorials, and educational training.

A **wiki** is a website specially designed to allow visitors to use their browser to add, edit, or delete the site's content. "Wiki" comes from the Hawaiian word for *fast,* which describes the simplicity of editing and publishing through wiki software. Wikis support collaborative writing in which there isn't a single expert author, but rather a community of interested people that builds knowledge over time. Perhaps the most famous example is **Wikipedia,** an online encyclopedia, written and edited by anyone who wants to contribute, that has millions of entries in over 20 languages. (See Figure 2-18.)

Creating blogs and wikis are examples of web authoring. We will discuss web authoring software in detail in Chapter 3.

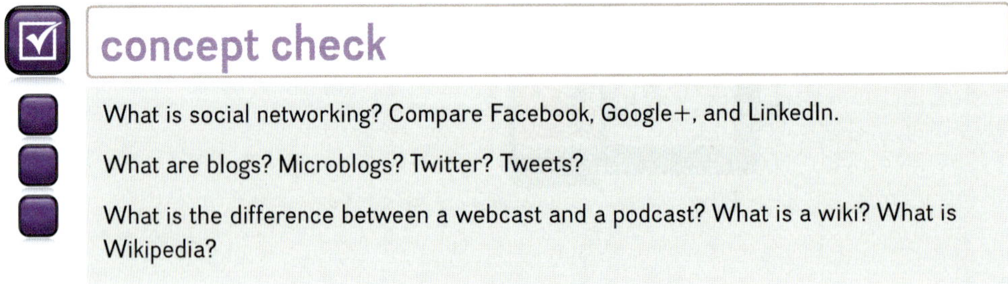

concept check

- What is social networking? Compare Facebook, Google+, and LinkedIn.
- What are blogs? Microblogs? Twitter? Tweets?
- What is the difference between a webcast and a podcast? What is a wiki? What is Wikipedia?

Search Tools

The web can be an incredible resource, providing information on nearly any topic imaginable. Are you interested in music? Writing a paper on the environment? Looking for a movie review? Trying to locate a long-lost friend? Information sources related to these questions, and much, much more, are available on the web.

With over 20 billion pages and more being added daily, the web is a massive collection of interrelated pages. With so much available information, locating the precise information you need can be difficult. Fortunately, a number of organizations called **search services** operate websites that can help you locate the information you need.

Search services maintain huge databases relating to information provided on the web and the Internet. The information stored at these databases includes addresses, content descriptions or classifications, and keywords appearing on web pages and other Internet informational resources. Special programs called **spiders** continually look for new information and update the search services' databases. Additionally, search services provide special programs called *search engines* that you can use to locate specific information on the web.

Search Engines

Search engines are specialized programs that assist you in locating information on the web and the Internet. To find information, you go to a search service's website and use its search engine. See Figure 2-19 for a list of commonly used search engines.

To use a search website, you enter a keyword or phrase reflecting the information you want. The search engine compares your entry against its database and returns a list of **hits,** or sites that contain the keywords. Each hit includes a link to the referenced web page (or other resource) along with a brief discussion of the information contained at that location. Many searches result in a large number of hits. For example, if you were to enter the keyword *music,* you would get billions of hits. Search engines order the hits according to those sites that most likely contain the information requested and present the list to you in that order, usually in groups of 10.

Since each search service maintains its own database, the hits returned by one search engine will not necessarily be the same hits returned by another search engine. Therefore, when researching a topic, it is best to use more than one search engine.

Search Service	Site
Bing	www.bing.com
Duckduckgo	www.duckduckgo.com
Google	www.google.com
Yahoo!	www.yahoo.com

Figure 2-19 **Search engines**

Specialized Search Engines

Specialized search engines focus on subject-specific websites. Specialized sites can potentially save you time by narrowing your search. For a list of just a few selected specialized search engines, see Figure 2-20. For example, let's say you are researching a paper about the environment. You could begin with a general search engine like Google. Or you could go to a search engine that specializes specifically on the environment, such as www.ecoearth.info.

To locate other specialized search engines, use a search service and enter the topic area followed by *specialized search engine.* For example, entering *sports specialized search engine* will return several search engines dedicated specifically to sports information.

Topic	Site
Cooking	www.recipebridge.com
Research	scholar.google.com
Fashion	www.shopstyle.com
History	www.historynet.com
Law	www.findlaw.com
Medicine	www.webmd.com

Figure 2-20 **Selected specialized search engines**

Content Evaluation

Search engines are excellent tools to locate information on the web. Be careful, however, how you use the information you find. Unlike most published material found in newspapers, journals, and textbooks, not all the information you find on the web has been subjected to strict guidelines to ensure accuracy. In fact, anyone can publish content on the web. Many sites, such as Wikipedia.org, allow anyone to post new material, sometimes anonymously and without critical evaluation.

To evaluate the accuracy of information you find on the web, consider the following:

- **Authority.** Is the author an expert in the subject area? Is the site an official site for the information presented, or is the site an individual's personal website?
- **Accuracy.** Has the information been critically reviewed for correctness prior to posting on the web? Does the website provide a method to report inaccurate information to the author?
- **Objectivity.** Is the information factually reported, or does the author have a bias? Does the author appear to have a personal agenda aimed at convincing or changing the reader's opinion?
- **Currency.** Is the information up to date? Does the site specify the date when the site was updated? Are the site's links operational? If not, the site is most likely not being actively maintained.

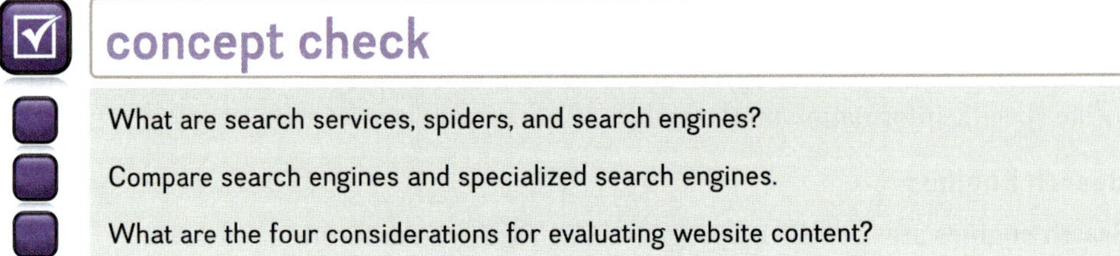

concept check

What are search services, spiders, and search engines?

Compare search engines and specialized search engines.

What are the four considerations for evaluating website content?

Electronic Commerce

Electronic commerce, also known as **e-commerce,** is the buying and selling of goods over the Internet. Electronic commerce is fast-growing and widely used in part because it provides incentives for both buyers and sellers. From the buyer's perspective, goods and services can be purchased at any time of day or night from any location that has an Internet connection. From the seller's perspective, the costs associated with owning and operating a retail outlet can be eliminated. Another advantage is reduced inventory. Traditional stores maintain an inventory of goods in their stores and periodically replenish this inventory from warehouses. With e-commerce, there is no in-store inventory and products are shipped directly from warehouses.

While there are numerous advantages to e-commerce, there are disadvantages as well. Some of these disadvantages include the inability to provide immediate delivery of goods, the inability to "try on" prospective purchases, and questions relating to the security of online payments. Although these issues are being addressed, very few observers suggest that e-commerce will replace bricks-and-mortar businesses entirely. It is clear that both will coexist and that e-commerce will continue to grow.

Just like any other type of commerce, electronic commerce involves two parties: businesses and consumers. There are three basic types of electronic commerce:

- **Business-to-consumer (B2C)** commerce involves the sale of a product or service to the general public or end users. It is the fastest-growing type of e-commerce. Whether large or small, nearly every existing corporation in the United States provides some type of B2C support as another means to connect to customers. Because extensive investments are not required to create traditional retail outlets and to maintain large marketing and sales staffs, e-commerce allows start-up companies to compete with larger established firms. The three most widely used B2C applications are for online banking, financial trading, and shopping. Amazon.com is one of the most widely used B2C sites.
- **Consumer-to-consumer (C2C)** commerce involves individuals selling to individuals. C2C often takes the form of an electronic version of the classified ads or an auction. **Web auctions** are similar to traditional auctions except that buyers and sellers seldom, if ever, meet face to face. Sellers post descriptions of products at a website, and buyers

submit bids electronically. Like traditional auctions, sometimes the bidding becomes highly competitive and enthusiastic. One of the most widely used auction sites is eBay.com. For a list of some of the most popular web auction sites, see Figure 2-21.

- **Business-to-business (B2B)** commerce involves the sale of a product or service from one business to another. This is typically a manufacturer-supplier relationship. For example, a furniture manufacturer requires raw materials such as wood, paint, and varnish.

Organization	Site
QuiBids	www.quibids.com
eBay	www.ebay.com
uBid	www.ubid.com

Figure 2-21 **Auction sites**

concept check

- What is electronic commerce?
- What are some of the advantages and disadvantages of electonic commerce?
- What are some of the differences among B2C, C2C, and B2B?

Security

The two greatest challenges for e-commerce are (1) developing fast, secure, and reliable payment methods for purchased goods and (2) providing convenient ways to submit required information such as mailing addresses and credit card information.

The two basic payment options are by credit card and by digital cash:

- Credit card purchases are faster and more convenient than check purchases. Credit card fraud, however, is a major concern for both buyers and sellers. We will discuss this and other privacy and security issues related to the Internet in Chapter 9.
- **Digital cash** is the Internet's equivalent to traditional cash. Buyers purchase digital cash from a third party (a bank that specializes in electronic currency) and use it to purchase goods. (See Figure 2-22.) Sellers convert the digital cash to traditional currency through the third party. Although not as convenient as credit card purchases, digital cash is more secure. For a list of digital cash providers, see Figure 2-23.

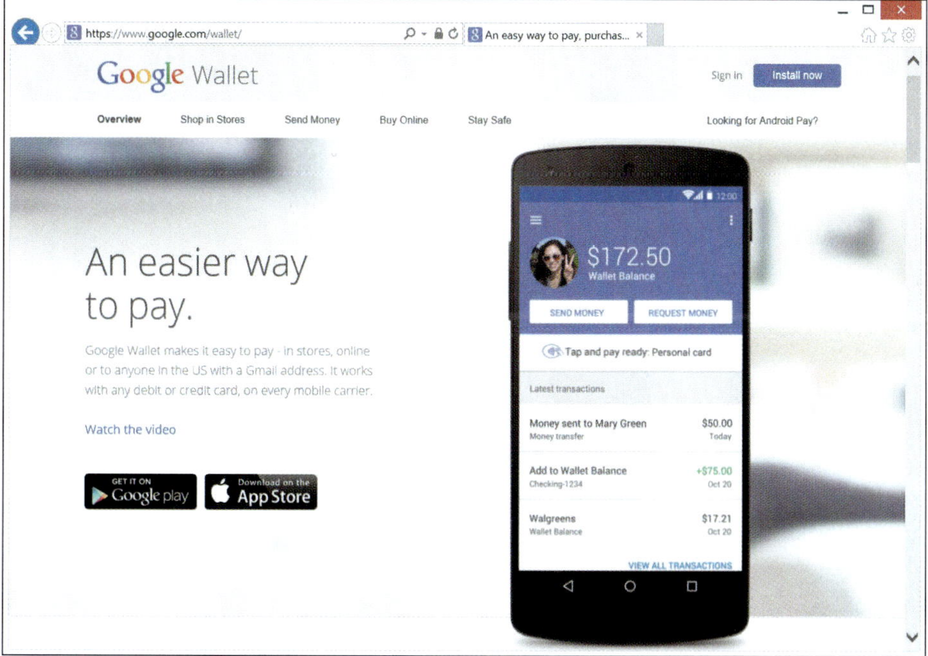

Figure 2-22 **Google Wallet offers digital cash**

Organization	Site
Amazon	payments.amazon.com
Google	wallet.google.com
Serve	www.serve.com
PayPal	www.paypal.com

Figure 2-23 **Digital cash providers**

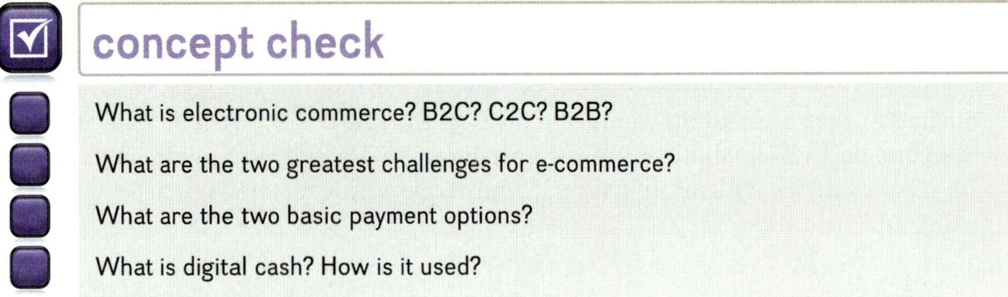

concept check

- What is electronic commerce? B2C? C2C? B2B?
- What are the two greatest challenges for e-commerce?
- What are the two basic payment options?
- What is digital cash? How is it used?

Cloud Computing

Typically, application programs are owned by individuals or organizations and stored on their computer system's hard disks. As discussed in Chapter 1, **cloud computing** uses the Internet and the web to shift many of these computer activities from the user's computer to other computers on the Internet.

While some suggest that cloud computing is merely a marketing term designed to promote new products, many others see cloud computing as a new model for computing that frees users from owning, maintaining, and storing software and data. It provides access to these services from anywhere through an Internet connection. Several prominent firms are aggressively pursuing this new concept. These firms include Google, IBM, Intel, and Microsoft to name just a few.

The basic components of cloud computing are clients, the Internet, and service providers. (See Figure 2-24.)

- Clients are corporations and end users who want access to data, programs, and storage. This access is to be available anywhere and anytime that a connection to the Internet is available. End users do not need to buy, install, and maintain application programs and data.

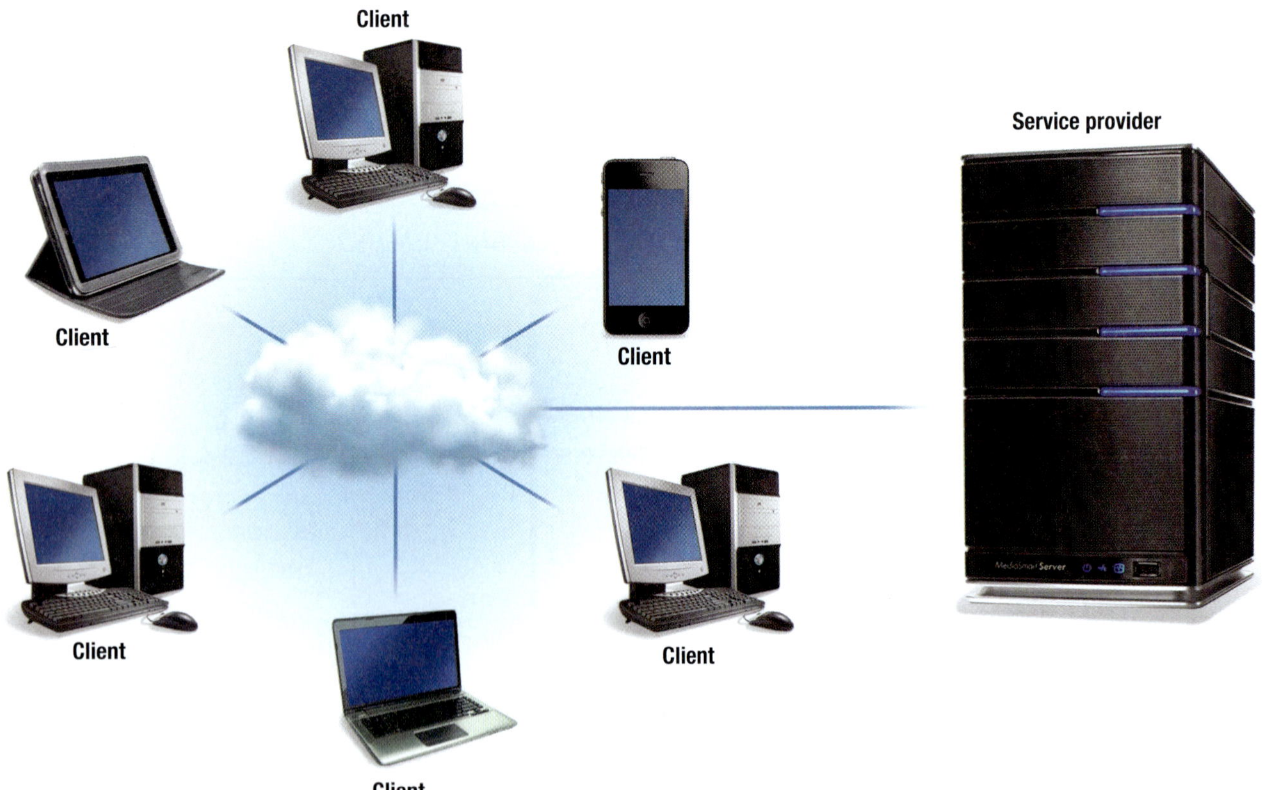

Figure 2-24 **Cloud computing**

- The Internet provides the connection between the clients and the providers. Two of the most critical factors determining the efficiency of cloud computing are (1) the speed and reliability of the user's access to the Internet and (2) the Internet's capability to provide safe and reliable transmission of data and programs.
- Service providers are organizations with computers connected to the Internet that are willing to provide access to software, data, and storage. These providers may charge a fee or may be free. For example, Google Drive Apps provide free access to programs with capabilities similar to Microsoft's Word, Excel, and PowerPoint. (See Figure 2-25.)

In the following chapters, you will learn more about the services provided through cloud computing. You will also learn about security and privacy challenges associated with cloud computing.

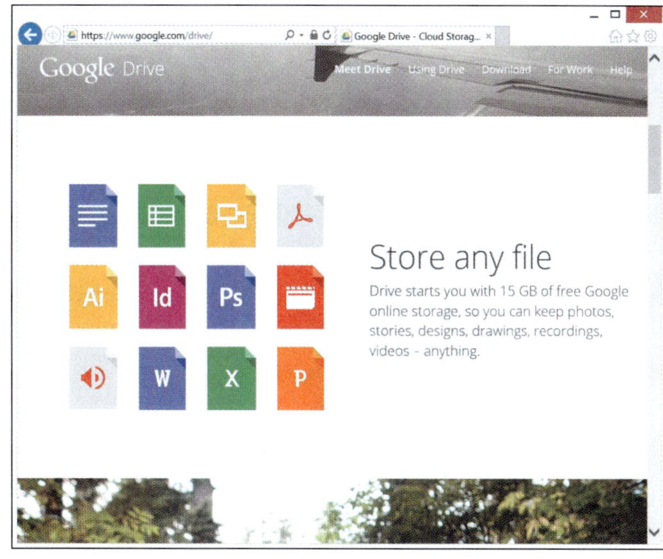

Figure 2-25 **Web-based service (Google Drive Apps)**

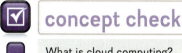

concept check

What is cloud computing?

What are the three basic components of cloud computing?

What are the two most critical factors that determine the efficiency of cloud computing?

The Internet of Things

The Internet is becoming more and more a part of our lives. As discussed in Chapter 1, the **Internet of Things (IoT)** is the continuing development of the Internet that allows everyday objects embedded with electronic devices to send and receive data over the Internet. These everyday objects include smartphones, wearable devices, and even coffeemakers. For example, the Fitbit is a bracelet that monitors health data and sends that data to your smartphone or personal web page. (See Figure 2-26.)

A Web 3.0 application can (1) access the Fitbit data, (2) combine that data with other data on the web, (3) process the data, and (4) send information back to another device. For example, Apple's Health App, a Web 3.0 application, can access your Fitbit data, combine it with other related health data, analyze the data, and report back to you through your smartphone. These reports provide information about your health including your heart rate, steps taken each day, and an estimate of daily calories burned. (See Figure 2-27.)

Figure 2-26 **Fitbit**

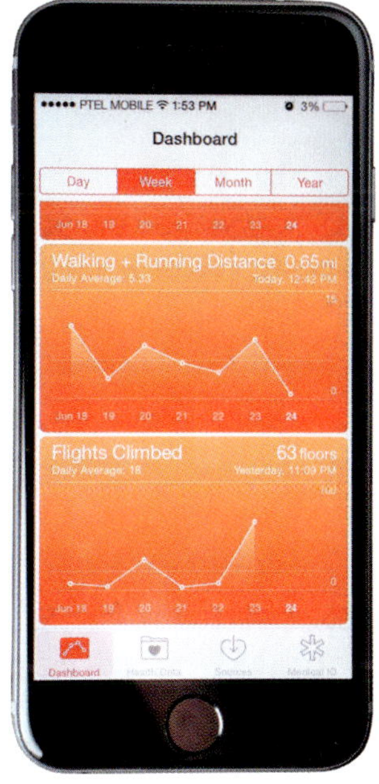

Figure 2-27 **Apple's Health App**

concept check

What is the Internet of Things?

What is Fitbit and Apple's Health App? How do they work together?

Discuss how Fitbit and Apple's Health App are examples of using IoT.

Careers in IT

"Now that you've learned about the Internet, the web, and electronic commerce, I'd like to tell you about my career as a webmaster."

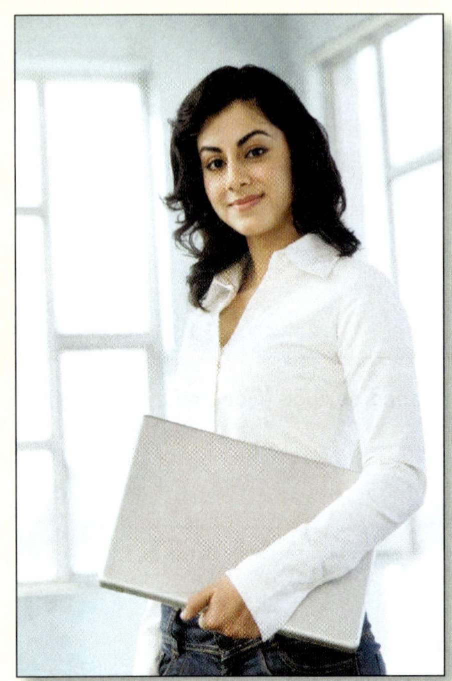

Webmasters develop and maintain websites and resources. The job may include backup of the company website, updating resources, or development of new resources. Webmasters are often involved in the design and development of the website. Some webmasters monitor traffic on the site and take steps to encourage users to visit the site. Webmasters also may work with marketing personnel to increase site traffic and may be involved in development of web promotions.

Employers look for candidates with a bachelor's or associate's degree in computer science or information systems and knowledge of common programming languages and web development software. Knowledge of HTML and CSS is considered essential. Those with experience using web authoring software and programs like Adobe Illustrator and Adobe Flash are often preferred. Good communication and organizational skills are vital in this position.

Webmasters can expect to earn an annual salary of $59,000 to $82,000. This position is relatively new in many corporations and tends to have fluid responsibilities. With technological advances and increasing corporate emphasis on a web presence, experience in this field could lead to managerial opportunities.

A LOOK TO THE FUTURE

Your Car's Dashboard as a Powerful, Internet-Connected Computing Device

Do you often wish that you could shop online or make dinner plans while your car drove itself? Would you like your car to use the Internet to suggest a better route, or stream a music list tailored to your likes? A computer located within the vehicle already governs many of your car's functions. That computer is responsible for various safety and diagnostic features. Recently, cars have begun offering Internet access for driving directions, streaming audio, and cell phone connectivity. In the future, cars will drive themselves and seamlessly integrate into our digital lives. Technology has been making better cars, and will continue to evolve to improve our lives as we look to the future.

Apple and Google have created partnerships with automobile manufacturers to place iPad or Android devices into the center of a vehicle's main console. Cars can connect to Wi-Fi access points or 4G networks to reach the Internet as the modern smartphone does. These developments allow your vehicle to provide many services that normally require a smartphone but in a safer and more integrated manner.

One of the immediate benefits involves quick access to information. Drivers get real-time traffic data, weather, store hours, and much more. Also available is access to all the apps that you expect to have. One example is the Pandora service, which allows you to stream free, ad-supported music from stations you create yourself. Why pay for satellite radio or listen to stations that you don't enjoy when you can access your favorite online music services right from your dashboard? Another benefit is the entertainment of your passengers or children. Some vehicles include screens that face the back seats, allowing parents to play DVDs for their children. Internet-connected vehicles allow individuals already paying for an online streaming video service to give their children access to this enormous library of cartoons and movies right in the vehicle. In fact, with a tabletlike interface, your child can choose from a preset selection of movies or educational games, depending on his or her mood.

Now, such a tool at your fingertips has the risk of becoming a distraction while you're driving. There is no question that safety features must be built in to prevent accidents from occurring. Luckily, there is already a piece of technology that prevents the driver from ever having to touch the dashboard: voice recognition.

In the same way that Apple's "Siri" has revolutionized the way individuals interact with their iPhones, similar systems are installed in the new dashboards. Drivers simply speak their commands to get the information they need and to use the vehicle's controls. Furthermore, this computer system uses existing technologies that recognize and speak English to the user. This will allow the driver to hear e-mail messages, social network updates, and today's news and weather while driving to work.

Some companies have already taken steps in implementing this technology. Ford uses voice recognition in some of its vehicles with a feature called Sync with MyFord Touch. Audi has added 3G connectivity in its new A7 model. However, the real breakthroughs will come when you can drive in safety while being as productive as when you are on your laptop. Advances in dictation software will one day allow users to easily dictate e-mail responses. Changes in sensors and automated driving will allow users to devote less attention to driving and more to getting things done. Google and Mercedes are currently testing self-driving cars, and they may be available in the next ten years. When it does, do you see yourself paying for this upgrade in your next car? Would you be comfortable allowing a car to drive itself while you worked on your laptop or tablet?

VISUAL SUMMARY The Internet, the Web, and Electronic Commerce

INTERNET AND WEB

Internet

Launched in 1969 with **ARPANET,** the **Internet** consists of the actual physical network.

Web

Introduced in 1991, the **web (World Wide Web, WWW)** provides a multimedia interface to Internet resources. Three generations: **Web 1.0** (existing information), **Web 2.0** (content creation and social interaction), and **Web 3.0** (automatic personalized content).

Common Uses

The most common uses of the Internet and the web include

- Communication–the most popular Internet activity.
- Shopping–one of the fastest-growing Internet activities.
- Searching–access libraries and local, national, and international news.
- Education–**e-learning** or taking online courses.
- Entertainment–music, movies, magazines, and computer games.

INTERNET ACCESS

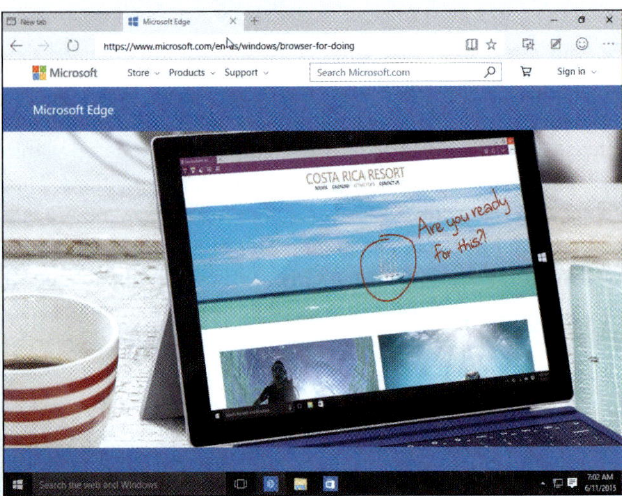

Once connected to the Internet, your computer seemingly becomes an extension of a giant computer that branches all over the world.

Providers

Internet service providers are connected to the Internet, providing a path for individuals to access the Internet. Connection technologies include **DSL, cable,** and **wireless modems.**

Browsers

Browsers provide access to web resources. Some related terms are

- **URLs–locations** or **addresses** to web resources; two parts are **protocol** and **domain name; top-level domain (TLD)** or **web suffix** identifies type of organization.
- **HTML**–commands to display **web pages; hyperlinks (links)** are connections.

Technologies providing interactive, animated websites include **cascading style sheets,** or **CSS** (to control the appearance of web pages); **JavaScript** (to trigger interactive features); **AJAX** (to create quick response interactive websites; and **applets** (to display graphics, provide interactive games, and more).

Mobile browsers run on portable devices.

To efficiently and effectively use computers, you need to be aware of resources available on the Internet and web, to be able to access these resources, to effectively communicate electronically, to efficiently locate information, to understand electronic commerce, and to use web utilities.

WEB UTILITIES

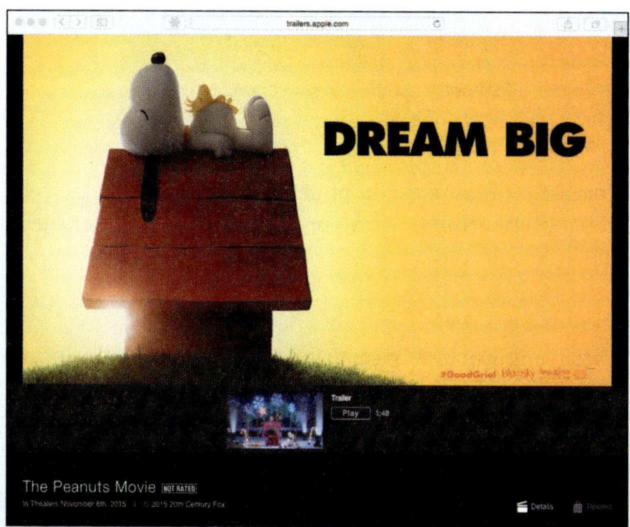

Web utilities are specialized utility programs that make using the Internet and the web easier and safer.

Plug-ins

Plug-ins are automatically loaded and operate as part of a browser. Many websites require specific plug-ins to fully experience their content. Some plug-ins are included in many of today's browsers; others must be installed.

Filters

Filters are used by parents and organizations to block certain sites and to monitor use of the Internet and the web.

File Transfer Utilities

File transfer utilities copy files to **(downloading)** and from **(uploading)** your computer. There are three types:

- **File transfer protocol (FTP)** and **secure file transfer protocol (SFTP)** allow you to efficiently copy files across the Internet.
- **BitTorrent** distributes file transfers across many different computers.
- **Web-based file transfer services** make use of a web browser to upload and download files.

Internet Security Suite

An **Internet security suite** is a collection of utility programs designed to protect your privacy and security on the Internet.

COMMUNICATION

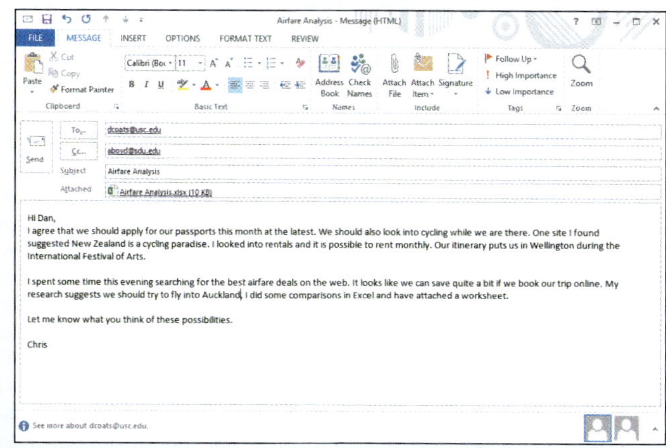

E-mail

E-mail (electronic mail) is the transmission of electronic messages. There are two basic types of e-mail systems:

- **Client-based e-mail systems** use **e-mail clients** installed on your computer.
- **Web-based e-mail systems** use **webmail clients** located on the e-mail provider's computer. This is known as **webmail.**

A typical e-mail has three basic elements: **header** (including **address, subject,** and perhaps **attachment**), **message,** and **signature.**

Spam is unwanted and unsolicited e-mail that may include a computer **virus** or destructive programs often attached to unsolicited e-mail. **Spam blockers,** also known as **spam filters,** are programs that identify and eliminate spam.

Messaging

While e-mail is the most widely used, there are two other messaging systems:

- **Text messaging,** also known as **texting** and **SMS (short message service),** is a process of sending short electronic messages typically less than 160 characters. Texting while driving is very dangerous and illegal in several states.
- **Instant messaging (IM)**—supports live communication between **friends.** Most instant messaging programs also include videoconferencing features, file sharing, and remote assistance.

COMMUNICATION

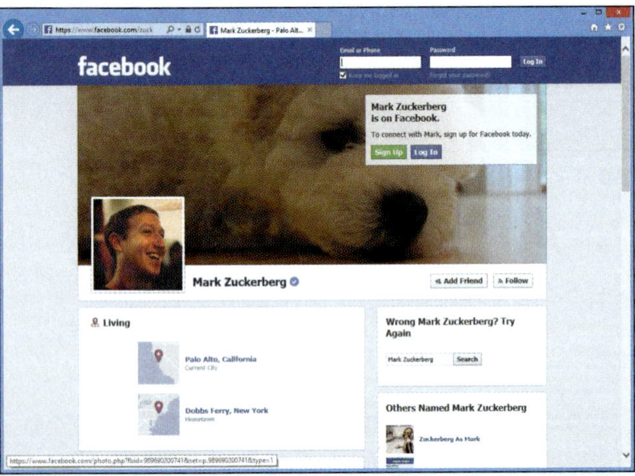

Social Networking

Social networks connect individuals to one another. Many sites support a variety of different activities. Three of the best known are Facebook, Google+, and LinkedIn.

- **Facebook** provides access to **Facebook Profiles, Facebook Pages,** and **Facebook groups.**
- **Google+** provides access to **Circles** and **Hangouts.**
- **LinkedIn** is a premier business-oriented social networking site.

Blogs, Webcasts, and Wikis

Other sites that help individuals communicate across the web are blogs, microblogs, webcasts, podcasts, and wikis.

- **Blogs (web logs)** are typically personal websites to keep in touch with friends and family. Some are like online diaries. Businesses, newspapers, and others also use blogs as a quick publishing method.
- **Microblogs,** unlike traditional blogs, use only short sentences that take only a few seconds to write. **Twitter** is the most popular microblogging site. A Twitter message is known as a **tweet.**
- **Webcasts** deliver media content over the Internet. Using **streaming** technology (audio and video files continuously downloaded while you are listening to and/or viewing the file content), no files remain on your computer at the conclusion of the webcast.
- **Podcasts,** like webcasts, deliver media content but do not use streaming technology. Before content can be accessed, the entire media file has to be downloaded and saved to your computer.
- A **wiki** is a website designed to allow visitors to use their browsers to add, edit, or delete the site's content. Wikis are often used to support collaborative writing. **Wikipedia** is one of the most popular wikis.

SEARCH TOOLS

Search Service	Site
Bing	www.bing.com
Duckduckgo	www.duckduckgo.com
Google	www.google.com
Yahoo!	www.yahoo.com

Search services maintain huge databases relating to website content. **Spiders** are programs that update these databases.

Search Engines

Search engines are specialized programs to help locate information. To use, enter a keyword or phrase and a list of **hits,** or links to references, is displayed.

Specialized Search Engines

Specialized search engines focus on subject-specific websites.

Topic	Site
Cooking	www.recipebridge.com
Research	scholar.google.com
Fashion	www.shopstyle.com
History	www.historynet.com
Law	www.findlaw.com
Medicine	www.webmd.com

Content Evaluation

To evaluate the accuracy of information found on the web, consider the following:

- Authority. Is the author an expert? Is the site official or does it present one individual's or organization's opinion.
- Accuracy. Has the information been critically reviewed? Does the site provide a method to report inaccurate information?
- Objectivity. Is the information factual or does the author have a bias? Does the author appear to have a personal agenda to convince or form a reader's opinion?
- Currency. Is the information up to date? Does the site specify when information is updated? Are the site's links operational?

ELECTRONIC COMMERCE

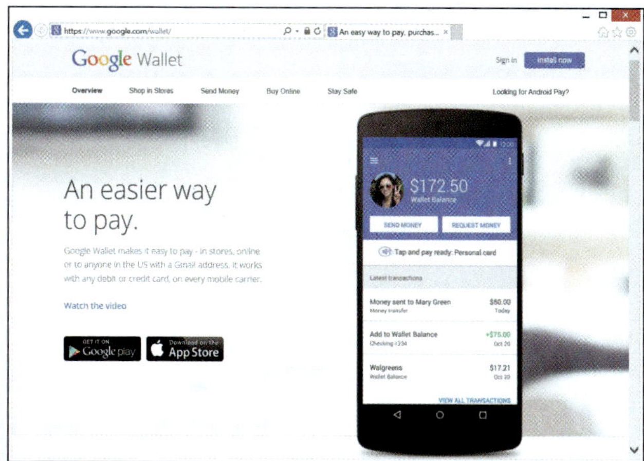

Electronic commerce, or **e-commerce,** is the buying and selling of goods over the Internet. Three basic types are

- **Business-to-consumer (B2C)** commerce, which involves sales from business to the general public.
- **Consumer-to-consumer (C2C)** commerce, which involves sales between individuals. **Web auctions** are similar to traditional auctions except buyers and sellers rarely, if ever, meet face to face.
- **Business-to-business (B2B)** commerce, which involves sales from one business to another, typically a manufacturer-supplier relationship.

CLOUD COMPUTING

Cloud computing uses the Internet and the web to shift many computer activities from the user's computer to other computers on the Internet.

Components

There are three basic components to cloud computing:

- Clients are corporations and end users who want access to data, programs, and storage.
- The Internet provides the connection between the clients and providers. Two critical factors are the speed and reliability of the user's access and the Internet's capability to provide safe and reliable access.
- Service providers are organizations with computers connected to the Internet that are willing to provide access to software, data, and storage.

Security

The two greatest challenges for e-commerce are the development of

- Safe, secure payment methods. Two types are credit cards and **digital cash.**
- Convenient ways to provide required information.

INTERNET OF THINGS

The **Internet of Things (IoT)** is a continuing development of the Internet allowing everyday objects embedded with electronic devices to send and receive data over the Internet. Objects include smartphones, wearable devices, and even coffeemakers. For example:

- The Fitbit is an IoT device (bracelet) that monitors health data and sends that data to a smartphone or personal web page.
- Apple's Health App is a Web 3.0 application that can access Fitbit data, combine it with other related health data, analyze the data, and report back to you through a smartphone.

The Apple Health App reports provide information about users' health including heart rate, steps taken each day, and an estimate of daily calories burned.

CAREERS in IT

Webmasters develop and maintain websites and web resources. A bachelor's or associate's degree in computer science or information systems and knowledge of common programming languages and web development software are required. Salary range is $59,000 to $82,000.

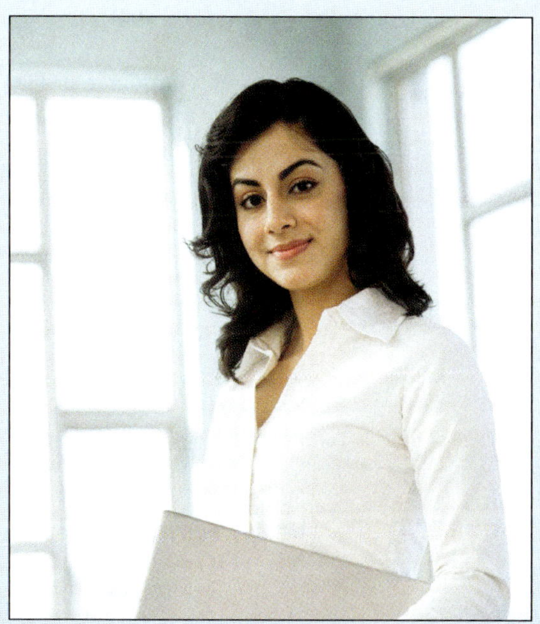

KEY TERMS

address (33, 37)
Advanced Research Project Agency Network (ARPANET) (28)
AJAX (33)
applets (33)
attachment (37)
BitTorrent (35)
blog (41)
browser (32)
business-to-business (B2B) (45)
business-to-consumer (B2C) (44)
cable (32)
cascading style sheets (CSS) (33)
Circles (40)
client-based e-mail system (38)
cloud computing (46)
consumer-to-consumer (C2C) (44)
digital cash (45)
domain name (33)
downloading (35)
DSL (32)
e-commerce (44)
e-learning (29)
electronic commerce (44)
electronic mail (37)
e-mail (37)
e-mail client (38)
Facebook (39)
Facebook groups (40)
Facebook Pages (40)
Facebook Profiles (40)
file transfer protocol (FTP) (35)
filter (34)
friend (39)
Google+ (40)
Google Plus (40)
Hangouts (40)
header (37)
hit (43)
hyperlink (33)
Hypertext Markup Language (HTML) (33)
instant messaging (IM) (39)
Internet (28)
Internet of Things (IoT) (47)
Internet security suite (36)
Internet service provider (ISP) (32)
JavaScript (33)
link (33)
LinkedIn (40)
location (33)
message (37)
microblog (41)
MMS (multimedia messaging service) (38)
mobile browser (33)
online (28)
plug-in (34)
podcast (42)
protocol (33)
search engine (43)
search service (43)
secure file transfer protocol (SFTP) (35)
signature (37)
SMS (short messaging service) (38)
social networking (39)
spam (38)
spam blocker (38)
spam filter (38)
specialized search engine (43)
spider (43)
streaming (41)
subject (37)
texting (38)
text messaging (38)
top-level domain (TLD) (33)
tweet (41)
Twitter (41)
uniform resource locator (URL) (33)
uploading (35)
virus (38)
web (28)
Web 1.0 (28)
Web 2.0 (28)
Web 3.0 (28)
web auction (44)
web-based e-mail system (38)
web-based file transfer services (35)
webcasts (41)
web log (41)
webmail (38)
webmail client (38)
webmaster (48)
web page (33)
web suffix (33)
web utility (34)
wiki (42)
Wikipedia (42)
wireless modem (32)
World Wide Web (28)
WWW (28)

MULTIPLE CHOICE

Circle the correct answer.

1. The network that connects computers all over the world.
   - a. ARPANET
   - b. Internet
   - c. LAN
   - d. web
2. The rules for exchanging data between computers.
   - a. DSL
   - b. protocols
   - c. web
   - d. WWW
3. Using file transfer utility software, you can copy files to your computer from specially configured servers on the Internet. This is called:
   - a. downloading
   - b. filtering
   - c. blogging
   - d. uploading
4. Communities of individuals who share a common interest typically create Facebook:
   - a. clients
   - b. groups
   - c. Pages
   - d. Profiles
5. Type of e-mail account that does not require an e-mail program to be installed on a user's computer is:
   - a. blog-based
   - b. client-based
   - c. utility-based
   - d. web-based
6. The most popular microblogging site:
   - a. LinkedIn
   - b. Google+
   - c. Twitter
   - d. Wikipedia
7. Using a keyword, a search engine returns a list of related sites known as:
   - a. blogs
   - b. hits
   - c. podcasts
   - d. strikes
8. This is the Internet's equivalent to traditional cash.
   - a. digital cash
   - b. e-commerce
   - c. ftp
   - d. Internet dollars
9. The continuing Internet development that allows objects to send and receive data over the Internet.
   - a. HTML
   - b. IoT
   - c. search engines
   - d. Web 2.0
10. Three basic components to cloud computing are clients, Internet, and _____.
    - a. CSS
    - b. service providers
    - c. streaming
    - d. Web 3.0

MATCHING

Match each numbered item with the most closely related lettered item. Write your answers in the spaces provided.

- **a.** chat
- **b.** C2C
- **c.** communicating
- **d.** e-mail
- **e.** Internet
- **f.** ISP
- **g.** LinkedIn
- **h.** microblog
- **i.** search services
- **j.** web log

___ **1.** The most popular Internet activity.

___ **2.** The most common way to access the Internet is through a(n) _____.

___ **3.** Transmission of electronic messages over the Internet.

___ **4.** Two popular instant messaging services are Google Talk and Facebook _____.

___ **5.** A business-oriented social networking site.

___ **6.** Another name for a blog.

___ **7.** Publishes short sentences that take only a few seconds to write.

___ **8.** Maintain huge databases relating to information provided on the web and the Internet.

___ **9.** Electronic commerce involving individuals selling to individuals.

___ **10.** The basic components of cloud computing are clients, service providers, and the _____.

OPEN-ENDED

On a separate sheet of paper, respond to each question or statement.

1. Discuss the Internet and web, including their origins, the three generations of the web, and the most common uses.
2. Describe how to access the Internet. What are providers? Define browsers, and discuss URLs, HTML, CSS, JavaScript, AJAX, applets, and mobile browsers.
3. What are web utilities? Discuss plug-ins, filters, file transfer utilities, and Internet security suites.
4. Discuss Internet communications including client-based and web-based e-mail, instant and text messaging, social networking, blogs, microblogs, webcasts, podcasts, and wikis.
5. Define search tools including search services. Discuss search engines and specialized search engines. Describe how to evaluate the content of a website.
6. Describe electronic commerce including business-to-consumer, consumer-to-consumer, and business-to-business e-commerce, and security.
7. Discuss the Internet of Things. Describe how Fitbit and Apple's Health App are examples of how an IoT device can interact with a Web 3.0 application.
8. What is cloud computing? Describe three basic components of cloud computing.

DISCUSSION

Respond to each of the following questions.

1 Making IT Work for You: ONLINE ENTERTAINMENT

Review the Making IT Work for You: Online Entertainment on pages 30–31, and then respond to the following: (a) Do you currently have a subscription to Netflix, Hulu Plus, or another service that allows you to stream movies and TV shows? If so, which ones? If not, do you plan on using one in the future? Why or why not? (b) What device do you use most often to watch video content from the web? Would you consider purchasing a dedicated streaming device such as the Roku? Why or why not? (c) Could ever see yourself canceling or "cutting the cord" from your current cable or satellite service? Why or why not?

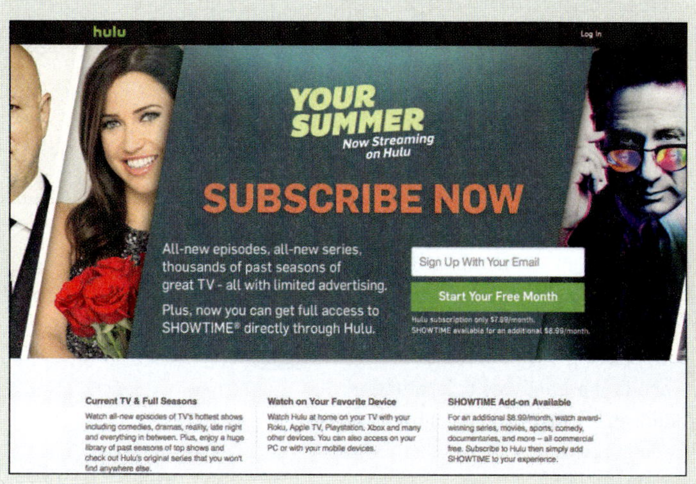

2 Privacy: SOCIAL NETWORKING

When a Facebook friend posts a picture, video, or text that includes you, who can view that post? Review the Privacy box on page 40, and respond to the following: (a) Who should be responsible for ensuring privacy on social networking sites? Defend your position. (b) Do you think that most people are aware of their privacy settings on Facebook? Have you ever checked your settings? Why or why not? (c) Investigate and then summarize the default security settings for a social networking website such as Facebook or Google+.

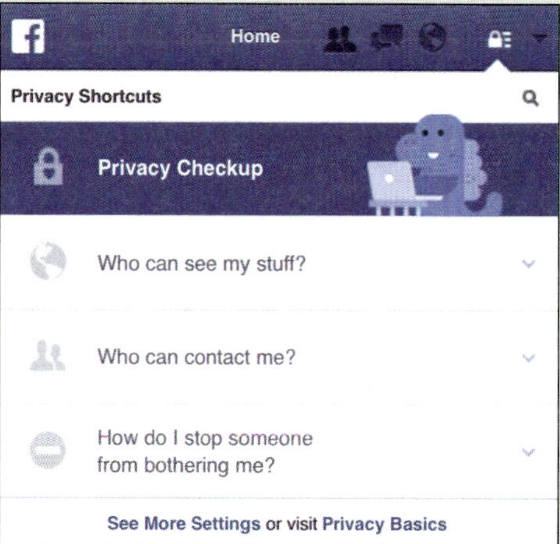

3 Ethics: FILTERING AND MONITORING

Parents can use content filters and monitoring software to restrict or monitor their child's Internet behavior. Review the Ethics box on page 35, and respond to the following: (a) Is it ethical for parents to filter or monitor Internet content for their children? Does your answer depend on the age of the child? Defend your position. (b) Should parents inform their children that Internet activity is being filtered or monitored? Why or why not? (c) Do you feel that filtering or monitoring software is the best way to protect children? Defend your position.

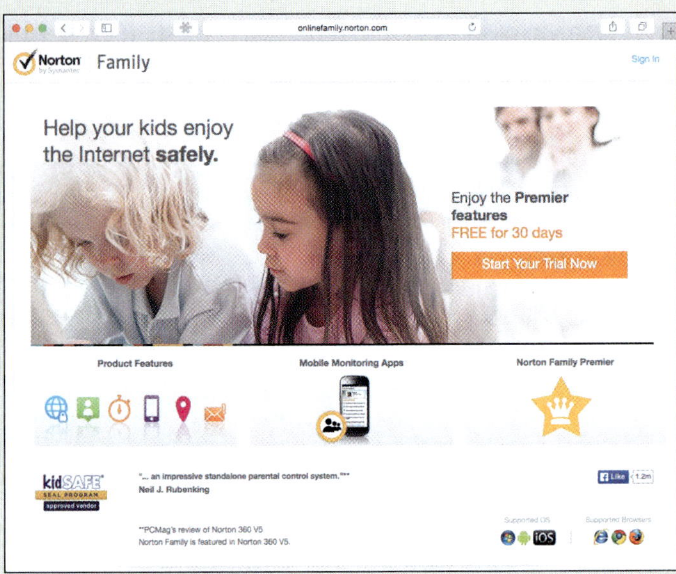

4 Environment: E-MAIL

Review the Environment box on page 37, and then respond to the following: (a) When it comes to sending letters, holiday cards, and invitations to friends and family, do you mostly use e-mail or postal mail? What are your reasons for choosing one over the other? (b) Are there any situations where you feel that using e-mail would be inappropriate? (c) Have you signed up for paperless billing from your financial institutions and utility companies? Why or why not? (d) Go through all the paper mail you have received in the last week or two. Is there anything there that you could receive via e-mail or view on the web? If so, list a few examples.

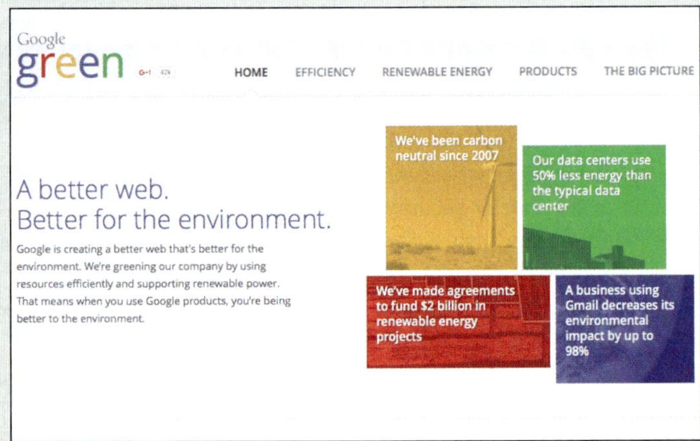

PHOTO CREDITS

CHAPTER 2

Opener: © liangpv/iStock Vectors/Getty Images RF; p. 27, 49: © epa european pressphoto agency b.v./Alamy; p. 28, 48, 53 (bottom): © Photosindia/Alamy; 2-1, 2-14, p. 50 (left), 58 (bottom): Google and the Google logo are registered trademarks of Google Inc., used with permission; p. 30 (top), 57 (top): © 2015 Hulu; p. 30 (bottom): Copyright © CNN, Inc.; p. 31 (top): Copyright © 2015 Pandora Media, Inc.; p. 31 (bottom): Copyright © 2015 Roku, Inc. All rights reserved; 2-2, 2-12, p. 50 (right), 51 (right): Microsoft product/screen shot(s) reprinted with permission from Microsoft Corporation; 2-5: © Allison Rocks! Photography RF; 2-6, p. 51 (left): Copyright © 2015 20th Century Fox; 2-8, 58 (top): © 2015 Symantec Corporation; 2-11: Copyright © 2012 McAfee, Inc. Used with permission; 2-14, 2-15, p. 52, 57 (bottom): Copyright © 2015 Facebook; 2-17: Copyright © 1999-2015 Google. Used with permission; 2-18: Screenshot credit to come; 2-22, p. 53 (top-left): Copyright © 2014 Google; 2-25: Copyright © 2015 Google; 2-26: Source: Becky Stern/Flickr/CC; 2-27: © picture alliance/Frank Duenzl/Newscom.

chapter 3 Application Software

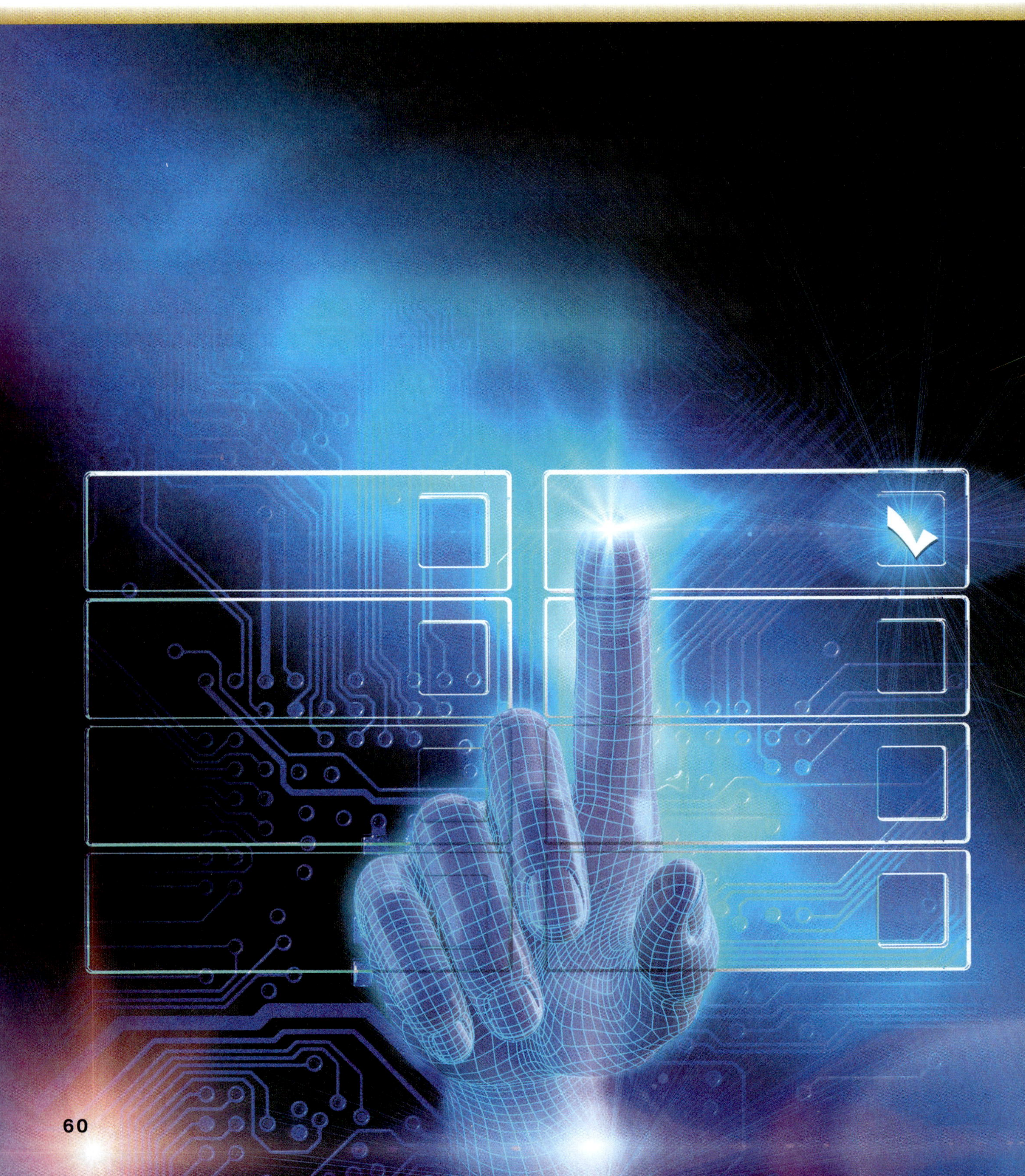

Why should I read this chapter?

The power and capability of application software is exploding. We can expect applications beyond our imagination and to control these applications entirely with our voice, gestures, and thoughts.

This chapter covers the things you need to know to be prepared for this ever-changing digital world, including:

- General-purpose applications—how to create documents, analyze data, make presentations, and organize information.
- Special-purpose applications—how to use graphics programs for image editing and creating web pages and how to locate and use mobile apps.
- Software suites—how to use suites and cloud-based applications.

Learning Objectives

After you have read this chapter, you should be able to:

1 Identify general-purpose applications.

2 Describe word processors, spreadsheets, presentation programs, and database management systems.

3 Identify specialized applications.

4 Describe graphics programs, web authoring programs, and other specialized professional applications.

5 Describe mobile apps and app stores.

6 Identify software suites.

7 Describe office suites, cloud suites, specialized suites, and utility suites.

Introduction

"Hi, I'm James, and I'm a software engineer. I'd like to talk with you about application software and how to access these traditional programs using cloud computing."

Not long ago, trained specialists were required to perform many of the operations you can now do with a personal computer. Market analysts used calculators to project sales. Graphic artists created designs by hand. Data processing clerks created electronic files to be stored on large computers. Now you can do all these tasks—and many others—with a personal computer and the appropriate application software.

Think of the personal computer as an electronic tool. You may not consider yourself very good at typing, calculating, organizing, presenting, or managing information. However, a personal computer can help you do all these things and much more. All it takes is the right kinds of software.

To efficiently and effectively use computers, you need to understand the capabilities of general-purpose application software, which includes word processors, spreadsheets, presentation programs, and database management systems. You also need to know about integrated packages and software suites.

Application Software

As we discussed in Chapter 1, there are two kinds of software. **System software** works with end users, application software, and computer hardware to handle the majority of technical details. **Application software** can be described as end user software and is used to accomplish a variety of tasks.

Application software can be divided into three categories. One category, **general-purpose applications,** includes word processing programs, spreadsheets, presentation graphics, and database management systems. Another category, **specialized applications,** includes thousands of other programs that tend to be more narrowly focused and used in specific disciplines and occupations. The third category, **mobile apps,** is add-on features or programs typically designed for smartphones and tablets.

User Interface

A **user interface** is the portion of the application that allows you to control and to interact with the program. Depending on the application, you can use a mouse, a pointer, a keyboard, and/or your voice to communicate with the application. Most general-purpose applications use a mouse and a **graphical user interface (GUI)** that displays graphical elements called **icons** to represent familiar objects. The mouse controls a **pointer** on the screen that is used to select items such as icons. Another feature is the use of windows to display information. A **window** is simply a rectangular area that can contain a document, program, or message. (Do not confuse the term *window* with the various versions of Microsoft's Windows operating systems, which are programs.) More than one window can be opened and displayed on the computer screen at one time.

Traditionally, most software programs use a system of menus, toolbars, and dialog boxes. (See Figure 3-1.)

- **Menus** present commands that are typically displayed in a **menu bar** at the top of the screen.
- **Toolbars** typically appear below the menu bar and include small graphic elements called **buttons** that provide shortcuts for quick access to commonly used commands.
- **Dialog boxes** provide additional information and request user input.

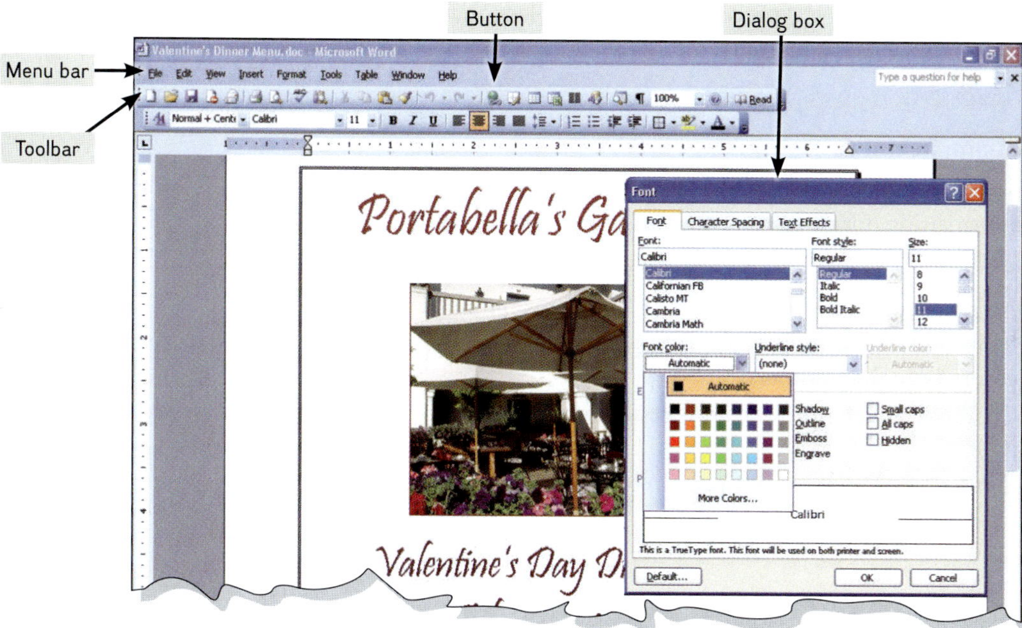

Figure 3-1 Traditional graphical user interface

Many applications, and Microsoft applications in particular, use an interface known as the **Ribbon GUI** to make it easier to find and use all the features of an application; this GUI uses a system of ribbons, tabs, and galleries. (See Figure 3-2.)

- **Ribbons** replace menus and toolbars by organizing commonly used commands into a set of tabs. These tabs display command buttons that are the most relevant to the tasks being performed by the user.
- **Tabs** are used to divide the ribbon into major activity areas. Each tab is then organized into **groups** that contain related items. Some tabs, called **contextual tabs,** appear only when they are needed and anticipate the next operation to be performed by the user.

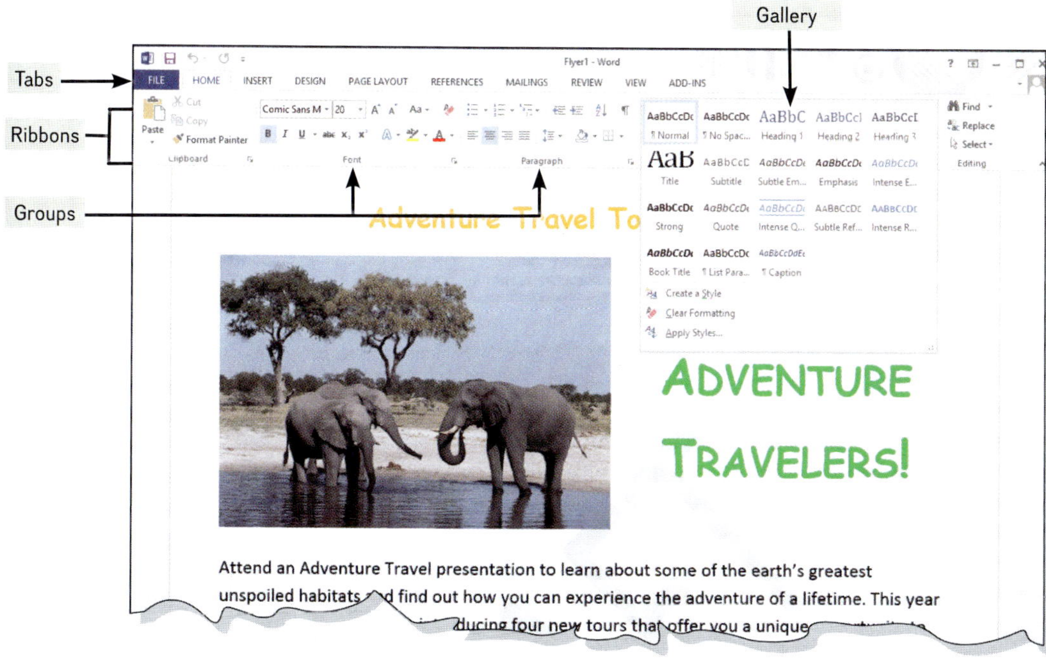

Figure 3-2 Ribbon GUI

- **Galleries** simplify the process of making a selection from a list of alternatives. This is accomplished by graphically displaying the effect of alternatives before being selected.

Common Features

Most applications provide a variety of features to make entering/presenting, editing, and formatting documents easy. Some of the most common features include

- Spell checker—looks for misspelled words.
- Alignment—centers, right-aligns, or left-aligns numbers and characters.
- Fonts and font sizes (perhaps using character effects)—specify the size and style of entered numbers and text.
- Character effects—provide a variety of different typefaces, such as bold or italics.
- Edit options—provide easy ways to edit text, such as cut, copy, and paste.

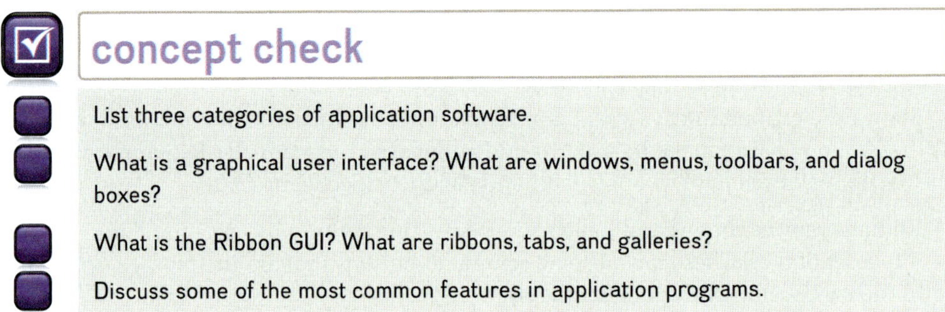

concept check

- List three categories of application software.
- What is a graphical user interface? What are windows, menus, toolbars, and dialog boxes?
- What is the Ribbon GUI? What are ribbons, tabs, and galleries?
- Discuss some of the most common features in application programs.

General-Purpose Applications

As mentioned previously, general-purpose applications include word processors, spreadsheets, presentation graphics, and database management systems.

Word Processors

Word processors create text-based **documents** and are one of the most flexible and widely used software tools. All types of people and organizations use word processors to create memos, letters, and faxes. Organizations create newsletters, manuals, and brochures to provide information to their customers. Students and researchers use word processors to create reports.

Microsoft Word is the most widely used word processor. Other popular word processors include Apple Pages, Google Docs, Corel WordPerfect, and OpenOffice Writer.

Assume that you have accepted a job as an advertising coordinator for Adventure Travel Tours, a travel agency specializing in active adventure vacations. Your primary responsibilities are to create and coordinate the company's promotional materials, including flyers and travel reports. To see how you could use Microsoft Word as the advertising coordinator for the Adventure Travel Tours, see Figures 3-3 and 3-4.

Creating a Flyer

You have been asked to create a promotional advertising flyer. After discussing the flyer's content and basic structure with your supervisor, you start to enter the flyer's text. As you enter the text, the spelling checker and grammar checker catch some spelling and grammatical errors. Once the text has been entered, you proofread the text and then focus your attention on enhancing the visual aspects of the flyer. You add a photograph and experiment with different character and paragraph formats, including fonts, font sizes, colors, and alignments.

Spelling Checker
Correcting spelling and typing errors identified by the **spelling checker** creates an error-free and professional-looking document.
Fonts and Font Size
Using interesting **fonts** and a large **font size** in the flyer's title grabs the reader's attention.
Adventure Travel Tours
New Adventures
Center-Aligning
Center-aligning all of the text in the flyer creates a comfortable, balanced appearance.
Attention adventure travelers! Attend an Adventure presentation to learn about some of the earth's greatest unspoiled habitats and find out how you can experience the adventure of a lifetime. This year we are offering four new tours:
India Wildlife Adventure
Inca Trail to Machu Picchu
Safari in Tanzania
Costa Rica Rivers and Rainforests
Call Student Name at 1-800-555-0004 for presentation locations, full color brochures, itinerary information , costs, and trip dates.
Character Effects
Adding **character effects** such as bold and color makes important information stand out and makes the flyer more visually interesting.
Grammar Checker
Incomplete sentences, awkward wording, and incorrect punctuation are identified and corrections are offered by the **grammar checker.**

Figure 3-3 **Flyer**

Creating a Report

Your next assignment is to create a report on Tanzania and Peru. After conducting your research, you start writing your paper. As you enter the text for the report, you notice that the AutoCorrect feature automatically corrects some grammar and punctuation errors. Your report includes several figures and tables. You use the captions feature to keep track of figure and table numbers, to enter the caption text, and to position the captions. You use the footnote feature to assist in adding notes to further explain or comment on information in the report.

Finally, you prepare the report for printing by adding header and footer information.

Tanzania & Peru

Tanzania

Geography and Climate

"In the midst of a great wilderness, full of wild beasts...I fancied I saw a summit...covered with a dazzlingly white cloud (qtd. in Cole 56). This is how Johann Krapf, the first outsider to witness the splendor of Africa's highest mountain, described Kilimanjaro. The peak was real, though the white clouds he "fancied" he saw were the dense layer of snow that coats the mountain.[1]

Figure1 GIRAFFE IN SERENGETI

Tanzania is primarily a plateau that slopes gently downward into the country's five hundred miles of Indian Ocean coastline. Nearly three-quarters of Tanzania is dry savannah, so much so that the Swahili word for the central plateau is *nyika*, meaning "wasteland." Winding through these flatlands is the Great Rift Valley, which forms narrow and shallow lakes in its long path. Several of these great lakes form a belt-like oasis of green vegetation. Contrasting with the severity of the plains are the coastal areas, which are lush with ample rainfall. In the north the plateau slopes dramatically into Mt. Kilimanjaro.

Ngorongoro Conservation Area

Some of Tanzania's most distinguishing geographical features are found in the Ngorongoro Conservation Area.[2] The park is composed of many craters and gorges, as well as lakes, forest, and plains. Among these features is the area's namesake, the Ngorongoro Crater. The Crater is a huge expanse, covering more than one hundred square miles. On the Crater's floor, grasslands blend into swamps, lakes, rivers, and woodland. Also within the Conservation Area's perimeter is the Olduvai Gorge, commonly referred to as the "Cradle of Mankind," where in 1931 the stone

[1] Mt. Kilimanjaro is 19,340 feet high, making it the fourth tallest mountain in the world.

[2] The Conservation Area is a national preserve spanning 3,196 square miles.

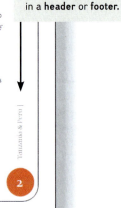

Tanzania & Peru |

2

AutoCorrect
As you enter text, you occasionally forget to capitalize the first word in a sentence. Fortunately, **AutoCorrect** recognizes the error and automatically capitalizes the word.

Captions
Identifying figures with **captions** in a report makes the report easier to read and more professional.

Header or Footer
Page numbers and other document-related information can be included in a **header** or **footer.**

Footnote
To include a note about Mt. Kilimanjaro, you use the footnote feature. This feature inserts the **footnote** superscript number and automatically formats the bottom of the page to contain the footnote text.

Figure 3-4 Report

Spreadsheets

Spreadsheets organize, analyze, and graph numeric data such as budgets and financial reports. Once used exclusively by accountants, spreadsheets are widely used by nearly every profession. Marketing professionals analyze sales trends. Financial analysts evaluate and graph stock market trends. Students and teachers record grades and calculate grade point averages.

The most widely used spreadsheet program is Microsoft Excel. Other spreadsheet applications include Apple Numbers, Corel Quattro Pro, Google Sheets, and OpenOffice Calc.

Assume that you have just accepted a job as manager of the Downtown Internet Café. This café provides a variety of flavored coffees as well as Internet access. One of your responsibilities is to create a financial plan for the next year. To see how you could use Microsoft Excel as the manager for the Downtown Internet Café, see Figures 3-5 and 3-6.

Creating a Sales Forecast

Your first project is to develop a first-quarter sales forecast for the café. You begin by studying sales data and talking with several managers. After obtaining sales and expense estimates, you are ready to create the first-quarter forecast. You start structuring the worksheet by inserting descriptive text entries for the row and column headings. Next, you insert numeric entries, including formulas and functions to perform calculations. To test the accuracy of the worksheet, you change the values in some cells and compare the recalculated spreadsheet results with hand calculations.

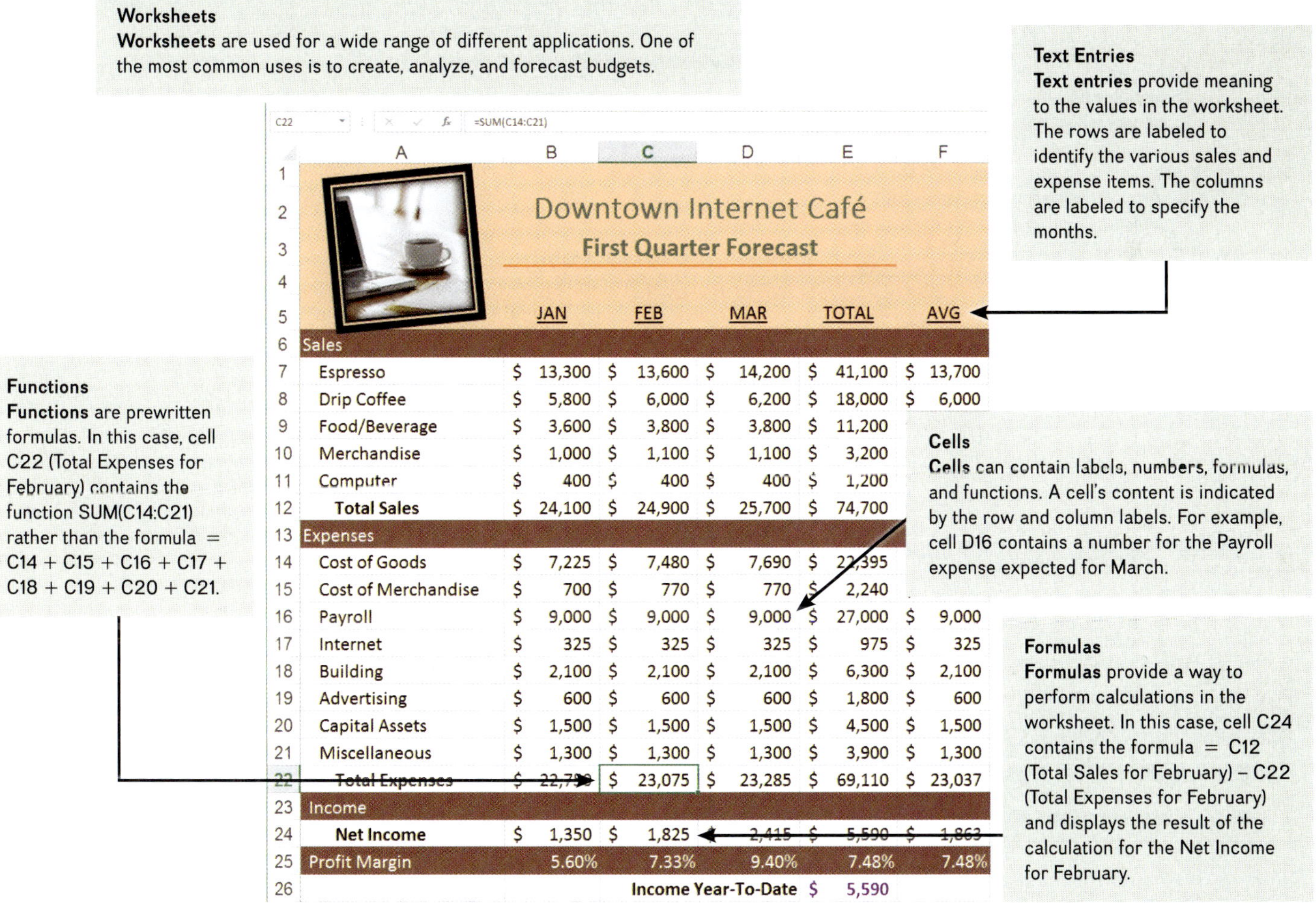

C22 =SUM(C14:C21)

Downtown Internet Café

First Quarter Forecast

	A	B	C	D	E	F
5		JAN	FEB	MAR	TOTAL	AVG
6	Sales					
7	Espresso	$ 13,300	$ 13,600	$ 14,200	$ 41,100	$ 13,700
8	Drip Coffee	$ 5,800	$ 6,000	$ 6,200	$ 18,000	$ 6,000
9	Food/Beverage	$ 3,600	$ 3,800	$ 3,800	$ 11,200	
10	Merchandise	$ 1,000	$ 1,100	$ 1,100	$ 3,200	
11	Computer	$ 400	$ 400	$ 400	$ 1,200	
12	**Total Sales**	$ 24,100	$ 24,900	$ 25,700	$ 74,700	
13	Expenses					
14	Cost of Goods	$ 7,225	$ 7,480	$ 7,690	$ 22,395	
15	Cost of Merchandise	$ 700	$ 770	$ 770	$ 2,240	
16	Payroll	$ 9,000	$ 9,000	$ 9,000	$ 27,000	$ 9,000
17	Internet	$ 325	$ 325	$ 325	$ 975	$ 325
18	Building	$ 2,100	$ 2,100	$ 2,100	$ 6,300	$ 2,100
19	Advertising	$ 600	$ 600	$ 600	$ 1,800	$ 600
20	Capital Assets	$ 1,500	$ 1,500	$ 1,500	$ 4,500	$ 1,500
21	Miscellaneous	$ 1,300	$ 1,300	$ 1,300	$ 3,900	$ 1,300
22	**Total Expenses**	$ 22,7[illegible]	$ 23,075	$ 23,285	$ 69,110	$ 23,037
23	Income					
24	**Net Income**	$ 1,350	$ 1,825	$ 2,415	$ 5,590	$ 1,863
25	Profit Margin	5.60%	7.33%	9.40%	7.48%	7.48%
26				**Income Year-To-Date**	$ 5,590	

Worksheets
Worksheets are used for a wide range of different applications. One of the most common uses is to create, analyze, and forecast budgets.
Text Entries
Text entries provide meaning to the values in the worksheet. The rows are labeled to identify the various sales and expense items. The columns are labeled to specify the months.
Functions
Functions are prewritten formulas. In this case, cell C22 (Total Expenses for February) contains the function SUM(C14:C21) rather than the formula = C14 + C15 + C16 + C17 + C18 + C19 + C20 + C21.
Cells
Cells can contain labels, numbers, formulas, and functions. A cell's content is indicated by the row and column labels. For example, cell D16 contains a number for the Payroll expense expected for March.
Formulas
Formulas provide a way to perform calculations in the worksheet. In this case, cell C24 contains the formula = C12 (Total Sales for February) – C22 (Total Expenses for February) and displays the result of the calculation for the Net Income for February.

Figure 3-5 **First-quarter forecast**

Analyzing Your Data

After presenting the First-Quarter Forecast to the owner, you revise the format and expand the workbook to include worksheets for each quarter and an annual forecast summary. You give each worksheet a descriptive sheet name. At the request of the owner, you perform a what-if analysis to test the effect of different estimates for payroll, and you use a chart to visualize the effect.

Workbook
The first worksheet in a **workbook** is often a summary of the following worksheets. In this case, the first worksheet presents the entire year's forecast. The subsequent worksheets provide the details.

Downtown Internet Café
Annual Forecast

	A	B	C	D	E	F	G	H	I	J
5		JAN	FEB	MAR	APR	MAY	JUN	JUL	AUG	SEP
6	**Sales**									
7	Espresso	$13,300	$13,600	$14,200	$14,400	$15,200	$15,500	$15,200	$15,300	$15,800
8	Drip Coffee	$5,800	$6,000	$6,200	$6,200	$6,200	$6,200	$6,000	$6,000	$6,500
9	Food/Beverage	$3,600	$3,800	$3,800	$3,600	$3,800	$3,800	$4,000	$4,000	$4,000
10	Merchandise	$1,000	$1,100	$1,100	$1,500	$1,500	$1,500	$2,000	$2,000	$2,000
11	Computer	$400	$400	$400	$600	$600	$800	$800	$800	$600
12	**Total Sales**	**$24,100**	**$24,900**	**$25,700**	**$26,300**	**$27,300**	**$27,800**	**$28,000**	**$28,100**	**$28,900**
13	**Expenses**									
14	Cost of Goods	$7,225	$7,480	$7,690	$7,620	$7,940	$8,015	$8,000	$8,025	$8,300
15	Cost of Merchandise	$700	$770	$770	$1,050	$1,050	$1,050	$1,400	$1,400	$1,400
16	Payroll	$9,000	$9,000	$9,000	$7,860	$8,390	$8,740	$9,000	$9,000	$9,000
17	Internet	$325	$325	$325	$325	$325	$325	$325	$325	$325
18	Building	$2,100	$2,100	$2,100	$2,100	$2,100	$2,100	$2,100	$2,100	$2,100
19	Advertising	$600	$600	$600	$600	$600	$600	$600	$600	$600
20	Capital Assets	$1,500	$1,500	$1,500	$1,500	$1,500	$1,500	$1,500	$1,500	$1,500
21	Miscellaneous	$1,300	$1,300	$1,300	$1,300	$1,300	$1,300	$1,300	$1,300	$1,300
22	**Total Expenses**	**$22,750**	**$23,075**	**$23,285**	**$22,355**	**$23,205**	**$23,630**	**$24,225**	**$24,250**	**$24,525**
23	**Income**									
24	**Net Income**	$1,350	$1,825	$2,415	$3,945	$4,095	$4,170	$3,775	$3,850	$4,375
25	**Profit Margin**	5.60%	7.33%	9.40%	15.00%	15.00%	15.00%	13.48%	13.70%	15.14%
26			**Quarter Profit Margin**	7.48%			15.00%			14.12%
27			**Income Year-To-Date**	$ 5,590			$ 17,800			$ 29,800

Year | First Quarter | Second Quarter | Third Quarter | Fourth Quarter

Sheet Name
Each worksheet has a unique **sheet name.** To make the workbook easy to navigate, it is a good practice to always use simple yet descriptive names for each worksheet.

What-If Analysis
What-if analysis is a very powerful and simple tool to test the effects of different assumptions in a spreadsheet.

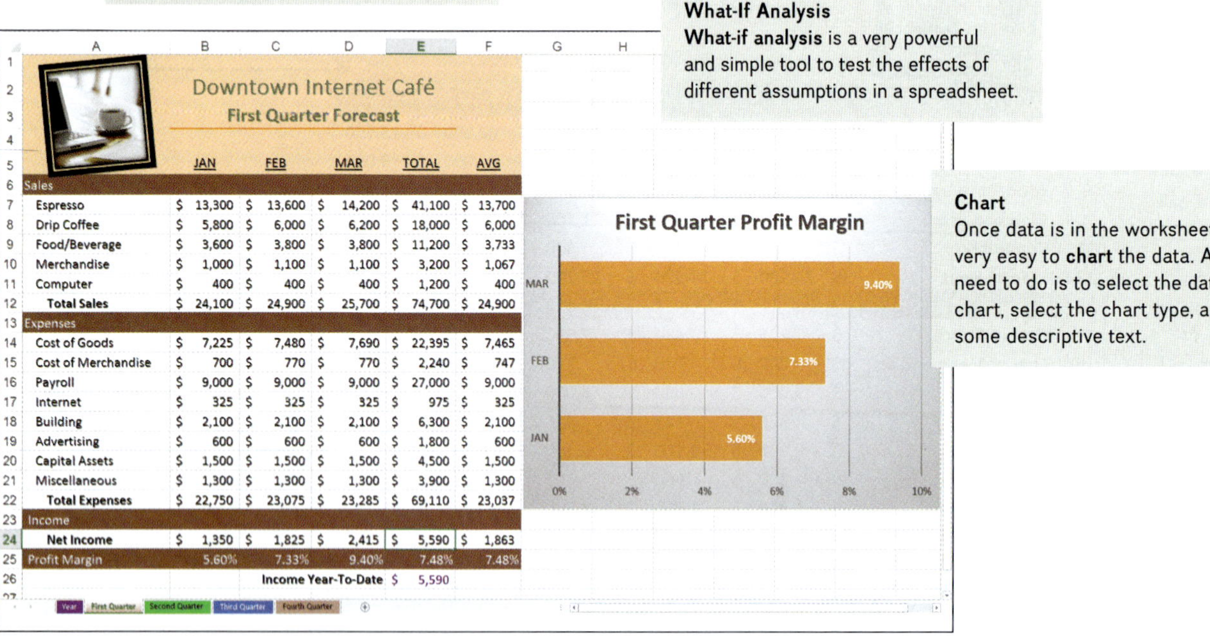

Downtown Internet Café
First Quarter Forecast

	A	B	C	D	E	F
5		JAN	FEB	MAR	TOTAL	AVG
6	Sales					
7	Espresso	$ 13,300	$ 13,600	$ 14,200	$ 41,100	$ 13,700
8	Drip Coffee	$ 5,800	$ 6,000	$ 6,200	$ 18,000	$ 6,000
9	Food/Beverage	$ 3,600	$ 3,800	$ 3,800	$ 11,200	$ 3,733
10	Merchandise	$ 1,000	$ 1,100	$ 1,100	$ 3,200	$ 1,067
11	Computer	$ 400	$ 400	$ 400	$ 1,200	$ 400
12	**Total Sales**	$ 24,100	$ 24,900	$ 25,700	$ 74,700	$ 24,900
13	Expenses					
14	Cost of Goods	$ 7,225	$ 7,480	$ 7,690	$ 22,395	$ 7,465
15	Cost of Merchandise	$ 700	$ 770	$ 770	$ 2,240	$ 747
16	Payroll	$ 9,000	$ 9,000	$ 9,000	$ 27,000	$ 9,000
17	Internet	$ 325	$ 325	$ 325	$ 975	$ 325
18	Building	$ 2,100	$ 2,100	$ 2,100	$ 6,300	$ 2,100
19	Advertising	$ 600	$ 600	$ 600	$ 1,800	$ 600
20	Capital Assets	$ 1,500	$ 1,500	$ 1,500	$ 4,500	$ 1,500
21	Miscellaneous	$ 1,300	$ 1,300	$ 1,300	$ 3,900	$ 1,300
22	**Total Expenses**	$ 22,750	$ 23,075	$ 23,285	$ 69,110	$ 23,037
23	Income					
24	**Net Income**	$ 1,350	$ 1,825	$ 2,415	$ 5,590	$ 1,863
25	Profit Margin	5.60%	7.33%	9.40%	7.48%	7.48%
26			**Income Year-To-Date**		$ 5,590	

Year | First Quarter | Second Quarter | Third Quarter | Fourth Quarter

Chart
Once data is in the worksheet, it is very easy to **chart** the data. All you need to do is to select the data to chart, select the chart type, and add some descriptive text.

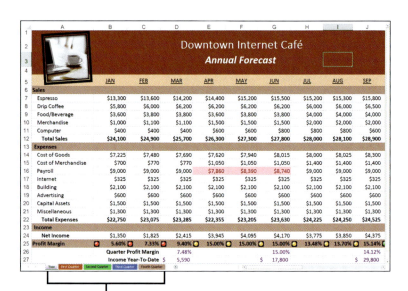

Figure 3-6 Annual forecast and analysis

Presentation Graphics

Research shows that people learn better when information is presented visually. **Presentation graphics** are programs that combine a variety of visual objects to create attractive, visually interesting presentations. They are excellent tools to communicate a message and to persuade people.

People in a variety of settings and situations use presentation graphics programs to make their presentations. For example, marketing managers use presentation graphics to present proposed marketing strategies to their superiors. Salespeople use these programs to demonstrate products and encourage customers to make purchases. Students use presentation graphics programs to create high-quality class presentations.

Six of the most widely used presentation graphics programs are Microsoft PowerPoint, Apple Keynote, Google Slides, Corel Presentations, OpenOffice Impress, and Prezi.

Assume that you have volunteered for the Animal Rescue Foundation, a local animal rescue agency. You have been asked to create a powerful and persuasive presentation to encourage other members from your community to volunteer. To see how you could use Microsoft PowerPoint, see Figure 3-7.

Creating a Presentation

You have been asked to create a powerful and persuasive presentation for the director of the foundation designed to encourage other members from your community to volunteer. The first step is to meet with the director of the foundation to determine the content of the presentation. Then using PowerPoint, you begin creating the presentation by selecting a presentation template and document theme. After entering the content, you add interest to the presentation by adding animation to selected objects and using slide transition effects.

Templates
Templates provide an excellent way to quickly create a presentation by providing predesigned styles and layouts as well as suggested content based on the type of template you select.

Document Theme
To make your presentation more professional and eye-catching, you select a **document theme**, built-in sets of colors, fonts, and effects that can be quickly applied to your entire presentation.

How Does the Foundation Help?
Provides temporary homes
Provides obedience training
Provides veterinary care
Finds loving permanent homes
Who Are Animal Angels?
Join Animal Angels
Animal Rescue Foundation
Volunteer Coordinator

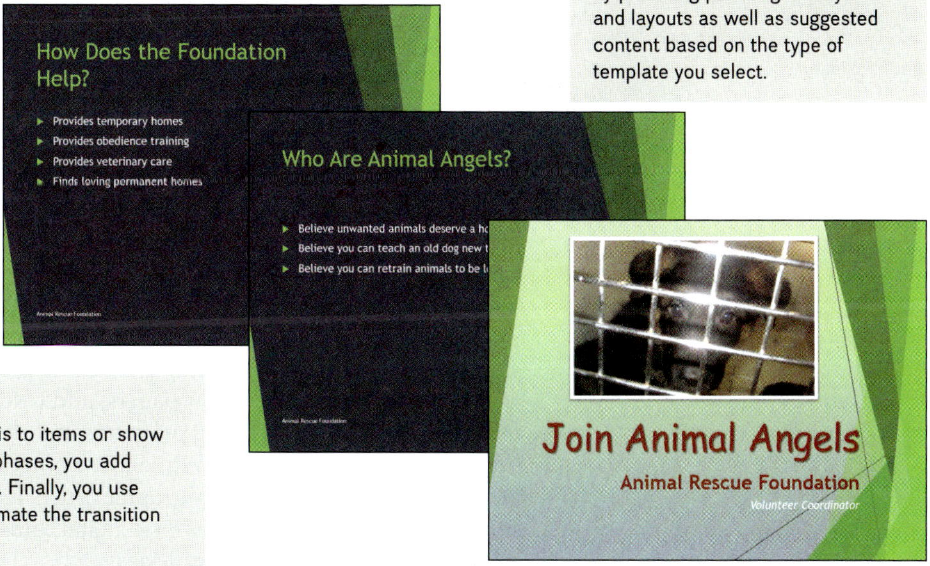

Animation
To provide additional emphasis to items or show the information on a slide in phases, you add **animation** to text and objects. Finally, you use slide **transition** effects to animate the transition from one slide to the next.

Figure 3-7 **Presentation**

Database Management Systems

A **database** is a collection of related data. It is the electronic equivalent of a file cabinet. A **database management system (DBMS)** or **database manager** is a program that sets up, or structures, a database. It also provides tools to enter, edit, and retrieve data from the database. All kinds of individuals use databases, from hospital administrators recording patient information to police officers checking criminal histories. Colleges and universities use databases to keep records on their students, instructors, and courses. Organizations of all types maintain employee databases.

Four widely used database management systems designed for personal computers are Microsoft Access, Apple FileMaker, Google Obvibase, and OpenOffice Base.

Assume that you have accepted a job as an employment administrator for the Lifestyle Fitness Club. To see how you could use Microsoft Access, see Figure 3-8.

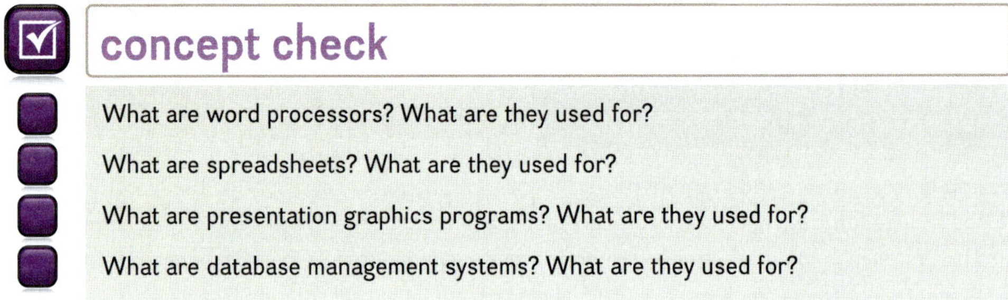

concept check
What are word processors? What are they used for?
What are spreadsheets? What are they used for?
What are presentation graphics programs? What are they used for?
What are database management systems? What are they used for?

Specialized Applications

While general-purpose applications are widely used in nearly every profession, specialized applications are widely used within specific professions. These programs include graphics programs and web authoring programs.

Graphics

Graphics are widely used by professionals in the graphic arts profession. They use desktop publishing programs, image editing programs, illustration programs, and video editors.

- **Desktop publishing programs,** or **page layout programs,** allow you to mix text and graphics to create publications of professional quality. While word processors focus on creating text and have the ability to combine text and graphics, desktop publishers focus on page design and layout and provide greater flexibility. Professional graphic artists use desktop publishing programs to create documents such as brochures, newsletters, newspapers, and textbooks.

  Popular desktop publishing programs include Adobe InDesign, Microsoft Publisher, and QuarkXPress. While these programs provide the capability to create text and graphics, typically graphic artists import these elements from other sources, including word processors, digital cameras, scanners, image editors, illustration programs, and image galleries.

Creating a Database

You have been asked to create an employee database to replace the club's manual system for recording employee data. The first step in creating the database management system is to plan. You study the existing manual system focusing on how and what data is collected and how it is used. Next, using Microsoft Access, one of the most widely used DBMS programs, you design the basic structure or organization of the new database system to include a table that will make entering data and using the database more efficient. You create the table structure by specifying the fields and primary key field. To make the process faster and more accurate, you create a form and enter the data for each employee as a record in the table.

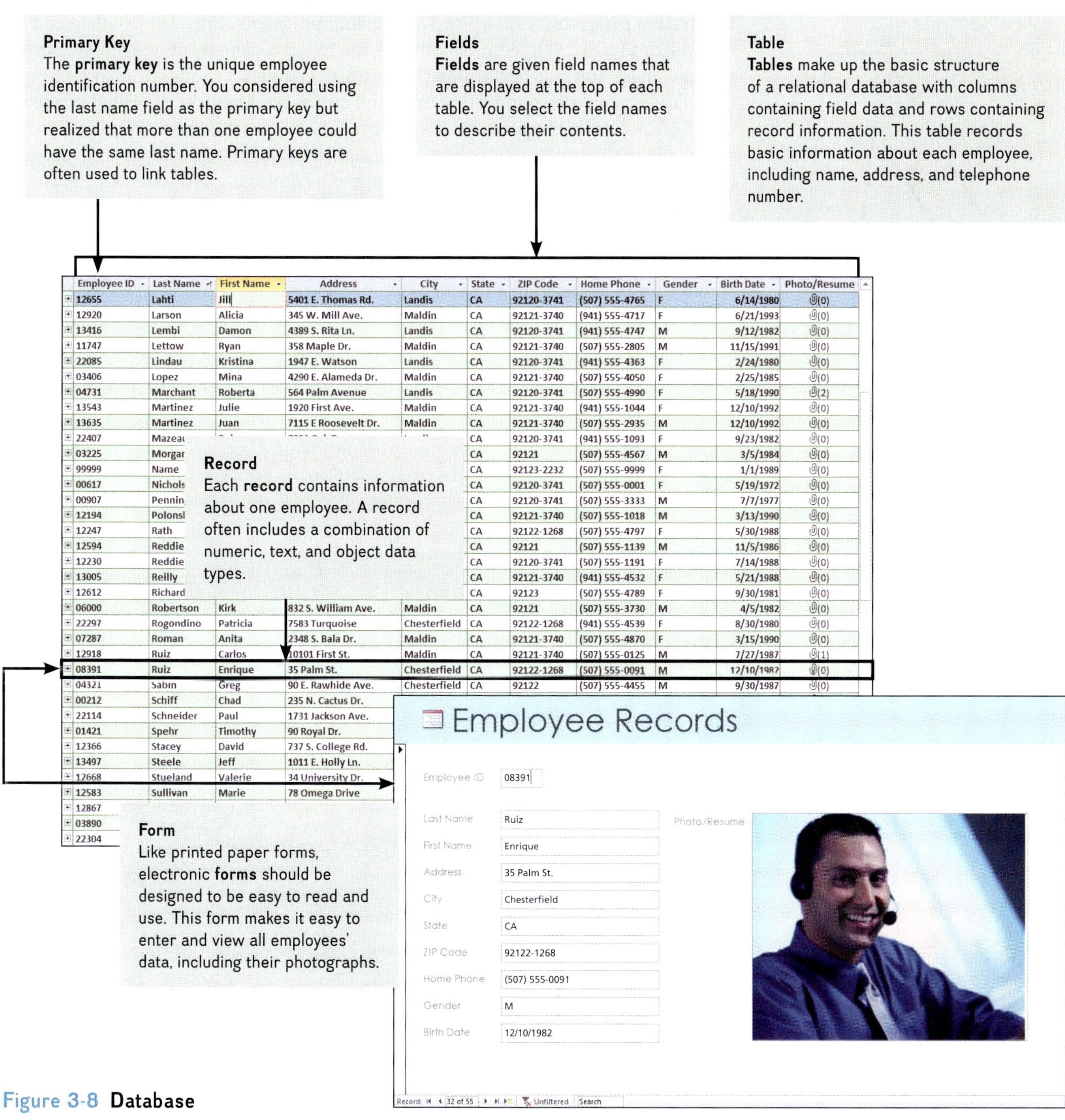

Primary Key
The **primary key** is the unique employee identification number. You considered using the last name field as the primary key but realized that more than one employee could have the same last name. Primary keys are often used to link tables.
Fields
Fields are given field names that are displayed at the top of each table. You select the field names to describe their contents.
Table
Tables make up the basic structure of a relational database with columns containing field data and rows containing record information. This table records basic information about each employee, including name, address, and telephone number.
Record
Each **record** contains information about one employee. A record often includes a combination of numeric, text, and object data types.
Form
Like printed paper forms, electronic **forms** should be designed to be easy to read and use. This form makes it easy to enter and view all employees' data, including their photographs.
Employee Records
Employee ID 08391
Last Name Ruiz
First Name Enrique
Address 35 Palm St.
City Chesterfield
State CA
ZIP Code 92122-1268
Home Phone (507) 555-0091
Gender M
Birth Date 12/10/1982
Photo/Resume

Figure 3-8 **Database**

Figure 3-9 **Bitmap image**

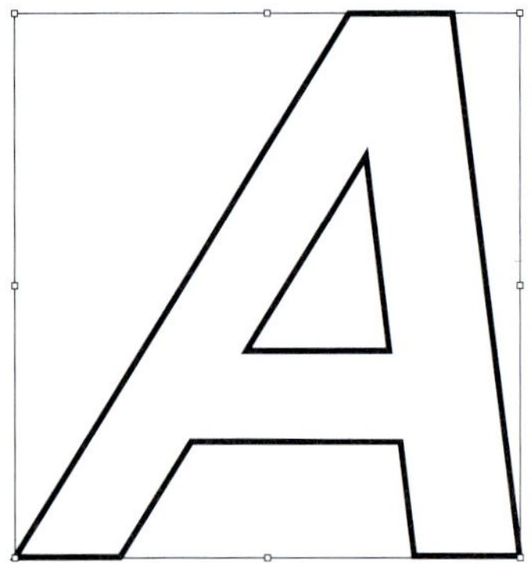

Figure 3-10 **Vector image**

- **Image editors,** also known as **photo editors,** are specialized graphics programs for editing or modifying digital photographs. They are often used to touch up photographs to remove scratches and other imperfections. The photographs consist of thousands of dots or **pixels** that form images often referred to as **bitmap** or **raster** images. One limitation of bitmap images, however, is that when they are expanded, the images can become pixelated, or jagged on the edges. For example, when the letter *A* in Figure 3-9 is expanded, the borders of the letter appear jagged, as indicated by the expanded view.

  Popular image editors include Adobe Photoshop, Corel PaintShop Pro, GIMP (GNU Image Manipulation Program), and Windows Photo Gallery.
- **Illustration programs,** also known as **drawing programs,** are used to create and edit vector images. While bitmap images use pixels to represent images, **vector images,** also known as **vector illustrations,** use geometric shapes or objects. These objects are created by connecting lines and curves avoiding the pixeleted or ragged edges created by bitmap images. (See Figure 3-10.) Because these objects can be defined by mathematical equations, they can be rapidly and easily resized, colored, textured, and manipulated. An image is a combination of several objects.

  Illustration programs are often used for graphic design, page layout, and creating sharp artistic images. Popular illustration programs include Adobe Illustrator, CorelDRAW, and Inkscape.
- **Video editors** are used to edit videos to enhance quality and appearance. Once used only by Hollywood professionals, video editors are now widely used to edit high-quality video captured using smartphones and other devices. You can readily add special effects, music tracks, titles, and on-screen graphics.

  Just a few years ago, video editors were used only by professionals with expensive specialized hardware and software. Now, there are several free or inexpensive editors designed to assist the amateur videographer. Three well-known video editors are Windows Live Movie Maker, Apple iMovie, and YouTube Video Editor. (See Figure 3-11.)

ethics

Image editing software has made it easy to alter any photo or video to correct for a variety of different imperfections. However, some professionals can use these programs to significantly manipulate the content or meaning of a photo or video. Such changes are often intended to influence the opinions or emotions of the viewer. Supporters argue that this type of editing is acceptable and is just another way to express an opinion or feeling from an editor. Critics note that this type of image and video manipulation is unethical because it intentionally misleads the viewer and often creates unobtainable or unhealthy definitions of beauty. What do you think?

Figure 3-11 **Video editor**

Figure 3-12 **Video game design software**

Video Game Design Software

Have you ever thought about designing a video game? While it may initially be unrealistic to create an immersive 3D world like Skyrim or BioShock, you can experiment and create some impressive games on your own with the right software. The first step is to visualize the game by thinking about the game's length and plot. The second step is to choose the right video game design software.

Video game design software will help you organize your thoughts and guide you through the game design process including character development and environmental design. There are many choices from free software to very expensive software designed for professional game designers. Some of the better-known free or inexpensive video game design software are YoYo GameMaker, Stencyl, Flixel, and Unity. (See Figure 3-12.)

Web Authoring Programs

There are over a billion websites on the Internet, and more are being added every day. Corporations use the web to reach new customers and to promote their products. Individuals create online diaries or commentaries, called **blogs.** Creating a site is called **web authoring.**

Almost all websites consist of interrelated web pages. As we mentioned in Chapter 2, web pages are typically HTML (Hypertext Markup Language) and CSS (cascading style sheets) documents. With knowledge of HTML and a simple text editor, you can create web pages. Even without knowledge of HTML, you can create simple web pages using a word processing package like Microsoft Word.

More specialized and powerful programs, called **web authoring programs,** are typically used to create sophisticated commercial sites. Also known as **web page editors** and **HTML editors,** these programs provide support for website design and HTML coding. Some web authoring programs are **WYSIWYG (what you see is what you get) editors,** which means you can build a page without interacting directly with HTML code. WYSIWYG editors preview the page described by HTML code. Widely used web authoring programs include Adobe Dreamweaver and Microsoft Expression Web.

Other Specialized Applications

There are numerous other specialized applications including accounting, personal finance, and project management applications. Accounting applications such as Intuit QuickBooks help companies record and report their financial operations. Personal financial applications such as Quicken Starter Edition help individuals track their personal finances and investments. Project management software like Microsoft Project is widely used in business to help coordinate and plan complicated projects.

concept check

What are desktop publishing programs? Image editors? Illustration programs? Video editors?

What is video game design software?

What are blogs? Web authoring? Web authoring programs? WYSIWYG?

Mobile Apps

Mobile apps or **mobile applications** are add-on programs for a variety of mobile devices including smartphones and tablets. Sometimes referred to simply as **apps,** mobile apps have been widely used for years. The traditional applications include address books, to-do lists, alarms, and message lists. With the introduction of smartphones, tablets, and wireless connections to the Internet, mobile capabilities have exploded. Now, any number of applications are available.

Apps

The breadth and scope of available mobile applications for smartphones and other mobile devices are ever expanding. There are over 500,000 apps just for Apple's iPhone alone. Some of the most widely used are for listening to music, viewing video, social networking, shopping, and game playing.

- Music. For many, their smartphone and/or tablet is their primary source for music. The mobile app Pandora offers free streaming music with ads and playlists that you can customize in a limited way. Spotify is another streaming music service that requires a monthly fee but offers direct control of what music you listen to and no ads.
- Video. With faster data speeds and higher resolution screens, smartphones and tablets are becoming a favorite way to watch TV shows, movies, or video clips. The YouTube app offers access to free online videos such as movie trailers and video blogs. The Netflix app provides access to more professional videos for a fee.
- Social networking. Mobile apps are ideal for sharing a picture while on vacation, checking in at your favorite coffee shop, or sending out invites to a last-minute party. The Facebook mobile app offers many of the features of the Facebook web-site, with additional features that take advantage of a mobile device's camera and GPS capability. The Instagram app provides a more specialized and artistic flair by focusing on sharing photos.

environment

Did you know that using mobile devices and apps can benefit the environment by reducing the production of paper? There are many apps that allow you to read electronic books and reference materials that would otherwise have been printed using a large amount of paper. Furthermore, many apps allow you to write digital notes so that you don't have to buy paper notebooks or notepads.

- Shopping. A recent poll concluded that well over half of all smartphone users in the United States regularly use their phones for shopping. By scanning a product's barcode, shopping apps search for the product and provide price comparisons as well as product reviews. Using Amazon's Price Check app, all you need to do is take a picture of the product.
- Games. One of the most popular activities on smartphones and tablets is game playing. Some of these games are quite basic, are free, and include in-app optional purchases. For example, Crossy Road challenges game players to assist a character across obstacles (roads, rivers, grass, and train tracks) without succumbing to obstacles such as rivers, trees, trains and cars. Players have the option to buy additional characters. Some other games are quite complex and are not free. For example, Dragon Quest V is a popular **role playing game (RPG)** where gamers create their own villages, fight off intruders, and form alliances with millions of other players online. (See Figure 3-13.)

Figure 3-13 **Crossy Road game**

Many apps are written for a particular type of mobile device and will not run on other types. For example, an app designed for Apple's iPhone may not work with Google's Android.

App Stores

An **app store** is typically a website that provides access to specific mobile apps that can be downloaded either for a nominal fee or free of charge. Two of the best-known stores are Apple's App Store and Google Play. (See Figure 3-14.) Although most of the best-known app stores specialize in applications for a particular line of mobile device, other less well-known stores provide apps for a wide variety of mobile devices. For a list of some more widely used app stores, see Figure 3-15.

privacy

Did you know that many mobile phone apps track a phone's physical location? For example, iOS's Siri and Android's Google Now use a smartphone's GPS to track locations to customize interactions with users. The smartphone's location is monitored, stored, and potentially used for a variety of different objectives. Privacy advocates argue that many people are unaware that they may be tracked in this manner and that their movements are recorded for possible later use. App developers argue that the objective is simply to improve users' interactions with their smartphones. What do you think?

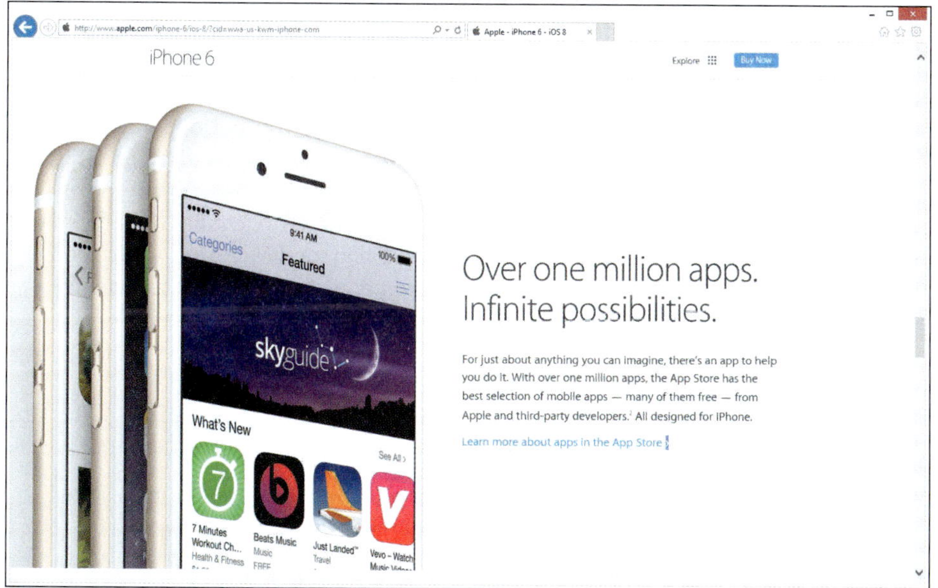

Figure 3-14 **Apple's App Store**

App Store	Focus	Site
Apple App Store	Apple devices	www.apple.com/itunes/charts
Google Play	Android devices	play.google.com/store/apps
Appszoom	Android and Apple devices	www.appszoom.com

Figure 3-15 App stores

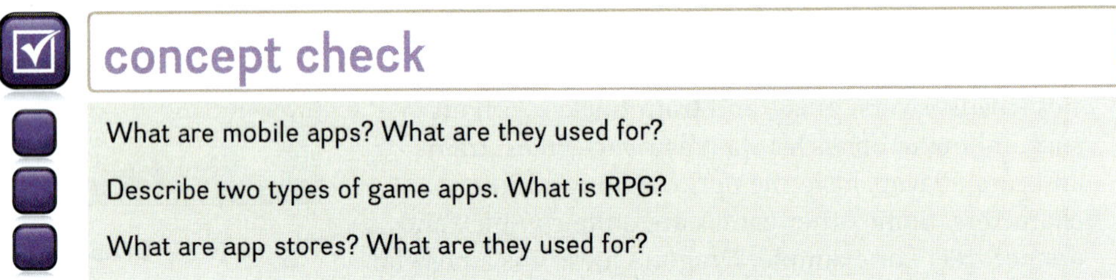

concept check

- What are mobile apps? What are they used for?
- Describe two types of game apps. What is RPG?
- What are app stores? What are they used for?

Software Suites

A **software suite** is a collection of separate application programs bundled together and made available as a group. Four types of suites are office suites, cloud suites, specialized suites, and utility suites.

Office Suites

Office suites, also known as **office software suites** and **productivity suites,** contain general-purpose application programs that are typically used in a business situation. Productivity suites commonly include a word processor, spreadsheet, database manager, and a presentation application. The best known is Microsoft Office. Other well-known productivity suites are Apple iWork and OpenOffice.

Cloud Computing

Cloud suites or **online office suites** are stored at a server on the Internet and are available anywhere you can access the Internet. Documents created using online applications can also be stored online, making it easy to share and collaborate on documents with others. One downside to cloud applications is that you are dependent on the server providing the application to be available whenever you need it. For this reason, when using online applications, it is important to have backup copies of your documents on your computer and to have a desktop office application available to use. Popular online office suites include Google Docs, Zoho, and Microsoft Office 365 and Office for iPad. (See Figure 3-16.) To learn more about one of the most widely used online office suites, see Making IT Work for You: Google Docs on page 78.

Specialized and Utility Suites

Two other types of suites that are more narrowly focused are specialized suites and utility suites.

- **Specialized suites** focus on specific applications. These include graphics suites like CorelDRAW Graphics Suite X6, financial planning suites like Moneytree Software's TOTAL Planning Suite, and many others.
- **Utility suites** include a variety of programs designed to make computing easier and safer. Two of the best known are Norton SystemWorks and Norton Internet Security Suite. (Utility suites will be discussed in detail in Chapter 4.)

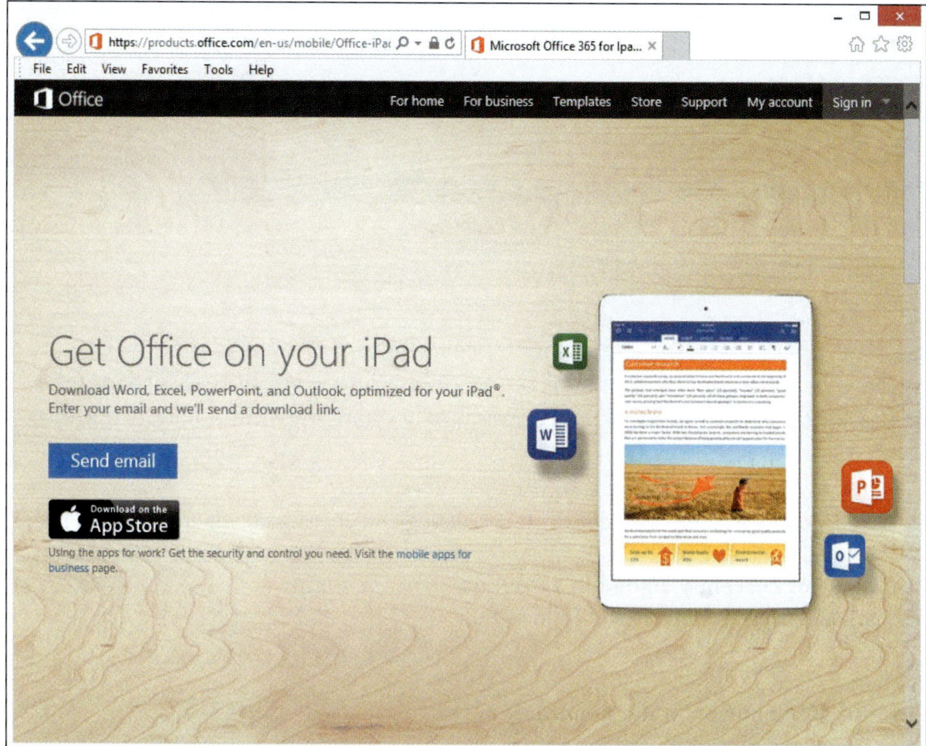

Figure 3-16 **Office for iPad**

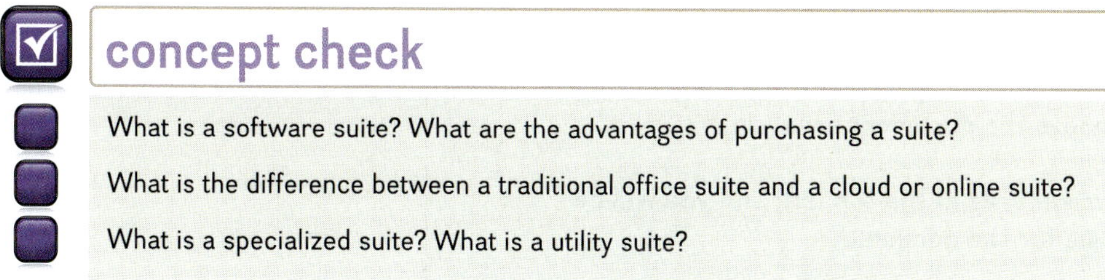

concept check

- What is a software suite? What are the advantages of purchasing a suite?
- What is the difference between a traditional office suite and a cloud or online suite?
- What is a specialized suite? What is a utility suite?

Careers in IT

"Now that you have learned about application software, I'd like to tell you about my career as a software engineer."

Software engineers analyze users' needs and create application software. Software engineers typically have experience in programming but focus on the design and development of programs using the principles of mathematics and engineering.

A bachelor's or an advanced specialized associate's degree in computer science or information systems and an extensive knowledge of computers and technology are required by most employers. Internships may provide students with the kinds of experience employers look for in a software engineer. Those with specific experience with web applications may have an advantage over other applicants. Employers typically look for software engineers with good communication and analytical skills.

Software engineers can expect to earn an annual salary in the range of $55,000 to $71,000. Starting salary is dependent on both experience and the type of software being developed. Experienced software engineers are candidates for many other advanced careers in IT.

GOOGLE DOCS

Do you need to create and collaborate with others on a document, presentation, or spreadsheet? Do you need access from different computers in different locations? If so, an online office suite, such as Google Docs, might be just what you need. (Please note that the web is continually changing, and some of the specifics presented below may have changed.)

Creating a Document You must have a free Google account in order to start creating and sharing documents. To get started:

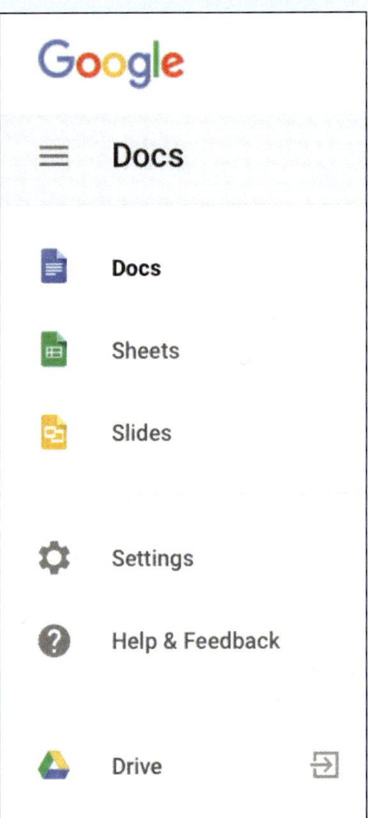

1. **Go to docs.google.com. If you are not currently signed in or you do not have a Google account, click the *Sign in* button and follow the appropriate instructions.**
2. **Once you are signed in, click the *Menu* button in the upper left of the page. Select *Docs* to see existing word processing documents.**
3. **Click the *Create New Documents* button in the lower right of the page (a red circle with a white + in the center).**
4. **Start typing in the blank document. You will notice many familiar buttons in the toolbar above the document area.**
5. **Click the *Untitled document* area at the top left, and you will be prompted to enter a name for the document.**
6. **Close the *browser* tab (or window) in order to close the document.**

You may have noticed that there is no save option. This is because your document is automatically being saved as you work on it.

Sharing a Document Any document that you create can be shared with one or more individuals. Those individuals can be granted read-only access, or they could be allowed to edit the document, even at the same time that you are working on it. To share a document:

1. **With the document open, click the *Share* button at the top right.**
2. **Type in the e-mail addresses of those with whom you wish to share the document.**
3. **To the right of this text box, select the permission these individuals will have for the document.**
4. **Click the *Done* button to finish.**

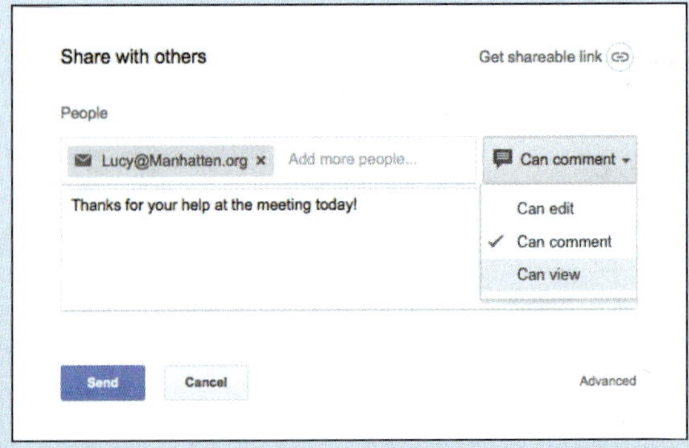

A LOOK TO THE FUTURE

Next-Generation User Interfaces

Have you ever given a presentation and wished you could interact with the whiteboard like a computer screen? Wouldn't it be great to be able to have a digital whiteboard with different pens for collaborating on projects? The traditional mouse and keyboard work great for interacting with a computer, but sometimes it would be nice to have more options. Recently, touch screens and voice recognition offer new ways to interface. In the future, larger touch screens that can identify different users will allow for multiple people to work on the same screen, and recent innovations in video capture technology may have computers leaving the desktop and entering the yoga studio. Technology has been making better interfaces, and will continue to evolve to improve our lives as we look to the future.

There are several challenges with designing interfaces. First is the simple fact that individuals have varying preferences. Some might prefer to interact with a friend through text messages, while others prefer voice communication. Therefore, it is doubtful that a single interface will become dominant. The second challenge is ergonomic in nature; that is, it must be comfortable to use.

Since tablets and smartphones have touch-screen interfaces, many people believe that all home and business computers will eventually have them too. In futuristic movies individuals use both hands to interact with a large screen. Such a setup allows a person to interact with multiple objects at the same time. The only problem with a multi-touch, multigesture screen is that it is not comfortable to extend our arms for prolonged periods. Knowing this, many companies are looking toward large, interactive surfaces that perform the same function while lying flat on a desk. Microsoft has already developed a product called "PixelSense" that acts like a large, interactive table. It responds to both human interactions and objects that are placed on top of it. Although costs prevent it from replacing the desktop of today, the strain on a person's neck from looking down could prevent it from being used for long periods of time.

The ideal use of PixelSense appears to be activities involving collaboration and teamwork. Voice recognition is another form of input that is already available, but much improvement is needed. Computers are becoming better at following specific voice commands, but they cannot engage in everyday conversation or follow complex requests. Researchers in the field of artificial intelligence are working to improve natural language processing to help computers understand our writing and speech. When that is fully developed, you will be able to speak to your computer in the same way you would speak to another person.

Both cameras and software are becoming sophisticated enough to observe and interpret our movements and gestures. The "Kinect" system for the Xbox One has the ability to use body movements to interact with various games and fitness programs, including ones that analyze and correct form during yoga routines. Researchers at MIT are also working with cameras that can observe our gestures and the physical objects we interact with in order to communicate with a computer. In the future, computers could become so attuned to our emotions and expressions that they will be able to see our frustration with the current operation and take various corrective actions to relieve that frustration.

The next step in computer interaction may be something called "Augmented Reality." Microsoft HoloLens offers glasses that you can see through but can also act as a monitor that can overlay text and images onto the real world. Through the HoloLens, and sophisticated body tracking cameras, your real world may become populated with virtual assistants, digital notes, and interactive how-to manuals.

Which type of interface do you currently enjoy using the most? Do you think that touch-screen interfaces will replace keyboards? Do you believe augmented reality will become the keyboard and mouse of the future?

VISUAL SUMMARY Application Software

APPLICATION SOFTWARE

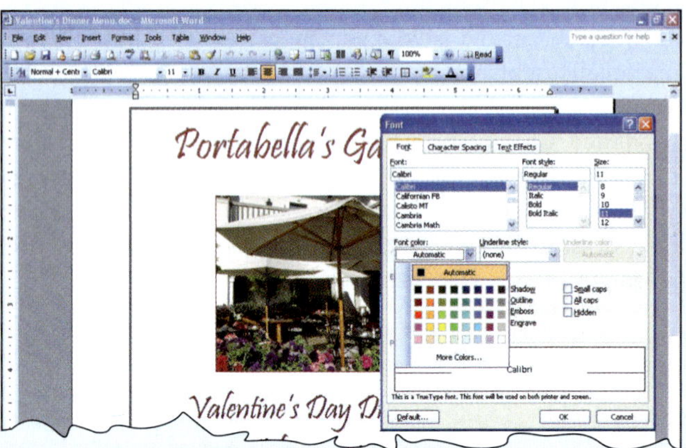

The three categories of application software are **general purpose, specialized,** and **mobile.**

User Interface

You control and interact with a program using a **user interface.** A **graphical user interface (GUI)** uses **icons** selected by a mouse-controlled **pointer.** A **window** contains a document, program, or message. Software programs with a traditional GUI have

- **Menus**—present commands listed on the **menu bar.**
- **Toolbars**—contain **buttons** for quick access to commonly used commands.
- **Dialog box**—provides additional information or requests user input.

Software programs with a **Ribbon GUI** have

- **Ribbons**—replace menus and toolbars.
- **Tabs**—divide ribbons into **groups. Contextual tabs** automatically appear when needed.
- **Galleries**—graphically display alternatives before they are selected.

Common Features

Common features include spell checkers, alignment, fonts and font sizes, character effects, and edit options.

GENERAL-PURPOSE APPLICATIONS

Adventure Travel Tours
New Adventures
Attention adventure travelers! Attend an Adventure presentation to learn about some of the earth's greatest unspoiled habitats and find out how you can experience the adventure of a lifetime. This year we are offering four new tours:
India Wildlife Adventure
Inca Trail to Machu Picchu
Safari in Tanzania
Costa Rica Rivers and Rainforests
Call Student Name at 1-800-555-0004 for presentation locations, full color brochures, itinerary information, costs, and trip dates.

General-purpose applications include word processors, spreadsheets, presentation graphics, and database management systems.

Word Processors

Word processors create text-based documents. Individuals and organizations use word processors to create memos, letters, and faxes. Organizations also create newsletters, manuals, and brochures to provide information to their customers. Microsoft Word is the most widely used word processor. Others include Apple Pages, Google Docs, Corel WordPerfect, and OpenOffice Writer.

Spreadsheets

Spreadsheets organize, analyze, and graph numeric data such as budgets and financial reports. They are widely used by nearly every profession. Microsoft Excel is the most widely used spreadsheet program. Others include Apple Numbers, Corel Quattro Pro, Google Sheets, and OpenOffice Calc.

To efficiently and effectively use computers, you need to understand the capabilities of general-purpose and specialized application software. Additionally, you need to know about mobile applications and software suites.

GENERAL-PURPOSE APPLICATIONS

Presentation Graphics

Presentation graphics are programs that combine a variety of visual objects to create attractive, visually interesting presentations. They are excellent tools to communicate a message and to persuade people. People in a variety of settings and situations use presentation graphics programs to make their presentations more interesting and professional. Six of the most widely used presentation graphics programs are Microsoft PowerPoint, Apple Keynote, Google Slides, Corel Presentations, OpenOffice Impress, and Prezi.

Database Management Systems

A **database** is a collection of related data. A **database management system (DBMS)** or **database manager** is a program that structures a database. It provides tools to enter, edit, and retrieve data from the database. Organizations use databases for many purposes including maintaining employee records. Four widely used database management systems designed for personal computers are Microsoft Access, Apple FileMaker, Google Obvibase, and OpenOffice Base.

SPECIALIZED APPLICATIONS

Specialized applications are widely used within specific professions. They include graphics programs, video game design software, and web authoring programs.

Graphics Programs

Graphics programs are used by graphic arts professionals.

- **Desktop publishing programs (page layout programs)** mix text and graphics to create professional-quality publications.
- **Image editors (photo editors)** edit digital photographs consisting of thousands of dots or **pixels** that form **bitmap** or **raster** images.
- **Illustration programs (drawing programs)** create and edit vector images. **Vector images (vector illustrations)** use geometric shapes.
- **Video editors** edit video to enhance quality and appearance.

Video Game Design Software

Video game design software helps to organize thoughts and guide users through the game design process including character development and environmental design.

Web Authoring Programs

Web authoring is the process of creating a website. Individuals create online diaries called **blogs. Web authoring programs (web page editors, HTML editors)** create sophisticated commercial websites. Some are **WYSIWYG (what you see is what you get) editors.**

MOBILE APPS

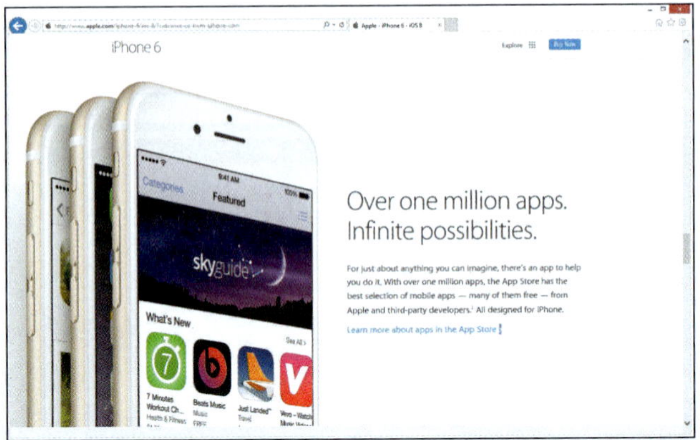

Mobile apps (mobile applications, apps) are add-on programs for a variety of mobile devices. Traditional applications include address books, to-do lists, alarms, and message lists. Recently, mobile capabilities have exploded.

Apps

Popular apps include those for music, videos, social networking, shopping, and game playing.

- Pandora and Spotify provide popular music apps.
- YouTube and Netflix provide streaming videos apps.
- Facebook and Instagram provide social networking apps.
- Crossy Road and Dragon Quest V are popular game playing apps. Crossy Road includes in-app optional purchases including the ability to purchase additional characters. Dragon Quest V is a **role playing game (RPG)** where gamers create their own villages, fight off intruders, and form alliances with millions of other players online.

App Stores

An **app store** is typically a website that provides access to specific mobile apps that can be downloaded either for a nominal fee or free of charge. Two of the best-known stores are Apple's App Store and Google Play. Most of the best-known app stores specialize in applications for a particular line of mobile device, other less well-known stores provide apps for a wide variety of mobile devices.

App Store	Focus	Site
Apple App Store	Apple devices	www.apple.com/itunes/charts
Google Play	Android devices	play.google.com/store/apps
Appszoom	Android and Apple devices	www.appszoom.com

SOFTWARE SUITES

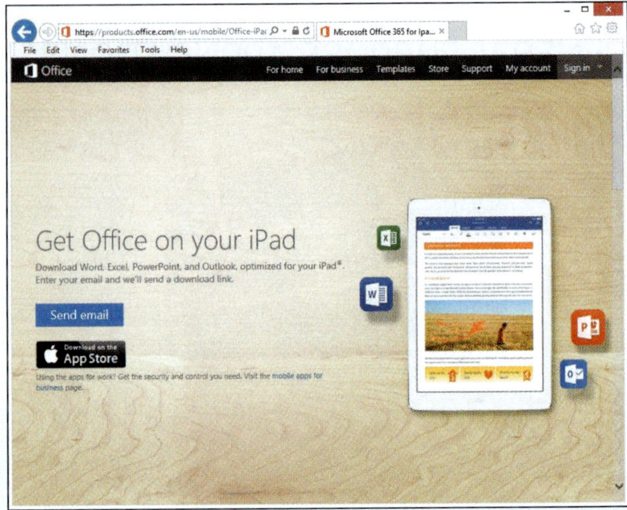

A **software suite** is a collection of individual application packages sold together.

- **Office suites (office software suites** or **productivity suites)** contain professional-grade application programs.
- **Cloud suites (online office suites)** are stored on servers and available through the Internet.
- **Specialized suites** focus on specific applications such as graphics.
- **Utility suites** include a variety of programs designed to make computing easier and safer.

CAREERS IN IT

Software engineers analyze users' needs and create application software. A bachelor's or advanced specialized associate's degree in computer science or information systems and extensive knowledge of computers and technology are required. Salary range is $55,000 to $71,000.

KEY TERMS

app (74)
application software (62)
app store (75)
bitmap (72)
blog (73)
button (62)
cloud suite (76)
contextual tab (63)
database (70)
database management system (DBMS) (70)
database manager (70)
desktop publishing program (70)
dialog box (62)
document (64)
drawing program (72)
gallery (64)
general-purpose application (62)
graphical user interface (GUI) (62)
group (63)
HTML editor (73)
icon (62)
illustration program (72)
image editor (72)
menu (62)
menu bar (62)
mobile app (62, 74)
mobile application (74)
office software suite (76)
office suite (76)
online office suite (76)
page layout program (70)
photo editor (72)
pixel (72)
pointer (62)
presentation graphics (69)
productivity suite (76)
raster (72)
ribbon (63)
Ribbon GUI (63)
role playing game (RPG) (75)
software engineer (77)
software suite (76)
specialized application (62)
specialized suite (76)
spreadsheet (67)
system software (62)
tab (63)
toolbar (62)
user interface (62)
utility suite (76)
video editor (72)
video game design software (73)
vector illustration (72)
vector image (72)
web authoring (73)
web authoring program (73)
web page editor (73)
window (62)
word processor (64)
WYSIWYG (what you see is what you get) editor (73)

MULTIPLE CHOICE

Circle the correct answer.

1. This type of software works with end users, application software, and computer hardware to handle the majority of technical details.
   a. application
   b. specialized
   c. system
   d. utility

2. A rectangular area that can contain a document, program, or message.
   a. dialog box
   b. form
   c. frame
   d. window

3. Programs that create text-based documents.
   a. DBMS
   b. suites
   c. spreadsheets
   d. word processors

4. Programs that organize, analyze, and graph numerical data such as budgets and financial reports.
   a. DBMS
   b. suites
   c. spreadsheets
   d. word processors

5. Program that allows you to mix text and graphics to create publications of professional quality.
   a. database
   b. desktop publishing
   c. presentation
   d. productivity

6. The type of image that consists of geometric shapes.
   a. bitmap
   b. raster
   c. ribbon
   d. vector

7. An online diary or commentary.
   a. bitmap
   b. blog
   c. HTML
   d. vector

8. Programs that combine a variety of visual objects to create attractive, visually interesting presentations.
   a. DBMS
   b. presentation graphics
   c. spreadsheet
   d. word processor

9. Programs typically used to create sophisticated commercial websites.
   a. game design programs
   b. illustration programs
   c. video editors
   d. web authoring programs

10. Also known as an online suite.
    a. cloud
    b. integrated
    c. office
    d. utility

MATCHING

Match each numbered item with the most closely related lettered item. Write your answers in the spaces provided.

- **a.** buttons
- **b.** cloud
- **c.** database
- **d.** galleries
- **e.** image editor
- **f.** pixels
- **g.** spreadsheet
- **h.** store
- **i.** utility
- **j.** word processor

___ **1.** Toolbars typically appear below the menu bar and include small graphic elements called _____.

___ **2.** Simplifies the process of making a selection from a list of alternatives by graphically displaying the effect of alternatives before being selected.

___ **3.** A general-purpose program that creates text-based documents.

___ **4.** Program that organizes, analyzes, and graphs numerical data.

___ **5.** A collection of related data.

___ **6.** Also known as a photo editor, this specialized graphics program edits or modifies digital photographs.

___ **7.** Image editors create images made up of thousands of dots known as _____.

___ **8.** A website that provides access to specific mobile apps is known as an app _____.

___ **9.** A type of suite that is stored at a server on the Internet and is available anywhere you can access the Internet.

___ **10.** A type of specialized suite that includes a variety of programs designed to make computing easier and safer.

OPEN-ENDED

On a separate sheet of paper, respond to each question or statement.

1. Explain the difference between general-purpose and specialized applications. Also discuss the common features of application programs, including those with traditional and ribbon graphical user interfaces.
2. Discuss general-purpose applications, including word processors, spreadsheets, database management systems, and presentation graphics.
3. Discuss specialized applications, including graphics programs, video game design software, web authoring programs, and other professional specialized applications.
4. Describe mobile apps, including popular apps and app stores.
5. Describe software suites, including office suites, cloud suites, specialized suites, and utility suites.

DISCUSSION

Respond to each of the following questions.

1 Making IT Work for You: GOOGLE DOCS

Would you like to try free alternatives to traditional office software suites? Review the Making IT Work for You: Google Docs on page 78, and then respond to the following: (a) Do you currently use Google Docs? If so, what types of documents do you typically create? If not, then list some possible benefits Google Docs could provide. (b) Do you share documents and/or collaborate with others? How do you do it? If you have used Google Docs, describe how you would share documents. (c) Using a search engine or your own research, list a few differences between Google Docs and Microsoft Office Web Apps. Which one do you prefer? Why?

2 Privacy: SMARTPHONE TRACKING

If you have a smartphone, then it is likely that your movements are recorded and stored. Review the Privacy box on page 75, and respond to the following: (a) Do you think that smartphone tracking is a violation of your privacy? If yes, what can be done? If no, explain your position. (b) Does a company that tracks your movements have the right to sell this information to other companies? Would your opinion change if the company sells your location information but does not reveal your identity? State and defend your position. (c) Does the government have the right to subpoena GPS information from an app maker? Why or why not? (d) Are there any circumstances in which it would be acceptable/justifiable for a company to reveal location data to the government or another company? If so, give some examples.

3 Ethics: IMAGE EDITING

Various image and video editing applications have made it easy for both professionals and amateurs to alter photographs and videos. Some of these edits raise ethical concerns when they are used inappropriately. Review the Ethics box on page 72. Research examples of digital photo or video editing that have resulted in controversy, and then respond to the following: (a) Do you see any ethical issues related to altering photographs or videos? (b) What do you consider the boundary to be between acceptable editing and deceptive or misleading practices? (c) How does such editing affect courtrooms where visual evidence is often presented? (d) Do you feel the old saying "seeing is believing" needs to be reconsidered for the digital age? Defend your answers.

4 Environment: APPS

Did you know that using mobile devices and apps can benefit the environment? Review the Environment box on page 74, and then respond to the following: (a) In what ways are mobile devices helping the environment? (b) Do you currently read any books on mobile devices? If so, list a few of your most recent ones. If you do not, name three of your traditional textbooks that are available as e-books. (c) List and briefly describe three apps that allow you to take notes on your mobile device. If you do not own a mobile device, research these apps for any mobile operating system. (d) Is it possible that mobile devices could actually be worse for the environment? Discuss your response.

PHOTO CREDITS

CHAPTER 3

Opener: © Oliver Burston/Getty Images; p. 61, 79: © Blend Images/Colin Anderson/Getty Images RF; p. 62, 77, 82 (bottom-right): © Hill Street Studios/Blend Images LLC RF; 3-1, 3-2, 3-5, 3-6, 3-7, 3-8, 3-16, p. 80 (both), 81 (left), 82 (top-right): Microsoft product screen shot(s) reprinted with permission from Microsoft Corporation; 3-11: Screenshot credit to come; 3-12, p. 81 (right): Screenshot of the Unity editor, courtesy of Unity Technologies; 3-13, p. 81 (top-right): Copyright © 2014 Hipster Whale. All rights reserved; 3-14, p. 82 (top-left): Copyright © 2015 Apple, Inc. All rights reserved; p. 78: Google and the Google logo are registered trademarks of Google Inc. Used with permission.

chapter 4 System Software

Why should I read this chapter?

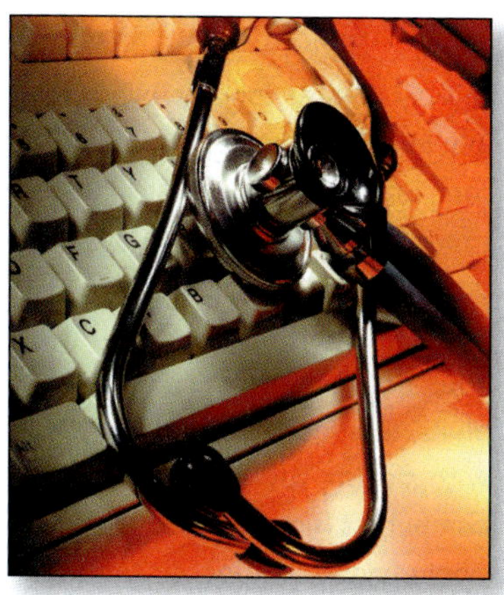

Someday soon, your computer will be able to automatically diagnose and repair problems, much like your body's immune system. For now, however, your electronics are at risk from dangerous viruses and software failures.

This chapter covers the things you need to know to protect your computer and data today and to prepare you for tomorrow, including:

- Desktop operating systems—discover how operating systems control and protect desktop and laptop computers.
- Mobile operating systems—learn the key features of the operating systems that control tablets and cell phones.
- Utilities—protect your computer from viruses and perform important maintenance tasks.

Learning Objectives

After you have read this chapter, you should be able to:

1. Describe the differences between system software and application software.
2. Identify the four types of system software programs.
3. Explain the basic functions, features, and categories of operating systems.
4. Compare mobile operating systems, including iOS, Android, and Windows Phone.
5. Compare desktop operating systems, including Windows, Mac OS, UNIX, Linux, and virtualization.
6. Explain the purpose of utilities and utility suites.
7. Identify the four most essential utilities.
8. Describe Windows utility programs.

Introduction

"Hi, I'm Ann, and I'm a computer support specialist. I'd like to talk with you about system software, programs that do a lot of the work behind the scenes so that you can run applications and surf the web. I'd also like to talk about the mobile operating systems that control smartphones and other small portable computers."

When most people think about computers, they think about surfing the web, writing papers, e-mailing friends, chatting online, making presentations, and any number of other valuable applications. We typically think about applications and application software. Computers and computer applications have become a part of the fabric of our everyday lives. Most of us agree that they are great . . . as long as they are working.

We usually do not think about the more mundane and behind-the-scenes computer activities: loading and running programs, coordinating networks that share resources, organizing files, protecting our computers from viruses, performing periodic maintenance to avoid problems, and controlling hardware devices so that they can communicate with one another. Typically, these activities go on behind the scenes without our help.

That is the way it should be, and the way it is, as long as everything is working perfectly. But what if new application programs are not compatible and will not run on our current computer system? What if we get a computer virus? What if our hard disk fails? What if we buy a new digital video camera and can't store and edit the images on our computer system? What if our computer starts to run slower and slower?

These issues may seem mundane, but they are critical. This chapter covers the vital activities that go on behind the scenes. A little knowledge about these activities can go a long way to making your computing life easier. To efficiently and effectively use computers, you need to understand the functionality of system software, including operating systems, utility programs, and device drivers.

System Software

End users use application software to accomplish specific tasks. For example, we use word processing programs to create letters, documents, and reports. However, end users also use system software. **System software** works with end users, application software, and computer hardware to handle the majority of technical details. For example, system software controls where a word processing program is stored in memory, how commands are converted so that the system unit can process them, and where a completed document or file is saved. (See Figure 4-1.)

System software is not a single program. Rather, it is a collection or a system of programs that handle hundreds of technical details with little or no user intervention. System software consists of four types of programs:

- **Operating systems** coordinate computer resources, provide an interface between users and the computer, and run applications.
- **Utilities** perform specific tasks related to managing computer resources.
- **Device drivers** are specialized programs that allow particular input or output devices to communicate with the rest of the computer system.
- **Language translators** convert the programming instructions written by programmers into a language that computers understand and process.

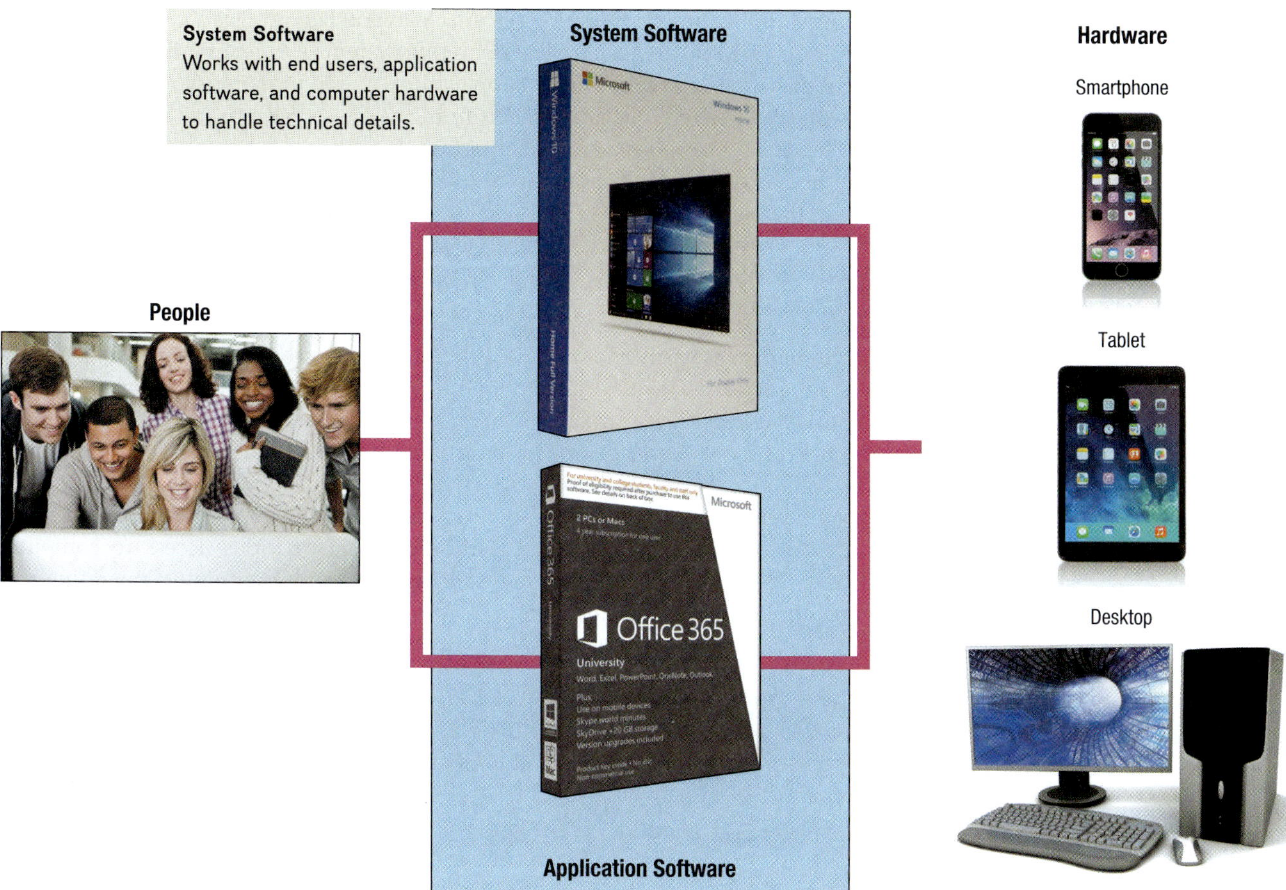

Figure 4-1 **System software handles technical details**

Operating Systems

An **operating system** is a collection of programs that handle many of the technical details related to using a computer. In many ways, an operating system is the most important type of computer program. Without a functioning operating system, your computer would be useless.

Functions

Every computer has an operating system, and every operating system performs a variety of functions. These functions can be classified into three groups:

- **Managing resources:** Operating systems coordinate all the computer's resources including memory, processing, storage, and devices such as printers and monitors. They also monitor system performance, schedule tasks, provide security, and start up the computer.
- **Providing user interface:** Operating systems allow users to interact with application programs and computer hardware through a **user interface.** Originally, operating systems used a character-based interface in which users communicated with the operating system through written commands such as "Copy A: report.txt C:". Today, most operating systems use a **graphical user interface (GUI).** As we discussed in Chapter 3, a graphical user interface uses graphical elements such as icons and windows. A new feature available with many operating systems is voice recognition. This allows users to interact with voice commands.

environment

Did you know that some operating systems help protect the environment? Recent versions of Microsoft's Windows operating system have various power management features that reduce energy consumption. For example, Windows will dim your screen and put your computer in sleep mode after a certain amount of time. The Energy Star program from the Environmental Protection Agency estimates that these features can save you up to $50 in electricity costs per year, which in turn helps reduce carbon emissions that affect the environment.

- **Running applications:** Operating systems load and run applications such as word processors and spreadsheets. Most operating systems support **multitasking,** or the ability to switch between different applications stored in memory. With multitasking, you could have Word and Excel running at the same time and switch easily between the two applications. The program that you are currently working on is described as running in the **foreground.** The other program or programs are running in the **background.**

Features

Starting or restarting a computer is called **booting** the system. There are two ways to boot a computer: a warm boot and a cold boot. A **warm boot** occurs when the computer is already on and you restart it without turning off the power. A warm boot can be accomplished in several ways. For many computer systems, they can be restarted by simply pressing a sequence of keys. Starting a computer that has been turned off is called a **cold boot.**

You typically interact with the operating system through the graphical user interface. Most provide a place, called the **desktop,** that provides access to computer resources. (See Figure 4-2.) Some important features common to most operating systems and application programs include:

- **Icons**—graphic representations for a program, type of file, or function.
- **Pointer**—controlled by a mouse, trackpad, or touch screen, the pointer changes shape depending on its current function. For example, when shaped like an arrow, the pointer can be used to select items such as an icon.

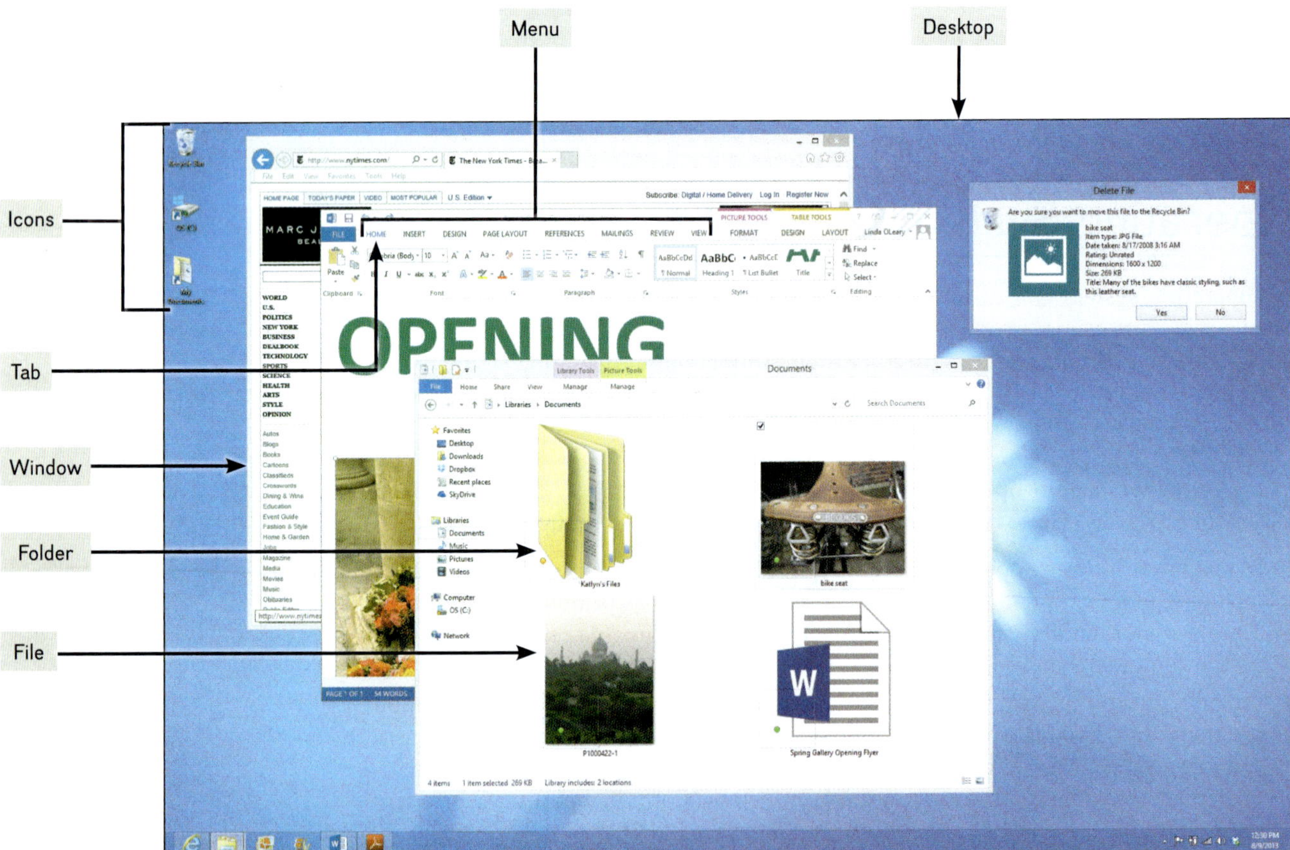

Figure 4-2 **Desktop**

- **Windows**—rectangular areas for displaying information and running programs.
- **Menus**—provide a list of options or commands that can be selected.
- **Tabs**—divide menus into major activity areas such as format and page layout.
- **Dialog boxes**—typically provide information or request input.
- **Help**—provides online assistance for operating system functions and procedures.
- **Gesture control**—ability to control operations with finger movements, such as swiping, sliding, and pinching.

Most offices have filing cabinets that store important documents in folders. Similarly, most operating systems store data and programs in a system of files and folders. **Files** are used to store data and programs. Related files are stored within a **folder,** and, for organizational purposes, a folder can contain other folders, or subfolders. For example, you might organize your electronic files in the *Documents* folder on your hard disk. This folder could contain other folders, each named to indicate its contents. One might be "Computer Class" and could contain all the files you have created (or will create) for this course.

Categories

While there are hundreds of different operating systems, there are only three basic categories: embedded, stand-alone, and network.

- **Embedded operating systems,** also known as **real-time operating systems** and **RTOS,** are entirely stored within (i.e., embedded in) a device. They control smartwatches, smartphones, video game systems, and thousands of other small electronic devices. Typically designed for a specific application, embedded operating systems are essential in the evolution of IoT where many everyday devices are able to communicate with one another as discussed in Chapter 1. For example, Watch OS was developed by Apple exclusively for the Apple Watch and Pebble OS was developed by Pebble Technology specifically for the Pebble Smartwatch. (See Figure 4-3.)
- **Stand-alone operating systems,** also called **desktop operating systems,** control a single desktop or laptop computer. (See Figure 4-4.) These operating systems are located on the computer's hard disk. Often desktop computers and laptops are part of a network. In these cases, the desktop operating system works with the network to share and coordinate resources.
- **Network operating systems (NOS)** are used to control and coordinate computers that are networked or linked together. Many networks are small and connect only a limited number of personal computers. Other networks, like those at colleges and universities, are very large and complex. These networks may include other smaller networks and typically connect a variety of different types of computers.

  Network operating systems are typically located on one of the connected computers' hard disks. Called the **network server,** this computer coordinates all communication between the other computers. Popular network operating systems Linux, Windows Server, and UNIX.

Figure 4-3 **Embedded operating systems control smartwatches**

Figure 4-4 **Laptops use stand-alone operating systems**

The operating system is often referred to as the **software environment** or **software platform.** Almost all application programs are designed to run with a specific platform. For example, Apple's iMovie software is designed to run with the Mac OS environment. Many applications, however, have different versions, each designed to operate with a particular platform. For example, one version of Microsoft Office is designed to operate with Windows. Another version is designed to operate with Mac OS.

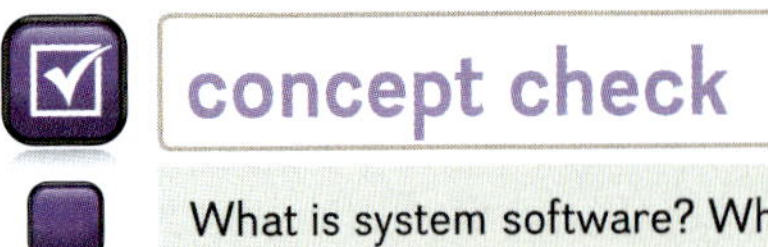

concept check

- What is system software? What are the four kinds of system software programs?
- What is an operating system? Discuss operating system functions and features.
- Describe each of the three categories of operating systems.

Figure 4-5 Apple's iPad and iPhone use iOS mobile operating system

Mobile Operating Systems

Mobile operating systems, also known as **mobile OS,** are a type of embedded operating system. Just like other computer systems, mobile computers including smartphones, tablets, and wearable computers require an operating system. These mobile operating systems are less complicated and more specialized for wireless communication.

While there are numerous mobile operating systems, some of the best known are Android, iOS, and Windows Phone.

- **Android** was introduced in 2007. It was originally developed by Android Inc. and later purchased by Google. Android is widely used in many of today's smartphones.
- **iOS,** formerly known as **iPhone OS,** was originally developed in 2007 by Apple. It is based on Mac OS and is used as the platform for Apple's iPad and iPhone. (See Figure 4-5.)
- **Windows Phone 8** was introduced in 2012 by Microsoft to support a variety of mobile devices, including smartphones. In 2015 Microsoft introduced a new mobile operating system, sometimes referred to as **Windows 10 Mobile** as a replacement for Windows Phone. It has the ability to run many powerful programs designed for desktop and laptop computers.

In the last chapter, we discussed that not all mobile applications will run on all smartphones. That is because an app is designed to run on a particular software platform or operating system. Before downloading an app, be sure that it is designed to run with the mobile operating system on your mobile device.

concept check

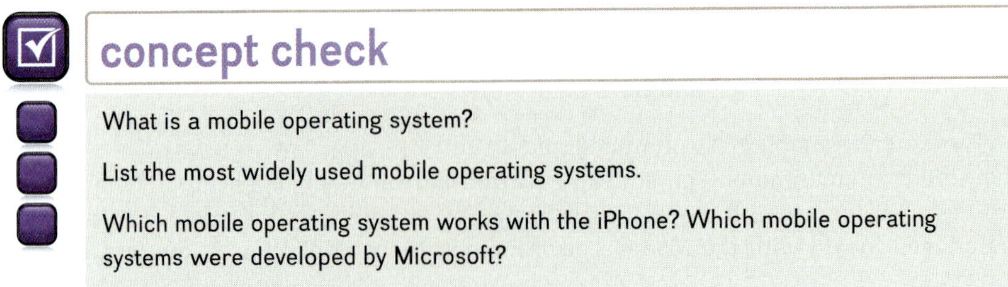

- What is a mobile operating system?
- List the most widely used mobile operating systems.
- Which mobile operating system works with the iPhone? Which mobile operating systems were developed by Microsoft?

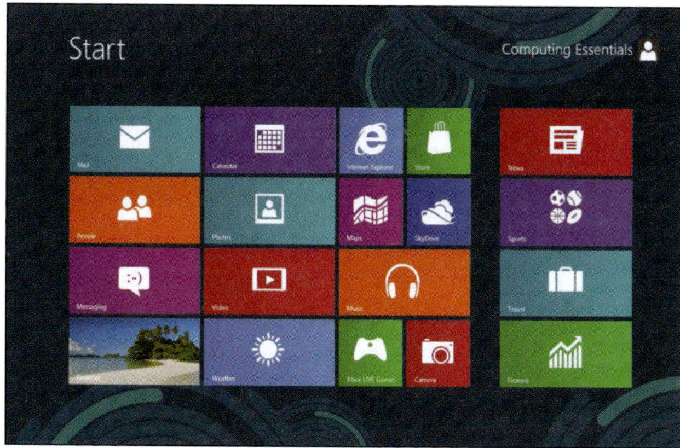

Figure 4-6 **Windows 8**

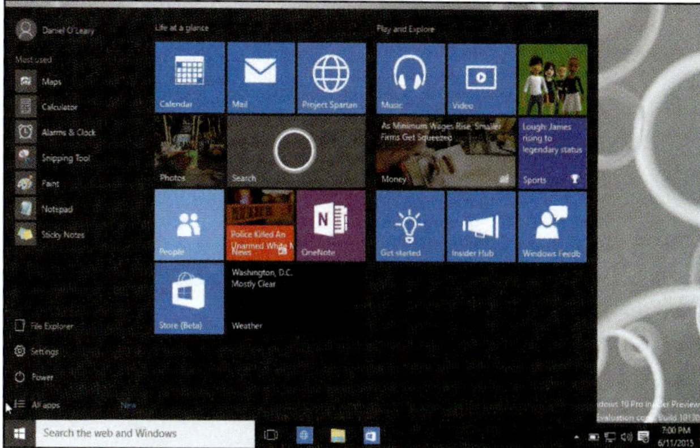

Figure 4-7 **Windows 10**

Desktop Operating Systems

Every personal computer has an operating system controlling its operations. The most widely used desktop operating systems are Windows, Mac OS, UNIX, and Linux.

Windows

Microsoft's **Windows** is the most widely used personal computer operating system. Because its market share is so large, more application programs have been developed to run under Windows than any other operating system. Windows comes in a variety of different versions and is designed to run with a variety of different microprocessors.

The two recent versions are Windows 8 and Windows 10.

- **Windows 8** was released in 2012 and was created to better integrate Microsoft's desktop operating systems with its mobile operating systems. (See Figure 4-6.) It provided support for gestures, cloud integration, and apps. Windows 8 also introduced a new interface. This interface is very similar to the interface for Microsoft's mobile operating system, Windows Phone, and is a dramatic shift from the traditional Windows interface. Windows 8 offers a **start screen** consisting of tiles. Each **tile** displays active content linked to an application. A desktop similar to the traditional Windows desktop can be accessed various ways. **Windows RT** is a version of Windows 8 designed to run with tablets using a particular microprocessor from ARM.
- **Windows 10** was announced in 2015. (See Figure 4-7.) It merges Windows' desktop and mobile operating systems. Unlike previous Windows versions, Windows 10 runs on all Windows devices, including desktops, tablets, and smartphones. This unification has brought several mobile OS innovations to the desktop OS, including **Cortana,** a digital assistant that can accept commands through text or speech, and Windows apps, such as Office, that can run on desktops, tablets, and smartphones. Other innovations include improved gaming with the Xbox gaming environment, a new web browser, and support for Microsoft HoloLens, an augmented reality tool.

Mac OS

Apple has been the leader in the development of powerful and easy-to-use personal computer operating systems since its introduction of the Macintosh personal computer in 1984. Designed to run only with Apple computers, **Mac OS** is not as widely used as the Windows operating system. As a result, fewer application programs have been written for it. However, with dramatically increasing sales of Apple computers, the use of Mac OS has been rapidly increasing and is widely recognized as one of the most innovative operating systems.

privacy

What information would you lose if a thief stole your computer or smartphone? If you use your computer or to shop on the Internet, check your bank balance, or read e-mail, then the thief would have access to your credit cards, bank accounts, and personal correspondence. The operating system on your computer or phone can be set up to require a password or secret code whenever the OS starts up. This could prevent a lost or stolen device from providing access to your private information.

Figure 4-8 **Mac OS X Yosemite**

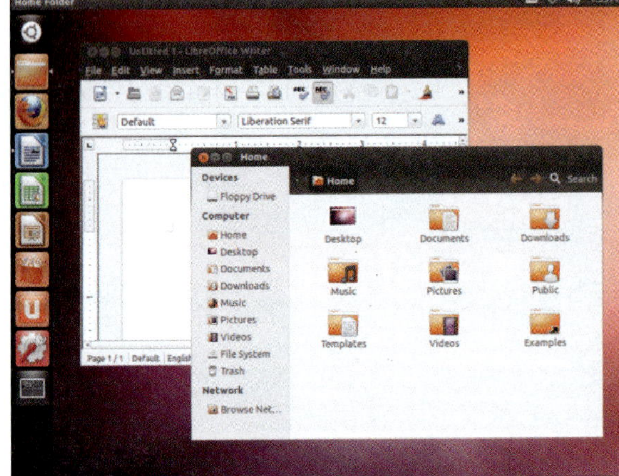

Figure 4-9 **Linux**

Mac OS X is the most widely used Mac desktop operating system. Its two most recent versions are

- **OS X Mavericks,** which was announced in 2013 and introduced several improvements, including better power management for longer laptop battery life, enhanced workflow options for multiple monitor setups, and better integration with cloud computing.
- **OS X Yosemite,** which was released in 2014. (See Figure 4-8.) It provided a new user interface similar to the iOS interface. Other innovations include greater use of Apple's cloud storage service, iCloud, and greater compatibility with Apple mobile devices. This compatibility includes the ability to send and receive text messages and phone calls from Apple's desktop computers and the ability to start e-mails and spreadsheets on one device and finish them on another.

UNIX and Linux

The **UNIX** operating system was originally designed in the late 1960s to run on minicomputers in network environments. Over the years, UNIX has evolved with numerous different versions. Now, it is widely used by servers on the web, mainframe computers, and very powerful personal computers. There are a large number of different versions of UNIX.

Linux is an operating system that extended one of the UNIX versions. It was originally developed by a graduate student at the University of Helsinki, Linus Torvalds, in 1991. He allowed free distribution of the operating system code and encouraged others to modify and further develop the code. Programs released in this way are called **open source.** Linux is a popular and powerful alternative to the Windows operating system. (See Figure 4-9.) Linux has been the basis of several other operating systems. For example, Google's **Chrome OS** is based on Linux.

Chrome OS integrates with web servers to run applications and to perform other traditional operating system functions. This capability has made Chrome OS a popular choice for inexpensive notebook computers that use cloud computing and cloud storage to do things that would normally require much more expensive hardware. One limitation of these computers is that their efficiency is dependent upon the speed of their Internet connection.

Virtualization

As we have discussed, application programs are designed to run with particular operating systems. What if you wanted to run two or more applications each requiring a different operating system? One solution would be to install each of the operating systems on a different computer. There is, however, a way in which a single physical computer can support multiple operating systems that operate independently. This approach is called **virtualization.**

When a single physical computer runs a special program known as **virtualization software,** it operates as though it were two or more separate and independent computers, known as **virtual machines.** Each virtual machine appears to the user as a separate independent computer with its own operating system. The operating system of the physical machine is known as the **host operating system.** The operating system for each virtual machine is known as the **guest operating system.** Users can readily switch between virtual computers and programs running on them. There are several programs that create and run virtual machines. One such program, Parallels, allows a user on a Mac to run Windows programs in OS X. (See Figure 4-10.)

Figure 4-10 **OS X Yosemite running Windows 10 in a virtual machine.**

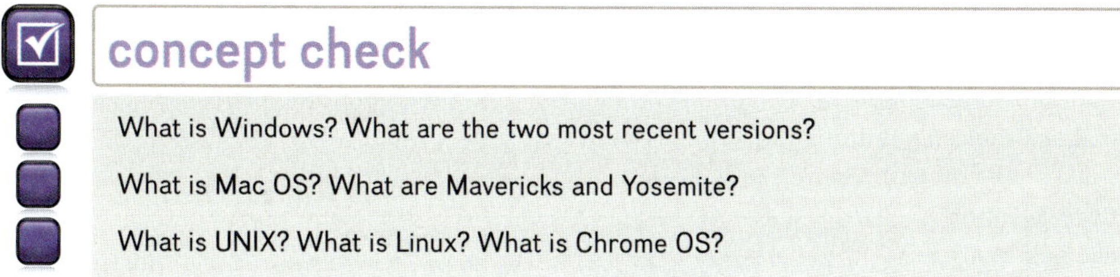

concept check

- What is Windows? What are the two most recent versions?
- What is Mac OS? What are Mavericks and Yosemite?
- What is UNIX? What is Linux? What is Chrome OS?

Utilities

Ideally, personal computers would continuously run without problems. However, that simply is not the case. All kinds of things can happen—internal hard disks can crash, computers can freeze up, operations can slow down, and so on. These events can make computing very frustrating. That's where utilities come in. **Utilities** are specialized programs designed to make computing easier. There are hundreds of different utility programs. The most essential are

- **Troubleshooting** or **diagnostic programs** that recognize and correct problems, ideally before they become serious. To learn more about using a troubleshooting program, see Making IT Work for You: Mac OS X Activity Monitor on pages 98–99.
- **Antivirus programs** that guard your computer system against viruses or other damaging programs that can invade your computer system. Popular antivirus programs include Norton AntiVirus and Webroot SecureAnywhere AntiVirus.
- **Backup programs** that make copies of files to be used in case the originals are lost or damaged. Windows 10 comes with a free backup program, the File History tool, and Mac OS X has a backup feature named Time Machine.
- **File compression programs** that reduce the size of files so they require less storage space and can be sent more efficiently over the Internet. Most operating systems handle unzipping files automatically when you open a .zip file.

Most operating systems provide some utility programs. Even more powerful utility programs can be purchased separately or in utility suites.

MAC OS X ACTIVITY MONITOR

Have you ever been working with a program when it simply stopped working and would not respond to you? Does your computer seem to be getting slower and slower? OS X Activity Monitor, which gives you a live view of every program that is currently in RAM, is designed to help with these and many other operational problems.

Starting Activity Monitor You can open Activity Monitor from anywhere by following these steps:

1. **Press and momentarily hold the command key (⌘) + space bar.**
2. **Type *Activity Monitor* and press return.**

As you can see, the Activity Monitor window provides a list of active programs; more information can be seen about an active program by clicking on the active program in the list and then clicking on the information button (the button with a lowercase "i" in a circle in the upper right of the window). This will open with more information about the process, including the CPU and Memory resources it uses. Click the red x button in the upper right to close this window.

Closing an Application Use Activity Monitor when a program you are using becomes stuck and stops responding.

1. **In the menu bar, click *view* → *Windowed Processes*. The Activity Monitor should show only the programs open on the desktop.**
2. **In the Activity Monitor window, find the program that is stuck. Next to the program name there should read, "(not responding)" in red.**
3. **Select the program and press the button in the upper left of the window with a gray octagon with a white "x" in it. This will force the process to quit.**

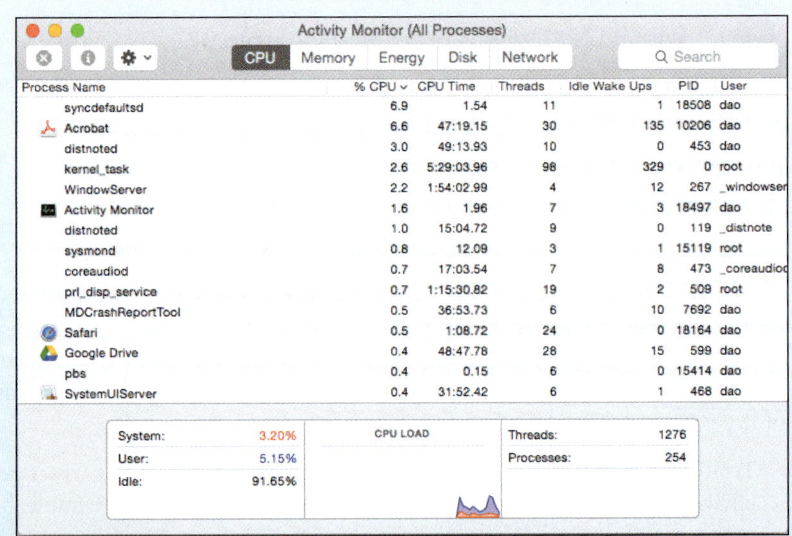

The program that was not responding has been closed, and you can now continue using OS X normally.

Viewing Processes This is the most powerful area of Activity Monitor. Here you will see a list of every process that is currently residing in your computer's RAM.

1. In the menu bar, click *view* → *All Processes*. The Activity Monitor should show all processes currently running on your computer.

2. In the Activity Monitor window, click the button labeled *Memory*. All the processes will be sorted from highest (occupying the most RAM) to the lowest.

3. Click the *CPU* button. This will show any process that the CPU is currently working on.

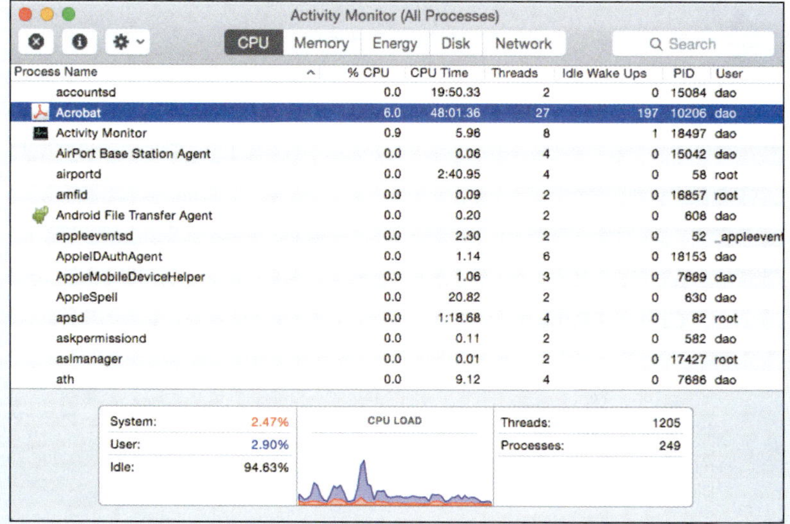

It is normal for the numbers to fluctuate, especially those for the CPU.

Ending a Process Some problematic processes could be spyware, while others represent background services you don't need. Other processes are crucial for your system and should never be ended. *Warning:* Before ending a process, you must truly understand the risks (or benefits) of doing so. Using a search engine, type the name of the process, and the result will list several websites that explain what it does. If you want to end a process:

1. In the Activity Monitor window, click the *Process Name* heading (to avoid the fluctuating positions of each process).

2. Click the process you want to end.

3. Select the program and press the button in the upper left of the window with a gray octagon with a white "x" in it. This will force the process to quit.

The particular program file will be removed from the list and from your computer's memory. Keep in mind that if this program is configured to load automatically, you will see it again when you restart your computer.

Monitoring CPU History If you are wondering what you may be doing that is taxing your computer, monitoring your CPU history can give you an idea. The Activity Monitor can open a small window where you can see the CPU load on your computer.

1. In the menu bar, click *Window* then select *CPU Usage*. A small window will open showing the load on each core in your CPU as a bar chart.

2. Keeping the CPU window visible, perform an action on your computer to see it impact the CPU load. For example, open a web page or a document.

3. When you are done viewing the CPU Usage, close the window.

tips **Have you ever experienced problems after installing a new program or changing system settings? If so, the System Restore utility can help by reversing the changes and bringing your computer to a previous point in time. For Windows 10:**

1. Go to the Windows 10 start screen and then type "recovery" in the search box.
2. Click on *Open System Restore* from the Advanced recovery tools list.
3. Follow the prompts, and choose a restore point.
4. Click the *Finish* button to start the process.

Windows Utilities

The Windows operating systems are accompanied by several utility programs, including File History, Disk Cleanup, and Disk Defragmenter.

File History is a utility program included with Windows 10 that makes a copy of all files that are in the libraries, contacts, and favorites and on the desktop. It helps protect you from the effects of a disk failure. For example, you can select *File History* from the Windows 10 System and Security window to create a backup for your hard disk as shown in Figure 4-11.

1

- **Click the Windows icon in the lower left of the screen, type "control panel," and select *Control Panel.***
- **In the Control Panel window, select *Systems and Security* and click on *File History.***
- **Choose the destination for the backup.**
- **Click the *Turn on* button.**

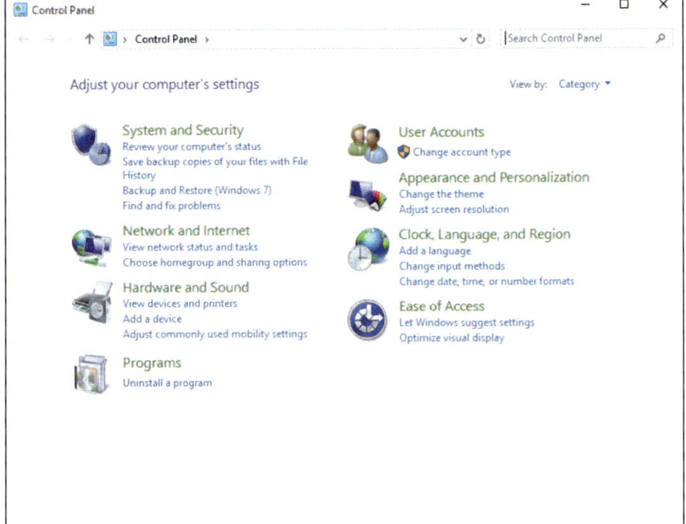

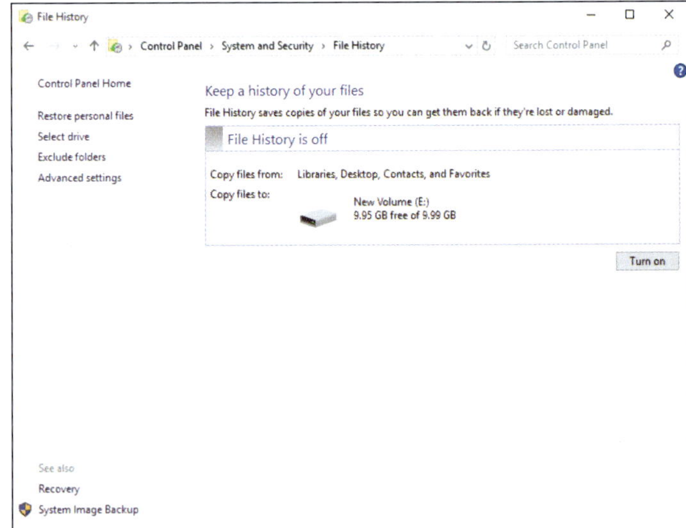

Figure 4-11 **File History utility**

When you surf the web, a variety of programs and files are saved on your hard disk. Many of these and other files are not essential. **Disk Cleanup** is a troubleshooting utility that identifies and eliminates nonessential files. This frees up valuable disk space and improves system performance.

For example, by opening Disk Cleanup from the Windows 10 search results, you can eliminate unneeded files on your hard disk as shown in Figure 4-12.

1. **Click the Windows icon in the lower left of the screen, type "disk cleanup," and select *Disk Cleanup*.**

   Review the files suggested for cleanup, and then click *OK*.

   Confirm that you want to permanently delete these files by clicking *Delete Files*.

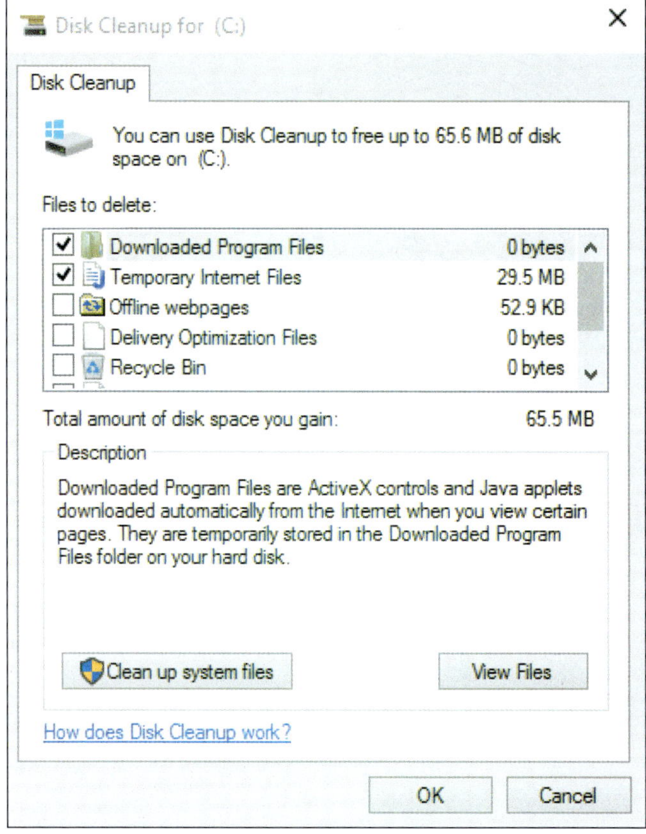

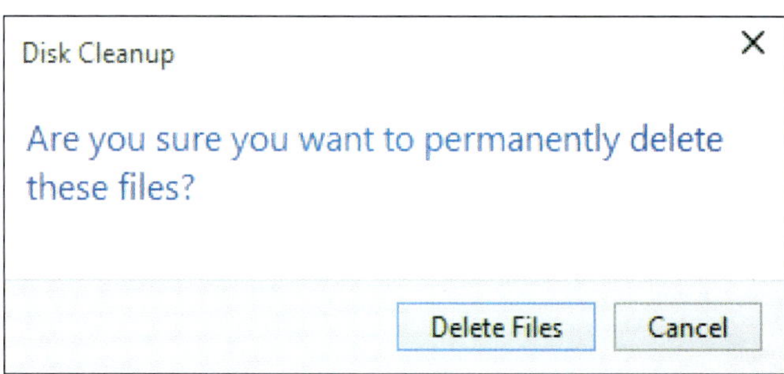

2. **The utility cleans the selected files.**

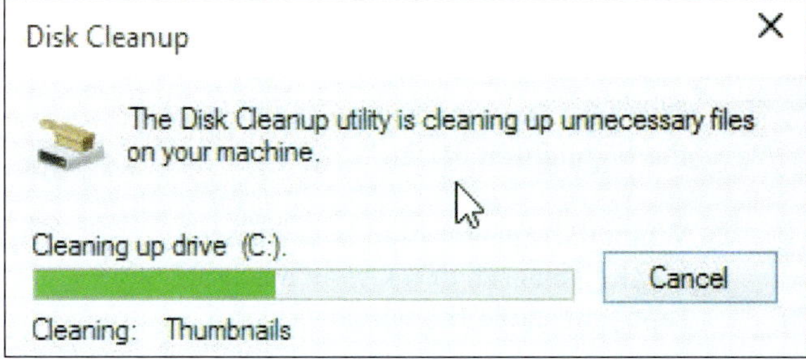

Figure 4-12 **Disk Cleanup utility**

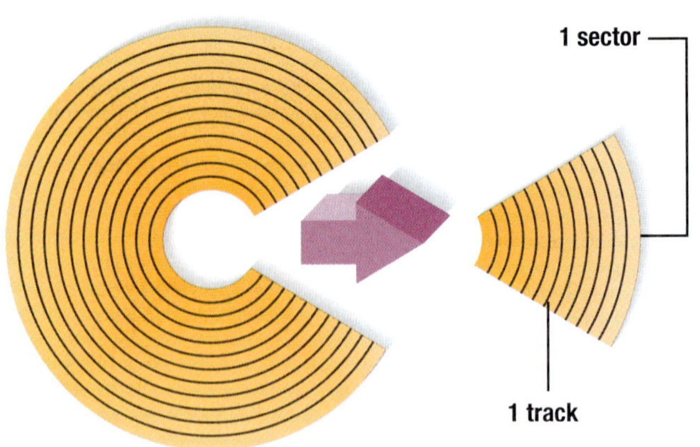

Figure 4-13 **Tracks and sectors**

As we will discuss in detail in Chapter 7, files are stored and organized on a disk according to tracks and sectors. A **track** is a concentric ring. Each track is divided into wedge-shaped sections called **sectors.** (See Figure 4-13.) The operating system tries to save a file on a single track across contiguous sectors. Often, however, this is not possible, and the file has to be broken up, or **fragmented,** into small parts that are stored wherever space is available. Whenever a file is retrieved, it is reconstructed from the fragments. After a period of time, a hard disk becomes highly fragmented, slowing operations.

Optimize Drives is a utility program that locates and eliminates unnecessary fragments and rearranges files and unused disk space to optimize operations. For example, by selecting Optimize Drives from the Windows 10 search results, you can defrag your hard disk as shown in Figure 4-14.

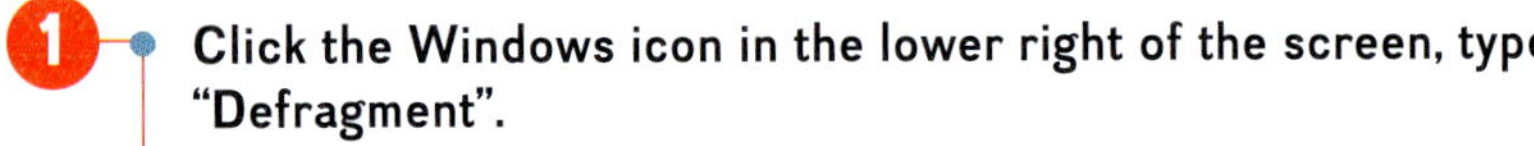

1

- **Click the Windows icon in the lower right of the screen, type "Defragment".**
- **From the search results, select *Defragment and optimize your drives.***

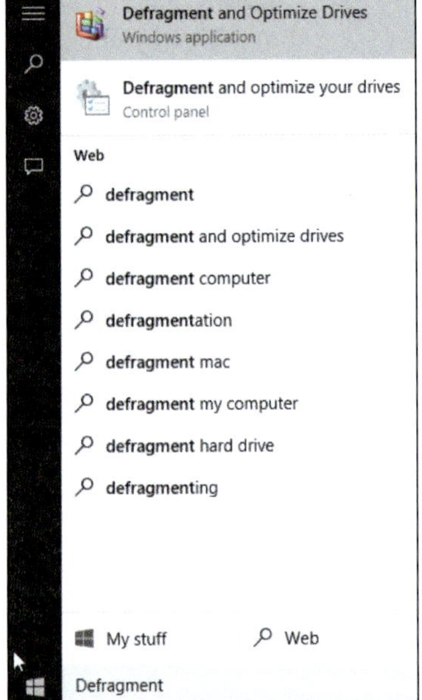

2

- **In the Optimize Drives window, in the section labeled Status, select the drive you would like to defrag.**
- **Click the *Optimize* button to defrag the highlighted drive.**
- **When defragmentation is complete for the selected drive, view the report or close the window.**

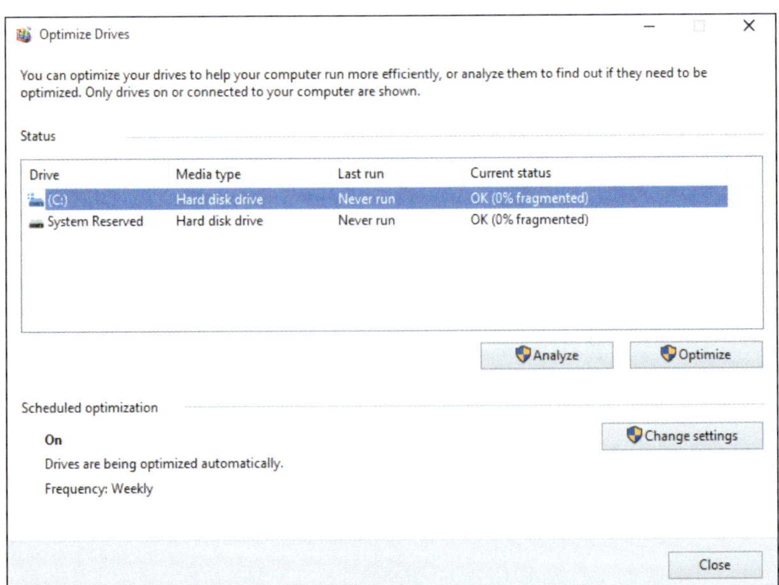

Figure 4-14 **Optimize Drives utility**

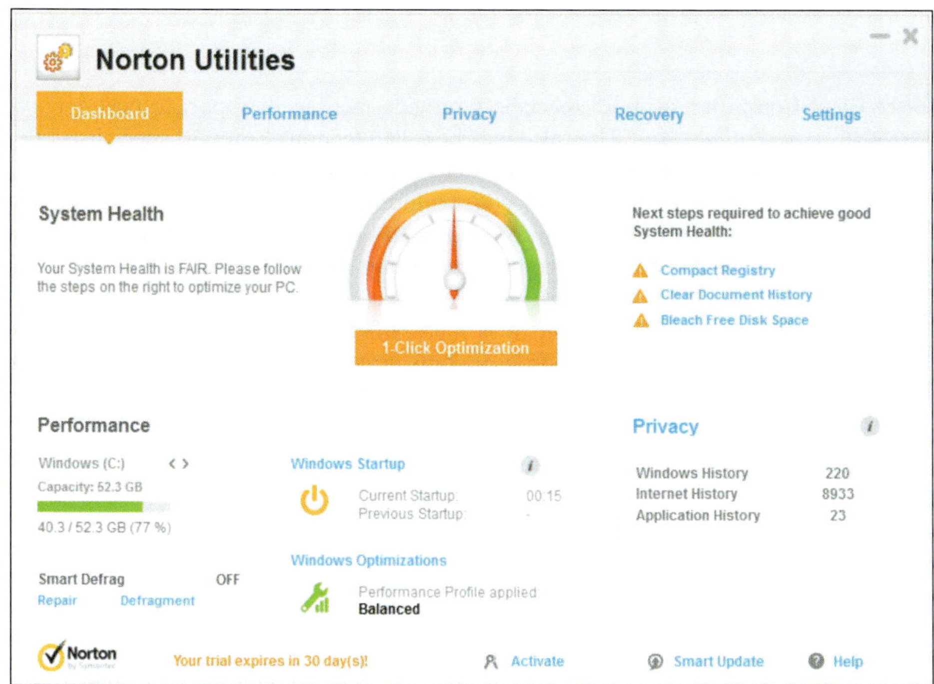

Figure 4-15 Utility suite

ethics

Everyone should worry about getting a computer virus that will corrupt or destroy files. Some suggest that software developers may be taking advantage of this fear by sending out misleading or fake virus alerts. One reported scam encourages users to download a free virus detection program. This free download begins by actually installing a virus onto the user's computer. It then performs a bogus scan, locating the virus and then offering to remove the virus for a fee. Obviously, this is unethical, not to mention illegal. How can you and legitimate antivirus manufacturers protect themselves against viruses and unethical software developers?

Utility Suites

Like application software suites, **utility suites** combine several programs into one package. Buying the package is less expensive than buying the programs separately. Some of the best-known utility suites are BitDefender, Kaspersky, and Norton. (See Figure 4-15.) These suites provide a variety of utilities. Some programs improve hard disk efficiency, while other programs will protect your system from dangerous computer **viruses.** You can "catch" a computer virus many ways, including by opening attachments to e-mail messages and downloading software from the Internet. (We will discuss computer viruses in detail in Chapter 9.)

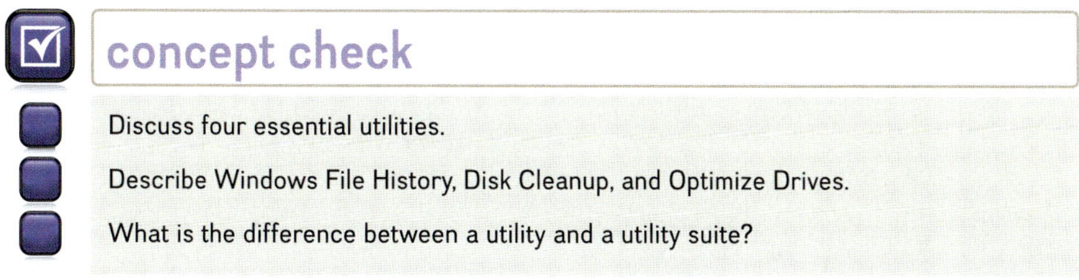

concept check

- Discuss four essential utilities.
- Describe Windows File History, Disk Cleanup, and Optimize Drives.
- What is the difference between a utility and a utility suite?

Careers in IT

"Now that you know about system software, I'd like to tell you about my career as a computer support specialist."

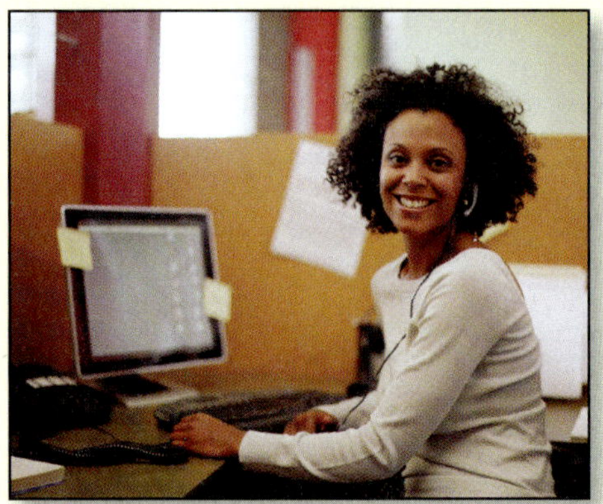

Computer support specialists provide technical support to customers and other users. They also may be called technical support specialists or help-desk technicians. Computer support specialists manage the every-day technical problems faced by computer users. They resolve common networking problems and may use troubleshooting programs to diagnose problems. Most computer support specialists are hired to work within a company and provide technical support for other employees and divisions. However, it is increasingly common for companies to provide technical support as an outsourced service.

Employers generally look for individuals with either an advanced associate's degree or a bachelor's degree to fill computer support specialist positions. Degrees in computer science or information systems may be preferred. However, because demand for qualified applicants is so high, those with practical experience and certification from a training program increasingly fill these positions. Employers seek individuals with customer service experience who demonstrate good analytical, communication, and people skills.

Computer support specialists can expect to earn an annual salary of $29,000 to $40,000. Opportunities for advancement are very good and may involve design and implementation of new systems.

A LOOK TO THE FUTURE

Self-Healing Computers Could Mean an End to Computer Crashes and Performance Problems

Wouldn't it be nice if computers could fix themselves? What if your computer could continually fine-tune its operations to maintain peak performance? Computers often perform performance improvements on a regular schedule, such as disk defragmentation. More recently, improvements in virus protection and eradication can identify and remove viruses before they impact performance. In the future, computers may not only fix software issues, but actually identify hardware problems and route functions around broken hardware. For many people, this sounds too good to be true. Maintenance and troubleshooting tasks like these can be time-consuming and frustrating. Technology has been making better self-fixing computers, and will continue to evolve to improve our lives as we look to the future.

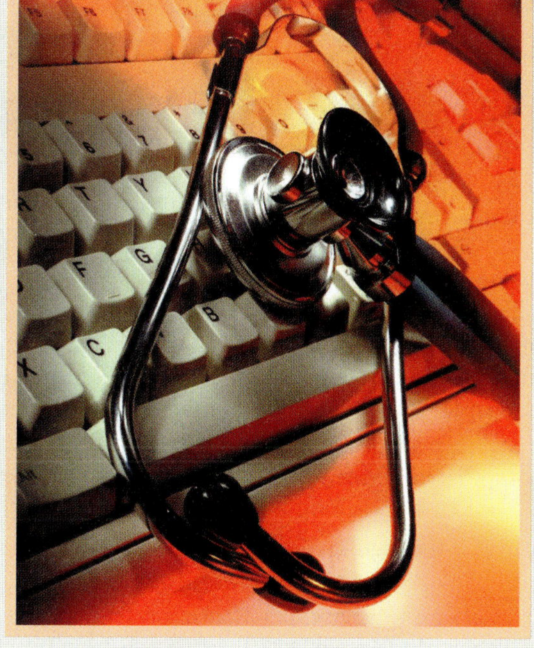

Now imagine you run a business, and unless these tasks are performed, you will lose time and money. It is not a pleasant daydream, and it quickly becomes a nightmare without properly trained systems administrators to keep servers running smoothly. Yet many experts predict that supercomputers and business systems are not far from becoming too complex for humans to manage and secure. Recent news from IBM makes the dream of a self-repairing, self-updating, and self-protecting server seem closer.

IBM has announced plans to concentrate research efforts on developing just such a server. The project, called the Autonomic Computing Initiative (ACI), hopes to free businesses from time-consuming computer maintenance. IBM hopes the new system will be self-regulating and virtually invisible. It believes autonomic computing has the potential to revolutionize the way businesses run.

Autonomic computing is a system that allows machines to run with little human intervention. Such computers would not have self-awareness but would be self-correcting. Autonomic processes in machines are modeled after autonomic processes in the human body. For example, you are not consciously breathing. Instead, your body monitors and maintains your respiration without your input. Scientists hope autonomic computing will behave in a similar manner and maintain systems without intervention.

Autonomic machines would be able to identify security flaws and repair them. They would be able to sense slow computer operations and take corrective action. They would be able to detect new equipment, format it, and test it. Computer usage will become less complex so that you can focus on getting work done instead of worrying about the machine's operation. These goals are impressive, and the autonomic computer is still in development.

It is important to note that autonomic computing is not artificial intelligence because autonomic machines do not have human cognitive abilities or intelligence. Instead, these machines have knowledge of their own systems and the capability to learn from experience to correct errors.

Given the potential for a self-maintaining server, the possibility of a similar system designed for a personal computer seems less like a dream and more like a reality. What do you think? Will personal computers ever care for themselves? Do you think it is possible to have a computer managing its own security? Will hackers find a way to outsmart these "intelligent" systems?

VISUAL SUMMARY System Software

SYSTEM SOFTWARE

System software works with end users, application programs, and computer hardware to handle many details relating to computer operations.

Not a single program but a collection or system of programs, these programs handle hundreds of technical details with little or no user intervention.

Four kinds of systems programs are operating systems, utilities, device drivers, and language translators.

- **Operating systems** coordinate resources, provide an interface between users and the computer, and run programs.
- **Utilities** perform specific tasks related to managing computer resources.
- **Device drivers** allow particular input or output devices to communicate with the rest of the computer system.
- **Language translators** convert programming instructions written by programmers into a language that computers can understand and process.

OPERATING SYSTEMS

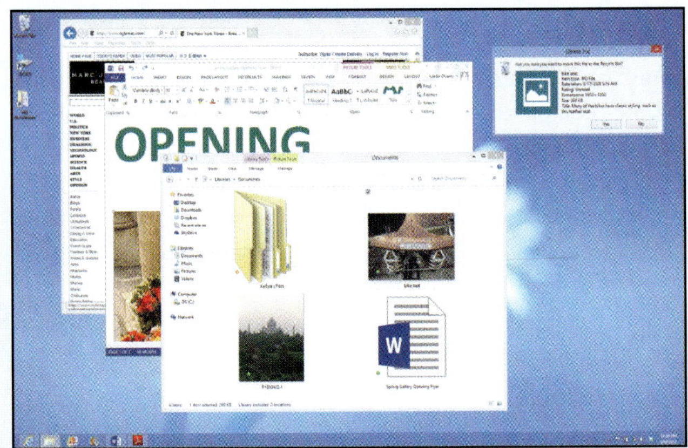

Operating systems (software environments, software platforms) handle technical details.

Functions

Functions include managing resources, providing a **user interface** (most operating systems use a **graphical user interface,** or **GUI**), and running applications. **Multitasking** allows switching between different applications stored in memory; current programs run in **foreground;** other programs run in **background.**

Features

Booting starts **(cold)** or restarts **(warm)** a computer system. The **desktop** provides access to computer resources. Common features include **icons, pointers, windows, menus, tabs, dialog boxes, Help,** and **gesture control.** Data and programs are stored in a system of **files** and **folders.**

Categories

Three categories of operating systems are

- **Embedded**—also known as **real-time operating systems (RTOS);** used with handheld computers; operating system stored within device.
- **Stand-alone (desktop)**—controls a single computer; located on the hard disk.
- **Network (NOS)**—controls and coordinates networked computers; located on the **network server.**

Operating systems are often called **software environments** or **software platforms.**

To efficiently and effectively use computers, you need to understand the functionality of system software, including operating systems and utility programs.

MOBILE OPERATING SYSTEMS

Mobile operating systems (mobile OS) are embedded in every smartphone and tablet. These systems are less complicated and more specialized for wireless communication than desktop operating systems.

Some of the best known are Android, iOS (iPhone OS), and Windows Phone.

- **Android** was originally developed by Android Inc. and later purchased by Google. It is a widely used mobile OS.
- **iOS (iPhone OS)** was developed by Apple to support iPhone and iPad.
- **Windows Phone 8** was introduced in 2012 by Microsoft to support a variety of mobile devices, including smartphones. **Windows 10 Mobile** was introduced in 2015 to replace Windows 8. It can run many powerful programs designed for laptop and desktop computers.

Not all mobile applications will run on all smartphones. That is because an app is designed to run on a particular software platform or operating system. Before downloading an app, be sure that it is designed to run with the mobile operating system on your mobile device.

DESKTOP OPERATING SYSTEMS

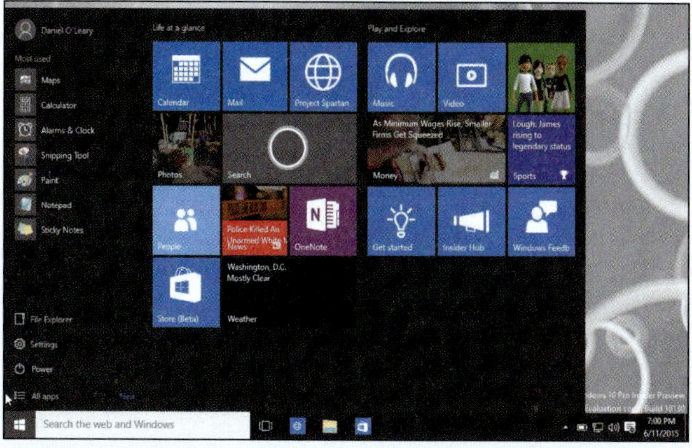

Windows

Windows is designed to run with many different microprocessors. The two recent versions are **Windows 8** and **Windows 10.** Windows 10 was introduced in 2015. It merged Windows' desktop and mobile operating systems. Innovations include **Cortana** (accepts commands through text or speech), support for Windows apps on desktops and mobile devices, improved gaming with the Xbox gaming environment, a new web browser, and support for Microsoft HoloLens, an augmented reality tool.

Mac OS

Mac OS, an innovative, powerful, easy-to-use operating system, runs on Macintosh computers. The two most recent versions are **Mavericks** and **Yosemite.** Yosemite was released in 2014. It provided a new user interface similar to the iOS interface. Innovations include greater use of Apple's cloud storage service (iCloud) and greater compatibility with Apple mobile devices. Compatibility includes the ability to send/receive text/phone messages from Apple's desktop computers and the ability to start e-mails/spreadsheets on one device and finish on another.

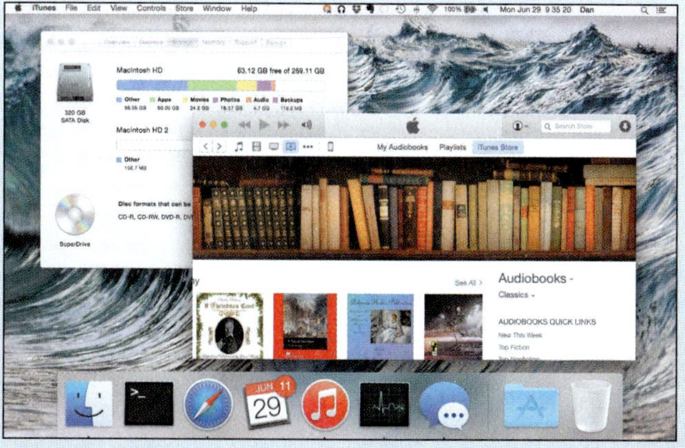

DESKTOP OPERATING SYSTEMS

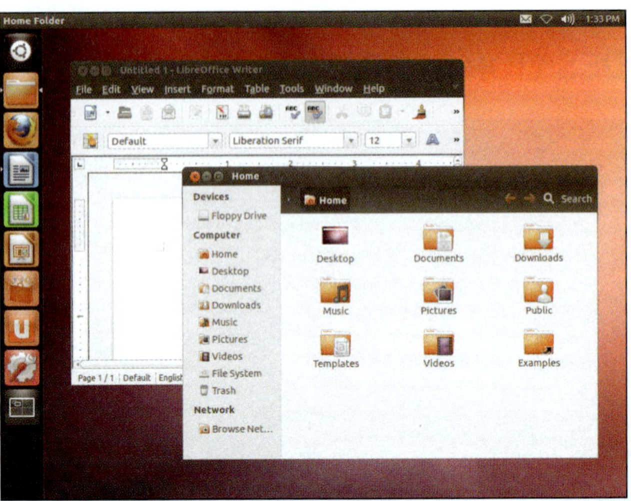

UNIX and Linux

UNIX was originally designed to run on minicomputers in network environments. Now, it is widely used by servers on the web, mainframe computers, and very powerful personal computers. There are many different versions of UNIX. One version, **Linux,** a popular and powerful alternative to the Windows operating system, is **open source** software. Google's **Chrome OS** is based on Linux. It integrates with web servers to run applications and to perform other traditional operating system functions. Chrome OS is a popular choice for inexpensive notebook computers using cloud computing and cloud storage. One limitation of these computers is that their efficiency is dependent upon the speed of their Internet connection.

Virtualization

Virtualization allows a single physical computer to support multiple operating systems. Using a special program **(virtualization software)** allows the single physical computer to operate as two or more separate and independent computers known as **virtual machines. Host operating systems** run on the physical machine. **Guest operating systems** operate on virtual machines. Parallels creates and runs virtual machines on Apple's Mac OS X.

UTILITIES

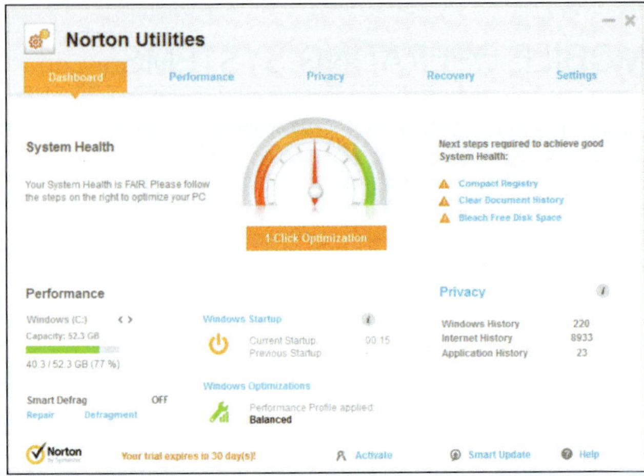

Utilities make computing easier. The most essential are **troubleshooting (diagnostic), antivirus, backup,** and **file compression.**

Windows Utilities

Windows operating systems are accompanied by several utility programs, including **File History, Disk Cleanup,** and **Optimize Drives** (eliminates unnecessary **fragments; tracks** are concentric rings; **sectors** are wedge-shaped).

Utility Suites

Utility suites combine several programs into one package. Computer **viruses** are dangerous programs.

CAREERS in IT

Computer support specialists provide technical support to customers and other users. Degrees in computer science or information systems are preferred plus good analytical and communication skills. Salary range is $29,000 to $40,000.

KEY TERMS

Android (94)
antivirus program (97)
background (92)
backup program (97)
booting (92)
Chrome OS (96)
cold boot (92)
computer support specialist (104)
Cortana (95)
desktop (92)
desktop operating system (93)
device driver (90)
diagnostic program (97)
dialog box (93)
Disk Cleanup (101)
embedded operating system (93)
file (93)
file compression program (97)
File History (100)
folder (93)
foreground (92)
fragmented (102)
gesture control (93)
graphical user interface (GUI) (91)
guest operating system (97)
Help (93)
host operating system (97)
icon (92)
iOS (94)
iPhone OS (94)
language translator (90)
Linux (96)
Mac OS (95)
Mac OS X (96)
menu (93)
mobile operating system (94)
mobile OS (94)
multitasking (92)
network operating system (NOS) (93)
network server (93)
open source (96)
operating system (90, 91)
Optimize Drives (102)
OS X Mavericks (96)
OS X Yosemite (96)
pointer (92)
real-time operating system (RTOS) (93)
sector (102)
software environment (93)
software platform (93)
stand-alone operating system (93)
start screen (95)
system software (90)
tab (93)
tile (95)
track (102)
troubleshooting program (97)
UNIX (96)
user interface (91)
utilities (90, 97)
utility suite (103)
virtual machine (97)
virtualization (97)
virtualization software (97)
virus (103)
warm boot (92)
window (93, 99)
Windows (95)
Windows 8 (95)
Windows 10 (95)
Windows 10 Mobile (94)
Windows Phone 8 (94)
Windows RT (95)

MULTIPLE CHOICE

Circle the correct answer.

1. What type of software works with users, application software, and computer hardware to handle the majority of technical details?
   a. application
   b. desktop
   c. Linux
   d. system
2. The programs that convert programming instructions written by programmers into a language that computers understand and process are language:
   a. converters
   b. linguists
   c. managers
   d. translators
3. The ability to switch between different applications stored in memory is called:
   a. diversion
   b. multitasking
   c. operational interference
   d. programming
4. Graphic representation for a program, type of file, or function:
   a. app
   b. icon
   c. image
   d. software
5. This operating system feature is controlled by a mouse and changes shape depending on its current function.
   a. dialog box
   b. menu
   c. mouse
   d. pointer
6. The operating system based on Linux, designed for notebook computers that use cloud computing and cloud storage:
   a. Chrome
   b. Mac
   c. UNIX
   d. Windows
7. The mobile operating system developed by Apple and originally called iPhone OS:
   a. Android
   b. iOS
   c. Mac OS
   d. Phone OS
8. A utility program that copies all files in the libraries, contacts, favorites, and on the desktop:
   a. File History
   b. Disk Cleanup
   c. Optimize Drives
   d. Compactor
9. A troubleshooting utility that identifies and eliminates nonessential files, frees up valuable disk space, and improves system performance:
   a. File History
   b. Disk Cleanup
   c. Optimize Drives
   d. Compactor
10. BitDefender, Kaspersky, and Norton are examples of:
    a. application packages
    b. apps
    c. operating systems
    d. utility suites

MATCHING

Match each numbered item with the most closely related lettered item. Write your answers in the spaces provided.

a. Android
b. antivirus
c. driver
d. fragmented
e. multitasking
f. NOS
g. platform
h. utilities
i. virtualization
j. warm boot

___ **1.** Programs that perform specific tasks related to managing computer resources.

___ **2.** Restarting a running computer without turning off the power.

___ **3.** Type of operating system that controls and coordinates networked computers.

___ **4.** An operating system is often referred to as the software environment or software _______.

___ **5.** Switching between different applications.

___ **6.** A type of software that allows a single physical computer to operate as though it were two or more separate and independent computers.

___ **7.** Mobile operating system that is owned by Google and is widely used in many smartphones.

___ **8.** Type of program that guards computer systems from viruses and other damaging programs.

___ **9.** If a file cannot be saved on a single track, it has to be _______.

___ **10.** Program that works with the operating system to allow communication between a device and the rest of a computer system is called a device _______.

OPEN-ENDED

On a separate sheet of paper, respond to each question or statement.

1. Describe system software. Discuss each of the four types of system programs.
2. Define operating systems. Describe the basic features and the three categories of operating systems.
3. What are mobile operating systems? Describe the leading mobile operating systems.
4. What are desktop operating systems? Compare Windows, Mac OS, Linux, and Chrome OS. Discuss virtualization.
5. Discuss utilities. What are the most essential utilities? What is a utility suite?

DISCUSSION

Respond to each of the following questions.

1 Making IT Work for You: MAC OS X ACTIVITY MONITOR

Have you ever been working with a program when it simply stopped working and would not respond to you? Review the Making IT Work for You: Mac OS X Activity Monitor on pages 98–99, and open Activity Monitor using a Mac computer. Then respond to the following: (a) List the top three processes in terms of memory usage. (b) List three processes that are using your CPU, even if it is only for a second or two as you look at that dialog box. (c) Find one process that you do not recognize. Using your favorite search engine, determine what the process does. Write down the name of the process, its description or purpose, and the URL of the website you used to research it.

2 Privacy: OPERATING SYSTEM SECURITY

Did you know that your computer or mobile device can provide others access to your personal information? Review the Privacy box on page 95, and respond to the following: (a) Have you ever lost a personal computer or mobile device? If so, what personal information was stored on it? If not, what personal information is stored on your current computer and/or mobile device? (b) Are you doing anything now that would make it difficult for someone to access personal information from your computing devices? If you are, discuss what you are doing. If not, what could/should you be doing? Be specific. (c) Investigate the privacy setting on your devices and describe them. (d) Do you think computer manufacturers have a responsibility to provide better security and privacy features? Why or why not?

3 Ethics: VIRUS PROTECTION SCAMS

Everyone should be concerned about viruses infecting computer systems. Some report that this fear is being used to manipulate users into purchasing new or upgraded antivirus programs. Some even report specific antivirus scams. Review the Ethics box on page 103, and then respond to the following: (a) Have you ever been offered a free virus alert program? If so, describe the offer and whether you accepted the offer. (b) Almost all legitimate antivirus software manufacturers issue new virus alerts. Do you think these alerts are motivated by greed or by good consumer service? Why or why not? (c) Is this an ethical issue for antivirus software manufacturers? If so, create some ethical guidelines for antivirus software manufacturers to follow when issuing virus alerts. (d) What can users do to protect themselves against antivirus scams and against unethical manufacturers of antivirus programs? Be specific and defend your suggestions.

4 Environment: OS POWER MANAGEMENT

Did you know that some operating systems help protect the environment? Review the Environment box on page 92, and then respond to the following: (a) In what ways do operating systems help the environment? (b) Do you leave your desktop or laptop computer on all day? Do you use sleep or hibernate modes? Explain the reasons behind your decision. (c) Find the power management options for your operating system. List a few options that you would consider adjusting in order to reduce your computer's energy consumption.

PHOTO CREDITS

CHAPTER 4

Opener: © Max Delson Martins Santos/Getty Images RF; p. 89, 105: © Brand X Pictures/Getty Images RF; p. 90, 104, 108 (bottom-right): © Thomas Barwick/Getty Images RF; 4-1 (right): © Image Source, all rights reserved, RF; 4-1 (middle), 4-7, p. 106 (top-left), 107 (top-right): Used with permission from Microsoft; 4-1 (top-right and middle-right), 4-5 (both): © Stanca Sanda/Alamy; 4-1 (bottom-right), p. 106 (bottom-left): © Maxim Kazmin/Getty Images RF; 4-1 (middle-top), p. 106 (top-left): © McGraw-Hill Education/Aaron Roeth, photographer; 4-2, 4-6, 4-10, 4-11, 4-12, 4-14, p. 106 (top-right), 108 (bottom-left): Microsoft product screen shot(s) reprinted with permission from Microsoft Corporation; 4-3: © Pawan Kumar/Alamy; 4-4: © Lenovo, used with permission; 4-5 (both), p. 107 (top-left): © Stanca Sanda/Alamy; 4-8, 4-10, p. 107 (bottom-right), 108 (bottom-left): Copyright © 2015 Apple Inc. All rights reserved; 4-9, p. 108 (top-left): © 2015 Linux.com. All rights reserved; 4-15, p. 108 (top-right): Copyright © 2015 Symantec Corporation. All rights reserved.

chapter 5 The System Unit

Why should I read this chapter?

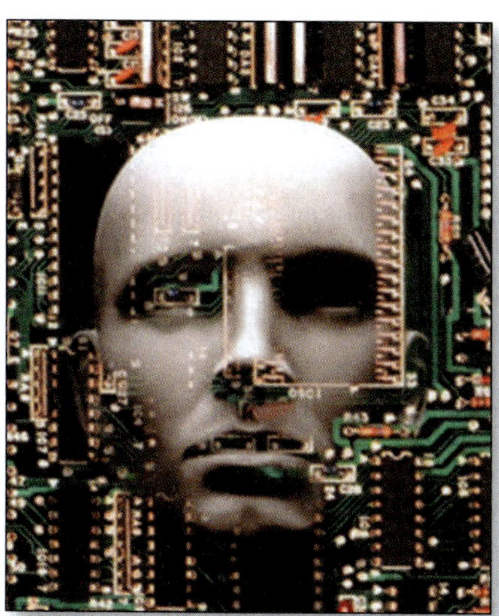

System units are getting smaller, faster, cheaper, and more powerful. These staggering improvements are resulting in microchips integrating with all aspects of our lives. For example, in the future we will see everything from microchips embedded in the brain that improve mental capacity to sensors that can literally read your mind.

This chapter covers the things you need to know to be prepared for this ever-changing digital world, including:

- Types of personal computers—learn the strengths and weaknesses of desktops, laptops, tablets, smartphones, and wearable computers.
- Computer components—understand the impact microprocessors and memory have on the power of a computer.
- Peripherals and upgrades—expand your computer's abilities and speed.

Learning Objectives

After you have read this chapter, you should be able to:

1. Differentiate between the five basic types of system units.
2. Describe system boards, including sockets, slots, and bus lines.
3. Recognize different microprocessors, including microprocessor chips and specialty processors.
4. Compare different types of computer memory, including RAM, ROM, and flash memory.
5. Explain expansion slots and cards.
6. Describe bus lines, bus widths, and expansion buses.
7. Describe ports, including standard and specialized ports.
8. Identify power supplies for desktop, laptop, tablet, and mobile devices.
9. Explain how a computer can represent numbers and encode characters electronically.

Introduction

"Hi, I'm Liz, and I'm a computer technician. I'd like to talk with you about the different types of system units for personal computers. I'd also like to talk about various electronic components that make your computer work."

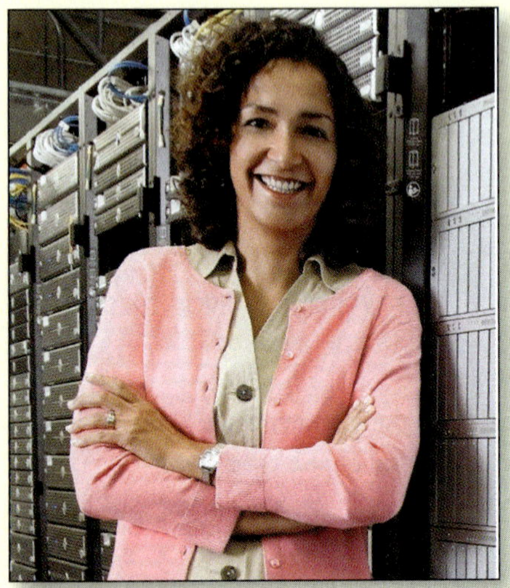

Why are some computers more powerful than others? The answer lies in three words: speed, capacity, and flexibility. After reading this chapter, you will be able to judge how fast, powerful, and versatile a particular personal computer is. As you might expect, this knowledge is valuable if you are planning to buy a new personal computer system or to upgrade an existing system. (The Computer Buyer's Guide at the end of this book provides additional information.) This knowledge will help you evaluate whether or not an existing system is powerful enough for today's new and exciting applications.

Sometime you may get the chance to watch when a technician opens up a personal computer. You will see that it is basically a collection of electronic circuitry. While there is no need to understand how all these components work, it is important to understand the principles. Armed with this knowledge, you will be able to confidently make sound purchasing and upgrading decisions.

To efficiently and effectively use computers, you need to understand the functionality of the basic components in the system unit, including the system board, microprocessor, memory, expansion slots and cards, bus lines, ports, cables, and power supply units.

System Unit

The **system unit,** also known as the **system chassis,** is a container that houses most of the electronic components that make up a computer system.

At one time all system units were in a separate case. Advances in the miniaturization of electronic components, however, have led to smaller and smaller computers with system units that share containers with other parts of the computer system.

As we have previously discussed, a **personal computer** is the most widely used type of computer. It is the most affordable and designed to be operated directly by an end user. The five most common types are desktop, laptop, tablet, smartphones, and wearable computers. Each has a unique type of system unit.

ethics

Labor costs are much less in China than in the United States. As a result, many computers and peripherals sold last year were manufactured there. While this has resulted in the loss of jobs elsewhere, it has also improved the standard of living for millions of Chinese. Unfortunately, working conditions in Chinese factories have been widely reported to be well below acceptable standards. Do you think consumers have an ethical responsibility regarding where and/or how products are manufactured?

Desktops

This is the most powerful type of personal computer. Most **desktops** have their system unit in a separate case. This case contains the system's electronic components and selected secondary storage devices. Input and output devices, such as a mouse, keyboard, and monitor, are located outside the system unit. This type of system unit is designed to be placed either horizontally or vertically. Desktop system units that are placed vertically are sometimes referred to as a **tower unit** or **tower computer.** (See Figure 5-1.)

Some desktop computers, like Apple's iMac, have their monitor and system unit housed together in the same case. These computers are known as an **all-in-one.** (See Figure 5-2.)

Laptops

Although typically not as powerful as desktops, **laptops** are portable and much smaller. Their system units are housed with selected secondary storage devices and input devices (keyboard and pointing device). Located outside the system unit, the monitor is attached by hinges.

Figure 5-1 Tower unit

Figure 5-2 All-in-one

There are several specialized laptops with features that make them unique. Some of them are:

- **Two-in-one laptops,** which include a touch screen and the ability to fold flat like a tablet computer. These laptops offer the advantages of a laptop with the convenience of a tablet. (See Figure 5-3.)
- **Gaming laptops,** which include high-end graphics hardware and very fast processors. At one time, most gamers preferred desktop computers. As laptops have become more powerful, gaming laptops have become the favorite primarily due to their portability.
- **Ultrabooks,** also known as **ultraportables** or **mini notebooks,** which are lighter and thinner with longer battery life than most laptops. They accomplish these advantages by leaving out components such as optical drives and using energy-efficient microprocessors. (See Figure 5-4.)

Figure 5-3 Two-in-one laptop

Tablets

Tablets, also known as **tablet computers,** are the newest and one of the most popular types of computer. They are effectively a thin slab that is almost all monitor with the system unit located behind the monitor.

Tablets are smaller, lighter, and generally less powerful than laptop computers. Like a laptop, tablets have a flat screen but typically do not have a standard keyboard. Instead, most tablets use a virtual keyboard that appears on the screen and is touch-sensitive. While tablets are very convenient for watching videos or surfing the web, inputting information can be difficult using their virtual keyboard. Some ways to overcome this limitation are with:

Figure 5-4 Ultrabook

- Keyboard attachments. Several manufacturers are offering keyboard options. For example, Apple and Logitech offer wireless keyboards for tablets.
- Digital pens. These devices assist in selecting options and entering handwritten notes. For example, both Microsoft and Samsung offer tablets with digital pens.
- Speech recognition. This advance allows direct verbal communication. For example, both Apple and Google feature excellent speech recognition features built into iOS and Chrome OS.

Mini tablets are a type of tablet with a smaller screen. While mini tablets operate like a traditional tablet, they typically do not have all the functionality of the bigger tablets. Their most significant advantage is that they are easier to transport in pockets and purses. (See Figure 5-5.)

Figure 5-5 Mini tablet

Smartphones

Smartphones are by far the most popular mobile device. Designed to comfortably fit into the palm of one hand, smartphones have become the indispensable handheld computer. They greatly extend the capabilities of a cell phone by providing computing power. In addition to capturing and sending audio and video, smartphones run apps, connect to the Internet, and more. Their system unit is located behind the display screen.

Wearable Computers

Figure 5-6 **Smartwatch**

Wearable computers, also known as **wearable devices,** are one of the first evolutionary steps to the IoT. These devices contain an embedded computer on a chip that is typically much smaller and less powerful than a smartphone's. The most common wearable computers are smartwatches and activity trackers. (See Figure 5-6.)

- **Smartwatches** like Apple's Watch. This device acts as a watch, fitness monitor, and communication device. For example, the Apple Watch connects to an iPhone to display e-mails, text messages, and calendar reminders on the user's wrist.
- **Activity trackers** like Fitbit's Flex. This device monitors daily exercise and sleep patterns. It also connects wirelessly to desktops, laptops, and smartphones to record and share data.

Components

Personal computers come in a variety of different sizes, shapes, and capabilities. While they look different and each has its own unique features, they share surprisingly similar components, including system boards, microprocessors, and memory. (See Figure 5-7.)

Desktop

Laptop

Tablet

Smartphone

Wearable

Figure 5-7 **System unit components**

Figure 5-8 **System board**

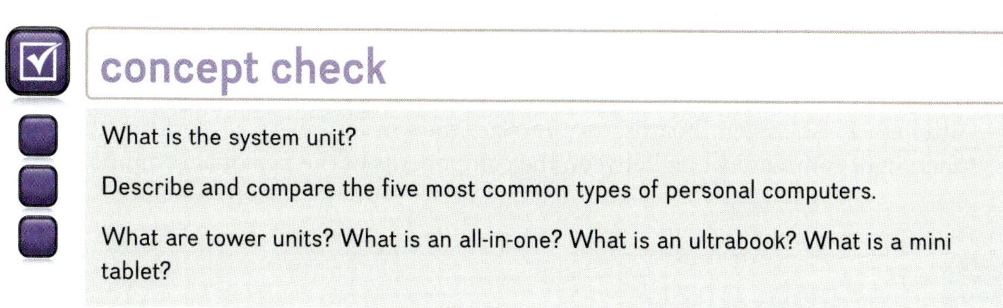

concept check
What is the system unit?
Describe and compare the five most common types of personal computers.
What are tower units? What is an all-in-one? What is an ultrabook? What is a mini tablet?

System Board

The **system board** is also known as the **mainboard** or **motherboard.** The system board controls communications for the entire computer system. All devices and components connect to the system board, including external devices like keyboards and monitors and internal components like hard-disk drives and microprocessors. The system board acts as a data path and traffic monitor, allowing the various components to communicate efficiently with one another.

On a desktop computer, the system board is typically located at the bottom of the system unit or along one side. It is a large flat circuit board covered with a variety of different electronic components including sockets, slots, and bus lines. (See Figure 5-8.)

- **Sockets** provide a connection point for small specialized electronic parts called chips. **Chips** consist of tiny circuit boards etched onto squares of sandlike material called silicon. These circuit boards can be smaller than the tip of your finger. (See Figure 5-9.) A chip is also called a **silicon chip, semiconductor,** or **integrated circuit.** Chips typically are mounted onto **chip carriers.** (See Figure 5-10.) These carriers plug either directly into sockets on the system board or onto cards that are then plugged into slots on the system board. Sockets are used to connect the system board to a variety of different types of chips, including microprocessor and memory chips.
- **Slots** provide a connection point for specialized cards or circuit boards. These cards provide expansion capability for a computer system. For example, a wireless

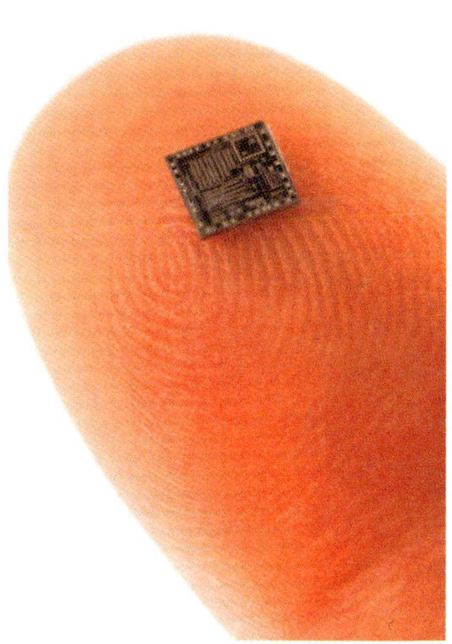

Figure 5-9 **Chip**

environment

Have you ever wondered what you should do with your old computers, monitors, and mobile devices? The last thing you want to do is throw them away. First, consider donating them to various charitable organizations that work with local schools and low-income families. Otherwise, recycle them. Many computer retailers near you accept used devices and components for recycling, even if they are broken. Alternatively, visit the website of your local government to find the electronics recycling center nearest you.

Figure 5-10 **Chip mounted onto a chip carrier**

networking card plugs into a slot on the system board to provide a connection to a local area network.

- Connecting lines called **bus lines** provide pathways that support communication among the various electronic components that are either located on the system board or attached to the system board.

Generally, the system board found on a desktop is larger than that found on a laptop, and much larger than one found on a tablet, smartphone, or wearable computer. Although these system boards vary in size, they nevertheless all perform the same function of communicating between the components of the personal computer.

concept check

 What is the system board, and what does it do?

 Define and describe sockets, slots, and bus lines.

 What are chips? How are chips attached to the system board?

Microprocessor

In most personal computer systems, the **central processing unit (CPU)** or **processor** is contained on a single chip called the **microprocessor.** The microprocessor is the "brains" of the computer system. It has two basic components: the control unit and the arithmetic-logic unit.

- **Control unit:** The **control unit** tells the rest of the computer system how to carry out a program's instructions. It directs the movement of electronic signals between memory, which temporarily holds data, instructions, and processed information, and the arithmetic-logic unit. It also directs these control signals between the CPU and input and output devices.
- **Arithmetic-logic unit:** The **arithmetic-logic unit,** usually called the **ALU,** performs two types of operations: arithmetic and logical. **Arithmetic operations** are the fundamental math operations: addition, subtraction, multiplication, and division. **Logical operations** consist of comparisons such as whether one item is equal to (=), less than (<), or greater than (>) the other.

Microprocessor Chips

Chip processing capacities are often expressed in word sizes. A **word** is the number of bits (such as 16, 32, or 64) that can be accessed at one time by the CPU. The more bits in a word, the more data a computer can process at one time. Eight bits group together to form a byte. A 32-bit-word computer can access 4 bytes at a time. A 64-bit-word computer can access 8 bytes at a time. Therefore, the computer designed to process 64-bit words has greater processing capacity. Other factors affect a computer's processing capability including how fast it can process data and instructions.

The processing speed of a microprocessor is typically represented by its **clock speed,** which is related to the number of times the CPU can fetch and process data or instructions in a second. Older personal computers typically process data and instructions in millionths of a second, or microseconds. Newer personal computers are much faster and process data and instructions in billionths of a second, or nanoseconds. Supercomputers, by contrast, operate at speeds measured in picoseconds—1,000 times as fast as personal computers. In the near future, we can expect processor speeds to be 1,000 times faster than that, operating at speeds measured in femtoseconds. (See Figure 5-11.) Logically, the higher a microprocessor's clock speed, the faster the microprocessor. However, some processors can handle multiple instructions per cycle or tick of the clock; this means that clock speed comparisons can only be made between processors that work the same way.

Unit	Speed
Microsecond	Millionth of a second
Nanosecond	Billionth of a second
Picosecond	Trillionth of a second
Femtosecond	Quadrillionth of a second

Figure 5-11 **Processing speeds**

At one time, personal computers were limited by microprocessors that could support a single CPU that controlled operations. These computers were limited to processing one program at a time. Now, many personal computers have **multicore processors** that can provide two or more separate and independent CPUs. For example, a quad-core processor could have one core computing a complex Excel spreadsheet, a second core creating a report using Word, a third core locating a record using Access, and a fourth core running a multimedia presentation all at the same time. More significantly, however, is the potential for personal computers to run very large, complex programs that previously required expensive and specialized hardware.

For multicore processors to be used effectively, computers must understand how to divide tasks into parts that can be distributed across each core—an operation called **parallel processing.** Operating systems such as Windows 8 and Mac OS X support parallel processing. Software developers use this technology for a wide range of applications from scientific programs to sophisticated computer games.

See Figure 5-12 for a table of popular microprocessors.

Processor	Manufacturer
A-Series	AMD
Cortex-A series	ARM
Edison	Intel
i7	Intel

Figure 5-12 **Popular microprocessors**

Specialty Processors

In addition to microprocessor chips, a variety of more specialized processing chips have been developed.

- **Coprocessors** are specialty chips designed to improve specific computing operations. One of the most widely used is the **graphics coprocessor,** also called a **GPU (graphics processing unit).** These processors are designed to handle a variety of specialized tasks such as displaying 3D images and encrypting data. Powerful GPUs are a standard feature in gaming computers to support fast processing of virtual environments.
- Many cars have more than 70 separate specialty processors to control nearly everything from fuel efficiency to satellite entertainment and tracking systems.

privacy

Did you know that one type of specialty processor is devoted exclusively to protecting your privacy? Called cryptoprocessors, these microchips perform encoding and decoding of data faster and more securely than a CPU. These specialized chips exist in ATMs, TV set-top boxes, and smartcards.

concept check

- Name and describe the two components of a microprocessor.
- Define word, clock speed, multicore chip, and parallel processing.
- What are specialty processors? Describe coprocessors.

Figure 5-13 RAM chips mounted on circuit board

Memory

Memory is a holding area for data, instructions, and information. Like microprocessors, **memory** is contained on chips connected to the system board. There are three well-known types of memory chips: random-access memory (RAM), read-only memory (ROM), and flash memory.

RAM

Random-access memory (RAM) chips hold the program (sequence of instructions) and data that the CPU is presently processing. (See Figure 5-13.) RAM is called temporary or volatile storage because everything in most types of RAM is lost as soon as the computer is turned off. It is also lost if there is a power failure or other disruption of the electric current going to the computer. Secondary storage, which we shall describe in Chapter 7, does not lose its contents. It is permanent or nonvolatile storage, such as the data stored on a hard disk. For this reason, as we mentioned earlier, it is a good idea to frequently save your work in progress to a secondary storage device. That is, if you are working on a document or a spreadsheet, every few minutes you should save, or store, the material.

Cache (pronounced "cash") **memory** improves processing by acting as a temporary high-speed holding area between the memory and the CPU. The computer detects which information in RAM is most frequently used and then copies that information into the cache. When needed, the CPU can quickly access the information from the cache.

Having enough RAM is important! For example, to use the standard version of Microsoft Office 2016, you need 2 GB, or 2 billion bytes, of RAM. Some applications, such as photo editing software, may require even more. Fortunately, additional RAM can be added to a computer system by inserting an expansion module called a **DIMM (dual in-line memory module)** into the system board. The capacity or amount of RAM is expressed in bytes. There are three commonly used units of measurement to describe memory capacity. (See Figure 5-14.)

Unit	Capacity
Megabyte (MB)	1 million bytes
Gigabyte (GB)	1 billion bytes
Terabyte (TB)	1 trillion bytes

Figure 5-14 Memory capacity

Even if your computer does not have enough RAM to hold a program, it might be able to run the program using **virtual memory.** Most of today's operating systems support virtual memory. With virtual memory, large programs are divided into parts and the parts are stored on a secondary device, usually a hard disk. Each part is then read into RAM only when needed. In this way, computer systems are able to run very large programs.

ROM

Read-only memory (ROM) chips have information stored in them by the manufacturer. Unlike RAM chips, ROM chips are not volatile and cannot be changed by the user. "Read only" means that the CPU can read, or retrieve, data and programs written on the ROM chip. However, the computer cannot write–encode or change–the information or instructions in ROM.

Not long ago, ROM chips were typically used to contain almost all the instructions for basic computer operations. For example, ROM instructions are needed to start a computer, to access memory, and to handle keyboard input. Recently, however, flash memory chips have replaced ROM chips for many applications.

Flash Memory

Flash memory offers a combination of the features of RAM and ROM. Like RAM, it can be updated to store new information. Like ROM, it does not lose that information when power to the computer system is turned off.

Flash memory is used for a wide range of applications. For example, it is used to store the start-up instructions for a computer. This information is called the system's

BIOS (basic input/output system). This information would include the specifics concerning the amount of RAM and the type of keyboard, mouse, and secondary storage devices connected to the system unit. If changes are made to the computer system, these changes are reflected in flash memory.

See Figure 5-15 for a summary of the three types of memory.

Type	Use
RAM	Programs and data
ROM	Fixed start-up instructions
Flash	Flexible start-up instructions

Figure 5-15 **Memory**

concept check

- What is memory? Name and describe three types.
- What are cache memory, DIMM, and virtual memory?
- Define ROM and flash memory.

Expansion Slots and Cards

As previously mentioned, many personal computers allow users to expand their systems by providing **expansion slots** on the system board. Users can insert optional devices known as **expansion cards** into these slots. (See Figure 5-16.) Ports on the cards allow cables to be connected from the expansion cards to devices outside the system unit. (See Figure 5-17.) There are a wide range of different types of expansion cards. Some of the most commonly used expansion cards are

Figure 5-16 **Expansion cards fit into slots on the system board**

- **Graphics cards,** which provide high-quality 3D graphics and animation for games and simulations. While many personal computer systems have a GPU connected directly to the system board, others connect through a graphics card. This card can contain one or more GPU chips and is standard for most gaming computers.
- **Network interface cards (NIC),** also known as **network adapter cards,** which are used to connect a computer to a network. (See Figure 5-18.) The network allows connected computers to share data, programs, and hardware. The network adapter card typically connects the system unit to a cable that connects to the network.

Figure 5-17 **Expansion card with three ports**

Figure 5-18 **Network interface card**

Figure 5-19 **SD card**

- **Wireless network cards** allow computers to be connected without cables. As we will discuss in Chapter 8, wireless networks in the home are widely used to share a common Internet connection. Each device on the network is equipped with a wireless network card that communicates with the other devices.

To meet the size constraints of laptop computers, tablets, and smartphones, fingernail-size expansion cards known as **SD cards** have been developed. These cards plug into expansion slots located within many laptops, tablets, and smartphones. (See Figure 5-19.)

concept check

What are expansion slots and cards? What are they used for?

List and describe three commonly used expansion cards.

What are SD cards? How are they used?

Bus Lines

As mentioned earlier, a **bus line**—also known simply as a **bus**—connects the parts of the CPU to each other. Buses also link the CPU to various other components on the system board. (See Figure 5-20.) A bus is a pathway for bits representing data and instructions. The number of bits that can travel simultaneously down a bus is known as the **bus width.**

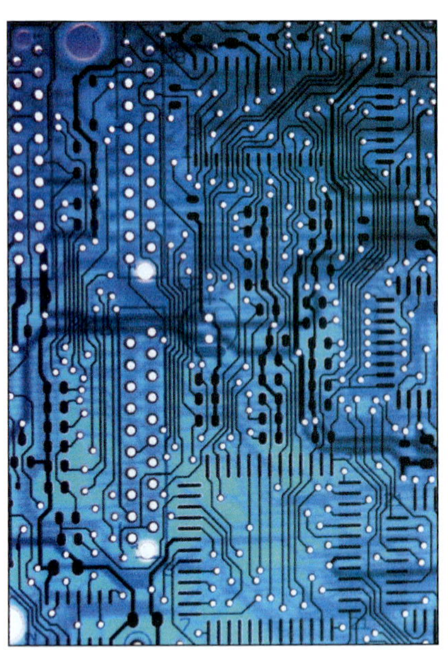

Figure 5-20 **Bus is a pathway for bits**

A bus is similar to a multilane highway that moves bits rather than cars from one location to another. The number of traffic lanes determines the bus width. A highway (bus line) with more traffic lanes (bus width) can move traffic (data and instructions) more efficiently. For example, a 64-bit bus can move twice as much information at a time as a 32-bit bus. Why should you even care about what a bus line is? Because as microprocessor chips have changed, so have bus lines. Bus design or bus architecture is an important factor relating to the speed and power for a particular computer. Additionally, many devices, such as expansion cards, will work with only one type of bus.

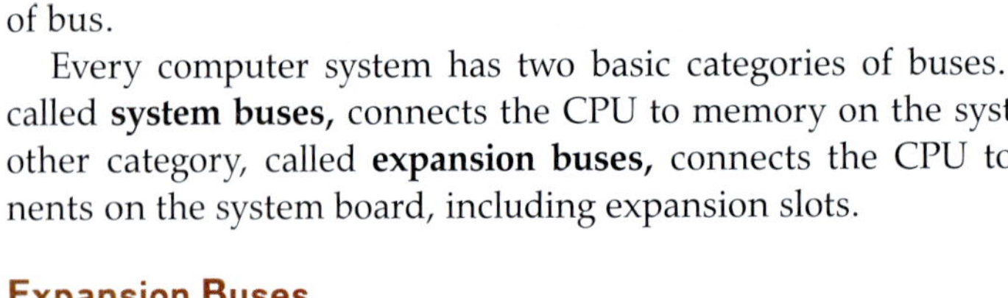

Every computer system has two basic categories of buses. One category, called **system buses,** connects the CPU to memory on the system board. The other category, called **expansion buses,** connects the CPU to other components on the system board, including expansion slots.

Expansion Buses

Computer systems typically have a combination of different types of expansion buses. The principal types are USB, FireWire, and PCIe.

- **Universal serial bus (USB)** is widely used today. External USB devices are connected from one to another or to a common point or hub and then onto the USB bus. The USB bus then connects to the PCI bus on the system board. The current USB standard is USB 3.1.
- **FireWire buses** are similar to USB buses but more specialized. They are used primarily to connect audio and video equipment to the system board.
- **PCI Express (PCIe)** is widely used in many of today's most powerful computers. Unlike most other buses that share a single bus line or path with several devices, the PCIe bus provides a single dedicated path for each connected device.

concept check

What is a bus, and what is bus width?

What is the difference between a system and an expansion bus?

Discuss three types of expansion buses.

Ports

A **port** is a socket for external devices to connect to the system unit. (See Figure 5-21.) Some ports connect directly to the system board, while others connect to cards that are inserted into slots on the system board. Some ports are standard features of most computer systems, and others are more specialized.

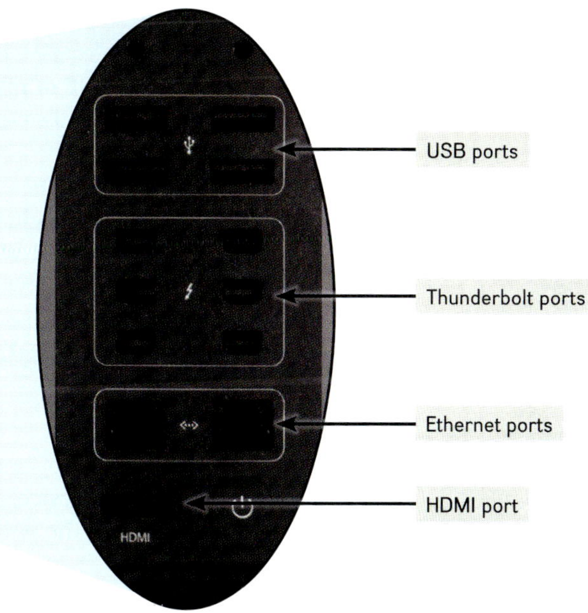

Figure 5-21 **Ports**

Standard Ports

Most desktop and laptop computers come with a standard set of ports for connecting a monitor, keyboard, and other peripheral devices. The most common ports follow.

- **Universal serial bus (USB) ports** can be used to connect several devices to the system unit and are widely used to connect keyboards, mice, printers, storage devices, and a variety of specialty devices. One such device, a USB TV tuner card, allows users to view and record television programs. To learn how you can use a TV tuner card, see Making IT Work for You: TV Tuners on page 127. A single USB port can be used to connect many USB devices to the system unit.
- **High Definition Multimedia Interface (HDMI) ports** provide high-definition video and audio, making it possible to use a computer as a video jukebox or an HD video recorder.
- **Thunderbolt ports,** first introduced in Apple's MacBook Pro computer, provide high-speed connections. A single port can connect up to seven separate devices connected one to another. Thunderbolt ports promise to replace a number of different types of ports including Mini DisplayPorts.
- **Ethernet ports** are a high-speed networking port that has become a standard for many of today's computers. Ethernet allows you to connect multiple computers for sharing files, or to a DSL or cable modem for high-speed Internet access.

Specialized Ports

In addition to standard ports, there are numerous specialty ports. The most common include:

- **External Serial Advanced Technology Attachment (eSATA) ports** provide high-speed connections for external hard-disk drives, optical discs, and other large secondary storage devices.
- **Musical instrument digital interface (MIDI) ports** are a special type of port for connecting musical instruments like an electronic keyboard to a sound card. The sound card converts the music into a series of digital instructions. These instructions can be processed immediately to reproduce the music or saved to a file for later processing.
- **Mini DisplayPort (MiniDP or mDP) ports** are audiovisual ports typically used to connect large monitors. These ports are used with many Apple Macintosh computers.
- **VGA (Video Graphics Adapter)** and **DVI (Digital Video Interface) ports** provide connections to analog and digital monitors, respectively. DVI has become the most commonly used standard, but VGA ports are still provided on almost all systems for compatibility with older/lower-cost monitors.
- **FireWire ports** provide high-speed connections to specialized FireWire devices such as camcorders and storage devices.

Cables

Cables are used to connect exterior devices to the system unit via the ports. One end of the cable is attached to the device, and the other end has a connector that is attached to a matching connector on the port. (See Figure 5-22.)

USB

HDMI

Thunderbolt

Ethernet

Figure 5-22 **Cables**

Making IT work for you

TV TUNERS

Do you already use a DVR (digital video recorder) in order to record your favorite TV shows? Although many cable and satellite companies offer this device, did you know that Windows Media Center can perform the same function? All you need is a device called a TV tuner that connects your antenna or cable to your computer. Below are the steps to turn your Windows-based computer into a DVR. (Please note that the following specifics do not apply to all versions of TV tuners and media players.)

Installing a TV Tuner A TV tuner is essentially a piece of hardware that allows your computer to process and display a cable or TV signal. Although some (usually pricey) PCs may include this technology, it is usually necessary to purchase it separately. The easiest ones to install are those that connect externally to a USB port, such as the Hauppauge Hybrid WinTV-HVR.

1. **Plug the TV tuner into an available USB port on your computer.**
2. **Connect a coaxial cable directly from your cable outlet or over-the-air antenna to the back of the TV tuner. If Windows does not automatically install the tuner, consult the user manual for instructions.**
3. **With your TV tuner installed, it will guide you through a setup process, including a long scan for all available channels from your cable or antenna.**

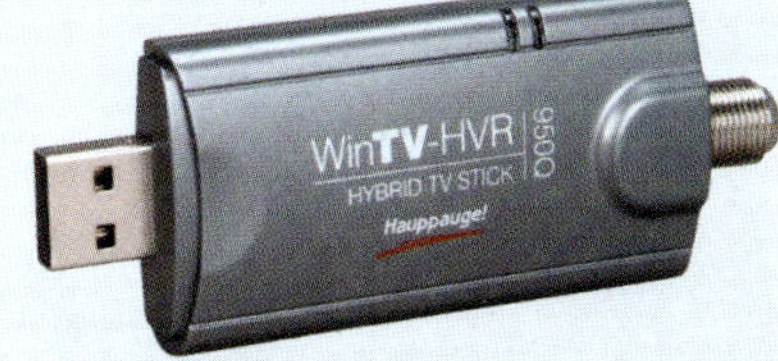

Using a Software Media Center The utility, Kodi, must be downloaded from the Internet. Although it contains many tools to manage your music, photos, and movies, we will focus on its DVR capabilities for TV and cable. (Please note that there are different versions of Kodi and that some of the specifics presented here may not apply to all versions.)

1. **Visit http://kodi.tv/download and click the *installer* for your operating system and download the program.**
2. **Run the installation file and follow the prompts.**
3. **Click on *Settings*, then *Add-ons*, then select *Disabled add-ons*, and enable the *MythTV PVR Client* add-on.**
4. **Click the *home* button located in the lower right of the window, then scroll right and click on *TV*, and then select *Channels*.**
5. **To record a program, locate the program and press *record*.**
6. **To view your recorded TV shows, return to the home screen and select the *TV* sub menu recordings. Click on the episode you wish to view.**

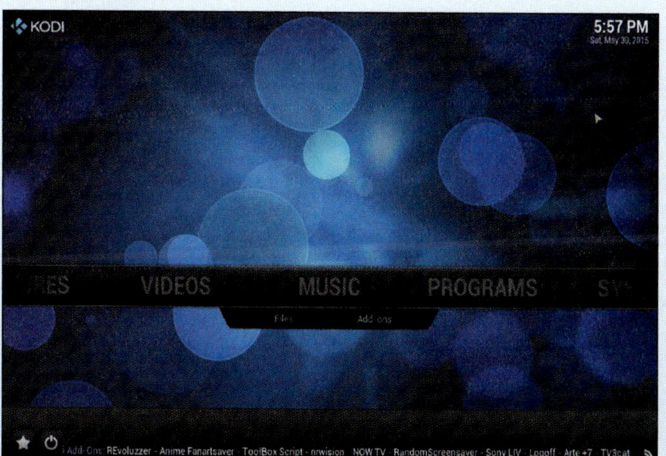

If you have a high-speed wireless network and several PCs in your home, you will have the capability to watch your recorded shows via Kodi's streaming ability.

Power Supply

Computers require direct current (DC) to power their electronic components and to represent data and instructions. DC power can be provided indirectly by converting alternating current (AC) from standard wall outlets or directly from batteries.

- Desktop computers have a **power supply unit** located within the system unit. (See Figure 5-23.) This unit plugs into a standard wall outlet, converts AC to DC, and provides the power to drive all of the system unit components.
- Laptops typically use **AC adapters** that are located outside the system unit. (See Figure 5-24.) AC adapters plug into a standard wall outlet, convert AC to DC, provide power to drive the system unit components, and can recharge the batteries. These computers can be operated either using an AC adapter plugged into a wall outlet or using battery power. Their batteries typically provide sufficient power for up to eight hours before they need to be recharged.
- Most tablets and mobile devices use internal AC adapters that use a cable to connect to a standard wall outlet. Some smartphones, however, use a **wireless charging platform** eliminating the cable. (See Figure 5-25.) Unlike most laptops, most tablets, mobile devices, and wearable computers can operate only using battery power. Their AC adapters or charging platforms are only used to recharge batteries.

tips **Does your laptop seem to be losing its charge sooner than it used to? These batteries do lose power over time; however, you can take some steps to slow down the aging process.**

1. **Balance adapter and battery use.** The best practice is to use the laptop on battery power for a little while without draining it completely (50 percent charge, for example), followed by charging it back to 100 percent. Modern batteries should not be drained to 0 percent each day.
2. **Calibrate it.** Your laptop's manufacturer will recommend that you calibrate, or reset, your battery every few months. Follow its guidelines on the web or in your instruction manual, as it will ensure that the battery meter in your operating system is accurate and that you are getting the expected charge time.
3. **Avoid excessive heat.** High temperatures can accelerate the deterioration of modern batteries. Therefore, avoid exposure to excessive heat and consider purchasing a laptop cooler or fan.
4. **Proper storage.** If you are not going to use your laptop for a few weeks, most manufacturers recommend that you remove the battery.

Figure 5-23 **Power supply unit**

Figure 5-24 **AC adapter**

Figure 5-25 **Wireless charging platform**

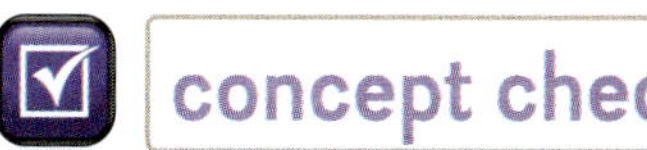

concept check

- What are ports? What do they do?
- Describe four standard ports and five specialized ports.
- What is a power supply unit? What is an AC adapter? What is a charging platform?

Electronic Data and Instructions

Have you ever wondered why it is said that we live in a digital world? It's because computers cannot recognize information the same way you and I can. People follow instructions and process data using letters, numbers, and special characters. For example, if we wanted someone to add the numbers 3 and 5 together and record the answer, we might say "please add 3 and 5." The system unit, however, is electronic circuitry and cannot directly process such a request.

Our voices create **analog,** or continuous, signals that vary to represent different tones, pitches, and volume. Computers, however, can recognize only **digital** electronic signals. Before any processing can occur within the system unit, a conversion must occur from what we understand to what the system unit can electronically process.

Numeric Representation

What is the most fundamental statement you can make about electricity? It is simply this: It can be either on or off. Indeed, there are many forms of technology that can make use of this two-state on/off, yes/no, present/absent arrangement. For instance, a light switch may be on or off, or an electric circuit open or closed. A specific location on a tape or disk may have a positive charge or a negative charge. This is the reason, then, that a two-state or binary system is used to represent data and instructions.

The decimal system that we are all familiar with has 10 digits (0, 1, 2, 3, 4, 5, 6, 7, 8, 9). The **binary system,** however, consists of only two digits—0 and 1. Each 0 or 1 is called a **bit**—short for binary digit. In the system unit, the 1 can be represented by a negative charge and the 0 by no electric charge. In order to represent numbers, letters, and special characters, bits are combined into groups of eight called **bytes.** Whenever you enter a number into a computer system, that number must be converted into a binary number before it can be processed.

Any number can be expressed as a binary number. Binary numbers, however, are difficult for humans to work with because they require so many digits. Instead, binary numbers are often represented in a format more readable by humans. The **hexadecimal system,** or **hex,** uses 16 digits (0, 1, 2, 3, 4, 5, 6, 7, 8, 9, A, B, C, D, E, F) to represent binary numbers. Each hex digit represents four binary digits, and two hex digits are commonly used together to represent 1 byte (8 binary digits). (See Figure 5-26.) You may have already seen hex when selecting a color in a website design or drawing application, or when entering the password for access to a wireless network.

Decimal	Binary	Hex
00	00000000	00
01	00000001	01
02	00000010	02
03	00000011	03
04	00000100	04
05	00000101	05
06	00000110	06
07	00000111	07
08	00001000	08
09	00001001	09
10	00001010	0A
11	00001011	0B
12	00001100	0C
13	00001101	0D
14	00001110	0E
15	00001111	0F

Figure 5-26 **Numeric representations**

Character Encoding

As we've seen, computers must represent all numbers with the binary system internally. What about text? How can a computer provide representations of the nonnumeric characters we use to communicate, such as the sentence you are reading now? The answer is character encoding schemes or standards.

Character encoding standards assign a unique sequence of bits to each character. Historically, personal computers used the **ASCII (American Standard Code for Information Interchange)** to represent characters, while mainframe computers used **EBCDIC (Extended Binary Coded Decimal Interchange Code).** These schemes were quite effective; however, they are limited. ASCII, for example, only uses 7 bits to represent each character, which means that only 128 total characters could be represented. This was fine for most characters in the English language but was not large enough to support other languages such as Chinese and Japanese. These languages have too many characters to be represented by the 7-bit ASCII code.

The explosion of the Internet and subsequent globalization of computing have led to a new character encoding called **Unicode,** which uses 16 bits. The Unicode standard is the most widely used character encoding standard and is recognized by virtually every computer system. The first 128 characters are assigned the same sequence of bits as ASCII to maintain compatibility with older ASCII-formatted information. However, Unicode uses a variable number of bits to represent each character, which allows non-English characters and special characters to be represented.

concept check

What is the difference between an analog and a digital signal?

What are decimal and binary systems? How are they different?

Compare EBCDIC, ASCII, and Unicode.

Careers in IT

"Now that you know about system units, I'd like to tell you about my career as a computer technician."

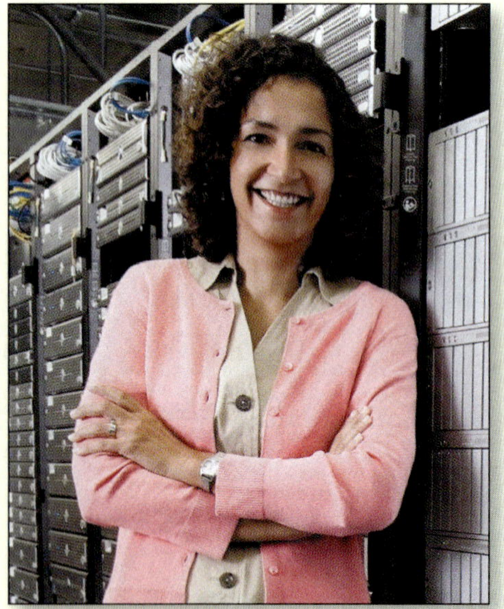

Computer technicians repair and install computer components and systems. They may work on everything from personal computers and mainframe servers to printers. Some computer technicians are responsible for setting up and maintaining computer networks. Experienced computer technicians may work with computer engineers to diagnose problems and run routine maintenance on complex systems. Job growth is expected in this field as computer equipment becomes more complicated and technology expands.

Employers look for those with certification in computer repair or associate's degrees from professional schools. Computer technicians also can expect to continue their education to keep up with technological changes. Good communication skills are important in this field.

Computer technicians can expect to earn an annual salary in the range of $37,000 to $47,000. Opportunities for advancement typically come in the form of work on more advanced computer systems. Some computer technicians move into customer service positions or go into sales.

A LOOK TO THE FUTURE

Chips inside Your Brain

Have you ever thought it would be possible to be able to communicate with a computer . . . by merely thinking? Simple computer implants are used on a regular basis to improve hearing or reduce the risk of heart attack. More recently, implants have been used to regulate drug intake and improve prosthetics. In the future you may use various devices (usually worn on the head) that can use your basic thoughts to move objects, such as wheelchairs. However, the future will lie in implanted microchips that can communicate directly with our nerve cells. Although their initial purpose will be to treat a variety of medical conditions, they could eventually (and controversially) be used to improve various brain functions of otherwise healthy individuals. Technology has been making better implants, and will continue to evolve to improve our lives as we look to the future.

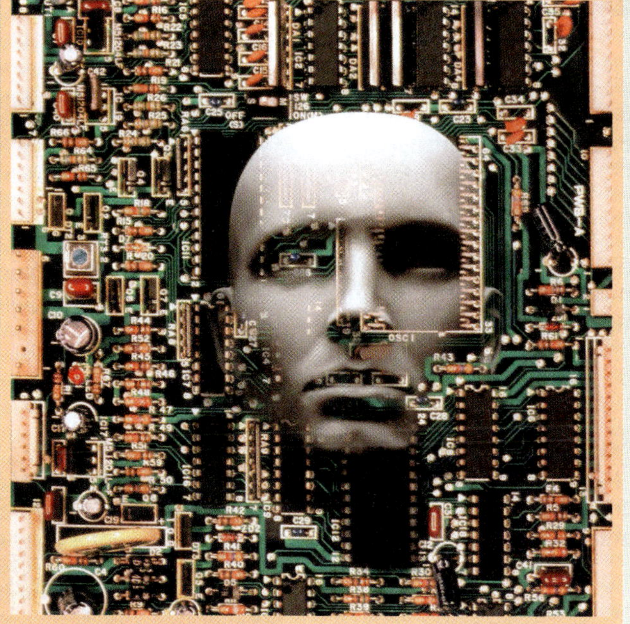

For over a decade, doctors have been able to use deep brain stimulation (DBS) to treat several disorders such as Parkinson's disease. As successful as it has been for many patients, those implants simply send preset electrical impulses to the brain. They do not involve an active communication between nerve cells and machines. Researchers working on a chip known as ReNaChip hope to change this by using a programmable computer chip that is responsive to what is going on in the patient's brain. This silicon chip can measure the brain's electrical activity and then deliver the appropriate stimulation when and where it is needed.

Another brain implant that is currently being developed aims to help the blind regain some sight. A microchip is implanted in the brain's visual cortex, which is responsible for processing images. This chip would communicate wirelessly with a camera located inside special eyeglasses worn by the individual. The images captured by that camera would be processed by the chip and then fed directly to the nerves in this area of the brain. Getting close to the world of the unbelievable, researchers are improving on the ability of computers to actually read human thoughts. Currently, one research team has been able to use a chip implant and computer to read the thoughts of a stroke victim in order to allow her to move a robotic hand. Although the success rate is not 100 percent and the processing is limited to basic movements, the patient has already been able to get the robotic arm to hold a cup of coffee by thinking about it. This research will hopefully lead to improved, thought-controlled prosthetic devices for millions of disabled individuals.

Many ethicists are concerned by the potential use of such chips to improve human abilities instead of treating medical conditions. For example, with tiny chips being able to store so much, people could use brain implants to improve their memory. This can lead to a variety of scenarios where the individual with the implants could have an unfair advantage over those who don't have them. However, others disagree, arguing that the integration of technology and biology is to be expected, and it is nothing more than the next step in human evolution. If such a technology became widespread and affordable, would you opt to receive a chip implant? Would you make a distinction between using one for a medical condition and simply for improving your mental abilities? Do you think the future of humanity lies in the merging of technology with human biology?

VISUAL SUMMARY The System Unit

SYSTEM UNIT

System unit (system chassis) contains electronic components. The most common **personal computers** are **desktop, laptop, tablet, smartphones,** and **wearable computers.**

Desktop

Desktop system units are located in a separate case; **tower unit (tower computer)** has vertical system unit; **all-in-one** computer combines system unit and monitor.

Laptop

Laptop system units contain secondary storage devices and input devices. Specialty laptops include **two-in-one laptops** (touch screen and fold flat), **gaming laptops** (high-end graphics and fast processors), **ultrabooks,** also known as **ultraportables,** and **mini notebooks** (lighter, thinner, longer battery life).

Tablet

Tablet system units are located behind the monitor. They are smaller, lighter, and generally less powerful than laptops and use a virtual keyboard. **Mini tablets** are a smaller version of a traditional tablet.

Smartphones

Smartphones are the most popular mobile device; extend cell phones by providing computing power to capture video, send audio and video, run apps, connect to the Internet, and more.

Wearable Computers

Wearable computers (wearable devices) contain an embedded computer on a chip. The most common wearable computers are **smartwatches** and **activity trackers.**

Components

Each type of system unit has the same basic components including system board, microprocessor, and memory.

SYSTEM BOARD

The **system board (mainboard** or **motherboard)** controls all communication for the computer system. All external and internal devices and components connect to it.

- **Sockets** provide connection points for **chips (silicon chips, semiconductors, integrated circuits).** Chips are mounted on **chip carriers.**
- **Slots** provide connection points for specialized cards or circuit boards.
- **Bus lines** provide pathways to support communication.

To efficiently and effectively use computers, you need to understand the functionality of the basic components in the system unit: system board, microprocessor, memory, expansion slots and cards, bus lines, ports, and cables. Additionally, you need to understand how data and programs are represented electronically.

MICROPROCESSOR

In most personal computers, the **central processing unit (CPU)** or **processor** is contained on a single chip called the **microprocessor.** It has two basic components: a **control unit** and **ALU.**

Microprocessor Chips

A **word** is the number of bits that can be accessed by the microprocessor at one time. **Clock speed** represents the number of times the CPU can fetch and process data or instructions in a second.

Multicore processors can provide multiple independent CPUs. **Parallel processing** requires programs that allow multiple processors to work together to run large complex programs.

Specialty Processors

Specialty processors include **graphics coprocessors,** also known as **GPU** or **graphics processing unit** (processes graphic images), and processors in automobiles (monitor fuel efficiency, satellite entertainment, and tracking systems).

MEMORY

Memory holds data, instructions, and information. There are three types of memory chips.

RAM

RAM (random-access memory) chips are called temporary or volatile storage because their contents are lost if power is disrupted.

- **Cache memory** is a high-speed holding area for frequently used data and information.
- **DIMM (dual in-line memory module)** is used to expand memory.
- **Virtual memory** divides large programs into parts that are read into RAM as needed.

ROM

ROM (read-only memory) chips are nonvolatile storage and control essential system operations.

Flash Memory

Flash memory does not lose its contents when power is removed.

EXPANSION SLOTS AND CARDS

Most computers allow users to expand their systems by providing **expansion slots** on their system boards to accept **expansion cards.**

Examples of expansion cards include **graphics cards, network interface cards (NIC; network adapter cards),** and **wireless network cards.**

SD cards are fingernail-size expansion cards used primarily for laptop computers, tablets, and smartphones. They connect to expansion slots within these devices.

BUS LINES

Bus lines, also known as **buses,** provide data pathways that connect various system components. **Bus width** is the number of bits that can travel simultaneously.

System buses connect CPU and memory. **Expansion buses** connect CPU and slots.

Expansion Buses

Three principal expansion bus types:

- **USB (universal serial bus)** can connect from one USB device to another or to a common point (hub) and then onto the system board.
- **FireWire bus** is similar to USB bus but more specialized.
- **PCI Express (PCIe) bus** is widely used; provides a single dedicated path for each connected device.

PORTS

Ports are connecting sockets on the outside of the system unit.

Standard Ports

Four standard ports are

- **USB (universal serial bus)**—widely used to connect keyboards, mice, printers, and storage devices; one port can connect several devices to system unit.
- **HDMI (high definition multimedia interface)**—provides high-definition video and audio.
- **Thunderbolt**—provides high-speed connections to up to seven Thunderbolt devices at once, such as external hard drives and monitors.
- **Ethernet**—high-speed networking port that has become a standard for many of today's computers.

Specialized Ports

Five specialty ports are **eSATA (external serial advanced technology attachment)** for high-speed connections to large secondary storage devices, **MIDI** for digital music, **Mini DisplayPort (MiniDP, mDP)** for large monitors, **VGA (Video Graphics Adapter)** and **DVI (Digital Video Interface)** for connecting to monitors, and **Firewire** for high-speed connection to devices such as camcorders and secondary storage.

Cables

Cables are used to connect external devices to the system unit via ports.

POWER SUPPLY

Power supply units convert AC to DC and power desktops. **AC adapters** power laptops and tablets and recharge batteries. Some smartphones use **wireless charging platforms.**

ELECTRONIC REPRESENTATION

Human voices create **analog** (continuous) signals; computers only recognize **digital** electronic signals.

Numeric Representation

Data and instructions can be represented electronically with a two-state or **binary system** of numbers (0 and 1). Each 0 or 1 is called a **bit.** A **byte** consists of 8 bits. **Hexadecimal system (hex)** uses 16 digits to represent binary numbers.

Character Encoding

Character encoding standards assign unique sequences of bits to each character. Three standards are

- **ASCII—American Standard Code for Information Interchange.** Historically used for personal computers.
- **EBCDIC—Extended Binary Coded Decimal Interchange Code.** Historically used for mainframe computers.
- **Unicode**—16-bit code, most widely used standard.

CAREERS IN IT

Computer technicians repair and install computer components and systems. Certification in computer repair or an associate's degree from professional schools is required. Salary range is $37,000 to $47,000.

KEY TERMS

AC adapter (128)
activity tracker (118)
all-in-one (116)
analog (129)
arithmetic-logic unit (ALU) (120)
arithmetic operation (120)
ASCII (130)
binary system (129)
BIOS (basic input/output system) (123)
bit (129)
bus (124)
bus line (124)
bus width (124)
byte (129)
cable (126)
cache memory (122)
central processing unit (CPU) (120)
character encoding standards (130)
chip (119)
chip carriers (119)
clock speed (121)
computer technician (130)
control unit (120)
coprocessor (121)
desktop (116)
digital (129)
DIMM (dual in-line memory module) (122)
DVI (Digital Video Interface) port (126)
EBCDIC (130)
Ethernet port (126)
expansion bus (124)
expansion card (123)
expansion slot (123)
external Serial Advanced Technology Attachment (eSATA) port (126)
FireWire bus (125)
FireWire port (126)
flash memory (122)
gaming laptops (117)
GPU (graphics processing unit) (121)
graphics card (123)
graphics coprocessor (121)
hexadecimal system (hex) (129)
High Definition Multimedia Interface (HDMI) port (126)
integrated circuit (119)
laptop (116)
logical operation (120)
mainboard (119)
memory (122)
microprocessor (120)
Mini DisplayPort (MiniDP, mDP) port (126)
mini notebook (117)
mini tablets (117)
motherboard (119)
multicore processor (121)
musical instrument digital interface (MIDI) port (126)
network adapter card (123)
network interface card (NIC) (123)
parallel processing (121)
PCI Express (PCIe) (125)
personal computer (116)
port (125)
power supply unit (128)
processor (120)
random-access memory (RAM) (122)
read-only memory (ROM) (122)
SD card (124)
semiconductor (119)
silicon chip (119)
slot (119)
smartphone (118)
smartwatch (118)
socket (119)
system board (119)
system bus (124)
system chassis (116)
system unit (116)
tablet (117)
tablet computer (117)
Thunderbolt port (126)
tower computer (116)
tower unit (116)
two-in-one laptops (117)
ultrabooks (117)
ultraportables (117)
Unicode (130)
universal serial bus (USB) (125)
universal serial bus (USB) port (126)
VGA (Video Graphics Adapter) port (126)
virtual memory (122)
wearable computer (118)
wearable device (118)
wireless charging platform (128)
wireless network card (124)
word (121)

MULTIPLE CHOICE

Circle the correct answer.

1. This container houses most of the electrical components for a computer system.
   - a. chip carrier
   - b. system board
   - c. system unit
   - d. Unicode
2. The most popular mobile device.
   - a. all-in-one
   - b. desktop
   - c. smartphone
   - d. ultrabook
3. The mainboard or motherboard is also known as the:
   - a. computer
   - b. board processor
   - c. mobile system
   - d. system board
4. How many bytes can a 32-bit-word computer access at one time?
   - a. 1
   - b. 4
   - c. 8
   - d. 16
5. In a personal computer system, the central processing unit is typically contained on a single:
   - a. bus
   - b. chip
   - c. module
   - d. RAM
6. This type of memory divides large programs into parts and stores the parts on a secondary storage device.
   - a. direct
   - b. expanded
   - c. random-access
   - d. virtual
7. Also known as NIC, this adapter card is used to connect a computer to a(n):
   - a. AIA
   - b. expansion
   - c. graphics
   - d. network
8. This provides a pathway to connect parts of the CPU to each other.
   - a. bus
   - b. cable
   - c. wired
   - d. wireless
9. The specialized port that connects musical instruments like an electronic keyboard to a sound card.
   - a. eSATA
   - b. HDMI
   - c. MIDI
   - d. Thunderbolt
10. Computers can only recognize this type of electronic signal.
    - a. analog
    - b. bus
    - c. digital
    - d. maximum

MATCHING

Match each numbered item with the most closely related lettered item. Write your answers in the spaces provided.

a. cache
b. flash
c. multicore
d. NIC
e. port
f. random-access
g. slots
h. sockets
i. system
j. USB

___ 1. A type of multiprocessor chip that provides two or more separate and independent CPUs.
___ 2. A type of memory that is volatile or loses its contents when power is turned off.
___ 3. System board component that provides a connection point for specialized cards or circuit boards.
___ 4. Provide connection points for chips.
___ 5. A type of memory that improves processing by acting as a temporary high-speed holding area between the memory and the CPU.
___ 6. A type of memory that provides a combination of features of RAM and ROM.
___ 7. Another name for a network adapter card.
___ 8. This bus connects the CPU to memory on the system board.
___ 9. This port can be used to connect many USB devices to the system.
___ 10. A socket for external devices to connect to the system unit.

OPEN-ENDED

On a separate sheet of paper, respond to each question or statement.

1. Describe the five most common types of personal computers.
2. Describe system boards including sockets, chips, chip carriers, slots, and bus lines.
3. Discuss microprocessor components, chips, and specialty processors.
4. Define computer memory including RAM, ROM, and flash memory.
5. Define expansion slots, cards, including graphics cards, network interface cards, wireless network cards, and SD cards.
6. Describe bus lines, bus width, system bus, and expansion bus.
7. Define ports including standard and specialized ports. Give examples of each.
8. Describe power supply including power supply units and AC adapters.
9. Discuss electronic data and instructions.

DISCUSSION

Respond to each of the following questions.

1 Making IT Work for You: TV TUNERS

Did you know that you can record your favorite TV shows with a computer? Review the Making IT Work for You: TV Tuners on page 127, and then respond to the following: (a) Do you currently have a DVR in your home? If so, who is the manufacturer? If not, have you considered purchasing one? Why or why not? (b) How do the Kodi Media Center DVR capabilities compare with the DVR offered by your cable or satellite company? Use a search engine to help you find these differences. (c) Find at least two USB-based TV tuners using any online store. Note their prices and specifications. What are their main differences?

2 Privacy: CRYPTOPROCESSORS

Did you know that some systems have specialty processors that automatically encrypt data before storing? Review the Privacy box on page 121, and respond to the following: (a) Who do you think would need a cryptoprocessor? Be specific. (b) Do think these processors would be worthwhile for you to protect your privacy? Why or why not? (c) Are there any reasons why you might not want all your data encrypted? Explain. (d) Do you think that all computer systems should be required to have cryptoprocessors? Defend your position.

3 Ethics: JOB LOSS AND WORKING CONDITIONS

Many computer-related products are produced in China, where working conditions are reported to be well below acceptable standards. Review the Ethics box on page 116, and then respond to the following: (a) What do you think about products produced in other countries like China? What are the advantages and disadvantages to consumers? Be specific. (b) What are the ethical issues? Be specific, and defend your list of issues. (c) Would you be willing to pay more for a computer produced entirely in the United States? More specifically, would you be willing to pay three times as much for a smartphone? Why or why not? (d) Do you think consumers have an ethical responsibility to know how goods are produced? More specifically, would your purchase decisions be affected by knowledge about the working conditions of those who make the product? Why or why not?

4 Environment: RECYCLING COMPUTER HARDWARE

Have you ever wondered what you should do with your old computers, monitors, and mobile devices? Review the Environment box on page 120, and then respond to the following: (a) What do you typically do with your used or broken computers and mobile devices? (b) What are three alternatives to throwing these devices in the trash? (c) Using a search engine, find one nonprofit organization near you that will accept used computers. List the name and URL. (d) Visit the waste management or recycling page of your local government's website. If it does not have a website, contact it. What is its recommended procedure for discarding your computers and other electronic devices?

PHOTO CREDITS

CHAPTER 5

Opener: © Ron Chapple Stock/FotoSearch/Glow Images RF; p. 115, 131: © Cusp/SuperStock; p. 116, 130: © Jetta Productions/Dana Neely/Blend Images/Corbis RF; 5-1: © Maxim Kazmin/Getty Images RF; 5-2: © Stanca Sanda/Alamy; 5-3, 5-4, page 132 (top-left): Courtesy of Dell Inc.; 5-5: © epa european pressphoto agency b.v./Alamy; 5-6: © PG Pictures/Alamy; 5-7 (top-left): © Godfried Edelman/iStock/Getty Images RF; 5-7 (top-right and bottom-left): Reproduced with permission Bill Detweiler/TechRepublic; 5-7 (bottom middle and bottom-right), 5-19: ifixit.com; 5-8, p. 132 (top-right): https://commons.wikimedia.org/wiki/User:Evan-Amos/Everyday#/media/File:A790GXH-128M-Motherboard.com; 5-9: © Lucidio Studio Inc/Photographer's Choice/Getty Images RF; 5-10, 5-13, 5-16, 5-20, 5-23, 5-24, p. 132 (bottom-right), 133: © Willis Technology; 5-17: Public Domain/Evan-Amos; 5-18: © 2015 D-Link Corporation/D-Link Systems, Inc.; 5-21, p. 134 (top-left): Adam Gasson/MacFormat Magazine via Getty Images; 5-22 (middle-left): © nikitabuida/Getty Images RF; 5-22 (right): © Chris Willson/Alamy; p. 127 (top): Courtesy of Hauppauge; p. 127 (bottom): KODI™ is a registered trademark of XBMC Foundation. Used with permission; 5-25, p. 134 (top-right): © Justin Sullivan/Getty Images.

chapter 6 Input and Output

Why should I read this chapter?

Input and output devices have seen staggering advances in recent years. A typical cell phone now has dozens of input sensors and display options. In the future, input devices such as tiny attachments to clothes or eyewear will be as common as cell phones. Augmented reality displays or wearable glasses will integrate what you see with extensive databases of relevant information.

This chapter covers the things you need to know to be prepared for this ever-changing digital world, including:

- Keyboard design—discover how wireless and virtual keyboards improve the speed and ease of typing.
- Intuitive input devices—learn about advances in touch screens and voice recognition systems.
- Display technology—discover how webcams and digital whiteboards can create videos and share presentations.
- Evolving output devices—learn about advances in UHDTVs, 3D printers, and e-books.

Learning Objectives

After you have read this chapter, you should be able to:

1 Define input.
2 Describe keyboard entry including types and features of keyboards.
3 Identify different pointing devices including game controllers and styluses.
4 Describe scanning devices including optical scanners, RFID readers, and recognition devices.
5 Recognize image capturing and audio-input devices.
6 Define output.
7 Identify different monitor features and types including flat panels and e-books.
8 Define printing features and types including inkjet and cloud printers.
9 Recognize different audio and video devices including portable media devices.
10 Define combination input and output devices including multifunctional devices, telephones, drones, robots, and VR headgear and gloves.
11 Explain ergonomics and ways to minimize physical damage.

Introduction

"Hi, I'm Marie, and I'm a technical writer. I'd like to talk with you about input and output devices . . . all those devices that help us to communicate with a computer. I'd also like to talk about emerging technologies such as virtual reality."

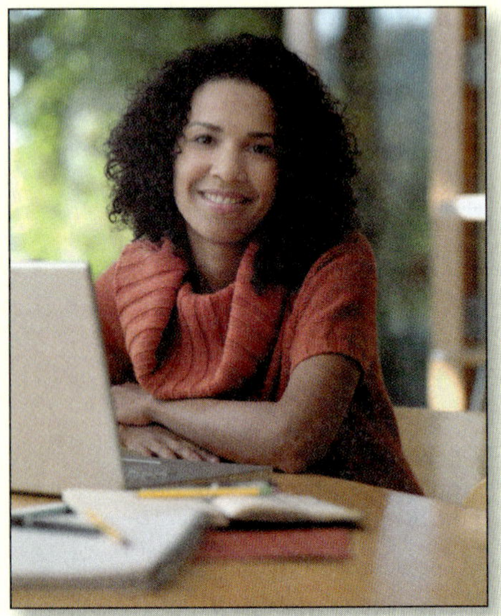

How do you send instructions and information to the CPU? How do you get information out? Here we describe one of the most important places where computers interface with people. We input text, music, and even speech, but we probably never think about the relationship between what we enter and what the computer processes. Input devices translate numbers, letters, special characters, and gestures that people understand into a form that computers can process.

Have you ever wondered how information processed by the system unit is converted into a form that you can use? That is the role of output devices. While input devices convert what we understand into what the system unit can process, output devices convert what the system unit has processed into a form that we can understand. Output devices translate machine language into letters, numbers, sounds, and images that people can understand.

To efficiently and effectively use computers, you need to know about the most commonly used input devices, including touch screens, game controllers, scanners, digital cameras, voice recognition, and audio-input devices. Additionally, you need to know about the most commonly used output devices, including monitors, printers, and audio and video output devices. You also need to be aware of combination input and output devices such as multifunctional devices and telephones.

What Is Input?

Input is any data or instructions that are used by a computer. They can come directly from you or from other sources. You provide input whenever you use system or application programs. For example, when using a word processing program, you enter data in the form of numbers and letters and issue commands such as to save and to print documents. You also can enter data and issue commands by pointing to items or using your voice. Other sources of input include scanned or photographed images.

Input devices are hardware used to translate words, numbers, sounds, images, and gestures that people understand into a form that the system unit can process. For example, when using a word processor, you typically use a keyboard to enter text and a mouse to issue commands. In addition to keyboards and mice, there are a wide variety of other input devices. These include pointing, scanning, image capturing, and audio-input devices.

Keyboard Entry

One of the most common ways to input data is by a **keyboard.** As mentioned in Chapter 5, keyboards convert numbers, letters, and special characters that people understand into electrical signals. These signals are sent to, and processed by, the system unit. Most keyboards use an arrangement of keys given the name QWERTY. This name reflects the keyboard layout by taking the letters of the first six alphabetic characters found on the top row of keys displaying letters.

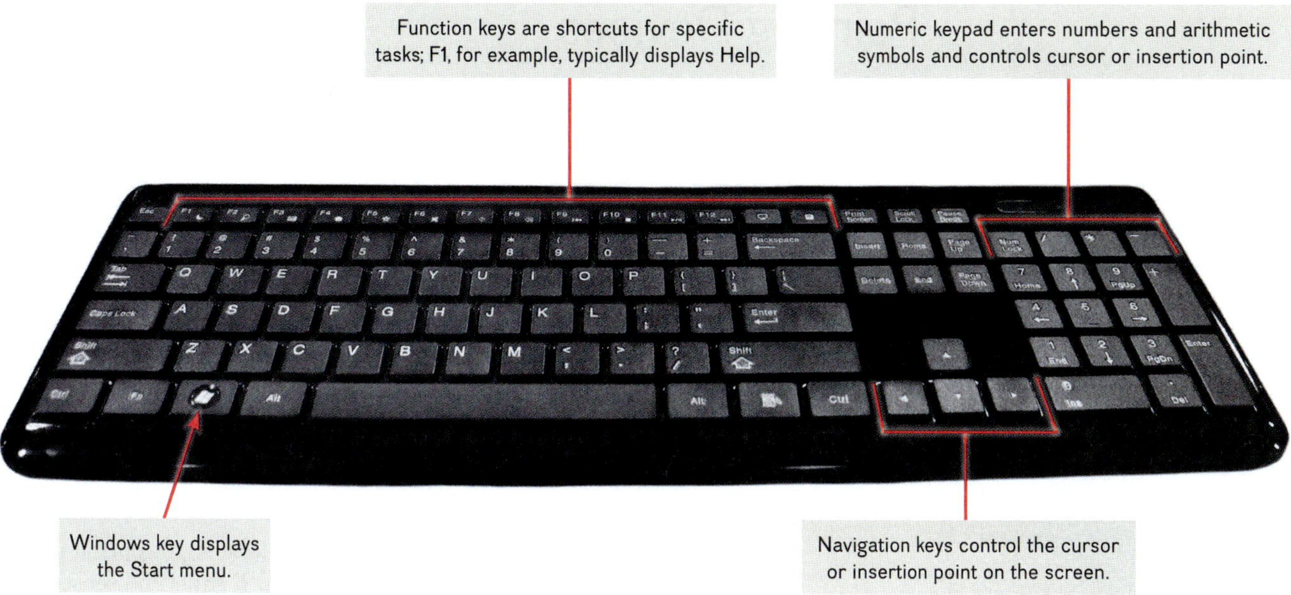

Function keys are shortcuts for specific tasks; F1, for example, typically displays Help.
Numeric keypad enters numbers and arithmetic symbols and controls cursor or insertion point.
Windows key displays the Start menu.
Navigation keys control the cursor or insertion point on the screen.

Figure 6-1 **Traditional keyboard**

Keyboards

There are a wide variety of keyboard designs. They range from the full-sized to miniature and can even be virtual. There are four basic categories of keyboards: traditional, laptop, virtual, and thumb.

- **Traditional keyboards**—these full-size keyboards are widely used on desktops and larger computers. The standard U.S. traditional keyboard has 101 keys. Some traditional keyboards include a few additional special keys. For example, the Windows keyboard includes a Windows key to directly access the Start menu. Traditional keyboards provide function keys, navigation keys, and a numeric keypad. Some keys, such as the Caps Lock key, are **toggle keys.** These keys turn a feature on or off. Others, such as the Ctrl key, are **combination keys,** which perform an action when held down in combination with another key. (See Figure 6-1.)

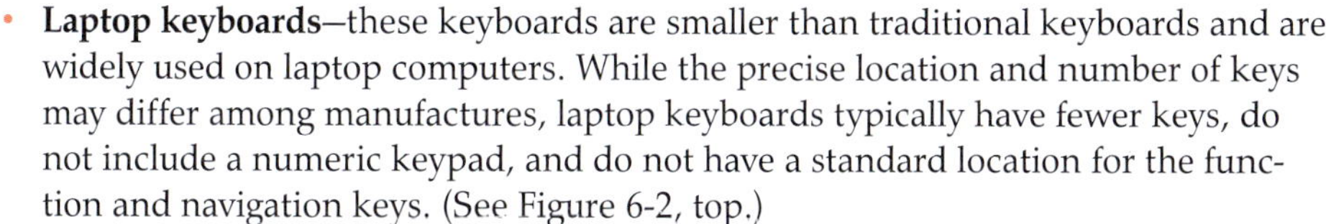

- **Laptop keyboards**—these keyboards are smaller than traditional keyboards and are widely used on laptop computers. While the precise location and number of keys may differ among manufactures, laptop keyboards typically have fewer keys, do not include a numeric keypad, and do not have a standard location for the function and navigation keys. (See Figure 6-2, top.)
- **Virtual keyboards**—these keyboards are used primarily with mobile devices and tablets. Unlike other keyboards, virtual keyboards do not have a physical keyboard. Rather, the keys are typically displayed on a screen and selected by touching their image on the screen. (See Figure 6-2, middle.)
- **Thumb keyboards**—these keyboards are used on smartphones and other small mobile devices. Designed primarily for communicating via texting and connecting to the web, these keyboards are very small. (See Figure 6-2, bottom.)

Laptop keyboard

Virtual keyboard

Thumb keyboard

Figure 6-2 **Keyboards**

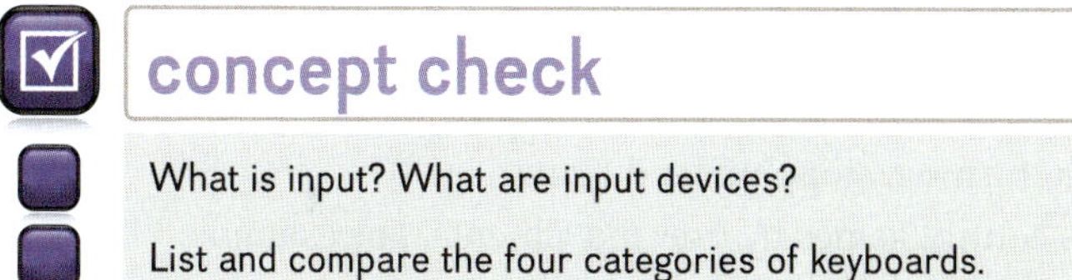

concept check

- What is input? What are input devices?
- List and compare the four categories of keyboards.
- What are toggle keys? What are combination keys?

Pointing Devices

Pointing is one of the most natural of all human gestures. **Pointing devices** provide an intuitive interface with the system unit by accepting physical movements or gestures such as a finger pointing or moving across a screen and converting these movements into machine-readable input. There are a wide variety of pointing devices, including the mouse, touch screen, game controller, and stylus.

Figure 6-3 **Optical mouse**

Mouse

A **mouse** controls a pointer that is displayed on the monitor. The **mouse pointer** usually appears in the shape of an arrow. It frequently changes shape, however, depending on the application. A mouse can have one, two, or more buttons, which are used to select command options and to control the mouse pointer on the monitor. Some mice have a **wheel button** that can be rotated to scroll through information that is displayed on the monitor.

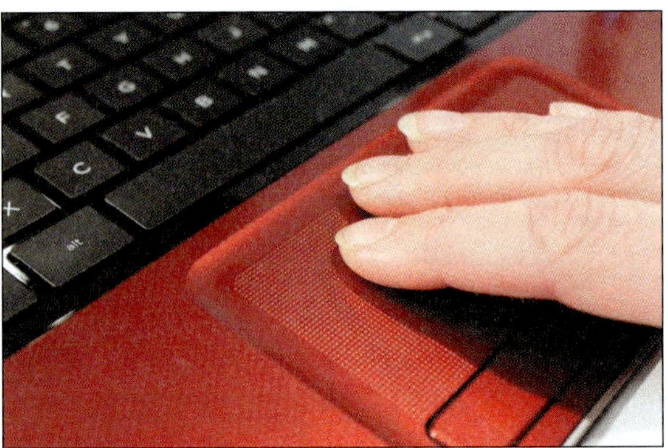

Figure 6-4 **Touch pad**

Although there are several different designs, the **optical mouse** is the most widely used. (See Figure 6-3.) It emits and senses light to detect mouse movement. Traditionally, the detected movements are communicated to the system unit through a cord. Alternatively, the **cordless** or **wireless mouse** uses radio waves or infrared light waves to communicate with the system unit. These devices eliminate the mouse cord and free up desk space.

Like a mouse, a **touch pad** is used to control the mouse pointer and to make selections. Unlike a mouse, however, a touch pad operates by moving or tapping your finger on the surface of a pad. These devices are widely used instead of a mouse with laptops and some types of mobile devices. (See Figure 6-4.)

Touch Screen

A **touch screen** allows users to select actions or commands by touching the screen with a finger or penlike device. **Multitouch screens** can be touched with more than one finger, which allows for interactions such as rotating graphical objects on the screen with your hand or zooming in and out by pinching and stretching your fingers. Multitouch screens are commonly used with tablets and smartphones, as well as some laptop computers and desktop monitors. (See Figure 6-5.)

Figure 6-5 **Multitouch screen**

Game Controllers

Game controllers are devices that provide input to computer games. While keyboards and traditional mice can be used as game controllers, the four most popular and specialized game controllers are joysticks, gaming mice, gamepads, and motion-sensing devices. (See Figure 6-6.)

- **Joysticks** control game actions by users varying the pressure, speed, and direction of a control stick.
- **Gaming mice** are similar to traditional mice with higher precision, faster responsiveness, programmable buttons, and better ergonomics.
- **Gamepads** are designed to be held by two hands and provide a wide array of inputs including motion, turning, stopping, and firing.
- **Motion-sensing devices** control games by user movements. For example, Microsoft's Kinect motion-sensing device accepts user movements and spoken commands to control games on the Xbox 360.

Joystick

Gaming mouse

Gamepad

Motion-sensing device

Figure 6-6 **Game controllers**

Stylus

A **stylus** is a penlike device typically used with tablets and mobile devices. (See Figure 6-7.) A stylus uses pressure to draw images on a screen. Often, a stylus interacts with the computer through handwriting recognition software. **Handwriting recognition software** translates handwritten notes into a form that the system unit can process.

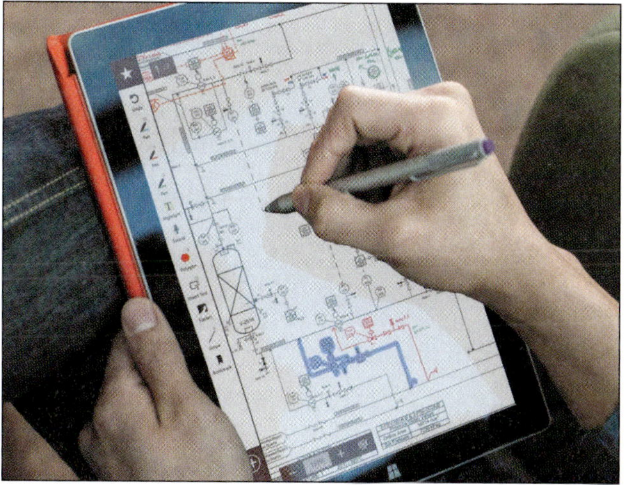

Figure 6-7 **Stylus**

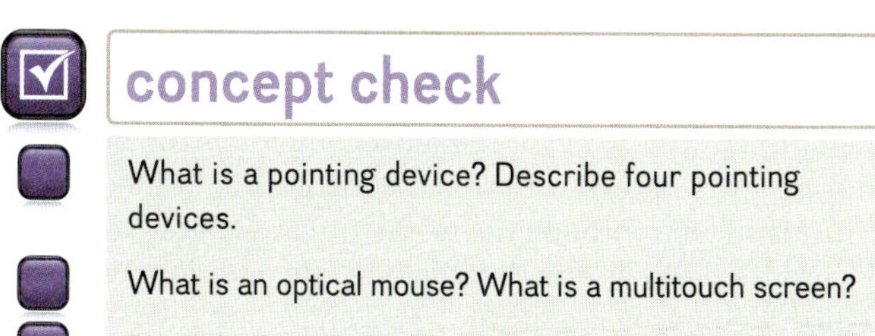

concept check

- What is a pointing device? Describe four pointing devices.
- What is an optical mouse? What is a multitouch screen?
- Describe four game controllers. What is a stylus?

Scanning Devices

Scanning devices convert scanned text and images into a form that the system unit can process. There are five types of scanning devices: optical scanners, card readers, bar code readers, RFID readers, and character and mark recognition devices.

Optical Scanners

An **optical scanner,** also known simply as a **scanner,** accepts documents consisting of text and/or images and converts them to machine-readable form. These devices do not recognize individual letters or images. Rather, they recognize light, dark, and colored areas that make up individual letters or images. Typically, scanned documents are saved in files that can be further processed, displayed, printed, or stored for later use.

Figure 6-8 **Document scanner**

Figure 6-9 **3D scanner**

There are four basic types of optical scanners: flatbed, document, portable, and 3D.

- **Flatbed scanner** is much like a copy machine. The image to be scanned is placed on a glass surface, and the scanner records the image.
- **Document scanner** is similar to a flatbed scanner except that it can quickly scan multipage documents. It automatically feeds one page of a document at a time through a scanning surface. (See Figure 6-8.)
- **Portable scanner** is typically a handheld device that slides across the image, making direct contact.
- **3D scanners** use lasers, cameras, or robotic arms to record the shape of an object. Like 2D scanners, most 3D scanners cannot recognize light, dark, and colored areas. (See Figure 6-9.)

Optical scanners are powerful tools for a wide variety of end users, including graphics and advertising professionals who scan images and combine them with text.

Card Readers

Nearly everyone uses a credit card, debit card, access (parking or building) card, and/or some type of identification card. These cards typically have the user's name, some type of identification number, and signature on the card. Additionally, encoded information is often stored on the card. **Card readers** interpret this encoded information.

Although there are several different types, by far the most common is the **magnetic card reader.** The encoded information is stored on a thin magnetic strip located on the back of the card. When the card is swiped through the magnetic card reader, the information is read. Many credit cards, known as **smart cards,** include additional security in the form of a microchip embedded in the credit card. This chip contains encrypted data that makes it nearly impossible for criminals to forge a duplicate card. Some chips require that you insert the card into a specialized reader, while others only require that you hold the card near the reader.

Bar Code Readers

You are probably familiar with **bar code readers** or **scanners** from grocery stores. These devices are either handheld **wand readers** or **platform scanners.** They contain photoelectric cells that scan or read **bar codes,** or the vertical zebra-striped marks printed on product containers.

There are a variety of different codes including **UPC** and **MaxiCode** codes.

- **UPCs (Universal Product Codes)** are widely used by retail stores to automate the processes to check out customers, to change product prices, and to maintain inventory records.
- **MaxiCode** is widely used by the United Parcel Service (UPS) and others to automate the process of routing packages, tracking in-transit packages, and locating lost packages.

Smartphones with the appropriate app can also scan codes. (See Figure 6-10.) For example, after scanning the bar code from a product you are thinking of buying, the app Price Check by Amazon will provide in-store and online price comparisons as well as provide other customer product reviews.

Figure 6-10 **Smartphone bar code reader**

RFID Readers

RFID (radio-frequency identification) tags are tiny chips that can be embedded in most everything. They can be found in consumer products, driver's licenses, passports, and any number of other items. (See Figure 6-11.) These chips contain electronically stored information that can be read using an **RFID reader** located several yards away. They are widely used to track and locate lost pets; to monitor production and update inventory; and to record prices, product descriptions, and locations of retail items.

Figure 6-11 **RFID reader**

Character and Mark Recognition Devices

Character and mark recognition devices are scanners that are able to recognize special characters and marks. They are specialty devices that are essential tools for certain applications. Three types are

- **Magnetic-ink character recognition (MICR)**—used by banks to automatically read those unusual numbers on the bottom of checks and deposit slips. A special-purpose machine known as a reader/sorter reads these numbers and provides input that allows banks to efficiently maintain customer account balances.
- **Optical-character recognition (OCR)**—uses special preprinted characters that can be read by a light source and changed into machine-readable code. A common OCR device is the handheld wand reader. (See Figure 6-12.) These are used in department stores to read retail price tags by reflecting light on the printed characters.
- **Optical-mark recognition (OMR)**—senses the presence or absence of a mark, such as a pencil mark. OMR is often used to score standardized multiple-choice tests.

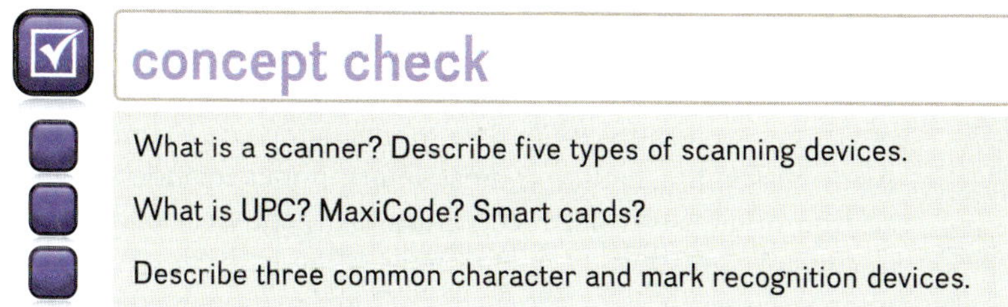

concept check

- What is a scanner? Describe five types of scanning devices.
- What is UPC? MaxiCode? Smart cards?
- Describe three common character and mark recognition devices.

Figure 6-12 **Wand reader**

Image Capturing Devices

Optical scanners, like traditional copy machines, can make a copy from an original. For example, an optical scanner can make a digital copy of a photograph. *Image capturing devices,* on the other hand, create or capture original images. These devices include digital cameras and webcams.

Figure 6-13 **Digital camera**

Figure 6-14 **Attached webcam**

Digital Cameras

Digital cameras capture images digitally and store the images on a memory card or in the camera's memory. Most digital cameras are also able to record video as well. (See Figure 6-13.) Almost all tablets and smartphones have built-in digital cameras capable of taking images and video. You can take a picture, view it immediately, and even place it on your own web page, within minutes.

Webcams

Webcams are specialized digital video cameras that capture images and send them to a computer for broadcast over the Internet. Webcams are built into most smartphones and tablets. Desktop and laptop webcams are either built in or attached to the computer's monitor. (See Figure 6-14.)

ethics

You may have heard of instances where webcams were used to broadcast the activities of individuals who did not know they were being recorded. For example, in a famous court case, a university student was prosecuted for using a webcam on an open laptop to secretly record his roommate's intimate activities. In other situations, public webcams have recorded embarrassing footage of people who were not aware of the camera. It has been argued that capturing and then broadcasting a person's image without his or her knowledge and consent is unethical. What do you think?

Audio-Input Devices

Audio-input devices convert sounds into a form that can be processed by the system unit. By far the most widely used audio-input device is the microphone. Audio input can take many forms, including the human voice and music.

Voice Recognition Systems

Voice recognition systems use a microphone, a sound card, and special software. These systems allow users to operate computers and other devices as well as to create documents using voice commands. As discussed in Chapter 4, most smartphones include a digital assistant that uses voice recognition to accept voice commands to control operations. Apple phones come with Siri, Windows phones come with Cortana, and Google phones come with Google Now. These voice recognition systems can perform any number of operations including scheduling events on your calendar, composing simple text messages, and looking up facts on the web. Specialized portable voice recorders are widely used by doctors, lawyers, and others to record dictation. These devices are able to record for several hours before connecting to a computer running voice recognition software to edit, store, and print the dictated information. Some systems are even able to translate dictation from one language to another, such as from English to Japanese.

tips

Have you ever had trouble communicating with someone who does not speak English? If so, Google Translate may be just what you need.

1. Go to translate.google.com.
2. Using the buttons at the top, select the language you will be speaking, followed by the language you want your words translated to.
3. Click the microphone icon in the box on the left, and begin speaking clearly into your microphone. In a few seconds, you will see the translated text in the box on the right.
4. Click the speaker icon in the box on the right to hear the translation.

concept check

How are image capturing devices different from an optical scanner?

Describe two image capturing devices.

What are voice recognition systems? Siri? Cortana? Google Now?

What Is Output?

Output is processed data or information. Output typically takes the form of text, graphics, photos, audio, and/or video. For example, when you create a presentation using a presentation graphics program, you typically input text and graphics. You also could include photographs, voice narration, and even video. The output would be the completed presentation.

Output devices are any hardware used to provide or to create output. They translate information that has been processed by the system unit into a form that humans can understand. There are a wide range of output devices. The most widely used are monitors, printers, and audio-output devices.

Monitors

The most frequently used output device is the **monitor.** Also known as **display screens,** monitors present visual images of text and graphics. The output is often referred to as **soft copy.** Monitors vary in size, shape, and cost. Almost all, however, have some basic distinguishing features.

Features

The most important characteristic of a monitor is its clarity. **Clarity** refers to the quality and sharpness of the displayed images. It is a function of several monitor features, including resolution, dot pitch, contrast ratio, size, and aspect ratio.

- **Resolution** is one of the most important features. Images are formed on a monitor by a series of dots or **pixels (picture elements).** (See Figure 6-15.) Resolution is expressed as a matrix of these dots or pixels. For example, many monitors today have a resolution 1,920 pixel columns by 1,080 pixel rows for a total of 2,073,600 pixels. The higher a monitor's resolution (the more pixels), the clearer the image produced. See Figure 6-16 for the most common monitor resolutions.
- **Dot (pixel) pitch** is the distance between each pixel. Most newer monitors have a dot pitch of 0.30 mm (30/100th of a millimeter) or less. The lower the dot pitch (the shorter the distance between pixels), the clearer the images produced.
- **Contrast ratios** indicate a monitor's ability to display images. It compares the light intensity of the brightest white to the darkest black. The higher the ratio, the better the monitor. Good monitors typically have contrast ratios between 500:1 and 2000:1.
- **Size,** or **active display area,** is measured by the diagonal length of a monitor's viewing area. Common sizes are 15, 17, 19, 21, and 24 inches.
- **Aspect ratio** indicates the proportional relationship between a display's width and height. Typically, this relationship is expressed by two numbers separated by a colon (:). Many older, more square-shaped monitors have a 4:3 aspect ratio. Almost all newer monitors have a 16:9 aspect ratio designed to display wide-screen content.

Figure 6-15 Monitor resolution

Standard	Pixels
HD 720	1,280 × 720
HD 1080	1,920 × 1,080
WQXGA	2,560 × 1,600
UHD 4K	3,840 × 2,160
UHD 5K	5,120 × 2,880

Figure 6-16 Resolution standards

Figure 6-17 Flat-panel monitor

Another important monitor feature is the ability to accept touch or gesture input such as finger movements including swiping, sliding, and pinching. While most older monitors do not support touch input, it is becoming a standard feature of newer monitors.

Flat-Panel Monitors

Flat-panel monitors are the most widely used type of monitor today. Compared to other types, they are thinner, are more portable, and require less power to operate. (See Figure 6-17.)

Almost all flat-panel displays are backlit, meaning that a common source of light is dispersed over all the pixels on the screen. There are three basic types of flat-panel monitors: LCD, LED, and OLED.

- **LCD (liquid crystal display)** is widely used for older monitors and is typically less expensive.
- **LED (light-emitting diode)** monitors use similar technology with a more advanced backlighting technology. They produce better-quality images, are slimmer, and are more environmentally friendly as they require less power and use fewer toxic chemicals to manufacture. Most new monitors are LED.
- **OLED (organic light-emitting diode)** monitors replace the LED monitor's backlighting technology with a thin layer of organic compound that produces light. By eliminating the backlight, OLED monitors can be even thinner with better power efficiency and contrast ratios.

Curved Monitors

One of the most recent developments is the **curved monitor.** It uses similar technology as flat-panel monitors except it has a concave screen that provides better viewing angles near the edges of the screen. Curved monitors are widely use for high-end televisions and for gamers searching for a highly immersive viewing experience. (See Figure 6-18.) Curved monitors are just beginning to appear in smartphones and wearable computers. For smartphones, curved monitors allow the screen to wrap around the edge of the phone for alternative display and button options. For smartwatches, a curved screen allows for large displays that contour to the shape of your wrist.

E-book Readers

E-books (electronic books) are traditional printed books in electronic format. These books are available from numerous sources including many public and private libraries, bookstore websites, and the cloud. **E-book readers (e-readers)** are dedicated mobile devices for storing and displaying e-books and other electronic media including electronic newspapers and magazines.

E-book readers have displays that are typically 6 inches and use a technology known as e-ink. **E-ink** produces images that reflect light like ordinary paper, making the display easy to read. Two well-known e-book readers are Amazon's Kindle and Barnes & Noble's Nook Simple Touch. (See Figure 6-19.)

Tablets can also display e-books. They are larger, heavier, and more expensive than e-book readers. They are also much more flexible, with displaying e-books

Figure 6-18 Curved monitor

Figure 6-19 E-book reader

Figure 6-20 **Digital whiteboard**

Figure 6-21 **3D UHDTV**

being only one of their any number of applications. Unlike dedicated e-book readers, these tablets use LCD displays that provide crisp, colorful images; however, they are difficult to read in bright light due to their reflective nature. Two well-known traditional tablets are Apple's iPad and Samsung's Galaxy Tab.

To learn more about e-books, see Making IT Work for You: E-books, on page 152.

Other Monitors

There are several other types of monitors. Some are used for more specialized applications, such as making presentations and watching television.

- **Digital** or **interactive whiteboards** are specialized devices with a large display connected to a computer or projector. The computer's desktop is displayed on the digital whiteboard and controlled using a special pen, a finger, or some other device. Digital whiteboards are widely used in classrooms and corporate boardrooms. (See Figure 6-20.)
- **Ultra-high-definition television (UHDTV)** delivers a much clearer and more detailed wide-screen picture than regular HDTV. Because the output is digital, users can readily freeze video sequences to create high-quality still images. The video and still images can then be edited and stored for later use. This technology is very useful to graphic artists, designers, and publishers. One of the most recent and dramatic advances is 3D UHDTV. (See Figure 6-21.) Using special viewing glasses, 3D UHDTV provides theater-quality three-dimensional viewing.
- **Digital projectors** project the images from a traditional monitor onto a screen or wall. This is ideal for presentations or meetings when several people need to see the screen at the same time. Further, projectors tend to be more portable and less expensive than a similarly sized monitor. Unfortunately, projected images can be difficult to see in bright rooms, so they are best used in dark rooms with curtains or no windows. (See Figure 6-22.)

Figure 6-22 **Digital projector**

concept check

 Define these monitor features: clarity, resolution, dot pitch, contrast ratios, size, and aspect ratio.

 Describe flat-panel, curved, LCD, LED, and OLED monitors.

 What are e-book readers, digital whiteboards, UHDTVs, and digital projectors?

Making IT work for you

E-BOOKS

Are you tired of carrying a book bag filled with textbooks? Have you ever wished you could have a reference book or text at your fingertips, instead of at home on a bookshelf? E-books are the solutions to these problems, and this guide will discuss their benefits, as well as various options on how to access and read them.

Benefits of E-books Because e-books are digital, they offer a wide range of benefits:

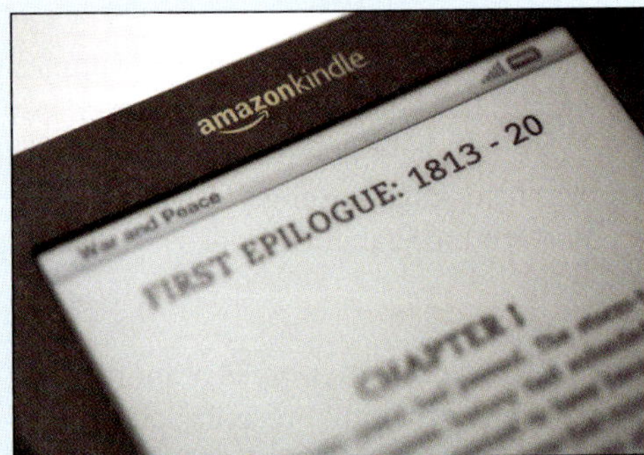

1. ***Transporting.*** **Books can take up a large volume of space in any home (or your school bag). With e-books, you can store over a thousand books in one small device!**

2. ***Searching.*** **Type any keyword, and you will be taken to the page(s) where that word appears. This is much faster than using an index.**

3. ***Bookmarking.*** **Mark any number of pages as important. This is an improvement over having countless physical bookmarks or folded pages.**

4. ***Adding highlights and notes.*** **All marks on an e-book are digital. They can be added and removed easily. The same could not be said for physical textbooks.**

5. ***Purchasing.*** **Buying an e-book can take less than a minute, as it is downloaded instantly to your device. Prices also tend to be lower than those for physical books.**

Reading E-books Once you decide to purchase an e-book, you may be surprised by the number of devices you can use to read it.

1. ***E-book reader.*** **Dedicated e-book readers, such as the Amazon Kindle and the Barnes & Noble Nook, can be purchased for less than $100. If it is important for you to read in direct sunlight or areas with heavy lighting, the e-ink used by these devices will be desirable.**

2. ***Smartphones and tablets.*** **Do you already own a smartphone or tablet that you take everywhere? If so, you may want to download the free apps from e-book sellers to avoid the cost of a separate e-book reader. The reading experience on these apps is excellent with the touch-screen interface present in these devices.**

3. ***Laptop and desktop computers.*** **Although many e-book retailers make apps for your computer, sellers such as Google allow you to read books purchased from its Google Play store with nothing more than a web browser.**

Most e-book sellers offer the synchronization of your e-books and notes with their cloud services. This allows you to start reading a book using your tablet, for example, and pick up where you left off with your smartphone.

Printers

Even as many individuals, schools, and businesses are trying to go paperless, printers remain one of the most used output devices. You probably use a printer to print homework assignments, photographs, and web pages. **Printers** translate information that has been processed by the system unit and present the information on paper. Printer output is often called **hard copy.**

environment

Have you considered the environmental impact of using your inkjet printer? Whenever possible, don't print. Use e-mail attachments, and encourage your school to use web technologies that let students upload their schoolwork. If you must print, buy ink cartridges that are made with mostly recycled plastic. And when your ink runs out, bring the cartridge to a retailer that will make sure it is recycled. Many retailers often offer a discount on a new cartridge when you turn in an empty one.

Features

There are many different types of printers. Almost all, however, have some basic distinguishing features, including resolution, color capability, speed, memory, and duplex printing.

- **Resolution** for a printer is similar to monitor resolution. It is a measure of the clarity of images produced. Printer resolution, however, is measured in **dpi (dots per inch).** (See Figure 6-23.) Most printers designed for personal use average 1,200 by 4,800 dpi. The higher the dpi, the better the quality of images produced.
- **Color** capability is provided by most printers today. Users typically have the option to print either with just black ink or with color. Because it is more expensive to print in color, most users select black ink for letters, drafts, and homework. The most common black ink selection is **grayscale,** in which images are displayed using many shades of gray. Color is used more selectively for final reports containing graphics and for photographs.
- **Speed** is measured in the number of pages printed per minute. Typically, printers for personal use average 15 to 19 pages per minute for single-color (black) output and 13 to 15 pages per minute for color output.
- **Memory** within a printer is used to store printing instructions and documents waiting to be printed. The more memory, the faster it will be able to print large documents.
- **Duplex printing** allows automatic printing on both sides of a sheet of paper. Although not currently a standard feature for all printers, it will likely become standard in the future as a way to reduce paper waste and to protect the environment.

Inkjet Printers

Inkjet printers spray ink at high speed onto the surface of paper. This process produces high-quality images in a variety of colors, making it ideal for printing photos.

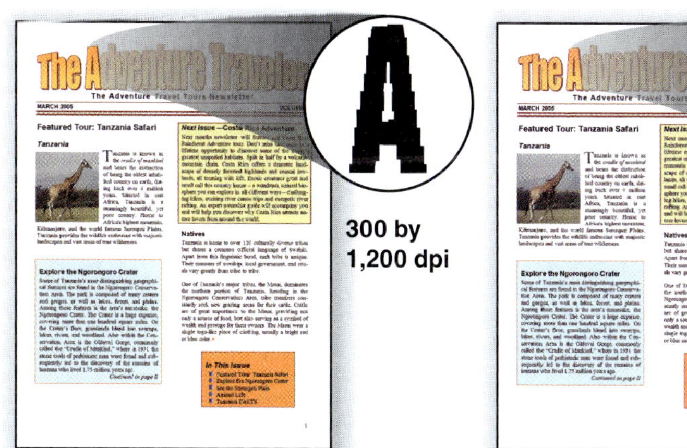

Figure 6-23 **DPI comparison**

Figure 6-24 **Inkjet printer**

(See Figure 6-24.) Inkjet printers are relatively inexpensive and are the most widely used printers. In addition, they are reliable and quiet. The most costly aspect of inkjet printers is replacing the ink cartridges. For this reason, most users specify black ink for the majority of print jobs and use the more expensive color printing for select applications. Typical inkjet printers produce 15 to 19 pages per minute of black-only output and 13 to 15 pages of color output.

Laser Printers

The **laser printer** uses a technology similar to that used in a photocopying machine. Laser printers use a laser light beam to produce images with excellent letter and graphics quality. More expensive than inkjet printers, laser printers are faster and are used in applications requiring high-quality output.

There are two categories of laser printers. **Personal laser printers** are less expensive and are used by a single user. They typically can print 15 to 17 pages a minute. **Shared laser printers** typically support color, are more expensive, and are used (shared) by a group of users. Shared laser printers typically print over 50 pages a minute.

3D Printers

3D printers, also known as **additive manufacturing,** create three-dimensional shapes by adding very thin layer after layer of material until the final shape is fully formed. (See Figure 6-25.) There are a variety of different processes and materials that can be used to create each layer. One of the most common sprays a liquid plastic or plasticlike substance through a nozzle similar to an inkjet printer.

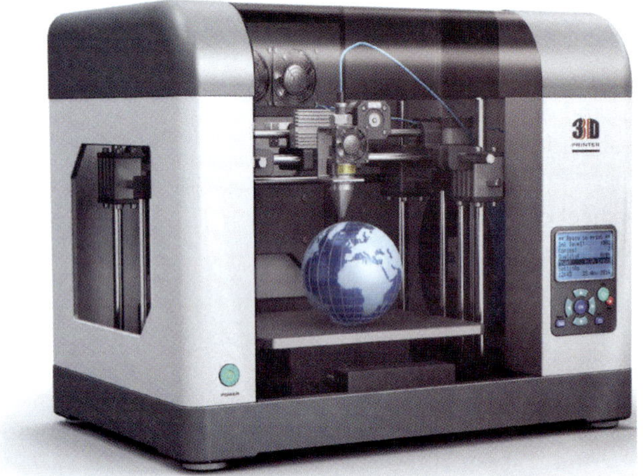

Figure 6-25 **3D printer**

3D printers are controlled by data describing the shape of the object to be created. This data typically comes from a file created by a 3D modeling program or from scanning a physical model using a 3D scanner. Specialized programs then take this data and further process it to create data describing hundreds or thousands of horizontal layers that when placed one on top of another form the shape of the intended object. The printer uses this data by extruding or cutting the first layer to very exact specifications. Successive layers are then created and attached to the layer below it until the product is finalized. The layers are so thin and so precise that they blend together, making a final product that shows no sign of the individual layers.

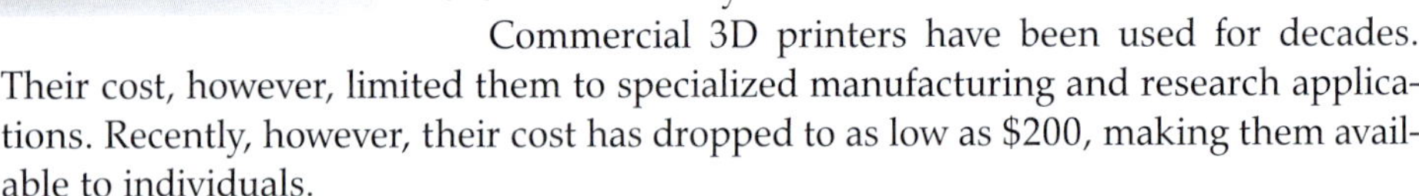

Commercial 3D printers have been used for decades. Their cost, however, limited them to specialized manufacturing and research applications. Recently, however, their cost has dropped to as low as $200, making them available to individuals.

Other Printers

There are several other types of printers. These printers include cloud printers, thermal printers, and plotters:

- **Cloud printers** are printers connected to the Internet that provide printing services to others on the Internet. **Google Cloud Print** is a service that supports cloud printing. Once a user activates a printer using the Google Chrome OS, the user can access that printer anywhere with a smartphone or any other type of computer that is connected to the Internet. For example, you could use a smartphone from almost anywhere to send documents to be printed on a printer located at your home or school.

- **Thermal printers** use heat elements to produce images on heat-sensitive paper. These printers are widely used with ATMs and gasoline pumps to print receipts.
- **Plotters** are special-purpose printers for producing a wide range of specialized output. Using output from graphics tablets and other graphical input devices, plotters create maps, images, and architectural and engineering drawings. Plotters are typically used by graphic artists, engineers, and architects to print out designs, sketches, and drawings.

privacy

Did you know that your printer may be identifying itself in every document that it creates? Some color printers print nearly invisible dots in the margins of all printed documents. These microscopic dots form a code that can be used to trace the printed page back to the printer that generated it. Printer manufacturers secretly developed this code with the U.S. Secret Service to assist in counterfeiting investigations. Some privacy experts suggest that it is inappropriate to track equipment without the owner's consent.

concept check

 Discuss these printer features: resolution, color capability, speed, memory, and duplex printing.

 Compare inkjet, laser, and 3D printers.

 Discuss cloud, thermal, and plotter printers.

Audio-Output Devices

Audio-output devices translate audio information from the computer into sounds that people can understand. The most widely used audio-output devices are **speakers** and **headphones.** (See Figure 6-26.) These devices connect to a sound card within the system unit. This connection can be by cable to an audio jack on the system unit, or the connection can be wireless. Wireless connections typically use **Bluetooth** technology. This type of connection requires special Bluetooth-enabled speakers and/or headphones. Bluetooth will be discussed further in Chapter 8. The sound card is used to capture as well as play back recorded sounds. Audio-output devices are used to play music, vocalize translations from one language to another, and communicate information from the computer system to users.

Creating voice output is not anywhere near as difficult as recognizing and interpreting voice input. In fact, voice output is quite common. It is used with many smartphones, cars, and soft drink machines. It is used as a reinforcement tool for learning, such as to help students study a foreign language. It also is used in many supermarkets at the checkout counter to confirm purchases. One of its most powerful capabilities is to assist the physically challenged.

Figure 6-26 **Headphones**

Combination Input and Output Devices

Many devices combine input and output capabilities. Sometimes this is done to save space. Other times it is done for very specialized applications. Common combination devices include headsets, multifunctional devices, telephones, drones, robots, and virtual reality headgear and gloves.

Headsets

Headsets combine the functionality of microphones and headphones. The microphone accepts audible input and headphones provide audio output. Headsets are an integral part of serious video game systems. (See Figure 6-27.)

Figure 6-27 **Headset**

Multifunctional Devices

Multifunctional devices (MFD) typically combine the capabilities of a scanner, printer, fax, and copy machine. These multifunctional devices offer a cost and space advantage. They cost about the same as a good printer or copy machine but require much less space than the single-function devices they replace. Their disadvantages are lower quality and unreliability. The output quality for any one function is often not quite as good as that of the separate single-purpose devices. The reliability of multifunctional devices suffers because problems with one of the functional parts can make the entire device inoperable. Even so, multifunctional devices are widely used in home and small business offices.

Telephones

Telephones are input and output devices for receiving and sending voice communication. **Voice over IP (VoIP)** is a set of standards or technologies that support voice and other types of communication over the Internet. **Telephony,** also known as **Internet Telephony,** is the VoIP application that uses Internet rather than traditional telephone lines to support voice communication.

There are many VoIP services available for free that do not require any dedicated hardware. Examples of these services are Skype from Microsoft, Hangouts from Google, and FaceTime from Apple. Once you subscribe to a service, you can use your smartphone or other type of computer to connect to any other subscriber. These services are free and support video as well as audio; however, both parties must have their computers on and be logged in to the service to send and receive calls. For an additional fee, Skype allows you to call non-Skype subscribers directly on their phone. To learn more about Skype, see Making IT Work for You: Skype, on pages 157–158.

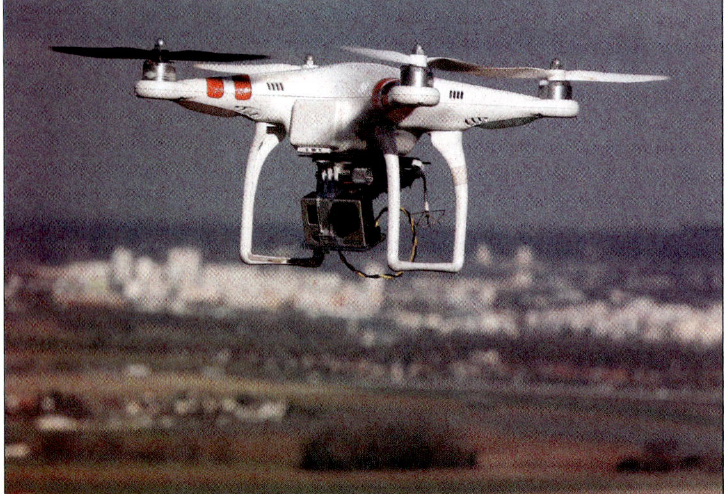

Figure 6-28 **Drone**

Drones

Drones, or **unmanned aerial vehicles (UAV),** were once too expensive for anything but military budgets. However, today's drones are inexpensive, faster, and smarter, making them a valuable tool and fun high-tech toy. (See Figure 6-28.) Most drones take input from a controller from either a radio joystick or a Wi-Fi connected tablet or laptop. The drones act as an output device, sending back video and sound to the user. The resulting combination of video and aerial maneuverability has made drones a popular choice for a wide variety of activities ranging from amateur cinematographers to civil engineers.

Robots

Like drones, robotics has become relatively inexpensive with expanding capabilities. **Robots** use cameras, microphones, and other sensors as inputs. Based on these inputs, robotic outputs can be as complex as exploring damaged nuclear reactors to as simple as taking a photo. Robots can be found almost everywhere including in a home vacuuming floors, in a factory assembling cars, on a farm sorting produce, and in hospitals assisting in surgery. (See Figure 6-29.)

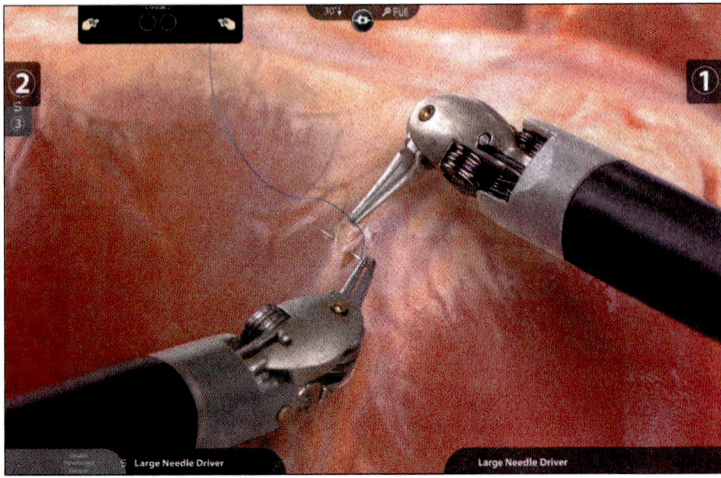

Figure 6-29 **Surgical robot**

SKYPE

Do you already use a communication tool that lets you keep in touch with your friends and family? Does that tool include the ability to have face-to-face conversations, share files and screens, and make calls to those not connected to the Internet? Skype is a well-known tool that offers all these services, most of them for free. This section will help you explore some of Skype's features. (Please note that the web is continually changing, and some of the specifics presented below may have changed.)

Getting Started In order to enjoy all the benefits of Skype, it is recommended that your computer have speakers, a microphone, and a webcam. If you have a laptop or tablet, these are all likely integrated. Follow these steps to create your account and install Skype on your machine:

1. **Visit www.skype.com, and click the Download Skype link.**
2. **Enter the required information to create your Skype account. When you are finished, the software will be downloaded automatically. Do not purchase any Skype credits at the moment.**
3. **Run the downloaded setup file, and follow the prompts to install Skype on your machine.**
4. **Log in to your Skype account on the welcome screen, and follow the prompts to make sure your audio and video are working.**

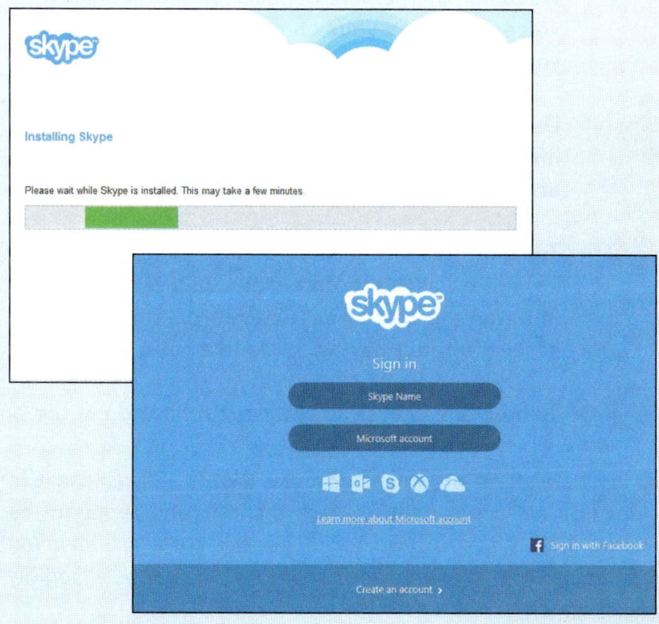

Adding Contacts You can find friends or other contacts manually, or you can import them from your address book on Facebook, Outlook, and several other services. To add a contact manually:

1. **Click next to the blue magnifying glass on the left of the window under your log-in information.**
2. **Enter the name, Skype name, or e-mail address you know about your contact, and hit Enter.**
3. **Skype will display matches. Click the one that matches your contact's details, and then click the *Add to Contacts* button.**

Your contact must accept your request before you can see his or her online status.

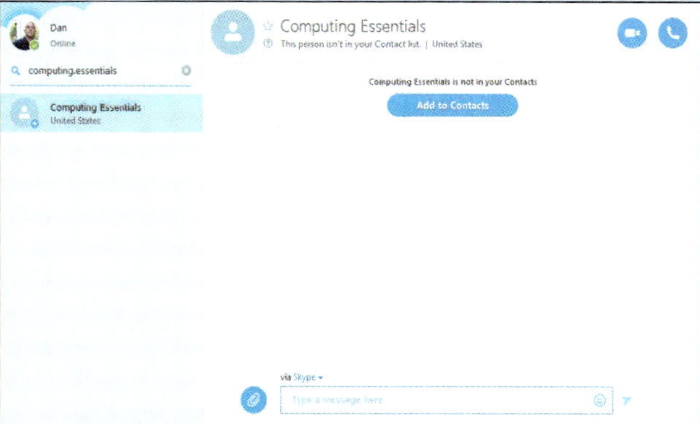

Skype-to-Skype Communication When two individuals have Skype accounts, they can contact each other (for free) using a variety of methods, from voice or video calls to instant messages. They can exchange files and share screens with each other. Please note that for videoconferencing between three or more people, you must have a premium or business account.

1. **From the main screen, click on the contact you wish to communicate with.**
2. **Click the blue video camera button to make a video call or the blue handset button to make a voice call. Once your contact accepts the call, your interface will change.**
3. **During the call, you have the ability to send instant messages and turn audio and/or video on or off by clicking the buttons at the bottom.**
4. **To send files or share screens, click the *Plus* (+) button at the bottom. You could also have initiated the *Send File* feature from the contact screen without having to place a call.**
5. **To hang up, press the red *handset* button at the bottom.**

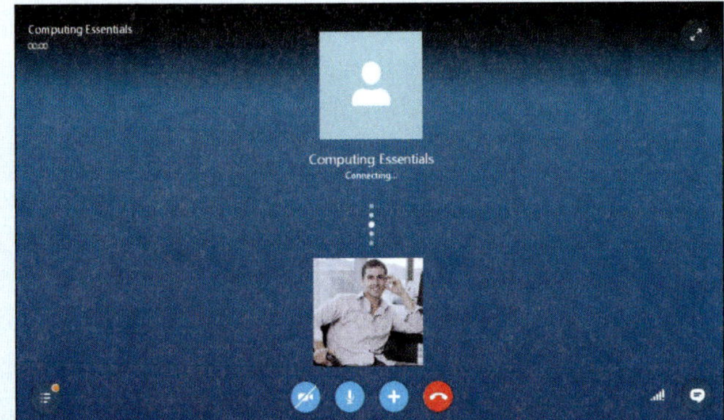

Calling Landline or Mobile Phones (VoIP) Skype can use your Internet connection to place a call to any phone in the world. This is not a free service, but the costs are low. You can pay as you go with Skype credits, or sign up for a monthly subscription.

1. **From the menu bar, select *Call*, and select *Call Phones*.**
2. **Click the *handset* button after entering the phone number.**

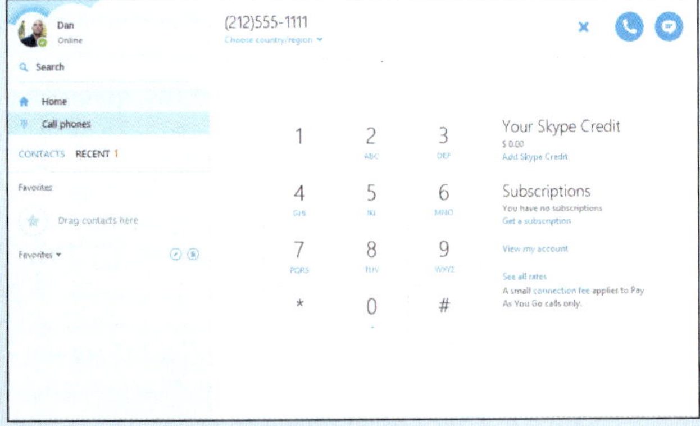

Virtual Reality Headgear and Gloves

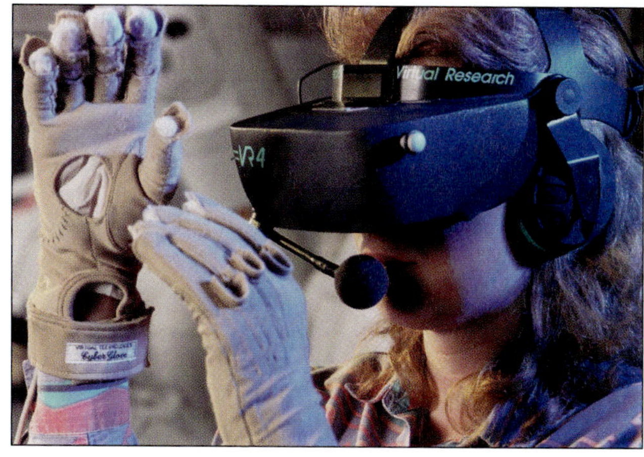

Figure 6-30 **Virtual reality headgear and gloves**

Virtual reality (VR) is an artificial, or simulated, reality created in 3D by computers. It strives to create a virtual or **immersive experience** by using specialized hardware that includes headgear and gloves. (See Figure 6-30.)

The **headgear** has earphones and three-dimensional stereoscopic screens. The **gloves** have sensors that collect data about your hand movements. Coupled with software, this interactive sensory equipment lets you immerse yourself in a computer-generated world.

There are any number of applications for virtual reality headgear and gloves. Automobile manufacturers use virtual reality to evaluate what it would be like to sit in the cars they have designed but not yet built. Virtual reality is becoming a standard for high-end video games and for immersive movies. Sony and Facebook have heavily invested in VR headsets as the future of computer interaction. Virtual reality promises to become commonplace in the near future.

concept check

What are the two most widely used audio-output devices? What is Bluetooth?

What are headsets? Multifunctional devices? VoIP? Telephony?

What are drones? Robots? Virtual reality? Headgear? Gloves?

Ergonomics

People use computers to enrich their personal and private lives. There are ways, however, that computers can make people less productive and even harm their health. Anyone who frequently uses a computer can be affected. As a result, there has been great interest in a field known as ergonomics.

Ergonomics (pronounced "er-guh-nom-ix") is defined as the study of human factors related to things people use. It is concerned with fitting the task to the user rather than forcing the user to contort to do the task. For computer users and manufacturers this means designing input and output devices to increase ease of use and to avoid health risks.

Sitting in front of a screen in awkward positions for long periods may lead to physical problems such as eyestrain, headaches, and back pain. Computer users can alleviate these problems by taking frequent rest breaks and by using well-designed computer furniture. Some recommendations by ergonomics experts are illustrated in Figure 6-31.

Other recommendations to avoid physical discomfort are

- **Eyestrain and headache:** To make the computer easier on the eyes, take a 15-minute break every hour or two. Keep everything you're focusing on at about the same distance. For example, the computer screen, keyboard, and a document holder containing your work might be positioned about 20 inches away. Clean the screen of dust from time to time.
- **Back and neck pain:** To help avoid back and neck problems, make sure your equipment is adjustable. You should be able to adjust your chair for height and angle, and the chair should have good back support. The monitor should be at eye level or slightly below eye level. Use a footrest, if necessary, to reduce leg fatigue.

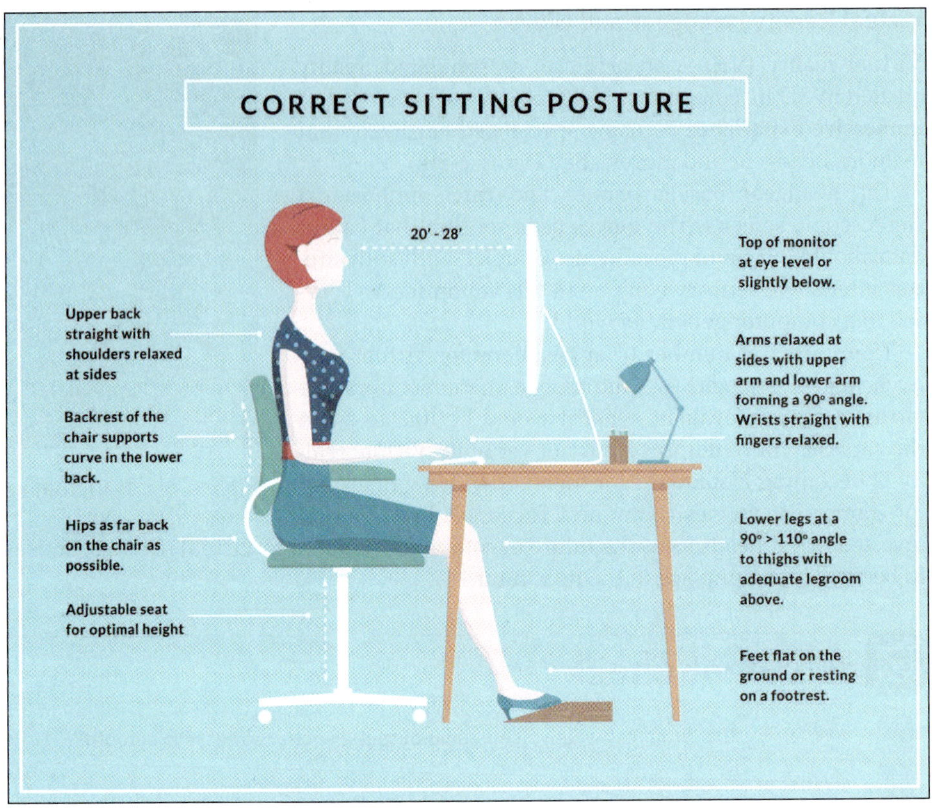

Figure 6-31 **Ergonomic recommendations**

- **Repetitive strain injury: Repetitive strain injury (RSI)** is any injury that is caused by fast, repetitive work that can generate neck, wrist, hand, and arm pain. RSI is by far the greatest cause of workplace illnesses, resulting in compensation claims totaling billions of dollars and lost productivity every year. One particular type of RSI, **carpal tunnel syndrome,** found among heavy computer users, consists of damage to nerves and tendons in the hands. Some victims report the pain is so intense that they cannot open doors or shake hands and that they require corrective surgery. Ergonomically correct keyboards have been developed to help prevent injury from heavy computer use. (See Figure 6-32.) In addition to using ergonomic keyboards, you should take frequent short rest breaks and gently massage your hands.

Figure 6-32 **Ergonomic keyboard**

Portable Computers

While the above recommendations apply to all personal computers, the design of portable computers including laptops, tablets, and smartphones presents some specific ergonomic challenges.

- **Laptops:** Almost all laptops have attached keyboards and screens. Unfortunately, it is impossible to optimally position either for safe ergonomic use. When the screen is positioned appropriately at eye level, the keyboard is too high. When the keyboard is appropriately positioned, the screen is too low. To minimize the negative impact, raise the level of the screen by using books or reams of paper under the laptop and attach an external keyboard to be used at waist level.
- **Tablets:** Almost all tablets use a virtual keyboard and are designed to be held in your hands, flat on a table, or slightly angled. These design features cause the user to improperly align his or her head to the viewing surface, often causing neck and back pain. This problem, sometimes referred to as *tablet hunch,* can be minimized by taking frequent breaks, moving around while working, using a tablet cover or stand that allows the screen to be tipped at various angles, and using an external keyboard.
- **Smartphones:** Today, smartphones are more likely to be used for texting than talking. As a result, thumbs are often used to type on a tiny keyboard. The result can be a pain at the base or in the muscles of the thumb or wrist. This problem, sometimes referred to as *BlackBerry thumb,* can be minimized by keeping wrists straight (not bent), head up, and shoulders straight and frequently resting thumbs by using other fingers.

In today's world, it is important to protect yourself by using computers appropriately.

concept check

What is ergonomics? How does it relate to input and output devices?

What can be done to minimize eyestrain, headache, back pain, and neck pain?

What is RSI? What is carpal tunnel syndrome?

Careers in IT

"Now that you've learned about input and output devices, I'd like to tell you about my career as a technical writer."

Technical writers prepare instruction manuals, technical reports, and other scientific or technical documents. Most technical writers work for computer software firms, government agencies, or research institutions. They translate technical information into easily understandable instructions or summaries. As new technology continues to develop and expand, the need for technical writers who can communicate technical expertise to others is expected to increase.

Technical writing positions typically require an associate's or a bachelor's degree in communications, journalism, or English and a specialization in, or familiarity with, a technical field. However, individuals with strong writing skills sometimes transfer from jobs in the sciences to positions in technical writing.

Technical writers can expect to earn an annual salary in the range of $44,000 to $58,000. Advancement opportunities can be limited within a firm or company, but there are additional opportunities in consulting.

A LOOK TO THE FUTURE

Augmented Reality Displays

Have you ever run into someone who looks familiar, but you cannot remember her name or where you know her from? What about finding yourself in an unfamiliar town, constantly having to look at your smartphone or GPS to get directions? Computers and the World Wide Web offer unrivaled information at the press of a button, but inputs have been limited to desktops and keyboards. Smartphone cameras, GPS, and screens now offer real-time, location-specific information to a user. In the future, with wearable augmented reality displays, information will appear instantly, right before your eyes. Data from your computer and the Internet will become instantly accessible and viewable without having to access another device. The reality you see in front of you is improved, or augmented, with additional visual information using projected images. Technology has been improving our interactions with the real world, and will continue to evolve to improve our lives as we look to the future.

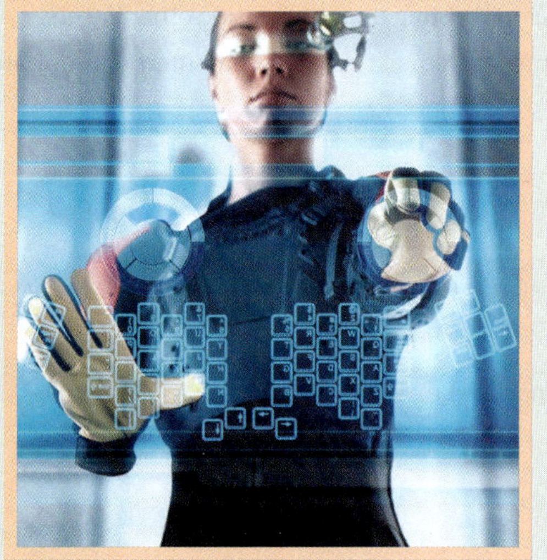

Bringing up information about a visual image is not new. Several search engines already have the ability to identify an image simply by looking for similar images in their databases. In addition, many types of software can recognize faces by looking at key points in the facial structure in order to identify the individual. These augmented reality displays will take that technology one step further by integrating it with wearable glasses or contact lenses. Whether you look at a landmark, textbook, or person, the computer connected to that display will be able to retrieve the information you need and place it in your field of vision. So if you forgot the name of the person greeting you in the coffee shop, do not worry. Her name and brief biography will be retrieved from her social networking account and be displayed in front of you in time to properly return the greeting.

Identification of people and objects is not the only use of augmented reality. As technology continues to shrink in size, the device will be able to perform all the tasks of your smartphone. You will be able to look at the sky and see information about today's weather. Text message and incoming call notifications can appear in front of you. Prices from various online stores will appear by the time you ask your friend where he got that new T-shirt. And, of course, integrated GPS will display arrows in front of you and guide you as you walk through unfamiliar city streets.

Although this technology will likely be available in the next few years, there are some challenges. First, you have the issue of powering the device. Some devices, such as a pair of glasses or contact lenses, may not be large enough to include a battery capable of powering for all day. Another issue involves limitations of human vision. Normally, our eyes find it difficult to focus on objects that are placed very close to them. Researchers have come up with various solutions to fix this problem, but they need to make it comfortable for the eyes to shift focus between the information being projected up close and the real-world object that could be far away. Lastly, there is the issue of comfort. Will these glasses or contact lenses be comfortable to wear all day? Will they make you look strange to those who do not know about augmented reality?

Many companies and universities are working on various types of augmented reality displays. There are a few that have received funding from the military in order to assist soldiers and pilots. The ones that seem closest to release for the general public are from Google. Prototype eyeglasses from its "Project Glass" division are already being tested by various Google employees. With the release of Windows 10, Microsoft introduced HoloLens, an augmented reality headset with embedded Windows software that allows the user to interact with the digital and real world through a pair of special glasses. Now that you have learned more about augmented reality, do you see yourself wearing these sorts of eyeglasses when they become affordable? Do you think that they can end up being a dangerous distraction?

VISUAL SUMMARY Input and Output

KEYBOARDS

Input is any data or instructions that are used by a computer. **Input devices** translate words, numbers, sounds, images, and gestures that people understand into a form that the system unit can process. These include keyboards and pointing, scanning, image capturing, and audio-input devices.

Keyboards convert numbers, letters, and special characters that people understand into electrical signals. These signals are sent to, and processed by, the system unit.

Keyboards

There are four basic categories of keyboards: traditional, laptop, virtual, and thumb.

- **Traditional keyboards,** used on desktop and larger computers. Standard keyboard has 101 keys. **Toggle keys** turn features on and off. **Combination keys** perform actions when combinations of keys are held down.
- **Laptop keyboards,** used on laptop computers. Smaller than traditional keyboard with fewer keys. Typically does not have numeric keypad or standard location for function and navigation keys.
- **Virtual keyboard,** primarily used on mobile devices and tablets. Does not have a physical keyboard. Keys displayed on screen and selected by pressing a key's image.
- **Thumb keyboard,** used on smartphones and other small mobile devices. Designed primarily for communicating via texting and connecting to the web.

POINTING DEVICES

Pointing devices provide an intuitive interface with the system unit by accepting physical movements or gestures and converting them into machine-readable input.

Mouse

A **mouse** controls a pointer that is displayed on the monitor. The **mouse pointer** usually appears in the shape of an arrow. Some mice have a **wheel button** that rotates to scroll through information on the monitor. **Optical mouse** is the most widely used. A **cordless** or **wireless mouse** uses radio waves or infrared light waves. A **touch pad** operates by touching or tapping a surface. It is widely used instead of a mouse with laptops and some types of mobile devices.

Touch Screens

Touch screens allow users to select actions by touching the screen with a finger or penlike device. **Multitouch screens** accept multiple-finger commands.

Game Controllers

Game controllers provide input to computer games. Widely used controllers include gaming mice, **joysticks, gamepads,** and **motion-sensing devices.**

Stylus

A **stylus** is typically used with tablets and mobile devices. Often, a stylus interacts with **handwriting recognition software** to translate handwritten notes into a form that the system unit can process.

To efficiently and effectively use computers, you need to be aware of the most commonly used input and output devices. These devices are translators for information into and out of the system unit. Input devices translate words, sounds, and actions into symbols the system unit can process. Output devices translate symbols from the system unit into words, images, and sounds that people can understand.

SCANNING DEVICES

Scanning devices move across text and images to convert them into a form that the system unit can process.

Optical Scanners

An **optical scanner (scanner)** converts documents into machine-readable form. The four basic types are **flatbed, document, portable,** and **3D.**

Card Readers

Card readers interpret encoded information located on a variety of cards. The most common is the **magnetic card reader** that reads information from a thin magnetic strip on the back of a card. **Smart cards** contain microchips to encrypt data and improve security.

Bar Code Readers

Bar code readers or **scanners** (either handheld **wand readers** or **platform scanners**) read **bar codes** on products. There are a variety of different codes including the **UPC** and **MaxiCode codes.**

RFID Readers

RFID readers read **RFID (radio-frequency identification) tags.** These tags are widely used for tracking lost pets, production, and inventory and for recording prices and product descriptions.

Character and Mark Recognition Devices

Character and mark recognition devices are scanners that are able to recognize special characters and marks. Three types are **magnetic-ink character recognition (MICR), optical-character recognition (OCR),** and **optical-mark recognition (OMR).**

IMAGE CAPTURING DEVICES

Image capturing devices create or capture original images. These devices include digital cameras and webcams.

Digital Cameras

Digital cameras record images digitally and store them on a memory card or in the camera's memory. Most digital cameras record video too.

Webcams

Webcams are specialized digital video cameras that capture images and send them to a computer for broadcast over the Internet. Webcams are built into many smartphones and tablets, while others are attached to the computer monitor.

AUDIO-INPUT DEVICES

Audio-input devices convert sounds into a form that can be processed by the system unit. By far the most widely used audio-input device is the microphone.

Voice Recognition Systems

Voice recognition systems use a microphone, a sound card, and special software. Siri, Cortana, and Google Now are digital assistants that use voice recognition. Specialized portable voice recorders are widely used by doctors, lawyers, and others to record dictation. Some systems are able to translate dictation from one language to another, such as from English to Japanese.

MONITORS

Output is processed data or information. **Output devices** are hardwareised to provide or create output. **Monitors (display screens)** are the most-used output device. Output is often referred to as **soft copy.**

Features

Monitor **clarity** is a function of **resolution** (matrix of **pixels,** or **picture elements), dot pitch, contrast ratio, size (active display area),** and **aspect ratio.**

Flat-Panel Monitors

Flat-panel monitors are the most widely used monitor. Three basic types are **LCD (liquid crystal display), LED (light-emitting diode),** and **OLED (organic light-emitting diode).**

Curved Monitors

Curved monitors have concave screens, provide better viewing angles, and are widely used for high-end televisions.

E-book Readers

E-books (electronic books) are traditional printed books in electronic format. **E-book readers (e-readers)** store and display e-books and other electronic media. They use **e-ink** technology.

Other Monitors

Other types of monitors include **digital (interactive) whiteboards, ultra-high-definition television (UHDTV),** and **digital projectors.**

PRINTERS

Printers translate information processed by the system unit and present the information on paper. Printer output is often called **hard copy.**

Features

Basic features include **resolution** measured in **dpi (dots per inch),** color capability (most common black ink selection is **grayscale**), speed, memory, and **duplex** (both sides of paper) **printing.**

Inkjet

Inkjet printers spray ink at high speed onto the surface of paper. They are the most widely used type of printer, reliable, quiet, and inexpensive. The most costly aspect of inkjet printers is replacing the ink cartridges.

Laser

Laser printers use technology similar to photocopying machine. There are two categories: **personal** and **shared.**

3D Printer

3D printers (additive manufacturing) create objects by adding layers of material onto one another. They have been available for decades; however, recent price reductions have increased their popularity.

Other Printers

There are several other types of printers, including **cloud printers** (**Google Cloud Print** is a cloud printing service), **thermal printers** (use heat elements to produce images on heat-sensitive paper), and **plotters** (use data from graphics tablets and other graphical devices).

AUDIO-OUTPUT DEVICES

Audio-output devices translate audio information from the computer into sounds that people can understand. The most widely used are **speakers** and **headphones.** These devices connect either by cable to an audio jack on the system unit or by a wireless connection. **Bluetooth** technology is widely used to connect wireless devices.

COMBINATION INPUT AND OUTPUT DEVICES

Combination devices combine input and output capabilities. Devices within this category include:

- **Multifunctional devices (MFD)** typically combine capabilities of scanner, printer, fax, and copy machine.
- **Headsets** combine the functionality of microphones and headphones; integral part of serious video game systems.
- **Telephones** are input and output devices. **Voice over IP (VoIP)** supports voice and other types of communication over the Internet. **Telephony (Internet Telephony)** is a VoIP application that uses Internet to support voice communication.
- **Drones (unmanned aerial vehicles, UAV)** take input from a controller and send output video and sound to the user.
- **Robots** use cameras, microphones, and other sensors as inputs; outputs can be as complex as exploring damaged nuclear reactors to as simple as taking a photo.
- **Virtual reality (VR)** creates 3D simulated **immersive experiences.** VR hardware includes **headgear** and **gloves.**

ERGONOMICS

Ergonomics is the study of human factors related to things people use.

Recommendations

Some recommendations to avoid physical discomfort associated with heavy computer use:

- To avoid eyestrain and headache, take a 15-minute break every hour; keep everything you're focusing on at the same distance; and clean the screen periodically.
- To avoid back and neck pain, use adjustable equipment; adjust chairs for height, angle, and back support; position monitors at eye level or slightly below. Use footrest, if necessary, to reduce leg fatigue.
- To avoid **repetitive strain injury (RSI)** and **carpal tunnel syndrome,** use ergonomically correct keyboards; take frequent, short rest breaks; and gently massage hands.

Portable Computers

The design of portable computers presents ergonomic challenges.

- Laptops do not allow correct positioning of keyboard and screen; raise level of laptop and use external keyboard.
- Tablets with virtual keyboards cause improper alignment of user's head; take frequent breaks, move while working, use cover or stand, use external keyboard.
- Smartphones require extensive use of thumbs; keep wrists straight, head up, and shoulders straight and use other fingers.

CAREERS IN IT

Technical writers prepare instruction manuals, technical reports, and other documents. An associate's or a bachelor's degree in communication, journalism, or English and a specialization in, or familiarity with, a technical field are required. Salary range is $44,000 to $58,000.

KEY TERMS

3D printer (154)
3D scanner (146)
active display area (149)
additive manufacturing (154)
aspect ratio (149)
bar code (146)
bar code reader (146)
bar code scanner (146)
Bluetooth (155)
card reader (146)
carpal tunnel syndrome (160)
clarity (149)
cloud printer (154)
combination key (143)
contrast ratio (149)
cordless mouse (144)
curved monitor (150)
digital camera (148)
digital projector (151)
digital whiteboard (151)
display screen (149)
document scanner (146)
dot pitch (149)
dots per inch (dpi) (153)
drones (156)
duplex printing (153)
e-book reader (150)
e-books (150)
e-ink (150)
e-reader (150)
electronic book (150)
ergonomics (159)
flat-panel monitor (150)
flatbed scanner (146)
game controller (144)
gamepads (144)
gaming mice (144)
gloves (159)
Google Cloud Print (154)
grayscale (153)
handwriting recognition software (145)
hard copy (153)
headgear (159)
headphone (155)
headset (155)
immersive experience (159)
inkjet printer (153)
input (142)
input device (142)
interactive whiteboard (151)
Internet telephony (156)
joystick (144)
keyboard (142)
laptop keyboard (143)
laser printer (154)
light-emitting diode (LED) (150)
liquid crystal display (LCD) (150)
magnetic card reader (146)
magnetic-ink character recognition (MICR) (147)
MaxiCode (146)
monitor (149)
motion-sensing device (144)
mouse (144)
mouse pointer (144)
multifunctional device (MFD) (156)
multitouch screen (144)
optical-character recognition (OCR) (147)
organic light-emitting diode (OLED) (150)
optical-mark recognition (OMR) (147)
optical mouse (144)
optical scanner (146)
output (149)
output device (149)
personal laser printer (154)
picture element (149)
pixel (149)
pixel pitch (149)
platform scanner (146)
plotter (155)
pointing device (144)
portable scanner (146)
printer (153)
repetitive strain injury (RSI) (160)
resolution (monitor) (149)
resolution (printer) (153)
RFID reader (147)
RFID (radio-frequency identification) tag (147)
robots (156)
scanner (146)
scanning device (146)
shared laser printer (154)
smart card (146)
soft copy (149)
speaker (155)
stylus (145)
technical writer (161)
telephone (156)
telephony (156)
thermal printer (155)
thumb keyboard (143)
toggle key (143)
touch pad (144)
touch screen (144)
traditional keyboard (143)
Universal Product Code (UPC) (146)
ultra-high-definition television (UHDTV) (151)
virtual keyboard (143)
virtual reality (VR) (159)
unmanned aerial vehicle (UAV) (156)
voice over IP (VoIP) (156)
voice recognition system (148)
wand reader (146)
webcam (148)
wheel button (144)
wireless mouse (144)

MULTIPLE CHOICE

Circle the correct answer.

1. Most keyboards use an arrangement of keys known as:

   a. Alpha
   b. Daisy
   c. OptiKey
   d. QWERTY

2. The device that controls a pointer displayed on the monitor.

   a. cord
   b. mouse
   c. printer
   d. scanner

3. The type of screen that can be touched with more than one finger and supports zooming in and out by pinching and stretching your fingers.

   a. digital
   b. dynamic
   c. multitouch
   d. OLED

4. Flatbed and document are types of:

   a. headsets
   b. MaxiCode
   c. monitors
   d. scanners

5. Device used by banks to automatically read those unusual numbers on the bottom of checks and deposit slips.

   a. MICR
   b. FDIC
   c. OMR
   d. UPC

6. The most widely used audio-input device.

   a. mouse
   b. VR
   c. microphone
   d. RFID

7. The monitor feature that indicates the ability to display colors.

   a. aspect ratio
   b. contrast ratio
   c. dot pitch
   d. resolution rate

8. Mobile devices able to store and display electronic media.

   a. e-book readers
   b. HDTV
   c. lasers
   d. whiteboards

9. Virtual reality strives to create this type of experience.

   a. electronic
   b. immersive
   c. LCD
   d. VoIP

10. The study of human factors related to things people use is:

    a. ergonomics
    b. RFID
    c. RSI
    d. telephony

MATCHING

Match each numbered item with the most closely related lettered item. Write your answers in the spaces provided.

a. active display area
b. digital camera
c. dot pitch
d. mouse
e. plotters
f. scanners
g. Skype
h. stylus
i. toggle key
j. UPC

___ 1. Pressing this key turns a feature on or off.
___ 2. Input device that controls a pointer that is displayed on the monitor.
___ 3. A penlike device commonly used with tablet PCs and PDAs.
___ 4. Bar code readers use either handheld wand readers or platform _____.
___ 5. Bar code system used by many electronic cash registers.
___ 6. Records images digitally on a memory card or in its memory.
___ 7. The distance between each pixel.
___ 8. A monitor feature that is measured by the diagonal length of the viewing area.
___ 9. Special-purpose printers for creating maps, images, and architectural and engineering drawings.
___ 10. A provider of lower-cost options for telephony.

OPEN-ENDED

On a separate sheet of paper, respond to each question or statement.

1. Define input and input devices.
2. Describe the different types of keyboard, pointing, scanning, image capturing, and audio-input devices.
3. Define output and output devices.
4. Describe the features and different types of monitors and printers.
5. Describe audio-output devices including Bluetooth technology.
6. Discuss combination input and output devices, including multifunctional devices, headsets, telephones, drones, robots, and virtual reality headgear and gloves.
7. Define ergonomics, describe ways to minimize physical discomfort, and discuss design issues with portable computers.

DISCUSSION

Respond to each of the following questions.

1 Making IT Work for You: E-BOOKS

Are you tired of carrying a book bag filled with textbooks? Review the Making IT Work for You: E-books on page 152, and then respond to the following: (a) Have you ever purchased or read an e-book? If so, what was your most recent one? If not, have you considered it? Why or why not? (b) Download and install an e-book app (desktop, tablet, or smartphone version), and then download a free e-book for that particular service. Identify the e-book you selected and describe your experience. (c) Based on your experience, will you be purchasing more e-books in the future? Why or why not? (d) Would you consider buying future textbooks as e-books? Discuss the advantages and disadvantages of e-book textbooks.

2 Making IT Work for You: SKYPE

Do you already use a communication tool that lets you keep in touch with your friends and family? Review the Making IT Work for You: Skype on pages 157–158, and then respond to the following: (a) Have you ever used Skype or a similar service? If so, what service have you used, and what do you typically use it for? If you have not used Skype or a similar service, do you expect to in the future? Why or why not? (b) If you do not have a Skype account, create a free one, and add one of your classmates as a contact. Try a few of Skype's features after connecting with your classmate, and then describe your experience with those features. (c) Discuss the advantages and disadvantages of using Skype or a similar service for communication.

3 Privacy: PRINTERS AND ANONYMITY

Did you know that your printer may print personally identifying information on every document you print without your knowledge or consent? Review the Privacy box on page 155, and respond to the following: (a) It's one thing that these codes can be used to identify a specific printer. But do you think the codes can lead to identifying the person who owns the printer? Why or why not? (b) Do you think the hidden codes are a violation of privacy? Explain your position. (c) Does a printer manufacturer have a duty to assist the government in criminal investigations? Justify your position. (d) Does a printer manufacturer have a duty to protect the privacy of its customers? Why or why not?

4 Ethics: WEBCAMS

Every day, thousands of webcams continuously broadcast images to the Internet. Review the Ethics box on page 148, and respond to the following: (a) Do you think recording and broadcasting images without permission is an ethical or a privacy concern? Why or why not? (b) Do you object to being recorded in public, within a retail store, or in a private home? Explain. (c) Do you think police should have access to webcam videos? Should concerned parents? Should jealous spouses? Why or why not? Defend your responses.

5 Environment: INKJET PRINTERS

Have you considered the environmental impact of using your inkjet printer? Review the Environment box on page 153, and then respond to the following: (a) How often do you use your printer at home? What sort of items do you typically print? (b) Have you considered any alternatives to printing? If so, what are those alternatives? Why would or wouldn't you use these alternatives? (c) Does the manufacturer of your ink cartridges use recycled plastic? Support your answer with details from the manufacturer's website. (d) Find a store near you that accepts used ink cartridges. Name the store, and provide details on the benefits it gives you for turning in cartridges.

PHOTO CREDITS

CHAPTER 6

Opener: © Colin Anderson/Blend Images LLC RF; p. 141, 162: © Blend Images/Colin Anderson/Getty Images RF; p. 142, 161: © Chris Ryan/Getty Images RF; 6-1: © Willis Technology; 6-2 (top), p. 163 (left): © Nick Koudis/Getty Images RF; 6-2 (middle) © CJG - Technology/Alamy; 6-2 (bottom): © tech gadgets/Alamy; 6-3: © Tetra Images/ Getty Images RF; 6-4: © cheekylorns/Getty Images RF; 6-5, p. 163 (right): © Ferran Traite Soler/ Getty Images/ RF; 6-6 (top-left): © Viacheslav Krisanov/Getty Images RF; 6-6 (top-right): Copyright © 2015 Razer Inc. All rights reserved; 6-6 (bottom-right), 6-7: Used with permission from Microsoft; 6-6 (bottom-left): © alehdats/Getty Images RF; 6-8, 6-13, p. 164 (right): Courtesy of Canon-Europe; 6-9: © 2015 MakerBot® Industries, LLC; 6-10, p. 164 (left): © Lisa-Blue/Getty Images RF; 6-11: Paul J. Richards/AFP/Getty Images/Newscom; 6-12: © Junior Gonzales/Getty Images RF; 6-14: © Medioimages/Photodisc/Getty Images RF; 6-15: © Maria Gritsai/Alamy RF; 6-17: © Stanca Sanda/Alamy Stock Photo RF; 6-18: © adventtr/iStock/Getty Images RF; 6-19: © JB Reed/Bloomberg via Getty Images; 6-20: Gerald Martineau/The Washington Post/Getty Images; 6-21, p. 165 (left): © scyther5/Getty Images RF; 6-22, 6-24, p. 165 (right): © Copyright 2015 Epson America, Inc.; p. 152 (top): © Kristoffer Tripplaar/Alamy Stock Photo; p. 152 (bottom): Photo by Simon Lees/PC Plus Magazine via Getty Images; 6-25: © scanrail/iStock/ Getty Images RF; 6-26, p. 166 (left): 2015 © Parrot SA. All rights reserved; 6-27: © Jesse Wild/PC Format Magazine via Getty Images; 6-28: © Francois Nascimbeni/AFP/Getty Images; 6-29: © 2015 Intuitive Surgical, Inc. Used with permission; p. 157 (all), 158 (both): Copyright © 2015 Skype and/or Microsoft; 6-30: © Chris Salvo/Getty Images; 6-31: © Wetcake Studio/Digital Vision Vectors/Getty Images; 6-32, p. 166 (right): Courtesy of Fellowes, Inc.

chapter 7 Secondary Storage

Why should I read this chapter?

If you don't have the right secondary storage, your computer will slow to a crawl, your digital camera won't take pictures, and your phone won't be able to run apps. In the future, that will likely not be a problem as we will see storage types that can hold the entire U.S. Library of Congress on a single disk the size of a coin and store information in holograms or even organic molecules.

This chapter covers the things you need to know to be prepared for this ever-changing digital world, including:

- Hard drives—get the right hard drive on your computer to meet all your needs.
- Optical discs—share digital information on Blu-ray, CD, or DVD.
- Solid-state storage—make your portable electronics faster and use less power.
- Cloud storage—store your information safely and securely on the Internet.

Learning Objectives

After you have read this chapter, you should be able to:

1 Distinguish between primary and secondary storage.

2 Identify the important characteristics of secondary storage including media, capacity, storage devices, and access speed.

3 Describe hard-disk platters, tracks, sectors, cylinders, and head crashes.

4 Compare internal and external hard drives.

5 Compare performance enhancements including disk caching, RAID, file compression, and file decompression.

6 Define optical storage including compact discs, digital versatile discs, and Blu-ray discs.

7 Define solid-state storage including solid-state drives, flash memory cards, and USB drives.

8 Define cloud storage and cloud storage services.

9 Describe mass storage, mass storage devices, enterprise storage systems, and storage area networks.

Introduction

"Hi, I'm James, and I'm a disaster recovery specialist. I'd like to talk with you about secondary storage, one of the most critical parts of any computer system. I'd also like to talk about various cloud storage services."

Secondary storage devices are used to save, back up, and even transport files consisting of data or programs from one location or computer to another. At one time, almost all files contained only numbers and letters. The demands for saving these files were easily met with low-capacity storage devices.

Data storage has expanded from text and numeric files to include digital music files, photographic files, video files, and much more. These new types of files require secondary storage devices that have much greater capacity.

Secondary storage devices have always been an indispensable element in any computer system. They have similarities to output and input devices. Like output devices, secondary storage devices receive information from the system unit in the form of the machine language of 0s and 1s. Rather than translating the information, however, secondary storage devices save the information in machine language for later use. Like input devices, secondary storage devices send information to the system unit for processing. However, the information, since it is already in machine form, does not need to be translated. It is sent directly to memory (RAM), where it can be accessed and processed by the CPU.

To efficiently and effectively use computers, you need to be aware of the different types of secondary storage. You need to know the capabilities, limitations, and uses of hard disks, solid-state drives, optical discs, cloud storage, and other types of secondary storage. Additionally, you need to be aware of specialty storage devices for portable computers and to be knowledgeable about how large organizations manage their extensive data resources.

Storage

An essential feature of every computer is the ability to save, or store, information. As discussed in Chapter 5, random-access memory (RAM) holds or stores data and programs that the CPU is presently processing. Before data can be processed or a program can be run, it must be in RAM. For this reason, RAM is sometimes referred to as **primary storage.**

Unfortunately, most RAM provides only temporary or volatile storage. That is, it loses all of its contents as soon as the computer is turned off. Its contents also are lost if there is a power failure that disrupts the electric current going into the system unit. This volatility results in a need for more permanent or nonvolatile storage for data and programs. We also need external storage because users need much more storage capacity than is typically available in a computer's primary or RAM memory.

Secondary storage provides permanent or nonvolatile storage. Using **secondary storage devices** such as a hard-disk drive, data and programs can be retained after the computer has been shut off. This is accomplished by *writing* files to and *reading* files from secondary storage devices. Writing is the process of saving information *to* the secondary storage device. Reading is the process of accessing information *from* secondary storage. This chapter focuses on secondary storage devices.

These are important characteristics of secondary storage:

- **Media** are the physical material that holds the data and programs. (See Figure 7-1.)
- **Capacity** measures how much a particular storage medium can hold.
- **Storage devices** are hardware that reads data and programs from storage media. Most also write to storage media.
- **Access speed** measures the amount of time required by the storage device to retrieve data and programs.

Most desktop personal computer systems have hard-disk and optical disc drives, as well as ports where additional storage devices can be connected.

Figure 7-1 **Secondary storage media**

Hard Disks

Hard disks save files by altering the magnetic charges of the disk's surface to represent 1s and 0s. Hard disks retrieve data and programs by reading these charges from the magnetic disk. Characters are represented by positive (+) and negative (−) charges using the ASCII, EBCDIC, or Unicode binary codes. For example, the letter A would require a series of 8 charges. (See Figure 7-2.) **Density** refers to how tightly these charges can be packed next to one another on the disk.

Hard disks use rigid metallic **platters** that are stacked one on top of another. Hard disks store and organize files using tracks, sectors, and cylinders. **Tracks** are rings of concentric circles on the platter. Each track is divided into invisible wedge-shaped sections called **sectors.** (See Figure 7-3.) A **cylinder** runs through each track of a stack of platters. Cylinders are necessary to differentiate files stored on the same track and sector of different platters. When a hard disk is formatted, tracks, sectors, and cylinders are assigned.

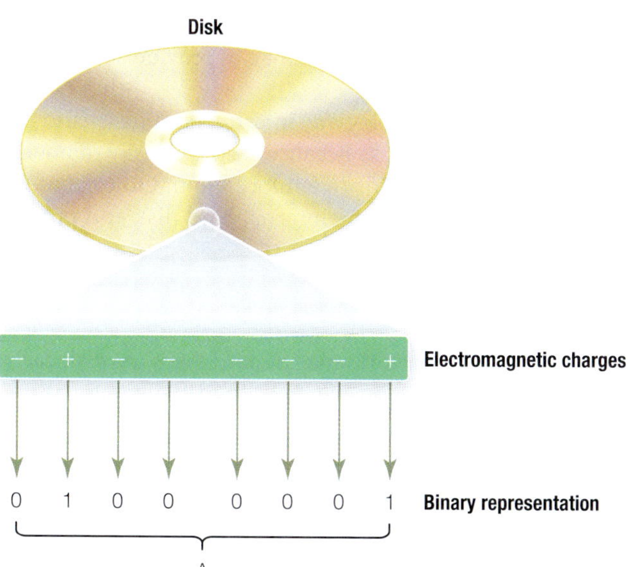

Figure 7-2 **How charges on a disk surface store the letter A**

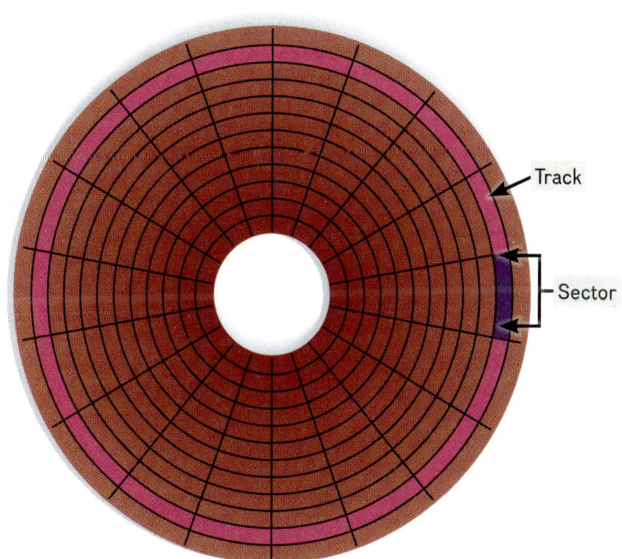

Figure 7-3 **Tracks and sectors**

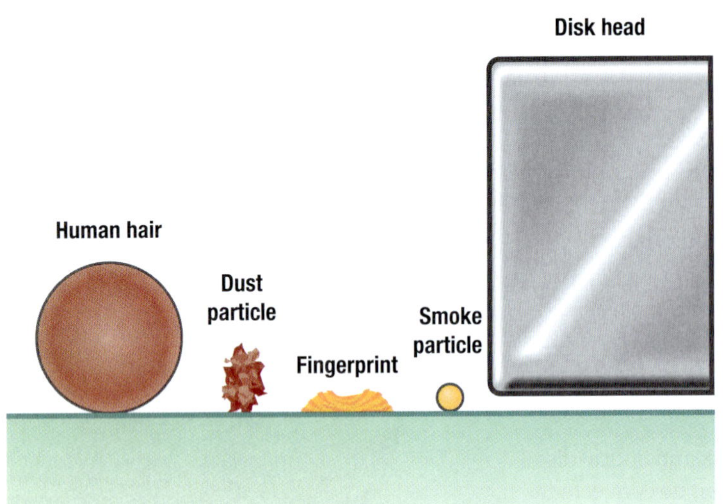

Figure 7-4 **Materials that can cause a head crash**

Hard disks are sensitive instruments. Their read/write heads ride on a cushion of air about 0.000001 inch thick. It is so thin that a smoke particle, fingerprint, dust, or human hair could cause what is known as a head crash. (See Figure 7-4.)

A **head crash** occurs when a read-write head makes contact with the hard disk's surface or with particles on its surface. A head crash is a disaster for a hard disk. The disk surface is scratched, and some or all of the data is destroyed. At one time, head crashes were commonplace. Now, fortunately, they are rare.

There are two basic types of hard disks: internal and external.

Internal Hard Disk

An **internal hard disk** is located inside the system unit. These hard disks are able to store and retrieve large quantities of information quickly. They are used to store programs and data files. For example, nearly every personal computer uses its internal hard disk to store its operating system and major applications such as Word and Excel.

To ensure adequate performance of your internal hard disk and the safety of your data, you should perform routine maintenance and periodically make backup copies of all important files. For hard-disk maintenance and backup procedures, refer to Chapter 4's coverage of the Windows utilities File History, Disk Cleanup, and Optimize Drives.

External Hard Drives

While internal hard disks provide fast access, they have a fixed amount of storage and cannot be easily removed from the system unit. External hard disks provide slower access and are typically connected to a USB or Thunderbolt port on the system unit and are easily removed. Like an internal hard disk, external hard disks have a fixed amount of storage. However, since each removable hard disk can be easily replaced by another removable hard disk, a single port on the system unit can provide access to an unlimited amount of storage. (See Figure 7-5.)

External hard drives use the same basic technology as internal hard disks and are used primarily to complement an internal hard disk. Because they are easily removed, they are particularly useful to protect or secure sensitive information. Other uses for external drives include backing up the contents of the internal hard disk and providing additional hard-disk capacity.

Figure 7-5 **External hard drive**

Performance Enhancements

Three ways to improve the performance of hard disks are disk caching, redundant arrays of inexpensive disks, and file compression/decompression.

Disk caching improves hard-disk performance by anticipating data needs. It performs a function similar to cache memory discussed in Chapter 5. While cache memory improves processing by acting as a temporary high-speed holding area between memory and the CPU, disk caching improves processing by acting as a temporary high-speed holding area between a secondary storage device and the CPU. Disk caching requires a combination of hardware and software. During idle processing time, frequently used data is automatically identified and read from the hard disk into the disk cache. When needed, the data is then accessed directly from memory. The transfer rate from memory is much faster than from the hard disk. As a result, overall system performance is often increased by as much as 30 percent.

Redundant arrays of inexpensive disks (RAID) improve performance by expanding external storage, improving access speed, and providing reliable storage. Several inexpensive hard-disk drives are connected to one another. These connections can be by a network or within specialized RAID devices. (See Figure 7-6.) The connected hard-disk drives are related or grouped together, and the computer system interacts with the RAID system as though it were a single large-capacity hard-disk drive. The result is expanded storage capability, fast access speed, and high reliability. For these reasons, RAID is often used by Internet servers and large organizations.

Figure 7-6 **RAID storage device**

privacy

Did you know that when you sell your computer, you might be selling all your data as well? When you delete a file, the computer does not remove the data. It simply makes that hard-disk space available to be written on in the future. If you accidentally delete a file, file recovery software is available to check the hard disk to see if the data is still there and has not been overwritten yet. In the same way that data can be recovered when accidentally deleted, thieves can recover data that was intentionally deleted. To confidently delete files, use a secure deletion utility before selling a computer.

File compression and **file decompression** increase storage capacity by reducing the amount of space required to store data and programs. File compression is not limited to hard-disk systems. It is frequently used to compress files on DVDs, CDs, and flash drives as well. File compression also helps to speed up transmission of files from one computer system to another. Sending and receiving compressed files across the Internet is a common activity.

File compression programs scan files for ways to reduce the amount of required storage. One way is to search for repeating patterns. The repeating patterns are replaced with a token, leaving enough tokens so that the original can be rebuilt or decompressed. These programs often shrink files to a quarter of their original size.

Windows and Mac operating systems provide compression and decompression utilities. For more advanced compression schemes, you can use specialized utilities such as WinZip. For a summary of performance enhancement techniques, see Figure 7-7.

Technique	Description
Disk caching	Uses cache and anticipates data needs
RAID	Linked, inexpensive hard-disk drives
File compression	Reduces file size
File decompression	Expands compressed files

Figure 7-7 **Performance enhancement techniques**

concept check

- Discuss four important characteristics of secondary storage.
- What are the two types of hard disks? Briefly describe each.
- What is density? What are tracks, sectors, cylinders, and head crashes?
- List and describe three ways to improve the performance of hard disks.

environment

Did you know that traditional, magnetic hard-disk storage requires more energy than solid-state storage? Unlike solid-state drives, which have no moving parts, hard drives have to rotate their magnetic disks in order to save or retrieve data. Fujitsu, which manufactures various storage devices, estimates that its high-end solid-state drives will consume 40 percent less power than comparable hard drives. For large data centers, this can result in a significant reduction in energy needs.

Solid-State Storage

Unlike hard disks, which rotate and have read/write heads that move in and out, **solid-state storage** devices have no moving parts. Data and information are stored and retrieved electronically directly from these devices much as they would be from conventional computer memory.

Solid-state storage devices provide access to **flash memory,** also known as **solid-state storage.** As we discussed in Chapter 5, flash memory offers a combination of features of RAM and ROM. Like RAM it can be updated and like ROM it does not lose information when a computer is turned off. Flash memory is a little slower than traditional memory but much faster than traditional hard disks.

Solid-State Drives

Solid-state drives (SSDs) are designed to be connected inside a personal computer system the same way an internal hard disk would be but contain solid-state memory instead of magnetic disks to store data. (See Figure 7-8.) SSDs are faster and more durable than hard disks. SSDs also require less power, which can lead to increased battery life for laptops and mobile devices. SSDs are more expensive and generally have a lower capacity than hard disks, but this is changing as the popularity of SSDs continues to increase. SSDs are widely used in tablets, smartphones, and other mobile devices. Computer manufacturers have developed hybrid systems that contain both SSDs and magnetic disks in an attempt to gain the speed and power benefits of SSDs while still having the low cost and large capacity of magnetic hard drives. Typically, these systems store the operating system and applications on the SSD drive and videos, music, documents, and folders on the magnetic hard drive.

Figure 7-8 **Solid-state drive**

Flash Memory Cards

Flash memory cards are small solid-state storage devices widely used in portable devices. Some of the cards are used within devices such as laptops, smartphones, and GPS navigation systems. (See Figure 7-9.) Other cards provide removable storage. For example, flash memory is used to store images captured from digital cameras and then to transfer the images to desktop and other computers. Flash memory is used in digital media players like the iPod to store and play music and video files.

USB Drives

USB drives, or **flash drives,** are so compact that they can be transported on a key ring. (See Figure 7-10.) These drives conveniently connect directly to a computer's USB port to transfer files and can have capacities ranging from 1 GB to 256 GB, with a broad price range to match. Due to their convenient size and large capacities, USB drives have become a very popular option for transporting data and information between computers, specialty devices, and the Internet.

tips

Have you ever accidentally deleted or lost important files from your flash drive? Do you have a USB flash drive that is no longer being recognized by your computer? Here are a few suggestions that might help:

1. **Recovery/undelete software.** If you accidentally deleted files from a USB drive, it is unlikely that you can recover them using your operating system or searching through your recycle bin. Fortunately, there are several recovery (or undelete) programs that might help, and some are even free. For example, two free programs are *Undelete 360* and *Recuva.* These programs will scan your flash drives for deleted files and offer you a chance to recover the ones you want back.
2. **Testing USB ports.** If your computer does not recognize your USB flash drive, there could be a problem with your USB port. Try plugging another device into that same port to see if it works. If this device does not work, then your computer's USB is most likely defective and needs to be replaced. If the device works, then most likely your USB flash drive is damaged and you should try the professional recovery services discussed in the next step.
3. **Professional recovery services.** For damaged flash drives, there is a possibility that your data could be recovered by several companies that are dedicated to data recovery. Although the fees are high, they can rescue data from the actual memory chip, even if the drive or supporting circuits are damaged.

Figure 7-9 **Flash memory card**

Figure 7-10 **USB drive**

concept check

- What is solid-state storage? How is it different from hard-disk drives?
- What are solid-state drives? What are they used for?
- What are flash memory cards? What are USB drives? What are they used for?

Optical Discs

Today's **optical discs** can hold over 128 gigabytes of data. (See Figure 7-11.) That is the equivalent of millions of typewritten pages or a medium-sized library all on a single disc. Optical discs are very common, with most software and many movies available on optical disc.

In optical disc technology, a laser beam alters the surface of a plastic or metallic disc to represent data. Unlike hard disks, which use magnetic charges to represent 1s and 0s, optical discs use reflected light. The 1s and 0s are represented by flat areas called **lands** and bumpy areas called **pits** on the disc surface. The disc is read by an **optical disc drive** using a laser that projects a tiny beam of light on these areas. The amount of reflected light determines whether the area represents a 1 or a 0.

Like hard disks, optical discs use tracks and sectors to organize and store files. Unlike the concentric tracks and wedge-shaped sectors used for hard disks, however, optical discs typically use a single track that spirals outward from the center of the disc. This single track is divided into equal-sized sectors.

The most widely used optical discs are CD, DVD, and Blu-ray discs.

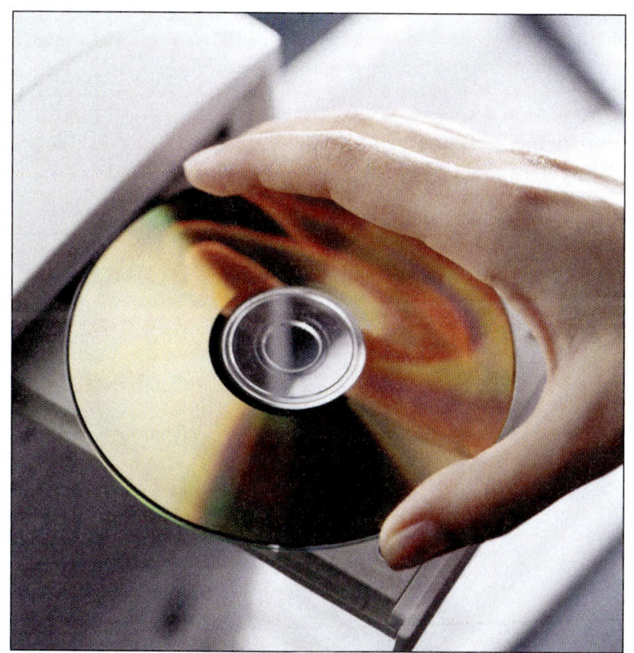

Figure 7-11 **Optical disc**

- **Compact discs** (**CD**s) were the first widely available optical format for PC users. Typically, CD drives store 700 MB (megabytes) of storage. Optical discs that store music are often CDs.
- **Digital versatile discs** (**DVD**s) are the standard optical discs in PCs. DVDs are very similar to CDs except that

typical DVD discs can store 4.7 GB (gigabytes)—seven times the capacity of CDs. Optical discs that store movies or software are often DVDs. DVD drives and CD drives look very similar.

- **Blu-ray discs (BDs)** are the newest form of optical storage designed to store **hi def (high definition)** video, which uses the HD 720 and HD 1080 resolutions discussed in Chapter 6. The name Blu-ray comes from a special blue-colored laser used to read the discs that gives them a typical capacity of 50 GB—ten times the capacity of DVDs. Optical discs that store hi def video and the newest video games are often Blu-ray discs.

Each of these optical discs has three basic formats: read only, write once, and rewritable.

- **Read-only** (**ROM** for **read-only memory**) **discs** are discs that cannot be written on or erased by the user. Optical discs that you buy in a store, such as music CDs, DVD movies, and Blu-ray video games, are often read only.
- **Write-once** (**R** for **recordable**) **discs** can be written on once. After that, the disc can be read many times but cannot be written on or erased. These discs are ideal for creating permanent archives, such as CD-R, often used for storing family photos, and DVD-R, often used to store home movies.
- **Rewritable** (**RW** for **rewritable** or **RAM** for **random-access memory**) **discs** are similar to write-once discs except that the disc surface is not permanently altered when data is recorded. These changeable, portable storage options are popular for storing and sharing audio, video, and large multimedia presentations.

Some optical discs, referred to as double-sided discs, contain information on both sides of the disc and need to be flipped over to read the other side, effectively doubling the storage capacity of the disk. For example, a double-sided DVD can store 9.4 GB, or twice as much as a single-sided DVD. Another way to add capacity to an optical disc is by adding multiple recording layers. These discs store information on several layers sandwiched together on one side of the disc. For example, some Blu-ray discs have multiple layers that increase storage capacity from 50 GB to 128 GB.

For a summary of the different types of optical discs, see Figure 7-12.

Format	Typical Capacity	Description
CD	700 MB	Once the standard optical disc
DVD	4.7 GB	Current standard
Blu-ray	50 GB	Hi-def format, large capacity

Figure 7-12 **Types of optical discs**

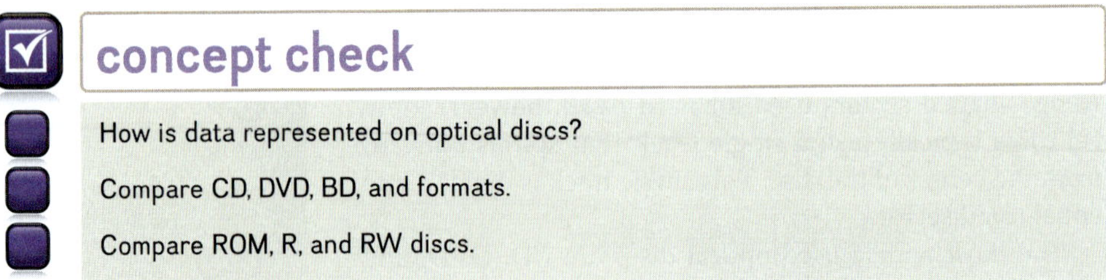

concept check
How is data represented on optical discs?
Compare CD, DVD, BD, and formats.
Compare ROM, R, and RW discs.

Cloud Storage

Recently, many applications that would have required installation on your computer to run have moved to the web. As we discussed in Chapter 2, this is known as **cloud computing,** where the Internet acts as a "cloud" of servers that supply applications

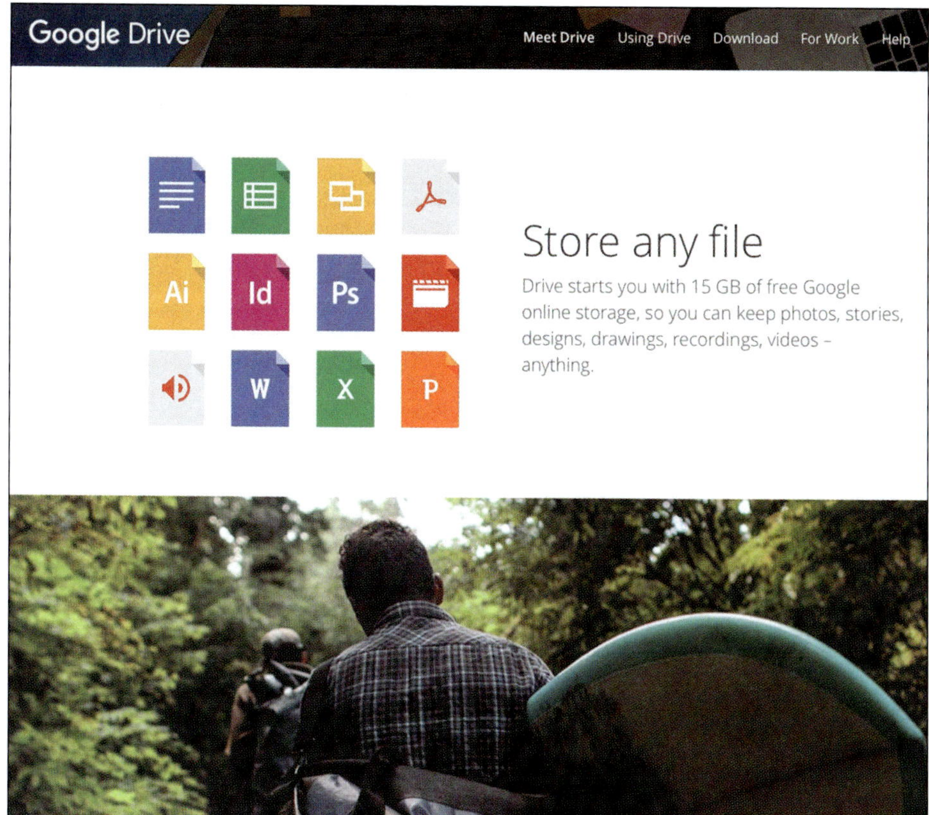

Figure 7-13 **Google Drive Docs**

to clients as a *service* rather than a *product.* Additionally, these servers provide **cloud storage,** also known as **online storage.**

If you have used Google Drive Docs to create a word processing document or a spreadsheet, you have already used cloud computing. (See Figure 7-13.) The service provider's server runs the applications and your computer displays results. The applications and data can be accessed from any Internet-ready device. This means that even devices with little storage, memory, or processing power, such as a smartphone, can run the same powerful applications as a desktop computer.

The benefits to this arrangement are numerous:

- Maintenance—The cloud service will take care of disk defragmentation, backups, encryption, and security.
- Hardware upgrades—The cloud service will never run out of disk space and can replace failed hard disks without interruption to the user.
- File sharing and collaboration—Users can share documents, spreadsheets, and files with others from anywhere with an Internet connection.

Of course, there are some disadvantages of cloud storage:

- Access speed—The data transfer rate is dependent upon the speed of your Internet connection, which most likely is not as fast as a user's internal network.
- File security—Users are dependent upon the cloud service's security procedures, which may not be as effective as your own.

There are numerous websites that provide cloud storage services. (See Figure 7-14.) To learn more about how you could use cloud storage, see Making IT Work for You: Cloud Storage on pages 182–183.

ethics

Cloud storage has created some interesting legal and ethical questions regarding the storage of sensitive and privileged information. Who is responsible for maintaining security and privacy of sensitive and confidential information? What if your attorney or doctor stored confidential information about you in the cloud and it somehow became widely distributed across the Internet? Clearly, you suffer any related consequences, but who is responsible? Is it your attorney, your doctor, the company providing the cloud service, or do you somehow have the responsibility to protect personal sensitive information?

Company	Location
Dropbox	www.dropbox.com
Google	drive.google.com
Microsoft	www.skydrive.com
Amazon	amazon.com/cloud
Apple	www.icloud.com

Figure 7-14 **Cloud storage services**

CLOUD STORAGE

Have you ever found yourself e-mailing files back and forth between two of your computers as a way to transport them? Do you keep forgetting your USB drive at school or work? Have you ever wished that you had some of your files readily available on your smartphone? If so, then you should sign up for Dropbox. (Please note that the web is continually changing, and some of the specifics presented below may have changed.)

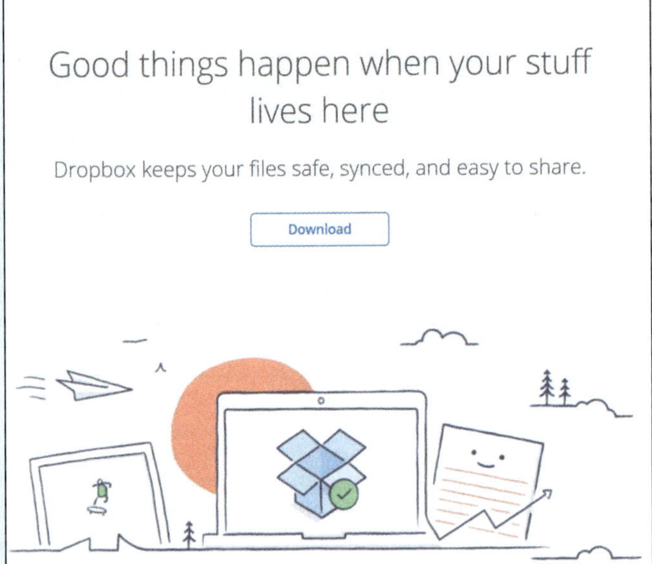

Getting Started To use Dropbox, you need to create an account. To take advantage of the synchronization feature, you will need to install the software on each of your computers.

1. **Go to www.dropbox.com, and click the *Download Dropbox* button.**
2. **Select the "I don't have a Dropbox account" option during the installation process (if this is your first installation).**
3. **Enter your information to create a new account.**
4. **Select the *Free* option when asked for a Dropbox size, and then choose the *Typical* setup.**
5. **Continue clicking the *Next* button to view the important tour.**

If you have a tablet or smartphone, be sure to install its free app in order to access your files.

The Dropbox Folder After installation, a folder named "Dropbox" will be created on your hard drive and connected to your computer's user account. This folder is the basis for all synchronization—any files placed here will immediately be uploaded to your Dropbox account and will be kept synchronized between all your computers. A good use of this folder would be to place all of your schoolwork and favorite photos, so that you can access them from any Internet-connected computer, tablet, or smartphone. Follow these steps to use your Dropbox folder:

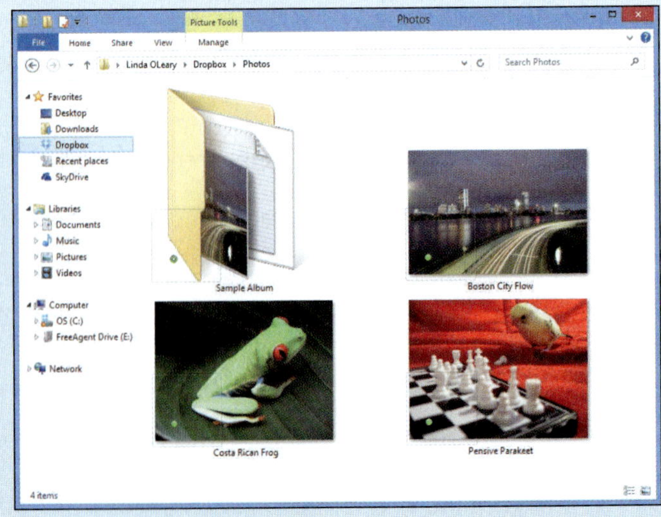

1. **Open Windows Explorer, and look at your *Favorites* area.**
2. **Click the *Dropbox* folder, and notice the files and folders already in there. Open the *Photos* subfolder.**
3. **Create a subfolder in this location named "Practice" (this will serve as a photo gallery or album).**
4. **Copy any photo from your computer, and paste it in this new folder.**

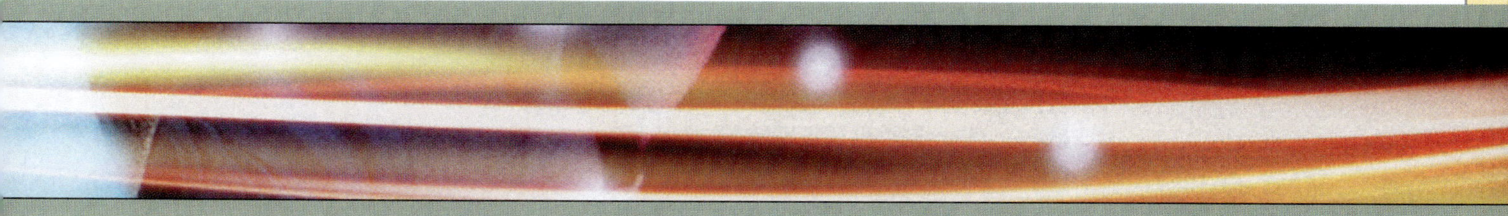

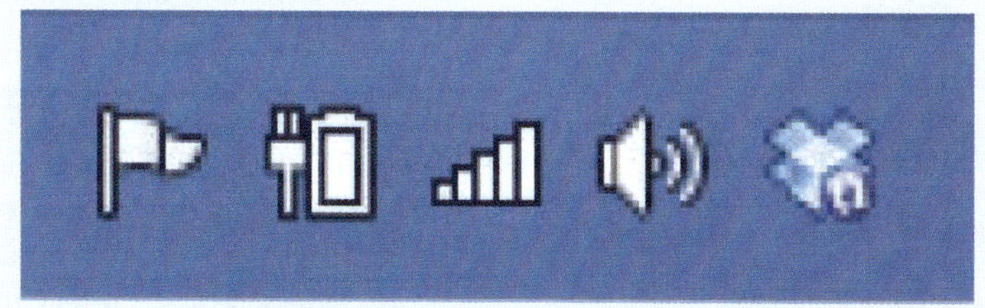

Notice the tiny, blue *synchronization icon* at the bottom left of your file. When this icon turns into a green check mark, it means that the file has finished uploading to the Dropbox server. The same system is used for the Dropbox icon in your Windows notification area.

Sharing Files Any file or folder in your Dropbox account can be shared with anyone via a unique link. This method is superior to sending large e-mail attachments that can be subject to the limits of the e-mail service. To share a file or folder:

1. **Go to your Dropbox folder using Windows Explorer.**
2. **Right-click any file or folder, and click *share Dropbox link.* A URL link to that file or folder will be copied to your clipboard.**
3. **Paste the link into an e-mail to share that file or folder with someone else. That individual will just follow the link in his or her Internet browser to get the file.**

Getting More Storage Space Dropbox's free service includes all its features, but with a limited amount of storage space. You can increase that space with a paid account or by inviting friends and colleagues to join. (Dropbox increases your storage each time one of them signs up.)

1. **Go to www.dropbox.com/getspace and log into your account.**
2. **Click the *Refer friends to Dropbox* and follow the instructions to invite others to use Dropbox.**

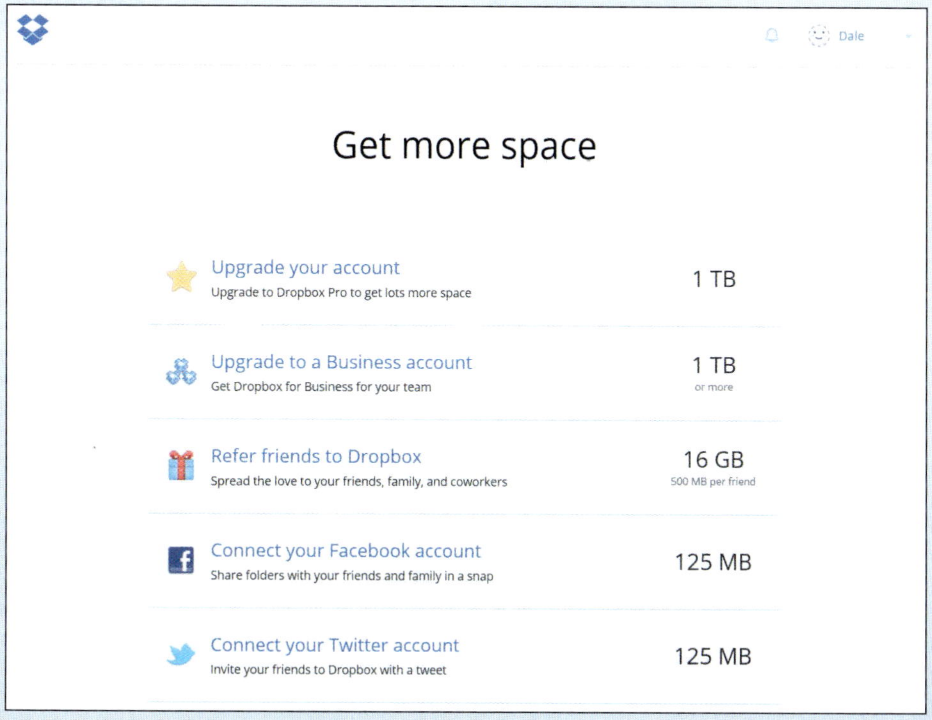

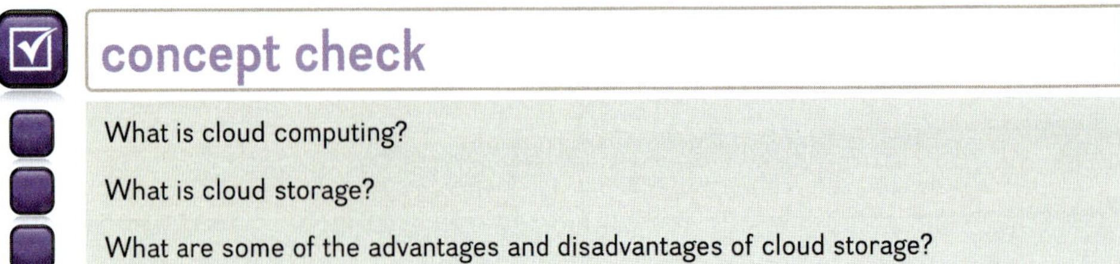

concept check

- What is cloud computing?
- What is cloud storage?
- What are some of the advantages and disadvantages of cloud storage?

Mass Storage Devices

It is natural to think of secondary storage media and devices as they relate to us as individuals. It may not be as obvious how important these matters are to organizations. **Mass storage** refers to the tremendous amount of secondary storage required by large organizations. **Mass storage devices** are specialized high-capacity secondary storage devices designed to meet organizational demands for data storage. These mass storage solutions allow large corporations and institutions to centralize their maintenance and security of data, thereby reducing costs and personnel.

Enterprise Storage System

Most large organizations have established a strategy called an **enterprise storage system** to promote efficient and safe use of data across the networks within their organizations. (See Figure 7-15.) Some of the mass storage devices that support this strategy are:

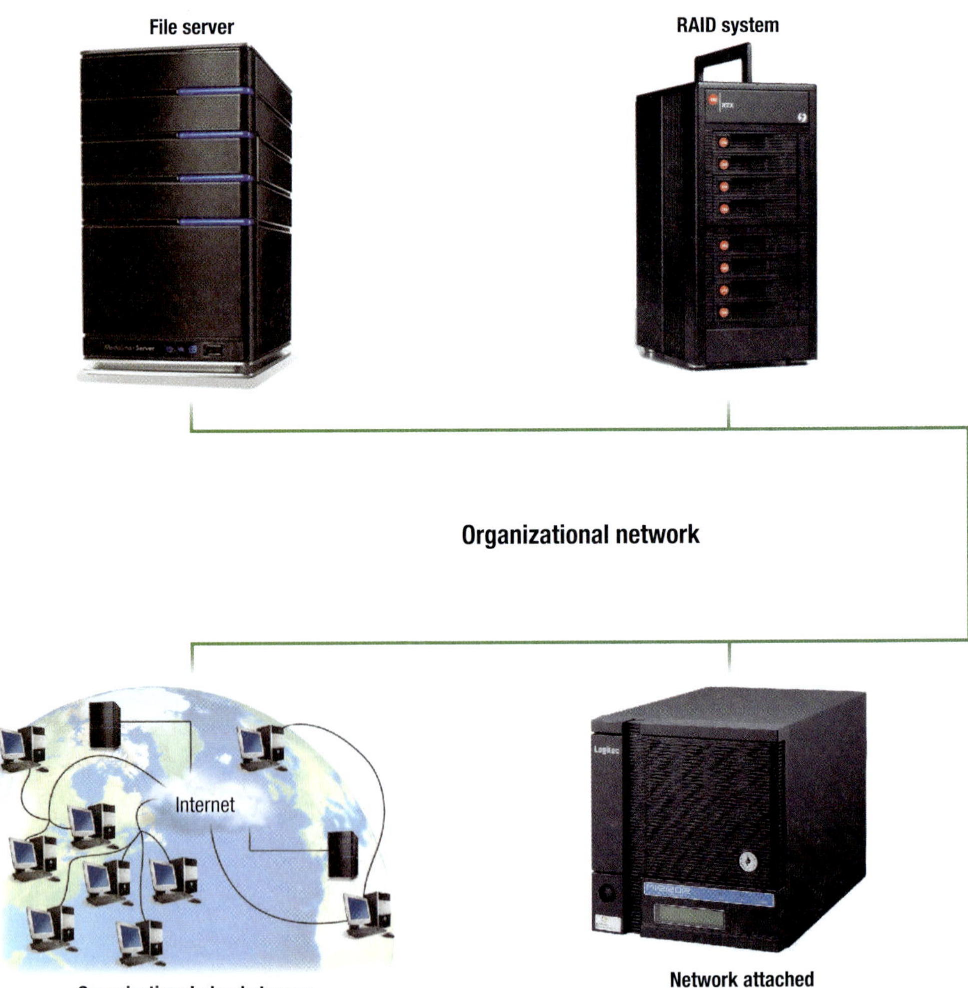

Figure 7-15 Enterprise storage system

- **File servers**—dedicated computers with very large storage capacities that provide users access to fast storage and retrieval of data.
- **Network attached storage (NAS)**—a type of file server designed for homes and small businesses. NAS is less expensive, easier to set up, and easier to manage than most file servers. However, it does not include powerful management tools and features found in many large-scale file servers.
- **RAID systems**—larger versions of the specialized devices discussed earlier in this chapter that enhance organizational security by constantly making backup copies of files moving across the organization's networks.
- **Organizational cloud storage**—high-speed Internet connection to a dedicated remote storage facility. These facilities contain banks of file servers to offer enormous amounts of storage.

Storage Area Network

A recent mass storage development is **storage area network (SAN)** systems. SAN is an architecture to link remote computer storage devices, such as enterprise storage systems, to computers such that the devices are as available as locally attached drives. In a SAN system, the user's computer provides the file system for storing data, but the SAN provides the disk space for data.

The key to a SAN is a high-speed network, connecting individual computers to mass storage devices. Special file systems prevent simultaneous users from interfering with each other. SANs provide the ability to house data in remote locations and still allow efficient and secure access.

concept check

Define mass storage and mass storage devices.

What is an enterprise storage system?

What is a storage area network system?

Careers in IT

"Now that you've learned about secondary storage, let me tell you a little bit about my career as a disaster recovery specialist."

Disaster recovery specialists are responsible for recovering systems and data after a disaster strikes an organization. In addition, they often create plans to prevent and prepare for such disasters. A crucial part of that plan is to use storage devices and media in order to ensure that all company data is backed up and, in some cases, stored off-site.

Employers typically look for candidates with a bachelor's or associate's degree in information systems or computer science. Experience in this field is usually required, and additional skills in the areas of networking, security, and database administration are desirable. Disaster recovery specialists should possess good communication skills and be able to handle high-stress situations.

Disaster recovery specialists can expect to earn an annual salary of $70,000 to $88,000. Opportunities for advancement typically include upper-management positions. With so many types of threats facing organizations, demand for these types of specialists is expected to grow.

A LOOK TO THE FUTURE

Next-Generation Storage

Have you already started to use a cloud storage service for your files? Have your friends and family members used one also? With millions of individuals and businesses all signing up for these services, how do these companies keep up with the amount of storage required to accommodate all these users? The answer is simple: They keep adding more hard drives. Although hard drives have been around a long time, the technology underlying these tools is undergoing incredible improvements. Recently, terabyte hard drives have become commonplace, using existing magnetic storage methods. In the future, your movies and photos may be stored using heat, organic compounds, or even holograms. Technology has been making better storage, and will continue to evolve to improve our lives as we look to the future.

The first product that will receive a huge improvement is the hard drive. When it comes to the primary storage of your computer and the millions of servers throughout the world, nothing beats hard drives. They are the most affordable solution when it comes to the price per gigabyte. Therefore, researchers are looking at ways of increasing their capacity without increasing their size. Current hard drive technology will max out at approximately 128 GB per square inch. Seagate, a manufacturer of hard drives, is working on two new technologies that hope to increase that limit: heat-assisted magnetic recording (HAMR) and bit-patterned media (BPM). The idea is to keep making the bits smaller so that more of them fit in the same area. Once these technologies are implemented, the capacity could reach 6.25 TB (or 6,250 GB) per square inch. With a density like that, Seagate estimates that you could hold the entire contents of the U.S. Library of Congress on a disk that is no bigger than a coin.

The latest optical disc, Blu-ray, is commercially available as 25- or 50-GB discs. Although several companies have achieved higher limits by adding more layers, a ceiling will soon be hit. GE Global Research is currently developing a disc made up of tiny holograms, stored over dozens of layers, that react to light. These discs will store 1 TB of data, and the drives that read them will also be able to read your DVD and Blu-ray discs.

Advancements in chemistry have led to the speculation that circuits and storage media could soon be working with carbon-containing molecules. Researchers have discovered that a group of compounds known as metallofullerenes can be oriented in various ways, allowing them to represent 0 and 1 bits just as other storage media currently do. The biggest advantage with organic molecules involves size. These molecules are so small that storage devices created with them could be extremely tiny, allowing the creation of much smaller computers and gadgets.

You may be wondering why solid-state storage, or flash memory, has not yet been mentioned. This type of media has definitely been improving over the years. Your flash drives and memory cards keep getting smaller and capacities keep going up. However, the price per gigabyte is still much higher than that of hard drives. In the past, they have a limited life span because they can support only approximately 10,000 write operations. These two issues may not be a problem for individuals, but they make it impossible for large businesses and cloud storage companies to rely on them. However, recent innovations in the way solid-state storage writes information has shown dramatic improvements and SSD stability concerns are likely to be a thing of the past.

Now that several types of future technologies have been explored, which do you see yourself using in five years? Do you believe that solid-state storage will completely replace the hard drive in desktop and laptop computers? Do you think that molecule-sized storage solutions will ever be affordable enough to be used in all computers?

VISUAL SUMMARY Secondary Storage

STORAGE

RAM is **primary storage.** Most RAM is volatile, meaning that it loses its contents whenever power is disrupted. **Secondary storage** provides nonvolatile storage. Secondary storage retains data and information after the computer system is turned off.

Writing is the process of saving information to **secondary storage devices.** Reading is the process of accessing information.

Important characteristics include

- **Media**—actual physical material that retains data and programs.
- **Capacity**—how much a particular storage medium can hold.
- **Storage devices**—hardware that reads and writes to storage media.
- **Access speed**—time required to retrieve data from a secondary storage device.

HARD DISKS

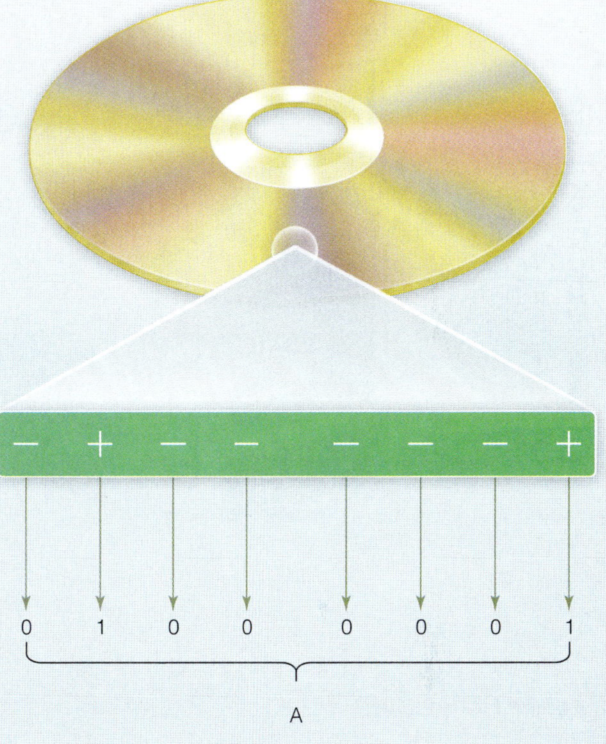

Hard disks use rigid metallic **platters** that provide a large amount of capacity. They store data and programs by altering the electromagnetic charges on the platter's surface. Files are organized according to

- **Tracks**—concentric rings on the platter.
- **Sectors**—wedge-shaped sections.
- **Cylinders**—run through each track of a stack of platters.

Density refers to how tightly electromagnetic charges can be packed next to one another on the disk.

A **head crash** occurs when the hard disk makes contact with the drive's read-write heads.

Two types are internal and external hard disks.

Internal Hard Disk

Internal hard disks are located within the system unit. Used to store programs and data files.

To efficiently and effectively use computers, you need to be aware of the different types of secondary storage. You need to know their capabilities, limitations, and uses. There are four widely used storage media: hard disk, solid state, optical disc, and cloud storage.

HARD DISKS

External Hard Drives

Unlike internal hard disks, **external hard drives** are removable. External drives use the same basic technology as internal disks.

Performance Enhancements

Three ways to improve hard-disk performance are disk caching, RAID, and file compression and decompression.

- **Disk caching**—provides a temporary high-speed holding area between a secondary storage device and the CPU; improves performance by anticipating data needs and reducing time to access data from secondary storage.
- **RAID (redundant array of inexpensive disks)**—several inexpensive hard-disk drives are connected together; improves performance by providing expanded storage, fast access, and high reliability.
- **File compression and decompression**—files are compressed before storing and then decompressed before being used again; improves performance through efficient storage.

SOLID-STATE STORAGE

Solid-state storage devices have no moving parts; provide access to **flash memory (solid-state storage).**

Solid-State Drives

Solid-state drives (SSDs) are similar to internal hard-disk drives except they use solid-state memory; are faster, more durable, and more expensive; and generally provide less capacity. Hybrid systems contain SSD and magnetic disks.

Flash Memory Cards

Flash memory cards are small solid-state storage devices that are widely used with portable devices. They are used with a variety of specialized input devices including digital cameras to store and transfer images and digital media players like the iPod to store and transfer music and video files.

USB Drives

USB drives (flash drives) are so small that they fit onto a key ring. These drives connect to a computer's USB port and are widely used to transfer data and information between computers, specialty devices, and the Internet.

OPTICAL DISCS

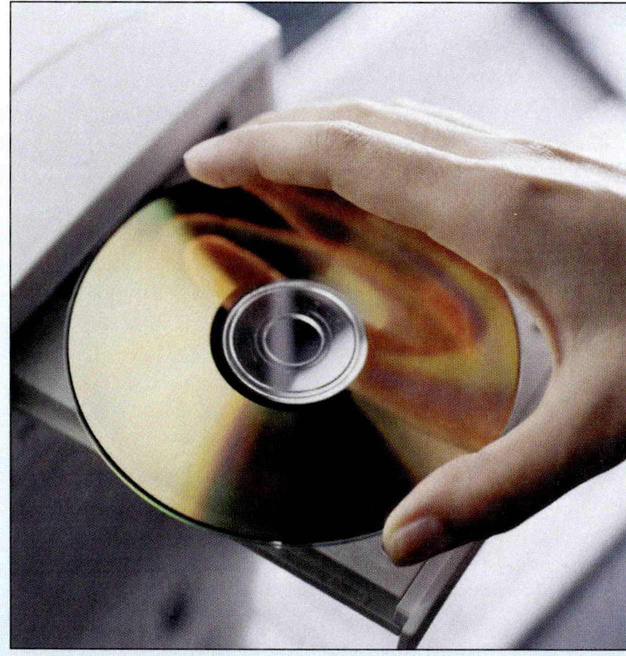

Optical discs use laser technology. 1s and 0s are represented by **pits** and **lands. Optical disc drives** project light and measure the reflected light.

The most widely used optical discs are:

- **Compact discs** (**CDs**) were the first; typical storage 700 MB; often used to store music.
- **Digital versatile discs** (**DVDs**); standard optical discs; typical storage 4.7 GB; often used to store movies and software.
- **Blu-ray discs (BDs**) are the newest; designed to store **hi def (high definition)** video; typical storage 50 GB; often used to store hi def video and video games.

Each of these optical discs has three basic formats:

- **Read-only** (**ROM** for **read-only memory**) discs cannot be written on or erased by the user.
- **Write-once** (**R** for **recordable**) discs can be written on once. After that, they can be read many times but cannot be written on or erased.
- **Rewritable** (**RW** for **rewritable** or **RAM** for **random-access memory**) discs are similar to write-once discs except that the disc surface is not permanently altered when data is recorded.

CLOUD STORAGE

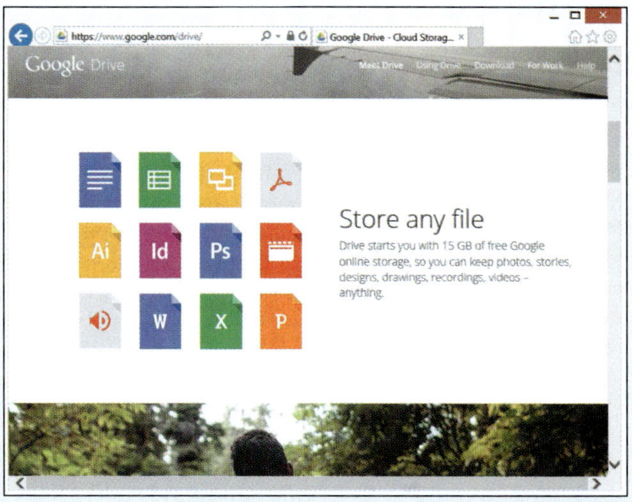

With **cloud computing,** the Internet acts as a "cloud" of servers. **Cloud storage (online storage)** is supplied by these servers.

- Cloud servers provide storage, processing, and memory.
- Advantages for users include less maintenance, fewer hardware upgrades, and easy file sharing and collaboration.
- Disadvantages for users include slower access speed and less control over file security.

MASS STORAGE DEVICES

Mass storage refers to the tremendous amount of secondary storage required by large organizations. **Mass storage devices** are specialized high-capacity secondary storage devices.

Most large organizations have established a strategy called an **enterprise storage system** to promote efficient and safe use of data.

Mass storage devices that support this strategy are **file servers, network attached storage (NAS), RAID systems,** and **organizational cloud storage.** A **storage area network (SAN)** is a method of using enterprise-level remote storage systems as if they were local to your computer.

CAREERS in IT

Disaster recovery specialists are responsible for recovering systems and data after a disaster strikes an organization. Bachelor's or associate's degree in information systems or computer science, experience, and additional skills in the areas of networking, security, and database administration are desirable. Salary range is $70,000 to $88,000.

KEY TERMS

access speed (175)
Blu-ray disc (BD) (180)
capacity (175)
compact disc (CD) (179)
cloud computing (180)
cloud storage (181)
cylinder (175)
density (175)
disaster recovery specialist (185)
disk caching (176)
digital versatile disc or digital video disc (DVD) (179)
enterprise storage system (184)
external hard drive (176)
file compression (177)
file decompression (177)
file server (185)
flash drive (178)
flash memory (178)
flash memory card (178)
hard disk (175)
head crash (176)
hi def (high definition) (180)
internal hard disk (176)
land (179)
mass storage (184)
mass storage devices (184)
media (175)
network attached storage (NAS) (185)
online storage (181)
optical disc (179)
optical disc drive (179)
organizational cloud storage (185)
pit (179)
platter (175)
primary storage (174)
recordable (R) disc (180)
RAID system (185)
random-access memory (RAM) disc (180)
read-only memory (ROM) disc (180)
redundant array of inexpensive disks (RAID) (177)
rewritable (RW) disc (180)
secondary storage (174)
secondary storage device (174)
sector (175)
solid-state drive (SSD) (178)
solid-state storage (178)
storage area network (SAN) (185)
storage device (175)
track (175)
USB drive (178)
write-once disc (180)

MULTIPLE CHOICE

Circle the letter of the correct answer.

1. RAM is sometimes referred to as:
   - **a.** primary storage
   - **b.** ratio active memory
   - **c.** read-only memory
   - **d.** secondary storage
2. The actual physical material that holds the data and programs.
   - **a.** primary storage
   - **b.** media
   - **c.** capacity
   - **d.** access
3. Measures how tightly the magnetic charges can be packed next to one another on the disk.
   - **a.** density
   - **b.** cylinders
   - **c.** tracks
   - **d.** sectors

4. When a read-write head makes contact with the hard disk's surface, it causes a head:
   a. crash
   b. land
   c. pit
   d. scratch
5. This hard-disk performance enhancement anticipates data needs.
   a. disk caching
   b. file compression
   c. file decompression
   d. RAID
6. This type of storage uses pits and lands to represent 1s and 0s.
   a. cloud
   b. hard disk
   c. optical
   d. solid state
7. DVD stands for:
   a. digital versatile disc
   b. digital video data
   c. dynamic versatile disc
   d. dynamic video disc
8. USB drives are also known as:
   a. flash drives
   b. optical drives
   c. ports
   d. universal state bus
9. An organizational strategy to promote efficient and safe use of data across the networks.
   a. cloud dynamic
   b. data mission statement
   c. enterprise storage system
   d. RAID
10. Specialized high-capacity secondary storage devices designed to meet organizational demands.
   a. CD devices
   b. flash drives
   c. mass storage devices
   d. platters

MATCHING

Match each numbered item with the most closely related lettered item. Write your answers in the spaces provided.

a. DVD
b. file compression
c. hi def
d. network attached storage
e. secondary storage
f. sectors
g. solid-state drives
h. storage area network
i. storage devices
j. tracks

___ 1. Provides permanent or nonvolatile storage.
___ 2. Hardware that reads data and programs from storage media.
___ 3. Concentric rings on a hard-disk platter.
___ 4. Each track is divided into invisible wedge-shaped sections called _____ .
___ 5. Increases storage capacity by reducing the amount of space required to store data and programs.
___ 6. Optical disc most common on today's personal computers.
___ 7. The next generation of optical discs.
___ 8. Similar to internal hard-disk drives except they use solid-state memory.
___ 9. Mass storage device widely used for home and small business storage.
___ 10. Architecture to link remote storage devices to computers such that the devices are as available as locally attached drives.

OPEN-ENDED

On a separate sheet of paper, respond to each question or statement.

1. Compare primary storage and secondary storage, and discuss the most important characteristics of secondary storage.
2. Discuss hard disks including density, platters, tracks, sectors, cylinders, head crashes, internal, external, and performance enhancements.
3. Discuss solid-state storage including solid-state drives, flash memory, and USB drives.
4. Discuss optical discs including pits, lands, CDs, DVDs, Blu-ray, and hi def.
5. Discuss cloud computing and cloud storage.
6. Describe mass storage devices including enterprise storage systems, file servers, network attached storage, RAID systems, organizational cloud storage, and storage area network systems.

DISCUSSION

Respond to each of the following questions.

1 Making IT Work for You: CLOUD STORAGE

Have you ever found yourself e-mailing files back and forth between two of your computers or with others as a way to transport them? Review the Making IT Work for You: Cloud Storage on pages 182–183. Then respond to the following: (a) Have you ever used Dropbox or a similar service? If so, what service have you used, and what do you typically use it for? If you have not used Dropbox or a similar service, describe how and why you might use one. (b) If you do not have a Dropbox account, set up a free one and create a Dropbox folder. Use Dropbox to either (1) access a file from another computer or (2) share a file with one of your classmates. Describe your experience. (c) Try a few of Dropbox's features, and describe your experience with these features. (d) Do you see yourself using Dropbox on an everyday basis? Why or why not?

2 Privacy: SECURE DATA DELETION

Once you've deleted a file it's gone forever, right? Wrong. Deleted files can often be recovered and your private information compromised. Review the Privacy box on page 177, and then respond to the following: (a) Have you ever used a secure deletion utility? If so, what one did you use? If not, do you think you might use one in the future? (b) What kinds of files would you consider deleting permanently? Be specific. (c) Even if you are not planning to sell your computer, do you think it would be a good practice to periodically use a secure deletion utility? Why or why not? (d) How would you find a secure deletion utility? Do you think there are any free ones?

3 Ethics: CLOUD STORAGE AND CONFIDENTIALITY

When individuals and businesses store files using cloud services, they expect the cloud company to behave ethically by providing adequate security to protect confidential files. What if this expectation is not met? Review the Ethics box on page 181, and then respond to the following: (a) Would you be comfortable if your attorney stored digital copies of your legal documents in the cloud? What about your doctor or psychologist? Why or why not? (b) Who should be responsible if files stored in the cloud are stolen or viewed by hackers or unethical employees? Who would suffer the consequences? Defend your position. (c) Should laws be created that require cloud storage companies to operate ethically and to assume responsibility for security and confidentiality of stored data? Why or why not? (d) Cloud computers are not necessarily located within the borders of the United States and therefore may not be subject to the same regulations as U.S.-based computers. Do you think that all U.S. companies should be required to keep their cloud servers in this country? Defend your response. (e) How do you feel about storing personal and confidential information in the cloud? Do you currently do it? Why or why not?

4 Environment: SOLID-STATE STORAGE

Did you know that traditional, magnetic hard-disk storage requires more energy than solid-state storage? Review the Environment box on page 178, and then respond to the following: (a) Why do you suppose that less energy is required for solid-state drives? (b) Why are not all hard drives being replaced with solid-state drives? (c) Do you think hard drives will become obsolete in the near future? Why or why not? (d) Would you be willing to pay more for a solid-state drive? If so, how much? If not, why not?

PHOTO CREDITS

CHAPTER 7

Opener: © Krishna Kumar/Getty Images RF; p. 173, 186: © Colin Anderson/Blend Images LLC RF; p. 174, 185: © ColorBlind Images/Getty Images RF; 7-1, p. 187 (top-left): © Nick Koudis/Getty Images RF; 7-5: Courtesy of LaCie; 7-6, p. 188 (top-left): Courtesy of CalDigit, Inc.; 7-8: © MacFormat Magazine/Contributor/ Getty Images; 7-9, p. 188 (top-right): © David Kilpatrick/Alamy; 7-10, p. 188 (bottom-right): Courtesy of Kingston Technology Company, Inc; 7-11, p. 189 (left): © PhotoDisc/Getty Images RF; 7-13, p. 189 (right): Google and the Google logo are registered trademarks of Google Inc. Used with permission; p. 182, 183: Copyright © 2015 Dropbox. Used with permission; 7-15 (top-right): © Copyright 2015, CRU Acquisition Group, LLC. All Rights Reserved; 7-15 (bottom-right): Source: Via Gallery/Flickr/CC.

chapter 8

Communications and Networks

Why should I read this chapter?

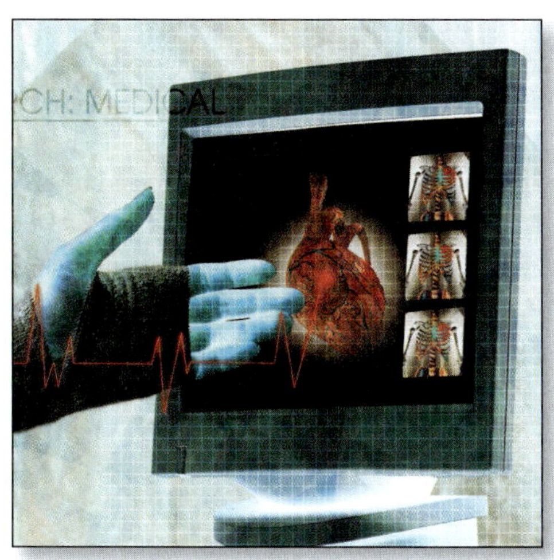

Communication networks are the backbone of nearly every aspect of modern digital life. In the future, telepresence (the ability to fully experience the reality of a different place without actually being there) will be commonplace. For example, doctors will routinely perform surgery on patients located halfway around the world!

This chapter covers the things you need to know to be prepared for this ever-changing digital world, including:

- Wired networks—learn about coaxial and fiber-optic cables so you can make smart decisions about home Internet connections.
- Wireless networks—use your digital devices in smarter and safer ways by understanding Wi-Fi, satellites and Bluetooth.
- Mobile computing—become a digital road warrior using 4G data networks and GPS.

Learning Objectives

After you have read this chapter, you should be able to:

1. Explain connectivity, the wireless revolution, and communication systems.
2. Describe physical and wireless communication channels.
3. Differentiate between connection devices and services including dial-up, DSL, cable, satellite, and cellular.
4. Describe data transmission factors, including bandwidth and protocols.
5. Define networks and key network terminology including network interface cards and network operating systems.
6. Describe different types of networks, including local, home, wireless, personal, metropolitan, and wide area networks.
7. Describe network architectures, including topologies and strategies.
8. Explain the organization issues related to Internet technologies and network security.

Introduction

"Hi, I'm Michael, and I'm a network administrator. I'd like to talk with you about computer communications and networks. I'd also like to talk about technologies that support mobile computing including global positioning systems, Wi-Fi, and 3G and 4G networks."

We live in a truly connected society. We can communicate almost instantaneously with others worldwide; changing events from the smallest of countries and places are immediately broadcast to the world; our e-mail messages are delivered to handheld devices; cars access the Internet to receive driving instructions and solve mechanical problems. Even household appliances can connect to the Internet and be remotely controlled. The communications and information options we have at our fingertips have changed how we react and relate to the world around us.

As the power and flexibility of our communication systems have expanded, the sophistication of the networks that support these systems has become increasingly critical and complex. The network technologies that handle our cellular, business, and Internet communications come in many different forms. Satellites, broadcast towers, telephone lines, even buried cables and fiber optics carry our telephone messages, e-mail, and text messages. These different networks must be able to efficiently and effectively integrate with one another.

To efficiently and effectively use computers, you need to understand the concept of connectivity, wireless networking, and the elements that make up network and communications systems. Additionally, you need to understand the basics of communications channels, connection devices, data transmission, network types, network architectures, and organizational networks.

Communications

Computer communications is the process of sharing data, programs, and information between two or more computers. We have discussed numerous applications that depend on communication systems, including

- **E-mail**—provides a fast, efficient alternative to traditional mail by sending and receiving electronic documents.
- **Texting**—provides very efficient direct text communication between individuals using short electronic messages.
- **Videoconferencing**—provides a very-low-cost alternative to long-distance telephone calls using electronic voice and video delivery.
- **Electronic commerce**—buying and selling goods electronically.

In this chapter, we will focus on the communication systems that support these and many other applications. Connectivity, the wireless revolution, and communication systems are key concepts and technologies for the 21st century.

Connectivity

Connectivity is a concept related to using computer networks to link people and resources. For example, connectivity means that you can connect your personal computer to other computers and information sources almost anywhere. With this connection, you are linked to the world of larger computers and the Internet. This includes hundreds of thousands of web servers and their extensive information resources. Thus, being able to efficiently and effectively use computers becomes a matter of knowing not only about connectivity through networks to personal computers but also about larger computer systems and their information resources.

The Wireless Revolution

Figure 8-1 Wireless revolution

The single most dramatic change in connectivity and communications in the past decade has been the widespread use of mobile devices like smartphones and tablets with wireless Internet connectivity. Students, parents, teachers, businesspeople, and others routinely talk and communicate with these devices. It is estimated that over 1.5 billion smartphones are in use worldwide. This wireless technology allows individuals to stay connected with one another from almost anywhere at any time.

So what's the revolution? While wireless technology was originally used primarily for voice communications, today's mobile computers support e-mail, web access, social networking, and a variety of Internet applications. In addition, wireless technology allows a wide variety of nearby devices to communicate with one another without any physical connection. Wireless communications allows you to share a high-speed printer, share data files, and collaborate on working documents with a nearby co-worker without having your computers connected by cables or telephone. High-speed Internet wireless technology allows individuals to connect to the Internet and share information from almost anywhere in the world. (See Figure 8-1.) But is it a revolution? Most experts say yes and that the revolution is just beginning.

Communication Systems

Communication systems are electronic systems that transmit data from one location to another. Whether wired or wireless, every communication system has four basic elements. (See Figure 8-2.)

- **Sending and receiving devices.** These are often a computer or specialized communication device. They originate (send) as well as accept (receive) messages in the form of data, information, and/or instructions.
- **Connection devices.** These devices act as an interface between the sending and receiving devices and the communication channel. They convert outgoing messages into packets that can travel across the communication channel. They also reverse the process for incoming messages.

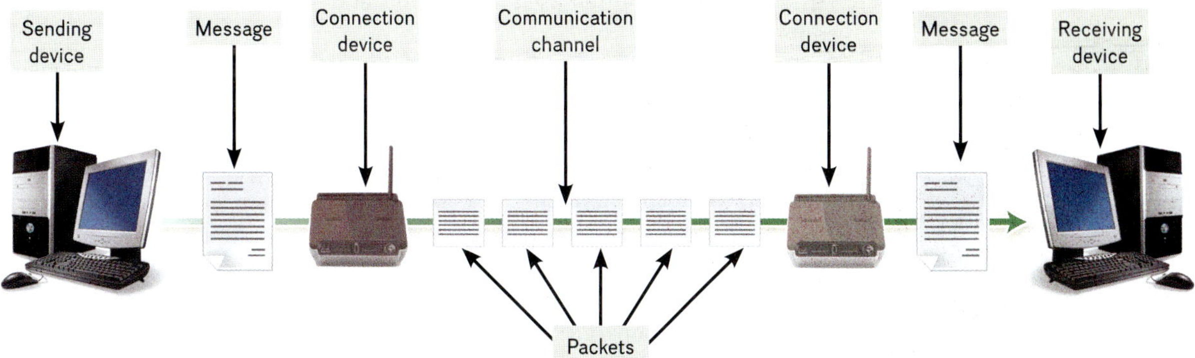

Figure 8-2 Basic elements of a communication system

ethics

As eavesdropping tools become more sophisticated, there is concern that law enforcement and government agencies will monitor everyone's Internet and cell phone activity. In the private sector, companies are increasingly using network tools and software to monitor the activity of their employees. Many websites also track your activity, and government officials have often requested these records during the course of an investigation. Some believe that it is unethical for government and businesses to engage in such monitoring and tracking. Do you agree?

- **Data transmission specifications.** These are rules and procedures that coordinate the sending and receiving devices by precisely defining how the message will be sent across the communication channel.
- **Communication channel.** This is the actual connecting or transmission medium that carries the message. This medium can be a physical wire or cable, or it can be wireless.

For example, if you wanted to send an e-mail to a friend, you could create and send the message using your computer, the *sending device.* Your modem, a *connection device,* would modify and format the message so that it could travel efficiently across *communication channels,* such as telephone lines. The specifics describing how the message is modified, reformatted, and sent would be described in the *data transmission specifications.* After your message traveled across the channel, the receiver's modem, a connection device, would reformat it so that it could be displayed on your friend's computer, the *receiving device.* (Note: This example presents the basic communication system elements involved in sending e-mail. It does not and is not intended to demonstrate all the specific steps and equipment involved in an e-mail delivery system.)

concept check

Define computer communications and connectivity.

What is the wireless revolution?

Describe the four elements of every communication system.

Communication Channels

Communication channels are an essential element of every communication system. These channels actually carry the data from one computer to another. There are two categories of communication channels. One category connects sending and receiving devices by providing a physical connection, such as a wire or cable. The other category is wireless.

Physical Connections

Physical connections use a solid medium to connect sending and receiving devices. These connections include twisted-pair, coaxial, and fiber-optic cables.

Figure 8-3 **Ethernet cable**

Figure 8-4 **Coaxial cable**

Figure 8-5 **Fiber-optic cable**

- **Twisted-pair cable** consists of pairs of copper wire that are twisted together. Both standard **telephone lines** and **Ethernet cables** use twisted pair. (See Figure 8-3.) Ethernet cables are often used in networks and to connect a variety of components to the system unit.
- **Coaxial cable,** a high-frequency transmission cable, replaces the multiple wires of telephone lines with a single solid-copper core. (See Figure 8-4.) In terms of the number of telephone connections, a coaxial cable has over 80 times the transmission capacity of twisted pair. Coaxial cable is used to deliver television signals as well as to connect computers in a network.
- **Fiber-optic cable** transmits data as pulses of light through tiny tubes of glass. (See Figure 8-5.) The data transmission speeds of fiber-optic cables are incredible; recently speeds of 1 petabit per second were measured (a petabit is 1 million gigabits). Compared to coaxial cable, it is lighter, faster, and more reliable at transmitting data. Fiber-optic cable is rapidly replacing twisted-pair cable telephone lines.

Wireless Connections

Wireless connections do not use a solid substance to connect sending and receiving devices. Rather, they move data through the air.

Most wireless connections use radio waves to communicate. For example, smartphones and many other Internet-enabled devices use radio waves to place telephone calls and to connect to the Internet. Primary technologies used for wireless connections are Bluetooth, Wi-Fi, microwave, WiMax, cellular, and satellite connections.

Standard	Maximum speed
802.11g	54 Mbps
802.11n	600 Mbps
802.11ac	2.6 Gbps
802.11ax	10.5 Gbps

Figure 8-6 Wi-Fi standards

- **Bluetooth** is a short-range radio communication standard that transmits data over short distances of up to approximately 33 feet. Bluetooth is widely used for wireless headsets, printer connections, and handheld devices.
- **Wi-Fi (wireless fidelity)** uses high-frequency radio signals to transmit data. A number of standards for Wi-Fi exist, and each can send and receive data at a different speed. (See Figure 8-6.) Most home and business wireless networks use Wi-Fi.
- **Microwave** communication uses high-frequency radio waves. It is sometimes referred to as line-of-sight communication because microwaves can only travel in a straight line. Because the waves cannot bend with the curvature of the earth, they can be transmitted only over relatively short distances. Thus, microwave is a good medium for sending data between buildings in a city or on a large college campus. For longer distances, the waves must be relayed by means of microwave stations with microwave dishes or antennas. (See Figure 8-7.)
- **WiMax (Worldwide Interoperability for Microwave Access)** is a new standard that extends the range of Wi-Fi networks using microwave connections. WiMax is commonly used by universities and others to extend the capability of existing Wi-Fi networks.
- **Cellular** communication uses multiple antennae **(cell towers)** to send and receive data within relatively small geographic regions **(cells).** Most cell phones and mobile devices use cellular networks.
- **Satellite** communication uses satellites orbiting about 22,000 miles above the earth as microwave relay stations. Many of these are offered by Intelsat, the International Telecommunications Satellite Consortium, which is owned by 114 governments and forms a worldwide communication system. Satellites orbit at a precise point and speed above the earth. They can amplify and relay microwave signals from one transmitter on the ground to another. Satellites can be used to send and receive large volumes of data. **Uplink** is a term relating to sending data to a satellite. **Downlink** refers to receiving data from a satellite. The major drawback to satellite communication is that bad weather can sometimes interrupt the flow of data.

  One of the most interesting applications of satellite communications is for global positioning. A network of satellites owned and managed by the Department of Defense continuously sends location information to earth. **Global positioning system (GPS)** devices use that information to uniquely determine the geographic location of the device. Available in many automobiles to provide navigational support, these systems are often mounted into the dash with a monitor to display maps and speakers to provide spoken directions. Most of today's smartphones and tablets use GPS technology for handheld navigation. (See Figure 8-8.)

Figure 8-7 Microwave dish

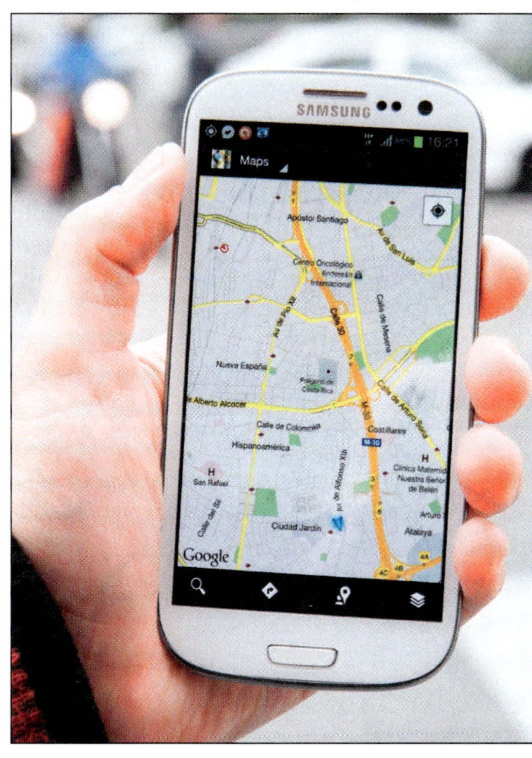

Figure 8-8 GPS navigation

environment

Did you know that GPS technology might help protect the environment? Many cars and mobile devices now have GPS capabilities, and these tools can help save fuel by providing drivers with the shortest route to a destination. Most devices now provide real-time traffic avoidance data, which will reduce the carbon emissions and pollution of cars stuck in traffic. By finding the best routes and avoiding congested areas, you can maximize your fuel efficiency and help protect the environment.

Unlike radio waves, **infrared** uses infrared light waves to communicate over short distances. Like microwave transmissions, infrared is a line-of-sight communication. Because light waves can only travel in a straight line, sending and receiving devices must be in clear view of one another without any obstructions blocking that view. One of the most common infrared devices is the TV remote control.

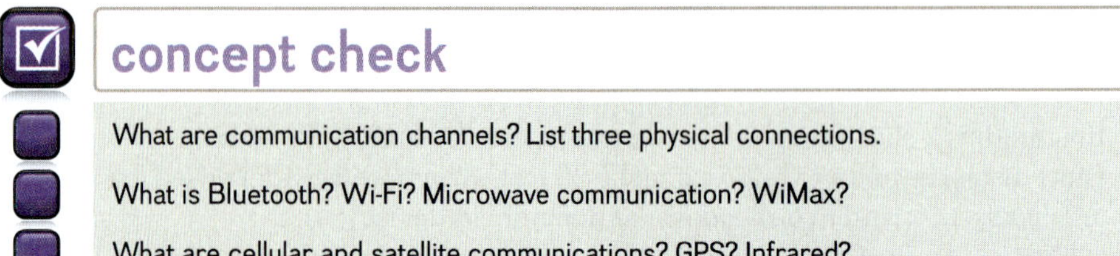

concept check

- What are communication channels? List three physical connections.
- What is Bluetooth? Wi-Fi? Microwave communication? WiMax?
- What are cellular and satellite communications? GPS? Infrared?

Connection Devices

At one time nearly all computer communication used telephone lines. However, because the telephone was originally designed for voice transmission, telephones typically send and receive **analog signals,** which are continuous electronic waves. Computers, in contrast, send and receive **digital signals.** (See Figure 8-9.) These represent the presence or absence of an electronic pulse—the on/off binary signals we mentioned in Chapter 5. To convert the digital signals to analog signals and vice versa, you need a modem.

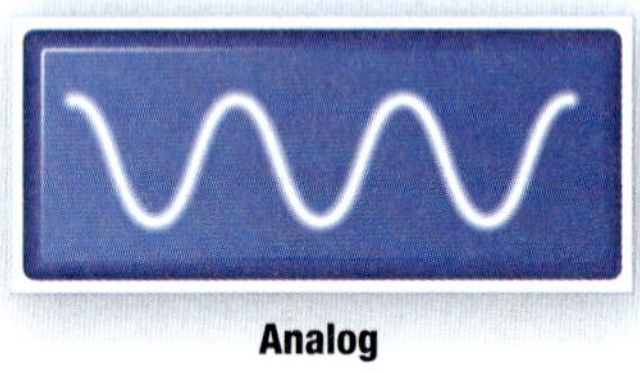

Analog

Digital

Figure 8-9 Analog and digital signals

Modems

The word **modem** is short for *modulator-demodulator.* **Modulation** is the name of the process of converting from digital to analog. **Demodulation** is the process of converting from analog to digital. The modem enables digital personal computers to communicate across different media, including telephone wires, cable lines, and radio waves.

The speed with which modems transmit data varies. This speed, called **transfer rate,** is typically measured in millions of bits **(megabits) per second (Mbps).** (See Figure 8-10.) The higher the speed, the faster you can send and receive information. For example, to download a complete full-length motion picture (700 MB) on a 1.5-Mbps modem would take about 1 hour. Using a 10.0-Mbps modem would take about 9 minutes.

There are three commonly used types of modems: DSL, cable, and wireless. (See Figure 8-11.)

- A **DSL (digital subscriber line)** modem uses standard phone lines to create a high-speed connection directly to your phone company's offices. These devices are usually external and connect to the system unit using either a USB or an Ethernet port.
- A **cable modem** uses the same coaxial cable as your television. Like a DSL modem, a cable modem creates high-speed connections using the system unit's USB or Ethernet port.
- A **wireless modem** is also known as a **WWAN (wireless wide area network) modem.** Almost all computers today have built-in wireless modems. For those that do not, wireless adapter cards are available that plug into USB or special card ports.

Unit	Speed
Mbps	Million bits per second
Gbps	Billion bits per second
Tbps	Trillion bits per second

Figure 8-10 Typical transfer rates

Connection Service

For years, large corporations have been leasing special high-speed lines from telephone companies. Originally, these were copper lines, known as **T1** lines, that could be combined to form higher-capacity options known as **T3** or **DS3** lines. These lines have largely been replaced by faster **optical carrier (OC)** lines.

While the special high-speed lines are too costly for most individuals, Internet service providers (as discussed in Chapter 2) do provide affordable connections.

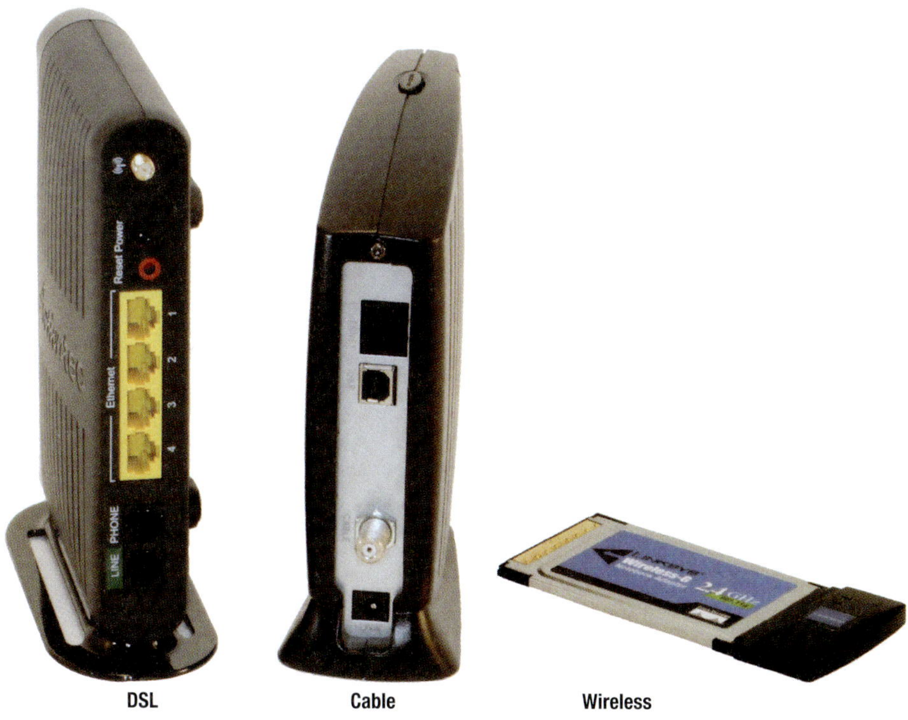

Figure 8-11 **Basic types of modems**

For years, individuals relied on **dial-up services** using existing telephones and telephone modems to connect to the Internet. This type of service has been replaced by higher-speed connection services including DSL, cable, satellite, and cellular services.

- **Digital subscriber line (DSL) service** is provided by telephone companies using existing telephone lines to provide high-speed connections. **ADSL (asymmetric digital subscriber line)** is one of the most widely used types of DSL. DSL is much faster than dial-up.
- **Cable service** is provided by cable television companies using their existing television cables. These connections are usually faster than DSL.
- **Fiber-optic service (FiOS)** is showing up in some areas, but it is a new technology and not widely available. Current providers of FiOS include Google and Verizon with speeds faster than cable or DSL connections.
- **Satellite connection services** use satellites to provide wireless connections. While slower than DSL and cable modem, satellite connections are available almost anywhere using a satellite-receiving disk.
- **Cellular service providers,** including Verizon, AT&T, Sprint, and T-Mobile, support voice and data transmission to wireless devices using cellular networks. These networks have gone through different generations. **First-generation mobile telecommunications (1G)** started in the 1980s using analog radio signals to provide analog voice transmission service. **Second-generation mobile telecommunications (2G)** started in the 1990s using digital radio signals. **Third-generation mobile telecommunications (3G)** started in the 2000s and provided services capable of effective connectivity to the Internet, marking the beginning of smartphones.

  Fourth-generation mobile telecommunications (4G) has begun to replace 3G networks in some areas with providers using **LTE (Long Term Evolution)**

connections to provide faster transmission speeds. While a user's experience with 4G will depend on several factors, including carrier, geography, and proximity to cell towers, 4G technologies can provide speeds up to 10 times faster than 3G.

To learn more about how you can use mobile communications, see Making IT Work for You: Mobile Internet on page 203.

concept check

What is the function of a modem? Compare the three types of modems.

What is a connection service? Compare the five high-speed connection services.

Describe the four generations of mobile communications.

Data Transmission

Several factors affect how data is transmitted. These factors include bandwidth and protocols.

Bandwidth

Bandwidth is a measurement of the width or capacity of the communication channel. Effectively, it means how much information can move across the communication channel in a given amount of time. For example, to transmit text documents, a slow bandwidth would be acceptable. However, to effectively transmit video and audio, a wider bandwidth is required. There are four categories of bandwidth.

- **Voiceband,** also known as **low bandwidth,** is used for standard telephone communication. Personal computers with telephone modems and dial-up service use this bandwidth. While effective for transmitting text documents, it is too slow for many types of transmission, including high-quality audio and video.
- **Medium band** is used in special leased lines to connect midrange computers and mainframes as well as to transmit data over long distances. This bandwidth is capable of very-high-speed data transfer.
- **Broadband** is widely used for DSL, cable, and satellite connections to the Internet. Several users can simultaneously use a single broadband connection for high-speed data transfer.
- **Baseband** is widely used to connect individual computers that are located close to one another. Like broadband, it is able to support high-speed transmission. Unlike broadband, however, baseband can only carry a single signal at a time.

Protocols

For data transmission to be successful, sending and receiving devices must follow a set of communication rules for the exchange of information. These rules for exchanging data between computers are known as **protocols.**

As discussed in Chapter 2, **https,** or **hypertext transfer protocol secure,** is widely used to protect the transfer of sensitive information. Another widely used Internet protocol is **TCP/IP (transmission control protocol/Internet protocol).** The essential features of this protocol involve (1) identifying sending and receiving devices

MOBILE INTERNET

Is your smartphone or tablet always connected to the Internet? Millions have this always-on connection to access their e-mail, favorite websites, cloud services, and apps from anywhere at any time. What can be confusing to many is the variety of connection devices, data plans, and penalties for exceeding usage limits.

Devices There are many devices that can help you get Internet access from wherever you are.

1. ***Smartphones.*** **Most modern smartphones are capable of accessing the Internet via Wi-Fi and 3G or 4G networks.**
2. ***Tablets.*** **Most tablets will provide Wi-Fi access, but to get 3G or 4G capabilities, you will generally have to purchase a higher-priced model.**
3. ***Laptops.*** **By inserting a USB modem, almost all laptops can access the Internet through a 3G or 4G network.**
4. ***Mobile hotspot device.*** **This is a stand-alone device that connects to a 3G or 4G network. It will then allow multiple devices near it to access the Internet via a Wi-Fi connection.**

Many smartphones can provide Wi-Fi sharing, or tethering, like a mobile hotspot device. However, you may have to pay an additional monthly fee.

Data Plans A data plan defines how much data you can download using your 3G or 4G connection. These plans can be very confusing, but for most individuals, the plan that gives you a few gigabytes per month is best. Although a few providers have unlimited data plans, they may slow down, or throttle, your connection speed significantly if they deem that your usage is excessive.

Overage Charges If you exceed the monthly data limit, wireless providers will start charging overage fees. For example, one provider charges $10 for every extra gigabyte used. To minimize overage charges, consider the following:

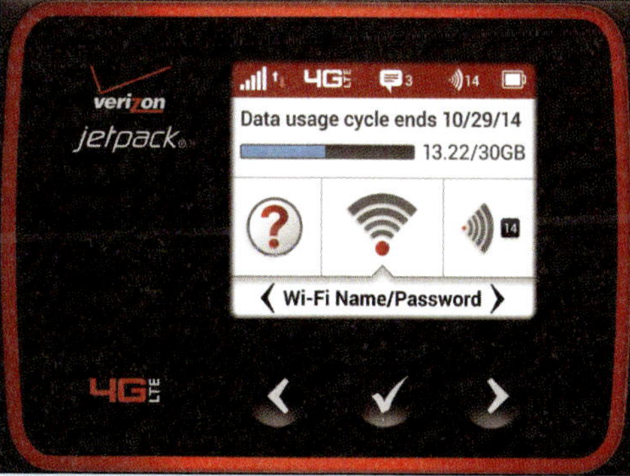

1. ***Wi-Fi access points.*** **Whenever possible, use a Wi-Fi connection. These connections are not subject to your data plan limits. So if you are in a coffee shop that offers free Wi-Fi, use it!**
2. ***Streaming music/video.*** **Streaming too much of any media can quickly become a problem. The solution: Be selective when watching TV shows, movies, and YouTube videos, and try to store some of your music on your device.**
3. ***Downloading.*** **Limit your downloading of new apps and music to Wi-Fi connections only. Many programs and MP3 files can reach (or even exceed) a size of 10 MB.**
4. ***Monitor your data usage.*** **Most wireless companies provide a free app that helps you monitor your minutes, text messages, and data. Keep an eye on this.**

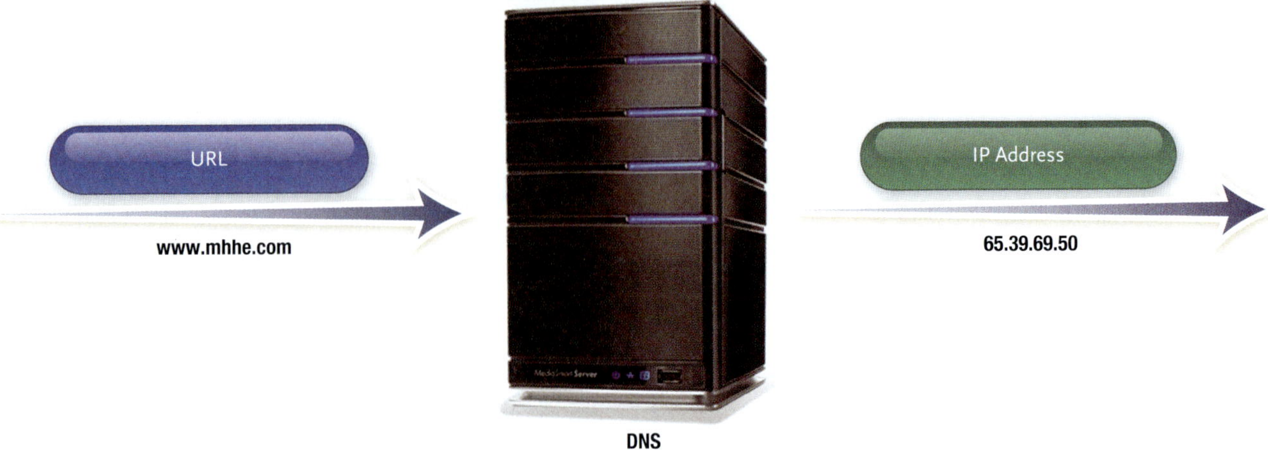

Figure 8-12 **DNS converts text-based addresses to numeric IP addresses**

and (2) breaking information into small parts, or packets, for transmission across the Internet.

- **Identification:** Every computer on the Internet has a unique numeric address called an **IP address (Internet protocol address).** Similar to the way a postal service uses addresses to deliver mail, the Internet uses IP addresses to deliver e-mail and to locate websites. Because these numeric addresses are difficult for people to remember and use, a system was developed to automatically convert text-based addresses to numeric IP addresses. This system uses a **domain name server (DNS)** that converts text-based addresses to IP addresses. For example, whenever you enter a URL, say www.mhhe.com, a DNS converts this to an IP address before a connection can be made. (See Figure 8-12.)
- **Packetization:** Information sent or transmitted across the Internet usually travels through numerous interconnected networks. Before the message is sent, it is reformatted or broken down into small parts called **packets.** Each packet is then sent separately over the Internet, possibly traveling different routes to one common destination. At the receiving end, the packets are reassembled into the correct order.

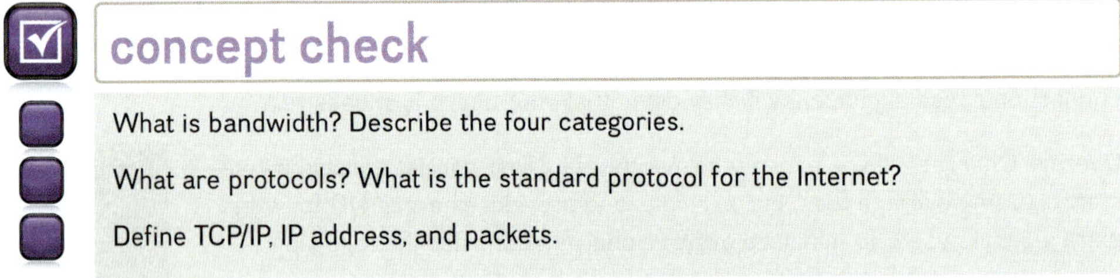

concept check
What is bandwidth? Describe the four categories.
What are protocols? What is the standard protocol for the Internet?
Define TCP/IP, IP address, and packets.

Networks

A **computer network** is a communication system that connects two or more computers so that they can exchange information and share resources. Networks can be set up in different arrangements to suit users' needs. (See Figure 8-13.)

Terms

There are a number of specialized terms that describe computer networks. These terms include

- **Node**—any device that is connected to a network. It could be a computer, printer, or data storage device.

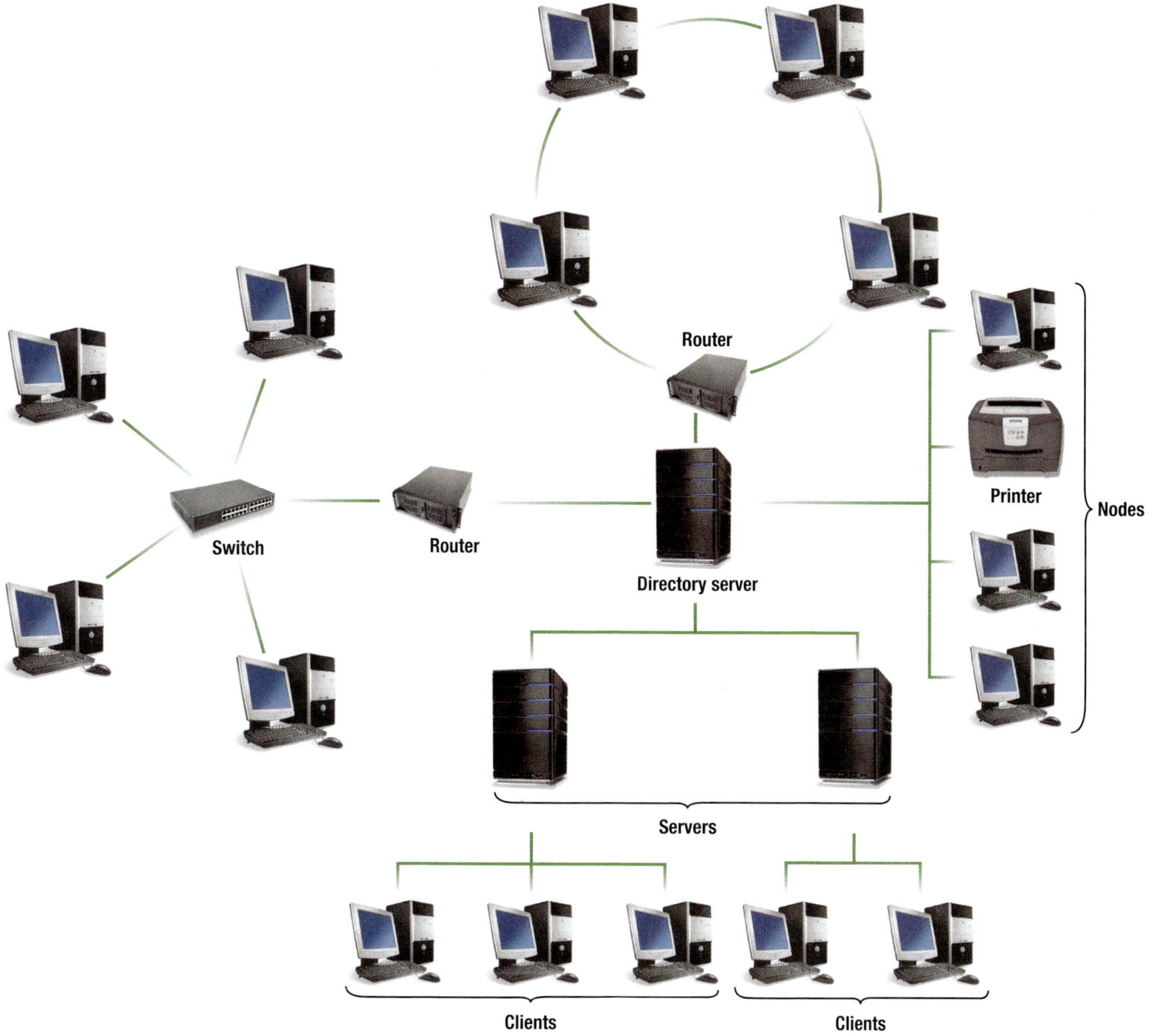

Figure 8-13 **Computer network**

- **Client**—a node that requests and uses resources available from other nodes. Typically, a client is a user's personal computer.
- **Server**—a node that shares resources with other nodes. Dedicated servers specialize in performing specific tasks. Depending on the specific task, they may be called an application server, communication server, database server, file server, printer server, or web server.
- **Directory server**—a specialized server that manages resources, such as user accounts, for an entire network.
- **Host**—any computer system connected to a network that provides access to its resources.
- **Router**—a node that forwards or routes data packets from one network to their destination in another network.
- **Switch**—central node that coordinates the flow of data by sending messages directly between sender and receiver nodes. A **hub** previously filled this purpose by sending a received message to all connected nodes, rather than just the intended node.
- **Network interface cards (NIC)**—as discussed in Chapter 5, these are expansion cards located within the system unit that connect the computer to a network. Sometimes referred to as a LAN adapter.

- **Network operating systems (NOS)**—control and coordinate the activities of all computers and other devices on a network. These activities include electronic communication and the sharing of information and resources.
- **Network administrator**—a computer specialist responsible for efficient network operations and implementation of new networks.

A network may consist only of personal computers, or it may integrate personal computers or other devices with larger computers. Networks can be controlled by all nodes working together equally or by specialized nodes coordinating and supplying all resources. Networks may be simple or complex, self-contained or dispersed over a large geographic area.

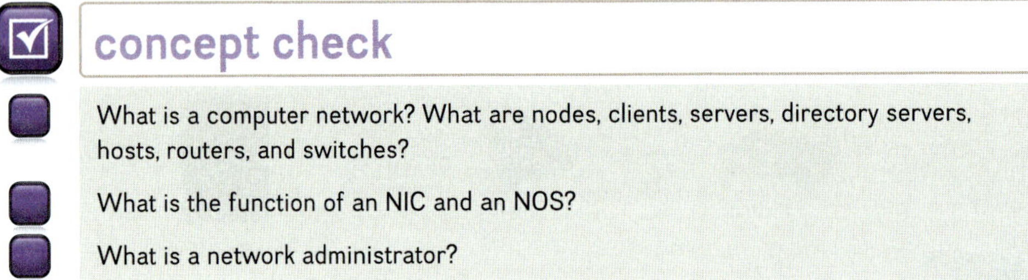

concept check
What is a computer network? What are nodes, clients, servers, directory servers, hosts, routers, and switches?
What is the function of an NIC and an NOS?
What is a network administrator?

Network Types

Clearly, different types of channels—wired or wireless—allow different kinds of networks to be formed. Telephone lines, for instance, may connect communications equipment within the same building or within a home. Networks also may be citywide and even international, using both cable and wireless connections. Local area, metropolitan area, and wide area networks are distinguished by the size of the geographic area they serve.

Local Area Networks

Networks with nodes that are in close physical proximity—within the same building, for instance—are called **local area networks (LANs).** Typically, LANs span distances less than a mile and are owned and operated by individual organizations. LANs are widely used by colleges, universities, and other types of organizations to link personal computers and to share printers and other resources. For a simple LAN, see Figure 8-14.

The LAN represented in Figure 8-14 is a typical arrangement and provides two benefits: economy and flexibility. People can share costly equipment. For instance, the four personal computers share the high-speed laser printer and the file server, which are expensive pieces of hardware. Other equipment or nodes also may be added to the LAN—for instance, more personal computers, a mainframe computer, or optical disc storage devices. Additionally, the **network gateway** is a device that allows one LAN to be linked to other LANs or to larger networks. For example, the LAN of one office group may be connected to the LAN of another office group.

There are a variety of different standards or ways in which nodes can be connected to one another and ways in which their communications are controlled in a LAN. The most common standard is known as **Ethernet.** LANs using this standard are sometimes referred to as Ethernet LANs.

Home Networks

While LANs have been widely used within organizations for years, they are now being commonly used by individuals in their homes and apartments. These LANs, called

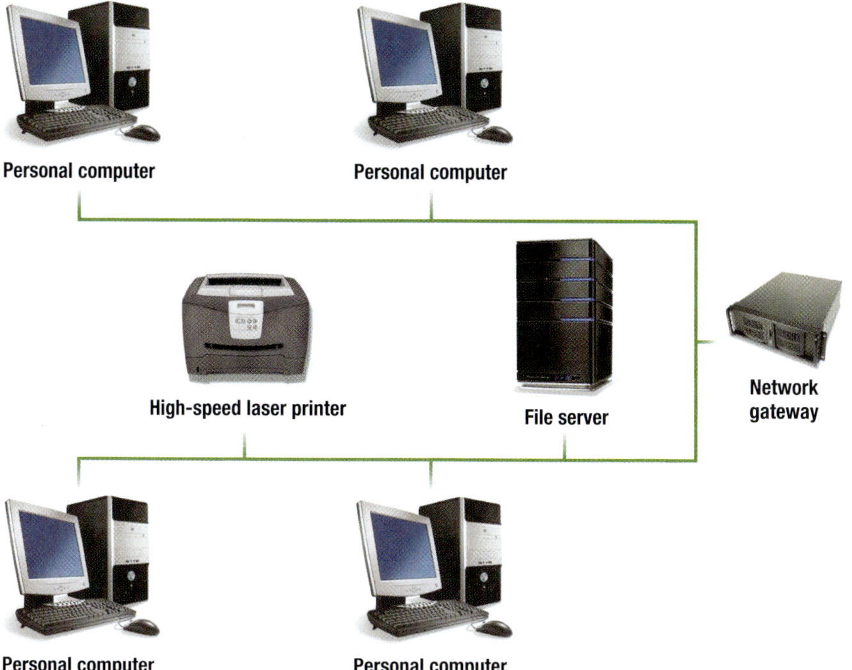

Figure 8-14 Local area network

home networks, allow different computers to share resources, including a common Internet connection. Computers can be connected in a variety of ways, including electrical wiring, telephone wiring, and special cables. One of the simplest ways, however, is without cables, or wireless.

Figure 8-15 Wireless adapter

Wireless LAN

A wireless local area network is typically referred to as a **wireless LAN (WLAN).** It uses radio frequencies to connect computers and other devices. All communications pass through the network's centrally located **wireless access point** or **base station.** This access point interprets incoming radio frequencies and routes communications to the appropriate devices.

Wireless access points that provide Internet access are widely available in public places such as coffee shops, libraries, bookstores, colleges, and universities. These access points are known as **hotspots** and typically use Wi-Fi technology. Many of these services are free and easy to find using free locator sites such as www.hotspot-locations.com. Most mobile computing devices have an internal wireless network card to connect to hotspots. If your mobile device does not have an internal wireless network card, you can use an external wireless adapter (see Figure 8-15) that plugs into your computer's USB port or PC card slot.

Personal Area Network

A **personal area network (PAN)** is a type of wireless network that works within a very small area–your immediate surroundings. PANs connect cell phones to headsets, keyboards to cell phones, and so on. These networks make it possible for wireless devices to interact with each other. The most popular PAN technology is Bluetooth, with a maximum range of around 33 feet. Virtually all wireless peripheral devices available today use Bluetooth, including the controllers on popular game systems like the PlayStation and Wii.

Type	Description
LAN	Local area network; located within close proximity
Home	Local area network for home and apartment use; typically wireless
WLAN	Wireless local area network; all communication passes through access point
PAN	Personal area network; connects digital devices, such as PDAs
MAN	Metropolitan area network; typically spans cities with coverage up to 100 miles
WAN	Wide area network for countrywide or worldwide coverage

Figure 8-16 **Types of networks**

tips **Do you use your laptop to connect to wireless networks at school or in public places such as coffee shops, airports, or hotels? If so, it is important to use caution to protect your computer and your privacy. Here are a few suggestions:**

1. **Use a firewall.** A personal firewall is essential when connecting your computer directly to public networks. Some firewalls, such as the one built into Windows 8 and Windows 10, will ask whether a new network should be treated as home, work, or a public network.
2. **Avoid fake hotspots.** Thieves are known to set up rogue (or fake) hotspots in popular areas where users expect free Wi-Fi, such as coffee shops and airports. Since many operating systems automatically connect to the access point with the strongest signal, you could be connecting to the one set up by the thief. Always confirm that you are connecting to the access point of that establishment. Ask an employee if you are unsure.
3. **Turn off file sharing.** Turning off file-sharing features in your operating system will ensure that no one can access or modify your files.
4. **Check if connection is encrypted.** If the hotspot you are using is protected with a password, then it is likely encrypted. If it is not, then be very careful with websites you visit and the information you provide.

Metropolitan Area Networks

Metropolitan area networks (MAN) span distances up to 100 miles. These networks are frequently used as links between office buildings that are located throughout a city.

Unlike a LAN, a MAN is typically not owned by a single organization. Rather, it is owned either by a group of organizations or by a single network service provider that provides network services for a fee.

Wide Area Networks

Wide area networks (WANs) are countrywide and worldwide networks. These networks provide access to regional service (MAN) providers and typically span distances greater than 100 miles. They use microwave relays and satellites to reach users over long distances—for example, from Los Angeles to Paris. Of course, the widest of all WANs is the Internet, which spans the entire globe.

The primary difference between a PAN, LAN, MAN, and WAN is the geographic range. Each may have various combinations of hardware, such as personal computers, midrange computers, mainframes, and various peripheral devices.

For a summary of network types, see Figure 8-16.

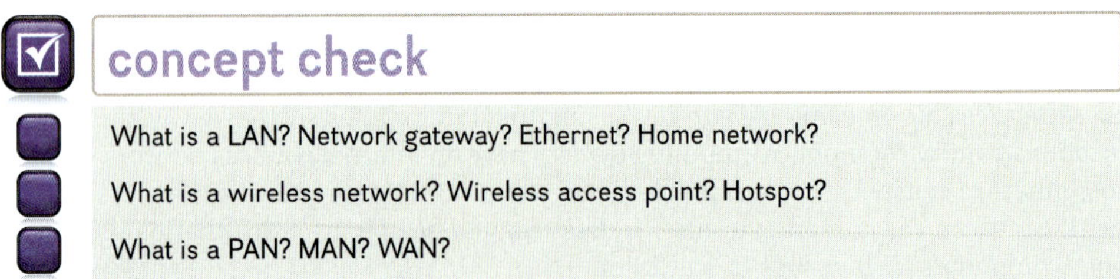

concept check
What is a LAN? Network gateway? Ethernet? Home network?
What is a wireless network? Wireless access point? Hotspot?
What is a PAN? MAN? WAN?

Network Architecture

Network architecture describes how a network is arranged and how resources are coordinated and shared. It encompasses a variety of different network specifics, including network topologies and strategies. Network topology describes the physical arrangement of the network. Network strategies define how information and resources are shared.

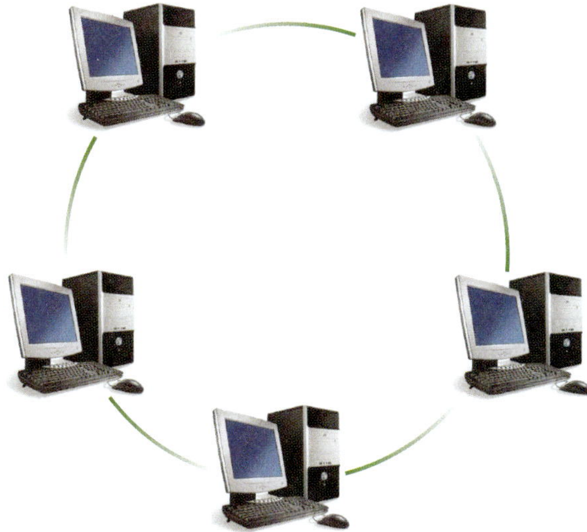
Figure 8-17 Ring network

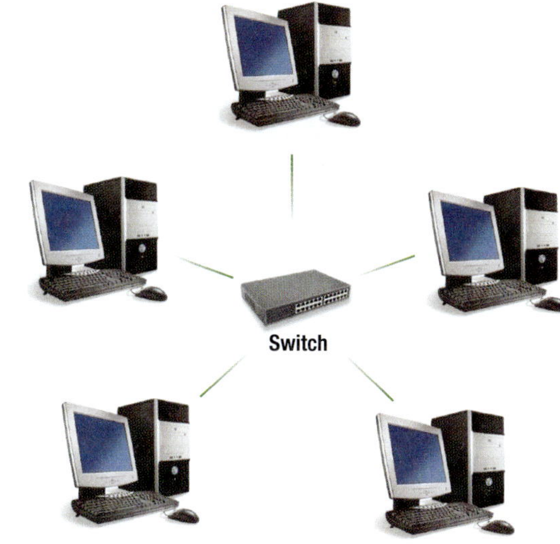

Figure 8-18 Star network

Topologies

A network can be arranged or configured in several different ways. This arrangement is called the network's **topology.** The most common topologies are

- **Bus network**—each device is connected to a common cable called a **bus** or **backbone,** and all communications travel along this bus.
- **Ring network**—each device is connected to two other devices, forming a ring. (See Figure 8-17.) When a message is sent, it is passed around the ring until it reaches the intended destination.
- **Star network**—each device is connected directly to a central network switch. (See Figure 8-18.) Whenever a node sends a message, it is routed to the switch, which then passes the message along to the intended recipient. The star network is the most widely used network topology today. It is applied to a broad range of applications from small networks in the home to very large networks in major corporations.
- **Tree network**—each device is connected to a central node, either directly or through one or more other devices. The central node is connected to two or more subordinate nodes that in turn are connected to other subordinate nodes, and so forth, forming a treelike structure. (See Figure 8-19.) This network, also known as a **hierarchical network,** is often used to share corporatewide data.
- **Mesh network**—this topology is the newest type and does not use a specific physical layout (such as a star or a tree). Rather, the mesh network requires that each node have more than one connection to the other nodes. (See Figure 8-20.) The resulting pattern forms the appearance of a mesh. If a path between two nodes is somehow disrupted, data can be

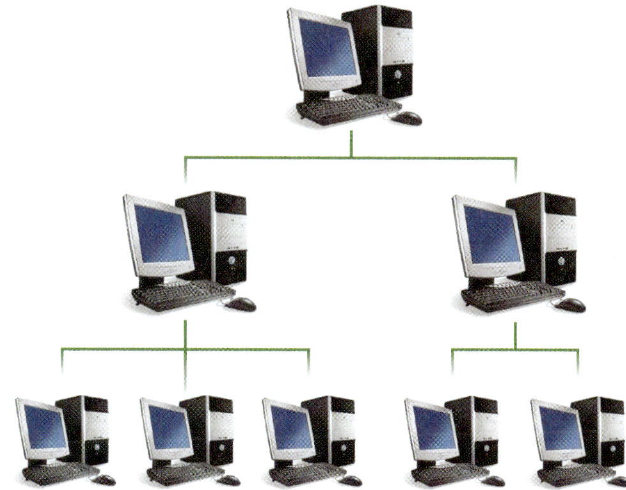
Figure 8-19 Tree network

Figure 8-20 Mesh network

automatically rerouted around the failure using another path. Wireless technologies are frequently used to build mesh networks.

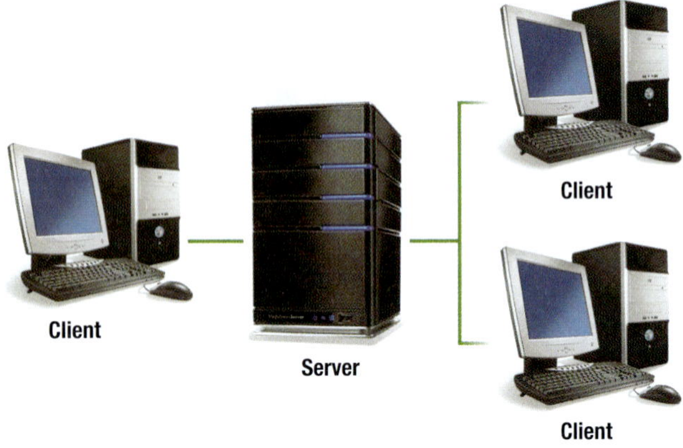

Figure 8-21 **Client/server network**

Strategies

Every network has a **strategy,** or way of coordinating the sharing of information and resources. Two of the most common network strategies are client/server and peer-to-peer.

Client/server networks use central servers to coordinate and supply services to other nodes on the network. The server provides access to resources such as web pages, databases, application software, and hardware. (See Figure 8-21.) This strategy is based on specialization. Server nodes coordinate and supply specialized services, and client nodes request the services. Commonly used server operating systems are Windows Server, Mac OS X Server, Linux, and Solaris.

Client/server networks are widely used on the Internet. For example, each time you open a web browser, your computer (the client) sends out a request for a specific web page. This request is routed over the Internet to a server. This server locates and sends the requested material back to your computer.

One advantage of the client/server network strategy is the ability to handle very large networks efficiently. Another advantage is the availability of powerful network management software to monitor and control network activities. The major disadvantages are the cost of installation and maintenance.

In a **peer-to-peer (P2P) network,** nodes have equal authority and can act as both clients and servers. The most common way to share games, movies, and music over the Internet is to use a P2P network. For example, special file-sharing software such as BitTorrent can be used to obtain files located on another personal computer and also can provide files to other personal computers.

P2P networks are rapidly growing in popularity as people continue to share information with others around the world. The primary advantage is that they are easy and inexpensive (often free) to set up and use. One disadvantage of P2P networks is the lack of security controls or other common management functions. For this reason, few businesses use this type of network to communicate sensitive information.

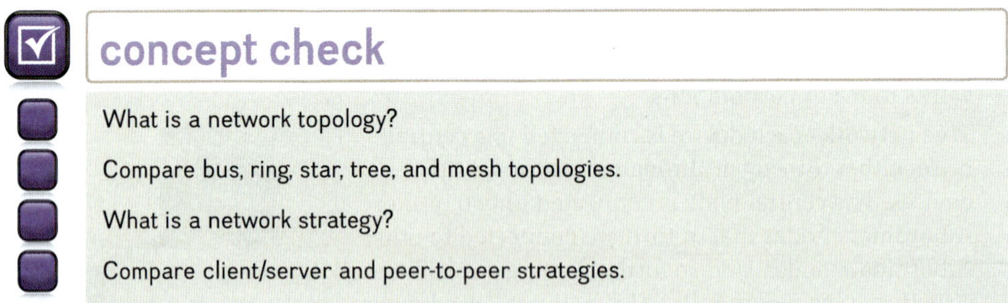

concept check

- What is a network topology?
- Compare bus, ring, star, tree, and mesh topologies.
- What is a network strategy?
- Compare client/server and peer-to-peer strategies.

Organizational Networks

Computer networks in organizations have evolved over time. Most large organizations have a complex and wide range of different network configurations, operating systems, and strategies. These organizations face the challenge of making these networks work together effectively and securely.

Internet Technologies

Many organizations today employ Internet technologies to support effective communication within and between organizations using intranets and extranets.

- An **intranet** is a *private* network within an organization that resembles the Internet. Like the *public* Internet, intranets use browsers, websites, and web pages. Typical applications include electronic telephone directories, e-mail addresses, employee benefit information, internal job openings, and much more. Employees find surfing their organizational intranets to be as easy and as intuitive as surfing the Internet.
- An **extranet** is a *private* network that connects *more than one* organization. Many organizations use Internet technologies to allow suppliers and others limited access to their networks. The purpose is to increase efficiency and reduce costs. For example, an automobile manufacturer has hundreds of suppliers for the parts that go into making a car. By having access to the car production schedules, suppliers can schedule and deliver parts as they are needed at the assembly plants. In this way, operational efficiency is maintained by both the manufacturer and the suppliers.

Network Security

Large organizations face the challenge of ensuring that only authorized users have access to network resources, sometimes from multiple geographic locations or across the Internet. Securing large computer networks requires specialized technology. Three technologies commonly used to ensure network security are firewalls, intrusion detection systems, and virtual private networks.

- A **firewall** consists of hardware and software that control access to a company's intranet and other internal networks. Most use software or a special computer called a **proxy server.** All communications between the company's internal networks and the outside world pass through this server. By evaluating the source and the content of each communication, the proxy server decides whether it is safe to let a particular message or file pass into or out of the organization's network. (See Figure 8-22.)
- **Intrusion detection systems (IDS)** work with firewalls to protect an organization's network. These systems use sophisticated statistical techniques to analyze all incoming and outgoing network traffic. Using advanced pattern matching and heuristics, an IDS can recognize signs of a network attack and disable access before an intruder can do damage.
- **Virtual private networks (VPN)** create a secure private connection between a remote user and an organization's internal network. Special VPN protocols create the equivalent of a dedicated line between a user's home or laptop computer and a company server. The connection is heavily encrypted, and, from the perspective of the user, it appears that the workstation is actually located on the corporate network.

Like organizations, end users have security challenges and concerns. We need to be concerned about the privacy of our personal information. In the next chapter, we will discuss personal firewalls and other ways to protect personal privacy and security.

privacy

Did you know that right now, people are attempting to access private networks that hold your private records and correspondence? Some individuals and governments are continually attempting to gain unauthorized access to networks and to obtain information stored on computers on those networks. Sometimes the objective is simply to create mischief; other times, to steal information or to test the security of a network. While some would say that any type of unauthorized intrusion is an unacceptable violation of privacy, others would say that under certain circumstances (such as homeland security), these intrusions can be essential.

concept check

 What are Internet technologies? Compare intranets and extranets.

 What is a firewall? What is a proxy server?

 What are intrusion detection systems?

 What are virtual private networks?

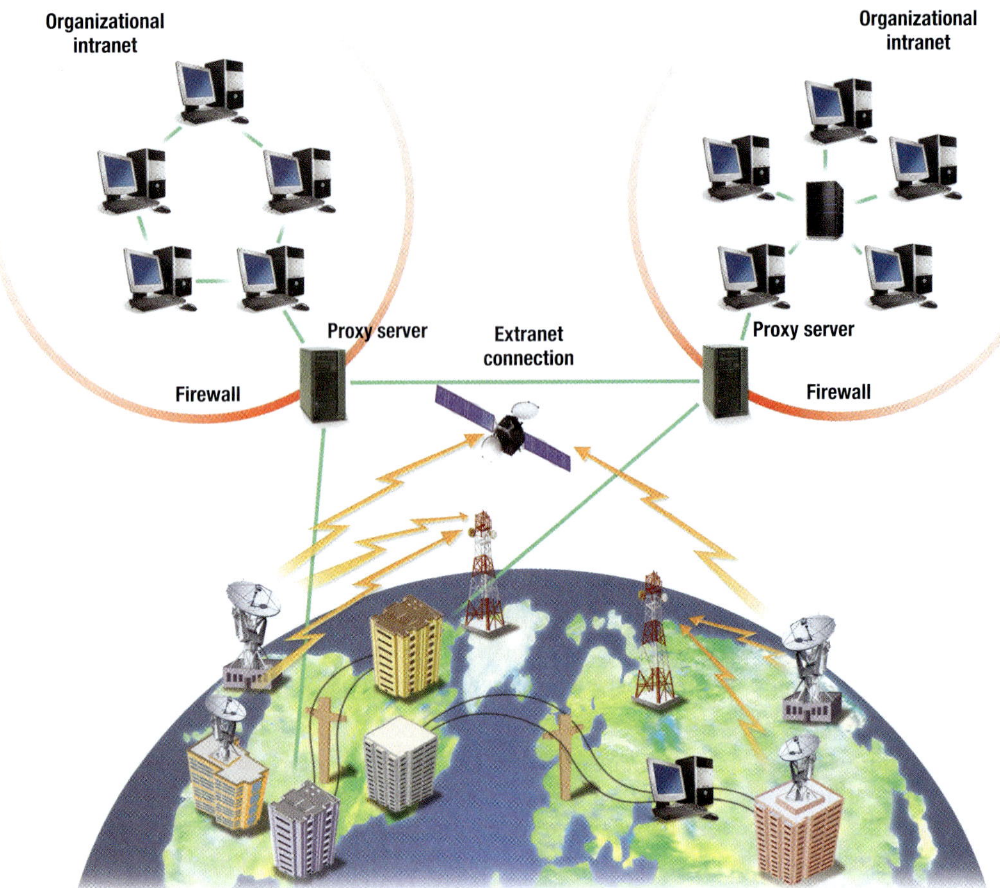

Figure 8-22 **Intranets, extranets, firewalls, and proxy servers**

Careers in IT

"Now that you have learned about computer communications and networks, let me tell you about my career as a network administrator."

Network administrators manage a company's LAN and WAN networks. They may be responsible for design, implementation, and maintenance of networks. Duties usually include maintenance of both hardware and software related to a company's intranet and Internet networks. Network administrators are typically responsible for diagnosing and repairing problems with these networks. Some network administrators' duties include planning and implementation of network security as well.

Employers typically look for candidates with a bachelor's or an associate's degree in computer science, computer technology, or information systems as well as practical networking experience. Experience with network security and maintenance is preferred. Also technical certification may be helpful in obtaining this position. Because network administrators are involved directly with people in many departments, good communication skills are essential.

Network administrators can expect to earn an annual salary of $47,000 to $64,000. Opportunities for advancement typically include upper-management positions. This position is expected to be among the fastest-growing jobs in the near future.

A LOOK TO THE FUTURE

Telepresence Lets You Be There without Actually Being There

How would you like to speak with distant friends or family as though they were in the same room at the touch of a button? Can you imagine receiving a physical examination from a doctor thousands of miles away? All this and more could be possible in the future thanks to the emerging technology known as telepresence. Telepresence can be considered the natural evolution of the phone call, from the analog telephone to the digital video chats of today. In the future, telepresence robots will allow video, audio, and manipulation of real-world objects. Technology has been making better telepresence, and will continue to evolve to improve our lives as we look to the future.

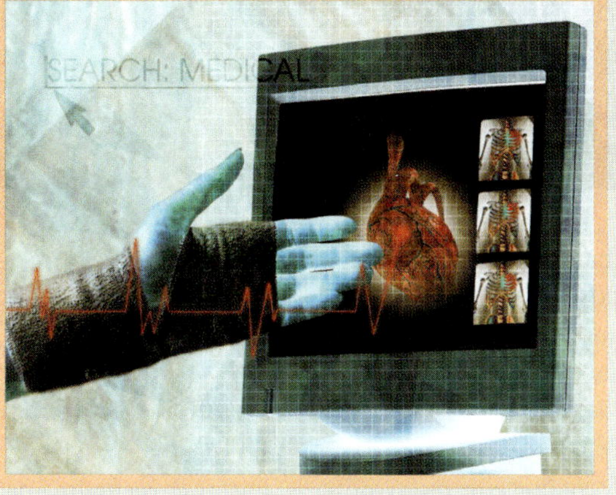

Telepresence seeks to create the illusion that you are actually at a remote location, seeing, hearing, and, someday maybe, even feeling as though you were really there. Today's early implementations, such as Cisco TelePresence, mainly focus on an extension of videoconferencing, allowing people in different locations to conduct meetings as though they are sitting across a table from one another. This illusion is created with very high-definition video, acoustically tuned audio systems, and high-speed networks. However, telepresence could someday go beyond the simple voice and videoconferencing available today, and the applications seem endless.

Robots are quickly becoming a key part of many telepresence applications. In addition to audio and video feeds from another location, robots will bring you the ability to manipulate objects at the remote location. Such robots are already being used in the medical field. In one system, a surgeon uses special controls and screens in one room to control robotic arms that operate on the patient in another room. This type of system could be used to allow expert surgeons to perform several procedures on various patients located throughout the world in just one day!

In addition to manipulating objects, users may one day wear special gloves and other sensors that permit them to feel the objects being touched by the robot. This technology might be used to allow people to work in hazardous areas or perform search and rescue operations from a safe, remote location. A more casual application may see individuals using telepresence as a substitute for traditional vacations. Imagine touring remote cities or touching objects from a shipwreck on a deep-sea diving expedition without the expense, hassle, or risk of travel.

Various research institutions are currently experiencing breakthroughs in the areas of holography, which is technology that creates 3D images, called holograms, that might pave the way to advanced telepresence. In the coming decade, you might be able to interact virtually with others via a projected, 3D hologram of yourself. How would you use telepresence? What benefits do you see from this technology? How might telepresence affect traveling? Do you see any disadvantages?

VISUAL SUMMARY Communications and Networks

COMMUNICATIONS

Communications is the process of sharing data, programs, and information between two or more computers. Applications include e-mail, texting, videoconferencing, and electronic commerce.

Connectivity

Connectivity is a concept related to using computer networks to link people and resources. You can link or connect to large computers and the Internet, providing access to extensive information resources.

The Wireless Revolution

Mobile devices like smartphones and tablets have brought dramatic changes in connectivity and communications. These wireless devices are becoming widely used for computer communication.

Communication Systems

Communication systems transmit data from one location to another. There are four basic elements:

- Sending and receiving devices originate or accept messages.
- Connection devices act as an interface between sending and receiving devices and the communication channel.
- Data transmission specifications are rules and procedures for sending and receiving data.
- Communication channel is the actual connecting or transmission medium for messages.

COMMUNICATION CHANNELS

Communication channels carry data from one computer to another.

Physical Connections

Physical connections use a solid medium to connect sending and receiving devices. Connections include **twisted-pair cable (telephone lines** and **Ethernet cables), coaxial cable,** and **fiber-optic cable.**

Wireless Connections

Wireless connections do not use a solid substance to connect devices. Most use radio waves.

- **Bluetooth**—transmits data over short distances; widely used for a variety of wireless devices.
- **Wi-Fi (wireless fidelity)**—uses high-frequency radio signals; most home and business wireless networks use Wi-Fi.
- **Microwave**—line-of-sight communication; used to send data between buildings; longer distances require microwave stations.
- **WiMax (Worldwide Interoperability for Microwave Access)**—extends the range of Wi-Fi networks using microwave connections.
- **Cellular**—uses **cell towers** to send and receive data within relatively small geographic regions or **cells.**
- **Satellite**—uses microwave relay stations; **GPS (global positioning system)** tracks geographic locations.
- **Infrared**—uses light waves over a short distance; line-of-sight communication.

To efficiently and effectively use computers, you need to understand the concepts of connectivity, the wireless revolution, and communication systems. Additionally, you need to know the essential parts of communication technology, including channels, connection devices, data transmission, networks, network architectures, and network types.

CONNECTION DEVICES

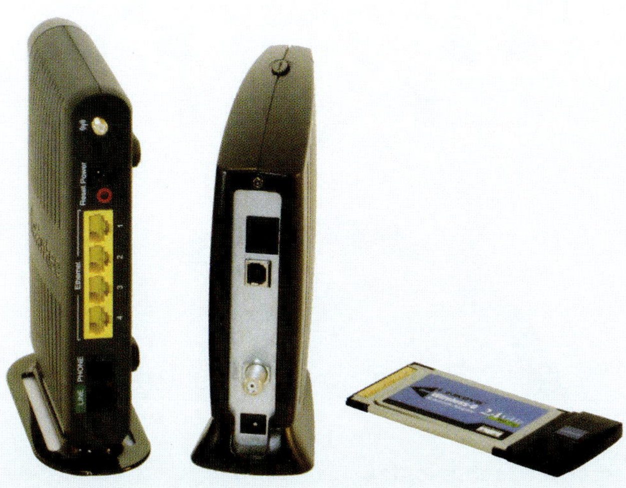

Many communication systems use standard telephone lines and **analog signals.** Computers use **digital signals.**

Modems

Modems modulate and **demodulate. Transfer rate** is measured in **megabits per second.** Three types are **DSL, cable,** and **wireless (wireless wide area network, WWAN).**

Connection Service

T1, T3 (DS3), and **OC (optical carrier)** lines provide support for very-high-speed, all-digital transmission for large corporations. More affordable technologies include **dial-up, DSL (digital subscriber line), ADSL** (widely used), **cable, fiber-optic service (FiOS), satellite,** and **cellular services. 4G (fourth-generation mobile telecommunications)** can provide 10 times faster speeds than **3G** using **LTE (Long Term Evolution)** connections.

DATA TRANSMISSION

Bandwidth measures a communication channel's width or capacity. Four bandwidths are **voiceband (low bandwidth), medium band, broadband** (high-capacity transmissions), and **baseband. Protocols** are rules for exchanging data. Widely used Internet protocols include **https** and **TCP/IP. IP addresses (Internet protocol addresses)** are unique numeric Internet addresses. **DNS (domain name server)** converts text-based addresses to and from numeric IP addresses. **Packets** are small parts of messages.

NETWORKS

Computer networks connect two or more computers. Some specialized network terms include

- **Node**—any device connected to a network.
- **Client**—node requesting resources.
- **Server**—node providing resources.
- **Directory server**—specialized node that manages resources.
- **Host**—any computer system that provides access to its resources over a network.
- **Router**—a node that forwards data packets from one network to another network.
- **Switch**—node that coordinates direct flow of data between other nodes. **Hub** is an older device that directed flow to all nodes.
- **NIC (network interface card)**—LAN adapter card for connecting to a network.
- **NOS (network operating system)**—controls and coordinates network operations.
- **Network administrator**—network specialist responsible for network operations.

NETWORK TYPES

Networks can be citywide or even international, using both wired and wireless connections.

- **Local area networks (LANs)** connect nearby devices. **Network gateways** connect networks to one another. **Ethernet** is a LAN standard. These LANs are called Ethernet LANs.
- **Home networks** are LANs used in homes.
- **Wireless LANs (WLANs)** use a **wireless access point (base station)** as a hub. Hotspots provide Internet access in public places.
- **Personal area networks (PANs)** are wireless networks for PDAs, cell phones, and other wireless devices.
- **Metropolitan area networks (MANs)** link office buildings within a city, spanning up to 100 miles.
- **Wide area networks (WANs)** are the largest type. They span states and countries or form worldwide networks. The Internet is the largest wide area network in the world.

NETWORK ARCHITECTURE

Network architecture describes how networks are arranged and resources are shared.

Topologies

A network's **topology** describes the physical arrangement of a network.

- **Bus network**—each device is connected to a common cable called a **bus** or **backbone.**
- **Ring network**—each device is connected to two other devices, forming a ring.
- **Star network**—each device is connected directly to a central network switch; most common type today.
- **Tree (hierarchical) network**—a central node is connected to subordinate nodes forming a treelike structure.
- **Mesh network**—newest; each node has two or more connecting nodes.

Strategies

Every network has a **strategy,** or way of sharing information and resources. Common network strategies include client/server and peer-to-peer.

- **Client/server (hierarchical) network**—central computers coordinate and supply services to other nodes; based on specialization of nodes; widely used on the Internet; able to handle very large networks efficiently; powerful network management software available.
- **Peer-to-peer network**—nodes have equal authority and act as both clients and servers; widely used to share games, movies, and music over the Internet; easy to set up and use; lacks security controls.

ORGANIZATIONAL NETWORKS

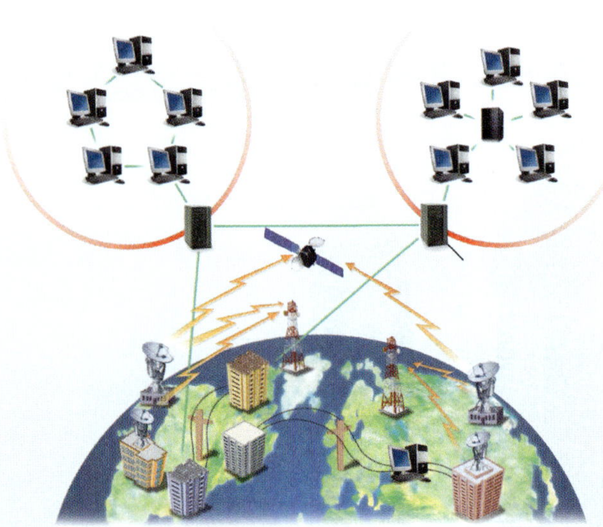

Internet Technologies

Internet technologies support effective communication using intranets and extranets.

- **Intranet**—private network within an organization; uses browsers, websites, and web pages. Typical applications include electronic telephone directories, e-mail addresses, employee benefit information, internal job openings, and much more.
- **Extranet**—like intranet except connects *more than one* organization; typically allows suppliers and others limited access to their networks.

Network Security

Three technologies commonly used to ensure network security are firewalls, intrusion detection systems, and virtual private networks.

- **Firewall**—controls access; all communications pass through **proxy server.**
- **Intrusion detection systems (IDS)**—work with firewalls; use sophisticated statistical techniques to recognize and disable network attacks.
- **Virtual private network (VPN)**—creates secure private connection between remote user and organization's internal network.

CAREERS in IT

Network administrators manage a company's LAN and WAN networks. Bachelor's or associate's degree in computer science, computer technology, or information systems and practical networking experience required. Salary range is $47,000 to $64,000.

KEY TERMS

1G (first-generation mobile telecommunications) (201)
2G (second-generation mobile telecommunications) (201)
3G (third-generation mobile telecommunications) (201)
4G (fourth-generation mobile telecommunications) (201)
analog signal (200)
asymmetric digital subscriber line (ADSL) (201)
backbone (209)
bandwidth (202)
base station (207)
baseband (202)
Bluetooth (199)
broadband (202)
bus (209)
bus network (209)
cable modem (200)
cable service (201)
cellular (199)
cellular service provider (201)
cell (199)
cell tower (199)
client (205)
client/server network (210)
coaxial cable (198)
communication channel (198)
communication system (197)
computer network (204)
connectivity (196)
demodulation (200)
dial-up service (201)
digital signal (200)
digital subscriber line (DSL) (200)
digital subscriber line (DSL) service (201)
directory server (205)
domain name server (DNS) (204)
downlink (199)
DS3 (200)
Ethernet (206)
Ethernet cable (198)
extranet (211)
fiber-optic cable (198)
fiber-optic service (FiOS) (201)
firewall (211)
global positioning system (GPS) (199)
hierarchical network (209)
home network (207)
host (205)
hotspot (207)
https (hypertext transfer protocol secure) (202)
hub (205)
infrared (200)
intranet (211)
intrusion detection system (IDS) (211)
IP address (Internet protocol address) (204)
local area network (LAN) (206)
low bandwidth (202)
LTE (Long Term Evolution) (201)
medium band (202)
megabits per second (Mbps) (200)
mesh network (209)
metropolitan area network (MAN) (208)
microwave (199)
modem (200)
modulation (200)
network administrator (206, 212)
network architecture (208)
network gateway (206)
network interface card (NIC) (205)
network operating system (NOS) (206)
node (204)
optical carrier (OC) (200)
packet (204)
peer-to-peer (P2P) network (210)
personal area network (PAN) (207)
protocol (202)
proxy server (211)
ring network (209)
router (205)
satellite (199)
satellite connection service (201)
server (205)
star network (209)
strategy (210)
switch (205)
T1 (200)
T3 (200)
telephone line (198)
topology (209)
transfer rate (200)
transmission control protocol/Internet protocol (TCP/IP) (202)
tree network (209)
twisted-pair cable (198)
uplink (199)
virtual private network (VPN) (211)
voiceband (202)
wide area network (WAN) (208)
Wi-Fi (wireless fidelity) (199)
WiMax (Worldwide Interoperability for Microwave Access) (199)
wireless access point (207)
wireless LAN (WLAN) (207)
wireless modem (200)
wireless wide area network (WWAN) modem (200)

MULTIPLE CHOICE

Circle the letter of the correct answer.

1. The concept related to using computer networks to link people and resources.
   a. connectivity
   b. GPS
   c. TCP/IP
   d. Wi-Fi
2. A high-frequency transmission cable that delivers television signals as well as connects computers in a network.
   a. coaxial
   b. hi def
   c. 3D
   d. twisted pair
3. A short-range radio communication standard that transmits data over short distances of up to approximately 33 feet.
   a. Bluetooth
   b. broadband
   c. DSL
   d. TCP/IP
4. The speed with which a modem transmits data is called its:
   a. digital velocity
   b. dynamic rate
   c. modular rating
   d. transfer rate
5. The bandwidth typically used for DSL, cable, and satellite connections to the Internet.
   a. baseband
   b. broadband
   c. medium band
   d. voiceband
6. Every computer on the Internet has a unique numeric address called a(n):
   a. IP address
   b. DNS
   c. broadcast
   d. packet
7. Sometimes referred to as a LAN adapter, these expansion cards connect a computer to a network.
   a. PCMCIA
   b. NIC
   c. server
   d. VPN
8. A device that allows one LAN to be linked to other LANs or to larger networks.
   a. IDS
   b. network gateway
   c. PAN
   d. switch
9. Typically using Wi-Fi technology, these wireless access points are available from public places such as coffee shops, libraries, bookstores, colleges, and universities.
   a. hotspots
   b. extranets
   c. PANs
   d. LANs
10. Bus, ring, star, tree, and mesh are five types of network:
   a. topologies
   b. protocols
   c. strategies
   d. devices

MATCHING

Match each numbered item with the most closely related lettered item. Write your answers in the spaces provided.

- **a.** analog
- **b.** bus
- **c.** intrusion detection systems
- **d.** microwave
- **e.** network administrator
- **f.** node
- **g.** peer-to-peer
- **h.** protocols
- **i.** TCP/IP
- **j.** tree

___ **1.** Type of network topology in which each device is connected to a common cable called a backbone.

___ **2.** A widely used Internet protocol.

___ **3.** Uses high-frequency radio waves.

___ **4.** Signals that are continuous electronic waves.

___ **5.** Rules for exchanging data between computers.

___ **6.** Any device that is connected to a network.

___ **7.** A computer specialist responsible for efficient network operations and implementation of new networks.

___ **8.** This network, also known as a hierarchical network, is often used to share corporatewide data.

___ **9.** In this network, nodes have equal authority and can act as both clients and servers.

___ **10.** Work with firewalls to protect an organization's network.

OPEN-ENDED

On a separate sheet of paper, respond to each question or statement.

1. Define communications including connectivity, the wireless revolution, and communication systems.
2. Discuss communication channels including physical connections and wireless connections.
3. Discuss connection devices including modems (DSL, cable, and wireless modems) and connection services (DSL, ADSL, cable, satellite, and cellular connection services).
4. Discuss data transmission including bandwidths (voiceband, medium band, broadband, and baseband) as well as protocols (IP addresses, domain name servers, and packetization).
5. Discuss networks by identifying and defining specialized terms that describe computer networks.
6. Discuss network types including local area, home, wireless, personal, metropolitan, and wide area networks.
7. Define network architecture including topologies (bus, ring, star, tree, and mesh) and strategies (client/server and peer-to-peer).
8. Discuss organization networks including Internet technologies (intranets and extranets) and network security (firewalls, proxy servers, intrusion detection systems, and virtual private networks).

DISCUSSION

Respond to each of the following questions.

1 Making IT Work for You: MOBILE INTERNET

Is your smartphone or tablet always connected to the Internet? Review the Making IT Work for You: Mobile Internet on page 203, and then respond to the following: (a) What mobile Internet devices do you currently use? If you do not own any, which device do you feel would be most beneficial to you? (b) Do you currently have a 3G or 4G data plan for your mobile device? If so, provide details on your plan and why you chose it. Otherwise, describe what your ideal data plan would include. (c) Have you, a friend, or a family member ever gone over the data limit and/or been throttled? What sorts of activities are typically responsible for excessive data usage? (d) Go to the websites of at least two wireless companies, and compare their data plans. How are they similar? How are they different?

2 Privacy: UNAUTHORIZED NETWORK INTRUSION

Unauthorized network access is common today. Review the Privacy box on page 211, and then respond to the following: (a) Some argue that some networks must be penetrated and that the loss in privacy is outweighed by other concerns. Others suggest that we have already sacrificed too much privacy. What do you think? Defend your position. (b) Are there any circumstances when unauthorized network access can be justified? Be specific. (c) Is it acceptable for the U.S. government to support unauthorized network access to obtain information about other countries including terrorist activities? (d) Is it acceptable for other countries to attempt to gain unauthorized access to U.S. government networks? Why or why not?

3 Ethics: ELECTRONIC MONITORING

Many companies, websites, and law enforcement and various government agencies engage in monitoring or tracking Internet activity. Review the Ethics box on page 198, and respond to the following: (a) Is it unethical for an organization or corporation to use programs to monitor communications on its network? Why or why not? (b) Is it unethical for a government agency (such as the FBI) to monitor communications on the Internet or gather your records from the websites you visit? Why or why not? (c) Do you feel that new laws are needed to handle these issues? How would you balance the needs of companies and the government with the needs of individuals? Explain your answers.

4 Environment: GPS

Did you know that GPS technology might help protect the environment? Review the Environment box on page 200, and then respond to the following: (a) Identify ways in which GPS could benefit the environment. You need not limit your response to applications in motor vehicles. (b) Have you used a GPS device or mobile navigation app? If so, describe what you used it for. If not, do you think that you will in the near future? (c) Do you think that GPS should be standard equipment for every new car? Why or why not? (d) Do you think that it should be required by law? Why or why not?

PHOTO CREDITS

CHAPTER 8

Opener: © Digital Vision/Punchstock RF; p. 195, 213: © Brand X Pictures/Punchstock RF; p. 196, 212: © Jetta Productions/The Image Bank/Getty Images; 8-1, p. 214 (left): © Alberto Pomares/Getty Images RF; 8-4, 8-5, 8-11 (all), p. 215 (both): © Willis Technology; 8-7, p. 214 (right): © Stuart Gregory/Photodisc/Getty Images RF; 8-8: © Alex Segre/Alamy; p. 203 (top): Holger Motzkau 2010, Wikipedia/Wikimedia Commons; p. 203 (bottom): © 2015 Verizon Wireless; 8-15: © Ilya Starikov/Alamy RF.

chapter 9 Privacy, Security, and Ethics

Why should I read this chapter?

Right now, criminals are trying to break into your e-mail, your online bank account, and even your cell phone. Organizations are recording and analyzing your every digital decision, leading many to believe that the future of the Internet will result in the end of privacy as we know it.

This chapter covers the things you need to know to be prepared for this ever-changing digital world, including:

- Cybercrime—protect yourself from viruses, Internet scams, and identity theft.
- Privacy rights—learn what companies can legally record about your Internet usage and how they use that information.
- Safe computing—avoid embarrassment and worse by knowing the way Facebook and social networking share your information.

Learning Objectives

After you have read this chapter, you should be able to:

1. Identify the most significant concerns for effective implementation of computer technology.
2. Discuss the primary privacy issues of accuracy, property, and access.
3. Describe the impact of large databases, private networks, the Internet, and the web on privacy.
4. Discuss online identity and the major laws on privacy.
5. Discuss cybercrimes including creation of malicious programs such as viruses, worms, Trojan horses, and zombies as well as denial of service attacks, Internet scams, identity theft, cyberbullying, rogue Wi-Fi hotspots, and data manipulation.
6. Detail ways to protect computer security including restricting access, encrypting data, anticipating disasters, and preventing data loss.
7. Discuss computer ethics including copyright law, software piracy, digital rights management, the Digital Millennium Copyright Act, as well as plagiarism and ways to identify plagiarism.

Introduction

"Hi, I'm Anthony, and I'm an IT security analyst. I'd like to talk with you about privacy, security, and ethics, three critical topics for anyone who uses computers today. I would also like to talk about how you can protect your privacy, ensure your security, and act ethically."

There are more than one billion personal computers in use today. What are the consequences of the widespread presence of this technology? Does technology make it easy for others to invade our personal privacy? When we apply for a loan or for a driver's license, or when we check out at the supermarket, is that information about us being distributed and used without our permission? When we use the web, is information about us being collected and shared with others?

This technology prompts lots of questions—very important questions. Perhaps these are some of the most important questions for the 21st century. To efficiently and effectively use computers, you need to be aware of the potential impact of technology on people and how to protect yourself on the web. You need to be sensitive to and knowledgeable about personal privacy and organizational security.

People

As we have discussed, information systems consist of people, procedures, software, hardware, data, and the Internet. This chapter focuses on people. While most everyone agrees that technology has had a very positive impact on people, it is important to recognize the negative, or potentially negative, impacts as well.

Effective implementation of computer technology involves maximizing its positive effects while minimizing its negative effects. The most significant concerns are

- **Privacy:** What are the threats to personal privacy, and how can we protect ourselves?
- **Security:** How can access to sensitive information be controlled, and how can we secure hardware and software?
- **Ethics:** How do the actions of individual users and companies affect society?

Let us begin by examining privacy.

Privacy

Technology makes it possible to collect and use data of all kinds, including information about people. The websites you visit, the stores where you shop, and the telephone calls you make are all examples of information about you. How would you feel if you learned such information was being collected or shared? Would it matter who was collecting it, or how it was being used, or whether it was even correct?

Privacy concerns the collection and use of data about individuals. There are three primary privacy issues:

- **Accuracy** relates to the responsibility of those who collect data to ensure that the data is correct.
- **Property** relates to who owns data.
- **Access** relates to the responsibility of those who have data to control who is able to use that data.

privacy

An Unmanned Aerial Vehicle (UAV or drone) is an aircraft without a human pilot. The U.S. military uses drones to take photographs, record videos, and run bombing missions without risk to American pilots. Drones are also used domestically to patrol the U.S. borders and to observe private locations in search of drugs. Opponents of drones say that they violate personal privacy rights; proponents of drones say that as long as the drone is in public air space, it does not violate personal privacy rights. What do you think? If a drone were to observe your backyard, would it be violating your privacy rights? What if a drone observed and/or took photographs through the windows in your home? Do drones have the right to track you when you go to public places? Should drones be used to follow and photograph individuals in public places?

Large Databases

Large organizations are constantly compiling information about us. The federal government alone has over 2,000 databases. Every day, data is gathered about us and stored in large databases. For example, telephone companies compile lists of the calls we make, the numbers called, locations from GPS-enabled smartphones, and so on. Credit card companies maintain user databases that track cardholder purchases, payments, and credit records. Supermarket scanners in grocery checkout counters record what we buy, when we buy it, how much we buy, and the price. Financial institutions, including banks and credit unions, record how much money we have, what we use it for, and how much we owe. Search engines record the search histories of their users including search topics and sites visited. Social networking sites collect every entry.

Effectively, every digital event—whether using a telephone or smartphone, buying a product or service, or sending or receiving any electronic communication—is collected and recorded. As a result, the size and the number of databases are exploding. In fact, it is widely reported that 90 percent of all of today's digitally stored data was collected in just the last two years. This ever-growing volume of data is often referred to as **big data.**

A vast industry of data gatherers known as **information resellers** or **information brokers** now exists that collects, analyzes, and sells such personal data. (See Figure 9-1.) Using publicly available databases and in many cases nonpublic databases, information resellers create **electronic profiles,** or highly detailed and personalized descriptions of individuals.

Almost certainly, you have an electronic profile that includes your name, address, telephone number, Social Security number, driver's license number, bank account numbers, credit card numbers, telephone records, shopping and purchasing patterns, and

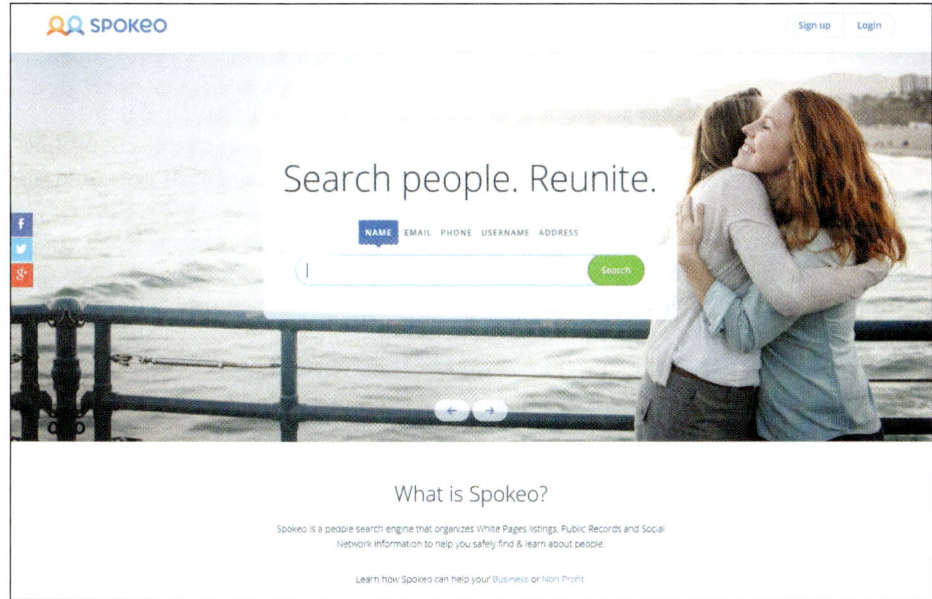

Figure 9-1 **Information reseller's website**

Figure 9-2 **Google Street View**

more. Information resellers sell these electronic profiles to direct marketers, fund-raisers, and others. Many provide these services on the web for free or for a nominal cost.

These profiles can reveal more than you might wish to make public and have an impact beyond what you might imagine. This raises many important issues, including

- **Collecting public, but personally identifying, information:** What if people anywhere in the world could view detailed images of you, your home, or your vehicle? Using detailed images captured with a specially equipped van, Google's Street View project allows just that. Street View makes it possible to take a virtual tour of many cities and neighborhoods from any computer with a connection to the Internet. (See Figure 9-2.) Although the images available on Street View are all taken in public locations, some have objected to the project as being an intrusion on their privacy.

  As digital cameras and webcams become cheaper and software becomes more sophisticated, it is likely that many more issues involving personal privacy in public spaces will need to be addressed. Such a combination of computing technologies could, for example, make real-time tracking of individuals in public places possible.
- **Spreading information without personal consent:** How would you feel if an employer were using your Facebook, Google+, or other social networking profiles to make decisions about hiring, placement, promotion, and firing? It is a common practice today for many organizations.

  As we have discussed in Chapter 2, social networking is designed for open sharing of information among individuals who share a common interest. Unfortunately, this openness can put individuals using social networking sites at risk. In fact, some have lost their jobs after posting unflattering remarks about their supervisor or after discussing their dislike of their current job. Deeper analysis of your social networking profile may reveal even more about yourself than you intend.

  The potential to inadvertently share personal information extends past what you might post to your social networking site. As an example, without your knowledge or permission, a social networking friend might tag or identify you in a photo on his or her site. Once tagged, that photo can become part of your electronic profile and available to others without your consent.

- **Spreading inaccurate information:** How would you like to be turned down for a home loan because of an error in your credit history? This is much more common than you might expect. What if you could not find a job or were fired from a job because of an error giving you a serious criminal history? This can and has happened due to simple clerical errors. In one case, an arresting officer while completing an arrest warrant incorrectly recorded the Social Security number of a criminal. From that time forward, this arrest and the subsequent conviction became part of another person's electronic profile. This is an example of **mistaken identity** in which the electronic profile of one person is switched with another.

  It's important to know that you have some recourse. The law allows you to gain access to those records about you that are held by credit bureaus. Under the **Freedom of Information Act,** you are also entitled to look at your records held by government agencies. (Portions may be deleted for national security reasons.)

Private Networks

Suppose you use your company's electronic mail system to send a co-worker an unflattering message about your supervisor or to send a highly personal message to a friend. Later you find the boss has been reading these e-mails. In fact, many businesses search employees' electronic mail and computer files using **employee-monitoring software.** These programs record virtually everything you do on your computer. One proposed law would not prohibit this type of electronic monitoring but would require employers to provide prior written notice. Employers also would have to alert employees during the monitoring with some sort of audible or visual signal. If you are employed and would like to know your company's current policy on monitoring electronic communication, contact your human relations department.

privacy

Sharing personal information on a social networking site like Facebook is a voluntary activity. However, many individuals do not fully understand the complex sharing and privacy policies of these networks. This often causes unintentional sharing with people outside their intended social circle. The social networks themselves have come under fire from privacy groups, who say that these companies use complex settings and policies to get users to share more information than intended. This information is in turn shared with advertisers. Do you think social networking companies are a threat to privacy?

concept check

Describe how large databases can effect our privacy.

What is big data? Information resellers? Electronic profiles?

List three important issues related to electronic profiles. What is mistaken identity? What is the Freedom of Information Act?

What are private networks? What is employee-monitoring software? Is it legal?

The Internet and the Web

When you send e-mail on the Internet or browse the web, do you have any concerns about privacy? Most people do not. They think that as long as they are using their own computer and are selective about disclosing their names or other personal information, then little can be done to invade their personal privacy. Experts call this the **illusion of anonymity** that the Internet brings.

As we discussed in Chapter 8, every computer on the Internet is identified by a unique number known as an IP address. IP addresses can be used to trace Internet activities to their origin, allowing computer security experts and law enforcement officers to investigate computer crimes such as unauthorized access to networks or sharing copyright files without permission.

When you browse the web, your browser stores critical information onto your hard disk, typically without you being aware of it. This information, which contains records about your Internet activities, includes history and temporary Internet files.

- **History files** include the locations, or addresses, of sites that you have recently visited. This history file can be displayed by your browser in various locations,

1 In the top-right corner of the browser window, select the *Chrome Menu* button.

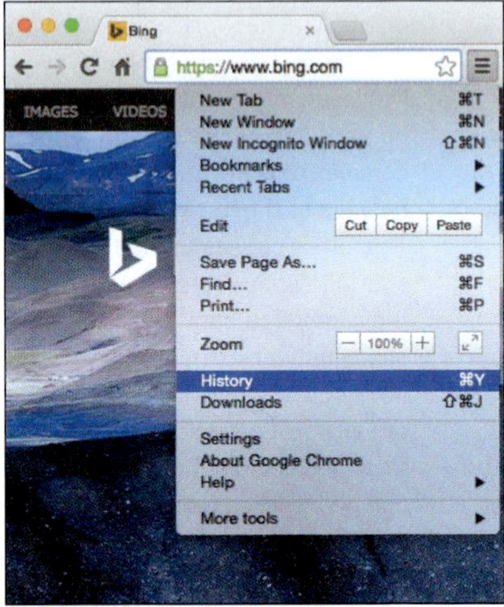

2 Select *History*.

Figure 9-3 Viewing history files

including the address bar (as you type) and the *History* page. To view your browsing history using Google Chrome, follow the steps in Figure 9-3.

- **Temporary Internet files,** also known as the **browser cache,** contain web page content and instructions for displaying this content. Whenever you visit a website, these files are saved by your browser. If you leave a site and then return later, these files are used to quickly redisplay web content.

Another way your web activity can be monitored is with **cookies.** Cookies are small data files that are deposited on your hard disk from websites you have visited. Based on your browser's settings, these cookies can be accepted or blocked. To see how to block cookies using Google Chrome, see Figure 9-4. Although you will generally not be aware when a website generates a cookie, the personalized experiences you enjoy on the web are often a result of those cookies. While cookies are harmless in and of themselves, what makes them a potential privacy risk is that they can store information about you, your preferences, and your browsing habits. The information stored generally depends on whether the cookie is a first-party or a third-party cookie.

- A **first-party cookie** is one that is generated (and then read) only by the website you are currently visiting. Many websites use first-party cookies to store information about the current session, your general preferences, and your activity on the site. The intention of these cookies is to provide a personalized experience on a particular site. For example, when you revisit a particular electronic commerce site, a previously deposited cookie can provide information so that you can be greeted by name and presented with sales and promotions that interest you.
- A **third-party cookie** is usually generated by an advertising company that is affiliated with the website you are currently visiting. These cookies are used by the advertising company to keep track of your web activity as you move from one site to the next. For this reason, they are often referred to as **tracking cookies.** Critics of this practice claim that your privacy is being violated because your activity is being recorded across multiple websites. Defenders of this practice argue that these cookies are beneficial because they help websites deliver ads that interest you. For example, suppose you visit four different websites that employ the same advertising agency. The first three sites are about cars, but the fourth is a search engine. When you visit the fourth site, you will likely see a car advertisement because your cookie showed that you had been visiting car-related websites.

Some users are not comfortable with the idea of web browsers storing so much information in the form of temporary Internet files, cookies, and history. For this reason, browsers now offer users an easy way to delete their browsing history. To see how to delete browsing histories using Google Chrome, see Figure 9-5. In addition, most browsers also offer a **privacy mode,** which ensures that your browsing activity is not recorded on your hard disk. For example, Google Chrome provides **Incognito Mode** accessible from the Chrome menu, and Safari provides **Private Browsing** accessible from the *Safari* option on the main menu.

Although these web browser files can concern many individuals, several other threats could potentially violate your privacy. **Web bugs,** which are invisible images or HTML code hidden within a web page or e-mail message, can be used to transmit

1. Select the *Chrome Menu* button.

   Choose *Settings*, then click *Show advanced settings*.

2. Select the *Content Settings* button in the Privacy section.

   Click the check box next to "Block third-party cookies and site data."

   Click *Done*.

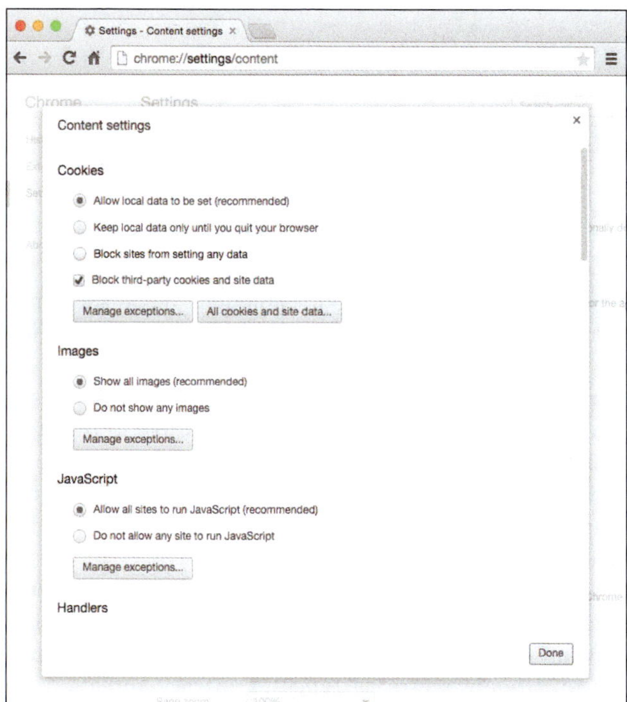

Figure 9-4 **Blocking cookies**

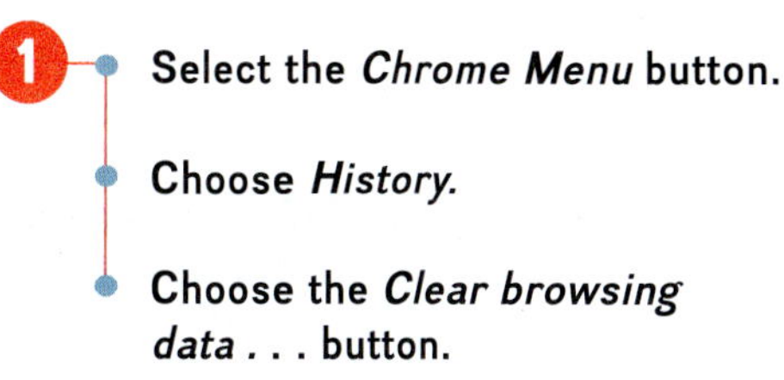

1. Select the *Chrome Menu* button.

   Choose *History*.

   Choose the *Clear browsing data . . .* button.

2. Select check boxes for items to be deleted.

   Choose the *Clear browsing data* button.

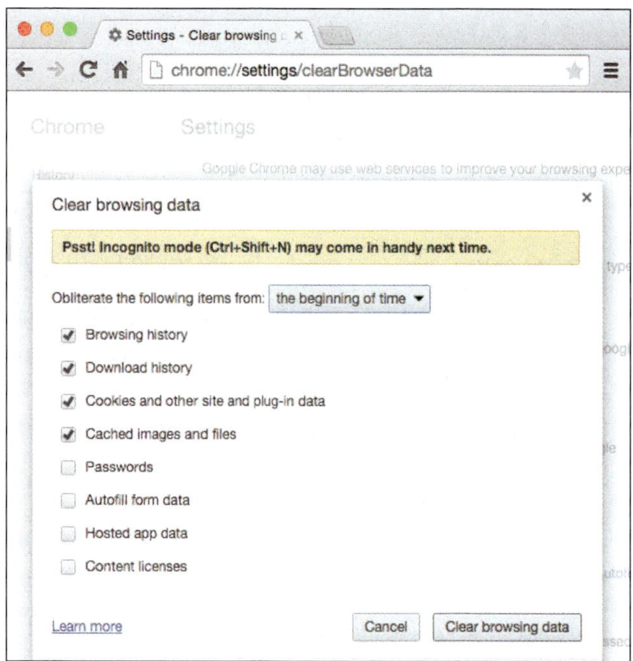

Figure 9-5 **Deleting browsing history**

information without your knowledge. When a user opens an e-mail containing a web bug, information is sent back to the source of the bug. The receiving server will now know that this e-mail address is active. One of the most common web bugs is used by companies that sell active mailing lists to spammers. Because of this deception, many e-mail programs now block images and HTML code from unknown senders. It is up to the user to decide whether or not to allow such content to be displayed for current and future messages.

The most dangerous type of privacy threat comes in the form of spyware. The term **spyware** is used to describe a wide range of programs that are designed to secretly record and report an individual's activities on the Internet. Some of these programs can even make changes to your browser in order to deceive you and manipulate what you see online. **Computer monitoring software** is perhaps the most invasive and dangerous type of spyware. One type of computer monitoring software, known as a **keystroke logger,** records every activity and keystroke made on your computer system, including credit card numbers, passwords, and e-mail messages. Computer monitoring software can be deposited onto your hard drive without your knowledge by a malicious website

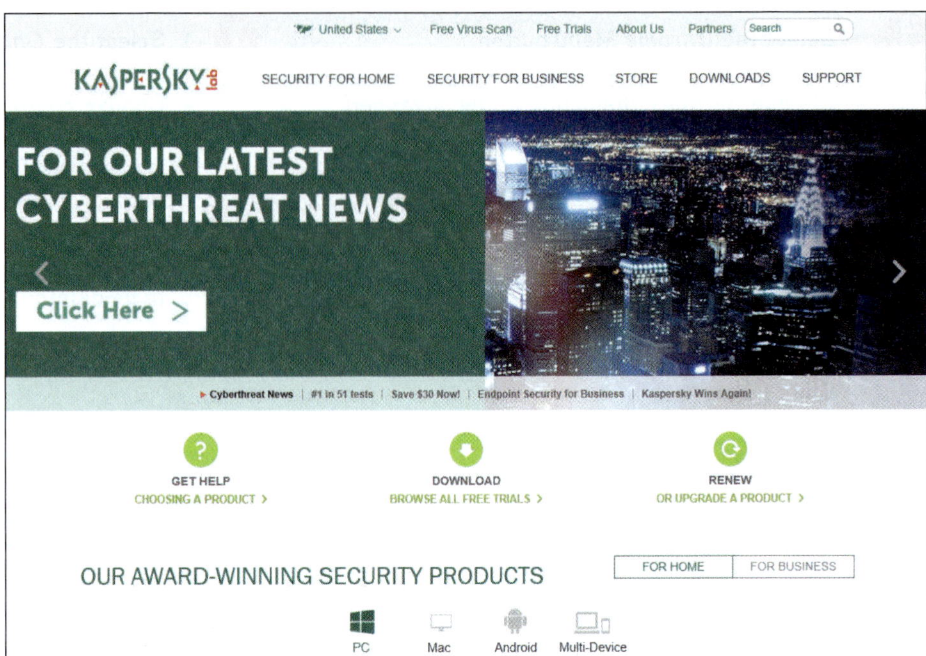

Figure 9-6 Antispyware

ethics

Lawmakers in Europe have created a "right to be forgotten" law. Under this law, a person can request that Google perform a search on their name and then remove any links to websites identified by the individual. In doing so, a person can remove an embarrassing past from Internet searches. Proponents of the law say that it allows people to live their lives without the stigma of a specific past action. Opponents of the law see it as in opposition to freedom of speech and an attack on others' right to know. Do you think a person has the right to keep people from discovering their past? Should the right to be forgotten apply to everyone, or would it be different for a politician, a movie star, or a criminal?

or by someone installing the program directly onto your computer. While such software is deadly in the hands of criminals, it can be legally used by companies monitoring employees or law enforcement officials who are collecting evidence.

Unfortunately, many spyware programs go undetected, largely because users have no idea they are infected. Spyware will run in the background, invisible to the average user. Other times, it disguises itself as useful software, such as a security program. Various studies have demonstrated that an alarming number of computers are infected with spyware. The financial impact to individuals, companies, and financial institutions is estimated at billions of dollars.

One of the best defenses against spyware is to exercise caution when visiting new websites and downloading software from an unknown source. Another defense involves using a category of software known as **antispyware** or **spy removal programs,** which are designed to detect and remove various types of privacy threats. (See Figure 9-6.) For a list of some of these programs, see Figure 9-7.

Online Identity

Another aspect of Internet privacy comes from **online identity,** the information that people voluntarily post about themselves online. With the popularity of social networking, blogging, and photo- and video-sharing sites, many people post intimate details of their lives without considering the consequences. Although it is easy to think of online identity as something shared between friends, the archiving and search features of the web make it available indefinitely to anyone who cares to look.

There are any number of cases of people who have lost their jobs on the basis of posts on social networking sites. These job losses range from a teacher (using off-color language and photos showing drinking) to a chief financial officer of a major corporation (discussing corporate dealings and financial data). The cases include college graduates being refused a job because of Facebook posts. How would you feel if information you posted about yourself on the web kept you from getting a job?

Program	Website
Ad-Aware	www.lavasoft.com
Kaspersky Anti-Virus	www.kaspersky.com
Windows Defender	www.microsoft.com

Figure 9-7 Antispyware programs

Major Laws on Privacy

Some federal laws governing privacy matters have been created. For example, the **Gramm-Leach-Bliley Act** protects personal financial information, the **Health Insurance Portability and Accountability Act (HIPAA)** protects medical records, and the **Family Educational Rights and Privacy Act (FERPA)** restricts disclosure of educational records.

Most of the information collected by private organizations is not covered by existing laws. However, as more and more individuals become concerned about controlling who has the right to personal information and how that information is used, companies and lawmakers will respond.

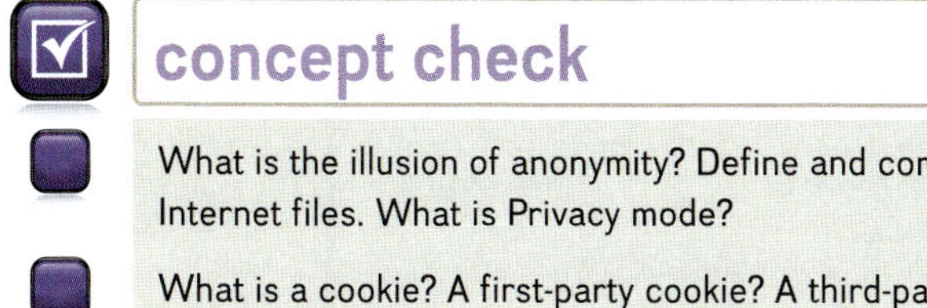

concept check

- What is the illusion of anonymity? Define and compare history files and temporary Internet files. What is Privacy mode?
- What is a cookie? A first-party cookie? A third-party cookie?
- What is a web bug? Spyware? Keystroke logger? Antispyware? Online identity?
- Describe three federal laws to protect privacy.

Security

We are all concerned with having a safe and secure environment to live in. We are careful to lock our car doors and our homes. We are careful about where we walk at night and whom we talk to. This is personal security. What about computer security? What if someone gains unauthorized access to our computer or other computers that contain information about us? These people are commonly known as computer **hackers.** It should be noted that not all hackers are intent on malicious actions and that not all are criminals. **Security** involves protecting individuals and organizations from theft and danger. Computer security specifically focuses on protecting information, hardware, and software from unauthorized use, as well as preventing or limiting the damage from intrusions, sabotage, and natural disasters.

Cybercrime

Cybercrime or **computer crime** is any criminal offense that involves a computer and a network. It was recently estimated that cybercrime affects over 400 million people and costs over $400 billion each year. Cybercrimes can take various forms including the creation of malicious programs, denial of service attacks, rogue Wi-Fi hotspots, data manipulation, identity theft, Internet scams, and cyberbullying.

Malicious Programs A **cracker** is a computer criminal who creates and distributes malicious programs. These programs are called **malware,** which is short for **malicious software.** They are specifically designed to damage or disrupt a computer system. The three most common types of malware are viruses, worms, and Trojan horses.

- **Viruses** are programs that migrate through networks and operating systems, and most attach themselves to different programs and databases. While some viruses are relatively harmless, many can be quite destructive. Once activated, these destructive viruses can alter and/or delete files. Creating and knowingly spreading a virus is a very serious crime and a federal offense punishable under the **Computer Fraud and Abuse Act.**

  Unfortunately, new computer viruses are appearing all the time. The best way to stay current is through services that keep track of viruses on a daily basis. For example, Symantec, McAfee, and Microsoft all track the most serious virus threats. (See Figure 9-8.)

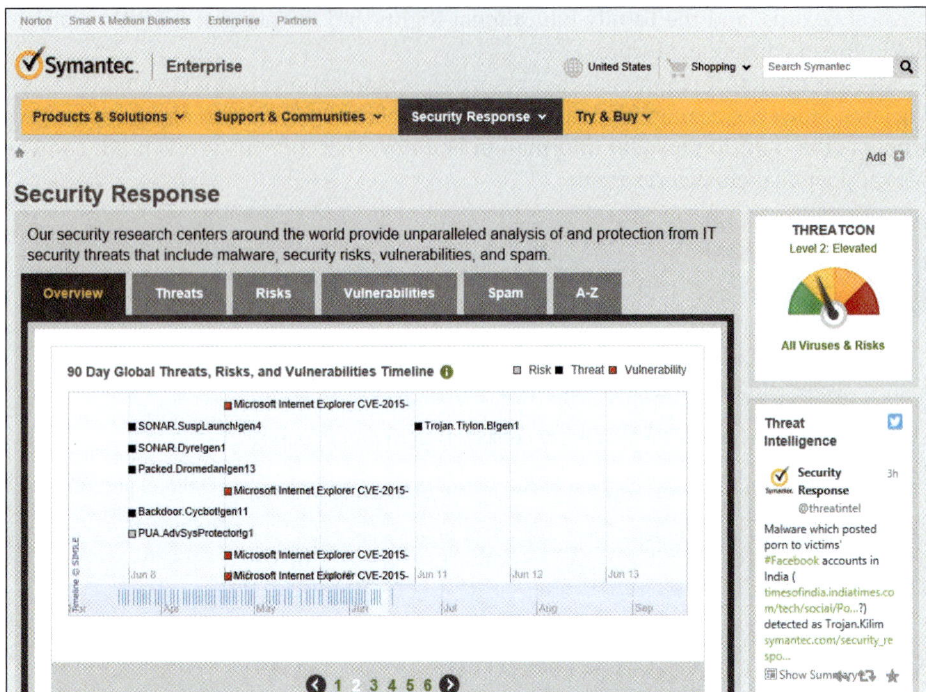

Figure 9-8 Tracking viruses

- **Worms** are programs that simply replicate themselves over and over again. Once active in a network, the self-replicating activity clogs computers and networks until their operations are slowed or stopped. A recent worm traveled across the world within hours, stopping tens of thousands of computers along its way. Unlike a virus, a worm typically does not attach itself to a program or alter and/or delete files. Worms, however, can carry a virus. Once a virus has been deposited by a worm onto an unsuspecting computer system, the virus will either activate immediately or lie dormant until some future time. For example, in 2010 the Stuxnet worm infected several networks in Iran. One of these networks was used by Iran's nuclear program. Soon after the infection, several key pieces of nuclear equipment became permanently disabled.

  Viruses and worms typically find their way into personal computers through e-mail attachments and programs downloaded from the Internet. Because viruses can be so damaging, computer users are advised to never open an e-mail attachment from an unknown source and to exercise great care in accepting new programs and data from any source.

  As we discussed in Chapter 4, antivirus programs alert users when certain kinds of viruses and worms enter their system. Two of the most widely used are Avast! Free Antivirus and Microsoft Security Essentials. Unfortunately, new viruses are being developed all the time, and not all viruses can be detected.

- **Trojan horses** are programs that appear to be harmless; however, they contain malicious programs. Trojan horses are not viruses. Like worms, however, they can be carriers of viruses. The most common types of Trojan horses appear as free computer games and free screensaver programs that can be downloaded from the Internet. When a user installs one of these programs, the Trojan horse also secretly installs a virus on the computer system. The virus then begins its mischief. One of the most dangerous types of Trojan horse claims to provide free antivirus programs. When a user downloads one of these programs, the Trojan horse first installs a virus that locates and disables any existing virus protection programs before depositing other viruses.

Zombies are computers infected by a virus, worm, or Trojan horse that allows them to be remotely controlled for malicious purposes. A collection of zombie computers is known as a **botnet,** or **robot network.** Botnets harness the combined power of many zombies for malicious activities like password cracking or sending junk e-mail. Because they are formed by many computers distributed across the Internet, botnets are hard to shut down even after they are detected. Unfortunately for individual computer owners, it also can be difficult to detect when a personal computer has been compromised.

Denial of Service A **denial of service (DoS) attack** attempts to slow down or stop a computer system or network by flooding a computer or network with requests for information and data. The targets of these attacks are usually Internet service providers (ISPs) and specific websites. Once under attack, the servers at the ISP or the website become overwhelmed with these requests for service and are unable to respond to legitimate users. As a result, the ISP or website is effectively shut down.

Rogue Wi-Fi Hotspots Free Wi-Fi networks are available almost everywhere from libraries to fast-food restaurants and coffee shops. **Rogue Wi-Fi hotspots** imitate these free networks. These rogue networks operate close to the legitimate free hotspots and typically provide stronger signals that many users unsuspectingly connect to. Once connected, the rogue networks capture any and all information sent by the users to legitimate sites including user names and passwords.

Data Manipulation Finding entry into someone's computer network and leaving a prankster's message may seem like fun, which is why hackers do it. It is still against the law. Moreover, even if the manipulation seems harmless, it may cause a great deal of anxiety and wasted time among network users.

The **Computer Fraud and Abuse Act** makes it a crime for unauthorized persons even to view—let alone copy or damage—data using any computer across state lines. It also prohibits unauthorized use of any government computer or a computer used by any federally insured financial institution. Offenders can be sentenced to up to 20 years in prison and fined up to $100,000.

Identity Theft **Identity theft** is the illegal assumption of someone's identity for the purposes of economic gain. It is one of the fastest-growing crimes in the country and can financially devastate its victim. Once an identity is stolen, the criminal applies for and obtains new credit cards in the victim's name and then uses the cards to purchase clothes, cars, and even a house.

To commit this crime, identity thieves look for anything that can help them steal your identity, from your Social Security number and date of birth, to account information and passwords. Sometimes they gain this information from social networking sites, where users often post detailed personal information such as their birth dates, family member names, home addresses, and photos of their children. As mentioned previously, always exercise caution when providing information on Facebook, Twitter, and other social networking sites, and use the privacy settings and controls that are provided at the social networking sites you use.

tips

Identity theft is a growing problem, and can be financially devastating if you are a victim. Thieves are after anything that can help them steal your identity, from your Social Security number and date of birth to account information and passwords. Here are some steps to help protect your identity:

1. Be careful what you write on the Internet. Never post personal information on forums or social networking areas that are public or in response to an e-mail from someone you do not know or trust.
2. Only do business on the Internet with companies you know to be legitimate.
3. When selling a computer, be sure to completely remove all personal information from the hard drive. To ensure that your personal information is erased, consider using a free erasure software tool, such as Dban (www.dban.com).
4. Monitor your credit. Each year, you are entitled to a free personal credit report from each of the three major credit reporting agencies. Monitor your credit by requesting a report every four months from a different reporting agency. The official site for this service is www.annualcreditreport.com.

privacy

Did you know that the World Wide Web contains websites purposely hidden from you? Some websites are designed to be hidden from standard search engines and allow people to communicate in a secure and anonymous manner. These hidden websites make up the Dark Web and require special software that makes it nearly impossible to identify who is using it. The ability to communicate anonymously attracts criminals who want to sell drugs, share child pornography, or profit from the poaching of endangered animals. This same anonymity allows people in countries where political dissent is dangerous and free speech is censored to communicate, plan, and organize toward a more free and open society without fear of jail or execution. Prior to reading this Privacy section, were you aware of the Dark Web? Do you think it should be stopped? Do you think it should be regulated?

Type	Description
Chain letter	Classic chain letter instructing recipient to send a nominal amount of money to each of five people on a list. The recipient removes the first name on the list, adds his or her name at the bottom, and mails the chain letter to five friends. This is also known as a pyramid scheme. Almost all chain letters are fraudulent and illegal.
Auction fraud	Merchandise is selected and payment is sent. Merchandise is never delivered.
Vacation prize	"Free" vacation has been awarded. Upon arrival at vacation destination, the accommodations are dreadful but can be upgraded for a fee.
Advance fee loans	Guaranteed low-rate loans available to almost anyone. After applicant provides personal loan-related information, the loan is granted subject to payment of an "insurance fee."

Figure 9-9 **Common Internet scams**

Internet Scams A **scam** is a fraudulent or deceptive act or operation designed to trick individuals into providing personal information or spending their time and money for little or no return. An **Internet scam** is simply a scam using the Internet. Internet scams are becoming a serious problem and have created financial and legal problems for many thousands of people. Almost all the scams are initiated by a mass mailing to unsuspecting individuals.

A technique often employed by scammers is **phishing** (pronounced "fishing"). Phishing attempts to trick Internet users into thinking a fake but official-looking website or e-mail is legitimate. Phishing has grown in sophistication, replicating entire websites like PayPal to try to lure users into divulging their financial information.

See Figure 9-9 for a list of common types of Internet scams.

Cyberbullying A fairly recent and all-too-common phenomenon, **cyberbullying** is the use of the Internet, smartphones, or other devices to send or post content intended to hurt or embarrass another person. Although not always a crime, it can lead to criminal prosecution. Cyberbullying includes sending repeated unwanted e-mails to an individual who has stated that he or she wants no further contact with the sender, ganging up on victims in electronic forums, posting false statements designed to injure the reputation of another, maliciously disclosing personal data about a person that could lead to harm to that person, and sending any type of communication that is threatening or harassing. Never participate in cyberbullying, and discourage others from participating in this dangerous and hateful activity.

For a summary of computer crimes, see Figure 9-10.

Computer Crime	Description
Malicious programs	Include viruses, worms, and Trojan horses
DoS	Causes computer systems to slow down or stop
Rogue Wi-Fi hotspots	Imitate legitimate Wi-Fi hotspot in order to capture personal information
Data manipulation	Involves changing data or leaving prank messages
Identity theft	Is illegal assumption of a person's identity for economic gain
Internet scams	Are scams over the Internet usually initiated by e-mail and involving phishing
Cyberbullying	Is using the Internet, smartphones, or other devices to send/post content intended to hurt or embarrass another person

Figure 9-10 **Computer crimes**

concept check

- What are hackers? What is cybercrime? What are malicious programs?
- Compare viruses, worms, and Trojan horses. What are zombies? What is a botnet?
- What are denial of service attacks? Rogue Wi-Fi hotspots? Data theft and manipulation?
- What is identity theft? Describe some common Internet scams. What is cyberbullying?

Measures to Protect Computer Security

There are numerous ways in which computer systems and data can be compromised and many ways to ensure computer security. Some of the principal measures to ensure computer security are restricting access, encrypting data, anticipating disasters, and preventing data loss.

Restricting Access Security experts are constantly devising ways to protect computer systems from access by unauthorized persons. Sometimes security is a matter of putting guards on company computer rooms and checking the identification of everyone admitted. Other times it is using **biometric scanning** devices such as fingerprint and iris (eye) scanners. (See Figure 9-11.) There are numerous applications that use face recognition to allow access to a computer system. For example, many personal computer systems use Dell's FastAccess face recognition application to prevent unauthorized access. There are also several face recognition apps for mobile devices including Face Recognition by iNFINITE Studios LLC.

Oftentimes it is a matter of being careful about assigning passwords to people and changing the passwords when people leave a company. **Passwords** are secret words or phrases (including numbers, letters, and special characters) that must be keyed into a computer system to gain access. For many applications on the web, users assign their own passwords. Windows 8 includes an application, Picture Password, that accepts a series of gestures over a picture of the user's choice to gain access.

Fingerprint scan

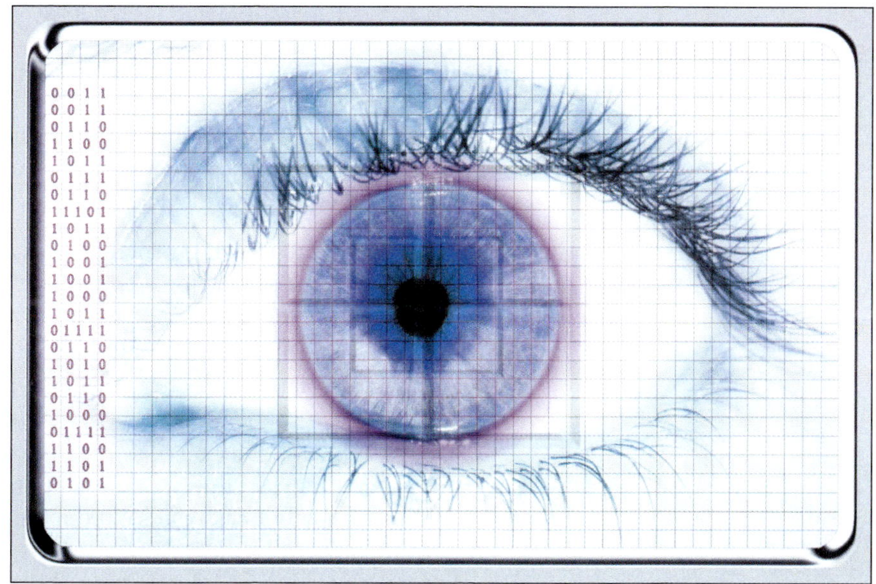

Iris scan

Figure 9-11 **Biometric scanning devices**

tips **Security professionals warn that most people use passwords that are too easily guessed. They categorize passwords as weak (easily guessed) or strong (difficult to guess). A weak password can be guessed in a matter of seconds, a strong one would take years to crack. Make sure you have a strong password by employing the following tips when creating a password.**

1. Use a password with at least eight characters. The fewer the characters, the easier it is to guess.
2. Do not use your user name, real name, or company name in your password. The first thing a cracker will try is variations of your personal information.
3. Do not use a complete word. Using a computer, a cracker can easily try every word in the dictionary as a password guess.
4. Do not reuse passwords. If a user's password for one account is compromised, hackers will attempt to use that password on the user's other accounts.
5. Create a password that contains at least one of each of the following characters: uppercase letter, lowercase letter, number, and symbol.

The strength of a password depends on how easily it can be guessed. A **dictionary attack** uses software to try thousands of common words sequentially in an attempt to gain unauthorized access to a user's account. For this reason, words, names, and simple numeric patterns make weak or poor passwords. Strong passwords have at least eight characters and use a combination of letters, numbers, and symbols. It is also important not to reuse passwords for different accounts. If one account is compromised, that password might be tried for access to other systems as well. For example, if a low-security account such as an online web forum is compromised, that password could also be tried on higher-security accounts such as banking websites.

As mentioned in previous chapters, individuals and organizations use a variety of ways to perform and automate important security tasks:

- **Security suites** provide a collection of utility programs designed to protect your privacy and security while you are on the web.
- **Firewalls** act as a security buffer between a corporation's private network and all external networks, including the Internet. All electronic communications coming into and leaving the corporation must pass through the company's firewall where it is evaluated. Security is maintained by denying access to unauthorized communications.
- **Password managers** help you create strong passwords. Additionally, they will store all your passwords in one location and automatically provide the appropriate password when requested from one of your favorite sites. This avoids many of the mistakes people make in generating and remembering passwords. However, this master list of passwords is protected by one "master" password. If you forget or reveal this master password, you open yourself up to considerable risk.

Encrypting Data Whenever information is sent over a network or stored on a computer system, the possibility of unauthorized access exists. The solution is **encryption,** the process of coding information to make it unreadable except to those who have a special piece of information known as an **encryption key,** or, simply, a **key.** Some common uses for encryption include

- **E-mail encryption:** Protects e-mail messages as they move across the Internet. One of the most widely used personal e-mail encryption programs is Pretty Good Privacy. (See Figure 9-12.)
- **File encryption:** Protects sensitive files by encrypting them before they are stored on a hard drive. Files can be encrypted individually, or specialized software can be used to encrypt all files automatically each time they are saved to a certain hard drive location. (See Figure 9-13.)
- **Website encryption:** Secures web transactions, especially financial transactions. Web pages that accept passwords or confidential information like a credit card number are often encrypted.

  As we discussed in Chapters 2 and 8, **https (hypertext transfer protocol secure)** is the most widely used Internet protocol. This protocol requires that the browser and the connecting site encrypt all messages, providing a safer and more secure transmission.

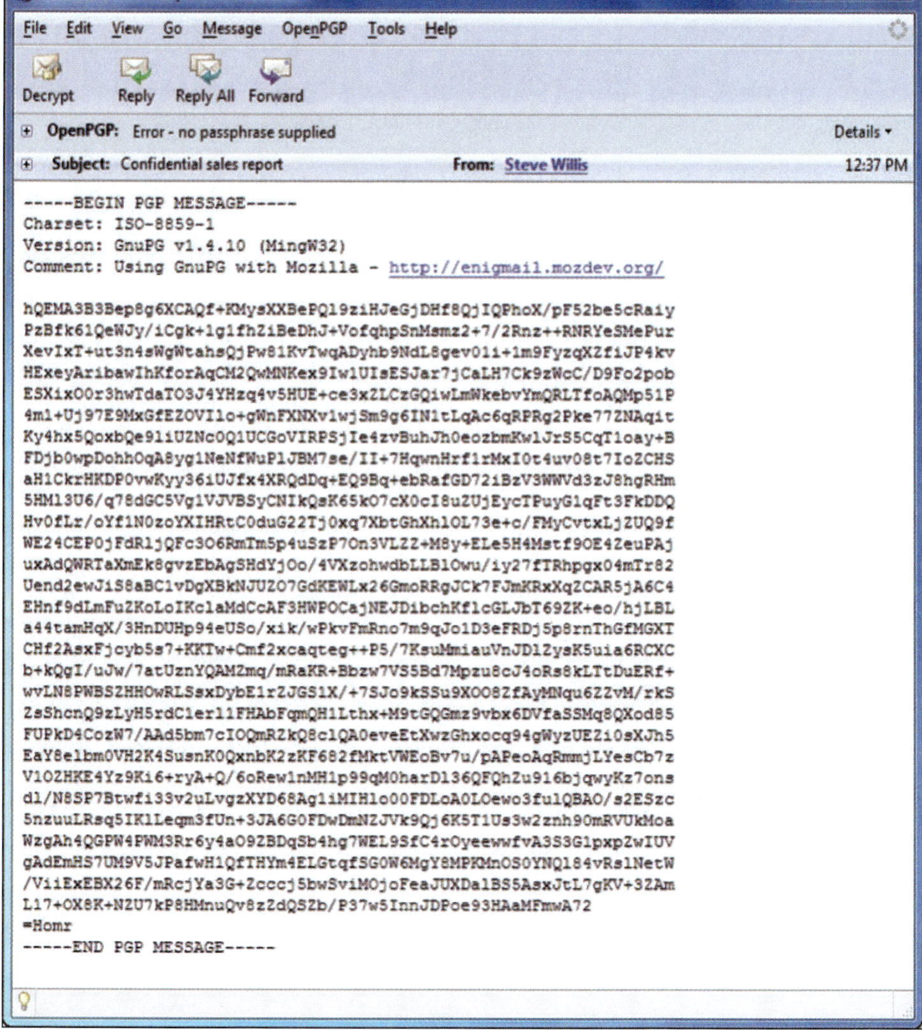

Figure 9-12 **Encrypted e-mail**

- **Virtual private networks: Virtual private networks (VPNs)** encrypt connections between company networks and remote users such as workers connecting from home. This connection creates a secure virtual connection to a company LAN across the Internet.
- **Wireless network encryption:** Restricts access to authorized users on wireless networks. **WPA2 (Wi-Fi Protected Access)** is the most widely used wireless network encryption for home wireless networks. WPA2 is typically established for a wireless network through the network's wireless router. While the specifics vary between routers, WPA2 is usually set through the router's settings options.

Anticipating Disasters Companies (and even individuals) should prepare themselves for disasters. **Physical security** is concerned with protecting hardware from possible human and natural

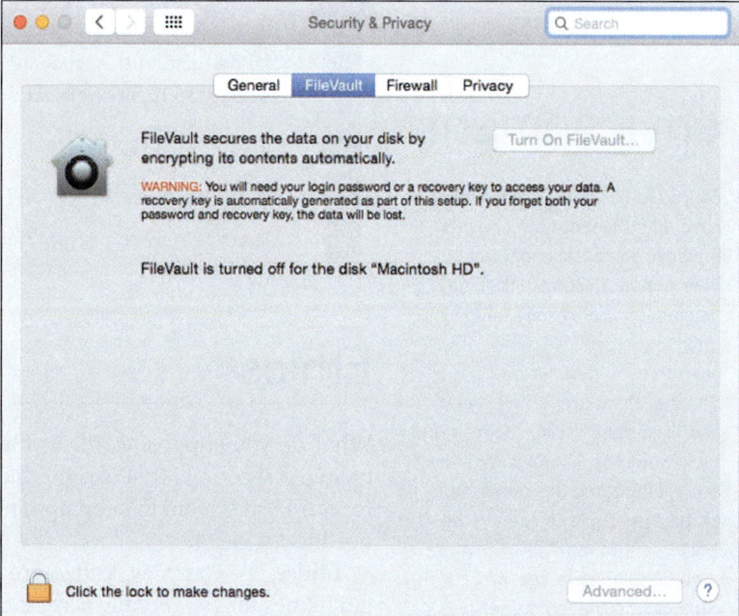

Figure 9-13 **File encryption**

Measure	Description
Restricting access	Limit access to authorized persons using such measures as passwords and firewalls.
Encrypting data	Code all messages sent over a network.
Anticipating disasters	Prepare for disasters by ensuring physical security and data security through a disaster recovery plan.
Preventing data loss	Routinely copy data and store it at a remote location.

Figure 9-14 **Measures to protect computer security**

disasters. **Data security** is concerned with protecting software and data from unauthorized tampering or damage. Most large organizations have **disaster recovery plans** describing ways to continue operating until normal computer operations can be restored.

Preventing Data Loss Equipment can always be replaced. A company's *data,* however, may be irreplaceable. Most companies have ways of trying to keep software and data from being tampered with in the first place. They include careful screening of job applicants, guarding of passwords, and auditing of data and programs from time to time. Some systems use redundant storage to prevent loss of data even when a hard drive fails. We discussed RAID in Chapter 7, which is a commonly used type of redundant storage. Backup batteries protect against data loss due to file corruption during unexpected power outages.

Making frequent backups of data is essential to prevent data loss. Backups are often stored at an off-site location to protect data in case of theft, fire, flood, or other disasters. Students and others often use flash drives and cloud storage as discussed in Chapter 7 to back up homework and important papers. Incremental backups store multiple versions of data at different points in time to prevent data loss due to unwanted changes or accidental deletion.

To see how you could use a cloud-based backup service, see Making IT Work for You: Cloud-Based Backup on page 239.

See Figure 9-14 for a summary of the different measures to protect computer security.

concept check

Define each of the following: biometric scanning, password, dictionary attack, security suite, firewalls, and password managers.

What are encryption and an encryption key? What is https? What is a VPN? WPA2?

Define physical security, data security, and disaster recovery plans.

Describe how to prevent data loss.

environment

Do you feel that IT professionals have an ethical duty to consider the environmental impact of their actions? Many technology companies are already taking their responsibility to the environment very seriously. Some of them are "going green" and promoting their practices on their websites. Other companies are encouraging the recycling of their products to reduce the waste sent to landfills. A few are even competing to see which can develop the most energy-efficient products.

Ethics

What do you suppose controls how computers can be used? You probably think first of laws. Of course, that is right, but technology is moving so fast that it is very difficult for our legal system to keep up. The essential element that controls how computers are used today is *ethics.*

Ethics, as you may know, are standards of moral conduct. **Computer ethics** are guidelines for the morally acceptable use of computers in our society. Ethical treatment is critically important to us all, and we are all entitled to ethical treatment. This includes the right to keep personal information, such as credit ratings and medical histories, from

CLOUD-BASED BACKUP

Do you remember to make frequent backups of your irreplaceable data files, such as photos and documents? Would you like a service that remembers to do the backups for you and places them in a very reliable location? If so, then a cloud-based backup service is a solution, and this guide will discuss their benefits, as well as various options on types of backups.

Benefits of Cloud-Based Backups

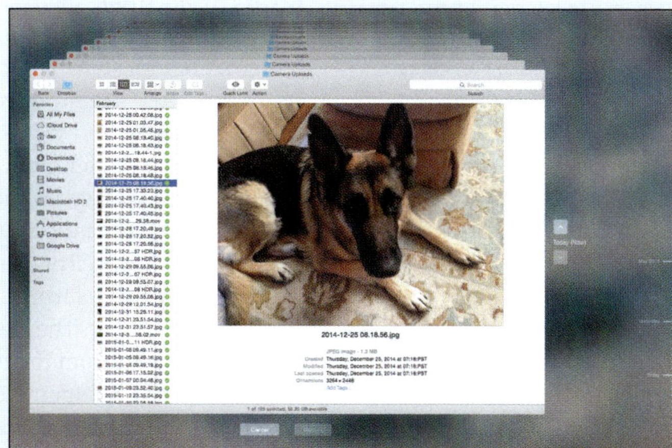

1. **Security.** Without a backup, you can lose data due to a hard drive failure, computer virus, laptop theft, or fire.
2. **Automation.** It is easy to forget to do a manual backup, and without frequent backups, you may lose important data when a restore is required.
3. **Cloud based.** Environmental events, such as a fire or flood, can damage both the local computer and the backup. By storing backups on a cloud server, a physical event that damages your local copy will not impact your cloud-based backup.

Backup Options Once you have decided to automate your backup procedure, you may be surprised at the number of options available to you.

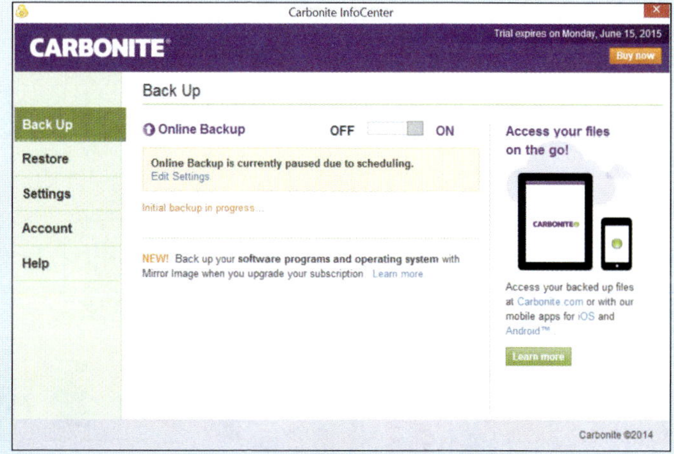

1. **Backup software.** Depending on your operating system and the level of customization you want, there are several options. Most operating systems come with free backup software; Microsoft Windows comes with File History and Apple OSX comes with Time Machine.
2. **Backup frequency and schedule.** A backup can tax the processor and hard drive of a system, slowing down a computer's performance. Depending on when your computer is turned on and how you use your machine, you will need to tune how often and when a backup is taken to best suit your needs.
3. **Which files to back up.** You may want to backup your entire hard drive, or you may choose to back up specific folders, such as photos and videos–most backup software allows you to choose which folders are backed up.
4. **Cloud services.** There are many cloud storage services available; depending on your operating system, backup software, and budget, you have several options. Popular choices include Apple's iCloud, Microsoft's Azure, and Google's Google Drive. There are also specialized backup programs with cloud storage plans bundled together, such as Carbonite's Personal Backup Plans.

ethics

Net neutrality is the policy that ISPs should deliver all data to customers at the same speed, regardless of the content. Opponents of net neutrality would allow ISPs to charge companies to deliver some websites faster, arguing that ISPs should be allowed to charge however they like. Proponents of net neutrality argue that the Internet has always had equal and unbiased access to information and that allowing ISPs to vary access to websites based on content is a new form of censorship. What do you think? Is net neutrality an important defense of Internet freedom of speech, or is it government overreach looking to hinder free markets?

getting into unauthorized hands. These issues, largely under the control of corporations and government agencies, were covered earlier in this chapter. These issues and many more have been addressed in the Ethics boxes throughout this book. Now we'll examine two important issues in computer ethics where average users have a role to play.

Copyright and Digital Rights Management

Copyright is a legal concept that gives content creators the right to control use and distribution of their work. Materials that can be copyrighted include paintings, books, music, films, and even video games. Some users choose to make unauthorized copies of digital media, which violates copyright. For example, making an unauthorized copy of a digital music file for a friend might be a copyright violation.

Software piracy is the unauthorized copying and/or distribution of software. According to a recent study, software piracy costs the software industry over $60 billion annually. To prevent copyright violations, corporations often use **digital rights management (DRM).** DRM encompasses various technologies that control access to electronic media and files. Typically, DRM is used to (1) control the number of devices that can access a given file and (2) limit the kinds of devices that can access a file. Although some companies see DRM as a necessity to protect their rights, some users feel they should have the right to use the media they buy—including movies, music, software, and video games—as they choose.

The **Digital Millennium Copyright Act** makes it illegal to deactivate or otherwise disable any antipiracy technologies including DRM technologies. The act also establishes that copies of commercial programs may not be legally resold or given away. It further makes it a crime to sell or to use programs or devices that are used to illegally copy software. This may come as a surprise to those who copy software, movies, or music from a friend or from the Internet. The law is clear: It is illegal to copy or download copyright-protected music and videos from the Internet without appropriate authorization.

Today, there are many legal sources for digital media. Television programs can be watched online, often for free, on television-network-sponsored sites. Sites like Pandora allow listeners to enjoy music at no cost. There are several online stores for purchasing music and video content. A pioneer in this area is Apple's iTunes Music Store. (See Figure 9-15.)

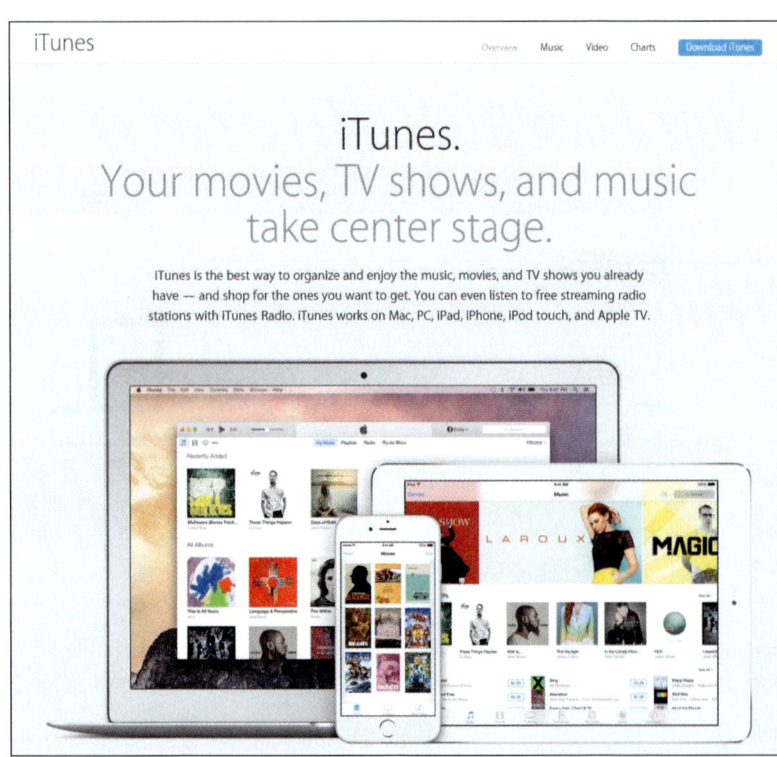

Figure 9-15 **iTunes Music Store**

Plagiarism

Another ethical issue is **plagiarism,** which means representing some other person's work and ideas as your own without giving credit to the original source. Although plagiarism was a problem long before the invention of computers, computer technology has made plagiarism easier. For example, simply cutting and pasting content from a web page into a report or paper may seem tempting to an overworked student or employee.

Correspondingly, computer technology has made it easier than ever to recognize and catch **plagiarists.** For example, services such as Turnitin are dedicated to preventing Internet plagiarism. This service will examine the content of a paper and compare it to a wide range of known public electronic documents including web page content. In this way, Turnitin can identify an undocumented paper or even parts of an undocumented paper. (See Figure 9-16.)

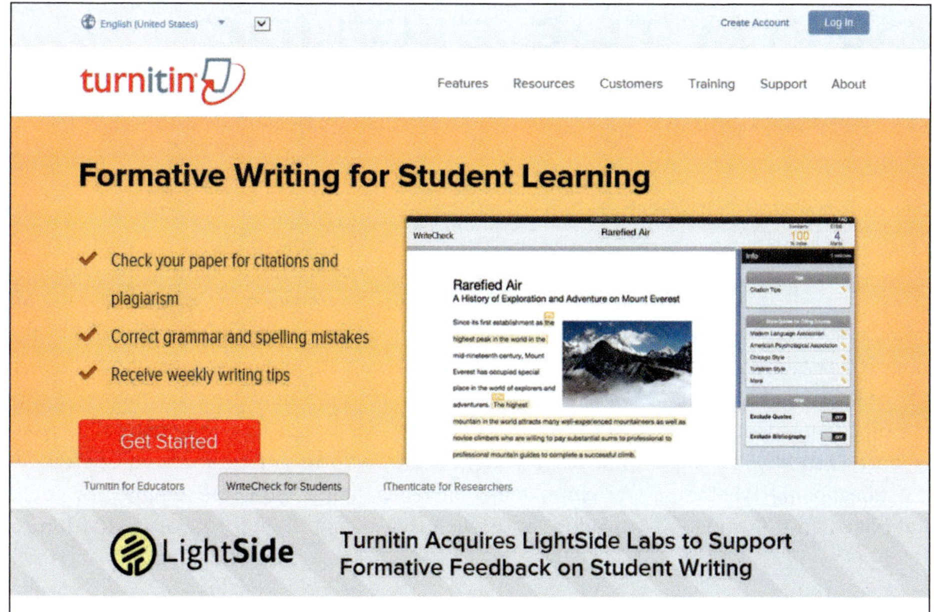

Figure 9-16 **Turnitin website**

ethics

Do you know of anyone who has copied parts of a web page from a variety of sites and combined the parts to form a term paper? Of course, such a practice is unethical and most likely illegal. Many schools and universities now use a program that can compare the content of a student's paper to published material on the web and to previously submitted papers. Do you think it is ethical for instructors to employ a program that checks for plagiarism? Is there a risk that the program may confuse proper citations from the web with obvious cases of plagiarism?

concept check

- What is the distinction between ethics and computer ethics?
- Define copyright, software privacy, digital rights management, and the Digital Millennium Copyright Act.
- What is plagiarism? What is Turnitin and what does it do?

Careers in IT

"Now that you have learned about privacy, security, and ethics, let me tell you about my career as an IT security analyst."

IT security analysts are responsible for maintaining the security of a company's networks, systems, and data. Their goal is to ensure the confidentiality, integrity, and availability of information. These analysts must safeguard information systems against a variety of external threats, such as hackers and viruses, as well as be vigilant of threats that may come from within the company.

Employers typically look for candidates with a bachelor's or associate's degree in information systems or computer science. Experience in this field or in network administration is usually required. IT security analysts should possess good communication and research skills, and be able to handle high-stress situations.

IT security analysts can expect to earn an annual salary of $46,000 to $64,000. Opportunities for advancement typically depend on experience. Demand for this position is expected to grow as malware, hackers, and other types of threats become more complex and prevalent.

A LOOK TO THE FUTURE

The End of Anonymity

Do you enjoy the ability to interact with others on the web anonymously? Is there a sense of comfort knowing that you can express yourself freely without others knowing your identity? Anonymity has been a way of life on the Internet since the very beginning. Recently, various organizations, ranging from advertisers to governments, are questioning whether the Internet can continue like this. And based on the amount of information currently shared by people online, one wonders whether anonymity will be valued at all in the future. Technology has been profoundly impacting our anonymity and public interactions, and will continue to evolve to impact our lives as we look to the future.

There are many factors that are causing many to question the value of anonymity. First is the issue of harassment. Most forums and comment areas on websites allow users to post messages anonymously. Some individuals use this ability to write abusive or threatening comments. Many children and teenagers have been victims of online harassment, or cyberbullying, at some point in their lives. Others have been stalked online to the point where they have experienced psychological harm. Experts feel that if anonymous comments were disallowed, those same individuals would not be willing to write those types of messages, as their anonymity would be stripped. The other area where anonymity has become a problem is the legal field. Some anonymous web users have posted lies about individuals or businesses that have damaged the target's reputation. In the real world, those types of false and damaging comments could lead to lawsuits. For these reasons, many legislators are proposing laws aimed at discouraging the sort of anonymity that allows various online crimes to occur. In the future, it may even be a requirement to provide a real-world ID in order to use the Internet.

Many online companies are also fighting to end anonymity. This is because they make most of their money off targeted advertising. For these companies to deliver the proper advertisement to you, they need to know quite a bit about you and your online activities. By having a profile with your real name and interests, they can follow your activity throughout the web to get to know you better. At present, many advertisements you see online are for a product or service that does not interest you. In the future, every advertisement you see will be selected just for you, as marketing companies develop a complete profile that lets them know everything about you.

Now, many online businesses do aim to protect your privacy, but this is only with respect to what the public knows about you. When it comes to their advertising partners, they don't hide much because it is not in their interest to do so. Essentially, it is a tradeoff for users, whether to give up some (or all) of your anonymity in return for targeted advertising. Although many organizations are working toward ending or severely limiting anonymity, some would like to keep the Internet the way it is.

Many civil rights groups and journalists support anonymity as a basic right. If you cannot be anonymous, then it would be difficult, for example, to post information that uncovers abuses in government or in a business. Some psychologists also support anonymity, stating that creating a separate online identity can be useful for personal development, allowing an individual to explore interests without leaving a record that is tied to his or her own life. How do you feel about the possible end to anonymity? Do you agree that there will be less negativity on the web if everyone had to provide real names? Since advertisements pay for free services, will you at least tolerate future ads more if they contain something that interests you?

VISUAL SUMMARY Privacy, Security, and Ethics

PRIVACY

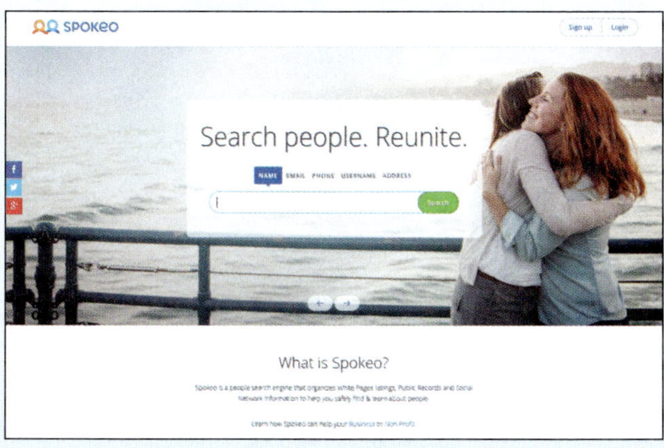

Privacy concerns the collection and use of data about individuals. There are three primary privacy issues: **accuracy** (who is responsible to ensure data is correct), **property** (who owns data), **access** (who controls access to data).

Large Databases

Large organizations are constantly compiling information about us. This ever-growing volume of data is often referred to as **big data. Information resellers (information brokers)** collect and sell personal data. **Electronic profiles** are compiled from databases to provide highly detailed and personalized descriptions of individuals.

Mistaken identity occurs when an electronic profile of one person is switched with another. **The Freedom of Information Act** entitles individuals access to governmental records relating to them.

Private Networks

Many organizations monitor employee e-mail and computer files using special software called **employee-monitoring software.**

The Internet and the Web

Many people believe that, while using the web, little can be done to invade their privacy. This is called the **illusion of anonymity.**

PRIVACY

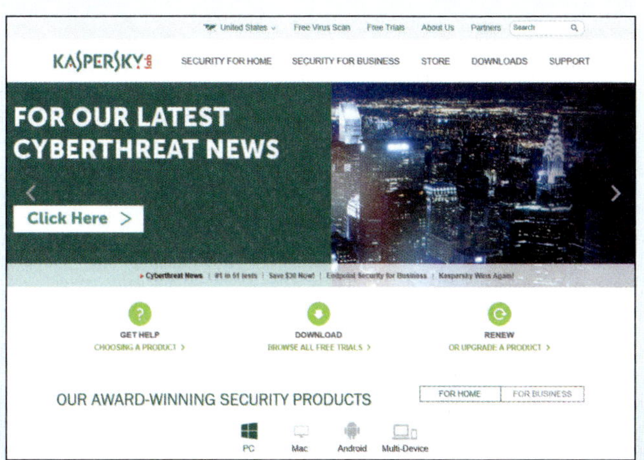

Information stored by browsers includes **history files** (record sites visited) and **temporary Internet files** or **browser cache** (contain website content and display instructions). **Cookies** store and track information. **Privacy mode (Private Browsing)** ensures that your browsing activity is not recorded.

Spyware secretly records and reports Internet activities. **Keystroke loggers** (one type of **computer monitoring software**) records every activity and keystroke. **Antispyware (spy removal programs)** detects and removes various privacy threats.

Online Identity

Many people post personal information and sometimes intimate details of their lives without considering the consequences. This creates an **online identity.** With the archiving and search features of the web, this identity is indefinitely available to anyone who cares to look for it.

Major Laws on Privacy

The **Gramm-Leach-Bliley Act** protects personal financial information; the **Health Insurance Portability and Accountability Act (HIPAA)** protects medical records; and the **Family Educational Rights and Privacy Act (FERPA)** restricts disclosure of educational records.

To efficiently and effectively use computers, you need to be aware of the potential impact of technology on people. You need to be sensitive to and knowledgeable about personal privacy, organizational security, and ethics.

SECURITY

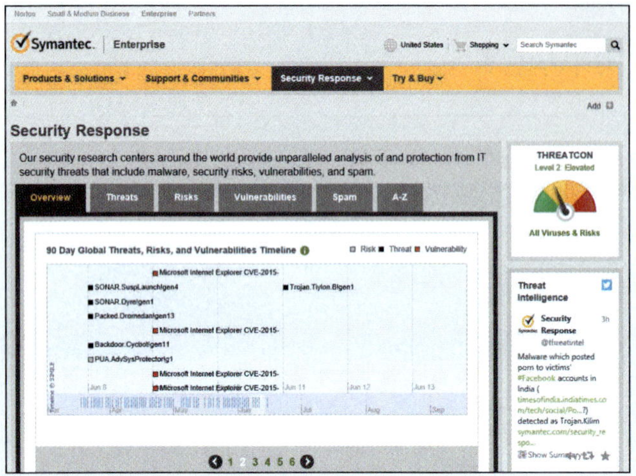

Computer **security** focuses on protecting information, hardware, and software from unauthorized use as well as preventing damage from intrusions, sabotage, and natural disasters. Someone who gains unauthorized access to computers that contain information about us is commonly known as a computer **hacker.** Not all hackers are intent on malicious actions and not all are criminals.

Cybercrime

Cybercrime (computer crime) is an illegal action involving special knowledge of computer technology.

- Malicious programs **(malware)** include **viruses** (the **Computer Fraud and Abuse Act** makes spreading a virus a federal offense), **worms,** and **Trojan horses. Zombies** are remotely controlled infected computers used for malicious purposes. A collection of zombie computers is known as a **botnet,** or **robot network.**
- **Denial of service (DoS) attack** is an attempt to shut down or stop a computer system or network.
- **Rogue Wi-Fi hotspots** imitate legitimate hotspots to capture personal information.
- Data manipulation involves changing data or leaving prank messages. The **Computer Fraud and Abuse Act** helps protect against data manipulation.
- **Identity theft** is the illegal assumption of someone's identity for the purposes of economic gain.

SECURITY

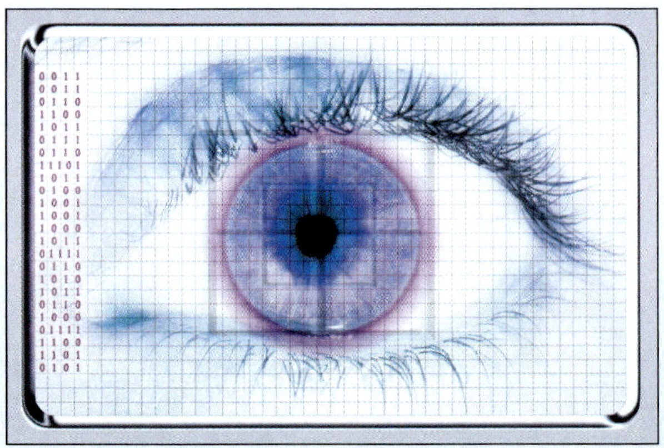

- **Scams** are designed to trick individuals into spending their time and money with little or no return. Common **Internet scams** are frequently coupled with **phishing** websites or e-mails.
- **Cyberbullying** is the use of the Internet, cell phones, or other devices to send or post content intended to hurt or embarrass another person.

Measures to Protect Computer Security

There are numerous ways in which computer systems and data can be compromised and many ways to protect computer security. These measures include

- Access can be restricted through **biometric scanning** devices and **passwords** (secret words or phrases; **dictionary attacks** use thousands of words to attempt to gain access); **security suites, firewalls,** and **password managers** help with security tasks.
- **Encrypting** is coding information to make it unreadable except to those who have the **encryption key. Hypertext transfer protocol secure (https)** requires browsers and websites to encrypt all messages. **Virtual private networks (VPNs)** encrypt connections between company networks and remote users. **WPA2 (Wi-Fi Protected Access)** is the most widely used wireless network encryption for home wireless networks.
- Anticipating disasters involves physical security, data security, and disaster recovery plans.
- Preventing data loss involves protecting data by screening job applicants, guarding passwords, and auditing and backing up data.

ETHICS

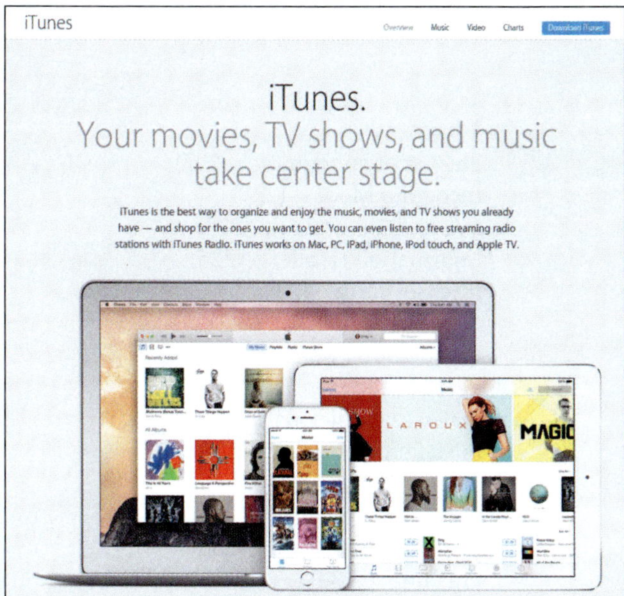

What do you suppose controls how computers can be used? You probably think first of laws. Of course, that is right, but technology is moving so fast that it is very difficult for our legal system to keep up. The essential element that controls how computers are used today is *ethics.*

Ethics are standards of moral conduct. **Computer ethics** are guidelines for the morally acceptable use of computers in our society. We are all entitled to ethical treatment. This includes the right to keep personal information, such as credit ratings and medical histories, from getting into unauthorized hands.

Copyright and Digital Rights Management

Copyright is a legal concept that gives content creators the right to control use and distribution of their work. Materials that can be copyrighted include paintings, books, music, films, and even video games.

Software piracy is the unauthorized copying and distribution of software. The software industry loses over $60 billion annually to software piracy. Two related topics are the Digital Millennium Copyright Act and digital rights management.

- **Digital Millennium Copyright Act** establishes the right of a program owner to make a backup copy of any program and disallows the creation of copies to be sold or given away. It is also illegal to download copyright-protected music and videos from the Internet.
- **Digital rights management (DRM)** is a collection of technologies designed to prevent copyright violations. Typically, DRM is used to (1) control the number of devices that can access a given file and (2) limit the kinds of devices that can access a file.

ETHICS

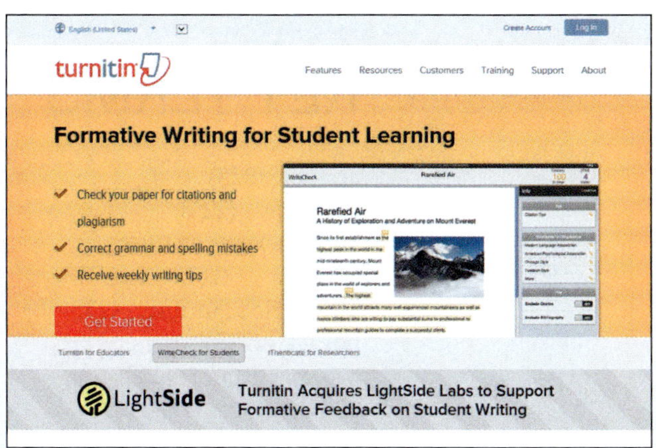

Today, many legal sources for digital media exist, including

- Television programs that can be watched online, often for free, on television-network-sponsored sites.
- Sites like Pandora that allow listeners to enjoy music at no cost.
- Online stores that legally sell music and video content. A pioneer in this area is Apple's iTunes Music Store.

Plagiarism

Plagiarism is the illegal and unethical representation of some other person's work and ideas as your own without giving credit to the original source. Examples of plagiarism include cutting and pasting web content into a report or paper.

Recognizing and catching **plagiarists** is relatively easy. For example, services such as Turnitin are dedicated to preventing Internet plagiarism. This service examines a paper's content and compares it to a wide range of known public electronic documents including web page content. Exact duplication or paraphrasing is readily identified.

CAREERS IN IT

IT security analysts are responsible for maintaining the security of a company's network, systems, and data. Employers look for candidates with a bachelor's or associate's degree in information systems or computer science and network experience. Salary range is $46,000 to $64,000.

KEY TERMS

access (225)
accuracy (225)
antispyware (230)
big data (225)
biometric scanning (235)
botnet (233)
browser cache (228)
computer crime (231)
computer ethics (238)
Computer Fraud and Abuse Act (231, 233)
computer monitoring software (229)
cookies (228)
copyright (240)
cracker (231)
cyberbullying (234)
cybercrime (231)
data security (238)
denial of service (DoS) attack (233)
dictionary attack (236)
Digital Millennium Copyright Act (240)
digital rights management (DRM) (240)
disaster recovery plan (238)
electronic profile (225)
employee-monitoring software (227)
encryption (236)
encryption key (236)
ethics (238)
Family Educational Rights and Privacy Act (FERPA) (231)
firewall (236)
first-party cookie (228)
Freedom of Information Act (227)
Gramm-Leach-Bliley Act (230)
hacker (231)
Health Insurance Portability and Accountability Act (HIPAA) (230)
history file (227)
https (hypertext transfer protocol secure) (236)
identity theft (233)
illusion of anonymity (227)
Incognito Mode (228)
information broker (225)
information reseller (225)
Internet scam (234)
IT security analyst (241)
key (236)
keystroke logger (229)
malware (malicious software) (231)
mistaken identity (227)
online identity (230)
password (235)
password managers (236)
phishing (234)
physical security (237)
plagiarism (240)
plagiarist (240)
privacy (225)
privacy mode (228)
Private Browsing (228)
property (225)
robot network (233)
rogue Wi-Fi hotspot (233)
scam (234)
security (231)
security suites (236)
software piracy (240)
spy removal program (230)
spyware (229)
temporary Internet file (228)
third-party cookie (228)
tracking cookies (228)
Trojan horse (232)
virtual private network (VPN) (237)
virus (231)
web bugs (228)
wireless network encryption (237)
worm (232)
WPA2 (Wi-Fi Protected Access 2) (237)
zombie (233)

MULTIPLE CHOICE

Circle the letter of the correct answer.

1. The three primary privacy issues are accuracy, property, and:
   - a. access
   - b. ethics
   - c. ownership
   - d. security
2. Highly detailed and personalized descriptions of individuals are electronic:
   - a. cookies
   - b. histories
   - c. profiles
   - d. web bugs
3. Browsers store the locations of sites visited in a:
   - a. history file
   - b. menu
   - c. tool bar
   - d. firewall
4. The browser mode that ensures your browsing activity is not recorded.
   - a. detect
   - b. insert
   - c. privacy
   - d. sleep
5. The information that people voluntarily post in social networking sites, blogs, and photo- and video-sharing sites is used to create their:
   - a. access approval
   - b. firewall
   - c. online identity
   - d. phish
6. Computer criminals who create and distribute malicious programs.
   - a. antispies
   - b. crackers
   - c. cyber traders
   - d. identity thieves
7. Programs that come into a computer system disguised as something else are called:
   - a. Trojan horses
   - b. viruses
   - c. web bugs
   - d. zombies
8. The use of the Internet, cell phones, or other devices to send or post content intended to hurt or embarrass another person is known as:
   - a. cyberbullying
   - b. online harassment
   - c. social networking discrimination
   - d. unethical communication
9. Special hardware and software used to control access to a corporation's private network is known as a(n):
   - a. antivirus program
   - b. communication gate
   - c. firewall
   - d. spyware removal program
10. To prevent copyright violations, corporations often use:
    - a. ACT
    - b. DRM
    - c. VPN
    - d. WPA2

MATCHING

Match each numbered item with the most closely related lettered item. Write your answers in the spaces provided.

a. accuracy
b. biometric
c. cookies
d. encryption
e. information brokers
f. malware
g. phishing
h. plagiarism
i. spyware
j. zombies

___ 1. Privacy concern that relates to the responsibility to ensure correct data collection.
___ 2. Individuals who collect and sell personal data.
___ 3. Small data files deposited on your hard disk from websites you have visited.
___ 4. Wide range of programs that secretly record and report an individual's activities on the Internet.
___ 5. Malicious programs that damage or disrupt a computer system.
___ 6. Infected computers that can be remotely controlled.
___ 7. Used by scammers to trick Internet users with official-looking websites.
___ 8. A type of scanning device such as fingerprint and iris (eye) scanner.
___ 9. Process of coding information to make it unreadable except to those who have a key.
___ 10. An ethical issue relating to using another person's work and ideas as your own without giving credit to the original source.

OPEN-ENDED

On a separate sheet of paper, respond to each question or statement.

1. Define privacy, and discuss the impact of large databases, private networks, the Internet, and the web.
2. Define and discuss online identity and the major privacy laws.
3. Define security. Define computer crime and the impact of malicious programs, including viruses, worms, Trojan horses, and zombies, as well as denial of service attacks, rogue Wi-Fi hotspots, data manipulation, identity theft, Internet scams, and cyberbullying.
4. Discuss ways to protect computer security including restricting access, encrypting data, anticipating disasters, and preventing data loss.
5. Define ethics, and describe copyright law and plagiarism.

DISCUSSION

Respond to each of the following questions.

1 Making IT Work for You: CLOUD-BASED BACKUP

Review the Making IT Work for You: Cloud-Based Backup on page 239, and then respond to the following: (a) How do you currently back up your important files? How often do you create these backups? (b) Have you ever used a cloud-based service? If so, which service have you used, and what do you typically use it for? If you have not used a cloud-based service, describe how and why you might use one. (c) Do you see yourself signing up for a paid, yearly subscription to a service such as Carbonite? Why or why not?

2 Privacy: DRONES

Review the Privacy box on page 225, and then answer the following: (a) Have you ever used a drone or seen one in operation? If so, describe the application. (b) Do you believe that drones are a threat to personal privacy? Why or why not? (c) If you used a drone to capture an aerial view of just your property, do you see any potential privacy violations? (d) If you used a drone to capture aerial views of your neighborhood, would that violate anyone's privacy? Why or why not?

3 Privacy: SOCIAL NETWORKING

Review the Privacy box on page 227, and then answer the following: (a) Do you use any social networking sites? If so, which ones and do you know their policy of sharing your posts and photos to others without your expressed consent? (b) Do you believe that social networks violate your privacy when they share information with advertisers? Why or why not? (c) Suppose that a high school teacher posts photos on her Facebook page showing her drinking at a party. When the school board becomes aware of these photos, the teacher is suspended. Is this a violation of her rights? Why or why not? (d) In late 2009, Facebook allowed users' names, pictures, and basic information to appear in Google search results. Do you think this is ethical? Why or why not?

4 Ethics: RIGHT TO BE FORGOTTEN

Review the Ethics box on page 230, and then answer the following: (a) What is your opinion regarding the right to be forgotten? Defend your position. (b) Do you think you should have the right and the ability to remove any embarrassing photos of you that have been posted on the Internet? Why or why not? (c) Do you think a person convicted of a crime should be able to remove any trace of that crime from the Internet? Defend your position. (d) Should the right to be forgotten apply to everyone, or would it be different for a politician, a movie star, or a criminal? Defend your position.

5 Privacy: DARK WEB

Review the Privacy box on page 234, and then respond to the following: (a) Before reading this Privacy box, were you aware of the Dark Web? If so, describe how you became aware of these hidden websites. (b) What do you think are the greatest risks associated with the Dark Web? Be specific. (c) Do you think elimination of the Dark Web is important? Why or why not? (d) Do you think elimination or control of the Dark Web is a privacy concern? Defend your position.

6 Environment: ENVIRONMENTAL ETHICS AND IT

Review the Environment box on page 238, and then respond to the following: (a) Do you feel that IT professionals should receive training or education in environmental issues? Why or why not? (b) Can a person be considered unethical if he or she fails to consider the environment in any decisions? Discuss your response. (c) Do you feel that governments should create laws that govern the energy consumption of computers and other electronic devices? Why or why not? (d) Using a search engine, find the website of the Energy Star program. Which government agencies are responsible for this program? What environmental benefits has this program already given us?

7 Ethics: NET NEUTRALITY

Review the Ethics box on page 240, and then respond to the following: (a) Do you think that government agencies should be allowed to regulate ISP pricing policies? Why or why not? (b) Do you think the speed or ease of access of web pages can be a form of censorship? Why or why not? (c) If a government made anti-government websites run slower, would that be censorship? Why or why not? (d) If a company made its competitions' websites run slower, would that be censorship? Why or why not? (e) Should an ISP be allowed to watch you browse the Internet to decide which web pages should download quickly and which should download slowly? Defend your position.

8 Ethics: PLAGIARISM

Review the Ethics box on page 241, and then respond to the following: (a) Do you think it is ethical for instructors to employ a program that checks for plagiarism? Why or why not? (b) Do you think it is ethical for students or any individuals to copy all or part of a web page's content and then present the information without crediting the source? Why or why not? (c) How would you distinguish between using the web for research and plagiarizing web content? Be specific. (d) Does your school have a policy specifically regarding plagiarism of web content? If yes, what is the policy? If not, what would you suggest would be an appropriate policy?

PHOTO CREDITS

CHAPTER 9

Opener: © Dimitri Vervits/ImageState RF; p. 223, 242: © Jasper James/Getty Images; p. 224, 241: © Peter M. Fisher/Corbis; 9-1, p. 243 (left): Copyright © 2015, Spokeo, Inc.; 9-2, 9-3 (bottom), 9-4, 9-5: Google and the Google logo are registered trademarks of Google Inc. Used with permission; 9-3 (top): Copyright © 2015 Microsoft, Inc.; 9-6, p. 243 (right): Copyright © 2015 Kaspersky Lab. All rights reserved; 9-8, p. 244 (left): Copyright © 2015 Symantec Corporation. All rights reserved; 9-11 (left): © Anatoliy Babiy/Getty Images RF; 9-11 (right), p. 244 (right): © Cristian Baitg/Getty Images; 9-12: Used with permission under Creative Commons License; 9-13, 9-15, p. 239 (top), 240, 245 (left): Copyright © 2015 Apple, Inc.; p. 239 (bottom): Copyright © 2015 Carbonite, Inc. All rights reserved; 9-16, p. 245 (right): Copyright © 2015. Used courtesy of www.turnitin.com.

chapter 10 Information Systems

Why should I read this chapter?

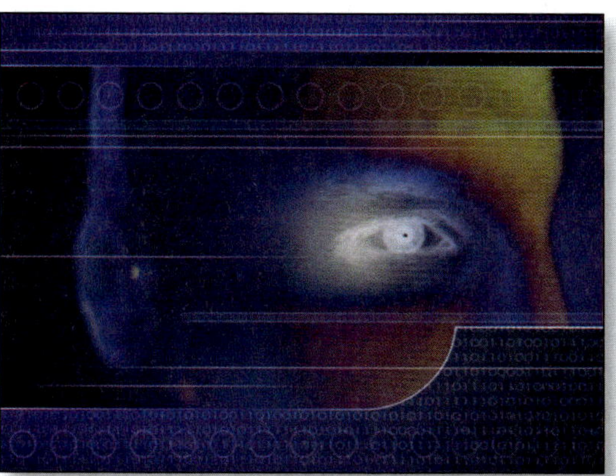

You hear an intruder in your home late at night and call the police; a fast response may save your life! Law enforcement use their information systems to organize resources and prioritize emergency calls—improving response times and saving lives. In the future, information systems of all types will automatically adjust to their environments and help organizations react to current and future changes.

This chapter covers the things you need to know to be prepared for this ever-changing digital world, including:

- Organizational flow—identify how information flows within an organization.
- Computer-based information systems—recognize the levels of information systems and how they help businesses make decisions.
- Other information systems—understand expert systems and how you can use them to make faster, smarter decisions.

Learning Objectives

After you have read this chapter, you should be able to:

1 Explain the functional view of an organization and describe each function.

2 Describe the management levels and the informational needs for each level in an organization.

3 Describe how information flows within an organization.

4 Describe computer-based information systems.

5 Distinguish among a transaction processing system, a management information system, a decision support system, and an executive support system.

6 Distinguish between office automation systems and knowledge work systems.

7 Explain the difference between data workers and knowledge workers.

8 Define expert systems and knowledge bases.

Introduction

"Hi, I'm Alice, and I'm an information systems manager. I'd like to talk with you about how organizations use computer information systems. I'd also like to talk about specialized knowledge work systems that assist managers, engineers, and scientists make decisions."

An **information system** is a collection of people, procedures, software, hardware, data, and connectivity (as we discussed in Chapter 1). They all work together to provide information essential to running an organization. This information is critical to successfully produce a product or service and, for profit-oriented enterprises, to derive a profit.

Why are computers used in organizations? No doubt you can easily state one reason: to keep records of events. However, another reason might be less obvious: to help make decisions. For example, point-of-sale terminals record sales as well as which salesperson made each sale. This information can be used for decision making. For instance, it can help the sales manager decide which salespeople will get year-end bonuses for doing exceptional work.

The Internet, communication links, and databases connect you with information resources as well as information systems far beyond the surface of your desk. The personal computer offers you access to a greater quantity of information than was possible a few years ago. In addition, you also have access to better-quality information. As we show in this chapter, when you tap into a computer-based information system, you not only get information—you also get help in making decisions.

To efficiently and effectively use computers within an organization, you need to understand how the information flows as it moves through an organization's different functional areas and management levels. You need to be aware of the different types of computer-based information systems, including transaction processing systems, management information systems, decision support systems, and executive support systems. You also need to understand the role and importance of databases to support each level or type of information system.

Organizational Information Flow

Computerized information systems do not just keep track of transactions and day-to-day business operations. They also support the vertical and horizontal flow of information within the organization. To understand this, we need to understand how an organization is structured. One way to examine an organization's structure is to view it from a functional perspective. That is, you can study the different basic functional areas in organizations and the different types of people within these functional areas.

As we describe these, consider how they apply to a hypothetical manufacturer of sporting goods, the HealthWise Group. This company manufactures equipment for sports and physical activities. Its products range from soccer balls to yoga mats. (See Figure 10-1.)

Like many organizations, HealthWise Group can be viewed from a functional perspective with various management levels. Effective operations require an efficient and coordinated flow of information throughout the organization.

Functions

Depending on the services or products they provide, most organizations have departments that specialize in one of five basic functions. These are accounting, marketing, human resources, production, and research. (See Figure 10-2.)

- **Accounting** records all financial activity from billing customers to paying employees. For example, at HealthWise, the accounting department tracks all sales, payments, and transfers of funds. It also produces reports detailing the financial condition of the company.
- **Marketing** plans, prices, promotes, sells, and distributes the organization's goods and services. At HealthWise, goods include a wide range of products related to sports and other types of physical activity.
- **Human resources** focuses on people—hiring, training, promoting, and any number of other human-centered activities within the organization. At HealthWise, human resources is responsible for implementing a new benefits package, for hiring new skilled workers, and much more.
- **Production** actually creates finished goods and services using raw materials and personnel. At HealthWise, this includes manufacturing a variety of sports equipment, including yoga mats.
- **Research** identifies, investigates, and develops new products and services. For example, at HealthWise, scientists are investigating a light, inexpensive alloy for a new line of weight-training equipment.

Figure 10-1 Yoga mats

Human resources is involved with all human-centered activities across the entire organization. At HealthWise, this department is implementing a new benefits package designed to attract new employees and retain current employees.

Functional perspective

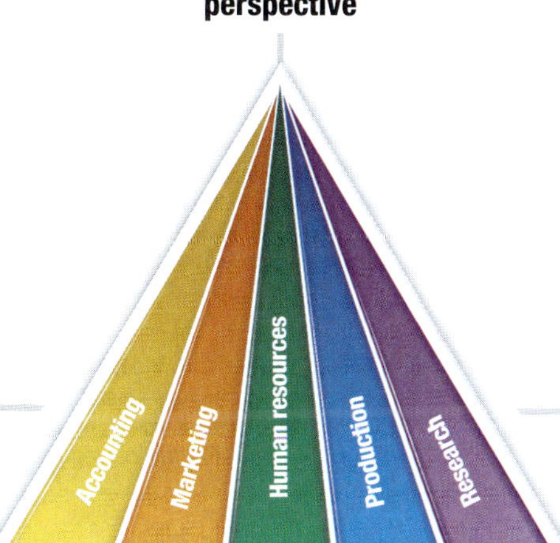

Accounting tracks all financial activity. At HealthWise, this department records bills and other financial transactions with sporting goods stores. It also produces financial statements, including budgets and forecasts of financial performance.

Research conducts basic research and relates new discoveries to the firm's current or new products department. Research people at HealthWise explore new ideas from exercise physiologists about muscle development. They use this knowledge to design new physical fitness machines.

Marketing handles planning, pricing, promoting, selling, and distributing goods and services to customers. At HealthWise, it even gets involved with creating a customer newsletter that is distributed via the corporate web page.

Production takes in raw materials and people work to turn out finished goods (or services). It may be a manufacturing activity or—in the case of a retail store—an operations activity. At HealthWise, this department purchases steel and aluminum to be used in weight-lifting and exercise machines.

Figure 10-2 The five functions of an organization

Although the titles may vary, nearly every large and small organization has departments that perform these basic functions. Whatever your job in an organization, it is likely to be in one of these functional areas.

Management Levels

Most people who work in an organization are not managers, of course. At the base of the organizational pyramid are the assemblers, painters, welders, drivers, and so on. These people produce goods and services. Above them are various levels of managers—people with titles such as supervisor, director, regional manager, and vice president. These are the people who do the planning, leading, organizing, and controlling necessary to see that the work gets done.

At HealthWise, for example, the northwest district sales manager directs and coordinates all the salespeople in her area. Other job titles might be vice president of marketing, director of human resources, or production manager. In smaller organizations, these titles are often combined.

Management in many organizations is divided into three levels. These levels are supervisors, middle management, and top management. (See Figure 10-3.)

- **Supervisors:** Supervisors manage and monitor the employees or workers. Thus, these managers have responsibility relating to *operational matters.* They monitor day-to-day events and immediately take corrective action, if necessary.
- **Middle management:** Middle-level managers deal with *control, planning* (also called *tactical planning*), and *decision making.* They implement the long-term goals of the organization.
- **Top management:** Top-level managers are concerned with *long-range planning* (also called *strategic planning*). They need information that will help them plan the future growth and direction of the organization.

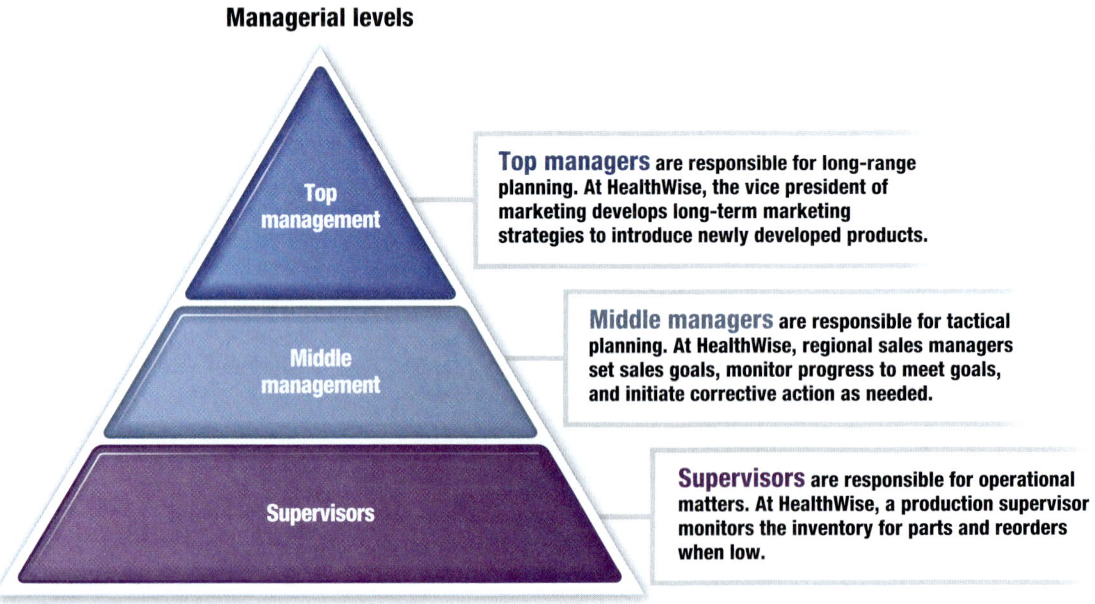

Managerial levels
Top management
Middle management
Supervisors
Top managers are responsible for long-range planning. At HealthWise, the vice president of marketing develops long-term marketing strategies to introduce newly developed products.
Middle managers are responsible for tactical planning. At HealthWise, regional sales managers set sales goals, monitor progress to meet goals, and initiate corrective action as needed.
Supervisors are responsible for operational matters. At HealthWise, a production supervisor monitors the inventory for parts and reorders when low.

Figure 10-3 Three levels of management

Information Flow

Figure 10-4 **Supervisors monitor day-to-day events**

Each level of management has different information needs. Top-level managers need summary information describing the overall operations of the business. They also need information from outside the organization because top-level managers need to forecast and plan for long-range events. Middle-level managers need summarized information—weekly or monthly reports. They need to develop budget projections and to evaluate the performance of supervisors. Supervisors need detailed, very current, day-to-day information on their units so that they can keep operations running smoothly. (See Figure 10-4.)

To support these different needs, information *flows* in different directions. (See Figure 10-5.) For top-level managers, the flow of information from within the organization is both vertical and horizontal. The top-level managers, such as the chief executive officer (CEO), need information from below and from all departments. They also need information from outside the organization. For example, at HealthWise, they are deciding whether to introduce a line of fitness trackers in the southwestern United States. The vice president of marketing must look at relevant data. Such data might include the number of people currently using the HealthWise fitness app and census data about the number of young people. It also might include sales histories on related fitness monitoring equipment.

For middle-level managers, the information flow is both vertical and horizontal across functional lines. For example, the regional sales managers at HealthWise set their sales goals by coordinating with middle managers in the production department. They are able to tell sales managers what products will be produced, how many, and when. The regional sales managers also must coordinate with the strategic goals set by the top managers. They must set and monitor the sales goals for the supervisors beneath them.

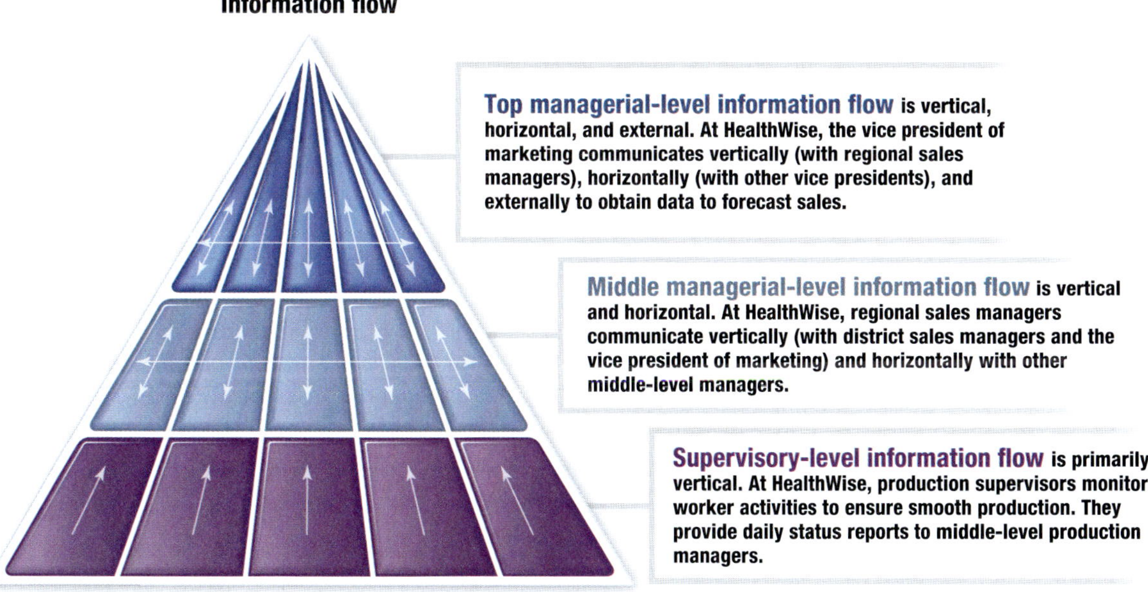

Information flow
Top managerial-level information flow is vertical, horizontal, and external. At HealthWise, the vice president of marketing communicates vertically (with regional sales managers), horizontally (with other vice presidents), and externally to obtain data to forecast sales.
Middle managerial-level information flow is vertical and horizontal. At HealthWise, regional sales managers communicate vertically (with district sales managers and the vice president of marketing) and horizontally with other middle-level managers.
Supervisory-level information flow is primarily vertical. At HealthWise, production supervisors monitor worker activities to ensure smooth production. They provide daily status reports to middle-level production managers.

Figure 10-5 **Information flow within an organization**

For supervisory managers, information flow is primarily vertical. That is, supervisors communicate mainly with their middle managers and with the workers beneath them. For instance, at HealthWise, production supervisors rarely communicate with people in the accounting department. However, they are constantly communicating with production-line workers and with their own managers.

Now we know how many organizations are structured and how information flows within the organization. But how is a computer-based information system likely to be set up to support its needs? And what do you need to know to use it?

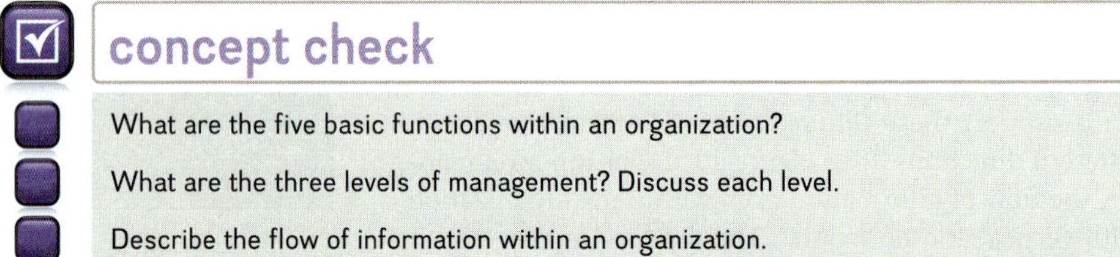

concept check
What are the five basic functions within an organization?
What are the three levels of management? Discuss each level.
Describe the flow of information within an organization.

Computer-Based Information Systems

Almost all organizations have computer-based information systems. Large organizations typically have formal names for the systems designed to collect and use the data. Although different organizations may use different names, the most common names are transaction processing, management information, decision support, and executive support systems. (See Figure 10-6.)

- **Transaction processing system:** The **transaction processing system (TPS)** records day-to-day transactions, such as customer orders, bills, inventory levels, and production output. The TPS helps supervisors by generating databases that act as the foundation for the other information systems.
- **Management information system:** The **management information system (MIS)** summarizes the detailed data of the transaction processing system in standard reports for middle-level managers. Such reports might include weekly sales and production schedules.
- **Decision support system:** The **decision support system (DSS)** provides a flexible tool for analysis. The DSS helps middle-level managers and others in the organization analyze a wide range of problems, such as the effect of events and trends outside the organization. Like the MIS, the DSS draws on the detailed data of the transaction processing system.
- **Executive support system:** The **executive support system (ESS),** also known as the **executive information system (EIS),** is an easy-to-use system that presents information in a very highly summarized form. It helps top-level managers oversee the company's operations and develop strategic plans. The ESS combines the databases generated from the TPS and the reports generated from the MIS with external data.

concept check

- What is a transaction processing system? How does it help supervisors?
- What is a management information system? Decision support system? How are they different?
- What is an executive support system? Who uses it? What is it used for?

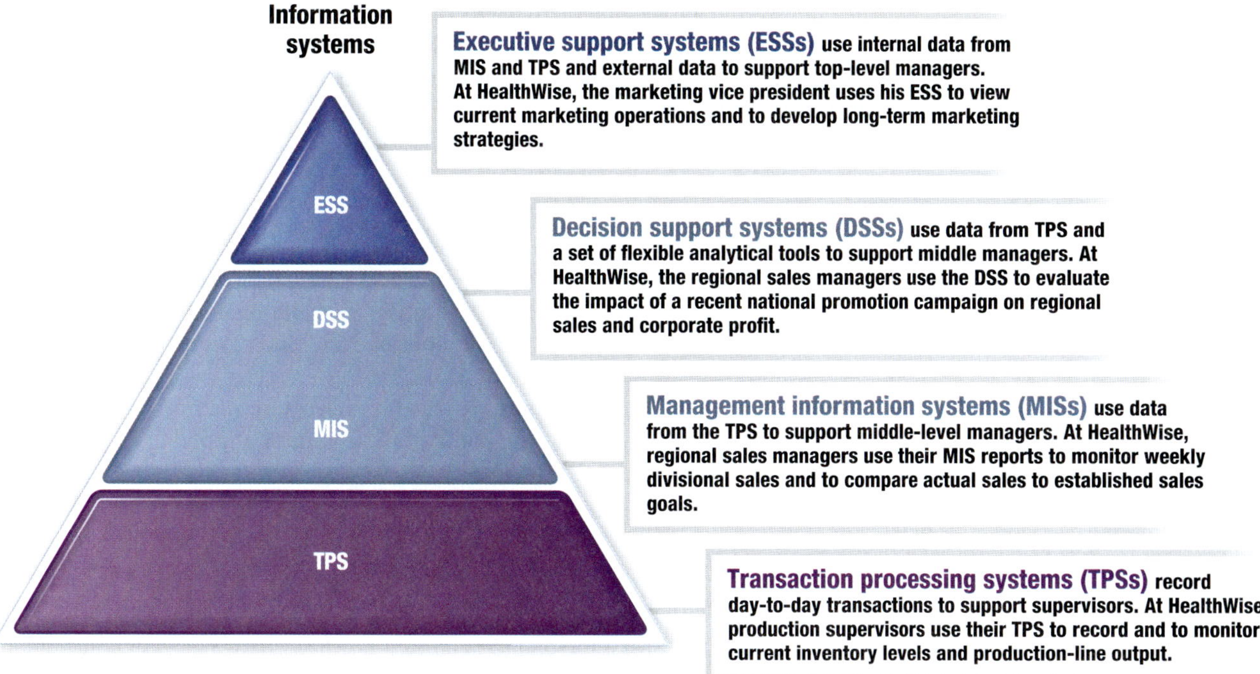

Information systems
Executive support systems (ESSs) use internal data from MIS and TPS and external data to support top-level managers. At HealthWise, the marketing vice president uses his ESS to view current marketing operations and to develop long-term marketing strategies.
ESS
Decision support systems (DSSs) use data from TPS and a set of flexible analytical tools to support middle managers. At HealthWise, the regional sales managers use the DSS to evaluate the impact of a recent national promotion campaign on regional sales and corporate profit.
DSS
MIS
Management information systems (MISs) use data from the TPS to support middle-level managers. At HealthWise, regional sales managers use their MIS reports to monitor weekly divisional sales and to compare actual sales to established sales goals.
TPS
Transaction processing systems (TPSs) record day-to-day transactions to support supervisors. At HealthWise, production supervisors use their TPS to record and to monitor current inventory levels and production-line output.

Figure 10-6 Types of computer-based information systems

Transaction Processing Systems

A **transaction processing system (TPS)** helps an organization keep track of routine operations and records these events in a database. For this reason, some firms call this the **data processing system (DPS).** The data from operations—for example, customer orders for HealthWise's products—makes up a database that records the transactions of the company. This database of transactions is used to support the MIS, DSS, and ESS.

One of the most essential transaction processing systems for any organization is in the accounting area. (See Figure 10-7.) Every accounting department handles six basic activities. Five of these are sales order processing, accounts receivable, inventory and purchasing, accounts payable, and payroll. All of these are recorded in the general ledger, the sixth activity.

Let us take a look at these six activities. They will make up the basis of the accounting system for almost any organization you might work in.

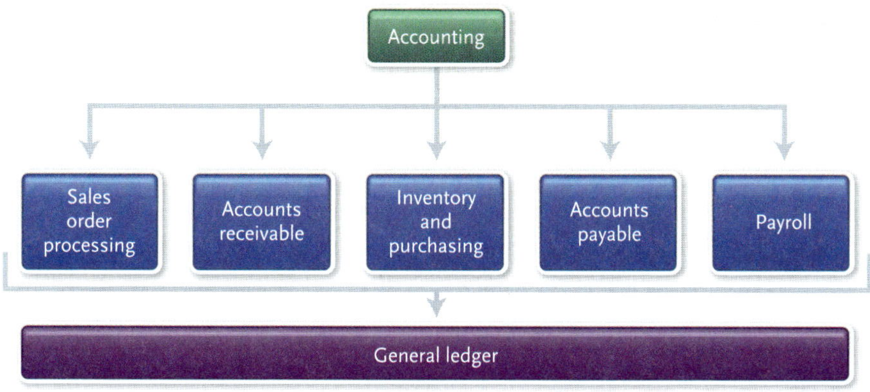

Figure 10-7 Transaction processing system for accounting

- The **sales order processing** activity records the customer requests for the company's products or services. At HealthWise when an order comes in—a request for a set of barbells, for example—the warehouse is alerted to ship a product.
- The **accounts receivable** activity records money received from or owed by customers. HealthWise keeps track of bills paid by sporting goods stores and by gyms and health clubs to which it sells directly.
- The parts and finished goods that the company has in stock are called **inventory.** At HealthWise this would include all exercise machines, footballs, soccer balls, and yoga mats ready for sale in the warehouse. (See Figure 10-8.) An **inventory control system** keeps records of the number of each kind of part or finished good in the warehouse.

  Purchasing is the buying of materials and services. Often a **purchase order** is used. This is a form that shows the name of the company supplying the material or service and what is being purchased.
- **Accounts payable** refers to money the company owes its suppliers for materials and services it has received. At HealthWise this would include materials such as steel and aluminum used to manufacture its exercise equipment.
- The **payroll** activity is concerned with calculating employee paychecks. Amounts are generally determined by the pay rate, hours worked, and deductions (such as taxes, Social Security, medical insurance). Paychecks may be calculated from employee time cards or, in some cases, supervisors' time sheets.
- The **general ledger** keeps track of all summaries of all the foregoing transactions. A typical general ledger system can produce income statements and balance sheets. **Income statements** show a company's financial performance—income, expenses, and the difference between them for a specific time period. **Balance sheets** list the overall financial condition of an organization. They include assets (for example, buildings and property owned), liabilities (debts), and how much of the organization (the equity) is owned by the owners.

There are many other transaction processing systems that you come into contact with every day. These include automatic teller machines, which record cash withdrawals; online registration systems, which track student enrollments; and supermarket discount cards, which track customer purchases.

Figure 10-8 **Inventory control systems manage the merchandise in the warehouse**

concept check

What is the purpose of a transaction processing system?

Describe the six activities of a TPS for accounting.

Other than TPS for accounting, describe three other TPSs.

Management Information Systems

A **management information system (MIS)** is a computer-based information system that produces standardized reports in summarized structured form. (See Figure 10-9.) It is used to support middle managers. An MIS differs from a transaction processing system in a significant way. Whereas a transaction processing system *creates* databases, an MIS *uses* databases. Indeed, an MIS can draw from the databases of several departments. Thus, an MIS requires a *database management system* that integrates the databases of the different departments. Middle managers often need summary data drawn from across different functional areas.

An MIS produces reports that are *predetermined.* That is, they follow a predetermined format and always show the same kinds of content. Although reports may differ from one industry to another, there are three common categories of reports: periodic, exception, and demand.

HealthWise Group Regional Sales Report			
Region	Actual Sales	Target	Difference
Central	$166,430	$175,000	($8,570)
Northern	137,228	130,000	7,228
Southern	137,772	135,000	2,772
Eastern	152,289	155,000	(2,711)
Western	167,017	160,000	7,017

Figure 10-9 **Management information system report**

- **Periodic reports** are produced at regular intervals—weekly, monthly, or quarterly, for instance. Examples are HealthWise's monthly sales and production reports. The sales reports from district sales managers are combined into a monthly report for the regional sales managers. For comparison purposes, a regional manager is also able to see the sales reports of other regional managers.
- **Exception reports** call attention to unusual events. An example is a sales report that shows that certain items are selling significantly above or below marketing department forecasts. For instance, if fewer exercise bicycles are selling than were predicted for the northwest sales region, the regional manager will receive an exception report. That report may be used to alert the district managers and salespeople to give this product more attention.
- The opposite of a periodic report, a **demand report** is produced on request. An example is a report on the numbers and types of jobs held by women and minorities. Such a report is not needed periodically, but it may be required when requested by the U.S. government. At HealthWise, many government contracts require this information. It is used to certify that HealthWise is within certain government equal-opportunity guidelines.

concept check

- What is the purpose of a management information system?
- What are predetermined reports?
- Describe the three common categories of MIS reports.

Decision Support Systems

Managers often must deal with unanticipated questions. For example, the Health-Wise manager in charge of manufacturing might ask how an anticipated labor strike would affect production schedules. A **decision support system (DSS)** enables managers to get answers to such unexpected and generally nonrecurring kinds of problems.

A DSS is quite different from a transaction processing system, which simply records data. It is also different from a management information system, which summarizes data in predetermined reports. A DSS is used to analyze data. Moreover, it produces reports that do not have a fixed format. This makes the DSS a flexible tool for analysis.

A DSS must be easy to use—or most likely it will not be used at all. A Health-Wise marketing manager might want to know which territories are not meeting their monthly sales quotas. To find out, the executive could ask or query the sales database for all "SALES < QUOTA." (See Figure 10-10.)

How does a decision support system work? Essentially, it consists of four parts: the user, system software, data, and decision models.

- The **user** could be you. In general, the user is someone who has to make decisions—a manager, often a middle-level manager.
- **System software** is essentially the operating system—programs designed to work behind the scenes to handle detailed operating procedures. In order to give the user a good, intuitive interface, the software typically is menu- or icon-driven. That is, the screen presents easily understood lists of commands or icons, giving the user several options.
- **Data** in a DSS is typically stored in a database and consists of two kinds. **Internal data**—data from within the organization—consists principally of transactions from the transaction processing system. **External data** is data gathered from outside the organization. Examples are data provided by marketing research firms, trade associations, and the U.S. government (such as customer profiles, census data, and economic forecasts).
- **Decision models** give the DSS its analytical capabilities. There are three basic types of decision models: strategic, tactical, and operational. **Strategic models** assist top-level managers in long-range planning, such as stating company

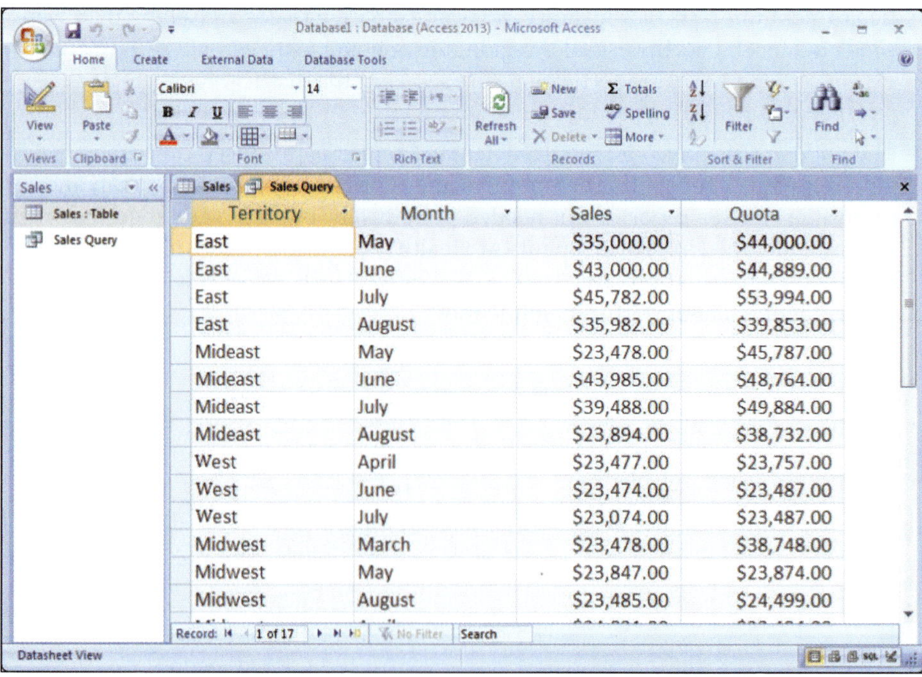

Territory	Month	Sales	Quota
East	May	$35,000.00	$44,000.00
East	June	$43,000.00	$44,889.00
East	July	$45,782.00	$53,994.00
East	August	$35,982.00	$39,853.00
Mideast	May	$23,478.00	$45,787.00
Mideast	June	$43,985.00	$48,764.00
Mideast	July	$39,488.00	$49,884.00
Mideast	August	$23,894.00	$38,732.00
West	April	$23,477.00	$23,757.00
West	June	$23,474.00	$23,487.00
West	July	$23,074.00	$23,487.00
Midwest	March	$23,478.00	$38,748.00
Midwest	May	$23,847.00	$23,874.00
Midwest	August	$23,485.00	$24,499.00

Figure 10-10 Decision support system query results for SALES < QUOTA

objectives or planning plant locations. **Tactical models** help middle-level managers control the work of the organization, such as financial planning and sales promotion planning. **Operational models** help lower-level managers accomplish the organization's day-to-day activities, such as evaluating and maintaining quality control.

Some DSSs are specifically designed to support more than one or a team of decision makers. These systems, known as **group decision support systems (GDSS),** include tools to support group meetings and collective work.

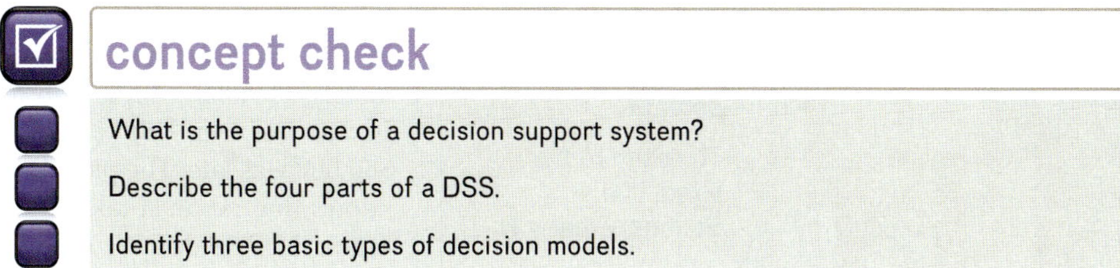

concept check

- What is the purpose of a decision support system?
- Describe the four parts of a DSS.
- Identify three basic types of decision models.

Executive Support Systems

Using a DSS requires some training. Many top managers have other people in their offices running DSSs and reporting their findings. Top-level executives also want something more concise than an MIS—something that produces very focused reports.

Executive support systems (ESSs) consist of sophisticated software that, like an MIS or a DSS, can present, summarize, and analyze data from an organization's databases. However, an ESS is specifically designed to be easy to use. This is so that a top executive with little spare time, for example, can obtain essential information without extensive training. Thus, information is often displayed in very condensed form with informative graphics.

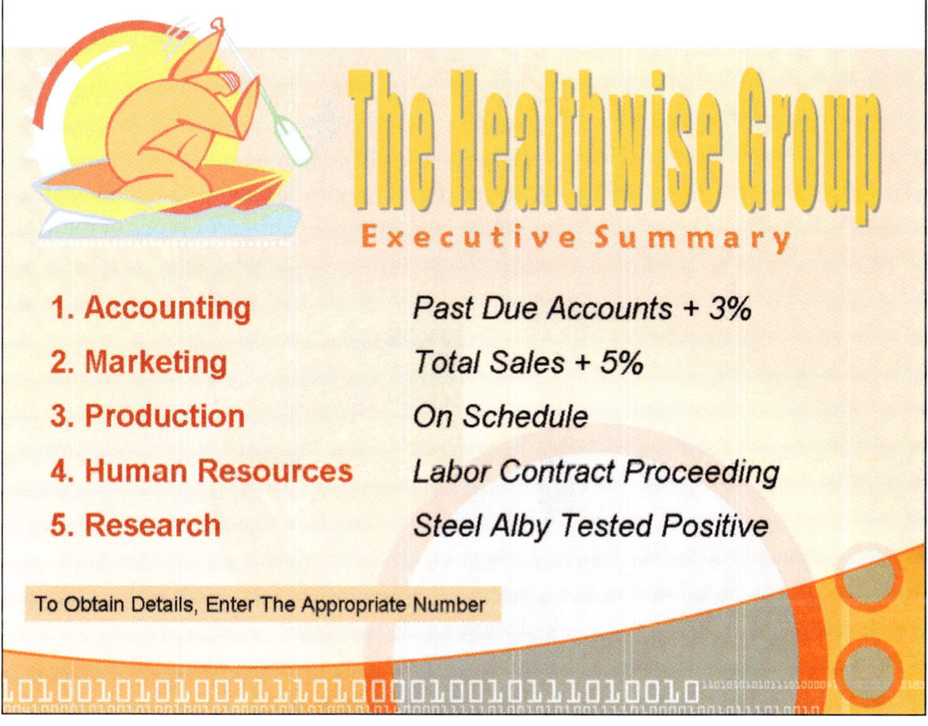

Figure 10-11 **Opening screen for an executive support system**

Consider an executive support system used by the president of HealthWise. It is available on his personal computer. The first thing each morning, the president calls up the ESS on his display screen, as shown in Figure 10-11. Note that the screen gives a condensed account of activities in the five different areas of the company. (These are Accounting, Marketing, Production, Human Resources, and Research.) On this particular morning, the ESS shows business in four areas proceeding smoothly. However, in the first area, Accounting, the percentage of late-paying customers—past due accounts—has increased by 3 percent. Three percent may not seem like much, but HealthWise has had a history of problems with late payers, which has left the company at times strapped for cash. The president decides to find out the details. To do so, he selects 1. Accounting.

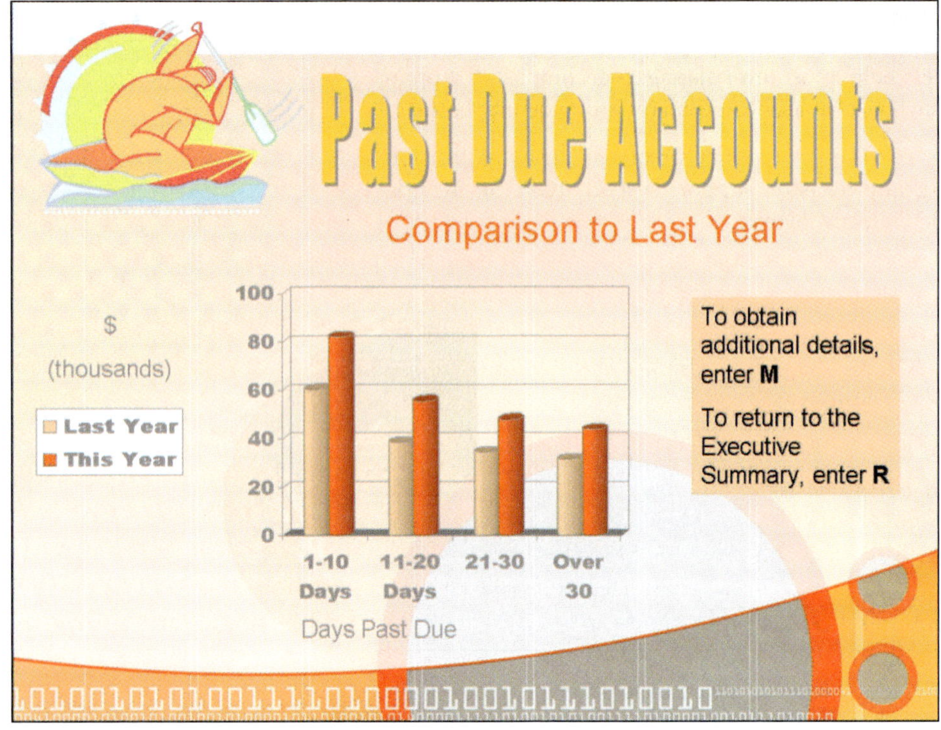
Past Due Accounts
Comparison to Last Year
$
(thousands)
100
80
60
40
20
0
Last Year
This Year
1-10 Days
11-20 Days
21-30
Over 30
Days Past Due
To obtain additional details, enter **M**
To return to the Executive Summary, enter **R**

Figure 10-12 Graphic representation of past due accounts

Within moments, the display screen displays a graph of the past due accounts. (See Figure 10-12.) The status of today's late payers is shown in red. The status of late payers at this time a year ago is shown in yellow. The differences between today and a year ago are significant and clearly presented. For example, approximately \$60,000 was late 1 to 10 days last year. This year, over \$80,000 was late. The president knows that he must take some action to speed up customer payments. (For example, he might call this to the attention of the vice president of accounting. The vice president might decide to implement a new policy that offers discounts to early payers or charge higher interest to late payers.)

ESSs permit a firm's top executives to gain direct access to information about the company's performance. Most provide direct electronic communication links to other executives. In addition, some ESSs have the ability to retrieve information from databases outside the company, such as business-news services. This enables a firm to watch for stories on competitors and stay current on relevant news events that could affect its business. For example, news of increased sports injuries caused by running and aerobic dancing, and the consequent decrease in people's interest in these activities, might cause HealthWise to alter its sales and production goals for its line of fitness-related shoes.

For a summary of the different types of information systems, see Figure 10-13.

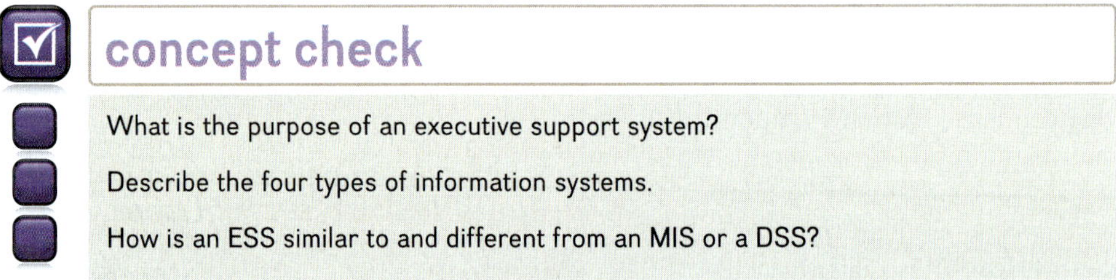
concept check
What is the purpose of an executive support system?
Describe the four types of information systems.
How is an ESS similar to and different from an MIS or a DSS?

Type	Description
TPS	Tracks routine operations and records events in databases; also known as data processing systems
MIS	Produces standardized reports (periodic, exception, and demand) using databases created by TPS
DSS	Analyzes unanticipated situations using data (internal and external) and decision models (strategic, tactical, and operational)
ESS	Presents summary information in a flexible, easy-to-use, graphical format designed for top executives

Figure 10-13 Summary of information systems

Other Information Systems

We have discussed only four information systems: TPSs to support lower-level managers, MISs and DSSs to support middle-level managers, and ESSs to support top-level managers. There are many other information systems to support different individuals and functions. The fastest growing are information systems designed to support information workers.

Information workers distribute, communicate, and create information. They are the organization's administrative assistants, clerks, engineers, and scientists, to name a few. Some are involved with distribution and communication of information (like administrative assistants and clerks; see Figure 10-14). They are called **data workers.** Others are involved with the creation of information (like the engineers and scientists). They are called **knowledge workers.**

Two systems to support information workers are

- **Office automation systems: Office automation systems (OASs)** are designed primarily to support data workers. These systems focus on managing documents, communicating, and scheduling. Documents are managed using word processing, web authoring, desktop publishing, and other image technologies. **Project managers** are programs designed to schedule, plan, and control project resources. Microsoft Project is the most widely used project manager. **Videoconferencing systems** are computer systems that allow people located at various geographic locations to communicate and have in-person meetings. (See Figure 10-15.)
- **Knowledge work systems:** Knowledge workers use OAS systems. Additionally, they use specialized information systems called **knowledge work systems (KWSs)** to create information in their areas of expertise. For example, engineers involved in product design and manufacturing use **computer-aided design/computer-aided manufacturing (CAD/CAM) systems.** (See Figure 10-16.) These KWSs consist of powerful personal computers running special programs that integrate the design and manufacturing activities. CAD/CAM is widely used in the manufacture of automobiles and other products.

Expert systems are another widely used knowledge work system.

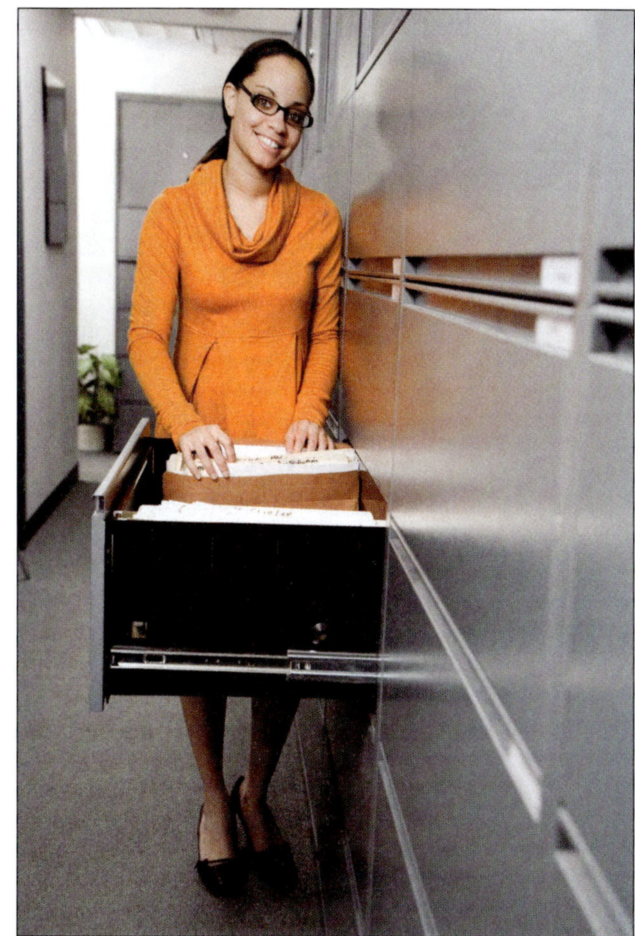

Figure 10-14 Administrative assistants and clerks are data workers

Figure 10-15 Videoconferencing: Individuals and groups can see and share information

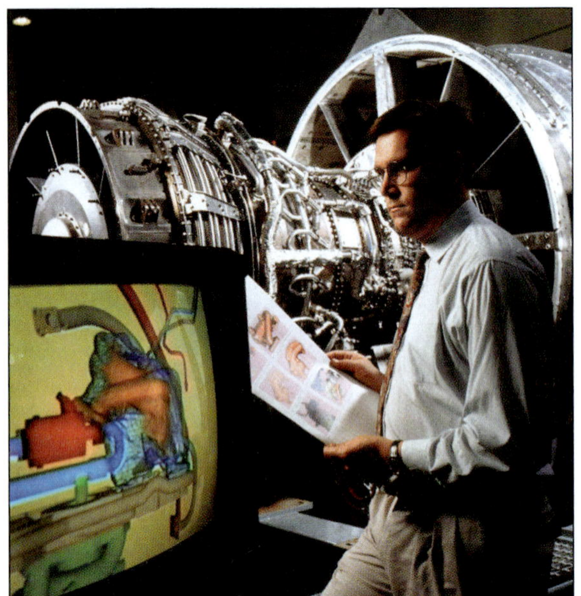

Figure 10-16 **CAD/CAM: Knowledge work systems used by design and manufacturing engineers**

Expert Systems

People who are expert in a particular area—certain kinds of medicine, accounting, engineering, and so on—are generally well paid for their specialized knowledge. Unfortunately for their clients and customers, these experts are expensive and not always available.

What if you were to somehow capture the knowledge of a human expert and make it accessible to everyone through a computer program? This is exactly what is being done with expert systems. **Expert systems**, also known as **knowledge-based systems,** are a type of artificial intelligence that uses a database to provide assistance to users. This database, known as a **knowledge base,** contains facts and rules to relate these facts distilled from a human expert. Users interact with an expert system by describing a particular situation or problem. The expert system takes the inputs and searches the knowledge base until a solution or recommendation is formulated.

Over the past decade, expert systems have been developed in areas such as medicine, geology, architecture, and nature. There are expert systems with such names as Oil Spill Advisor, Bird Species Identification, and even Midwives Assistant.

concept check

What is an information worker?

Who are data workers? What type of information system is designed to support them?

Who are knowledge workers? What type of information system is designed to support them?

What are expert systems? What is a knowledge base?

Careers in IT

"Now that you have learned about information systems, let me tell you about my career as an information systems manager."

Information systems managers oversee the work of programmers, computer specialists, systems analysts, and other computer professionals. They create and implement corporate computer policy and systems.

Most companies look for individuals with strong technical backgrounds, sometimes as consultants, with a master's degree in business. Employers seek individuals with strong leadership and excellent communication skills. Information systems managers must be able to communicate with people in technical and nontechnical terms. Information systems management positions are often filled by individuals who have been consultants or managers in previous positions. Those with experience in computer and network security will be in demand as businesses and society continue to struggle with important security issues.

Information systems managers can expect an annual salary of $95,000 to $125,000. Advancement opportunities typically include leadership in the field.

A LOOK TO THE FUTURE

IBM's Watson: The Ultimate Information-Finding Machine

Have you noticed how much information is out there, from books and journals in your library to the millions of articles on the web? Do you ever wonder how professionals manage to read through all that research in order to stay up to date in their field? Recently, as the amount of information increases, those professionals are finding it difficult to keep up. In the future, IBM hopes to change that through its information-finding supercomputer known as Watson. Technology has been making better information tools, and will continue to evolve to improve our lives as we look to the future.

You may have already heard of Watson. In 2011, this computer defeated the two best contestants in the game show *Jeopardy*. What made the achievement so remarkable was that the computer had to read the question, understand what was being asked, search through 200 million pages of text, figure out what the best answer would be, and then hit a buzzer before the other contestants to deliver the answer. It accomplished all these steps in about 3 seconds.

With this skill, IBM predicts that Watson could be the ultimate researcher, helping professionals in various industries find the information they are looking for in a matter of seconds. Several organizations have already "hired" Watson. One health care company will be using Watson to help suggest options based on a patient's unique circumstances. It assists physicians and nurses by looking through millions of pages of medical research and then quickly identifying the most likely diagnosis and treatment options for the patient. To help Watson learn more about the medical field, IBM has partnered with a cancer center in order to "teach" Watson how to process the massive amount of cancer-related research and case studies. In the finance field, Watson has recently been learning about the complexities of Wall Street, with the hopes that it can help financial firms identify risks and rewards to improve the advice given to their customers.

In the future, IBM envisions Watson's technology being an integral part of these two industries. In addition, it also sees practical applications in call centers and technical support services. There are countless organizations and consumers that would all benefit if access to this type of information technology became widespread. It would transform the way all of us do research and seek answers for our toughest problems.

What do you think about Watson's powerful services? Do you think you could one day have access to this powerful technology on your favorite search engine? How about at home? Do you believe it will be a beneficial support tool or a machine that threatens to take jobs away from professionals?

VISUAL SUMMARY Information Systems

ORGANIZATIONAL INFORMATION FLOW

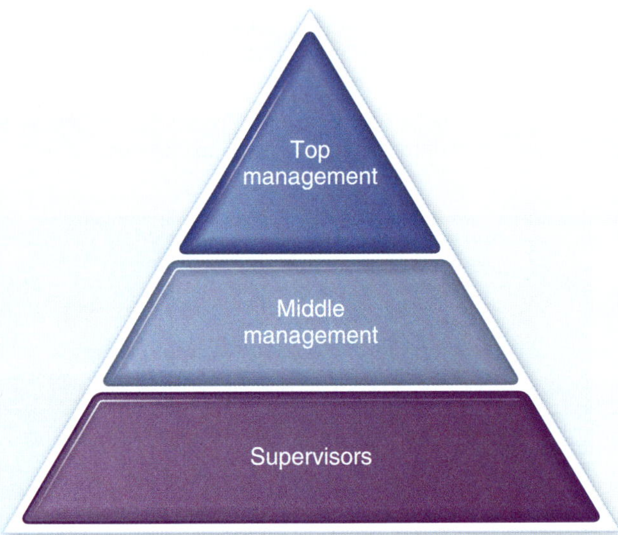

Information flows in an organization through functional areas and between management levels.

Functions

Most organizations have separate departments to perform five functions:

- **Accounting**—tracks all financial activities and generates periodic financial statements.
- **Marketing**—advertises, promotes, and sells the product (or service).
- **Production**—makes the product (or service) using raw materials and people to turn out finished goods.
- **Human resources**—finds and hires people; handles such matters as sick leave, retirement benefits, evaluation, compensation, and professional development.
- **Research**—conducts product research and development; monitors and troubleshoots new products.

Management Levels

The three basic management levels are

- **Top level**—concerned with long-range planning and forecasting.
- **Middle level**—deals with control, planning, decision making, and implementing long-term goals.
- **Supervisors**—control operational matters, monitor day-to-day events, and supervise workers.

Information Flow

Information flows within an organization in different directions.

- For **top-level managers,** the information flow is primarily upward from within the organization and into the organization from the outside.
- For **middle-level managers,** the information flow is horizontal and vertical within departments.
- For **supervisors,** the information flow is primarily vertical.

To efficiently and effectively use computers within an organization, you need to understand how information flows through functional areas and management levels. You need to be aware of the different types of computer-based information systems, including transaction processing systems, management information systems, decision support systems, and executive support systems.

INFORMATION SYSTEMS

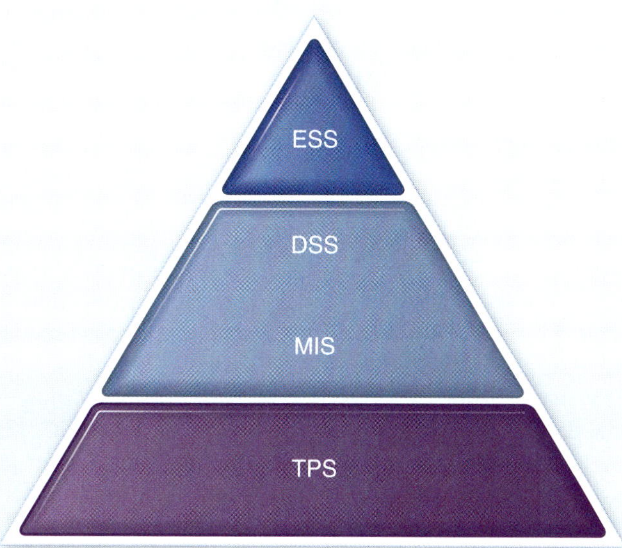

Transaction Processing Systems

Transaction processing systems (TPSs), sometimes called **data processing systems (DPSs),** record day-to-day transactions. Accounting activities include **sales order processing, accounts receivable, inventory** and **purchasing, accounts payable, payroll,** and **general ledger.** General ledger is used to produce **income statements** and **balance sheets.**

Management Information Systems

Management information systems (MISs) produce predetermined reports **(periodic, exception, demand).**

Decision Support Systems

Decision support systems (DSSs) focus on unanticipated questions; consist of the **user, system software, data (internal** and **external)** and **decision models.** Three types are **strategic, tactical,** and **operational. Group decision support systems (GDSS)** support a team of decision makers.

Executive Support Systems

Executive support systems (ESSs) are similar to MIS or DSS but easier to use. ESSs are designed specifically for top-level decision makers.

Other Information Systems

Many other systems are designed to support **information workers** who create, distribute, and communicate information. Three such systems are

- **Office automation systems (OASs),** which support **data workers** who are involved with distribution and communication of information. **Project managers** and **videoconferencing systems** are **OASs.**
- **Knowledge work systems (KWSs),** which support **knowledge workers,** who create information. Many engineers use **computer-aided design/computer-aided manufacturing (CAD/CAM) systems.**
- **Expert (knowledge-based) systems,** which are a type of **knowledge work system.** They use **knowledge bases** to apply expert knowledge to specific user problems.

CAREERS in IT

Information systems managers oversee a variety of other computer professionals. Strong leadership and communication skills are required; experience as a consultant and/or manager is desired. Salary range is $95,000 to $125,000.

KEY TERMS

accounting (255)
accounts payable (260)
accounts receivable (260)
balance sheet (260)
computer-aided design/computer-aided manufacturing (CAD/CAM) system (265)
data (262)
data processing system (DPS) (259)
data worker (265)
decision model (262)
decision support system (DSS) (258, 262)
demand report (261)
exception report (261)
executive information system (EIS) (258)
executive support system (ESS) (258, 263)
expert system (266)
external data (262)
general ledger (260)
group decision support system (GDSS) (263)
human resources (255)
income statement (260)
information system (254)
information systems manager (266)
information worker (265)
internal data (262)
inventory (260)
inventory control system (260)
knowledge base (266)
knowledge-based system (266)
knowledge work system (KWS) (265)
knowledge worker (265)
management information system (MIS) (258, 261)
marketing (255)
middle management (256)
office automation system (OAS) (265)
operational model (263)
payroll (260)
periodic report (261)
production (255)
project manager (265)
purchase order (260)
purchasing (260)
research (255)
sales order processing (260)
strategic model (262)
supervisor (256)
system software (262)
tactical model (263)
top management (256)
transaction processing system (TPS) (258, 259)
user (262)
videoconferencing system (265)

MULTIPLE CHOICE

Circle the letter of the correct answer.

1. Which of the basic organizational functions records all financial activity from billing customers to paying employees?
   - a. accounting
   - b. marketing
   - c. production
   - d. research
2. What managerial level has information flow that is vertical, horizontal, and external?
   - a. top
   - b. supervisory
   - c. middle
   - d. foreman
3. Which computer-based information system uses data from TPS and analytical tools to support middle managers?
   - a. ESS
   - b. MIS
   - c. DSS
   - d. TPS
4. Accounts payable refers to money the company owes its suppliers for materials and services it has:
   - a. created
   - b. exported
   - c. inventoried
   - d. received
5. What accounting activity keeps track of all summaries of all transactions?
   - a. balance sheet
   - b. general ledger
   - c. income statement
   - d. inventory control
6. What accounting statement lists the overall financial condition of an organization?
   - a. balance sheet
   - b. general ledger
   - c. income statement
   - d. inventory control
7. What type of report is produced at regular intervals?
   - a. demand
   - b. exception
   - c. inventory
   - d. periodic
8. A DSS consists of four parts: user, system software, decision models, and:
   - a. application software
   - b. data
   - c. operating system
   - d. spreadsheets
9. What type of worker is involved with the distribution, communication, and creation of information?
   - a. executive
   - b. foreman
   - c. information
   - d. knowledge
10. What type of program is designed to schedule, plan, and control project resources?
    - a. auditing
    - b. dtp
    - c. project managers
    - d. schedulers

MATCHING

Match each numbered item with the most closely related lettered item. Write your answers in the spaces provided.

a. data
b. exception
c. marketing
d. middle
e. MIS
f. payroll
g. processing
h. standardized
i. system
j. videoconferencing

___ **1.** Function that plans, prices, promotes, sells, and distributes the organization's goods and services.
___ **2.** Managerial level where information flow is vertical and horizontal.
___ **3.** Computer-based information system that uses data from TPS to support middle-level managers.
___ **4.** The accounting activity that records the customer requests for the company's products or services is sales order _____.
___ **5.** The accounting activity concerned with calculating employee paychecks.
___ **6.** MIS produces this type of report.
___ **7.** A type of report that calls attention to unusual events.
___ **8.** Type of software that works behind the scenes to handle detailed operating procedures.
___ **9.** Type of worker who is involved with the distribution and communication of information.
___ **10.** Computer system that allows people located at various geographic locations to communicate and have in-person meetings.

OPEN-ENDED

On a separate sheet of paper, respond to each question or statement.

1. Name and discuss the five common functions of most organizations.
2. Discuss the roles of the three kinds of management in a corporation.
3. What are the four most common computer-based information systems?
4. Describe the different reports and their roles in managerial decision making.
5. What is the difference between an office automation system and a knowledge work system?

DISCUSSION

Respond to each of the following questions.

1 Expanding Your Knowledge: EXECUTIVE SUPPORT SYSTEMS

Research at least three different executive support systems using a web search. Review each, and then answer the following questions: (a) Which ESSs did you review? (b) What are the common features of ESSs? (c) What specific types of decisions were each ESS designed to aid in? (d) What type of company is likely to use each? Provide some examples.

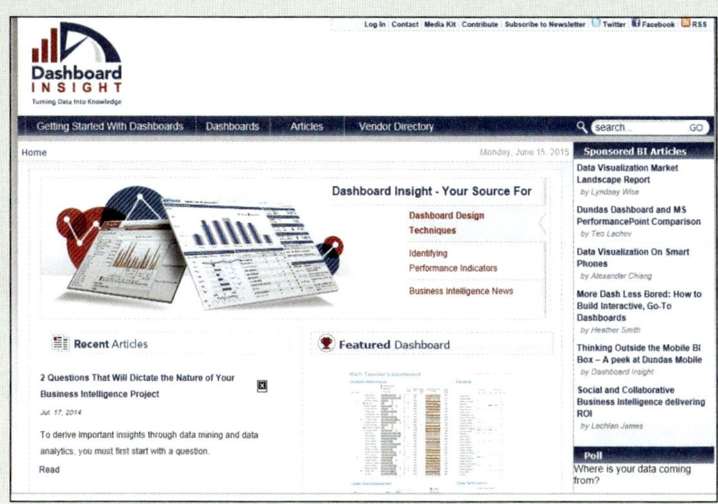

2 Writing about Technology: IDENTITY THEFT

Identity theft occurs when someone acquires your personal information and uses it to hijack your finances. A common scenario is a thief using your Social Security number to open a credit card account in your name. When the thief does not pay, it is your credit history that is blemished. Consider this scam thoroughly, and then respond to the following: (a) List three steps an individual should take to avoid identity theft. (b) List three steps a corporation that maintains your personal data in its information system should take to safeguard your data. (c) How can Internet activities contribute to the likelihood of identity theft? How can this be prevented?

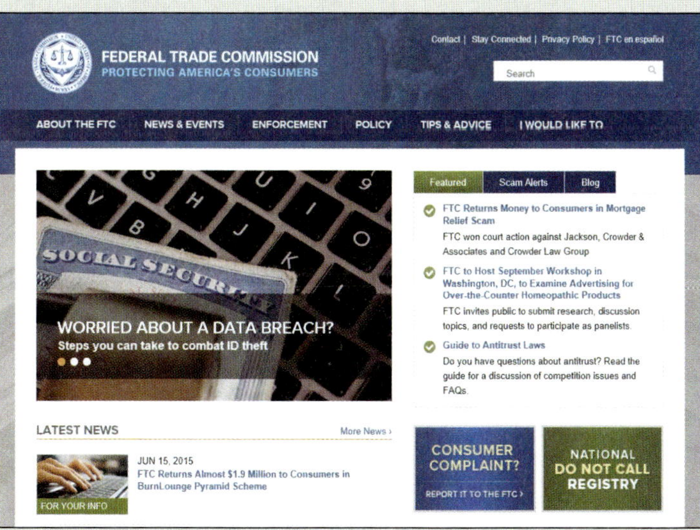

PHOTO CREDITS

CHAPTER 10:

Opener: © nadla/Getty Images RF; p. 253, 267: © Chad Baker/Ryan McVay/Getty Images RF; p. 254, 266: © Radius Images/Getty Images RF; 10-1: © Ryan McVay/Getty Images RF; 10-4: © Flying Colours Ltd/Getty Images RF; 10-8: © Erik Isakson/Getty Images RF; 10-10, 10-11, 10-12: Microsoft product screen shot(s) reprinted with permission from Microsoft Corporation; 10-14: © DCA Productions/Taxi/Getty Images; 10-15: © Tom Merton/OJO Images/Getty Images; 10-16: © Brownie Harris/Corbis, p. 273 (top): Dashboard Insight @2015.

chapter 11 Databases

Why should I read this chapter?

Giant databases are recording your every digital action, from credit card purchases to Facebook check-ins. These databases can be used to tailor advertisements to your interests, predict your credit score, and even assess your safety at home. In the future, databases with DNA records of all U.S. citizens and every digital activity of a city may be able to predict crime and even identify likely criminals.

This chapter covers the things you need to know to be prepared for this ever-changing digital world, including:

- Different data-organization methods—understand the significance of relational, multidimensional, and hierarchical databases.
- Types of databases—identify the right database for an individual, company, distributed, or commercial situation.

Learning Objectives

After you have read this chapter, you should be able to:

1. Distinguish between the physical and logical views of data.
2. Describe how data is organized: characters, fields, records, tables, and databases.
3. Define key fields and how they are used to integrate data in a database.
4. Define and compare batch processing and real-time processing.
5. Describe databases, including the need for databases and database management systems (DBMSs).
6. Describe the five common database models: hierarchical, network, relational, multidimensional, and object-oriented.
7. Distinguish among individual, company, distributed, and commercial databases.
8. Describe strategic database uses and security concerns.

Introduction

"Hi, I'm Henry. I'm a database administrator, and I'd like to talk with you about databases. I'd also like to talk about how organizations are using data warehouses and data mining to perform complex analyses and discover new information."

Like a library, secondary storage is designed to store information. How is this stored information organized? What are databases, and why do you need to know anything about them?

Only a few decades ago, a computer was considered to be an island with only limited access to information beyond its own hard disk. Now, through communication networks and the Internet, individual computers have direct electronic access to almost unlimited sources of information.

In today's world, almost all information is stored in databases. They are an important part of nearly every organization including schools, hospitals, and banks. To effectively compete in today's world, you need to know how to find information and understand how it is stored.

To efficiently and effectively use computers, you need to understand data fields, records, tables, and databases. You need to be aware of the different ways in which a database can be structured and the different types of databases. Also, you need to know the most important database uses and issues.

Data

As we have discussed throughout this book, information systems consist of people, procedures, software, hardware, data, and the Internet. This chapter focuses on **data,** which can be defined as facts or observations about people, places, things, and events. More specifically, this chapter focuses on how databases store, organize, and use data.

Not long ago, data was limited to numbers, letters, and symbols recorded by keyboards. Now, data is much richer and includes:

- Audio captured, interpreted, and saved using microphones and voice recognition systems.
- Music downloaded from the Internet and saved on smartphones, tablets, and other devices.
- Photographs captured by digital cameras, edited by image editing software, and shared with others over the Internet.
- Video captured by digital video cameras, TV tuner cards, and webcams.

There are two ways or perspectives to view data. These perspectives are the *physical view* and the *logical view.* The **physical view** focuses on the actual format and location of the data. As discussed in Chapter 5, data is recorded as digital bits that are typically grouped together into bytes that represent characters using a coding scheme such as Unicode. Typically, only very specialized computer professionals are concerned with the physical view. The other perspective, the **logical view,** focuses on the meaning, content, and context of the data. End users and most computer professionals are concerned with this view. They are involved with actually using the data with application programs. This chapter presents the logical view of data and how data is stored in databases.

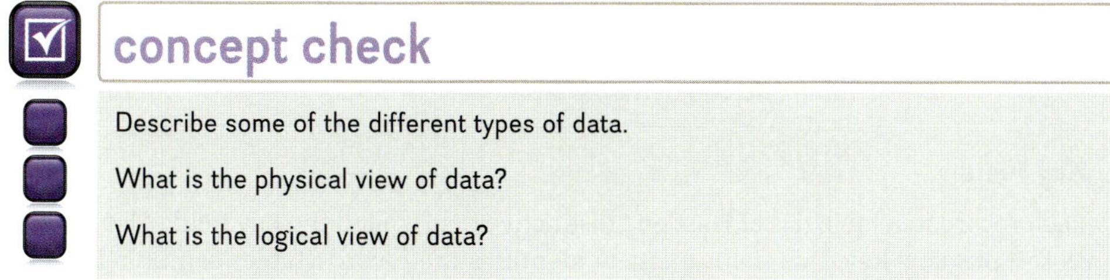

Describe some of the different types of data.

What is the physical view of data?

What is the logical view of data?

Data Organization

The first step in understanding databases is to learn how data is organized. In the logical view, data is organized into groups or categories. Each group is more complex than the one before. (See Figure 11-1.)

- **Character:** A **character** is the most basic logical data element. It is a single letter, number, or special character, such as a punctuation mark, or a symbol, such as $.
- **Field:** The next higher level is a **field** or group of related characters. In our example, Brown is in the data field for the Last Name of an employee. It consists of the individual letters (characters) that make up the last name. A data field represents an **attribute** (description or characteristic) of some **entity** (person, place, thing, or object). For example, an employee is an entity with many attributes, including his or her last name.
- **Record:** A **record** is a collection of related fields. A record represents a collection of attributes that describe an entity. In our example, the payroll record for an employee consists of the data fields describing the attributes for one employee. These attributes are First Name, Last Name, Employee ID, and Salary.
- **Table:** A **table** is a collection of related records. For example, the Payroll Table would include payroll information (records) for the employees (entities).

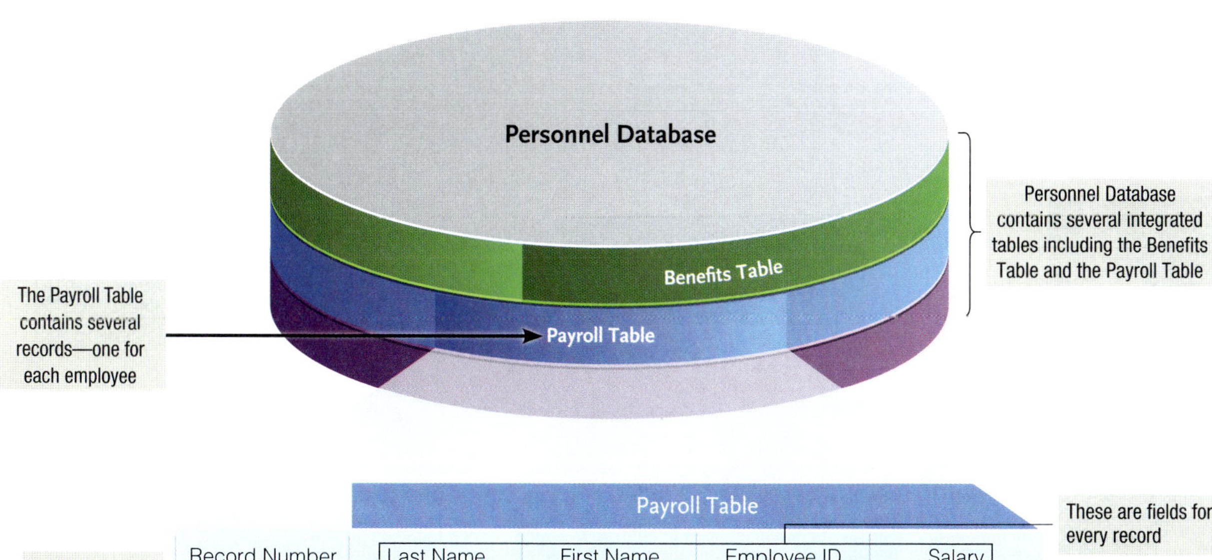

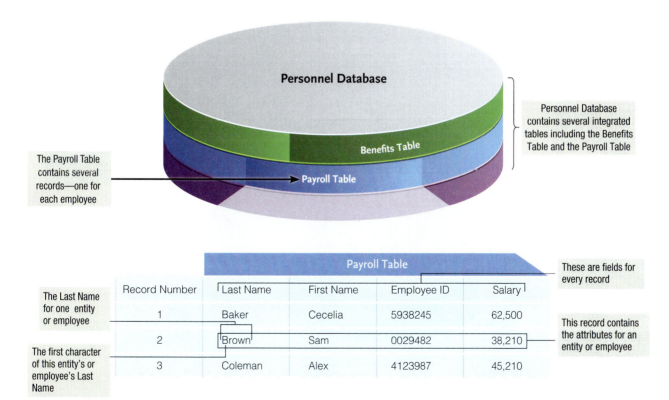

Record Number	Last Name	First Name	Employee ID	Salary
1	Baker	Cecelia	5938245	62,500
2	Brown	Sam	0029482	38,210
3	Coleman	Alex	4123987	45,210

Figure 11-1 **Logical data organization**

- **Database:** A **database** is an integrated collection of logically related tables. For example, the Personnel Database would include all related employee tables including the Payroll Table and the Benefits Table.

Key Field

Each record in a table has at least one distinctive field, called the **key field.** Also known as the **primary key,** this field uniquely identifies the record. Tables can be related or connected to other tables by common key fields.

For most employee databases, a key field is an employee identification number. Key fields in different tables can be used to integrate the data in a database. For example, in the Personnel Database, both the Payroll and the Benefits tables include the field Employee ID. Data from the two tables could be related by combining all records with the same key field (Employee ID).

Batch versus Real-Time Processing

Traditionally, data is processed in one of two ways. These are batch processing, or what we might call "later," and real-time processing, or what we might call "now." These two methods have been used to handle common record-keeping activities such as payroll and sales orders.

- **Batch processing:** In **batch processing,** data is collected over several hours, days, or even weeks. It is then processed all at once as a "batch." If you have a credit card, your bill probably reflects batch processing. That is, during the month, you buy things and charge them to your credit card. Each time you charge something, an electronic copy of the transaction is sent to the credit card company. At some point in the month, the company's data processing department puts all those transactions (and those of many other customers) together and processes them at one time. The company then sends you a single bill totaling the amount you owe. (See Figure 11-2.)

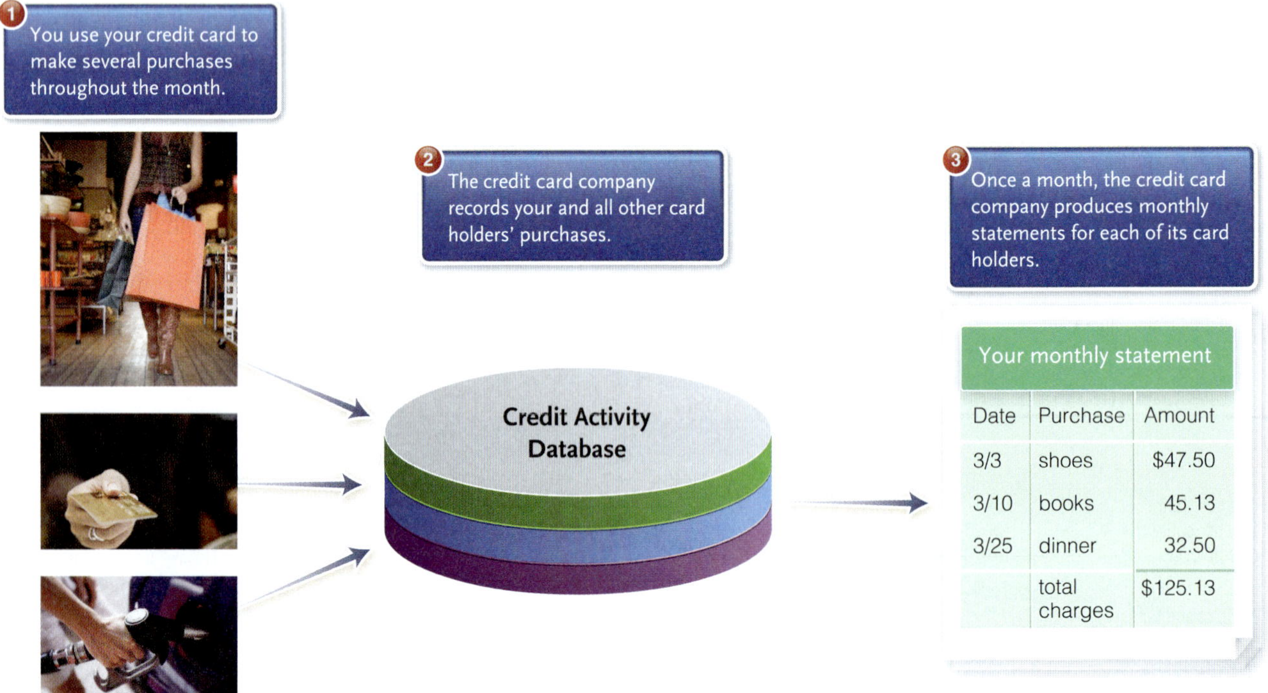

Figure 11-2 **Batch processing: Monthly credit card statements**

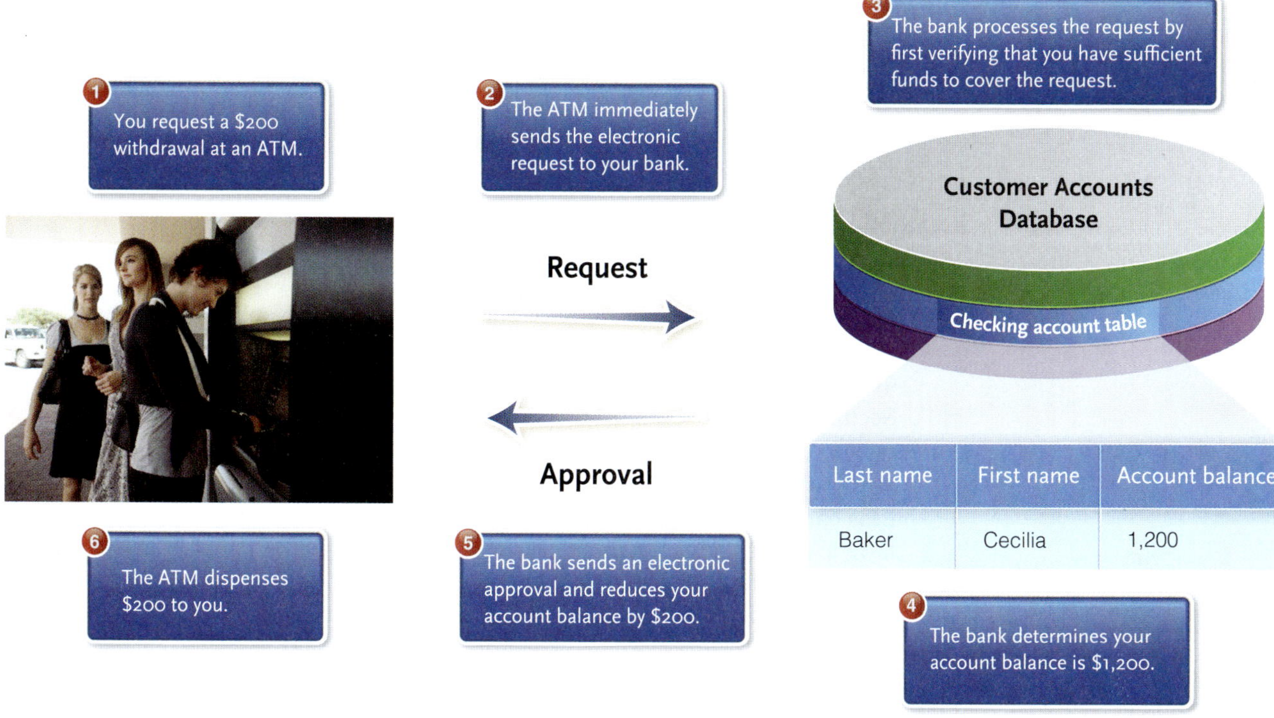

Figure 11-3 **Real-time processing: ATM withdrawal**

- **Real-time processing: Real-time processing,** also known as **online processing,** occurs when data is processed at the same time the transaction occurs. For example, whenever you request funds at an ATM, real-time processing occurs. After you have provided account information and requested a specific withdrawal, the bank's computer verifies that you have sufficient funds in your account. If you do, then the funds are dispensed to you, and the bank immediately updates the balance of your account. (See Figure 11-3.)

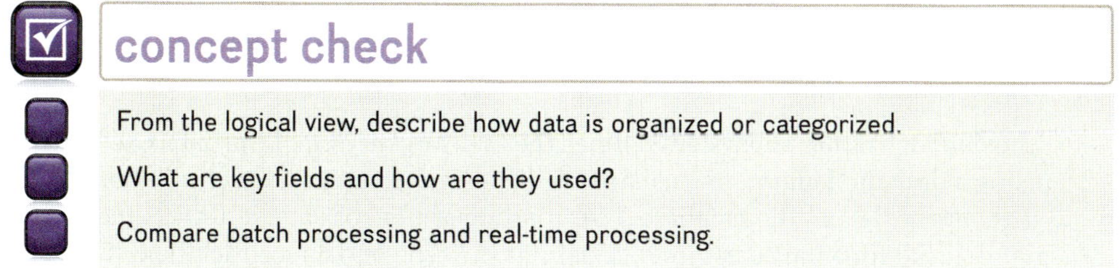

concept check

- From the logical view, describe how data is organized or categorized.
- What are key fields and how are they used?
- Compare batch processing and real-time processing.

Databases

Many organizations have multiple files on the same subject or person. For example, a customer's name and address could appear in different files within the sales department, billing department, and credit department. This is called **data redundancy.** If the customer moves, then the address in each file must be updated. If one or more files are overlooked, problems will likely result. For example, a product ordered might be sent to the new address, but the bill might be sent to the old address. This situation results from a lack of **data integrity.**

Moreover, data spread around in different files is not as useful. The marketing department, for instance, might want to offer special promotions to customers who order large quantities of merchandise. To identify these customers, the marketing department would need to obtain permission and access to files in the billing department. It would be much more efficient if all data were in a common database. A database can make the needed information available.

Need for Databases

For an organization, there are many advantages to having databases:

- **Sharing:** In organizations, information from one department can be readily shared with others. Billing could let marketing know which customers ordered large quantities of merchandise.
- **Security:** Users are given passwords or access only to the kind of information they need. Thus, the payroll department may have access to employees' pay rates, but other departments would not.
- **Less data redundancy:** Without a common database, individual departments have to create and maintain their own data, and data redundancy results. For example, an employee's home address would likely appear in several files. Redundant data causes inefficient use of storage space and data maintenance problems.
- **Data integrity:** When there are multiple sources of data, each source may have variations. A customer's address may be listed as "Main Street" in one system and "Main St." in another. With discrepancies like these, it is probable that the customer would be treated as two separate people.

Database Management

In order to create, modify, and gain access to a database, special software is required. This software is called a **database management system,** which is commonly abbreviated **DBMS.**

Some DBMSs, such as Microsoft Access, are designed specifically for personal computers. Other DBMSs are designed for specialized database servers. DBMS software is made up of five parts or subsystems: *DBMS engine, data definition, data manipulation, application generation,* and *data administration.*

- The **DBMS engine** provides a bridge between the logical view of the data and the physical view of the data. When users request data (logical perspective), the DBMS engine handles the details of actually locating the data (physical perspective).
- The **data definition subsystem** defines the logical structure of the database by using a **data dictionary** or **schema.** This dictionary contains a description of the structure of data in the database. For a particular item of data, it defines the names used for a particular field. It defines the type of data for each field (text, numeric, time, graphic, audio, and video). An example of an Access data dictionary form is presented in Figure 11-4.
- The **data manipulation subsystem** provides tools for maintaining and analyzing data. Maintaining data is known as **data maintenance.** It involves adding new data, deleting old data, and editing existing data. Analysis tools support viewing all or selected parts of the data, querying the database, and generating reports. Specific tools include **query-by-example** and a specialized programming language called **structured query language (SQL).** (Structured query language and other types of programming languages will be discussed in Chapter 13.)
- The **application generation subsystem** provides tools to create data entry forms and specialized programming languages that interface or work with

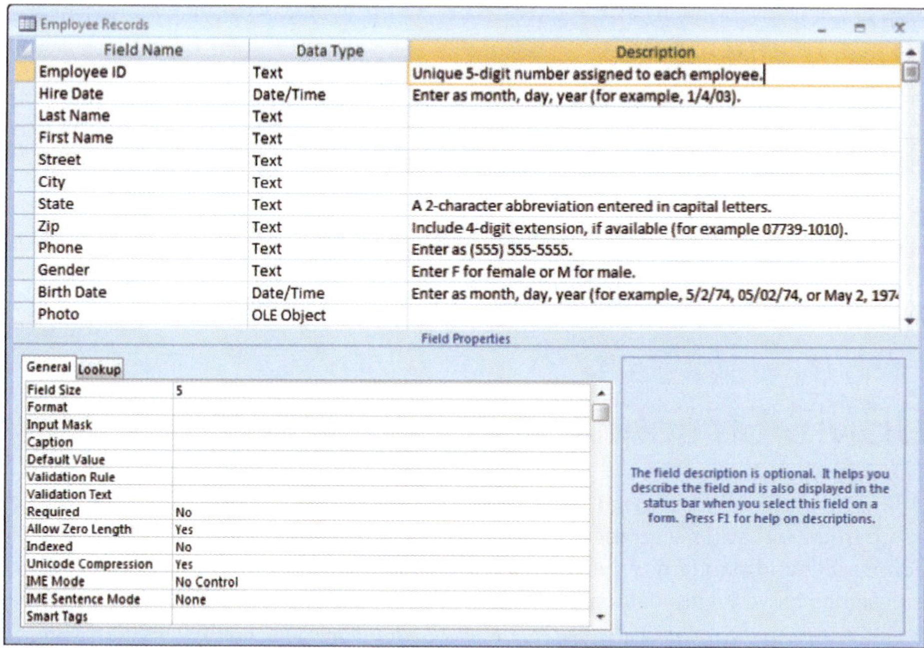

Figure 11-4 **Access data dictionary form**

common and widely used programming languages such as C++ or Visual Basic. See Figure 11-5 for a data entry form created by the application generation subsystem in Access.

- The **data administration subsystem** helps to manage the overall database, including maintaining security, providing disaster recovery support, and monitoring the overall performance of database operations. Larger organizations typically employ highly trained computer specialists, called **database administrators (DBAs),** to interact with the data administration subsystem. Additional duties of database administrators include determining **processing rights** or determining which people have access to what kinds of data in the database.

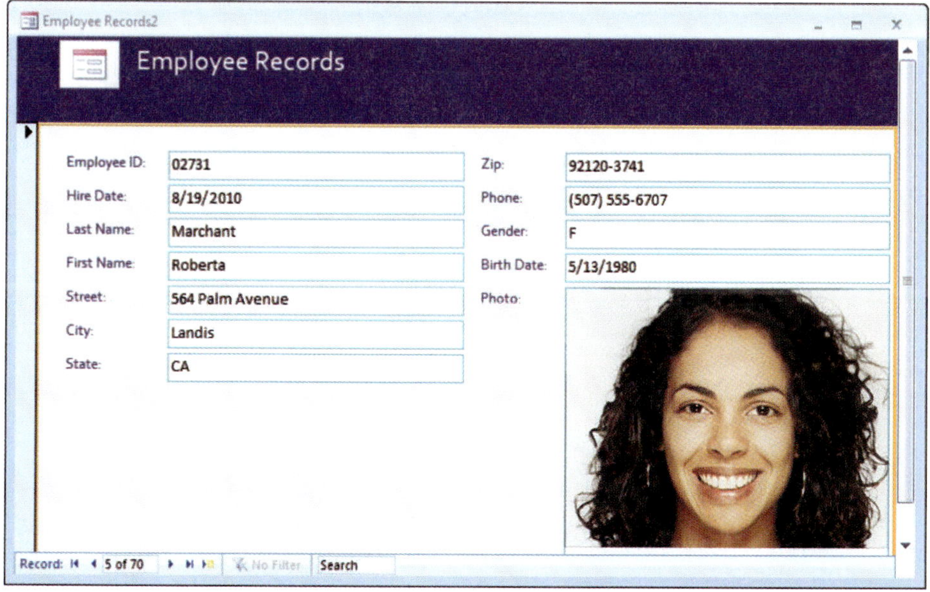

Figure 11-5 **Access data entry form**

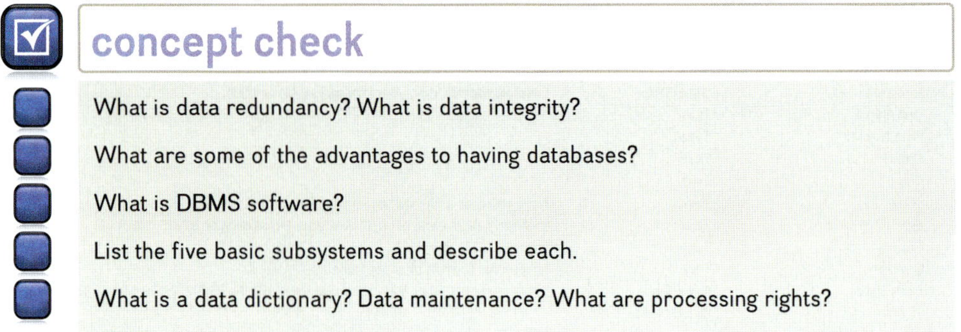

concept check
What is data redundancy? What is data integrity?
What are some of the advantages to having databases?
What is DBMS software?
List the five basic subsystems and describe each.
What is a data dictionary? Data maintenance? What are processing rights?

DBMS Structure

DBMS programs are designed to work with data that is logically structured or arranged in a particular way. This arrangement is known as the **database model.** These models define rules and standards for all the data in a database. For example, Microsoft Access is designed to work with databases using the relational data model. Five common database models are *hierarchical, network, relational, multidimensional,* and *object-oriented.*

Hierarchical Database

At one time, nearly every DBMS designed for mainframes used the hierarchical data model. In a **hierarchical database,** fields or records are structured in nodes. **Nodes** are points connected like the branches of an upside-down tree. Each entry has one **parent node,** although a parent may have several **child nodes.** This is sometimes described as a **one-to-many relationship.** To find a particular field, you have to start at the top with a parent and trace down the tree to a child.

The nodes farther down the system are subordinate to the ones above, like the hierarchy of managers in a corporation. An example of a hierarchical database is a system to organize music files. (See Figure 11-6.) The parent node is the music library

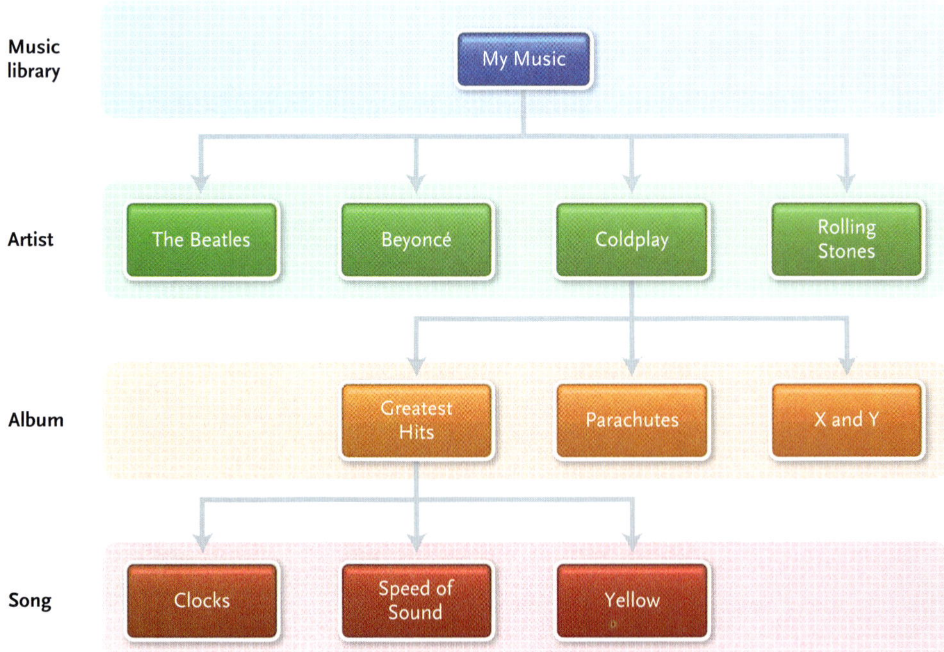

Figure 11-6 **Hierarchical database**

for a particular user. This parent has four children, labeled "artist." Coldplay, one of the children, has three children of its own. They are labeled "album." The *Greatest Hits* album has three children, labeled "song."

The problem with a hierarchical database is that if one parent node is deleted, so are all the subordinate child nodes. Moreover, a child node cannot be added unless a parent node is added first. The most significant limitation is the rigid structure: one parent only per child, and no relationships or connections between the child nodes themselves.

Network Database

Responding to the limitations of the hierarchical data model, network models were developed. A **network database** also has a hierarchical arrangement of nodes. However, each child node may have more than one parent node. This is sometimes described as a **many-to-many relationship.** There are additional connections—called **pointers**—between parent nodes and child nodes. Thus, a node may be reached through more than one path. It may be traced down through different branches.

For example, a university could use this type of organization to record students taking classes. (See Figure 11-7.) If you trace through the logic of this organization, you can see that each student can have more than one teacher. Each teacher also can teach more than one course. Students may take more than a single course. This demonstrates how the network arrangement is more flexible and in many cases more efficient than the hierarchical arrangement.

Relational Database

A more flexible type of organization is the **relational database.** In this structure, there are no access paths down a hierarchy. Rather, the data elements are stored in different tables, each of which consists of rows and columns. A table and its data are called a **relation.**

An example of a relational database is shown in Figure 11-8. The Vehicle Owner Table contains license numbers, names, and addresses for all registered drivers. Within the table, a row is a record containing information about one driver. Each column is a field. The fields are License Number, Last Name, First Name, Street, City, State, and Zip. All related tables must have a **common data item** enabling information stored in one table to be linked with information stored in another. In this case, the three tables are related by the License Number field.

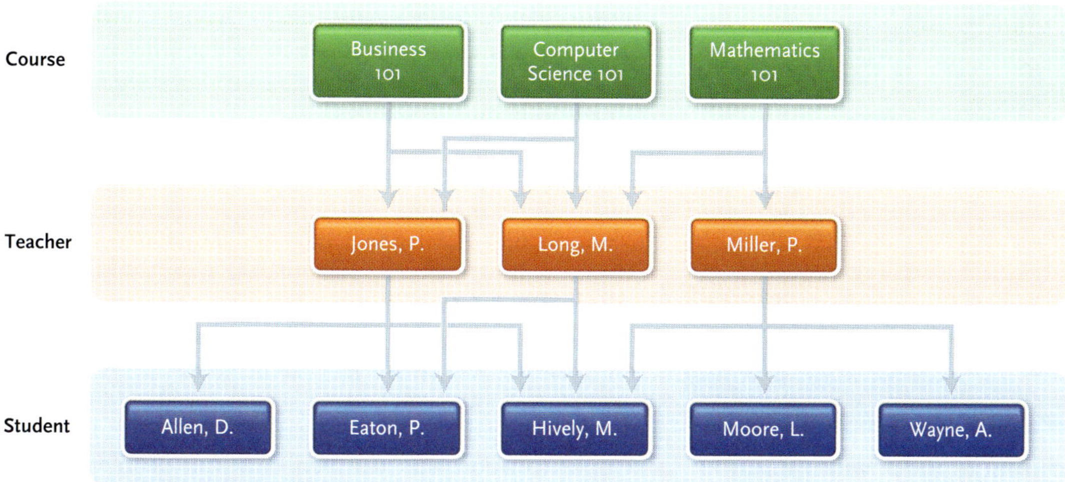

Figure 11-7 **Network database**

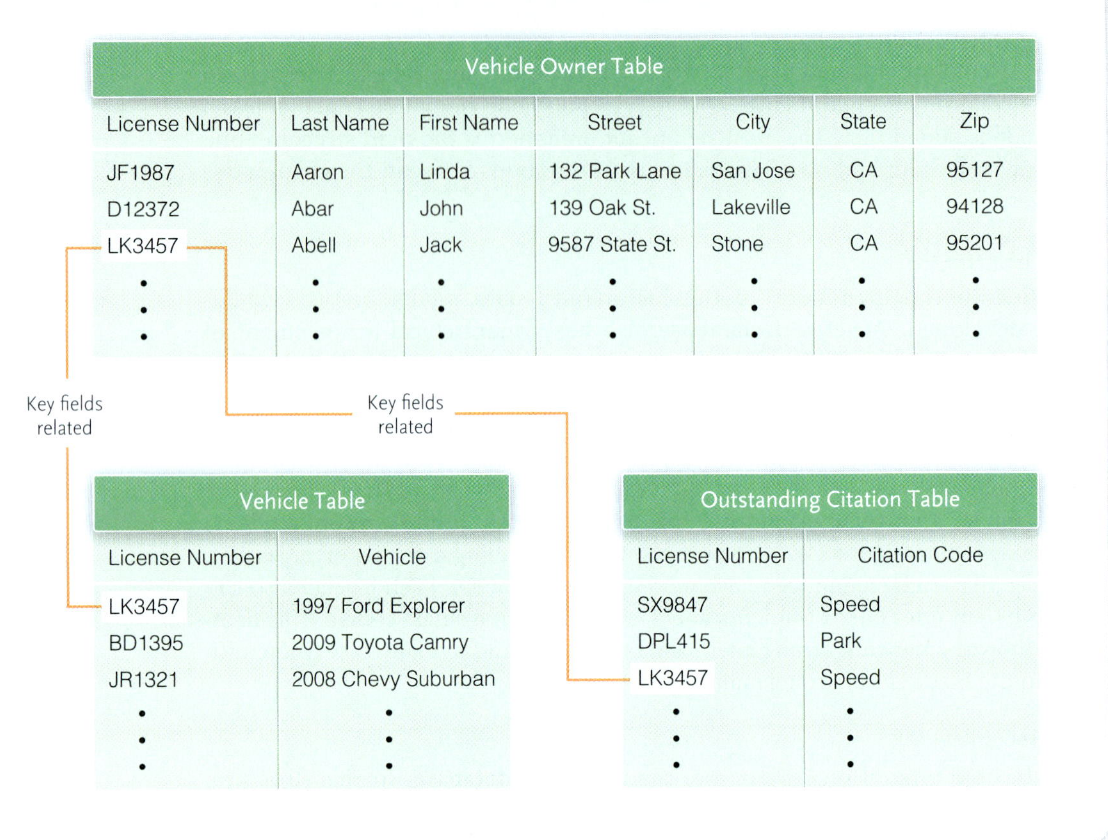

Vehicle Owner Table

License Number	Last Name	First Name	Street	City	State	Zip
JF1987	Aaron	Linda	132 Park Lane	San Jose	CA	95127
D12372	Abar	John	139 Oak St.	Lakeville	CA	94128
LK3457	Abell	Jack	9587 State St.	Stone	CA	95201
⋮	⋮	⋮	⋮	⋮	⋮	⋮

Vehicle Table

License Number	Vehicle
LK3457	1997 Ford Explorer
BD1395	2009 Toyota Camry
JR1321	2008 Chevy Suburban
⋮	⋮

Outstanding Citation Table

License Number	Citation Code
SX9847	Speed
DPL415	Park
LK3457	Speed
⋮	⋮

Figure 11-8 Relational database

Police officers who stop a speeding car look up the driver's information in the Department of Motor Vehicles database (Figure 11-9) using the driver's license number. They also can check for any unpaid traffic violations in the Outstanding Citations Table. Finally, if the officers suspect that the car is stolen, they can look up what vehicles the driver owns in the Vehicle Table.

The most valuable feature of relational databases is their simplicity. Entries can be easily added, deleted, and modified. The hierarchical and network databases are more rigid. The relational organization is common for personal computer DBMSs such as Access. Relational databases are also widely used for mainframe and midrange systems.

Figure 11-9 The Department of Motor Vehicles may use a relational database

Multidimensional Database

The multidimensional data model is a variation and an extension of the relational data model. While relational databases use tables consisting of rows and columns, **multidimensional databases** extend this two-dimensional data model to include additional or multiple dimensions, sometimes called a **data cube.** Data can be viewed as a cube having three or more sides and consisting of cells. Each side of the cube is considered a dimension of the data. In this way, complex relationships between data can be represented and efficiently analyzed.

Multidimensional databases provide several advantages over relational databases. Two of the most significant advantages are

- **Conceptualization.** Multidimensional databases and data cubes provide users with an intuitive model in which complex data and relationships can be conceptualized.
- **Processing speed.** Analyzing and querying a large multidimensional database can be much faster. For example, a query requiring just a few seconds on a multidimensional database could take minutes or hours to perform on a relational database.

Object-Oriented Database

The other data structures are primarily designed to handle structured data such as names, addresses, pay rates, and so on. **Object-oriented databases** are more flexible and store data as well as instructions to manipulate the data. Additionally, this structure is ideally designed to provide input for object-oriented software development, which is described in Chapter 13.

Object-oriented databases organize data using classes, objects, attributes, and methods.

- **Classes** are general definitions.
- **Objects** are specific instances of a class that can contain both data and instructions to manipulate the data.
- **Attributes** are the data fields an object possesses.
- **Methods** are instructions for retrieving or manipulating attribute values.

For example, a health club might use an object-oriented employment database. (See Figure 11-10.) The database uses a class, Employee, to define employee objects that are stored in the database. This definition includes the attributes First name, Last name, Address, and Wage and the method Pay. Bob, Sarah, and Omar are objects each with specific attribute values. For example, the object Bob has the stored values Bob, Larson, 191 Main St., 18. While hierarchical and network databases are still widely used, the relational, multidimensional, and object-oriented data models are more popular today.

For a summary of DBMS organization, see Figure 11-11.

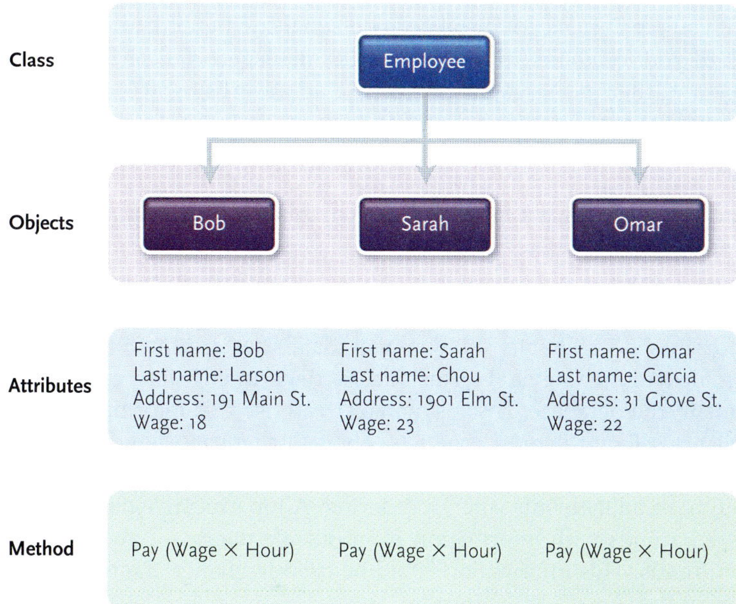

Figure 11-10 Object-oriented database

Organization	Description
Hierarchical	Data structured in nodes organized like an upside-down tree; each parent node can have several children; each child node can have only one parent
Network	Like hierarchical except that each child can have several parents
Relational	Data stored in tables consisting of rows and columns
Multidimensional	Data stored in data cubes with three or more dimensions
Object-oriented	Organizes data using classes, objects, attributes, and methods

Figure 11-11 Summary of DBMS organization

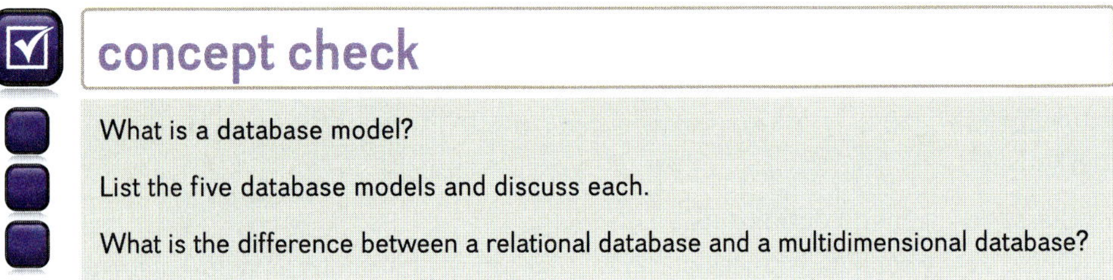

concept check

- What is a database model?
- List the five database models and discuss each.
- What is the difference between a relational database and a multidimensional database?

Types of Databases

Databases may be small or large, limited in accessibility or widely accessible. Databases may be classified into four types: *individual, company, distributed,* and *commercial.*

Individual

The **individual database** is also called a **personal computer database.** It is a collection of integrated files primarily used by just one person. Typically, the data and the DBMS are under the direct control of the user. They are stored either on the user's hard-disk drive or on a LAN file server.

There may be many times in your life when you will find this kind of database valuable. If you are in sales, for instance, a personal computer database can be used to keep track of your customers. If you are a sales manager, you can keep track of your salespeople and their performance. If you are an advertising account executive, you can keep track of your different projects and how many hours to charge each client.

Company

Companies, of course, create databases for their own use. The **company database** may be stored on a central database server and managed by a database administrator. Users throughout the company have access to the database through their personal computers linked to local or wide area networks.

As we discussed in Chapter 10, company databases are the foundation for management information systems. For instance, a department store can record all sales transactions in the database. A sales manager can use this information to see which salespeople are selling the most products. The manager can then determine year-end sales bonuses. Or the store's buyer can learn which products are selling well or not selling and make adjustments when reordering. A top executive might combine overall store sales trends with information from outside databases about consumer and population trends. This information could be used to change the whole merchandising strategy of the store.

Distributed

Many times the data in a company is stored not in just one location but in several locations. It is made accessible through a variety of communications networks. The database, then, is a **distributed database.** That is, not all the data in a database is physically located in one place. Typically, database servers on a client/server network provide the link between the data.

For instance, some database information can be at regional offices. Some can be at company headquarters, some down the hall from you, and some even overseas. Sales figures for a chain of department stores, then, could be located at the various stores. But executives at district offices or at the chain's headquarters could have access to all these figures.

Commercial

A **commercial database** is generally an enormous database that an organization develops to cover particular subjects. It offers access to this database to the public or selected outside individuals for a fee. Sometimes commercial databases also are called **information utilities** or **data banks.** An example is LexisNexis, which offers a variety of information-gathering and reporting services. (See Figure 11-12.)

Some of the most widely used commercial databases are:

- **Dialog Information Services**–offers business information, as well as technical and scientific information.
- **Dow Jones Interactive Publishing**–provides world news and information on business, investments, and stocks.
- **LexisNexis**–offers news and information on legal news, public records, and business issues.

Most of the commercial databases are designed for organizational as well as individual use. Organizations typically pay a membership fee plus hourly use fees. Often, individuals are able to search the database to obtain a summary of available information without charge. They pay only for those items selected for further investigation.

See Figure 11-13 for a summary of the four types of databases.

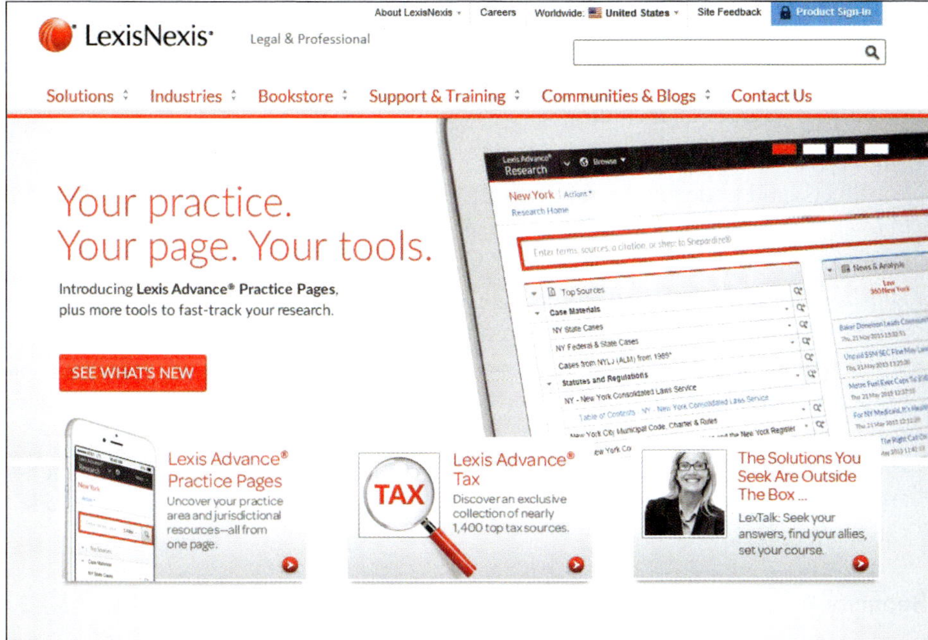

Figure 11-12 **Commercial database (LexisNexis)**

Type	Description
Individual	Integrated files used by just one person
Company	Common operational or commonly used files shared in an organization
Distributed	Database spread geographically and accessed using database server
Commercial	Information utilities or data banks available to users on a wide range of topics

Figure 11-13 Summary of the four types of databases

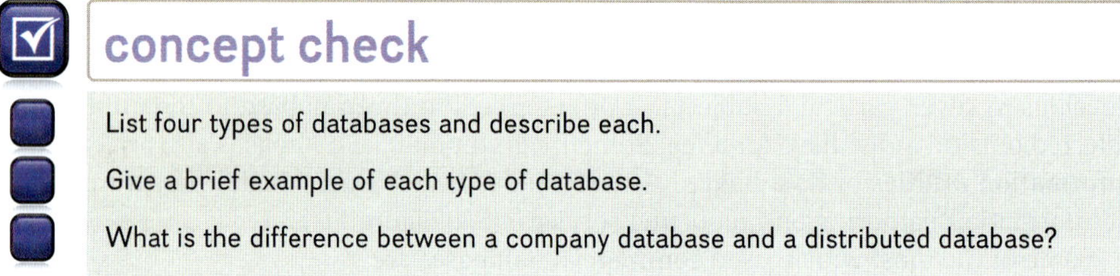

concept check
List four types of databases and describe each.
Give a brief example of each type of database.
What is the difference between a company database and a distributed database?

Database Uses and Issues

Databases offer great opportunities for productivity. In fact, in corporate libraries, electronic databases are now considered more valuable than books and journals. However, maintaining databases means users must make constant efforts to keep them from being tampered with or misused.

Strategic Uses

Databases help users to keep up to date and to plan for the future. To support the needs of managers and other business professionals, many organizations collect data from a variety of internal and external databases. This data is then stored in a special type of database called a **data warehouse.** A technique called **data mining** is often used to search these databases to look for related information and patterns.

There are hundreds of databases available to help users with both general and specific business purposes, including

- *Business directories* providing addresses, financial and marketing information, products, and trade and brand names.
- *Demographic data,* such as county and city statistics, current estimates on population and income, employment statistics, census data, and so on.
- *Business statistical information,* such as financial information on publicly traded companies, market potential of certain retail stores, and other business data and information.
- *Text databases* providing articles from business publications, press releases, reviews on companies and products, and so on.
- *Web databases* covering a wide range of topics, including all of the above. As mentioned earlier, web search sites like Google maintain extensive databases of available Internet content.

Security

Precisely because databases are so valuable, their security has become a critical issue. As we discussed in Chapter 9, there are several database security concerns. One concern is that personal and private information about people stored in databases may be used for the wrong purposes. For instance, a person's credit history or medical records might be used to make hiring or promotion decisions. Another concern is unauthorized users gaining access to a database. For example, there have been numerous instances in which a computer virus has been launched into a database or network.

Security may require putting guards in company computer rooms and checking the identification of everyone admitted. Some security systems electronically check fingerprints. (See Figure 11-14.) Security is particularly important to organizations using WANs. Violations can occur without actually entering secured areas. As mentioned in previous chapters, most major corporations today use special hardware and software called **firewalls** to control access to their internal networks.

Figure 11-14 **Security: electronic fingerprint scanner**

concept check

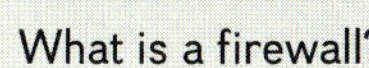

- What is a data warehouse? What is data mining?
- What are some database security concerns?
- What is a firewall?

Careers in IT

"Now that you have learned about databases, let me tell you about my career as a database administrator."

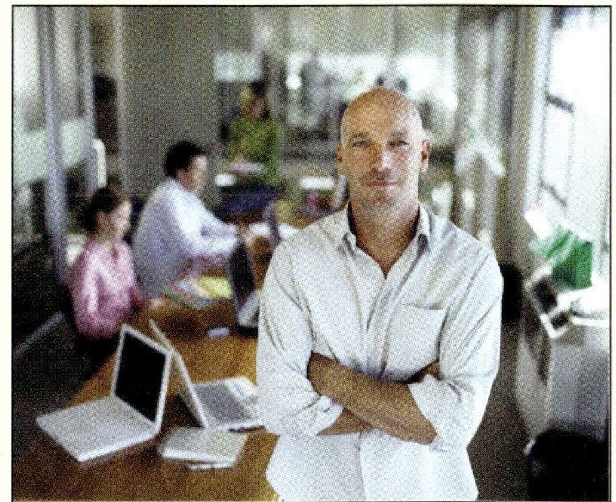

Database administrators use database management software to determine the most efficient ways to organize and access a company's data. Additionally, database administrators are typically responsible for maintaining database security and backing up the system. Database administration is a fast-growing industry and substantial job growth is expected.

Database administrator positions normally require a bachelor's degree in computer science or information systems and technical experience. Internships and prior experience with the latest technology are a considerable advantage for those seeking jobs in this industry. It is possible to transfer skills learned in one industry, such as finance, to a new career in database administration. In order to accomplish this objective, many people seek additional training in computer science.

Database administrators can expect to earn an annual salary of $76,000 to $98,000. Opportunities for advancement include positions as a chief technology officer or other managerial opportunities.

A LOOK TO THE FUTURE

The Future of Crime Databases

Have you ever imagined a world without violent crime? What would you be willing to do (or give up) if your government could guarantee that all potential criminals could be stopped before they commit their crime? Recently, we are close to making this possible through large and powerful databases, along with computer programs that can analyze data and make predictions. The tricky part is that the databases require a significant amount of personal information from everyone who lives in the country. Technology has been making better crime databases, and will continue to evolve to improve our lives as we look to the future.

Currently, national crime databases in several countries, such as the United States, focus on keeping data about individuals that have committed crimes. Not only do these databases contain basic information such as name and date of birth, they also contain fingerprints, photos, and even DNA samples. This makes it easier to figure out who committed a crime after it happens, assuming the criminal is already in the database. Although the offender will eventually be caught, it is too late for the innocent victim. For this reason, researchers are currently looking into the possibility of expanding the collection of data and then using powerful programs to figure out who is capable of committing violent crimes in the future.

Over the last few years, various research institutions have been looking into patterns that could predict criminal behavior. They analyze data ranging from childhood abuse to current employment status. Their goal is to find a combination of factors that usually leads to violent, criminal behavior. Other researchers are looking deep into human DNA, looking for any sequences that could be connected to antisocial or violent behavior. If such patterns could be found, then all we need to do is find the individuals who have these characteristics. The problem is that not all these individuals have an entry in the national crime database. Furthermore, these databases do not contain data about every aspect of a person's life. That, however, could change.

Over the years, criminal databases have been expanding. However, in the United States, each state has the ability to determine the data to be collected and from whom it will be collected. While one state might take a DNA sample from only violent criminals and sex offenders, another state might collect that data from someone who committed a misdemeanor. If a future crime database is to make predictions, law enforcement will have to take DNA samples from every person living in the United States. Furthermore, the government will need access to all databases that contain information about that person—including databases from schools, businesses, insurance companies, and medical practices. Only then can these future programs be able to predict which individuals have the sort of patterns that may lead to future criminal behavior. Once those individuals are spotted, law enforcement could be authorized to monitor them closely or perhaps even intervene with psychological or medical assistance.

Supposing a crime-predicting program could be developed, there will be legal challenges to the type of data collection required. Individuals will be asked to weigh their privacy against the possibility of reducing crime. Inevitably, our trust of the government will also come into play. What do you think about this sort of future database? Would you trust the government with all this personal and biological information? Do you believe it is worth giving up privacy for the sake of having security?

DATA ORGANIZATION

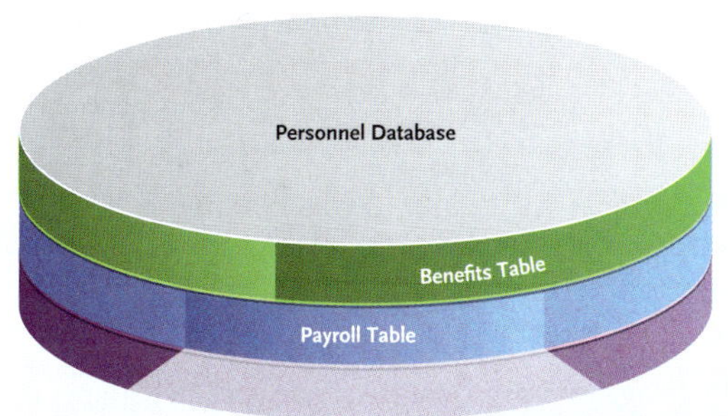

Payroll Table				
Record Number	Last Name	First Name	Employee ID	Salary
1	Baker	Cecelia	5938245	62,500
2	Brown	Sam	0029482	38,210
3	Coleman	Alex	4123987	45,210

Data is organized by the following groups:

- **Character**—the most basic logical element, consisting of individual numbers, letters, and special characters.
- **Field**—next level, consisting of a set of related characters, for example, a person's last name. A data field represents an **attribute** (description or characteristic) of some **entity** (person, place, thing, or object).
- **Record**—a collection of related fields; for example, a payroll record consisting of fields of data relating to one employee.
- **Table**—a collection of related records; for example, a payroll table consisting of all the employee records.
- **Database**—an integrated collection of related tables; for example, a personnel database contains all related employee tables.

Key Field

A **key field (primary key)** is the field in a record that uniquely identifies each record.

- Tables can be related (connected) to other tables by key fields.
- Key fields in different files can be used to integrate the data in a database.
- Common key fields are employee ID numbers and driver's license numbers.

DATA ORGANIZATION

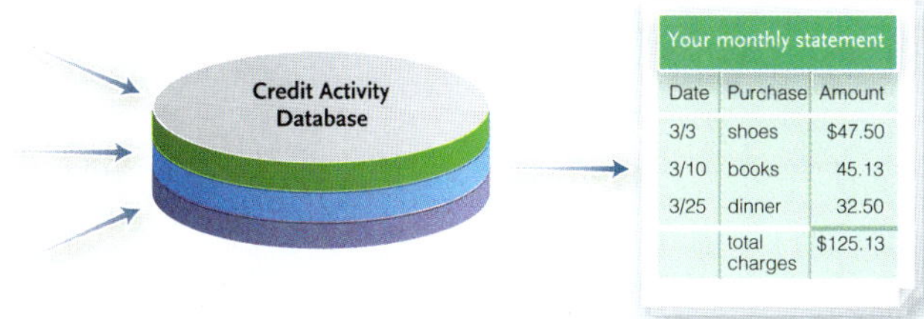

Batch versus Real-Time Processing

Traditionally, data is processed in one of two ways: batch or real-time processing.

- **Batch processing**—data is collected over time and then processed later all at one time (batched). For example, monthly credit card bills are typically created by processing credit card purchases throughout the past month.
- **Real-time processing (online processing)**—data is processed at the same time the transaction occurs; direct access storage devices make real-time processing possible. For example, a request for cash using an ATM machine initiates a verification of funds, approval or disapproval, disbursement of cash, and an update of the account balance.

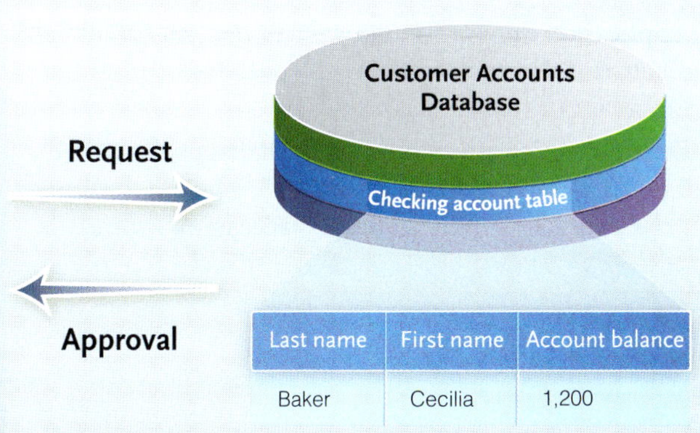

To efficiently and effectively use computers, you need to understand data fields, records, tables, and databases. You need to be aware of the different ways in which a database can be structured and the different types of databases. Also, you need to know the most important database uses and issues.

DATABASES

A **database** is a collection of integrated data–logically related files and records.

Need for Databases

Advantages of databases are sharing data, improved security, reduced **data redundancy,** and higher **data integrity.**

Database Management

A **database management system (DBMS)** is the software for creating, modifying, and gaining access to the database. A DBMS consists of five subsystems:

- **DBMS engine** provides a bridge between logical and physical data views.
- **Data definition subsystem** defines the logical structure of a database using a **data dictionary** or **schema.**
- **Data manipulation subsystem** provides tools for **data maintenance** and data analysis; tools include **query-by-example** and **structured query language (SQL).**
- **Application generation subsystem** provides tools for creating data entry forms with specialized programming languages.
- **Data administration subsystem** manages the database; **database administrators (DBAs)** are computer professionals who help define **processing rights.**

DBMS STRUCTURE

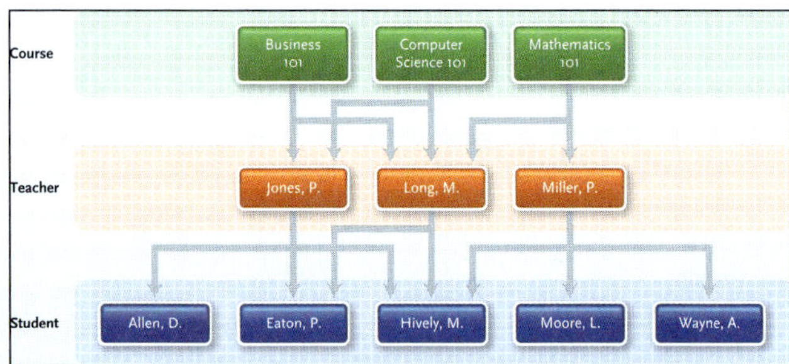

DBMS programs are designed to work with specific data structures or **database models.** These models define rules and standards for all the data in the database. Five principal database models are *hierarchical, network, relational, multidimensional,* and *object-oriented.*

Hierarchical Database

Hierarchical database uses **nodes** to link and structure fields and records; entries may have one **parent node** with several **child nodes** in a **one-to-many relationship.**

Network Database

Network database is like hierarchical except a child node may have more than one parent in a **many-to-many relationship;** additional connections are called **pointers.**

Relational Database

Relational database data is stored in tables **(relations);** related tables must have a **common data item** (key field). A table and its data are called a **relation.**

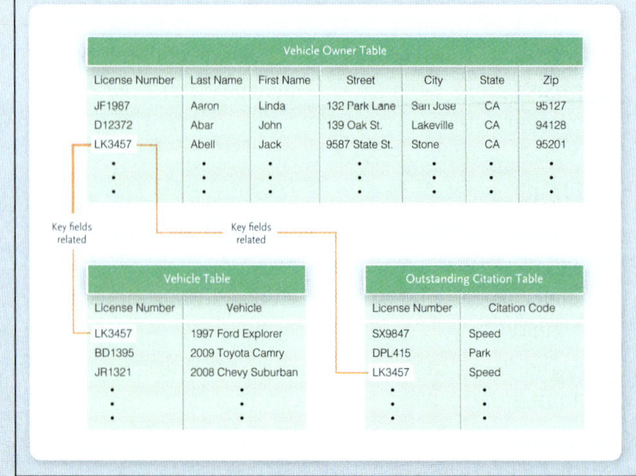

Vehicle Owner Table

License Number	Last Name	First Name	Street	City	State	Zip
JF1987	Aaron	Linda	132 Park Lane	San Jose	CA	95127
D12372	Abar	John	139 Oak St.	Lakeville	CA	94128
LK3457	Abell	Jack	9587 State St.	Stone	CA	95201
⋮	⋮	⋮	⋮	⋮	⋮	⋮

Vehicle Table

License Number	Vehicle
LK3457	1997 Ford Explorer
BD1395	2009 Toyota Camry
JR1321	2008 Chevy Suburban
⋮	⋮

Outstanding Citation Table

License Number	Citation Code
SX9847	Speed
DPL415	Park
LK3457	Speed
⋮	⋮

DBMS STRUCTURE

Multidimensional Database

Multidimensional databases extend two-dimensional relational tables to three or more dimensions, sometimes called a **data cube.**

Multidimensional databases offer more flexible structures than relational databases, providing a more intuitive way of modeling data.

Object-Oriented Database

Object-oriented databases store data, instructions, and unstructured data. Data is organized using *classes, objects, attributes,* and *methods.*

- **Classes** are general definitions.
- **Objects** are specific instances of a class that can contain both data and instructions to manipulate the data.
- **Attributes** are the data fields an object possesses.
- **Methods** are instructions for retrieving or manipulating attribute values.

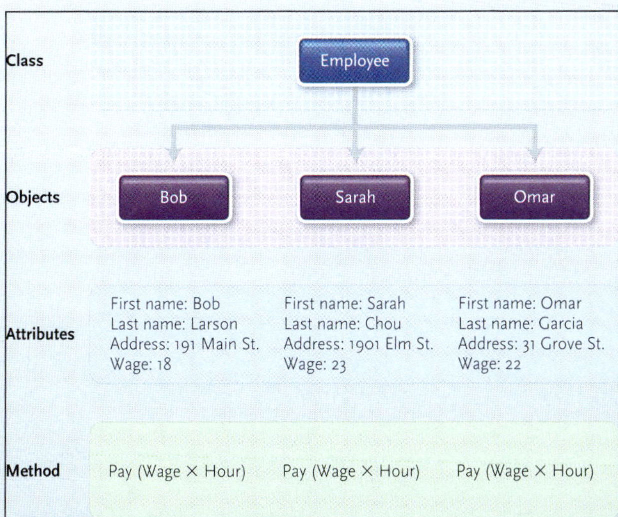

TYPES OF DATABASES

There are four types of databases:

- **Individual (personal computer) database:** Used by one person.
- **Company database:** Stored on central server; accessed by multiple people.
- **Distributed database:** Spread out geographically; accessed by communications links.
- **Commercial databases (information utilities** and **data banks):** Enormous; for particular subjects.

DATABASE USES AND ISSUES

Databases offer a great opportunity for increased productivity; however, security is always a concern.

Strategic Uses

Data warehouses support data mining. **Data mining** is a technique for searching and exploring databases for related information and patterns.

Security

Two important security concerns are illegal use of data and unauthorized access. Most organizations use **firewalls** to protect their internal networks.

CAREERS in IT

Database administrators use database management software to determine the most efficient ways to organize and access a company's data. They are also responsible for database security and system backup. A bachelor's degree in computer science or information systems and technical experience are required. Salary range is $76,000 to $98,000.

KEY TERMS

application generation subsystem (282)
attribute (279, 287)
batch processing (280)
character (279)
child node (284)
class (287)
commercial database (289)
common data item (285)
company database (288)
data (278)
data administration subsystem (283)
data bank (289)
data cube (286)
data definition subsystem (282)
data dictionary (282)
data integrity (281)
data maintenance (282)
data manipulation subsystem (282)
data mining (290)
data redundancy (281)
data warehouse (290)
database (280)
database administrator (DBA) (283, 291)
database management system (DBMS) (282)
database model (284)
DBMS engine (282)
distributed database (289)
entity (279)
field (279)
firewall (291)
hierarchical database (284)
individual database (288)
information utility (289)
key field (280)
logical view (278)
many-to-many relationship (285)
method (287)
multidimensional database (286)
network database (285)
node (284)
object (287)
object-oriented database (287)
one-to-many relationship (284)
online processing (281)
parent node (284)
personal computer database (288)
physical view (278)
pointers (285)
primary key (280)
processing rights (283)
query-by-example (282)
real-time processing (281)
record (279)
relation (285)
relational database (285)
schema (282)
structured query language (SQL) (282)
table (279)

MULTIPLE CHOICE

Circle the letter of the correct answer.

1. Facts or observations about people, places, things, and events are:
   a. data
   b. occurrences
   c. records
   d. tables
2. The most basic logical data element such as a single letter, number, or special character is known as a(n):
   a. character
   b. element
   c. phrase
   d. record
3. Each record in a database has at least one distinctive field, called the:
   a. key field
   b. structure
   c. type
   d. view
4. One element of database security is to provide only authorized users with:
   a. classes
   b. nodes
   c. passwords
   d. relations
5. The bridge between the logical and physical views of the data is provided by:
   a. DBMS
   b. records
   c. SQL
   d. tables
6. Highly trained computer specialists who interact with the data administration subsystem are known as:
   a. DBMS
   b. data modelers
   c. database administrators
   d. relational specialists
7. In a network database, each child node may have more than one parent node; this is known as a:
   a. hierarchy
   b. many-to-many relationship
   c. parent relationship
   d. relational relationship
8. Connections between parent nodes and child nodes are provided by:
   a. characters
   b. DBA
   c. objects
   d. pointers
9. Two of the most significant advantages of multidimensional databases over relational databases are processing speed and:
   a. conceptualization
   b. control
   c. format
   d. objectification
10. Object-oriented databases organize data by classes, attributes, methods, and:
    a. objects
    b. relations
    c. space
    d. time

MATCHING

Match each numbered item with the most closely related lettered item. Write your answers in the spaces provided.

- **a.** attributes
- **b.** batch
- **c.** distributed
- **d.** field
- **e.** hierarchical
- **f.** physical
- **g.** redundancy
- **h.** relational
- **i.** schema
- **j.** speed

___ **1.** View that focuses on the actual format and location of the data.

___ **2.** Group of related characters.

___ **3.** Type of processing in which data is collected over several hours, days, or even weeks and then processed all at once.

___ **4.** A data problem that often occurs when individual departments create and maintain their own data.

___ **5.** Another name for a data dictionary.

___ **6.** Type of database structure where fields or records are structured in nodes that are connected like the branches of an upside-down tree.

___ **7.** Type of database structure where the data elements are stored in different tables.

___ **8.** Two of the most significant advantages of multidimensional databases are conceptualization and processing _____.

___ **9.** Object-oriented databases organize data by classes, objects, methods, and _____.

___ **10.** Type of database that uses communication networks to link data stored in different locations.

OPEN-ENDED

On a separate sheet of paper, respond to each question or statement.

1. Describe the five logical data groups or categories.
2. What is the difference between batch processing and real-time processing?
3. Identify and define the five parts of DBMS programs.
4. Describe each of the five common database models.
5. What are some of the benefits and limitations of databases? Why is security a concern?

DISCUSSION

Respond to each of the following questions.

1 Applying Technology: INTERNET MOVIE DATABASE

One popular commercial database is the Internet Movie Database, or IMDb. Connect to its website, explore its content, search for a few movies, and then answer the following questions: (a) What types of information does the IMDb contain? (b) What searches did you try? What were the results? (c) Based on your knowledge of databases, would you expect the IMDb to be relational or hierarchical? Justify your answer.

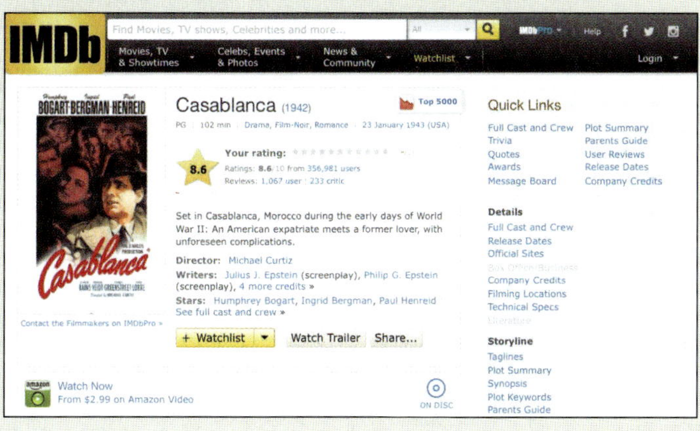

2 Writing about Technology: INFORMATION SHARING

Corporations currently collect information about the purchases you make and your personal spending habits. Sometimes corporations will share information to build a more informative profile about you. There have been proposals for legislation to regulate or halt this type of exchange. Consider how you feel about this exchange of information, and then respond to the following: (a) What ethics and privacy concerns are related to corporations sharing personal data? (b) How might the consumer benefit from this? (c) Could this harm the consumer? What could happen if your grocery store shared information about your purchases with your life insurance carrier? (d) What rights do you feel consumers should have with regard to privacy of information collected about them? How should these rights be enforced? Defend your answer.

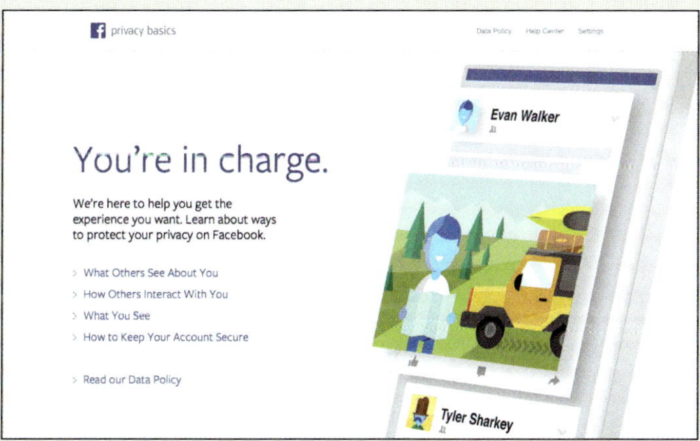

3 Writing about Technology: DATABASE SECURITY

Securing the data in a database is typically as important a concern as is its design. Research database security on the web, and then respond to the following: (a) Describe a few security risks that databases must be protected against. (b) Describe some steps that can be taken to ensure that a database is secured.

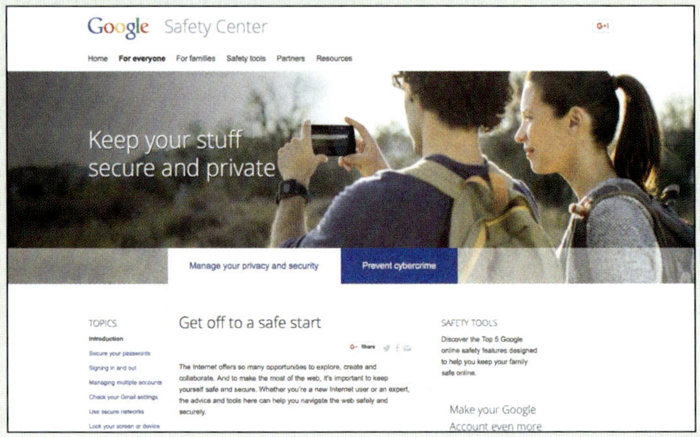

PHOTO CREDITS

CHAPTER 11:

Opener: © Colin Anderson/Getty Images RF; p. 277, 292: © Brand X Pictures/Jupiterimages RF; p. 278, 291: © David Lees/Taxi/Getty Images; 11-2 (top): © UpperCut Images/Getty Images RF; 11-2 (middle): © Ned Frisk/ Getty Images RF; 11-2 (bottom): © Jack Star/PhotoLink/Getty Images RF; 11-3: © amana productions/Getty Images RF; 11-4: Microsoft product screen shot(s) reprinted with permission from Microsoft Corporation; 11-5, p. 294: © Digital Vision/Getty Images RF; 11-9, p. 295 (left): Aaron Roeth Photography RF; 11-12, p. 295 (right): Copyright 2010 LexisNexis, a division of Reed Elsevier Inc. All Rights Reserved. LexisNexis and the Knowledge Burst logo are registered trademarks of Reed Elsevier Properties Inc. and are used with the permission of LexisNexis; 11-14: Peter Macdiarmid/Getty Images I, p. 299 (top): © 2015 IMDb.com, Inc.; p. 299 (bottom): Facebook © 2015; p. 300: Google and the Google logo are registered trademarks of Google, Inc., used with permission.

chapter 12

Systems Analysis and Design

Why should I read this chapter?

When an organization designs and implements a new system, jobs are on the line. A well-designed system can make a career; a poor one can destroy a company. Systems analysis and design details the framework for creating new systems. In the future, information systems will rely on cloud-based services, giving easier upgrades, improved security, and higher reliability.

This chapter covers the things you need to know to be prepared for this ever-changing digital world, including:

- The systems life cycle—understand the phases of information systems development and avoid confusion, missteps, and inefficiency.
- Prototyping and rapid development—learn the newest alternatives to the systems life cycle to respond quickly and effectively to unexpected systems design challenges.

Learning Objectives

After you have read this chapter, you should be able to:

1. Describe the six phases of the systems life cycle.
2. Identify information needs and formulate possible solutions.
3. Analyze existing information systems and evaluate the feasibility of alternative systems.
4. Identify, acquire, and test new system software and hardware.
5. Switch from an existing information system to a new one with minimal risk.
6. Perform system audits and periodic evaluations.
7. Describe prototyping and rapid applications development.

Introduction

"Hi, I'm Nicole, and I'm a systems analyst. I'd like to talk with you about analyzing and designing information systems for organizations."

Most people in an organization are involved with an information system of some kind. For an organization to create and effectively use a system requires considerable thought and effort. Fortunately, there is a six-step process for accomplishing this. It is known as systems analysis and design.

Big organizations can make big mistakes. For example, a large automobile manufacturer once spent $40 billion putting in factory robots and other high technology in its automaking plants. Unfortunately, the manufacturer could never make these new changes work and removed much of the equipment and reinstalled its original production systems. Why did the high-tech production systems fail? The probable reason was that not enough energy was devoted to training its workforce in using the new systems.

The government also can make big mistakes. In one year, the Internal Revenue Service computer system was so overwhelmed it could not deliver tax refunds on time. How did this happen? Despite extensive testing of much of the system, not all testing was completed. Thus, when the new system was phased in, the IRS found it could not process tax returns as quickly as it had hoped.

Both of these examples show the necessity for thorough planning—especially when an organization is trying to implement a new kind of system. Systems analysis and design reduces the chances for such spectacular failures.

To efficiently and effectly use computers, you need to understand the importance of systems analysis and design. You need to be aware of the relationship of an organization's chart to its managerial structure. Additionally, you need to know the six phases of the systems development life cycle: preliminary investigation, systems analysis, systems design, systems development, systems implementation, and systems maintenance.

Systems Analysis and Design

We described different types of information systems in the last chapter. Now let us consider: What, exactly, is a **system?** We can define it as a collection of activities and elements organized to accomplish a goal. As we saw in Chapter 10, an *information system* is a collection of hardware, software, people, procedures, data, and the Internet. These work together to provide information essential to running an organization. This information helps produce a product or service and, for profit-oriented businesses, derive a profit.

Information about orders received, products shipped, money owed, and so on, flows into an organization from the outside. Information about what supplies have been received, which customers have paid their bills, and so on, also flows within the organization. To avoid confusion, the flow of information must follow a route that is defined by a set of rules and procedures. However, from time to time, organizations need to change their information systems. Reasons include organizational growth, mergers and acquisitions, new marketing opportunities, revisions in governmental regulations, and availability of new technology.

Systems analysis and design is a six-phase problem-solving procedure for examining and improving an information system. The six phases make up the **systems life cycle.** (See Figure 12-1.) The phases are as follows:

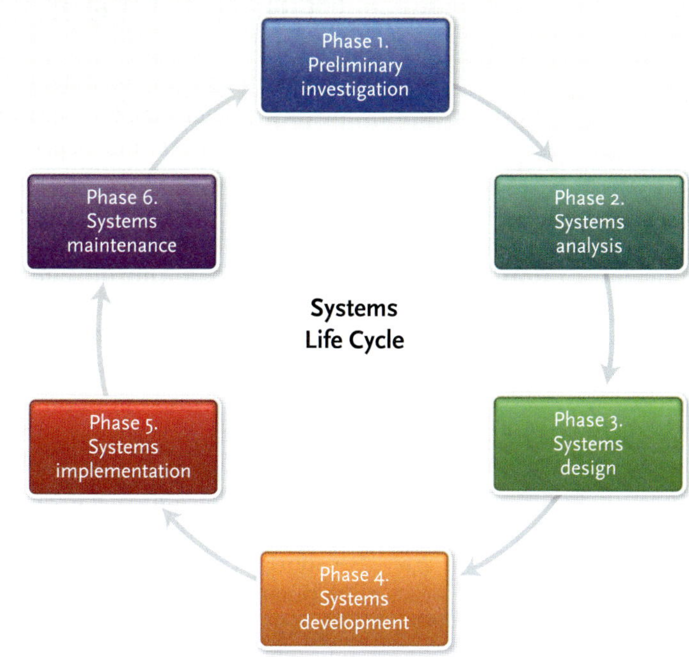

Figure 12-1 **The six-phase systems life cycle**

1. *Preliminary investigation:* The organization's problems or needs are identified and summarized in a short report.
2. *Systems analysis:* The present system is studied in depth. New requirements are specified and documented.
3. *Systems design:* A new or alternative information system is designed and a design report created.
4. *Systems development:* New hardware and software are acquired, developed, and tested.
5. *Systems implementation:* The new information system is installed, and people are trained to use it.
6. *Systems maintenance:* In this ongoing phase, the system is periodically evaluated and updated as needed.

In organizations, this six-phase systems life cycle is used by computer professionals known as **systems analysts.** These people study an organization's systems to determine what actions to take and how to use computer technology to assist them.

As an end user, working alone or with a systems analyst, it is important that you understand how the systems life cycle works. In fact, you may *have* to use the procedure.

More and more end users are developing their own information systems. This is because in many organizations there is a three-year backlog of work for systems analysts. For instance, suppose you recognize that there is a need for certain information within your organization. Obtaining this information will require the introduction of new hardware and software. You go to seek expert help from systems analysts in studying these information needs. At that point you discover that the systems analysts are so overworked it will take them three years to get to your request! You can see, then, why many managers are learning to do these activities themselves.

In any case, learning the six steps described in this chapter will raise your computer efficiency and effectiveness. It also will give you skills to solve a wide range of problems. These skills can make you more valuable to an organization.

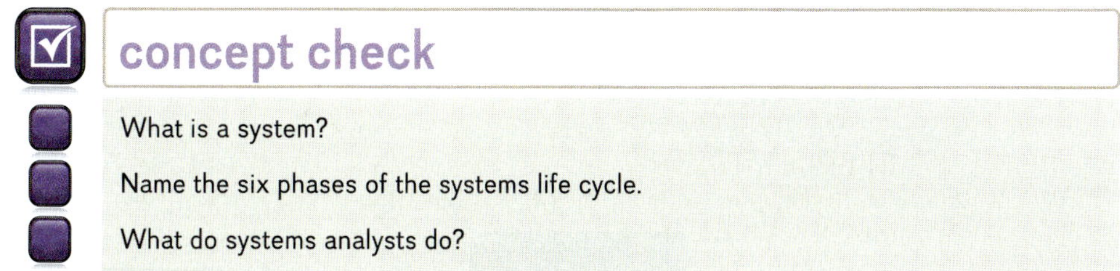

concept check

- What is a system?
- Name the six phases of the systems life cycle.
- What do systems analysts do?

Phase 1: Preliminary Investigation

The first phase of the systems life cycle is a **preliminary investigation** of a proposed project to determine the need for a new information system. This usually is requested by an end user or a manager who wants something done that is not presently being done. For example, suppose you work for Advantage Advertising, a fast-growing advertising agency. Advantage Advertising produces a variety of different ads for a wide range of different clients. The agency employs both regular staff workers and on-call freelancers. One of your responsibilities is keeping track of the work performed for each client and the employees who performed the work. In addition, you are responsible for tabulating the final bill for each project.

How do you figure out how to charge which clients for which work done by which employees? This kind of problem is common to many service organizations (such as lawyers' and contractors' offices). Indeed, it is a problem in any organization where people charge for their time and clients need proof of hours worked.

In Phase 1, the systems analyst—or the end user—is concerned with three tasks: (1) briefly defining the problem, (2) suggesting alternative solutions, and (3) preparing a short report. (See Figure 12-2.) This report will help management decide whether to pursue the project further. (If you are an end user, you may not produce a written report. Rather, you might report your findings directly to your supervisor.)

Defining the Problem

Defining the problem means examining whatever current information system is in use. Determining what information is needed, by whom, when, and why is accomplished by interviewing and making observations. If the information system is large, this survey is done by a systems analyst. If the system is small, the survey can be done by the end user.

For example, suppose Advantage Advertising account executives, copywriters, and graphic artists currently record the time spent on different jobs on their desk calendars. (Examples might be "Client A, telephone conference, 15 minutes"; "Client B, design layout, 2 hours.") After interviewing several account executives

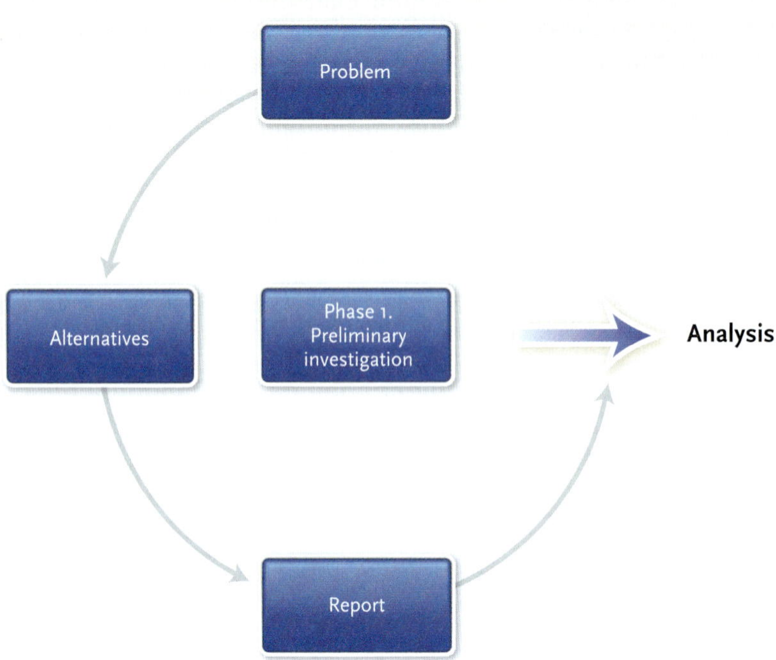

Figure 12-2 **Phase 1: Preliminary investigation**

and listening to their frustrations, it becomes clear that the approach is somewhat disorganized. (See Figure 12-3.) Written calendar entries are too unprofessional to be shown to clients. Moreover, a large job often has many people working on it. It is difficult to pull together all their notations to make up a bill for the client. Some freelancers work at home, and their time slips are not readily available. These matters constitute a statement of the problem: The company has a manual time-and-billing system that is slow and difficult to use.

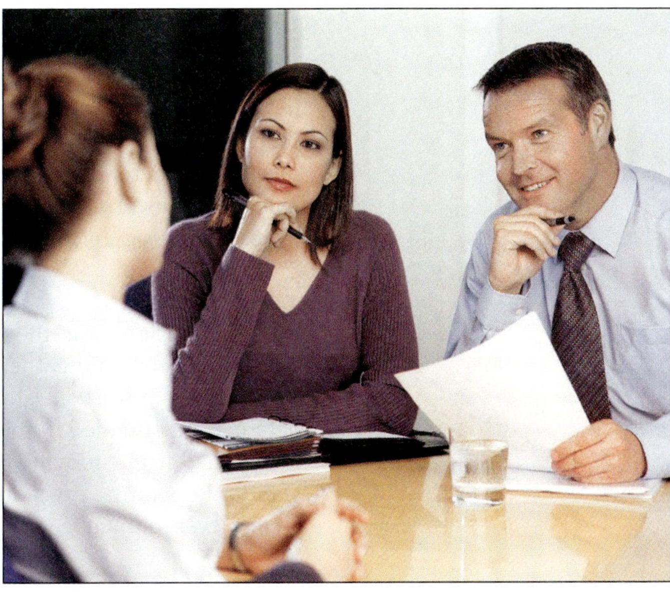

Figure 12-3 **One step in defining problems with the current system is to interview executives**

As an end user, you might experience difficulties with this system yourself. You're in someone else's office, and a telephone call comes in for you from a client. Your desk calendar is back in your own office. You have two choices. You can always carry your calendar with you, or you can remember to note the time you spent on various tasks when you return to your office. The administrative assistant reporting to the account executive is continually after you (and everyone else at Advantage) to provide photocopies of your calendar. This is so that various clients can be billed for the work done on various jobs. Surely, you think, there must be a better way to handle time and billing.

Suggesting Alternative Systems

This step is simply to suggest some possible plans as alternatives to the present arrangement. For instance, Advantage could hire more administrative assistants to collect the information from everyone's calendars (including telephoning those working at home). Or it could use the existing system of network-linked personal computers that staffers and freelancers presently use. Perhaps, you think, there is already some off-the-shelf packaged software available that could be used for a time-and-billing system. At least there might be one that would make your own job easier.

Preparing a Short Report

For large projects, the systems analyst writes a report summarizing the results of the preliminary investigation and suggesting alternative systems. The report also may include schedules for further development of the project. This document is presented to higher management, along with a recommendation to continue or discontinue the project. Management then decides whether to finance the second phase, the systems analysis.

For Advantage Advertising, your report might point out that billing is frequently delayed. It could say that some tasks may even "slip through the cracks" and not get charged at all. Thus, as the analyst has noted, you suggest the project might pay for itself merely by eliminating lost or forgotten charges.

concept check

What is the purpose of the preliminary investigation phase?

What are the three tasks the systems analyst is concerned with during this phase?

Who determines whether to finance the second phase?

Phase 2: Systems Analysis

In Phase 2, **systems analysis,** data is collected about the present system. This data is then analyzed, and new requirements are determined. We are not concerned with a new design here, only with determining the *requirements* for a new system. Systems analysis is concerned with gathering and analyzing the data. This usually is completed by documenting the analysis in a report. (See Figure 12-4.)

Gathering Data

When gathering data, the systems analyst—or the end user doing systems analysis—expands on the data gathered during Phase 1. He or she adds details about how the current system works. Data is obtained from observation and interviews. In addition, data may be obtained from questionnaires given to people using the system. Data also is obtained from studying documents that describe the formal lines of authority and standard operating procedures. One such document is the **organization chart,** which shows levels of management as well as formal lines of authority.

Analyzing the Data

In the data analysis step, the idea is to learn how information currently flows and to pinpoint why it isn't flowing appropriately. The whole point of this step is to apply logic to the existing arrangement to see how workable it is. Many times, the current system is not operating correctly because prescribed procedures are not being followed. That is, the system may not really need to be redesigned. Rather, the people in it may need to be shown how to follow correct procedures.

Many different tools are available to assist systems analysts and end users in the analysis phase. Some of the most important are the top-down analysis method, grid charts, system flow charts, data flow diagrams, and automated design tools.

- **Top-down analysis method:** The top-down analysis method is used to identify the top-level components of a complex system. Each component is then broken down into smaller and smaller components. This approach makes each component easier to analyze and deal with.

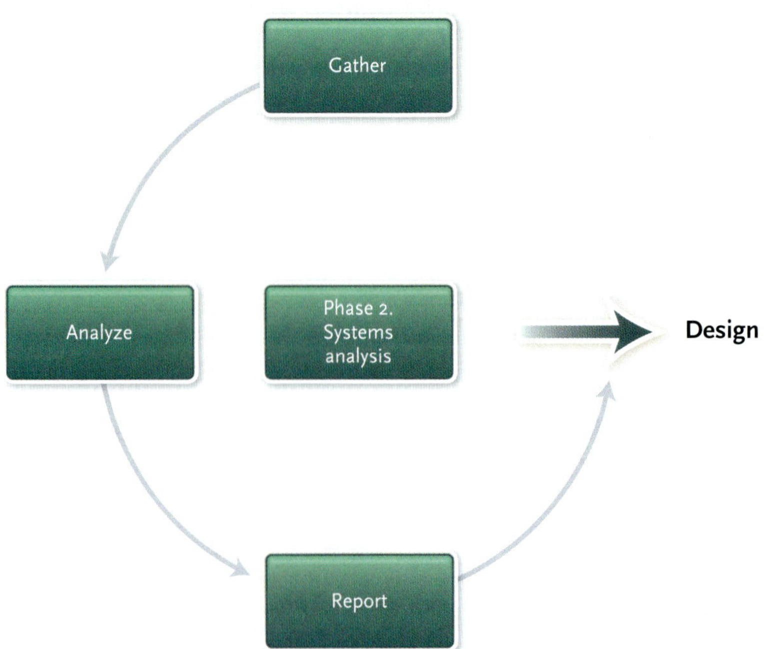

Figure 12-4 **Phase 2: Systems analysis**

	Reports (output)		
Forms (input)	Client billing	Personnel expense	Support cost
Time sheet	✓	✓	
Telephone log	✓		✓
Travel log	✓		✓

Figure 12-5 Example of a grid chart

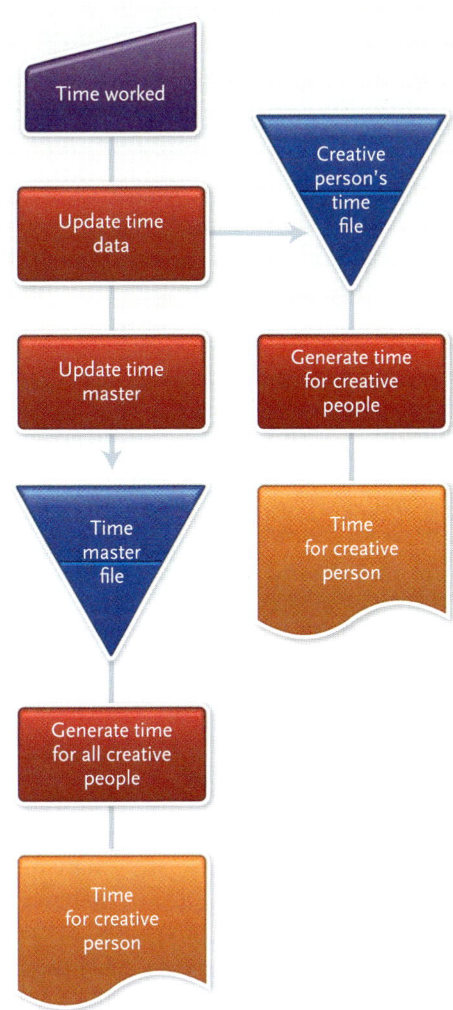

Figure 12-6 Example of a system flowchart

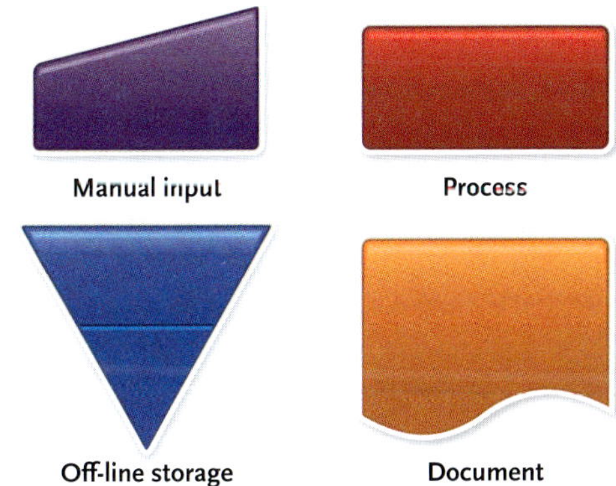

Figure 12-7 System flowchart symbols

For instance, the systems analyst might look at the present kind of bill submitted to a client for a complex advertising campaign. The analyst might note the categories of costs—employee salaries, telephone and mailing charges, travel, supplies, and so on.

- **Grid charts:** A grid chart shows the relationship between input and output documents. An example is shown in Figure 12-5 that indicates the relationship between the data input and the outputs.

  For instance, a time sheet is one of many inputs that produces a particular report, such as a client's bill. Other inputs might be forms having to do with telephone conferences and travel expenses. On a grid sheet, rows represent inputs, such as time sheet forms. Columns represent output documents, such as different clients' bills. A check mark at the intersection of a row and column means that the input document is used to create the output document.
- **System flowcharts:** System flowcharts show the flow of input data to processing and finally to output, or distribution of information. An example of a system flowchart keeping track of time for advertising "creative people" is shown in Figure 12-6. The explanation of the symbols used appears in Figure 12-7. Note that this describes the present manual, or noncomputerized, system. (A system flowchart is not the same as a program flowchart, which is very detailed. Program flowcharts are discussed in Chapter 13.)
- **Data flow diagrams:** Data flow diagrams show the data or information flow within an information system. The data is traced from its origin through processing, storage, and output. An example of a data flow diagram is shown in Figure 12-8. The explanation of the symbols used appears in Figure 12-9.
- **Automated design tools:** Automated design tools are software packages that evaluate hardware and software alternatives according to requirements given by the systems analyst. They are also called **computer-aided software engineering (CASE) tools.** These tools are not limited to systems analysis. They are used in systems design and development as well. CASE tools relieve the systems analysts of many repetitive tasks, develop clear documentation, and, for larger projects, coordinate team member activities.

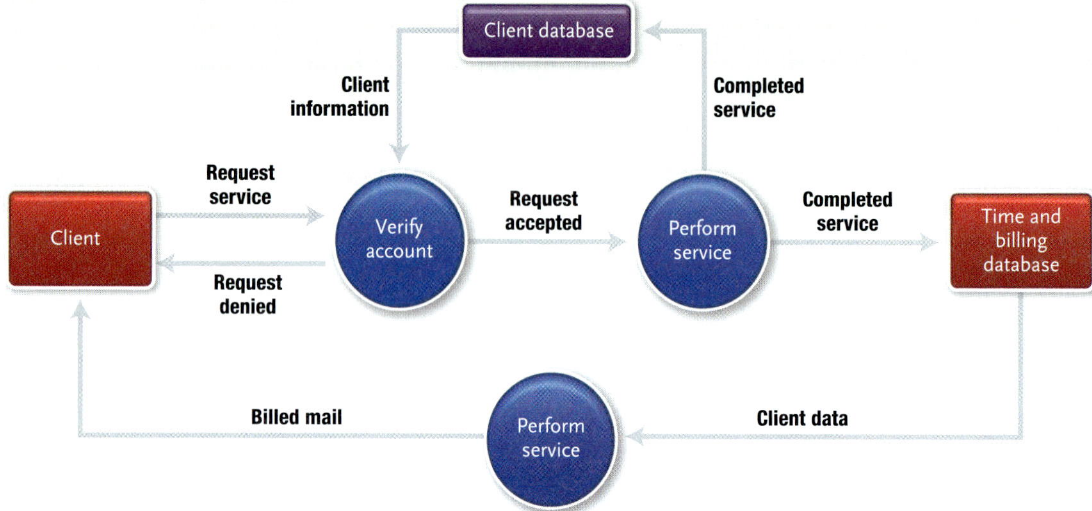

Figure 12-8 **Example of a data flow diagram**

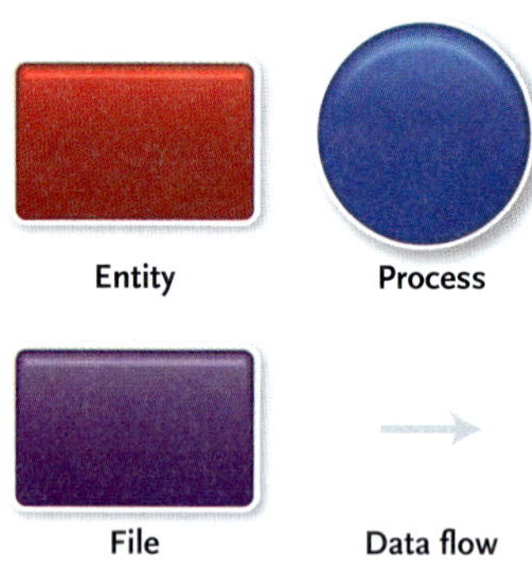

Figure 12-9 **Data flow diagram symbols**

Documenting Systems Analysis

In larger organizations, the systems analysis stage is typically documented in a report for higher management. The **systems analysis report** describes the current information system, the requirements for a new system, and a possible development schedule. For example, at Advantage Advertising, the system flowcharts show the present flow of information in a manual time-and-billing system. Some boxes in the system flowchart might be replaced with symbols showing where a computerized information system could work better.

Management studies the report and decides whether to continue with the project. Let us assume your boss and higher management have decided to continue. You now move on to Phase 3, systems design.

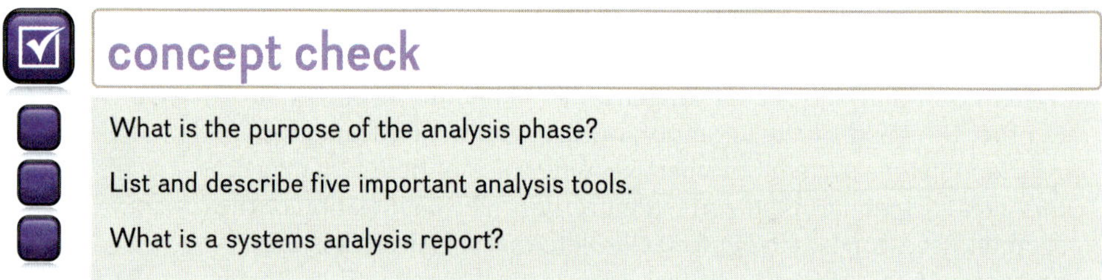

concept check

- What is the purpose of the analysis phase?
- List and describe five important analysis tools.
- What is a systems analysis report?

Phase 3: Systems Design

Phase 3 is **systems design.** It consists of three tasks: (1) designing alternative systems, (2) selecting the best system, and (3) writing a systems design report. (See Figure 12-10.)

Designing Alternative Systems

In almost all instances, more than one design can be developed to meet the information needs. Systems designers evaluate each alternative system for feasibility. By feasibility we mean three things:

- **Economic feasibility:** Will the costs of the new system be justified by the benefits it promises? How long will it take for the new system to pay for itself?

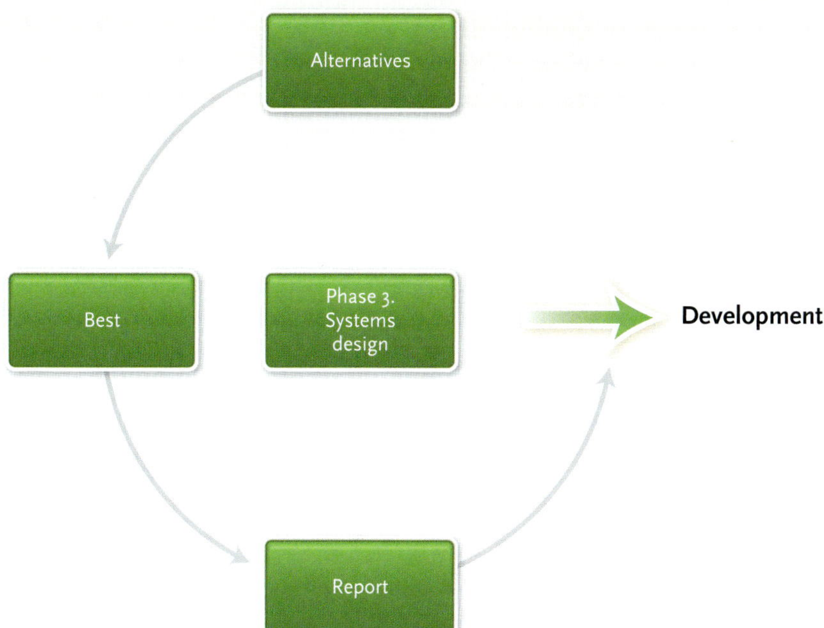

Figure 12-10 **Phase 3: Systems design**

- **Technical feasibility:** Are reliable hardware, software, and training available to make the system work? If not, can they be obtained?
- **Operational feasibility:** Can the system actually be made to operate in the organization, or will people—employees, managers, clients—resist it?

Selecting the Best System

When choosing the best design, managers must consider these four questions: (1) Will the system work with the organization's overall information system? (2) Will the system be flexible enough so it can be modified in the future? (3) Can it be made secure against unauthorized use? (4) Are the benefits worth the costs?

For example, one aspect you have to consider at Advantage Advertising is security. Should freelancers and outside vendors enter data directly into a computerized time-and-billing system, or should they keep submitting time sheets manually? In allowing these outside people to input information directly, are you also allowing them access to files they should not see? Do these files contain confidential information, perhaps information of value to rival advertising agencies?

Writing the Systems Design Report

The **systems design report** is prepared for higher management and describes the alternative designs. It presents the costs versus the benefits and outlines the effect of alternative designs on the organization. It usually concludes by recommending one of the alternatives.

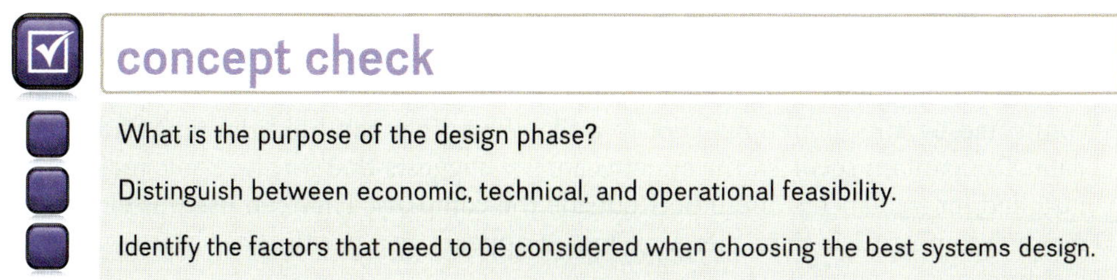

concept check
What is the purpose of the design phase?
Distinguish between economic, technical, and operational feasibility.
Identify the factors that need to be considered when choosing the best systems design.

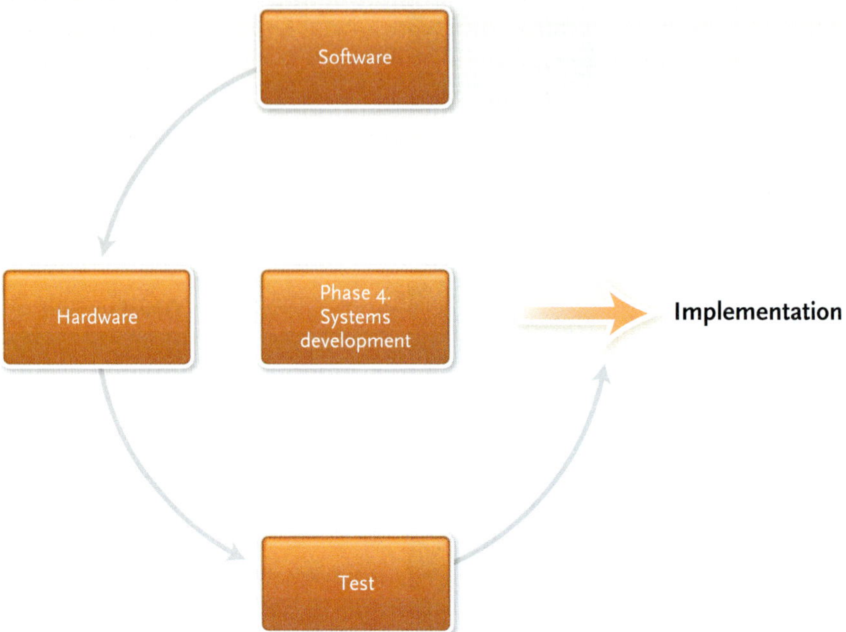

Figure 12-11 **Phase 4: Systems development**

Phase 4: Systems Development

Phase 4 is **systems development.** It has three steps: (1) acquiring software, (2) acquiring hardware, and (3) testing the new system. (See Figure 12-11.)

Acquiring Software

Application software for the new information system can be obtained in two ways. It can be purchased as off-the-shelf packaged software and possibly modified, or it can be custom-designed. If any of the software is being specially created, the programming steps we will outline in Chapter 13 should be followed.

With the systems analyst's help, you have looked at time-and-billing packaged software designed for service organizations. Unfortunately, you find that none of the packaged software will do. Most of the packages seem to work well for one person (you). However, none seems to be designed for many people working together. It appears, then, that software will have to be custom-designed. (We discuss the process of developing software in Chapter 13, on programming.)

Acquiring Hardware

Some new systems may not require new computer equipment, but others will. The equipment needed and the places where they are to be installed must be determined. This is a very critical area. Switching or upgrading equipment can be a tremendously expensive proposition. Will a personal computer system be sufficient as a company grows? Are networks expandable? Will people have to undergo costly training?

The systems analyst tells you that there are several different makes and models of personal computers currently in use at Advantage Advertising. Fortunately, all are connected by a local area network to a file server that can hold the time-and-billing data. To maintain security, the systems analyst suggests that an electronic mailbox be installed for freelancers and others outside the company. They can use this electronic mailbox to post their time charges. Thus, it appears that existing hardware will work just fine.

Testing the New System

After the software and equipment have been installed, the system should be tested. Sample data is fed into the system. The processed information is then evaluated to see whether results are correct. Testing may take several months if the new system is complex.

For this step, you ask some people in Creative Services to test the system. (See Figure 12-12.) You observe that some of the people have problems knowing where to enter their times. To solve the problem, the software is modified to display an improved user entry screen. After the system has been thoroughly tested and revised as necessary, you are ready to put it into use.

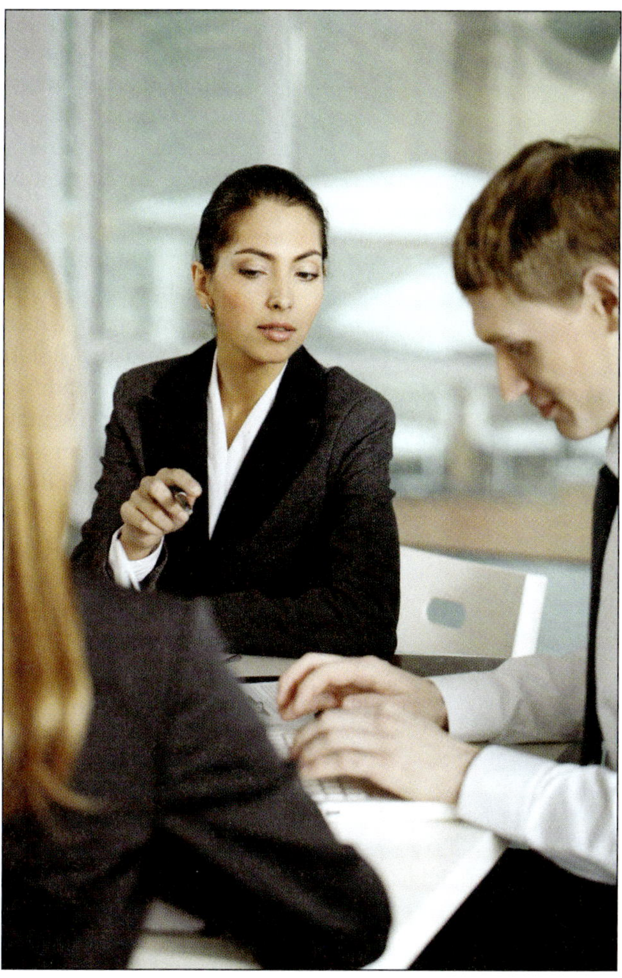

Figure 12-12 **To test a system, sample data is entered and problems are resolved**

concept check

What is the purpose of the development phase?

What are the ways by which application software can be obtained?

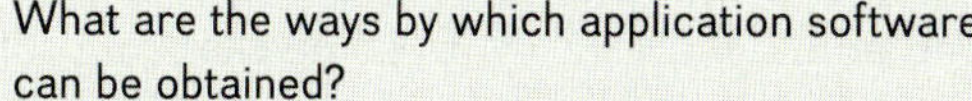

Phase 5: Systems Implementation

Another name for Phase 5, **systems implementation,** is **conversion.** It is the process of changing–converting–from the old system to the new one and training people to use the new system.

Types of Conversion

There are four approaches to conversion: *direct, parallel, pilot,* and *phased.*

- In the **direct approach,** the conversion is done simply by abandoning the old and starting up the new. This can be risky. If anything is still wrong with the new system, the old system is no longer available to fall back on.

  The direct approach is not recommended precisely because it is so risky. Problems, big or small, invariably crop up in a new system. In a large system, a problem might just mean catastrophe.
- In the **parallel approach,** old and new systems are operated side by side until the new one proves to be reliable.

  This approach is low risk. If the new system fails, the organization can just switch to the old system to keep going. However, keeping enough equipment and people active to manage two systems at the same time can be very expensive. Thus, the parallel approach is used only in cases in which the cost of failure or of interrupted operation is great.
- In the **pilot approach,** the new system is tried out in only one part of the organization. Once the system is working smoothly in that part, it is implemented throughout the rest of the organization.

  The pilot approach is certainly less expensive than the parallel approach. It also is somewhat riskier. However, the risks can be controlled because problems will be confined to only certain areas of the organization. Difficulties will not affect the entire organization.

- In the **phased approach,** the new system is implemented gradually over a period of time. The entire implementation process is broken down into parts or phases. Implementation begins with the first phase, and once it is successfully implemented, the second phase begins. This process continues until all phases are operating smoothly. Typically, this is an expensive proposition because the implementation is done slowly. However, it is certainly one of the least risky approaches.

In general, the pilot and phased approaches are the favored methods. Pilot is preferred when there are many people in an organization performing similar operations—for instance, all salesclerks in a department store. Phased is more appropriate for organizations in which people are performing different operations.

You and the systems analyst, with top management support, have decided on a pilot implementation. This approach was selected in part based on cost and the availability of a representative group of users. The Creative Services department previously tested the system and has expressed enthusiastic support for it. A group from this department will pilot the implementation of the time-and-billing system.

Training

Training people is important, of course. Unfortunately, it is one of the most commonly overlooked activities. Some people may begin training early, even before the equipment is delivered, so that they can adjust more easily. In some cases, a professional software trainer may be brought in to show people how to operate the system. However, at Advantage Advertising, the time-and-billing software is simple enough that the systems analyst can act as the trainer.

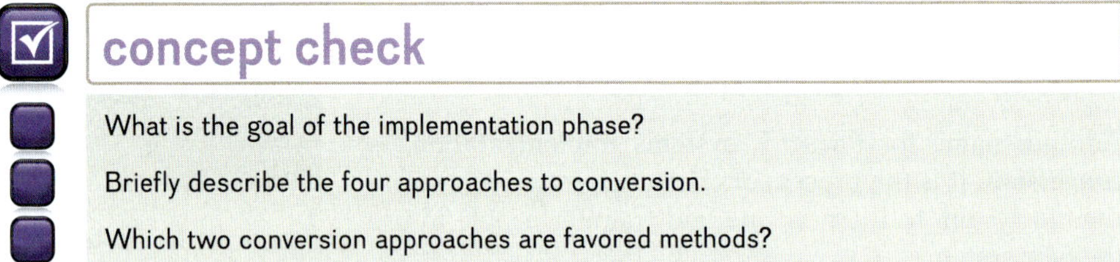

concept check

- What is the goal of the implementation phase?
- Briefly describe the four approaches to conversion.
- Which two conversion approaches are favored methods?

Phase 6: Systems Maintenance

After implementation comes **systems maintenance,** the last step in the systems life cycle. This phase is a very important, ongoing activity. Most organizations spend more time and money on this phase than on any of the others. Maintenance has two parts: a *systems audit* and a *periodic evaluation.*

In the **systems audit,** the system's performance is compared to the original design specifications. This is to determine whether the new procedures are actually furthering productivity. If they are not, some redesign may be necessary.

After the systems audit, the new information system is further modified, if necessary. All systems should be evaluated from time to time to determine whether they are meeting the goals and providing the service they are supposed to.

The six-step systems life cycle is summarized in Figure 12-13.

concept check

- What is the purpose of the maintenance phase?
- Name the two parts of the maintenance phase.

Phase	Activity
1. Preliminary investigation	Define problem, suggest alternatives, prepare short report
2. Systems analysis	Gather data, analyze data, document
3. Systems design	Design alternatives, select best alternative, write report
4. Systems development	Develop software, acquire hardware, test system
5. Systems implementation	Convert, train
6. Systems maintenance	Perform systems audit, evaluate periodically

Figure 12-13 Summary of systems life cycle

Prototyping and Rapid Applications Development

Is it necessary to follow every phase of the systems life cycle? It may be desirable, but often there is no time to do so. For instance, hardware may change so fast that there is no opportunity for evaluation, design, and testing as just described. Two alternative approaches that require much less time are *prototyping* and *rapid applications development.*

Prototyping

Prototyping means to build a *model* or *prototype* that can be modified before the actual system is installed. For instance, the systems analyst for Advantage Advertising might develop a proposed or prototype menu as a possible screen display for the time-and-billing system. Users would try it out and provide feedback to the systems analyst. The systems analyst would revise the prototype until the users felt it was ready to put into place. Typically, the development time for prototyping is shorter; however, it is sometimes more difficult to manage the project and to control costs. (See Figure 12-14.)

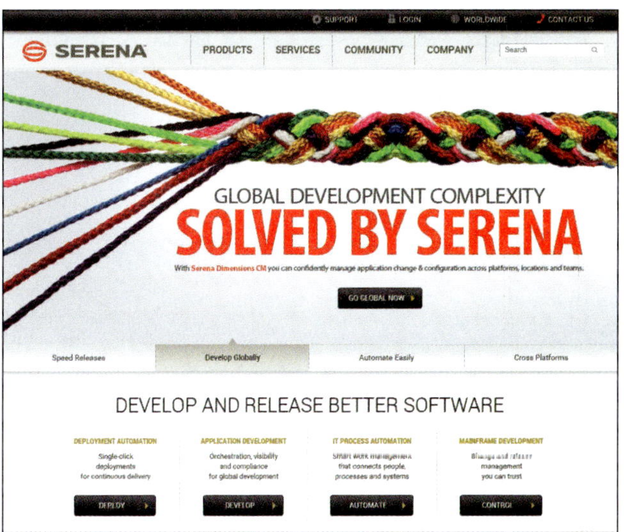

Figure 12-14 Serena offers prototyping software

Rapid Applications Development

Rapid applications development (RAD) involves the use of powerful development software, small specialized teams, and highly trained personnel. For example, the systems analyst for Advantage Advertising would use specialized development software like CASE, form small teams consisting of select users and managers, and obtain assistance from other highly qualified analysts. Although the resulting time-and-billing system would likely cost more, the development time would be shorter and the quality of the completed system would be better.

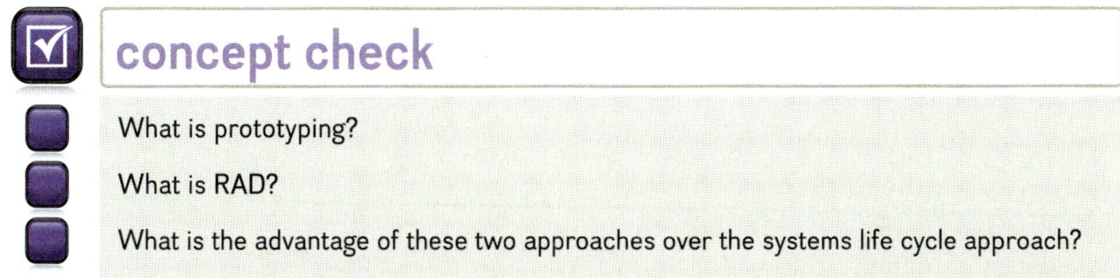

concept check

- What is prototyping?
- What is RAD?
- What is the advantage of these two approaches over the systems life cycle approach?

Careers in IT

"Now that you have learned about systems analysis and design, let me tell you about my career as a systems analyst."

A **systems analyst** follows the steps described in the systems life cycle. Analysts plan and design new systems or reorganize a company's computer resources to best utilize them. Analysts follow the systems life cycle through all its steps: preliminary investigation, analysis, design, development, implementation, and maintenance.

Systems analyst positions normally require either an advanced associate's degree or a bachelor's degree in computer science or information systems and technical experience. Internships and prior experience with the latest technology are a considerable advantage for those seeking jobs in this industry. Systems analysts can expect to earn an annual salary of $50,000 to $64,000. Opportunities for advancement include positions as a chief technology officer or other managerial opportunities.

A LOOK TO THE FUTURE

The Challenge of Keeping Pace

Have you noticed the speed with which new (or competing) products and services are being released? Does your favorite website change often to keep up with its competitors? Most observers firmly believe that the pace of business is accelerating. The time to develop a product and bring it to market, in many cases, is now months rather than years. Internet technologies, in particular, have provided tools to support the rapid introduction of new products and services. Technology has been making better business tools, and will continue to evolve to improve our lives as we look to the future.

To stay competitive, corporations must integrate these new technologies into their existing ways of doing business. In many cases, the traditional systems life cycle approach takes too long—sometimes years—to develop a system. Many organizations are responding by aggressively implementing prototyping and RAD. Others are enlisting the services of outside consulting groups that specialize in systems development. However, many experts believe that the future of life cycle management lies in relying on the cloud: businesses will turn to companies that offer both processing and software as a service, rather than hosting these systems on their own.

In the future, many companies will no longer have large servers and database systems under their own roof. They will instead pay a monthly fee to a company, such as Amazon, that has large data centers that are accessible via the Internet. These data centers offer security and reliability, and they can grow, or scale, based on the needs of the business. The systems analyst of the future will not have to worry about the hardware requirements of a new piece of software or database management system. The implementation of new systems will be much easier, for both the business and its customers. All hardware upgrades will now be managed by the company offering the cloud service, and the software will be hosted there. Of course, all this requires a good communications infrastructure—one that is being improved each year by telecommunications companies.

What do you think about moving so many aspects of a system to the cloud? Is there a danger in trusting another company with your business's data? Do you think cloud computing will enable a business to release reliable products more quickly and at a lower cost?

VISUAL SUMMARY Systems Analysis and Design

SYSTEMS ANALYSIS AND DESIGN

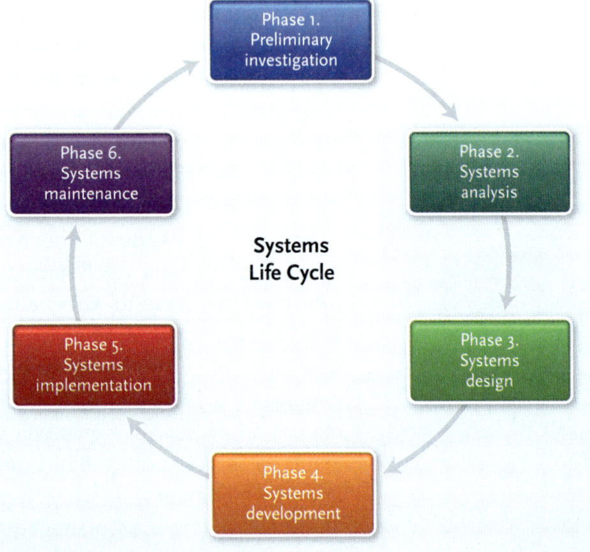

A **system** is a collection of activities and elements organized to accomplish a goal. **Systems analysis and design** is a six-phase problem-solving procedure that makes up the **systems life cycle.** The phases are

- Preliminary investigation—identifying organization's problems or needs and summarizing in short report.
- Systems analysis—studying present system in depth, specifying new requirements, and documenting findings.
- Systems design—designing new or alternative system to meet new requirements and creating a design report.
- Systems development—acquiring, developing, and testing needed hardware and software.
- Systems implementation—installing new system and training people.
- Systems maintenance—periodically evaluating and updating system as needed.

Systems analysts are the computer professionals who typically follow the six-phase systems life cycle.

PHASE 1: PRELIMINARY INVESTIGATION

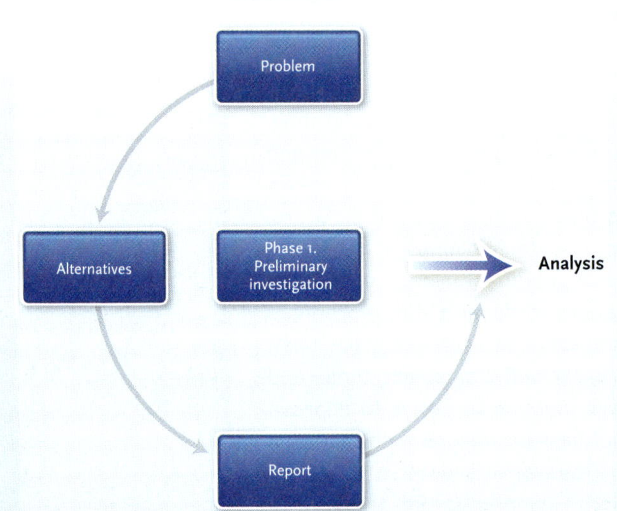

The **preliminary investigation** determines the need for a new information system. It is typically requested by an end user or a manager. Three tasks of this phase are defining the problem, suggesting alternative systems, and preparing a short report.

Defining the Problem

The current information system is examined to determine who needs what information, when the information is needed, and why it is needed.

If the existing information system is large, then a *systems analyst* conducts the survey. Otherwise, the end user conducts the survey.

Suggesting Alternative Systems

Some possible alternative systems are suggested. Based on interviews and observations made in defining the problem, alternative information systems are identified.

Preparing a Short Report

To document and communicate the findings of Phase 1, preliminary investigation, a short report is prepared and presented to management.

To efficiently and effectively use computers, you need to understand the importance of systems analysis and design. You need to know the six phases of the systems development life cycle: preliminary investigation, analysis, design, development, implementation, and maintenance. Additionally, you need to understand prototyping and RAD.

PHASE 2: SYSTEMS ANALYSIS

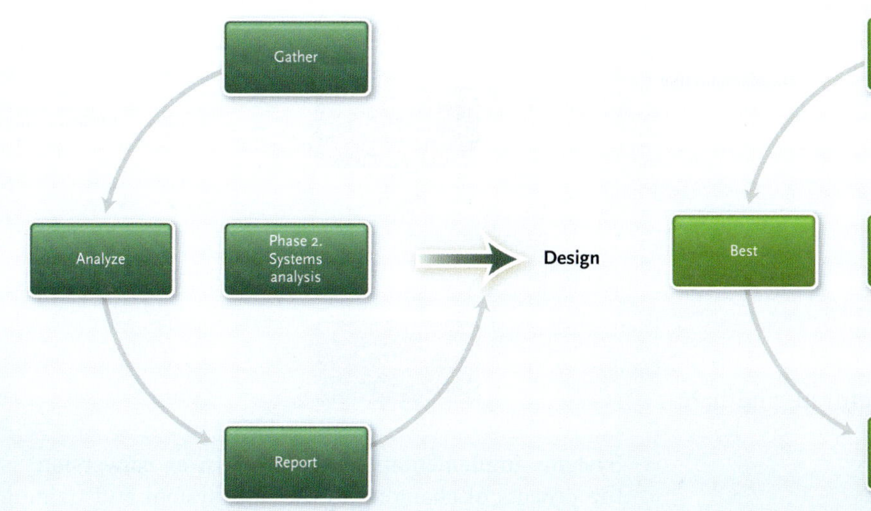

In **systems analysis,** data is collected about the present system. The focus is on determining the requirements for a new system. Three tasks of this phase are gathering data, analyzing the data, and documenting the analysis.

Gathering Data

Data is gathered by observation, interviews, questionnaires, and looking at documents. One helpful document is the **organization chart,** which shows a company's functions and levels of management.

Analyzing the Data

There are several tools for the analysis of data, including **top-down analysis, grid charts,** and **system flowcharts.**

Documenting Systems Analysis

To document and communicate the findings of Phase 2, a **systems analysis report** is prepared for higher management.

	Reports (output)		
Forms (input)	**Client billing**	**Personnel expense**	**Support cost**
Time sheet	✓	✓	
Telephone log	✓		✓
Travel log	✓		✓

PHASE 3: SYSTEMS DESIGN

In the **systems design** phase, a new or alternative information system is designed. This phase consists of three tasks:

Designing Alternative Systems

Alternative information systems are designed. Each alternative is evaluated for

- **Economic feasibility**–cost versus benefits; time for the system to pay for itself.
- **Technical feasibility**–hardware and software reliability; available training.
- **Operational feasibility**–will the system work within the organization?

Selecting the Best System

Four questions should be considered when selecting the best system:

- Will the system fit into an overall information system?
- Will the system be flexible enough to be modified as needed in the future?
- Will it be secure against unauthorized use?
- Will the system's benefits exceed its costs?

Writing the Systems Design Report

To document and communicate the findings of Phase 3, a **systems design report** is prepared for higher management.

PHASE 4: SYSTEMS DEVELOPMENT

Software

Hardware

Phase 4. Systems development

Implementation

Test

In the **systems development** phase, software and hardware are acquired and tested.

Acquiring Software

Two ways to acquire software are purchasing off-the-shelf packaged software and designing custom programs.

Acquiring Hardware

Acquiring hardware involves consideration for future company growth, existing networks, communication capabilities, and training.

Testing the New System

Using sample data, the new system is tested. This step can take several months for a complex system.

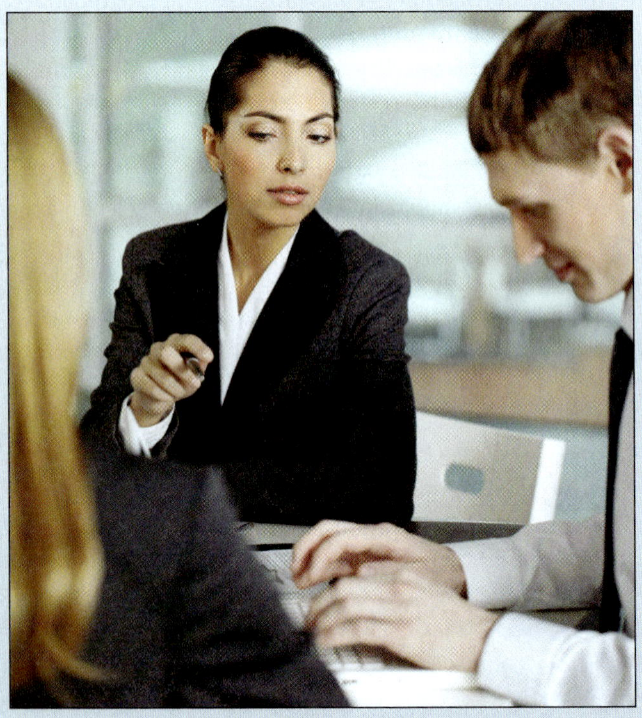

PHASE 5: SYSTEMS IMPLEMENTATION

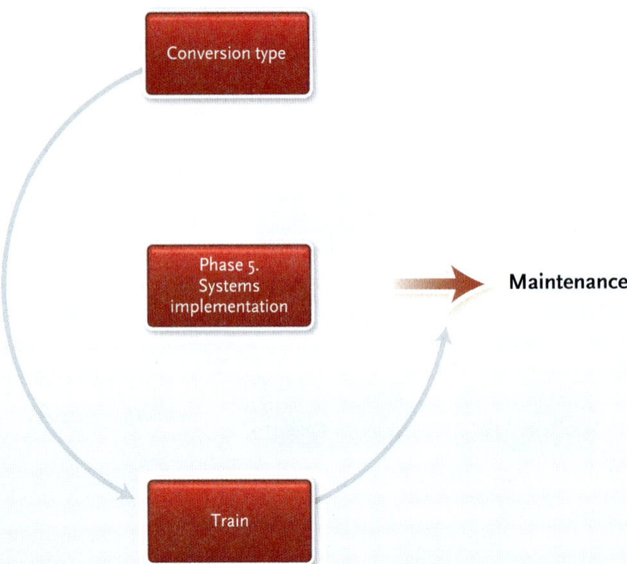

Systems implementation, also known as **conversion,** is the process of changing to the new system and training people.

Types of Conversion

Four ways to convert are direct, parallel, pilot, and phased approaches.

- **Direct approach**—abandoning the old system and starting up the new system; can be very risky and not recommended.
- **Parallel approach**—running the old and new side by side until the new system proves its worth; very low risk; however, very expensive; not generally recommended.
- **Pilot approach**—converting only one part of the organization to the new system until the new system proves its worth; less expensive but riskier than parallel conversion; recommended for situations with many people performing similar operations.
- **Phased approach**—gradually implementing the new system to the entire organization; less risky but more expensive than parallel conversion; recommended for situations with many people performing different operations.

Training

Training is important, however, often overlooked. Some people may train early as the equipment is being delivered so that they can adjust more easily. Sometimes a professional trainer is used; other times the systems analyst acts as the trainer.

PHASE 6: SYSTEMS MAINTENANCE

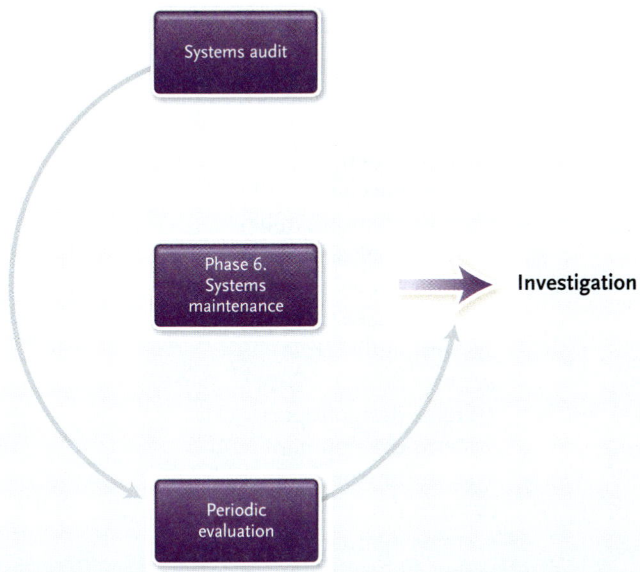

Systems maintenance consists of a systems audit followed by periodic evaluation.

Systems Audit

Once the system is operational, the systems analyst performs a **systems audit** by comparing the new system to its original design specifications.

Periodic Evaluation

The new system is periodically evaluated to ensure that it is operating efficiently.

Phase	Activity
1. Preliminary investigation	Define problem, suggest alternatives, prepare short report
2. Systems analysis	Gather data, analyze data, document
3. Systems design	Design alternatives, select best alternative, write report
4. Systems development	Develop software, acquire hardware, test system
5. Systems implementation	Convert, train
6. Systems maintenance	Perform systems audit, evaluate periodically

PROTOTYPING AND RAD

Due to time pressures, it is not always feasible to follow every phase of the systems life cycle. Two alternatives that require less time are *prototyping* and *RAD.*

Prototyping

Prototyping means to build a model or prototype that can be modified before the actual system is installed. Typically, the development time for prototyping is shorter; however, it can be more difficult to manage the project and to control costs.

Rapid Applications Development

Rapid applications development (RAD) uses powerful development software, small specialized teams, and highly trained personnel. Typically, the development costs more. However, the time is much less and the quality is often better.

CAREERS in IT

Systems analysts plan and design new systems or reorganize a company's computer resources to better utilize them. They follow the systems life cycle through all its steps. Either an advanced associate's degree or a bachelor's degree in computer science or information systems and technical experience are required. Salary range is $50,000 to $64,000.

KEY TERMS

automated design tools (309)
computer-aided software engineering (CASE) tools (309)
conversion (313)
data flow diagram (309)
direct approach (313)
economic feasibility (310)
grid chart (309)
operational feasibility (311)
organization chart (308)
parallel approach (313)
phased approach (314)
pilot approach (313)
preliminary investigation (306)
prototyping (315)
rapid applications development (RAD) (315)
system (304)
system flowchart (309)
systems analysis (308)
systems analysis and design (305)
systems analysis report (310)
systems analyst (305, 316)
systems audit (314)
systems design (310)
systems design report (311)
systems development (312)
systems implementation (313)
systems life cycle (305)
systems maintenance (314)
technical feasibility (311)
top-down analysis method (308)

MULTIPLE CHOICE

Circle the letter of the correct answer.

1. An information system is a collection of hardware, software, people, procedures, the Internet, and:
   - **a.** data
   - **b.** DBMS
   - **c.** specialists
   - **d.** systems analysts
2. What is the first phase in the systems life cycle?
   - **a.** needs analysis
   - **b.** preliminary investigation
   - **c.** systems analysis
   - **d.** systems design
3. Which phase involves installing the new system and training people?
   - **a.** preliminary investigation
   - **b.** systems analysis
   - **c.** systems design
   - **d.** systems implementation
4. This phase is concerned about determining system requirements not in design.
   - **a.** preliminary investigation
   - **b.** systems analysis
   - **c.** systems design
   - **d.** systems implementation
5. Which systems analysis tool shows the relationship between input and output documents?
   - **a.** automated design tool
   - **b.** data flow diagram
   - **c.** grid chart
   - **d.** system flow chart
6. These tools relieve the systems analysts of many repetitive tasks, develop clear documentation, and, for larger projects, coordinate team member activities.
   - **a.** automated systems life cycle
   - **b.** CASE
   - **c.** data flow analyzers
   - **d.** flowcharts
7. Which phase is concerned with economic, technical, and operational feasibility?
   - **a.** preliminary investigation
   - **b.** systems analysis
   - **c.** systems design
   - **d.** systems implementation
8. What type of feasibility evaluates whether the people within the organization will embrace or resist a new system?
   - **a.** behavioral
   - **b.** economic
   - **c.** operational
   - **d.** technical
9. Which approach to conversion begins by trying out a new system in only one part of an organization?
   - **a.** direct
   - **b.** pilot
   - **c.** parallel
   - **d.** phased
10. An alternative to the systems life cycle approach using powerful development software, small specialized teams, and highly trained personnel.
    - **a.** AAD
    - **b.** CASE
    - **c.** prototyping
    - **d.** RAD

MATCHING

Match each numbered item with the most closely related lettered item. Write your answers in the spaces provided.

a. analysis
b. conversion
c. direct
d. implementation
e. maintenance
f. phased
g. solutions
h. system
i. systems design
j. organization chart

___ 1. Systems analysis and design is a six-phase problem-solving procedure for examining and improving an information _____.

___ 2. Systems life cycle phase that studies the present system in depth.

___ 3. Systems analysis involves suggesting alternative _____.

___ 4. The last and ongoing phase of the systems life cycle is systems _____.

___ 5. The document that shows the levels of management and formal lines of authority is an _____.

___ 6. This phase begins with designing alternative systems.

___ 7. Another name for systems implementation.

___ 8. The phase in which the old system is replaced and training begins.

___ 9. The four approaches to conversion are parallel, pilot, phased, and _____.

___ 10. The approach in which the new system is implemented gradually over a period of time.

OPEN-ENDED

On a separate sheet of paper, respond to each question or statement.

1. What is a system? What are the six phases of the systems life cycle? Why do corporations undergo this process?
2. What are the tools used in the analysis phase? What is top-down analysis? How is it used?
3. Describe each type of system conversion. Which is the most commonly used?
4. What is systems maintenance? When does it occur?
5. Explain prototyping and RAD. When might they be used by corporations?

DISCUSSION

Respond to each of the following questions.

1 Applying Technology: SYSTEMS ANALYSIS SOFTWARE

There are several companies that specialize in systems analysis support software. Using the Internet, search for and connect to one of these companies. Then answer the following: (a) Describe the products designed to enhance systems analysis. (b) For each product you described, list the phase or phases of the systems life cycle it applies to. (c) Select the product that you would prefer to use and justify your selection.

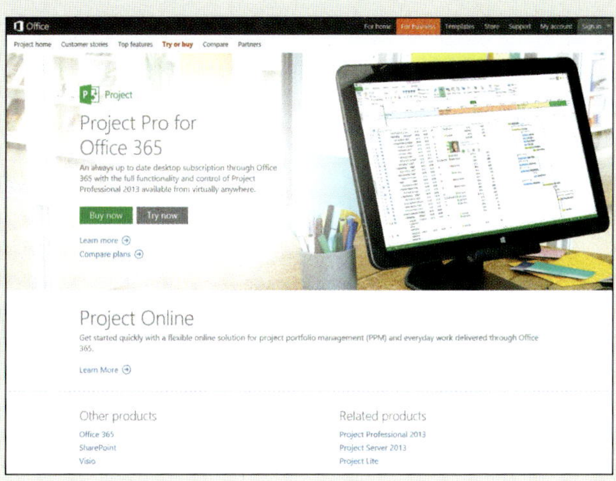

2 Writing about Technology: MANAGING CHOICES

Consider the following scenario, and then respond to the following: You're a manager who comes up with a new system that will make your company more efficient. However, implementing this system would make several tasks obsolete and cost many of your co-workers their jobs. (a) What is your ethical obligation to your company in this situation? (b) What is your ethical obligation to your co-workers? (c) What would you do in this situation? Defend your answer.

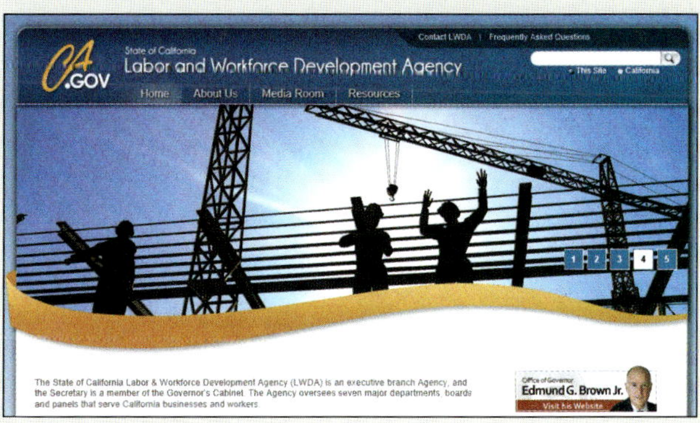

PHOTO CREDITS

CHAPTER 12:

Opener: © Digital Vision/Punchstock RF; p. 303, 317: © Brand X Pictures/Punchstock RF; p. 304, 316: © Thomas Northcut/Digital Vision/Getty Images RF; 12-3: © Digital Vision RF; 12-12, p. 320: © Image Source/Getty Images RF; 12-14, p. 321: Copyright © 2012 serena.com. Used with permission; p. 325 (top): Microsoft product screen shot(s) reprinted with permission from Microsoft Corporation.; p. 325 (bottom): Copyright © 2014 State of California.

chapter 13 Programming and Languages

Why should I read this chapter?

Poorly designed software has destroyed companies in the blink of an eye. From stock purchase to pacemakers, our lives are increasingly dependent on digital devices and the programs that run them. In the future, robots with sophisticated artificial intelligence will handle everyday chores and you will program these robots using conversational English instruction.

This chapter covers the things you need to know to be prepared for this ever-changing digital world, including:

- The software development life cycle—understand the steps of software development to be prepared to assist or manage software development projects.
- Programming languages—understand the differences between assembly, procedural, and natural languages to choose the best language for your needs.

Learning Objectives

After you have read this chapter, you should be able to:

1. Define programming and describe the six steps of programming.
2. Compare design tools including top-down design, pseudocode, flowcharts, and logic structures.
3. Describe program testing and the tools for finding and removing errors.
4. Describe CASE tools and object-oriented software development.
5. Explain the five generations of programming languages.

Introduction

“Hi, I'm Ray, and I'm a computer programmer. I'd like to talk with you about programming and programming languages.”

In the previous chapter, we discussed systems analysis and design. We discussed the six-phase systems life cycle approach for examining and improving an information system. One of the phases is systems development, or the acquisition of new hardware and software. This chapter relates to this phase, systems development. More specifically, this chapter focuses on developing new software or programming. We will describe programming in two parts: (1) the steps in the programming process and (2) some of the programming languages available.

Why should you need to know anything about programming? The answer is simple. You might need to deal with programmers in the course of your work. You also may be required to do some programming yourself in the future. A growing trend is toward end user software development. This means that end users, like you, are developing their own application programs.

To efficiently and effectively use computers, you need to understand the relationship between systems development and programming. Additionally, you need to know the six steps of programming, including program specification, program design, program code, program test, program documentation, and program maintenance.

Programs and Programming

What exactly is programming? Many people think of it as simply typing words into a computer. That may be part of it, but that is certainly not all of it. Programming, as we've hinted before, is actually a *problem-solving procedure.*

What Is a Program?

To see how programming works, think about what a program is. A **program** is a list of instructions for the computer to follow to accomplish the task of processing data into information. The instructions are made up of statements used in a programming language, such as C++, Java, or Visual Basic.

You are already familiar with some types of programs. As we discussed in Chapters 1 and 3, application programs are widely used to accomplish a variety of different types of tasks. For example, we use word processors to create documents and spreadsheets to analyze data. These can be purchased and are referred to as prewritten or packaged programs. Programs also can be created or custom-made. In Chapter 12, we saw that the systems analyst looked into the availability of time-and-billing software for Advantage Advertising. Will off-the-shelf software do the job, or should it be custom-written? This is one of the first things that needs to be decided in programming.

What Is Programming?

A program is a list of instructions for the computer to follow to process data. **Programming,** also known as **software development,** typically follows a six-step process known as the **software development life cycle (SDLC).** (See Figure 13-1.)

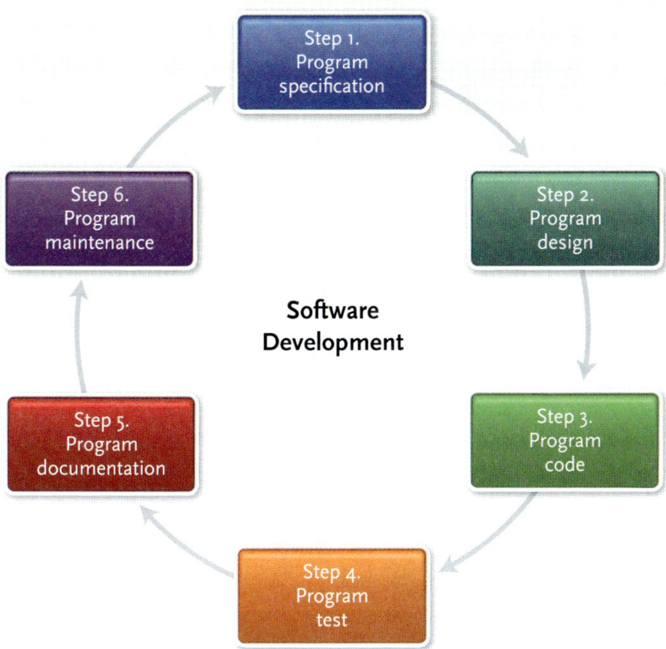

Figure 13-1 **Software development**

The six steps are as follows:

1. *Program specification:* The program's objectives, outputs, inputs, and processing requirements are determined.
2. *Program design:* A solution is created using programming techniques such as top-down program design, pseudocode, flowcharts, and logic structures.
3. *Program code:* The program is written or coded using a programming language.
4. *Program test:* The program is tested or debugged by looking for syntax and logic errors.
5. *Program documentation:* Documentation is an ongoing process throughout the programming process. This phase focuses on formalizing the written description and processes used in the program.
6. *Program maintenance:* Completed programs are periodically reviewed to evaluate their accuracy, efficiency, standardization, and ease of use. Changes are made to the program's code as needed.

In organizations, computer professionals known as **software engineers** or **programmers** use this six-step procedure. In a recent survey by *Money* magazine, software engineers were ranked near the top of over 100 widely held jobs based on salary, prestige, and security.

You may well find yourself working directly with a programmer or indirectly through a systems analyst. Or you may actually do the programming for a system that you develop. Whatever the case, it's important that you understand the six-step programming procedure.

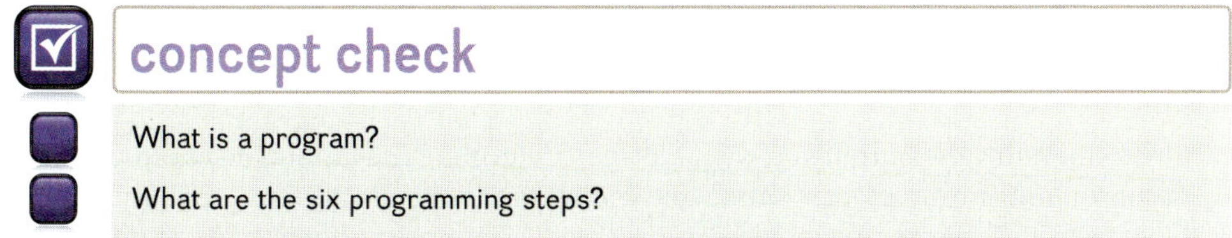

concept check

- What is a program?
- What are the six programming steps?

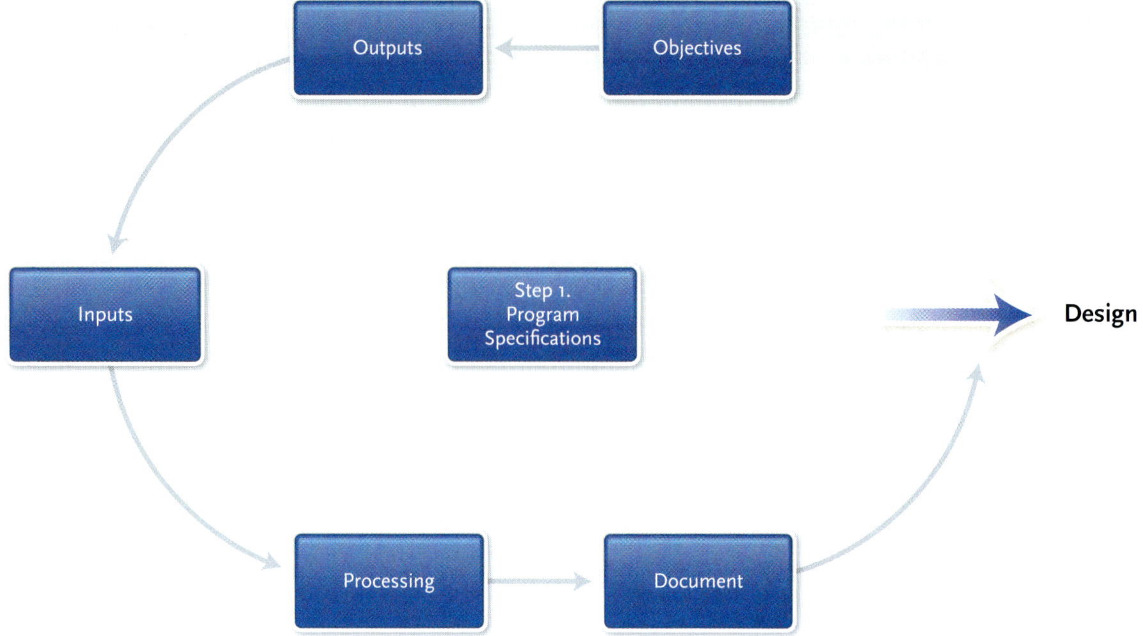

Figure 13-2 **Step 1: Program specification**

Step 1: Program Specification

Program specification is also called **program definition** or **program analysis.** It requires that the programmer—or you, the end user, if you are following this procedure—specify five items: (1) the program's objectives, (2) the desired output, (3) the input data required, (4) the processing requirements, and (5) the documentation. (See Figure 13-2.)

Program Objectives

You solve all kinds of problems every day. A problem might be deciding how to commute to school or work or which homework or report to do first. Thus, every day you determine your **objectives**—the problems you are trying to solve. Programming is the same. You need to make a clear statement of the problem you are trying to solve. An example would be "I want a time-and-billing system to record the time I spend on different jobs for different clients of Advantage Advertising."

Desired Output

It is best always to specify outputs before inputs. That is, you need to list what you want to *get out* of the computer system. Then you should determine what will *go into it.* The best way to do this is to draw a picture. You—the end user, not the programmer—should sketch or write how you want the output to look when it's done. It might be printed out or displayed on the monitor.

For example, if you want a time-and-billing report, you might write or draw something like Figure 13-3. Another form of output from the program might be bills to clients.

Input Data

Once you know the output you want, you can determine the input data and the source of this data. For example, for a time-and-billing report, you can specify that one source of data to be processed should be time cards. These are usually logs or statements

Client name: Allen Realty | **Month and Year:** Jan. '16

Date	Worker	Regular Hours & Rate	Overtime Hours & Rate	Bill
1/2	M. Jones	5 @ $10	1 @ $15	$65.00
	K. Williams	4 @ $30	2 @ $45	$210.00

Figure 13-3 End user's sketch of desired output

of hours worked submitted either electronically or on paper forms. The log shown in Figure 13-4 is an example of the kind of input data used in Advantage Advertising's manual system. Note that military time is used. For example, instead of writing "5:45 P.M.," people would write "1745."

Processing Requirements

Here you define the processing tasks that must happen for input data to be processed into output. For Advantage, one of the tasks for the program will be to add the hours worked for different jobs for different clients.

Program Specifications Document

As in the systems life cycle, ongoing documentation is essential. You should record program objectives, desired outputs, needed inputs, and required processing. This leads to the next step, program design.

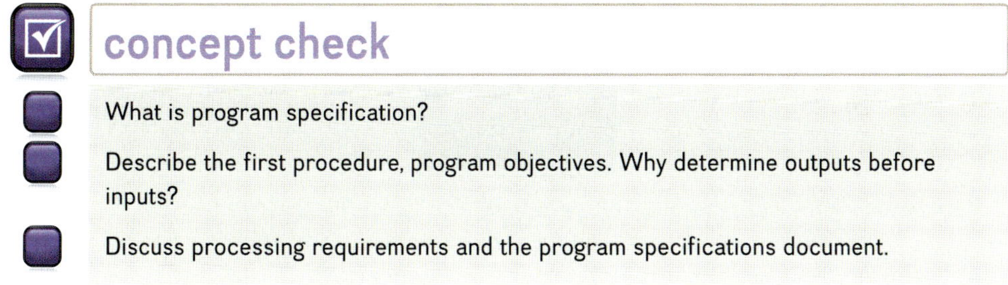

concept check

- What is program specification?
- Describe the first procedure, program objectives. Why determine outputs before inputs?
- Discuss processing requirements and the program specifications document.

Daily Log

Worker:

Date:

Client	Job	Time in	Time out
A	TV commercial	800	915
B	Billboard ad	935	1200
C	Brochure	1315	1545
D	Magazine ad	1600	1745

Figure 13-4 Example of input data for hours worked expressed in military time

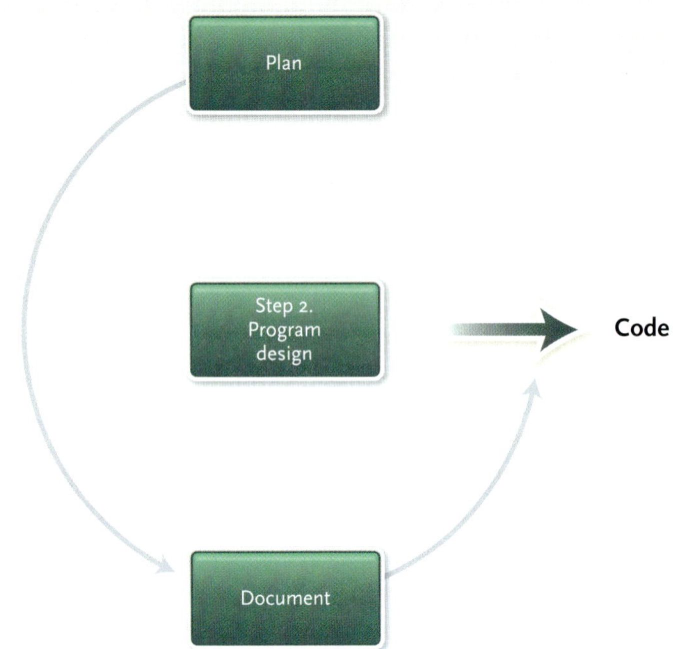

Figure 13-5 **Step 2: Program design**

Step 2: Program Design

After program specification, you begin **program design.** (See Figure 13-5.) Here you plan a solution, preferably using **structured programming techniques.** These techniques consist of the following: (1) top-down program design, (2) pseudocode, (3) flowcharts, and (4) logic structures.

Top-Down Program Design

First determine the outputs and inputs for the program. Then use **top-down program design** to identify the program's processing steps. Such steps are called **program modules** (or just **modules**). Each module is made up of logically related program statements.

An example of a top-down program design for a time-and-billing report is shown in Figure 13-6. Each of the boxes shown is a module. Under the rules of top-down design, each module should have a single function. The program must pass in sequence from one module to the next until all modules have been processed by the computer. Three of the boxes—"Obtain input," "Compute hours for billing," and "Produce output"—correspond to the three principal computer system operations: *input, process,* and *output.*

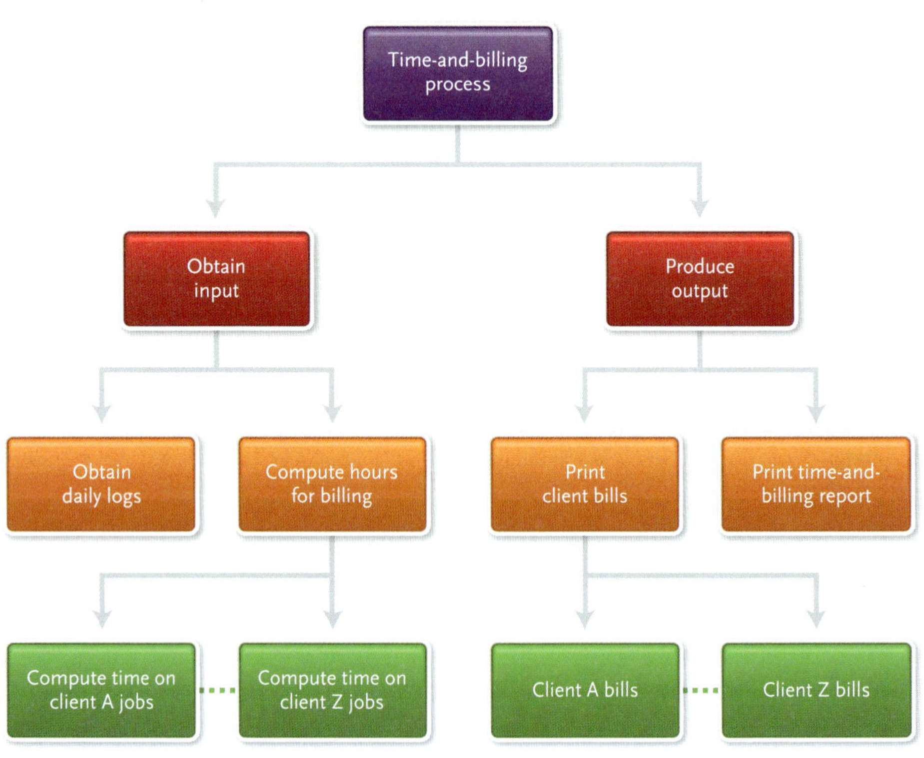

Figure 13-6 **Example of top-down program design**

Compute time for Client A

Set total regular hours and total overtime hours to zero.
Get time in and time out for a job.
If worked past 1700 hours, then compute overtime hours.
Compute regular hours.
Add regular hours to total regular hours.
Add overtime hours to total overtime hours.
If there are more jobs for that client, go back and compute for that job as well.

Figure 13-7 **Example of pseudocode**

Pseudocode

Pseudocode (pronounced "soo-doh-code") is an outline of the logic of the program you will write. It is like doing a summary of the program before it is written. Figure 13-7 shows the pseudocode you might write for one module in the time-and-billing program. This shows the reasoning behind determining hours–including overtime hours–worked for different jobs for one client, Client A. Again, note this expresses the *logic* of what you want the program to do.

Flowcharts

We mentioned system flowcharts in the previous chapter. Here we are concerned with **program flowcharts.** These graphically present the detailed sequence of steps needed to solve a programming problem. Figure 13-8 presents several of the standard flowcharting symbols. An example of a program flowchart is presented in Figure 13-9. This flowchart expresses all the logic for just one module–"Compute time on Client A jobs"–in the top-down program design.

Perhaps you can see from this flowchart why a computer is a computer, and not just an adding machine. One of the most powerful capabilities of computers is their ability to make logical comparisons. For example, a computer can compare two items to determine if one is less than, greater than, or equal to the other item.

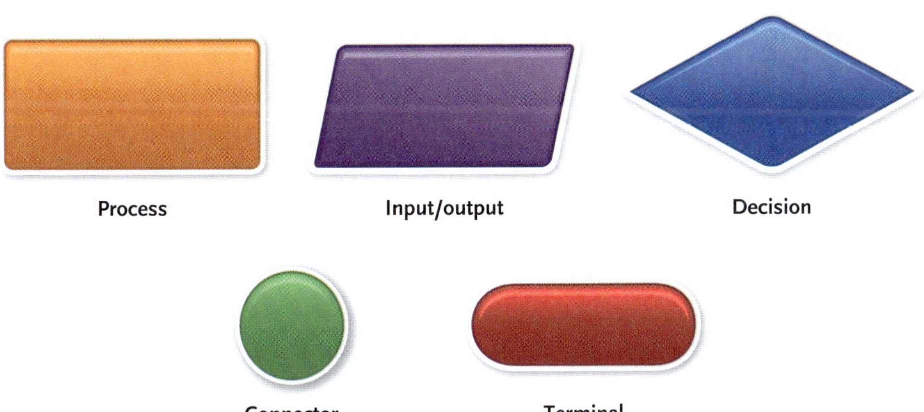

Figure 13-8 **Flowchart symbols**

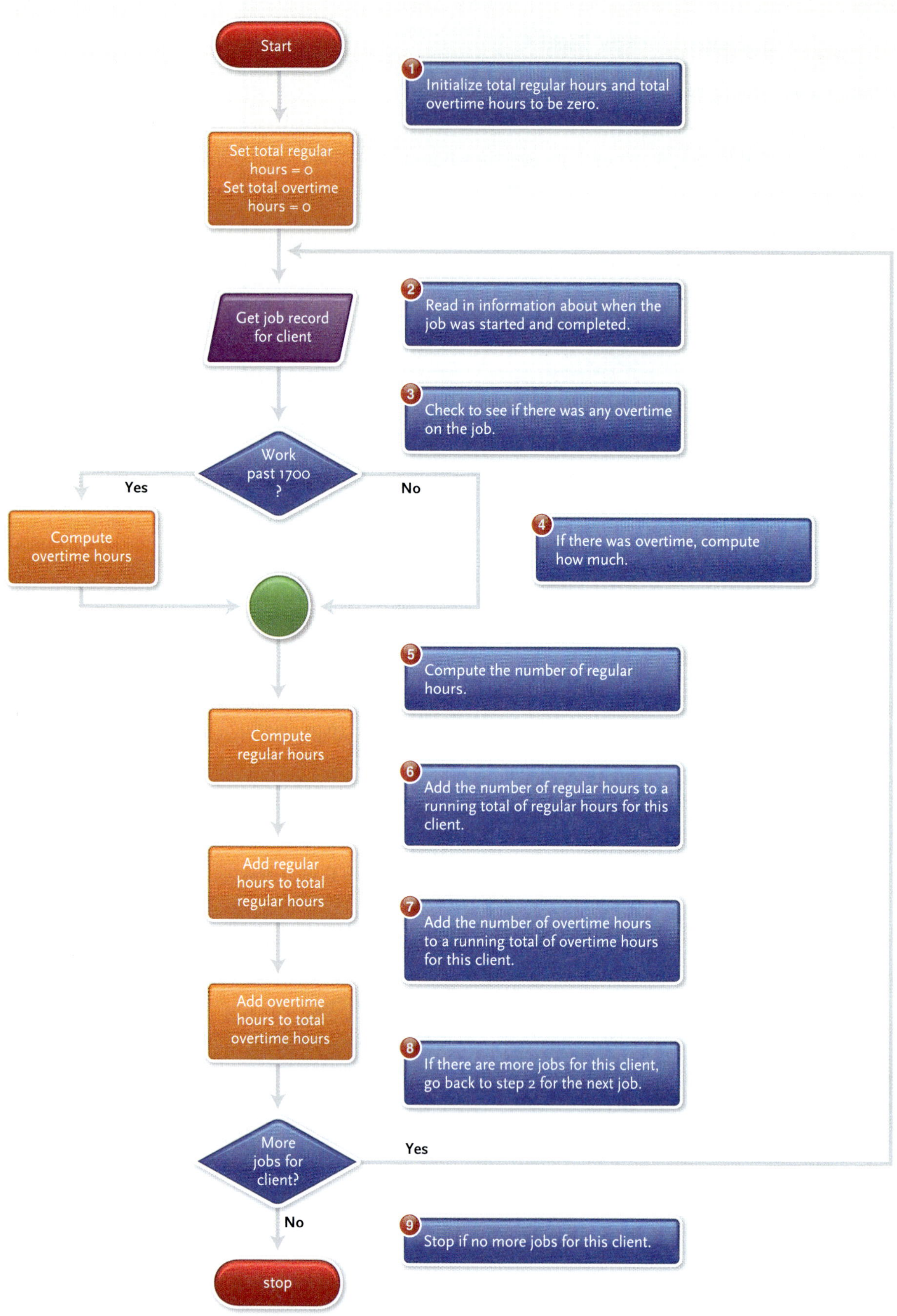

Figure 13-9 Flowchart for "Compute time on Client A jobs"

But have we skipped something? How do we know which kind of twists and turns to put in a flowchart so that it will work logically? The answer is based on the use of logic structures, as we will explain.

Logic Structures

How do you link the various parts of the flowchart? The best way is a combination of three **logic structures** called *sequential, selection,* and *repetition.* Using these arrangements enables you to write structured programs, which take much of the guesswork out of programming. Let us look at the logic structures.

- In the **sequential structure,** one program statement follows another. Consider, for example, the "compute time" flowchart. (Refer back to Figure 13-9.) *Add regular hours to total regular hours* and *Add overtime hours to total overtime hours* form a sequential structure. They logically follow each other. There is no question of "yes" or "no," or a decision suggesting other consequences. See Figure 13-10.
- The **selection structure** occurs when a decision must be made. The outcome of the decision determines which of two paths to follow. (See Figure 13-11.) This structure is also known as an **IF-THEN-ELSE structure** because that is how you can formulate the decision. Consider, for example, the selection structure in the "compute time" flowchart, which is concerned about computing overtime hours (*Work past 1700?*). (Refer back to Figure 13-9.) It might be expressed in detail as follows:

  IF hour finished for this job is later than 1700 hours (5:00 p.m.), THEN overtime hours equal the number of hours past 1700 hours, ELSE overtime hours equal zero.

  See Figure 13-11.
- The **repetition** or **loop structure** describes a process that may be repeated as long as a certain condition remains true. The structure is called a "loop" or "iteration" because the program loops around (iterates or repeats) again and again. Consider the loop structure in the "compute time" flowchart, which is concerned with testing if there are more jobs (*More jobs for clients?*). It might be expressed in detail as follows:

  DO read in job information WHILE (that is, as long as) there are more jobs.

  See Figure 13-12.

The last thing to do before leaving the program design step is to document the logic of the design. This report typically includes pseudocode, flowcharts, and logic structures. Now you are ready for the next step, program code.

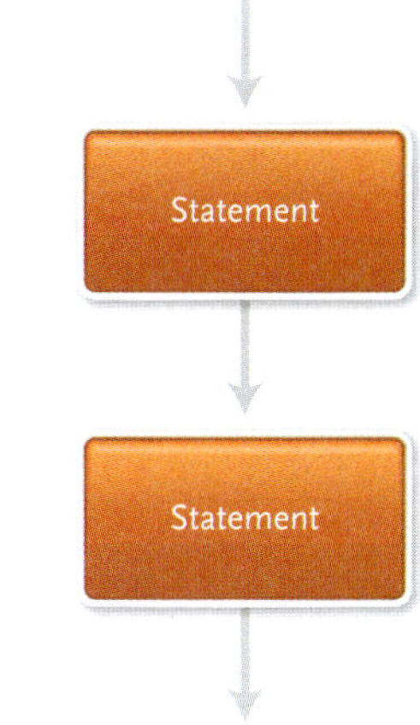

Figure 13-10 **Sequential logic structure**

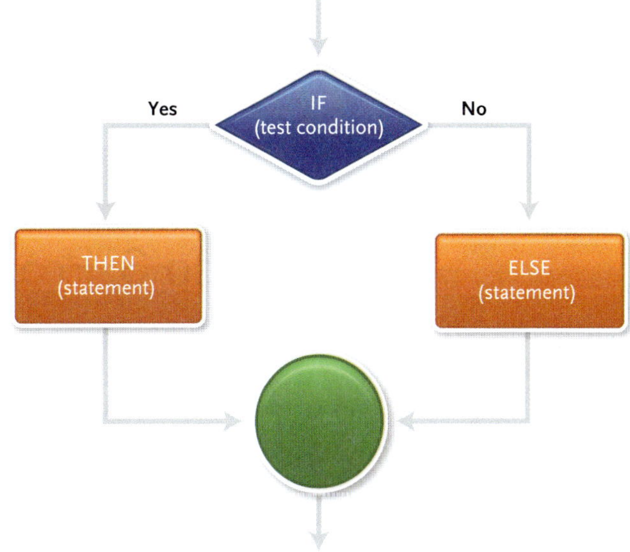

Figure 13-11 **Selection (IF-THEN-ELSE) logic structure**

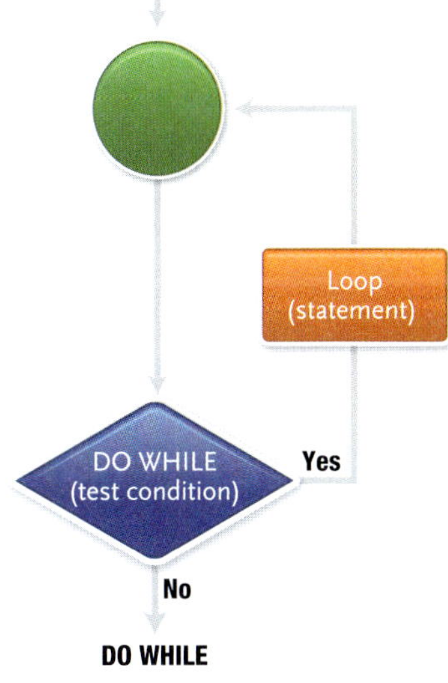

Figure 13-12 **Repetition logic structure**

concept check

 Define the goal of the program design step.

 Discuss top-down program design, pseudocode, flowcharts, and logic structures.

 Describe three logic structures.

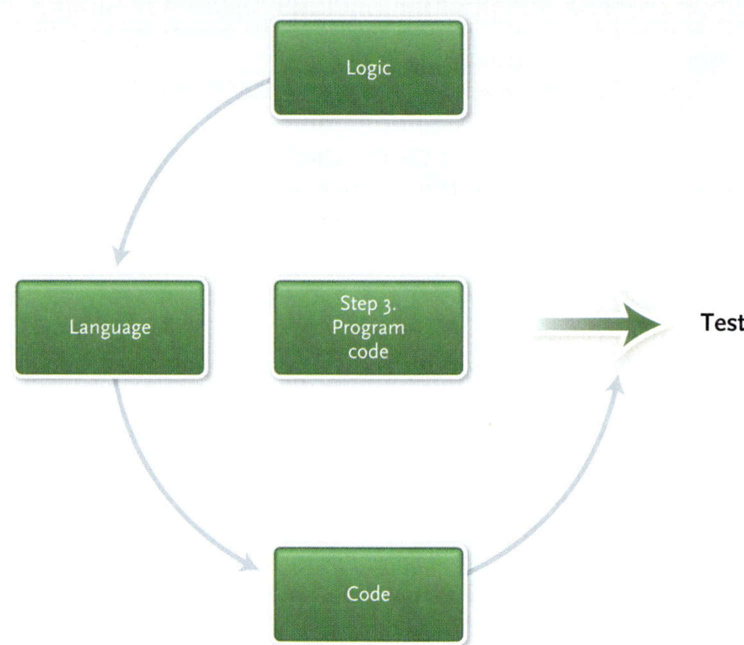

Figure 13-13 **Step 3: Program code**

Step 3: Program Code

Writing the program is called **coding.** Here you use the logic you developed in the program design step to actually write the program. (See Figure 13-13.) This is the "program code" that instructs the computer what to do. Coding is what many people think of when they think of programming. As we've pointed out, however, it is only one of the six steps in the programming process.

The Good Program

What are the qualities of a good program? Above all, it should be reliable—that is, it should work under most conditions and produce correct output. It should catch obvious and common input errors. It also should be well documented and understandable by programmers other than the person who wrote it. After all, someone may need to make changes in the program in the future. One of the best ways to code effective programs is to write so-called **structured programs,** using the logic structures described in Step 2: Program Design.

Coding

After the program logic has been formulated, the next step is to **code,** or write the program using the appropriate computer language.

A **programming language** uses a collection of symbols, words, and phrases that instruct a computer to perform specific operations. Programming languages process data and information for a wide variety of different types of applications. Figure 13-14 presents the programming code using C++, a widely used programming language, to calculate the compute time module. For a description of C++ and some other widely used programming languages, see Figure 13-15.

Once the program has been coded, the next step is testing, or debugging, the program.

```
#include <fstream.h>

void main (void)
{
    ifstream input_file;

    float total_regular, total_overtime, regular, overtime;
    int hour_in, minute_in, hour_out, minute_out;
    input_file.open("time.txt",ios::in);

    total_regular = 0;
    total_overtime = 0;

    while (input_file != NULL)
    {
        input_file >> hour_in >> minute_in >> hour_out >> minute_out;

        if (hour_out > 17)
            overtime = (hour_out-17) +(minute_out/(float)60);
        else
            overtime = 0;
            regular = ((hour_out - hour_in) +(minute_out
                        - minute_in)/(float)60)    - overtime;
        total_regular += regular;
        total_overtime += overtime;
    }

    cout <<"Regular: " << total_regular <<endl;
    cout <<"Overtime " << total_overtime <<endl;
}
```

Figure 13-14 **C++ code for computing regular and overtime hours**

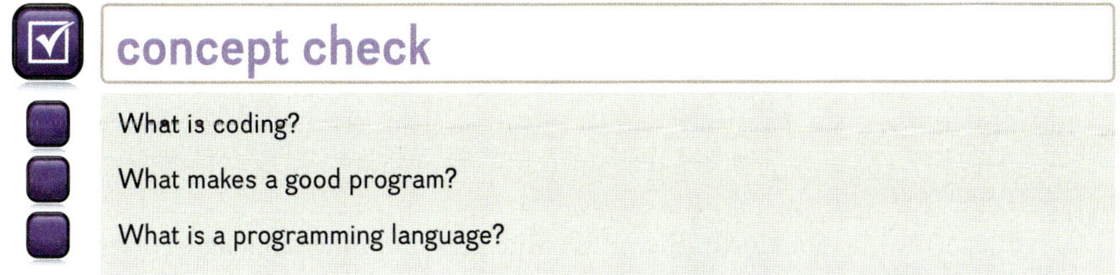
concept check
What is coding?
What makes a good program?
What is a programming language?

Language	Description
C++	Extends C to use objects or program modules that can be reused and interchanged between programs
Java	Primarily used for Internet applications; similar to C++; runs with a variety of operating systems
JavaScript	Embedded into web pages to provide dynamic and interactive content
Visual Basic	Uses a very graphical interface, making it easy to learn and to rapidly develop Windows and other applications
Swift	Uses graphical user interface and special code for touchscreen interfaces to create apps for Apple iOS devices

Figure 13-15 **Widely used programming languages**

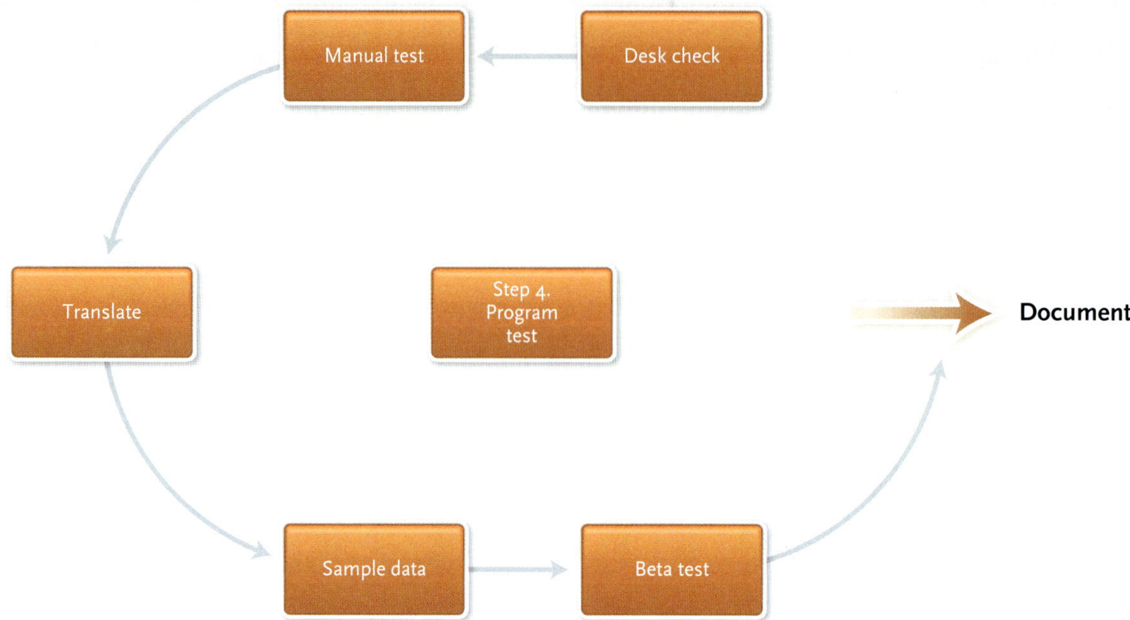

Figure 13-16 **Step 4: Program test**

Step 4: Program Test

Debugging refers to the process of testing and then eliminating errors ("getting the bugs out"). (See Figure 13-16.) It means running the program on a computer and then fixing the parts that do not work. Programming errors are of two types: *syntax errors* and *logic errors.*

Syntax Errors

A **syntax error** is a violation of the rules of the programming language. For example, in C++, each statement must end with a semicolon (;). If the semicolon is omitted, then the program will not run or execute due to a syntax error. For example, Figure 13-17 shows testing of the compute time module in which a syntax error was identified.

Logic Errors

A **logic error** occurs when the programmer uses an incorrect calculation or leaves out a programming procedure. For example, a payroll program that did not compute overtime hours would have a logic error.

Testing Process

Several methods have been devised for finding and removing both types of errors including desk checking, manually testing, translating, running, and beta testing.

- **Desk checking:** In **desk checking** or **code review,** a programmer sitting at a desk checks (proofreads) a printout of the program. The programmer goes through the listing line by line carefully looking for syntax errors and logic errors.

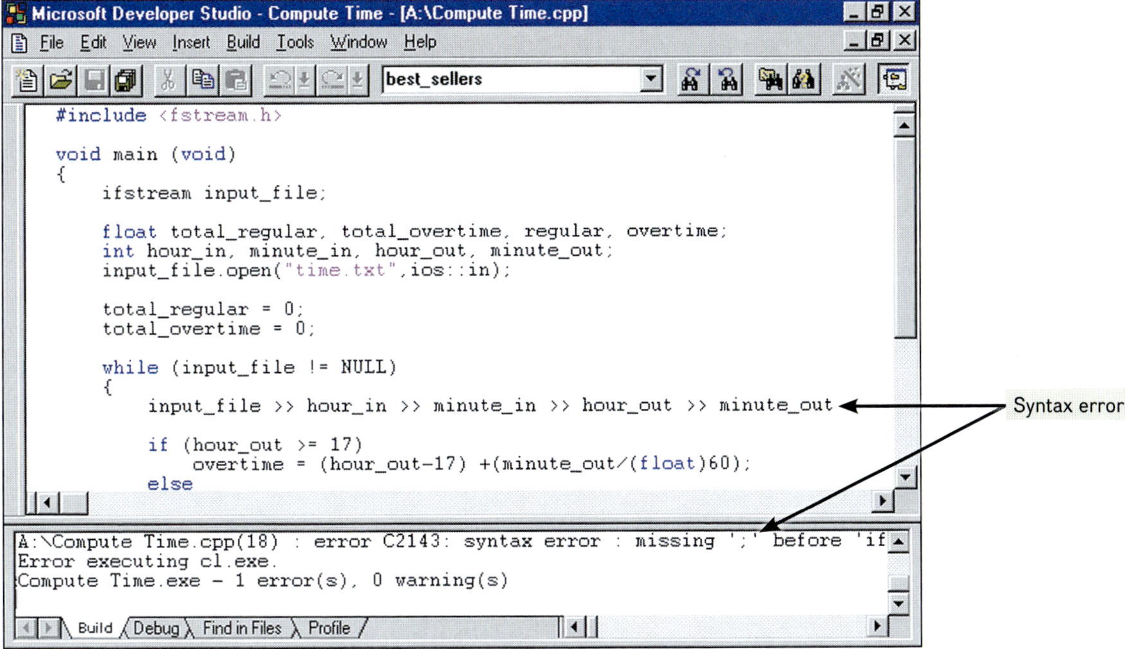

Figure 13-17 Syntax error identified

- **Manually testing with sample data:** Using a calculator and sample data, a programmer follows each program statement and performs every calculation. Looking for programming logic errors, the programmer compares the manually calculated values to those calculated by the programs.
- **Attempt at translation:** The program is run through a computer, using a translator program. The translator attempts to translate the written program from the programming language (such as C++) into the machine language. Before the program will run, it must be free of syntax errors. Such errors will be identified by the translating program. (See Figure 13-17.)
- **Testing sample data on the computer:** After all syntax errors have been corrected, the program is tested for logic errors. Sample data is used to test the correct execution of each program statement.
- **Testing by a select group of potential users:** This is sometimes called **beta testing.** It is usually the final step in testing a program. Potential users try out the program and provide feedback.

For a summary of Step 4: Program test, see Figure 13-18.

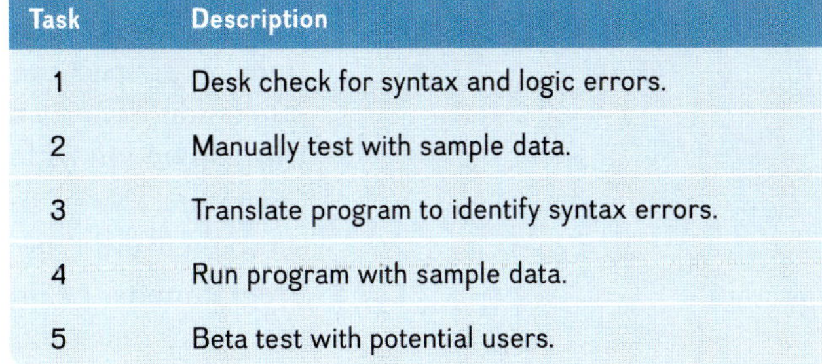

Task	Description
1	Desk check for syntax and logic errors.
2	Manually test with sample data.
3	Translate program to identify syntax errors.
4	Run program with sample data.
5	Beta test with potential users.

Figure 13-18 Step 4: Program testing process

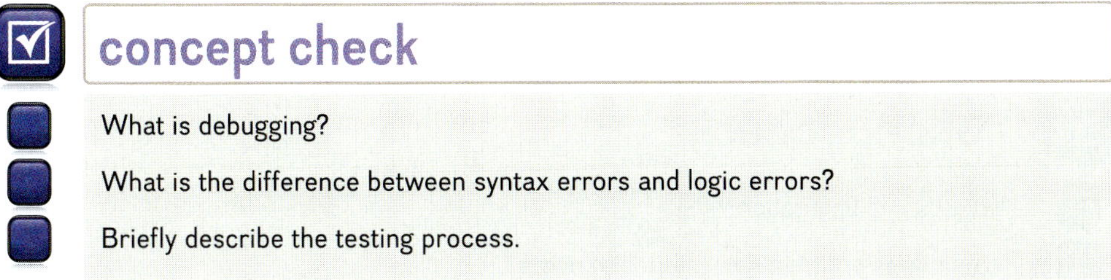

concept check

- What is debugging?
- What is the difference between syntax errors and logic errors?
- Briefly describe the testing process.

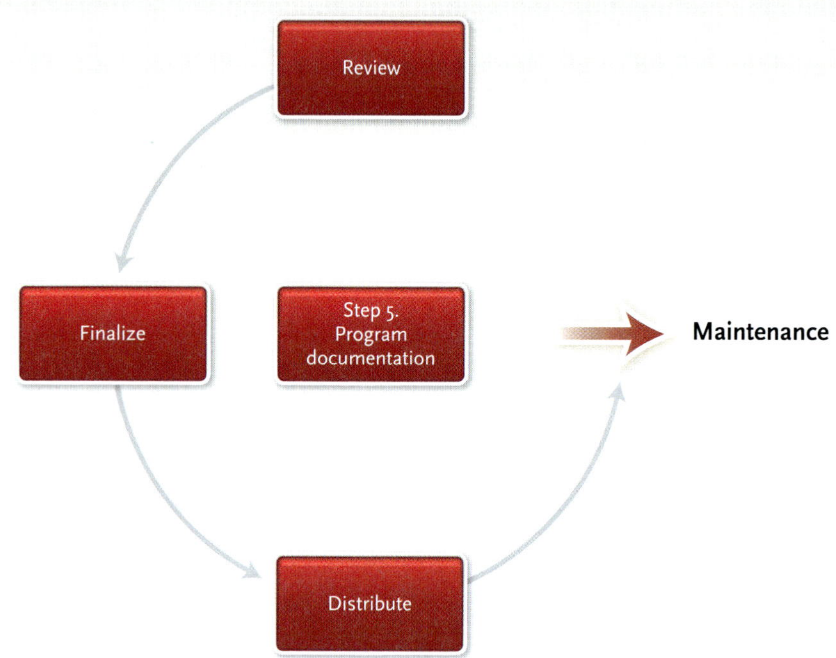

Figure 13-19 **Step 5: Program documentation**

Step 5: Program Documentation

Documentation consists of written descriptions and procedures about a program and how to use it. (See Figure 13-19.) It is not something done just at the end of the programming process. **Program documentation** is carried on throughout all the programming steps. In this step, all the prior documentation is reviewed, finalized, and distributed. Documentation is important for people who may be involved with the program in the future. These people may include the following:

- **Users.** Users need to know how to use the software. Some organizations may offer training courses to guide users through the program. However, other organizations may expect users to be able to learn a package just from the written documentation. Two examples of this sort of documentation are printed manuals and the help option within most applications.
- **Operators.** Documentation must be provided for computer operators. If the program sends them error messages, for instance, they need to know what to do about them.
- **Programmers.** As time passes, even the creator of the original program may not remember much about it. Other programmers wishing to update and modify it—that is, perform program maintenance—may find themselves frustrated without adequate documentation. This kind of documentation should include text and program flowcharts, program listings, and sample output. It also might include system flowcharts to show how the particular program relates to other programs within an information system.

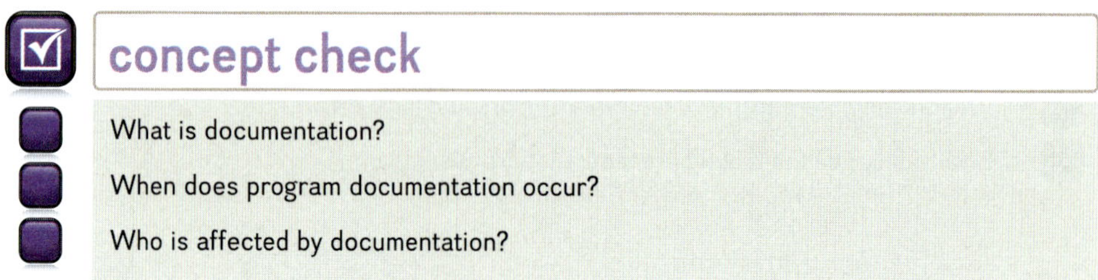

concept check

- What is documentation?
- When does program documentation occur?
- Who is affected by documentation?

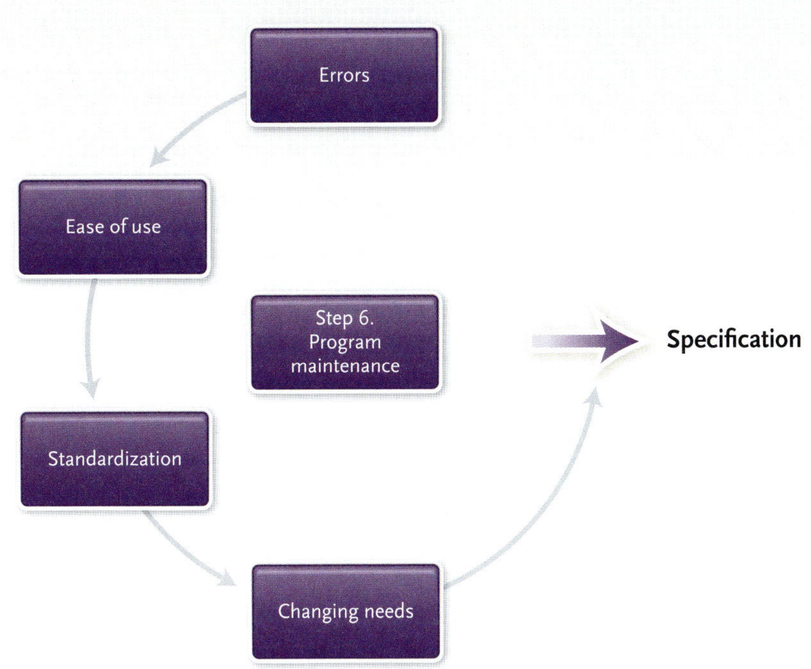

Figure 13-20 **Step 6: Program maintenance**

Step 6: Program Maintenance

The final step is **program maintenance.** (See Figure 13-20.) As much as 75 percent of the total lifetime cost for an application program is for maintenance. This activity is so commonplace that a special job title, **maintenance programmer,** exists.

The purpose of program maintenance is to ensure that current programs are operating error-free, efficiently, and effectively. Activities in this area fall into two categories: operations and changing needs.

Operations

Operations activities concern locating and correcting operational errors, making programs easier to use, and standardizing software using structured programming techniques. For properly designed programs, these activities should be minimal.

Programming modifications or corrections are often referred to as **patches.** For software that is acquired, it is common for the software manufacturer to periodically send patches or updates for its software. If the patches are significant, they are known as **software updates.**

Changing Needs

All organizations change over time, and their programs must change with them. Programs need to be adjusted for a variety of reasons, including new tax laws, new information needs, and new company policies. Significant revisions may require that the entire programming process begin again with program specification.

Ideally, a software project sequentially follows the six steps of software development. However, some projects start before all requirements are known. In these cases, the SDLC becomes a more cyclical process, repeated several times throughout the development of the software. For example, **agile development,** a popular development methodology, starts by getting core functionality of a program working,

Step	Primary Activity
1. Program specification	Determine program objectives, desired output, required input, and processing requirements.
2. Program design	Use structured programming techniques.
3. Program code	Select programming language; write the program.
4. Program test	Perform desk check (code review) and manual checks; attempt translation; test using sample data; beta test with potential users.
5. Program documentation	Write procedure for users, operators, and programmers.
6. Program maintenance	Adjust for errors, inefficient or ineffective operations, nonstandard code, and changes over time.

Figure 13-21 Summary of six steps in programming

then expands on it until the customer is satisfied with the results. All six steps are repeated over and over as quickly as possible to create incrementally more functional versions of the application.

Figure 13-21 summarizes the six steps of the programming process.

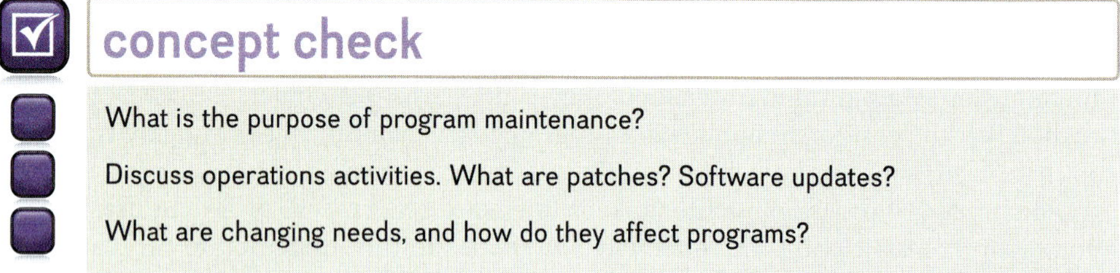

concept check
What is the purpose of program maintenance?
Discuss operations activities. What are patches? Software updates?
What are changing needs, and how do they affect programs?

CASE and OOP

You hear about efficiency and productivity everywhere. They are particularly important for software development. Two resources that promise to help are *CASE tools* and *object-oriented software development.*

CASE Tools

Professional programmers are constantly looking for ways to make their work easier, faster, and more reliable. One tool we mentioned in Chapter 12, CASE, is meeting this need. **Computer-aided software engineering (CASE) tools** provide some automation and assistance in program design, coding, and testing. (See Figure 13-22.)

Object-Oriented Software Development

Traditional systems development is a careful, step-by-step approach focusing on the procedures needed to complete a certain objective. **Object-oriented software**

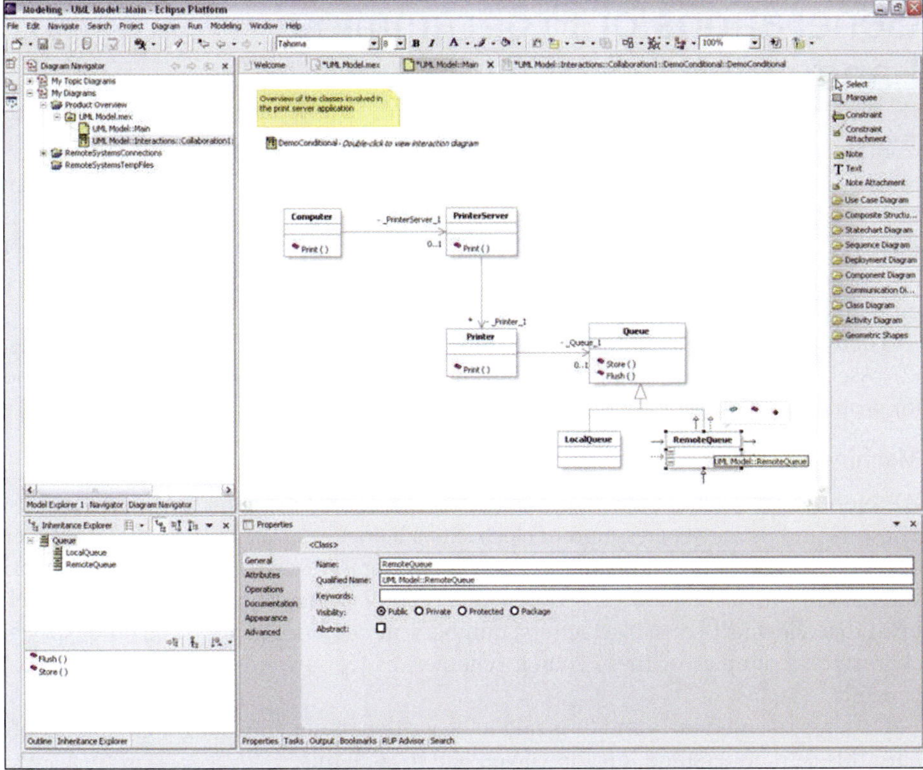

Figure 13-22 **CASE tool: Providing code-generation assistance**

development focuses less on the procedures and more on defining the relationships between previously defined procedures or "objects." **Object-oriented programming (OOP)** is a process by which a program is organized into objects. Each **object** contains both the data and processing operations necessary to perform a task. Let's explain what this means.

In the past, programs were developed as giant entities, from the first line of code to the last. This has been compared to building a car from scratch. Object-oriented programming is like building a car from prefabricated parts—carburetor, alternator, fenders, and so on. Object-oriented programs use objects that are reusable, self-contained components. Programs built with these objects assume that certain functions are the same. For example, many programs, from spreadsheets to database managers, have an instruction that will sort lists of names in alphabetical order. A programmer might use this object for alphabetizing in many other programs. There is no need to invent this activity anew every time. C++ is one of the most widely used object-oriented programming languages.

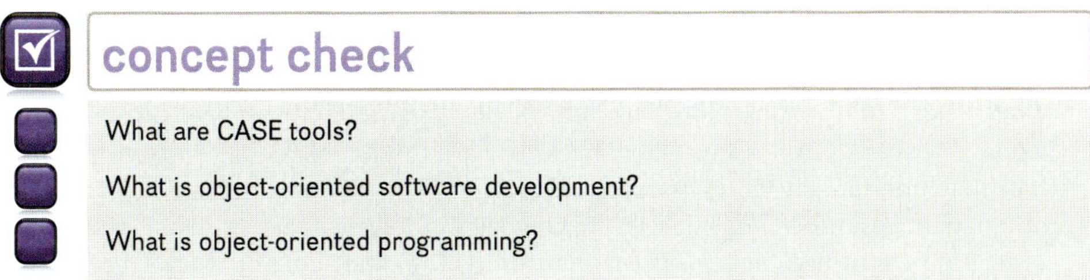

concept check

- What are CASE tools?
- What is object-oriented software development?
- What is object-oriented programming?

Generations of Programming Languages

Computer professionals talk about **levels** or **generations** of programming languages, ranging from "low" to "high." Programming languages are called **lower level** when they are closer to the language the computer itself uses. The computer understands the 0s and 1s that make up bits and bytes. Programming languages are called **higher level** when they are closer to the language humans use—that is, for English speakers, more like English.

There are five generations of programming languages: (1) machine languages, (2) assembly languages, (3) procedural languages, (4) task-oriented languages, and (5) problem and constraint languages.

Machine Languages: The First Generation

We mentioned in Chapter 5 that a byte is made up of bits, consisting of 1s and 0s. These 1s and 0s may correspond to electricity's being on or off in the computer. They also may correspond to a magnetic charge being present or absent on storage media such as disc or tape. From this two-state system, coding schemes have been developed that allow us to construct letters, numbers, punctuation marks, and other special characters. Examples of these coding schemes, as we saw, are ASCII, EBCDIC, and Unicode.

Data represented in 1s and 0s is said to be written in **machine language.** To see how hard this is to understand, imagine if you had to code this:

```
111100100111001111010010000100000111000000101011
```

Machine languages also vary according to make of computer—another characteristic that makes them hard to work with.

Assembly Languages: The Second Generation

Before a computer can process or run any program, the program must be converted or translated into machine language. **Assembly languages** use abbreviations or mnemonics such as ADD that are automatically converted to the appropriate sequence of 1s and 0s. Compared to machine languages, assembly languages are much easier for humans to understand and to use. The machine language code we gave above could be expressed in assembly language as

```
ADD 210(8,13),02B(4,7)
```

This is still pretty obscure, of course, and so assembly language is also considered low level.

Assembly languages also vary from computer to computer. With the third generation, we advance to high-level languages, many of which are considered **portable languages.** That is, they can be run on more than one kind of computer—they are "portable" from one machine to another.

High-Level Procedural Languages: The Third Generation

People are able to understand languages that are more like their own (e.g., English) than machine languages or assembly languages. These more English-like programming languages are called "high-level" languages. However, most people still require some training to use higher-level languages. This is particularly true of procedural languages.

Procedural languages, also known as **3GLs (third-generation languages),** are designed to express the logic—the procedures—that can solve general problems.

Procedural languages, then, are intended to solve general problems and are the most widely used languages to create software applications. C++ is a procedural language widely used by today's programmers. For example, C++ was used in Advantage Advertising's time-and-billing report. (See again Figure 13-14 for the compute time module of this program.)

Consider the following C++ statement from a program that assigns letter grades based on the score of an exam:

```
if (score > = 90) grade = 'A';
```

This statement tests whether the score is greater than or equal to 90. If it is, then the letter grade of A is assigned.

Like assembly languages, procedural languages must be translated into machine language so that the computer processes them. Depending on the language, this translation is performed by either a *compiler* or an *interpreter.*

- A **compiler** converts the programmer's procedural language program, called the **source code,** into a machine language code, called the **object code.** This object code can then be saved and run later. Examples of procedural languages using compilers are the standard versions of C++ and Visual Basic.
- An **interpreter** converts the procedural language one statement at a time into machine code just before it is to be executed. No object code is saved. An example of a procedural language using an interpreter is the standard version of BASIC.

What is the difference between using a compiler and using an interpreter? When a program is run, the compiler requires two steps. The first step is to convert the entire program's source code to object code. The second step is to run the object code. The interpreter, in contrast, converts and runs the program one line at a time. The advantage of a compiler language is that once the object code has been obtained, the program executes faster. The advantage of an interpreter language is that programs are easier to develop.

Task-Oriented Languages: The Fourth Generation

Third-generation languages are valuable, but they require training in programming. Task-oriented languages, also known as **4GLs (fourth-generation languages)** and **very high level languages,** require little special training on the part of the user.

Unlike general-purpose languages, **task-oriented languages** are designed to solve specific problems. While 3GLs focus on procedures and how logic can be combined to solve a variety of problems, 4GLs are nonprocedural and focus on specifying the specific tasks the program is to accomplish. 4GLs are more English-like, easier to program, and widely used by nonprogrammers. Some of these fourth-generation languages are used for very specific applications. For example, **IFPS (interactive financial planning system)** is used to develop financial models. Many 4GLs are part of a database management system. 4GLs include query languages and application generators:

- **Query languages: Query languages** enable nonprogrammers to use certain easily understood commands to search and generate reports from a database. One of the most widely used query languages is SQL (structured query language). For example, let's assume that Advantage Advertising has a database containing all customer calls for service and that its management would like a listing of all clients who incurred overtime charges. The SQL command to create this list is

  ```
  SELECT client FROM dailyLog WHERE serviceEnd >17
  ```

  This SQL statement selects or identifies all clients (a field name from the dailyLog table) that required service after 17 (military time for 5:00 P.M.). Microsoft Access can generate SQL commands like this one by using its Query wizard.

- **Application generators:** An **application generator** or a **program coder** is a program that provides modules of prewritten code. When using an application generator, a programmer can quickly create a program by referencing the module(s) that performs certain tasks. This greatly reduces the time to create an application. For example, Access has a report generation application and a Report wizard for creating a variety of different types of reports using database information.

Problem and Constraint Languages: The Fifth Generation

As they have evolved through the generations, computer languages have become more humanlike. Clearly, the fourth-generation query languages using commands that include words like SELECT, FROM, and WHERE are much more humanlike than the 0s and 1s of machine language. However, 4GLs are still a long way from the natural languages such as English and Spanish that people use.

The next step in programming languages will be the **fifth-generation language (5GL),** or computer languages that incorporate the concepts of artificial intelligence to allow a person to provide a system with a problem and some constraints, and then request a solution. Additionally, these languages would enable a computer to *learn* and to *apply* new information as people do. Rather than coding by keying in specific commands, we would communicate more directly to a computer using **natural languages.**

Consider the following natural language statement that might appear in a 5GL program for recommending medical treatment:

Get patientDiagnosis from patientSymptoms "sneezing", "coughing", "aching"

When will fifth-generation languages become a reality? That's difficult to say; however, researchers are actively working on the development of 5GL languages and have demonstrated some success.

See Figure 13-23 for a summary of the generations of programming languages.

Generation	Sample Statement
First: Machine	111100100111001111010010000100000111000000101011
Second: Assembly	ADD 210(8,13),02B(4,7)
Third: Procedural	if (score > = 90) grade = 'A';
Fourth: Task	SELECT client FROM dailyLog WHERE serviceEnd > 17
Fifth: Problems and Constraints	Get patientDiagnosis from patientSymptoms "sneezing", "coughing", "aching"

Figure 13-23 Summary of five programming generations

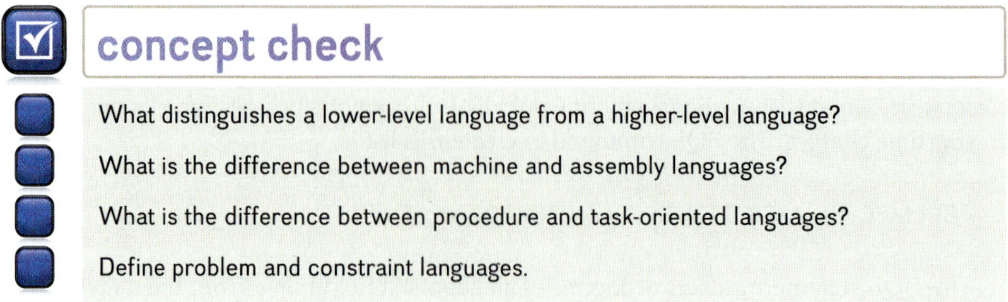

concept check

- What distinguishes a lower-level language from a higher-level language?
- What is the difference between machine and assembly languages?
- What is the difference between procedure and task-oriented languages?
- Define problem and constraint languages.

Careers in IT

"Now that you have learned about programming and programming languages, let me tell you about my career as a programmer."

Computer **programmers** create, test, and troubleshoot programs used by computers. Programmers also may update and repair existing programs. Most computer programmers are employed by companies that create and sell software, but programmers also may be employed in various other businesses. Many computer programmers work on a project basis as consultants, meaning they are hired by a company only to complete a specific program. As technology has developed, the need for programmers to work on the most basic computer functions has decreased. However, demand for computer programmers with specializations in advanced programs continues.

Jobs in programming typically require a bachelor's degree in computer science or information systems. However, there are positions available in the field for those with a two-year degree. Employers looking for programmers typically put an emphasis on previous experience. Programmers who have patience, think logically, and pay attention to detail are continually in demand. Additionally, programmers who can communicate technical information to nontechnical people are preferred.

Computer programmers can expect to earn an annual salary in the range of $51,000 to $64,000. Advancement opportunities for talented programmers include a lead programmer position or supervisory positions. Programmers with specializations and experience also may have an opportunity to consult.

A LOOK TO THE FUTURE

Your Own Programmable Robot

Have you ever dreamed of having your own robot that could help you with all your chores? Wouldn't it be nice if that robot understood every word you said and required no complex programming from you? Such a robot will be possible in the future as the field of robotics keeps advancing. Currently robots are used in many manufacturing roles, making everything from cars to frozen pancakes. Recently, there are already several companies that are mass-producing programmable robots for individuals and educational institutions. It is just a matter of time before these robots can understand human instructions instead of complex programming languages. Technology has been making better programming tools, and will continue to evolve to improve our lives as we look to the future.

One of the earliest robots that was made available to consumers was the Roomba from iRobot which is essentially an automated, intelligent vacuum cleaner. Since then, the same company has released robots that wash floors, clean pools, and clear gutters. The programming is handled by the robot's developers, with the end user doing very little except turning the robot on. As well as these robots perform, their function is limited to their programmed task.

A company named Aldebaran Robotics has taken a different approach, creating small, humanoid robots, called Nao, which the end user can program. Although the Nao robots are being mass-produced, they are a bit too expensive for the average home. Currently, they are being marketed toward schools and research institutions. Using a GUI, students can create programs that the robot will follow. Alternatively, programmers can use one of several supported languages to write their own custom scripts for Nao.

In the future, it will not be necessary for someone to use software or know a programming language to communicate with a robot. Developers will use sophisticated programming to give the robot the artificial intelligence necessary to understand natural language. This software will be embedded in a chip within the robot. When you purchase a robot, all you will have to do is speak the commands in normal, conversational English. If you want the robot to help you clean the pool or lift a heavy box, you can tell the robot in the same manner you would tell another person.

The hardware components needed to make robots are becoming cheaper. However, the software remains a challenge. Human languages and conversations remain very difficult for a computer to fully understand. Speech recognition continues to improve, and we are seeing this technology embedded in the latest smartphones. Nevertheless, many improvements are necessary before a humanoid robot will be able to converse with us.

Do you think you will be able to own a humanoid robot in your lifetime? Do you believe that programmers will be able to make these robots intelligent enough to carry on conversations and perform a wide variety of tasks?

VISUAL SUMMARY Programming and Languages

PROGRAMS AND PROGRAMMING

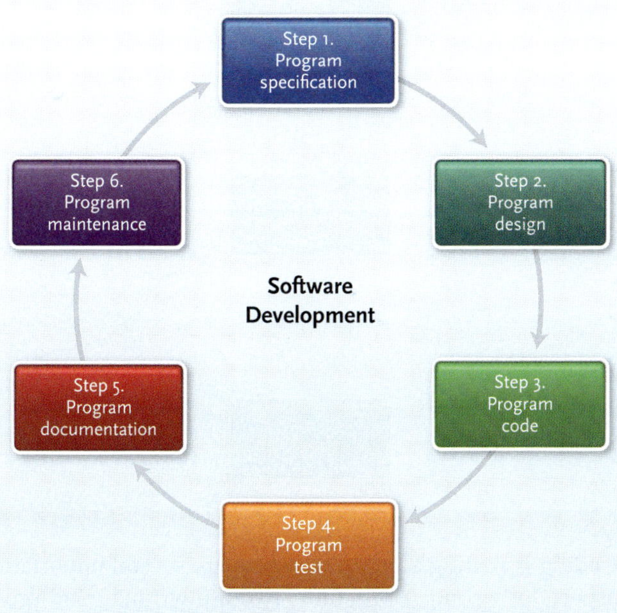

A **program** is a list of instructions for a computer to follow. **Programming (software development)** is a six-step procedure for creating programs.

The steps are

- Program specification—defining objectives, inputs, outputs, and processing requirements.
- Program design—creating a solution using structured programming tools and techniques such as **top-down program design, pseudocode, program flowcharts,** and **logic structures.**
- Program code—writing or coding the program using a **programming language.**
- Program test—testing or debugging the program by looking for **syntax** and **logic errors.**
- Program documentation—ongoing process throughout the programming process.
- Program maintenance—periodically evaluating programs for accuracy, efficiency, standardization, and ease of use and modifying program code as needed.

STEP 1: PROGRAM SPECIFICATION

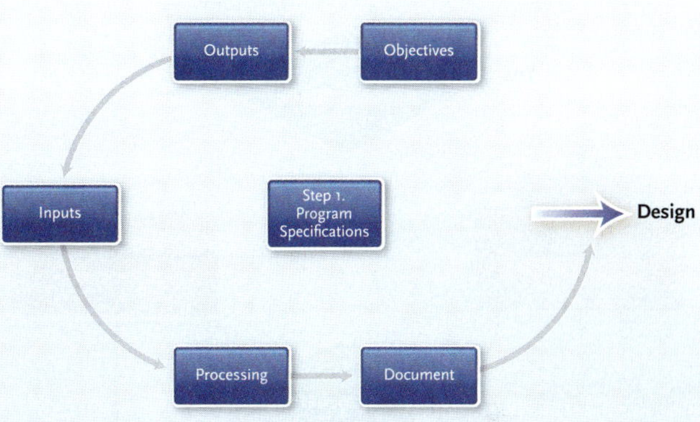

Program specification, also called **program definition** or **program analysis,** consists of specifying five tasks related to objectives, outputs, inputs, requirements, and documentation.

Program Objectives

The first task is to clearly define the problem to solve in the form of program **objectives.**

Desired Output

Next, focus on the desired output before considering the required inputs.

Input Data

Once outputs are defined, determine the necessary input data and the source of the data.

Processing Requirements

Next, determine the steps necessary (processing requirements) to use input to produce output.

Program Specifications Document

The final task is to create a specifications document to record this step's program objectives, outputs, inputs, and processing requirements.

To efficiently and effectively use computers, you need to understand the six steps of programming: program specification, program design, program coding, program test, program documentation, and program maintenance. Additionally, you need to be aware of CASE, OOP, and the generations of programming languages.

STEP 2: PROGRAM DESIGN

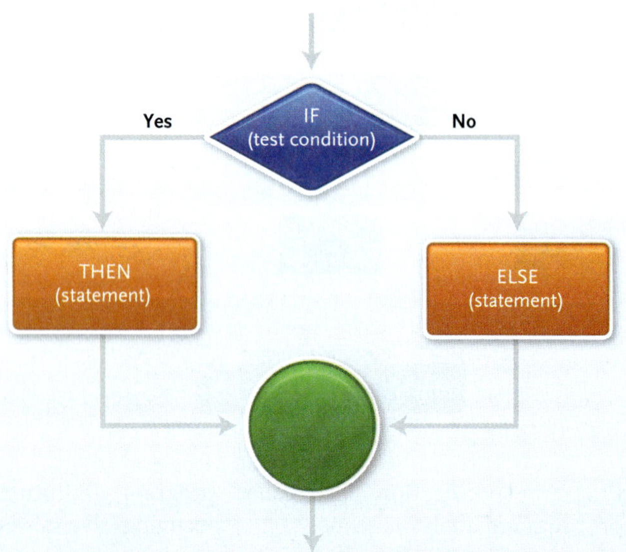

In **program design,** a solution is designed using, preferably, **structured programming techniques,** including the following.

Top-Down Program Design

In **top-down program design,** major processing steps, called **program modules (or modules),** are identified.

Pseudocode

Pseudocode is an outline of the logic of the program you will write.

Flowcharts

Program flowcharts are graphic representations of the steps necessary to solve a programming problem.

Logic Structures

Logic structures are arrangements of programming statements. Three types are

- **Sequential**—one program statement followed by another.
- **Selection (IF-THEN-ELSE)**—when a decision must be made.
- **Repetition (loop)**—when a process is repeated until condition is true.

STEP 3: PROGRAM CODE

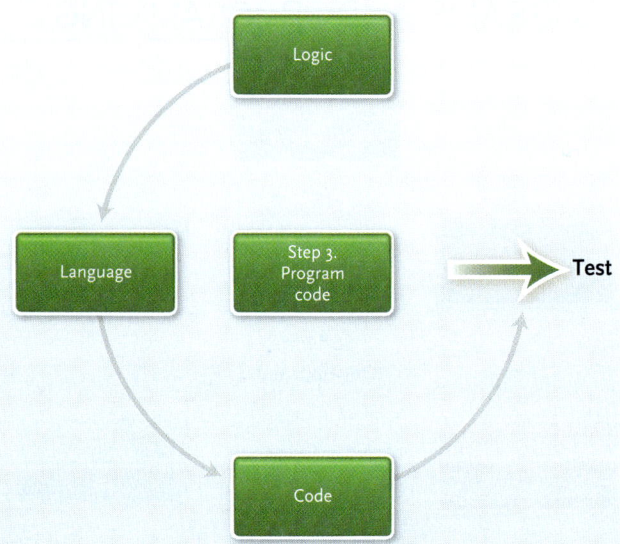

Coding is writing a program. There are several important aspects of writing a program. Two are writing good programs and actually writing or coding.

Good Programs

Good programs are reliable, detect obvious and common errors, and are well documented. The best way to create good programs is to write **structured programs** using the three basic logic structures presented in Step 2.

Coding

There are hundreds of different programming languages. **Programming languages** instruct a computer to perform specific operations. C++ is a widely used programming language.

```
#include <fstream.h>

void main (void)
{
    ifstream input_file;

    float total_regular, total_overtime, regular, overtime;
    int hour_in, minute_in, hour_out, minute_out;
    input_file.open("time.txt",ios::in);

    total_regular = 0;
    total_overtime = 0;

    while (input_file != NULL)
    {
        input_file >> hour_in >> minute_in >> hour_out >> minute_out;

        if (hour_out > 17)
            overtime = (hour_out-17) +(minute_out/(float)60);
        else
            overtime = 0;
            regular = ((hour_out - hour_in) +(minute_out
                      - minute_in)/(float)60)    - overtime;
        total_re  lar += regular;
                     = overtime;
```

STEP 4: PROGRAM TEST

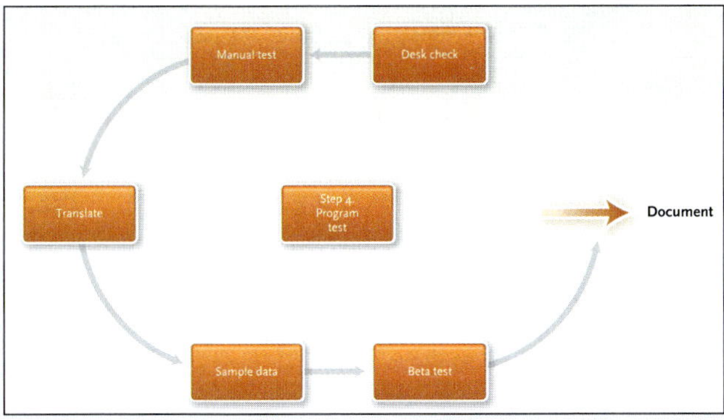

Debugging is a process of testing and eliminating errors in a program. Syntax and logic are two types of programming errors.

Syntax Errors

Syntax errors are violations of the rules of a programming language. For example, omitting a semicolon at the end of a C++ statement is a syntax error.

Logic Errors

Logic errors are incorrect calculations or procedures. For example, failure to include calculation of overtime hours in a payroll program is a logic error.

Testing Process

Five methods for testing for syntax and logic errors are

- **Desk checking (code review)**—careful reading of a printout of the program.
- **Manual testing**—using a calculator and sample data to test for correct programming logic.
- **Attempt at translation**—running the program using a translator program to identify syntax errors.
- **Testing sample data**—running the program and testing the program for logic errors using sample data.
- **Testing by users (beta testing)**—final step in which potential users try the program and provide feedback.

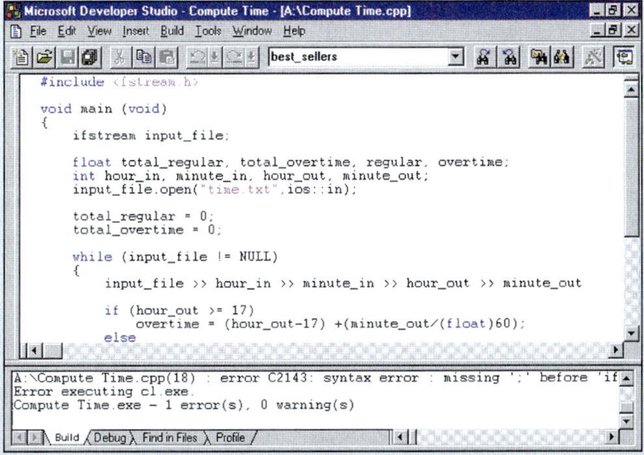

STEP 5: PROGRAM DOCUMENTATION

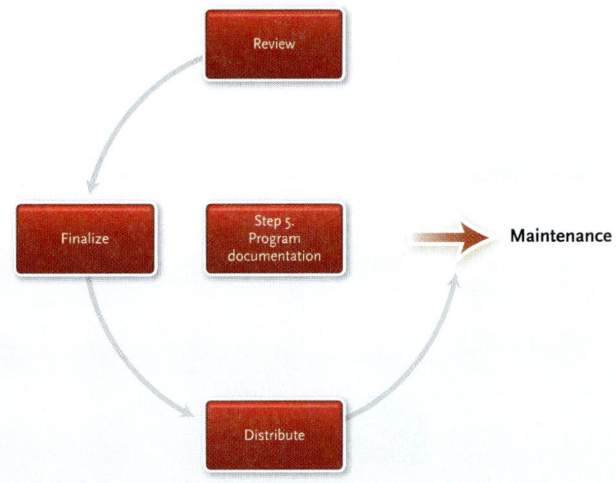

Program documentation consists of a written description of the program and the procedures for running it. People who use documentation include

- **Users,** who need to know how to use the program. Some organizations offer training courses; others expect users to learn from written documentation.
- **Operators,** who need to know how to execute the program and how to recognize and correct errors.
- **Programmers,** who may need to update and maintain the program in the future. Documentation could include text and program flowcharts, program listings, and sample outputs.

STEP 6: PROGRAM MAINTENANCE

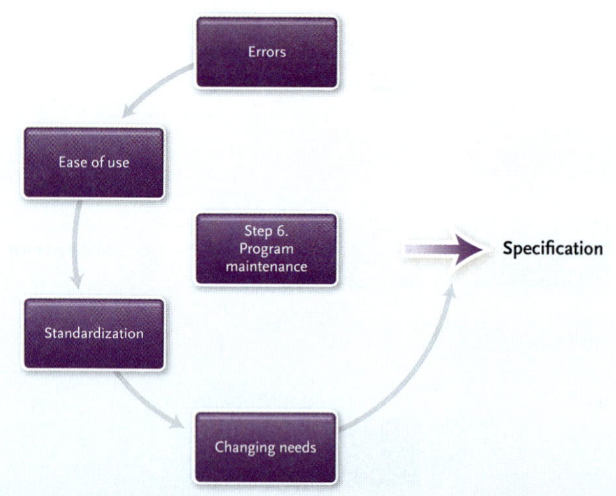

Program maintenance is designed to ensure that the program operates correctly, efficiently, and effectively. Two categories of maintenance activities are the following.

Operations

Operations activities include locating and correcting errors, improving usability, and standardizing software. Software updates are known as **patches.** Significant patches are called **software updates.**

Changing Needs

Organizations change over time, and their programs must change with them. **Agile development** starts with core program functionality and expands until the customer is satisfied with the results.

CASE AND OOP

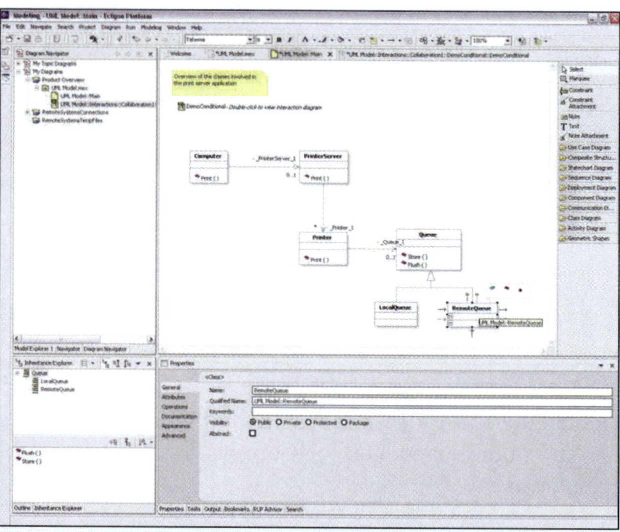

CASE

Computer-aided software engineering (CASE) tools provide automation and assistance in program design, coding, and testing.

OOP

Traditional systems development focuses on procedures to complete a specific objective.

Object-oriented software development focuses less on procedures and more on defining relationships between previously defined procedures or objects. **Object-oriented programming (OOP)** is a process by which a program is divided into modules called **objects.** Each object contains both the data and processing operations necessary to perform a task.

PROGRAMMING LANGUAGE GENERATIONS

Programming languages have **levels** or **generations** ranging from low to high. **Lower-level** languages are closer to the 0s and 1s language of computers. **Higher-level** languages are closer to the languages of humans.

CAREERS in IT

Programmers create, test, and troubleshoot programs. They also update and repair existing programs. Requirements include a bachelor's or specialized two-year degree in computer science or information systems. Salary range is $51,000 to $64,000.

KEY TERMS

agile development (343)
application generator (348)
assembly language (346)
beta testing (341)
code (338)
code review (340)
coding (338)
compiler (347)
computer-aided software engineering (CASE) tools (344)
debugging (340)
desk checking (340)
documentation (342)
fifth-generation language (5GL) (348)
fourth-generation language (4GL) (347)
generation (346)
higher level (346)
IF-THEN-ELSE structure (337)
IFPS (interactive financial planning system) (347)
interpreter (347)
level (346)
logic error (340)
logic structure (337)
loop structure (337)
lower level (346)
machine language (346)
maintenance programmer (343)
module (334)
natural language (348)
object (345)
object code (347)
object-oriented programming (OOP) (345)
object-oriented software development (344, 345)
objective (332)
operator (342)
patches (343)
portable language (346)
procedural language (346)
program (330)
program analysis (332)
program coder (348)
program definition (332)
program design (334)
program documentation (342)
program flowchart (335)
program maintenance (343)
program module (334)
program specification (332)
programmer (331, 342, 349)
programming (330)
programming language (338)
pseudocode (335)
query language (347)
repetition structure (337)
selection structure (337)
sequential structure (337)
software development (330)
software development life cycle (SDLC) (330)
software engineer (331)
software updates (343)
source code (347)
structured program (338)
structured programming technique (334)
syntax error (340)
task-oriented language (347)
third-generation language (3GL) (346)
top-down program design (334)
user (342)
very high level language (347)

MULTIPLE CHOICE

Circle the letter of the correct answer.

1. A program is a list of instructions for the computer to follow to process:
   - a. data
   - b. direct logic
   - c. hardware
   - d. software
2. The major processing steps identified in a top-down program design are called:
   - a. assembly
   - b. instructions
   - c. modules
   - d. logic
3. The programming logic structure in which one program statement follows another.
   - a. loop
   - b. repetition
   - c. selection
   - d. sequential
4. One of the best ways to code effective programs is to use the three basic logic structures to create:
   - a. code reviews
   - b. modular languages
   - c. pseudocode
   - d. structured programs
5. Which step in the six-step programming procedure involves desk checking and searching for syntax and logic errors?
   - a. program design
   - b. program documentation
   - c. program maintenance
   - d. program test
6. Which step in the six-step programming procedure is the final step?
   - a. program design
   - b. program documentation
   - c. program test
   - d. program maintenance
7. Unlike traditional systems development, this software development approach focuses less on the procedures and more on defining the relationships between previously defined procedures.
   - a. 2GL
   - b. context-markup
   - c. module
   - d. object-oriented
8. Natural languages are considered to be a:
   - a. high-level language
   - b. low-level language
   - c. midlevel language
   - d. procedural language
9. A compiler converts the programmer's procedural language program, called the source code, into a machine language code, called the:
   - a. interpreter code
   - b. object code
   - c. structured code
   - d. top-down code
10. The 4GL languages that enable nonprogrammers to use certain easily understood commands to search and generate reports from a database.
    - a. query
    - b. application generator
    - c. C++
    - d. COBOL

MATCHING

Match each numbered item with the most closely related lettered item. Write your answers in the spaces provided.

a. debugging
b. documentation
c. higher level
d. interpreter
e. machine
f. natural language
g. programming
h. pseudocode
i. selection
j. 5GL

___ 1. Six-step procedure also known as software development.

___ 2. An outline of the logic of the program to be written.

___ 3. Logic structure, also known as IF-THEN-ELSE, that controls program flow based on a decision.

___ 4. Programming languages that are closer to the language of humans.

___ 5. The process of testing and then eliminating program errors.

___ 6. Program step that involves creating descriptions and procedures about a program and how to use it.

___ 7. The first-generation language consisting of 1s and 0s.

___ 8. Converts a procedural language one statement at a time into machine code just before it is to be executed.

___ 9. Generation of computer languages that allows a person to provide a system with a problem and some constraints, and then request a solution.

___ 10. 5GL that allows more direct human communication with a program.

OPEN-ENDED

On a separate sheet of paper, respond to each question or statement.

1. Identify and discuss each of the six steps of programming.
2. Describe CASE tools and OOP. How does CASE assist programmers?
3. What is meant by "generation" in reference to programming languages? What is the difference between low-level and high-level languages?
4. What is the difference between a compiler and an interpreter?
5. What are logic structures? Describe the differences between the three types.

DISCUSSION

Respond to each of the following questions.

1 Expanding Your Knowledge: SOURCE CODE GENERATORS

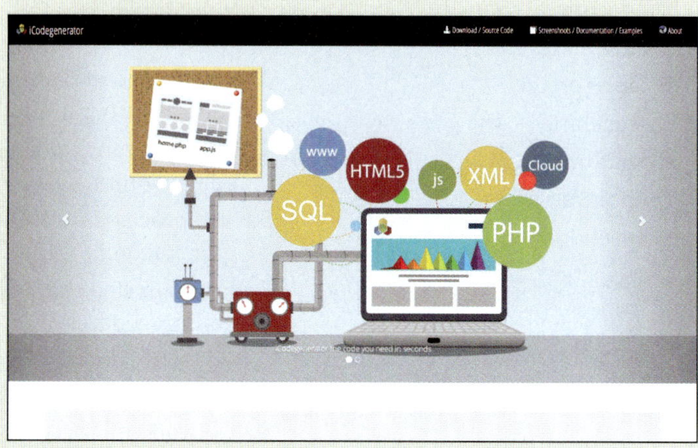

Generally, the human resources that are devoted to a successful software project are its greatest single expense. Programming and testing applications are time-consuming tasks. Recently, source code generators have become popular for handling some of the more routine programming tasks. Research source code generators on the web, and answer the following questions: (a) What are source code generators? (b) How do source code generators work? (c) What programming tasks are source code generators best for? Why? (d) What programming tasks are beyond what source code generators can accomplish? Why?

2 Writing about Technology: BUGS

Several years ago, two people died and a third was maimed after receiving excessive radiation from a medical machine. It was only after the second incident that the problem was located—a bug in the software that controlled the machine. Consider the possible consequences of software failure in situations where life is at stake, and then respond to the following: (a) Are there situations when software bugs are unethical? Explain your answer. (b) No program of any significant complexity can reasonably be fully tested. When is it ethical to say that software is "tested enough"? (c) What responsibility does a programmer have in situations where a program fails in the field? What about the software company he or she works for? Does the consumer share any responsibility? Justify your answers.

3 Writing about Technology: SECURITY AND PRIVACY

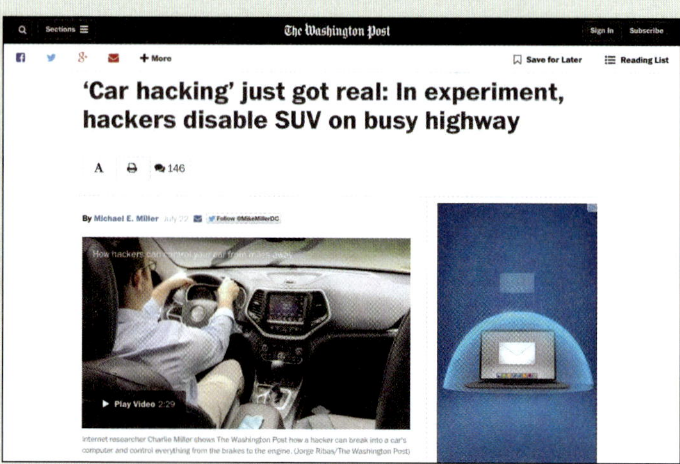

Security and privacy are important concerns in the development of any information system. Respond to the following: (a) In the development process, who would you expect to have the responsibility of identifying security and privacy concerns? (b) In what phase of the software development life cycle would security and privacy concerns be identified?

PHOTO CREDITS

CHAPTER 13:

Opener: © loops7/Getty Images RF; p. 329, 350: © Blutgruppe/Corbis; p. 330, 349: © ERproductions Ltd/Getty Images RF; 13-17, 13-22, p. 353 (bottom-left), p. 354 (top-right): Microsoft product screen shot(s) reprinted with permission from Microsoft Corporation; p. 354 (bottom-left): Lucas Lenci Photo/Getty Images RF; p. 358 (top): icodegenerator.com; p. 358 (bottom): washingtonpost.com © 2015 The Washington Post. p. 353 (bottom-right): Michael Poehlman/The Image Bank/Getty Images.

The Evolution of the Computer Age

Many of you probably can't remember a world without computers, but for some of us, computers were virtually unknown when we were born and have rapidly come of age during our lifetime.

Although there are many predecessors to what we think of as the modern computer—reaching as far back as the 18th century, when Joseph Marie Jacquard created a loom programmed to weave cloth and Charles Babbage created the first fully modern computer design (which he could never get to work)—the computer age did not really begin until the first computer was made available to the public in 1951.

The modern age of computers thus spans slightly more than 65 years (so far), which is typically broken down into five generations. Each generation has been marked by a significant advance in technology.

- **First Generation (1951–57):** During the first generation, computers were built with vacuum tubes—electronic tubes that were made of glass and were about the size of lightbulbs.

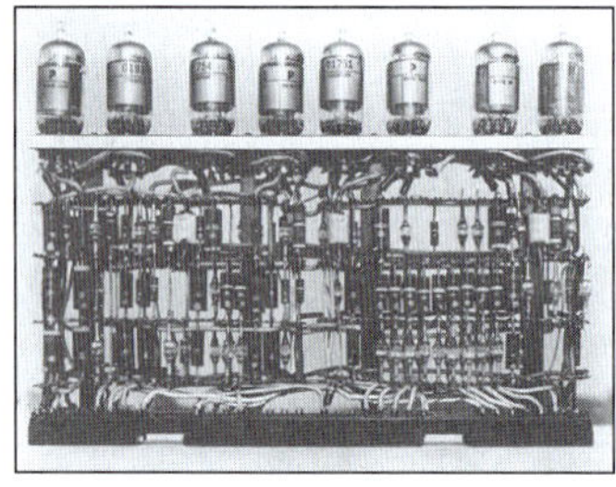

- **Second Generation (1958–63):** This generation began with the first computers built with transistors—small devices that transfer electronic signals across a resistor. Because transistors are much smaller, use less power, and create less heat than vacuum tubes, the new computers were faster, smaller, and more reliable than the first-generation machines.

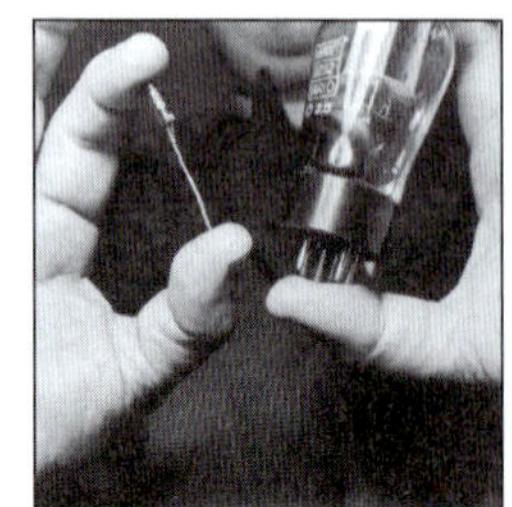

- **Third Generation (1964–69):** In 1964, computer manufacturers began replacing transistors with integrated circuits. An integrated circuit (IC) is a complete electronic circuit on a small chip made of silicon (one of the most abundant elements in the earth's crust). These computers were more reliable and compact than computers made with transistors, and they cost less to manufacture.

- **Fourth Generation (1970–90):** Many key advances were made during this generation, the most significant being the microprocessor—a specialized chip developed for computer memory and logic. Use of a single chip to create a smaller "personal" computer (as well as digital watches, pocket calculators, copy machines, and so on) revolutionized the computer industry.

- **Fifth Generation (1991–2017 and beyond):** Our current generation has been referred to as the "Connected Generation" because of the industry's massive effort to increase the connectivity of computers. The rapidly expanding Internet, World Wide Web, and intranets have created an information superhighway that has enabled both computer professionals and home computer users to communicate with others across the globe.

This appendix provides you with a timeline that describes in more detail some of the most significant events in each generation of the computer age.

First Generation: The Vacuum Tube Age

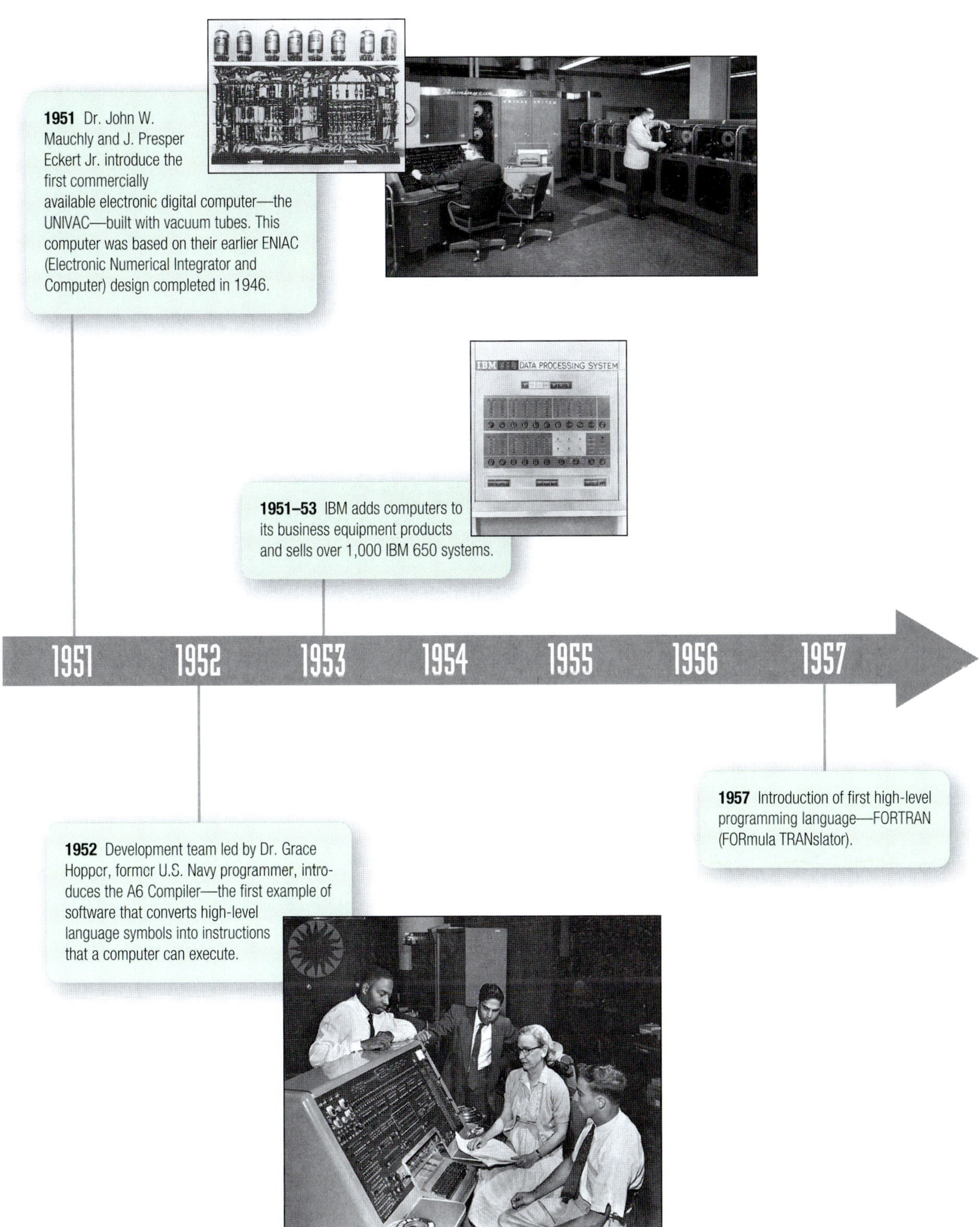

1951 Dr. John W. Mauchly and J. Presper Eckert Jr. introduce the first commercially available electronic digital computer—the UNIVAC—built with vacuum tubes. This computer was based on their earlier ENIAC (Electronic Numerical Integrator and Computer) design completed in 1946.
IBM DATA PROCESSING SYSTEM
1951–53 IBM adds computers to its business equipment products and sells over 1,000 IBM 650 systems.
1951
1952
1953
1954
1955
1956
1957
1957 Introduction of first high-level programming language—FORTRAN (FORmula TRANslator).
1952 Development team led by Dr. Grace Hopper, former U.S. Navy programmer, introduces the A6 Compiler—the first example of software that converts high-level language symbols into instructions that a computer can execute.

Second Generation: The Transistor Age

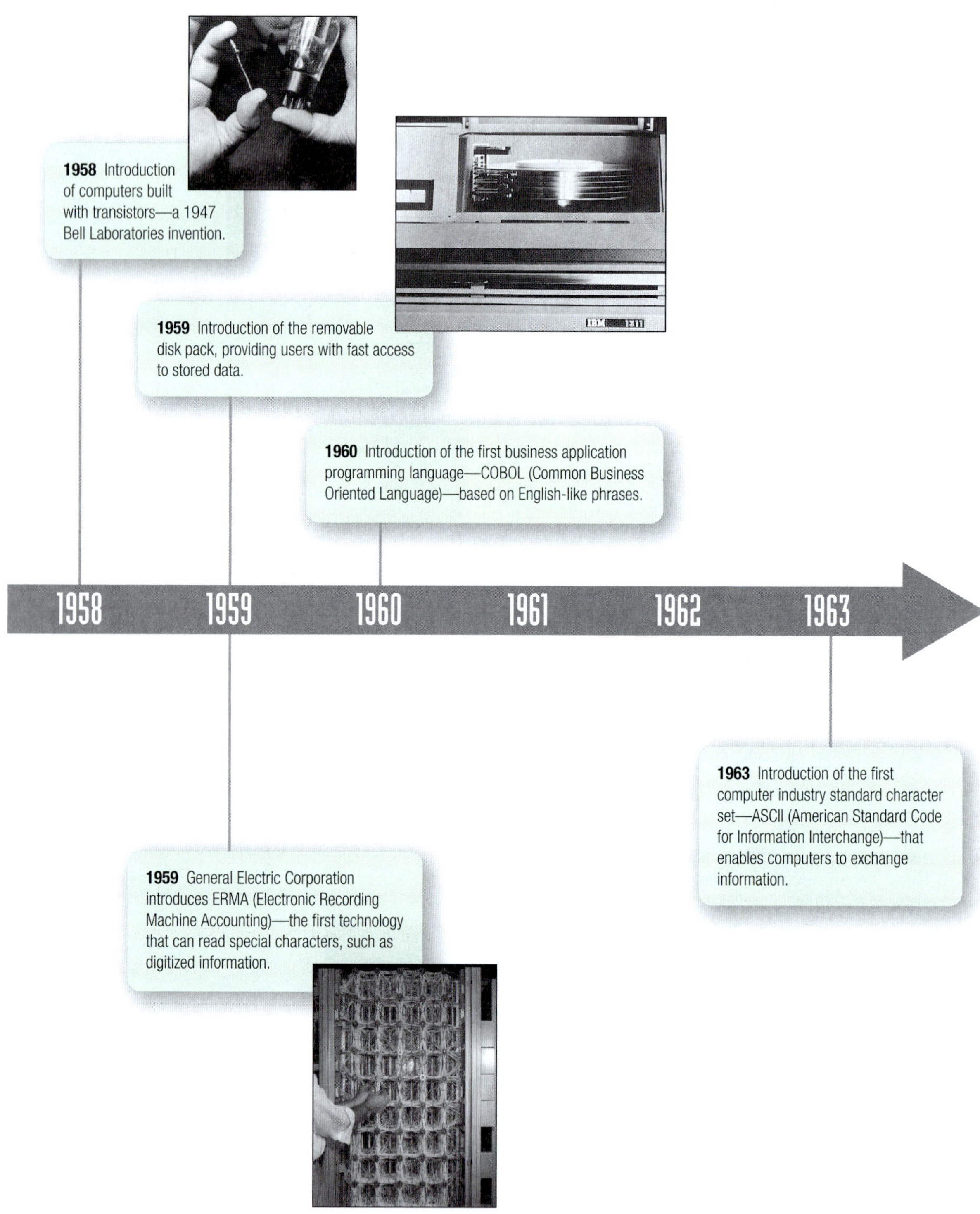

1958 Introduction of computers built with transistors—a 1947 Bell Laboratories invention.
1959 Introduction of the removable disk pack, providing users with fast access to stored data.
1960 Introduction of the first business application programming language—COBOL (Common Business Oriented Language)—based on English-like phrases.
1958
1959
1960
1961
1962
1963
1963 Introduction of the first computer industry standard character set—ASCII (American Standard Code for Information Interchange)—that enables computers to exchange information.
1959 General Electric Corporation introduces ERMA (Electronic Recording Machine Accounting)—the first technology that can read special characters, such as digitized information.

Third Generation: The Integrated Circuit Age

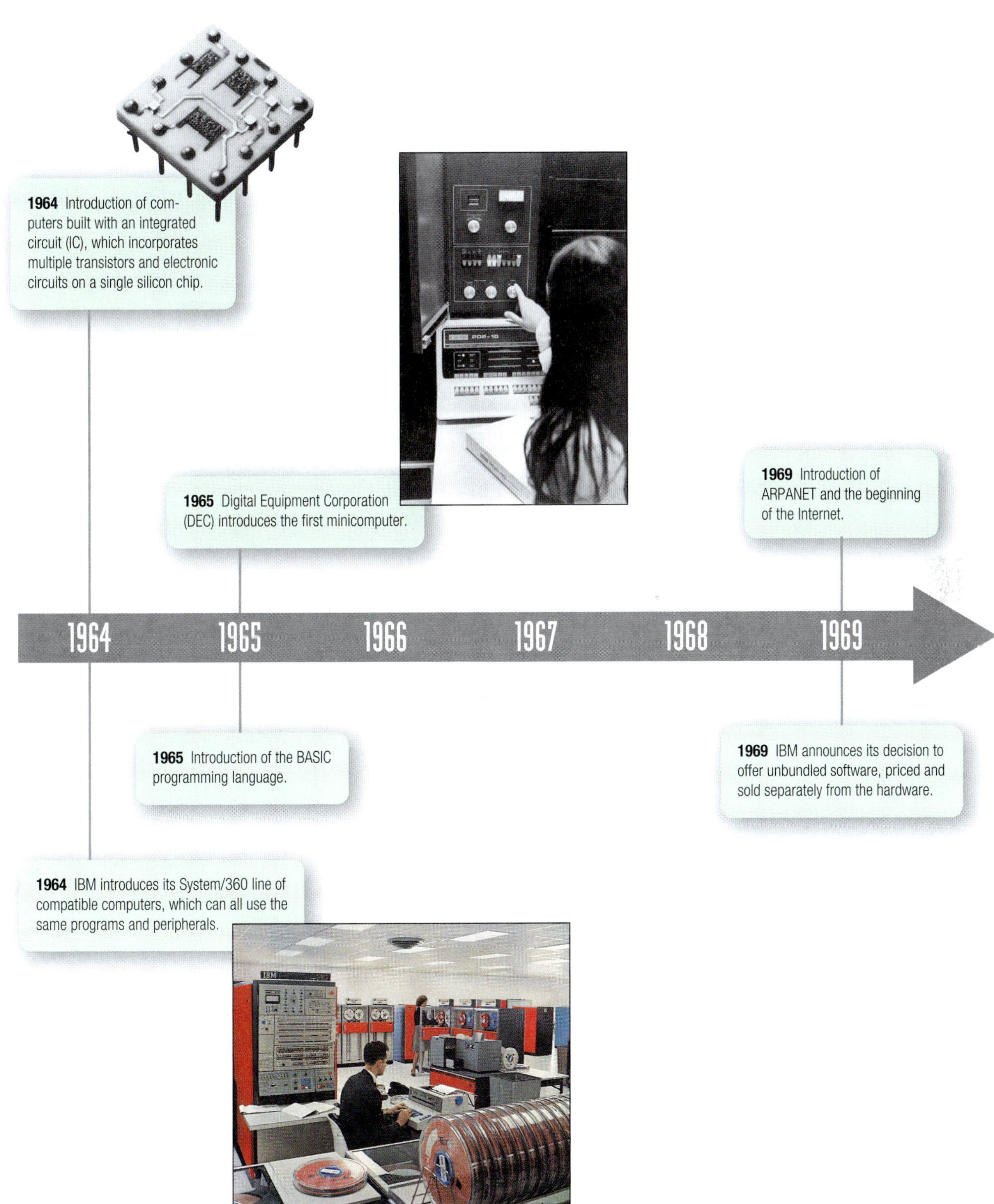

1964 Introduction of computers built with an integrated circuit (IC), which incorporates multiple transistors and electronic circuits on a single silicon chip.
1965 Digital Equipment Corporation (DEC) introduces the first minicomputer.
1969 Introduction of ARPANET and the beginning of the Internet.
1964
1965
1966
1967
1968
1969
1965 Introduction of the BASIC programming language.
1969 IBM announces its decision to offer unbundled software, priced and sold separately from the hardware.
1964 IBM introduces its System/360 line of compatible computers, which can all use the same programs and peripherals.
PDP-10
IBM

Fourth Generation: The Microprocessor Age

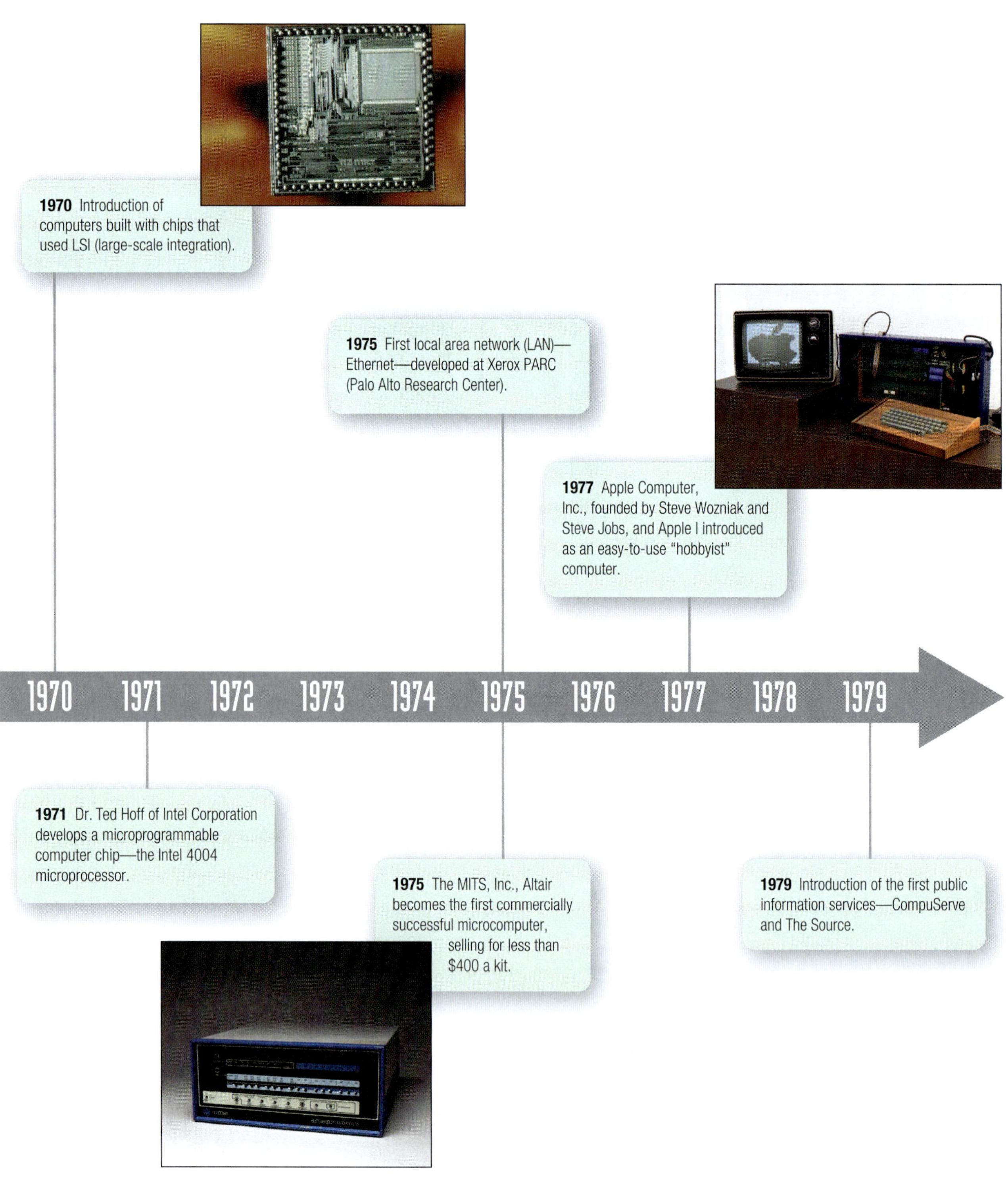

1970 Introduction of computers built with chips that used LSI (large-scale integration).
1975 First local area network (LAN)—Ethernet—developed at Xerox PARC (Palo Alto Research Center).
1977 Apple Computer, Inc., founded by Steve Wozniak and Steve Jobs, and Apple I introduced as an easy-to-use "hobbyist" computer.
1970
1971
1972
1973
1974
1975
1976
1977
1978
1979
1971 Dr. Ted Hoff of Intel Corporation develops a microprogrammable computer chip—the Intel 4004 microprocessor.
1975 The MITS, Inc., Altair becomes the first commercially successful microcomputer, selling for less than $400 a kit.
1979 Introduction of the first public information services—CompuServe and The Source.

1980 IBM asks Microsoft founder, Bill Gates, to develop an operating system—MS-DOS—for the soon-to-be-released IBM personal computer.

1981 Introduction of the IBM PC, which contains an Intel microprocessor chip and Microsoft's MS-DOS operating system.

1989 Introduction of Intel 486—the first 1,000,000-transistor microprocessor.

1980 1981 1982 1983 1984 1985 1986 1987 1988 1989 1990

1984 Apple introduces the Macintosh Computer, with a unique, easy-to-use graphical user interface.

1985 Microsoft introduces its Windows graphical user interface.

1990 Microsoft releases Windows 3.0, with an enhanced graphical user interface and the ability to run multiple applications.

Fifth Generation: The Age of Connectivity

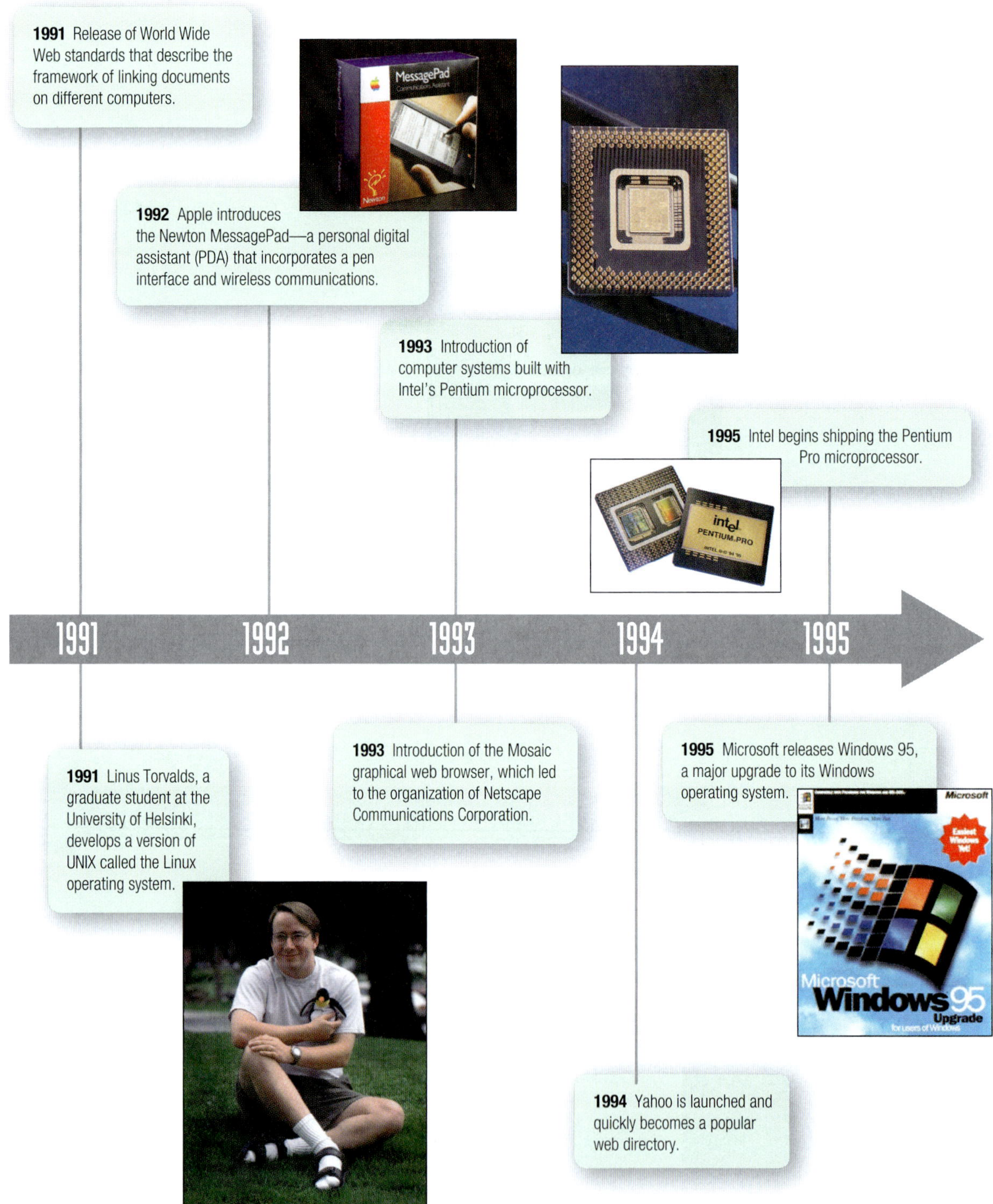

1991 Release of World Wide Web standards that describe the framework of linking documents on different computers.
1992 Apple introduces the Newton MessagePad—a personal digital assistant (PDA) that incorporates a pen interface and wireless communications.
1993 Introduction of computer systems built with Intel's Pentium microprocessor.
1995 Intel begins shipping the Pentium Pro microprocessor.
1991
1992
1993
1994
1995
1991 Linus Torvalds, a graduate student at the University of Helsinki, develops a version of UNIX called the Linux operating system.
1993 Introduction of the Mosaic graphical web browser, which led to the organization of Netscape Communications Corporation.
1995 Microsoft releases Windows 95, a major upgrade to its Windows operating system.
1994 Yahoo is launched and quickly becomes a popular web directory.

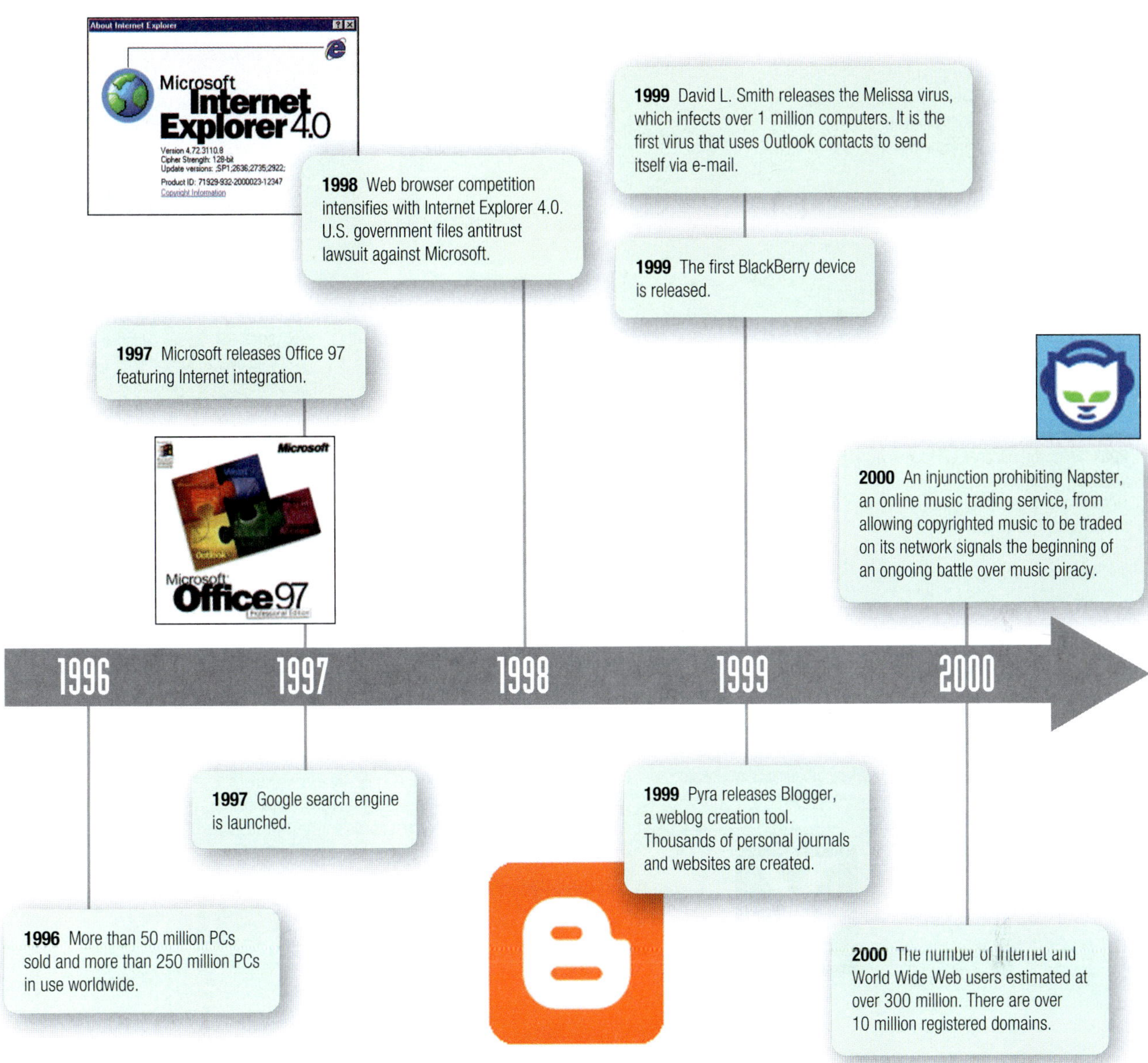
Microsoft Internet Explorer 4.0
1998 Web browser competition intensifies with Internet Explorer 4.0. U.S. government files antitrust lawsuit against Microsoft.
1999 David L. Smith releases the Melissa virus, which infects over 1 million computers. It is the first virus that uses Outlook contacts to send itself via e-mail.
1999 The first BlackBerry device is released.
1997 Microsoft releases Office 97 featuring Internet integration.
Microsoft
Microsoft Office 97
2000 An injunction prohibiting Napster, an online music trading service, from allowing copyrighted music to be traded on its network signals the beginning of an ongoing battle over music piracy.
1996
1997
1998
1999
2000
1997 Google search engine is launched.
1999 Pyra releases Blogger, a weblog creation tool. Thousands of personal journals and websites are created.
1996 More than 50 million PCs sold and more than 250 million PCs in use worldwide.
2000 The number of Internet and World Wide Web users estimated at over 300 million. There are over 10 million registered domains.

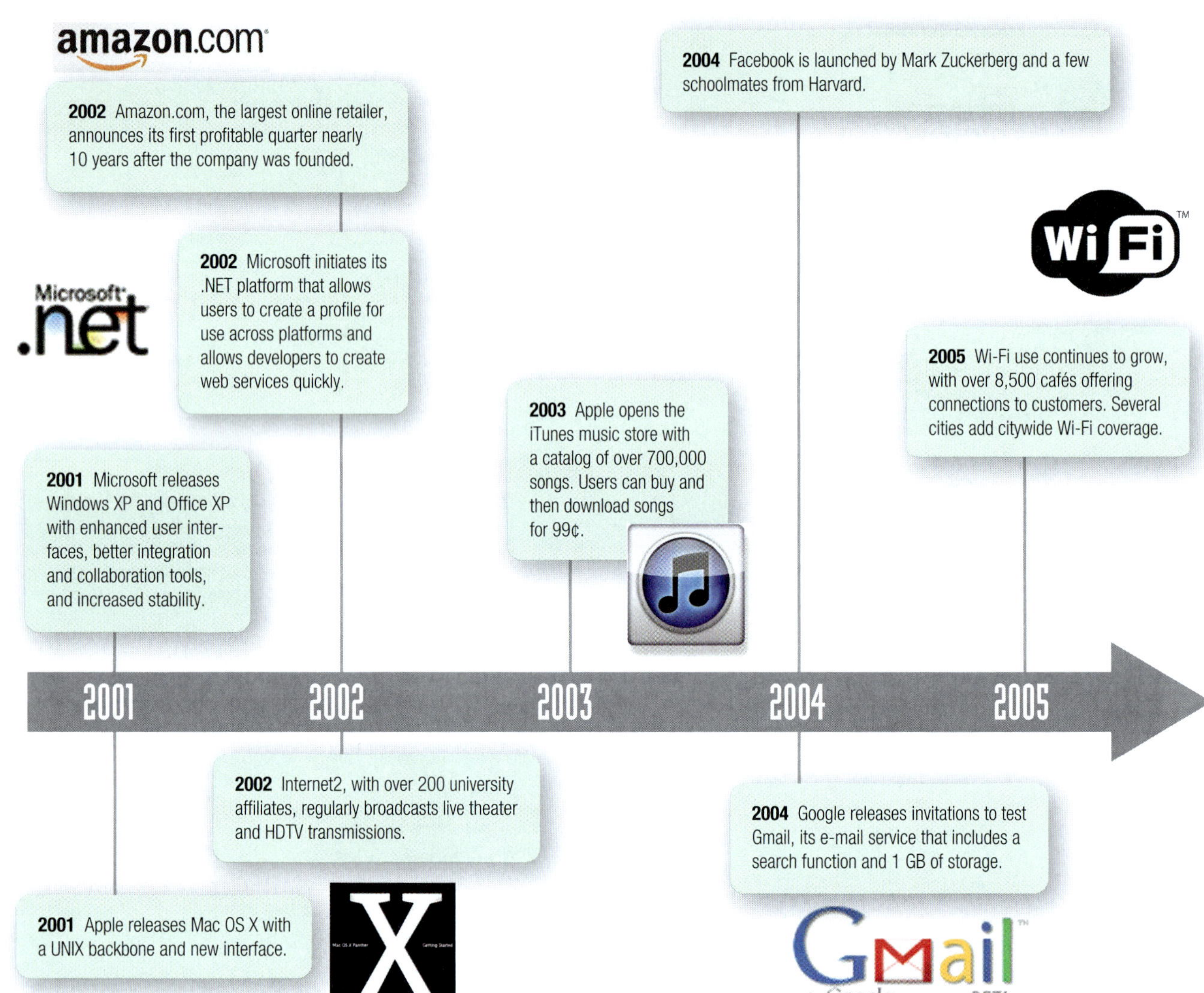
amazon.com
2002 Amazon.com, the largest online retailer, announces its first profitable quarter nearly 10 years after the company was founded.
2004 Facebook is launched by Mark Zuckerberg and a few schoolmates from Harvard.
Wi Fi
Microsoft .net
2002 Microsoft initiates its .NET platform that allows users to create a profile for use across platforms and allows developers to create web services quickly.
2005 Wi-Fi use continues to grow, with over 8,500 cafés offering connections to customers. Several cities add citywide Wi-Fi coverage.
2003 Apple opens the iTunes music store with a catalog of over 700,000 songs. Users can buy and then download songs for 99¢.
2001 Microsoft releases Windows XP and Office XP with enhanced user interfaces, better integration and collaboration tools, and increased stability.
2001
2002
2003
2004
2005
2002 Internet2, with over 200 university affiliates, regularly broadcasts live theater and HDTV transmissions.
2004 Google releases invitations to test Gmail, its e-mail service that includes a search function and 1 GB of storage.
2001 Apple releases Mac OS X with a UNIX backbone and new interface.
X
Gmail by Google BETA

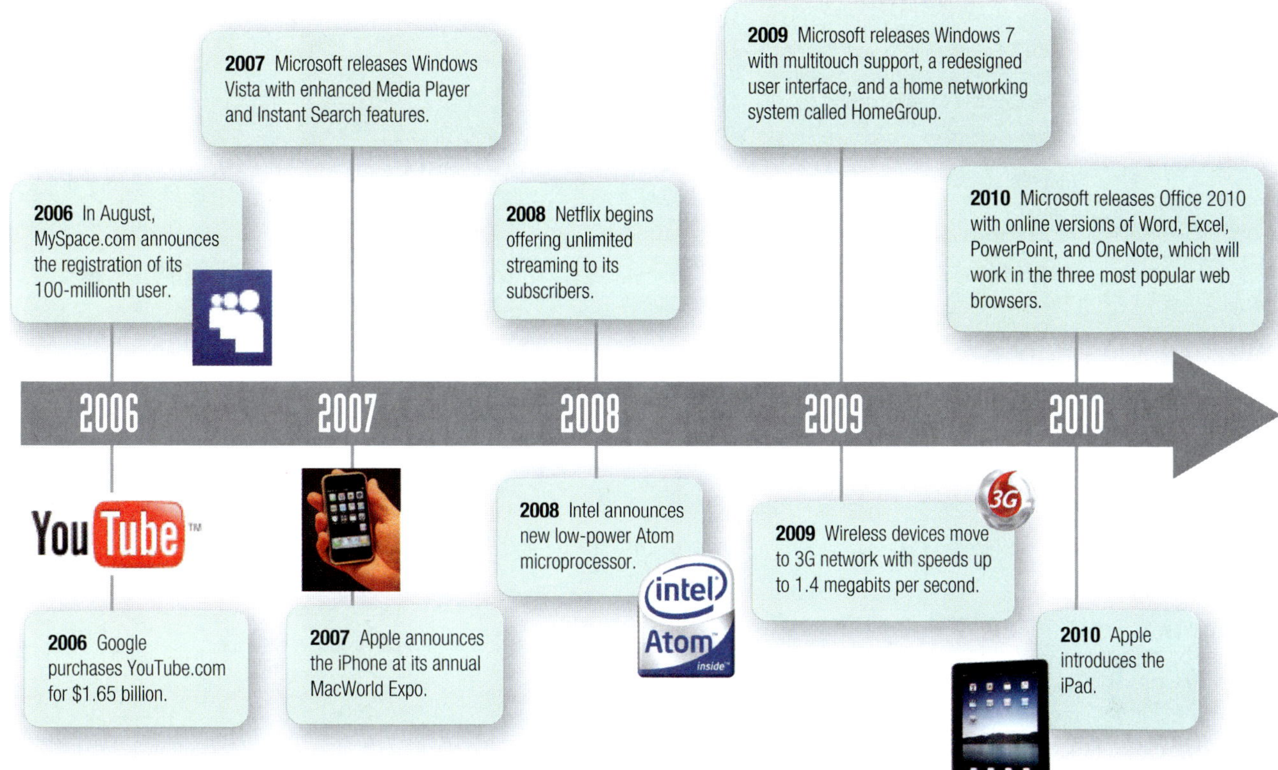
2007 Microsoft releases Windows Vista with enhanced Media Player and Instant Search features.
2009 Microsoft releases Windows 7 with multitouch support, a redesigned user interface, and a home networking system called HomeGroup.
2006 In August, MySpace.com announces the registration of its 100-millionth user.
2008 Netflix begins offering unlimited streaming to its subscribers.
2010 Microsoft releases Office 2010 with online versions of Word, Excel, PowerPoint, and OneNote, which will work in the three most popular web browsers.
2006
2007
2008
2009
2010
YouTube
2008 Intel announces new low-power Atom microprocessor.
intel
Atom
inside
3G
2009 Wireless devices move to 3G network with speeds up to 1.4 megabits per second.
2006 Google purchases YouTube.com for $1.65 billion.
2007 Apple announces the iPhone at its annual MacWorld Expo.
2010 Apple introduces the iPad.

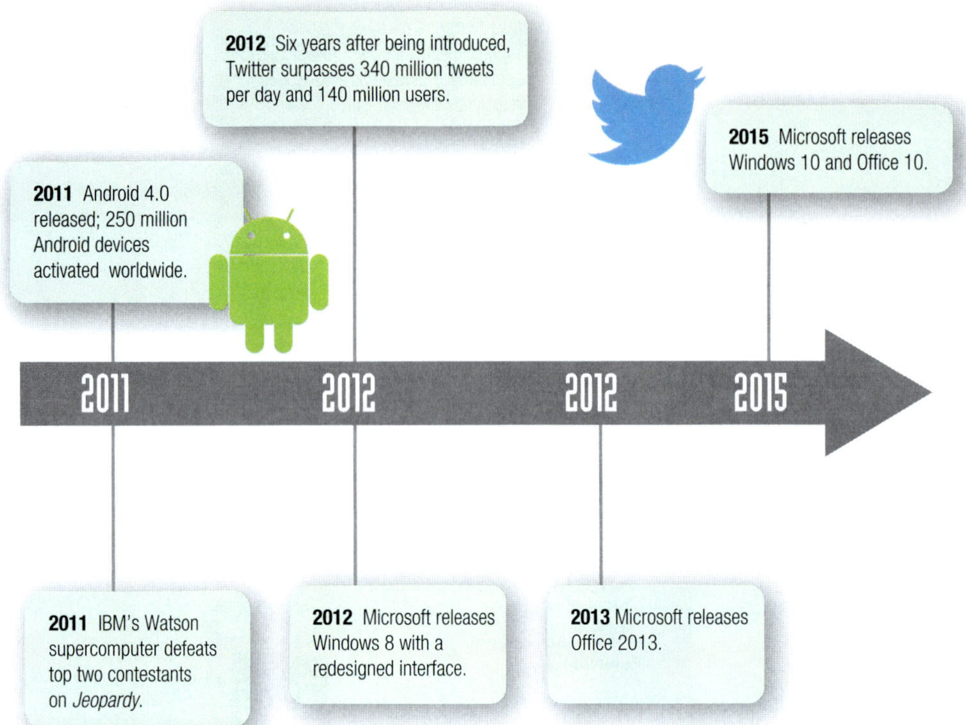
2012 Six years after being introduced, Twitter surpasses 340 million tweets per day and 140 million users.
2015 Microsoft releases Windows 10 and Office 10.
2011 Android 4.0 released; 250 million Android devices activated worldwide.
2011
2012
2012
2015
2011 IBM's Watson supercomputer defeats top two contestants on *Jeopardy*.
2012 Microsoft releases Windows 8 with a redesigned interface.
2013 Microsoft releases Office 2013.

The Computer Buyer's Guide

PART 1: WHICH TYPES OF COMPUTERS SHOULD YOU PURCHASE?

Many individuals feel confused and overwhelmed when it comes to buying a new computer. In today's market, there are various categories of computers ranging from desktops and laptops to ultraportable tablets and smartphones. And within each category, there are countless choices and a wide range of prices. This buying guide will help you choose the best combination of computers for your needs, as well as point out some key specifications that they should have.

LAPTOP COMPUTERS: TODAY'S STANDARD

Typical Recommendation: Buy a $700 to $1000 laptop with a 13-inch screen.

The laptop computer has become the must-have device that can do everything you need, wherever you need it. They are powerful enough to be your primary home computer (replacing desktops) while portable enough to take to school, work, the local coffee shop, and even on your next trip. Many students are bringing them to classes to take notes and perform research. If you can own only one computer, make it a laptop. Affordable ones start at under $700.

If you have decided that you want to buy a laptop computer, be sure to read Part 2 for additional tips and recommendations.

SMARTPHONES: COMPUTERS IN YOUR POCKET

Typical Recommendation: Obtain a free or low-cost smartphone by signing a two-year wireless contract with a data plan.

For many individuals, the smartphone has become much like a wallet, purse, or keys–you don't leave home without it. This single, pocket-sized device fills many roles. It is a mobile phone, digital camera, video recorder, gaming device, and personal digital assistant. Most individuals purchase a smartphone because they need to access information quickly and easily, regardless of where they are.

With many smartphones now available for free with two-year contracts, it is easier than ever to replace your older cell phone. The biggest drawback to owning a smartphone is that its "use anywhere" benefit is limited if it is not paired with a wireless data plan, which can often cost around $30 per month.

Although Apple's iPhone was once the clear leader in the smartphone market, various Android devices include competitive features and are enjoying favorable reviews. If you have decided that you want to buy a smartphone, be sure to read Part 2 for additional tips and recommendations.

TABLETS: THE RISING STARS

Typical Recommendation: Buy a 10-inch tablet with 64 GB of storage.

The release of the iPad has revived this category of computers. With an attractive, 10-inch touch-screen surface, it has quickly become a popular device for watching videos, playing games, reading e-books, and browsing the web. Tablets are light enough to hold comfortably for many hours, yet powerful enough to use a variety of apps. They generally have a much longer battery life than laptop computers.

If you are a typical computer user, then you may not benefit much from purchasing a tablet computer. Most of your computing time will be spent on your laptop computer (at home and at school, for example) or on your smartphone. Although tablets are very popular right now, you must remember that they cost several hundred dollars. You should have a very clear need for this sort of device before you decide to spend the money on it.

Many students consider buying tablets because the low weight makes a tablet easy to carry around. Although this is true, there are lightweight laptop computers that weigh only one or two pounds more and are much more versatile than tablets. Such versatility is crucial for various types of software that are not available as apps and require installation on a Windows or Mac computer. Before you decide between a tablet and lightweight laptop, consider the type of software you will need for your schoolwork, business, or personal use. If everything you need is available as a mobile app, then a tablet (paired with a wireless keyboard) will be more affordable than a lightweight laptop computer.

In conclusion, purchase a tablet computer only if you see yourself using it often. The touch-screen interface, low weight, and long battery life do indeed make it easy to carry around and use almost anywhere you go. However, the price tag does not make the decision an obvious one if you already own a laptop computer and smartphone. If you have decided that you want to buy a tablet, be sure to read Part 2 for additional tips and recommendations.

DESKTOPS

Typical Recommendation: Buy a tower system with a 20- to 24-inch monitor for approximately $800.

Desktop (or tower) computers have been around for a long time. You will still find them in many offices and homes. However, they are steadily losing popularity because laptop computers have become very powerful and affordable. Why have a computer that remains stuck in your home or office when you can have a laptop that can be taken almost anywhere?

Although laptop computers seem to be the better choice, there are several reasons why you might want to purchase a desktop computer. First, the use of a laptop computer as your primary computer can be uncomfortable. After prolonged use, it can place stress on your neck, back, and wrists. Desktops typically come with large monitors, and various types of ergonomic keyboards are available. However, desktop critics will point out that laptop computers can be connected to external monitors and keyboards as well. The only downside is that a laptop requires the purchase of extra equipment.

The other reason to get a desktop is if you have a specific need that cannot be addressed by a laptop computer. For example, some families have a media center computer that holds all the videos, photos, and music for the entire home network. Another example involves gamers, who often seek to build or customize extremely powerful computers. They often choose desktops for this endeavor.

Most users will not need to purchase a desktop computer. In fact, they are currently the least popular of the four categories in this buying guide. However, if you have decided that you want to buy a desktop, be sure to read Part 2 for additional tips and recommendations.

PART 2: PERSONALIZED BUYING GUIDE

Now that you have decided which types of computers you need, it is time to explore computer specifications. The areas below explore the decision-making process from the perspective of various buyers.

LAPTOPS

There are two basic categories of laptop: the traditional laptop and the ultrabook. Although these two categories of laptop computers have the same general appearance, they vary greatly in power, storage capacity, weight, and battery life. The following section helps you find the device that best meets your needs.

User #1: *I am a power user. I need a portable computer that can handle the latest video games or process-intensive operations such as video editing, engineering, and design.*

Response #1: Purchase a traditional laptop computer that includes the following minimum specs:

- **The fastest categories of processors with large number of cores and high GHz count**
- **A graphics processor (GPU) outside of the main CPU**
- **16-GB RAM**
- **1-TB hard drive**
- **17-inch screen**

Expect to pay approximately $1500, perhaps more. For games, many individuals choose Windows-based PCs. The video and design industries usually use Macs.

User #2: *I am a regular user. I need a desktop replacement and portable computer. I typically run office software, use the Internet, and listen to music.*

Response #2: Purchase an affordable traditional laptop computer that includes the following specs:

- **Middle-tier processors—not the fastest but not the slowest either**
- **4- to 8-GB RAM**
- **500-GB hard drive**
- **15-inch screen**

Expect to pay approximately $800 to $1000. For maximum savings, as well as compatibility with most software, many buyers choose Windows-based PCs. Be sure to purchase an external monitor, keyboard, and mouse if you plan on heavy use while at home.

User #3: *I want a small, lightweight computer that I can carry anywhere. I would like long battery life for extended use.*

Response #3: Purchase an ultrabook with

- **11- to 13-inch screen**
- **Solid-state hard drive**
- **4-GB RAM**
- **Weight under 4 pounds**

Expect to pay $700 to $1000. Many ultrabooks will not include a DVD drive. Windows-based ultrabooks tend to be more affordable. The MacBook Air is slightly more expensive, but it has always been considered a leader in the lightweight laptop field.

SMARTPHONES

Shopping for a smartphone involves three separate processes: (1) choosing an operating system, such iOS, Android, or Windows; (2) choosing a device; and (3) choosing a wireless carrier. Although the following section does not review different wireless companies or data plans, it presents a list of smartphone features that you should always consider before making your choice. In addition, it presents each smartphone operating system from the perspective of typical users.

Features to Consider

- *Screen and device size:* **Consider a size (and weight) that is comfortable for you to use and carry around. Four-inch screens are now typical.**
- *Screen resolution:* **Some devices deliver HD quality for sharp photos and videos.**
- *Integrated keyboard:* **Consider one if you type often on these devices.**
- *Storage:* **Having 8 GB is enough for most users. Choose 16 GB or more if you plan to store large quantities of music, photos, and videos. Some devices allow you to increase storage by using memory cards.**
- *Battery life:* **About 7 to 8 hours is typical. Some devices have removable batteries.**
- *Cameras:* **Many include front- and rear-facing cameras. Compare megapixels and photo quality.**
- *App market:* **Consider the number of apps, and ensure that any apps you need are available for this operating system.**

Operating Systems

- *iOS:* **The iPhone is considered by many to be the standard against which all smartphones are measured. Buyers typically choose the iPhone if they are Mac owners or prefer a tightly controlled "ecosystem" from Apple where stability and ease of use are favored over heavy customization.**
- *Android:* **There are many Android devices available from various manufacturers, some free with a wireless contract. Buyers who enjoy customizing their interface typically choose Android. In addition, this operating system is tightly integrated with many of Google's products and services.**
- *Windows 10 Phone:* **The newcomer to the smartphone market features an interface that will seem familiar to those using Windows 8 laptop and tablets. Users enjoy the "live tiles," which constantly update information, such as social network activity.**

Remember that smartphones can cost very little when you sign a two-year contract with a wireless company. Consider whether you want to make that sort of commitment.

TABLET COMPUTERS

Because of their increased popularity, tablets are available in several sizes from many different companies. The following section helps you find the device that best meets your needs.

User #1: *I want to watch videos, play games, create notes, and browse websites.*

Response #1: Purchase a 10-inch tablet. Expect to pay $400 to $500. Most weigh about 1.5 pounds. Apple's iPad was very popular when first released, and it continues to be a popular choice among buyers today. Other things to consider:

- **For greater customization, consider an Android-based tablet. There are several models that are comparable to the iPad, which is considered by many reviewers to be the standard bearer.**
- **The Microsoft Surface tablet includes a keyboard that is integrated into the cover. However, any tablet can be paired with a Bluetooth keyboard, which is crucial if you plan to type often.**
- **Make sure the apps you plan on using are available for the tablet's operating system.**
- **Having 16 GB of storage is typical. Some tablets let you expand this by using flash memory cards.**

User #2: *I want to read e-books, browse websites, and have a lightweight device that I can hold with one hand.*

Response #2: Purchase a 7-inch tablet. Expect to pay around $200. Most weigh less than 1 pound. Google's Nexus 7 and Amazon's Kindle Fire are popular Android-based tablets.

DESKTOP COMPUTERS

Desktops remain popular for offices, both at home and in many companies. In addition, many power users require them for graphics-intensive tasks. The following section helps you find the device that best meets your needs.

User #1: *I need a powerful computer that can handle the latest video games or process-intensive operations such as video editing, engineering, and design.*

Response #1: Purchase a tower-based computer with the following minimum specs:

- **The fastest categories of processors with large number of cores and high GHz count**
- **High-performance video card**

- **16-GB RAM**
- **2-TB hard drive**
- **24-inch monitor**
- **Specialty peripherals (such as game controllers) when needed**

Expect to pay at least $1500 for these powerful computers. For games, many individuals choose Windows-based PCs. The video and design industries usually use Macs.

User #2: *I would like a computer that can be used by the entire family for many years.*

Response #2: Purchase a tower or all-in-one computer with the following minimum specs:

- **Middle-tier processor**
- **8-GB RAM**
- **500-GB hard drive (increase to 2 TB if you plan to store a large number of videos)**
- **20- to 24-inch monitor**
- **Ergonomic keyboard**

Tower-based systems are usually offered in a package that includes the monitor and several peripherals. All-in-one systems will, of course, include the monitor, some of which are touch screens. Spending approximately $700 to $1000 will help ensure that the components remain relevant for several years. For a stylish and powerful all-in-one computer, consider the slightly more expensive iMac from Apple.

PHOTO CREDITS

Appendix:

Page 360 (top-left, top-right), 361 (1951-left, 1953), 362 (1959-top), 363 (1964-top, bottom), 365 (1981): IBM Corporate Archives; p. 360 (bottom-left), 362 (1958): © Keystone-France/Gamma-Keystone via Getty Images; p. 360 (bottom-right): © John Foxx/Stockbyte/Getty Images RF; p. 361 (1951-right): © Bettman/Corbis; p. 361 (1952): Smithsonian Institute/Public.Resource.Org/Flickr; p. 362 (1959-bottom): SRI International/Flickr/CC; p. 363 (1965): © Underwood Archives/Getty Images; p. 364 (1970): © Bill Pierce/Time Life Pictures/Getty Images; p. 364 (1977): © Timothy A. Clary/AFP/Getty Images; p. 364 (1975), 365 (1984, 1989), 366 (1992): © Science & Society Picture Library/Getty Images; p. 365 (1980), 366 (1995-bottom), 367 (1997, 1998), 368 (2002-middle): Used with permission from Microsoft; p. 366 (1993, 1995-top): Courtesy Intel; p. 366 (1991): © Chuck Nacke/Alamy Stock Photo; p. 367 (2000): Reprinted by permission of Rhapsody International, Inc.; p. 367 (1999): © 2015 Google, Inc., used with permission. Blogger and the Blooger logo are registered trademarks of Google Inc.; p. 368 (2002-top): © Anatolii Babii/Alamy Stock Photo; p. 368 (2003): © PSL Images/Alamy Stock Photo; p. 368 (2005): © TP/Alamy Stock Photo; p. 368 (2002-bottom): © David Gee/Alamy Stock Photo; p. 368 (2004): © 2015 Google, Inc., used with permission. Gmail and the Gmail logo are registered trademarks of Google Inc.; p. 369 (2006-top): © 2015 Myspace LLC. Used with permission; p. 369 (2006-bottom): © 2015 Google, Inc., used with permission. YouTube and the YouTube logo are registered trademarks of Google Inc.; p. 369 (2007): © Shaun Curry/AFP/Getty Images; p. 369 (2008): Intel Atom is a trademark of Intel Corporation in the U.S. and/or other countries. Used with permission; p. 369 (2009): © 2015 Vodafone Group; p. 369 (2010): © Daniel Acker/Bloomberg via Getty Images; p. 370 (2011): The Android robot is reproduced or modified from work created and shared by Google and used according to terms described in the Creative Commons 3.0 Attribution License.; p. 370 (2012): © 2015 Twitter, Inc. Used with permission.

1G (first-generation mobile telecommunications): Started in 1980s using analog signals to provide voice transmission service.

2G (second-generation mobile telecommunications): Started in the 1990s using digital radio signals.

3D printer: A printer that creates objects by adding layers of material onto one another. Also known as additive manufacturing.

3D scanner: Scanner that uses lasers, cameras, or robotic arms to record the shape of an object.

3G (third-generation mobile telecommunications): Started in the 2000s and provided services capable of effective connectivity to the Internet, marking the beginning of smartphones.

3GLs (third-generation languages): High-level procedural language. *See also* Procedural language.

4G (fourth-generation mobile telecommunications): Replacing 3G networks in some areas with providers using WiMax and LTE connections to provide faster transmission speeds.

4GLs (fourth-generation languages): Very high level or problem-oriented languages. *See also* Task-oriented language.

5GLs (fifth-generation languages): *See* Fifth-generation language.

802.11: *See* Wi-Fi (wireless fidelity).

a

AC adapter: Notebook computers use AC adapters that are typically outside the system unit. They plug into a standard wall outlet, convert AC to DC, provide power to drive the system components, and can recharge batteries.

Access: Refers to the responsibility of those who have data to control who is able to use that data.

Access speed: Measures the amount of time required by the storage device to retrieve data and programs.

Accounting: The organizational department that records all financial activity from billing customers to paying employees.

Accounts payable: The activity that shows the money a company owes to its suppliers for the materials and services it has received.

Accounts receivable: The activity that shows what money has been received or is owed by customers.

Accuracy: Relates to the responsibility of those who collect data to ensure that the data is correct.

Active display area: The diagonal length of a monitor's viewing area.

Activity tracker: A wearable computer that typically monitors daily exercise and sleep patterns.

Additive manufacturing: *See* 3D printer.

Address: Located in the header of an e-mail message; the e-mail address of the persons sending, receiving, and, optionally, anyone else who is to receive copies.

Advanced Research Project Agency Network (ARPANET): A national computer network from which the Internet developed.

Agile development: A development methodology that starts by getting core functionality of a program working, then expands on it until the customer is satisfied with the results.

AJAX: An advanced use of JavaScript found on many interactive sites. This technology is used to create interactive websites that respond quickly like traditional desktop application software.

All-in-one: A desktop computer that has the monitor and system unit housed together in the same case (e.g., Apple's iMac).

Analog: Continuous signals that vary to represent different tones, pitches, and volume.

Analog signals: Signals that represent a range of frequencies, such as the human voice. They are a continuous electronic wave signal as opposed to a digital signal that is either on or off.

Android: Mobile operating system originally developed by Android Inc. and later purchased by Google.

Antispyware: *See* Spy removal programs.

Antivirus program: A utility program that guards a computer system from viruses or other damaging programs.

App: *See* Application software.

App store: A website that provides access to specific mobile apps that can be downloaded either for a nominal fee or free of charge.

Applets: Web pages contain links to programs called applets, which are written in a programming language called Java. These programs are used to add interest to a website by presenting animation, displaying graphics, providing interactive games, and so forth.

Application generation subsystem: Provides tools to create data entry forms and specialized programming languages that interface or work with common languages, such as C or Visual Basic.

Application generator: Also called program coder; provides modules of prewritten code to accomplish various tasks, such as calculation of overtime pay.

Application software: Also referred to as apps. Software that can perform useful work, such as word processing, cost estimating, or accounting tasks. The user primarily interacts with application software.

Arithmetic-logic unit (ALU): The part of the CPU that performs arithmetic and logical operations.

Arithmetic operation: Fundamental math operations: addition, subtraction, multiplication, and division.

Artificial intelligence (AI): A field of computer science that attempts to develop computer systems that can mimic or simulate human thought processes and actions.

Artificial reality: *See* Virtual reality.

ASCII (American Standard Code for Information Interchange): Binary coding scheme widely used on all computers, including personal computers. Eight bits form each byte, and each byte represents one character.

Aspect ratio: The width of a monitor divided by its height. Common aspect ratios for monitors are 4:3 (standard) and 16:9 (wide screen).

Assembly language: A step up from machine language, using names instead of numbers. These languages use abbreviations or mnemonics, such as ADD, that are automatically converted to the appropriate sequence of 1s and 0s.

Asymmetric digital subscriber line (ADSL): One of the most widely used types of telephone high-speed connections (DSL).

Attachment: A file, such as a document or worksheet, that is attached to an e-mail message.

Attribute: A data field represents an attribute (description or characteristic) of some entity (person, place, thing, or object). For example, an employee is an entity with many attributes, including his or her last name, address, phone, etc.

Automated design tool: Software package that evaluates hardware and software alternatives according to requirements given by the systems analyst. Also called computer-aided software engineering (CASE) tools.

b

Backbone: *See* Bus.

Background: Other programs running simultaneously with the program being used in an operating system. *See also* Foreground.

Backup: A Windows utility program. *See* Backup program.

Backup program: A utility program that helps protect you from the effects of a disk failure by making a copy of selected or all files that have been saved onto a disk.

Balance sheet: Lists the overall financial condition of an organization.

Bandwidth: Bandwidth determines how much information can be transmitted at one time. It is a measurement of the communication channel's capacity. There are three bandwidths: voice band, medium band, and broadband.

Bar code: Code consisting of vertical zebra-striped marks printed on product containers, read with a bar code reader.

Bar code reader: Photoelectric scanner that reads bar codes for processing.

Bar code scanner: *See* Bar code reader.

Base station: *See* Wireless access point.

Baseband: Bandwidth used to connect individual computers that are located close to one another. Though it supports high-speed transmission, it can only carry a single signal at a time.

Batch processing: Processing performed all at once on data that has been collected over time.

BD (Blu-ray disc): A type of high-definition disc with a capacity of 25 to 50 gigabytes.

Beta testing: Testing by a select group of potential users in the final stage of testing a program.

Big data: Term given to describe the ever-growing volume of data currently being collected.

Binary system: Numbering system in which all numbers consist of only two digits: 0 and 1.

Biometric scanning: Devices that check fingerprints or retinal scans.

BIOS (basic input/output system): Information including the specifics concerning the amount of RAM and the type of keyboard, mouse, and secondary storage devices connected to the system unit.

Bit (binary digit): Each 1 or 0 is a bit; short for binary digit.

Bitmap image: Graphic file in which an image is made up of thousands of dots (pixels).

BitTorrent: A peer-to-peer file-sharing protocol used for distributing large amounts of data over the Internet.

Blog: *See* Web log.

Bluetooth: A wireless technology that allows nearby devices to communicate without the connection of cables or telephone systems.

Booting: Starting or restarting your computer.

Botnet: A collection of zombie computers.

Broadband: Bandwidth that includes microwave, satellite, coaxial cable, and fiber-optic channels. It is used for very-high-speed computers.

Browser: Special Internet software connecting you to remote computers; opens and transfers files, displays text and images, and provides an uncomplicated interface to the Internet and web documents. Examples of browsers are Internet Explorer, Mozilla Firefox, and Google Chrome.

Browser cache: A collection of temporary Internet files that contain web page content and instructions for displaying this content.

Bus: All communication travels along a common connecting cable called a bus or a backbone. As information passes along the bus, it is examined by each device on the system board to see if the information is intended for that device. *See also* Bus line *and* Ethernet.

Bus line: Electronic data roadway, along which bits travel; connects the parts of the CPU to each other and links the CPU with other important hardware. The common connecting cable in a bus network.

Bus network: Each device is connected to a common cable called a bus or backbone, and all communications travel along this bus.

Bus width: The number of bits traveling simultaneously down a bus is the bus width.

Business suite: *See* Productivity suites.

Business-to-business (B2B): A type of electronic commerce that involves the sale of a product or service from one business to another. This is typically a manufacturer-supplier relationship.

Business-to-consumer (B2C): A type of electronic commerce that involves the sale of a product or service to the general public or end users.

Button: A special area you can click to make links that "navigate" through a presentation.

Byte: Unit consisting of eight bits. There are 256 possible bit combinations in a byte, and each byte represents one character.

Cable: Cords used to connect input and output devices to the system unit.

Cable modem: Type of modem that uses coaxial cable to create high-speed computer connections.

Cable service: Service provided by cable television companies using existing television cables.

Cache memory: Area of random-access memory (RAM) set aside to store the most frequently accessed information. Cache memory improves processing by acting as a temporary high-speed holding area between memory and the CPU, allowing the computer to detect which information in RAM is most frequently used.

Capacity: Capacity is how much data a particular storage medium can hold and is another characteristic of secondary storage.

Card reader: A device that interprets the encoded information contained on credit, debit, access, and identification cards.

Carpal tunnel syndrome: A repetitive strain injury consisting of damage to the nerves and tendons in the hands.

Cascading style sheets (CSS): Files inserted into an HTML document that control the appearance of web pages including layout, colors, and fonts.

CD: *See* Compact disc.

CD-R: Stands for CD-recordable. This optical disc can be written to only once. After that it can be read many times without deterioration but cannot be written on or erased. Used to create custom music CDs and to archive data.

CD-ROM (compact disc–read-only memory): CD format that allows data to be read but not recorded. Used to distribute large databases, references, and software application packages.

CD-RW (compact disc rewritable): A reusable, optical disc that is not permanently altered when data is recorded. Used to create and edit large multimedia presentations.

Cell: The space created by the intersection of a vertical column and a horizontal row within a worksheet in a program like Microsoft Excel. A cell can contain text or numeric entries.

Cell tower: Antennae that support cellular communication.

Cellular: Type of wireless connection that uses multiple antennae (cell towers) to send and receive data within relatively small geographic regions (cells).

Cellular service provider: Supports voice and data transmission to wireless devices.

Central processing unit (CPU): The part of the computer that holds data and program instructions for processing the data. The CPU consists of the control unit and the arithmetic-logic unit. In a personal computer, the CPU is on a single electronic component called a microprocessor chip.

Character: A single letter, number, or special character, such as a punctuation mark or $.

Character encoding standards: Assign unique sequence of bits to each character.

Child node: A node one level below the node being considered in a hierarchical database or network. *See also* Parent node.

Chip: A tiny circuit board etched on a small square of sand-like material called silicon. A chip is also called a silicon chip, semiconductor, or integrated circuit.

Chip carrier: The device onto which chips are mounted and plugged into the system board.

Chrome OS: An operating system designed by Google for netbook computers and Internet connectivity through cloud computing.

Circles: A service offered through Google Plus, for grouping individuals according to common interests or other criteria.

Clarity: Indicated by the resolution, or number of pixels, on a monitor. The greater the resolution, the better the clarity.

Class: In an object-oriented database, classes are similar objects grouped together.

Client: A node that requests and uses resources available from other nodes. Typically, a client is a user's personal computer.

Client-based e-mail system: A system that requires a special program known as an e-mail client to be installed on your computer.

Client/server network: Network in which one powerful computer coordinates and supplies services to all other nodes on the network. Server nodes coordinate and supply specialized services, and client nodes request the services.

Clock speed: Also called clock rate. It is measured in gigahertz, or billions of beats per second. The faster the clock speed, the faster the computer can process information and execute instructions.

Cloud computing: Data stored at a server on the Internet and available anywhere the Internet can be accessed.

Cloud printer: A printer connected to the Internet that provides printing services to others on the Internet.

Cloud storage: Also known as online storage. An Internet-based space for storing data and files.

Cloud suite: Suite stored at a server on the Internet and available anywhere from the Internet.

Coaxial cable: High-frequency transmission cable that replaces the multiple wires of telephone lines with a single solid-copper core. It is used to deliver television signals as well as to connect computers in a network.

Code: Writing a program using the appropriate computer language.

Code review: *See* Desk checking.

Coding: Actual writing of a computer program, using a programming language.

Cold boot: Starting the computer after it has been turned off.

Combination key: Keys such as the Ctrl key that perform an action when held down in combination with another key.

Commercial database: Enormous database an organization develops to cover certain particular subjects. Access to this type of database is usually offered for a fee or subscription. Also known as data bank and informational utility.

Common data item: In a relational database, all related tables must have a common data item or key field.

Communication channel: The actual connecting medium that carries the message between sending and receiving devices. This medium can be a physical wire, cable, or wireless connection.

Communication device: Computer systems that communicate with other computer systems using modems. For example, it modifies computer output into a form that can be transmitted across standard telephone lines.

Communication system: Electronic system that transmits data over communication lines from one location to another.

Compact disc (CD): Widely used optical disc format. It holds 650 MB (megabytes) to 1 GB (gigabyte) of data on one side of the CD.

Compact disc–read-only memory: *See* CD-ROM.

Compact disc rewritable: *See* CD-RW.

Company database: Also called shared database. Stored on a mainframe, users throughout the company have access to the database through their personal computers linked by a network.

Compiler: Software that converts the programmer's procedural language program (source code) into machine language (object code). This object code can then be saved and run later.

Computer-aided design/computer-aided manufacturing (CAD/CAM) system: Knowledge work systems that run programs to integrate the design and manufacturing activities. CAD/CAM is widely used in manufacturing automobiles.

Computer-aided software engineering (CASE) tool: A type of software development tool that helps provide some automation and assistance in program design, coding, and testing. *See also* Automated design tool.

Computer crime: *See* Cybercrime.

Computer ethics: Guidelines for the morally acceptable use of computers in our society.

Computer Fraud and Abuse Act: Law allowing prosecution of unauthorized access to computers and databases.

Computer monitoring software: The most invasive and dangerous type of spyware. These programs record every activity made on your computer, including credit card numbers, bank account numbers, and e-mail messages.

Computer network: Communications system connecting two or more computers and their peripheral devices to exchange information and share resources.

Computer support specialist: Specialists include technical writers, computer trainers, computer technicians, and help-desk specialists who provide technical support to customers and other users.

Computer technician: Specialist who installs hardware and software and troubleshoots problems for users.

Connectivity: Capability of the personal computer to use information from the world beyond one's desk. Data and information can be sent over telephone or cable lines and through the air so that computers can talk to each other and share information.

Consumer-to-consumer (C2C): A type of electronic commerce that involves individuals selling to individuals.

Contextual tab: A type of tab found in Microsoft Word that appears only when needed and anticipates the next operations to be performed by the user.

Contrast ratio: Indicates a monitor's ability to display colors. It compares the light intensity of the brightest white to the darkest black.

Control unit: Section of the CPU that tells the rest of the computer how to carry out program instructions.

Conversion: Also known as systems implementation; four approaches to conversion: direct, parallel, pilot, and phased. *See also* Systems implementation.

Cookies: Small data files that are deposited on your hard disk from websites you have visited.

Coprocessor: Specialized processing chip designed to improve specific computer operations, such as the graphics coprocessor.

Copyright: A legal concept that gives content creators the right to control use and distribution of their work.

Cordless mouse: A battery-powered mouse that typically uses radio waves or infrared light waves to communicate with the system unit. Also known as wireless mouse.

Cortana: A digital assistant that accepts commands through text or speech. Introduced in 2015 as a part of Windows 10.

Cracker: One who gains unauthorized access to a computer system for malicious purposes.

Curved monitor: Uses similar technology as flat panel monitors except it has a concave screen that provides better viewing angles near the edges of the screen.

Cyberbullying: The use of the Internet, a cell phone, or other device to deliver content intended to hurt or embarrass another person.

Cybercash: *See* Digital cash.

Cybercrime: Any criminal offense that involves a computer and a network. Criminals may be employees, outside users, hackers and crackers, or organized crime members.

Cylinder: Hard disks store and organize files using tracks, sectors, and cylinders. A cylinder runs through each track of a stack of platters. Cylinders differentiate files stored on the same track and sector of different platters.

Data: Raw, unprocessed facts that are input to a computer system that will give compiled information when the computer processes those facts. Data is also defined as facts or observations about people, places, things, and events.

Data administration subsystem: Helps manage the overall database, including maintaining security, providing disaster recovery support, and monitoring the overall performance of database operations.

Data bank: *See* Commercial database.

Data cube: A multidimensional data model. *See also* Multidimensional database.

Data definition subsystem: This system defines the logical structure of the database by using a data dictionary.

Data dictionary: Dictionary containing a description of the structure of data in a database.

Data flow diagram: Diagram showing data or information flow within an information system.

Data integrity: Database characteristics relating to the consistency and accuracy of data.

Data maintenance: Maintaining data includes adding new data, deleting old data, and editing existing data.

Data manipulation subsystem: Provides tools to maintain and analyze data.

Data mining: Technique of searching data warehouses for related information and patterns.

Data processing system (DPS): Transaction processing system that keeps track of routine operations and records these events in a database. Also called transaction processing system (TPS).

Data redundancy: A common database problem in which data is duplicated and stored in different files.

Data security: Protection of software and data from unauthorized tampering or damage.

Data warehouse: Data collected from a variety of internal and external databases and stored in a database called a data warehouse. Data mining is then used to search these databases.

Data worker: Person involved with the distribution and communication of information, such as administrative assistants and clerks.

Database: A collection of related information, like employee names, addresses, and phone numbers. It is organized so that a computer program can quickly select the desired pieces of information and display them for you.

Database administrator (DBA): Uses database management software to determine the most efficient way to organize and access data.

Database file: File containing highly structured and organized data created by database management programs.

Database management system (DBMS): To organize, manage, and retrieve data. DBMS programs have five subsystems: DBMS engine, data definition, data manipulation, applications generation, and data administration. An example of a database management system is Microsoft Access. *See also* Database manager.

Database manager: Software package used to set up, or structure, a database such as an inventory list of supplies. It also provides tools to edit, enter, and retrieve data from the database.

Database model: Defines rules and standards for all data in a database. There are five database models: hierarchical, network, relational, multidimensional, and object-oriented. For example, Access uses the relational data model.

DBMS engine: Provides a bridge between the logical view of data and the physical view of data.

Debugging: Programmer's word for testing and then eliminating errors in a program. Programming errors are of two types: syntax and logic errors.

Decision model: The decision model gives the decision support system its analytical capabilities. There are three types of models included in the decision model: tactical, operational, and strategic.

Decision support system (DSS): Flexible analysis tool that helps managers make decisions about unstructured problems, such as effects of events and trends outside the organization.

Demand report: A demand report is produced on request. An example is a report on the numbers and types of jobs held by women and minorities done at the request of the government.

Demodulation: Process performed by a modem in converting analog signals to digital signals.

Denial of service (DoS) attack: A variant virus in which websites are overwhelmed with data and users are unable to access the website. Unlike a worm that self-replicates, a DoS attack floods a computer or network with requests for information and data.

Density: Refers to how tightly the bits (electromagnetic charges) can be packed next to one another on a disk.

Desk checking: Process of checking out a computer program by studying a printout of the program line by line, looking for syntax and logic errors.

Desktop: (1) The screen that is displayed on the monitor when the computer starts up. All items and icons on the screen are considered to be on your desktop and are used to interact with the computer. (2) A system unit that typically contains the system's electronic components and selected secondary storage devices. Input and output devices, such as the mouse, keyboard, and monitor, are located outside the system unit.

Desktop computer: Computer small enough to fit on top of or along the side of a desk and yet too big to carry around.

Desktop operating system: *See* Stand-alone operating system.

Desktop publisher: One who creates and formats publication-ready material.

Desktop publishing program: Program that allows you to mix text and graphics to create publications of professional quality.

Device driver: Every device that is connected to the computer has a special program associated with it called a device driver that allows communication between the operating system and the device.

Diagnostic program: *See* Troubleshooting program.

Dial-up service: Antiquated method of connecting to the Internet using telephones and telephone modems, which has been replaced with higher-speed connection services.

Dialog box: Provides additional information and requests user input.

Dictionary attack: Uses software to try thousands of common words sequentially in an attempt to gain unauthorized access to a user's account.

Digital: Computers are digital machines because they can only understand 1s and 0s. For example, a digital watch states the exact time on the face, whereas an analog watch has the second hand moving in constant motion as it tells the time.

Digital camera: Similar to a traditional camera except that images are recorded digitally in the camera's memory rather than on film.

Digital cash: Currency for Internet purchases. Buyers purchase digital cash from a third party (a bank that specializes in electronic currency) by transferring funds from their banks.

Digital Millennium Copyright Act: Law that makes it legal for a program owner to make only his or her own backup copies of a software program. However, it is illegal for those copies to be resold or given away.

Digital projector: A type of monitor that projects images from a traditional monitor onto a screen or wall.

Digital rights management (DRM): Encompasses various technologies that control access to electronic media and files.

Digital signal: Computers can only understand digital signals. Before processing can occur within the system unit, a conversion must occur from what we understand (analog) to what the system unit can electronically process (digital). *See also* Analog signals.

Digital subscriber line (DSL): Provides high-speed connection using existing telephone lines.

Digital subscriber line (DSL) service: Service provided by telephone companies using existing telephone lines to provide high-speed connections.

Digital versatile disc (DVD): A type of optical disc similar to CD-ROMs except that more data can be packed into the same amount of space. *See also* DVD (digital versatile disc).

Digital video disc: *See* DVD (digital versatile disc).

Digital wallet: Information to make online shopping more convenient. A digital wallet typically resides on a user's smartphone and contains an individual's mailing address, credit card, and other information typically required to make an online purchase.

Digital whiteboard: A specialized device with a large display connected to a computer or projector.

DIMM (dual in-line memory module): An expansion module used to add memory to the system board.

Direct approach: Approach for systems implementation whereby the old system is simply abandoned for the new system.

Directory server: A specialized server that manages resources such as user accounts for an entire network.

Disaster recovery plan: Plan used by large organizations describing ways to continue operations following a disaster until normal computer operations can be restored.

Disaster recovery specialist: Worker responsible for recovering systems and data after a disaster strikes an organization.

Disk caching: Method of improving hard-disk performance by anticipating data needs. Frequently used data is read from the hard disk into memory (cache). When needed, data is then accessed directly from memory, which has a much faster transfer rate than from the hard disk. Increases performance by as much as 30 percent.

Disk Cleanup: A Windows troubleshooting utility that eliminates nonessential files.

Display: Output device like a television screen that displays data processed by the computer.

Display screen: *See* Display.

Distributed database: Database that can be made accessible through a variety of communications networks, which allow portions of the database to be located in different places.

Document: Any kind of text material.

Document file: File created by a word processor to save documents such as letters, research papers, and memos.

Document scanner: Similar to a flatbed scanner except that it can quickly scan multipage documents. It automatically feeds one page of a document at a time through a scanning surface.

Documentation: Written descriptions and procedures about a program and how to use it. *See also* Program documentation.

Domain name: The second part of the URL; it is the name of the server where the resource is located. For example, www.mtv.com.

Domain name server (DNS): Internet addressing method that assigns names and numbers to people and computers. Because the numeric IP addresses are difficult to remember, the DNS server was developed to automatically convert text-based addresses to numeric IP addresses.

Dot pitch: Distance between each pixel. The lower the dot pitch, the shorter the distance between pixels, and the higher the clarity of images produced.

Dots per inch (dpi): Printer resolution is measured in dpi. The higher the dpi, the better the quality of images produced.

Downlink: To receive data from a satellite.

Downloading: Process of transferring information from a remote computer to the computer one is using.

Drawing program: Program used to help create artwork for publications. *See also* Illustration program.

Driver: *See* Device driver.

Drones: Unmanned aerial vehicles (UAV) that act as an output device, sending back video and sound to the user.

DS3: Provides support for very high speed, all-digital transmission for large corporations.

DSL: *See* Digital subscriber line.

Duplex printing: Allows automatic printing on both sides of a sheet of paper.

DVD (digital versatile disc or **digital video disc):** Similar to CD-ROMs except that more data can be packed into the same amount of space. DVD drives can store a typical capacity of 4.7 GB on one side.

DVI (Digital Video Interface) port: A type of port that provides a connection to a digital monitor.

e

E-book: *See* E-book reader.

E-book reader: Handheld, book-sized device that displays text and graphics. Using content downloaded from the web or special cartridges, these devices are used to read newspapers, magazines, and books.

E-commerce: Buying and selling goods over the Internet.

E-ink: A black-and-white output from some e-book readers producing images that reflect light like ordinary paper.

E-learning: A web application that allows one to take educational courses online.

E-mail: Allows you to communicate with anyone in the world who has an Internet address or e-mail account with a system connected to the Internet. You can include a text message, graphics, photos, and file attachments.

E-mail client: A special program that communicates with the e-mail service provider and must be installed on the computer first.

E-reader: Dedicated mobile devices for storing and displaying e-books and other electronic media including electronic newspapers and magazines.

EBCDIC (Extended Binary Coded Decimal Interchange Code): Binary coding scheme that is a standard for minicomputers and mainframe computers.

Economic feasibility: Comparing the costs of a new system to the benefits it promises.

Electronic books: Traditional printed books in electronic format.

Electronic commerce (e-commerce): Buying and selling goods over the Internet.

Electronic mail: Transmission of electronic messages over the Internet. Also known as e-mail.

Electronic profile: Using publicly and privately available databases, information resellers create electronic profiles, which are highly detailed and personalized descriptions of individuals.

Embedded operating system: An operating system that is completely stored within the ROM (read-only memory) of the device that it is in; used for handheld computers and smaller devices like PDAs. Also known as a real- time operating system (RTOS).

Employee-monitoring software: Programs that record virtually every activity on a computer system.

Encryption: Coding information so that only the user can read or otherwise use it.

Encryption key: A number used to gain access to encrypted information.

End user: Person who uses personal computers or has access to larger computers.

Enterprise storage system: Using mass storage devices, a strategy designed for organizations to promote efficient and safe use of data across the networks within their organizations.

Entity: In an object-oriented database, a person, place, thing, or event that is to be described.

Ergonomics: The study of human factors related to things people use.

Ethernet: Otherwise known as Ethernet bus or Ethernet LAN. The Ethernet bus is the pathway or arterial to which all nodes (PCs, file servers, print servers, web servers, etc.) are connected. All of this is connected to a local area network (LAN) or a wide area network (WAN). *See also* Bus network.

Ethernet cable: Twisted-pair cable commonly used in networks and to connect a variety of components to the system unit.

Ethernet port: A high-speed networking port that allows multiple computers to be connected for sharing files or for high-speed Internet access.

Ethics: Standards of moral conduct.

Exception report: Report that calls attention to unusual events.

Executive information system (EIS): Sophisticated software that can draw together data from an organization's databases in meaningful patterns and highly summarized forms.

Executive support system (ESS): *See* Executive information system.

Expansion bus: Connects the CPU to slots on the system board. There are different types of expansion buses such as industry standard architecture (ISA), peripheral component interconnect (PCI), accelerated graphics port (AGP), universal serial bus (USB), and FireWire buses. *See also* System bus.

Expansion card: Optional device that plugs into a slot inside the system unit to expand the computer's abilities. Ports on the system board allow cables to be connected from the expansion board to devices outside the system unit.

Expansion slots: Openings on a system board. Users can insert optional devices, known as expansion cards, into these slots, allowing users to expand their systems. *See also* Expansion card.

Expert system: Computer program that provides advice to decision makers who would otherwise rely on human experts. It's a type of artificial intelligence that uses a database to provide assistance to users.

External data: Data gathered from outside an organization. Examples are data provided by market research firms.

External hard drive: Uses the same technology as an internal hard disk but is used primarily to complement an internal hard disk by providing additional storage. It is typically connected to a USB or FireWire port on the system unit and is easily removed.

External Serial Advanced Technology Attachment (eSATA) port: A port that provides high speed connections for external hard-disk drives, optical discs, and other large secondary storage devices.

Extranet: Private network that connects more than one organization.

Facebook: One of the best-known social networking sites.

Facebook groups: Communities of individuals who share common interest on Facebook.

Facebook Pages: Often used by businesses and public figures to promote ideas, products, and services.

Facebook Profile: An individual's Facebook page, which may include photos, lists of personal interests, contact information, and other personal information.

Family Educational Rights and Privacy Act (FERPA): A federal law that restricts disclosure of educational records.

Fiber-optic cable: Special transmission cable made of glass tubes that are immune to electronic interference. Data is transmitted through fiber-optic cables in the form of pulses of light.

Fiber-optic service (FiOS): An Internet connection service that is not yet widely available. Current providers of FiOS include Google and Verizon with speeds faster than cable or DSL connections.

Field: Each column of information within a record is called a field. A field contains related information on a specific item like employee names within a company department.

Fifth-generation language (5GL): Computer language that incorporates the concept of artificial intelligence to allow direct human communication.

File: A collection of related records that can store data and programs. For example, the payroll file would include payroll information (records) for all of the employees (entities).

File compression: Process of reducing the storage requirements for a file.

File compression program: Utility program that reduces the size of files so they require less storage on the computer and can be sent more efficiently over the Internet. Examples of such programs are WinZip and Wizard.

File decompression: Process of expanding a compressed file.

File History: A utility program included with many versions of Windows that makes a copy of all files or selected files that have been saved onto a disk.

File server: Dedicated computer with large storage capacity providing users access to shared folders or fast storage and retrieval of information used in that business.

File transfer protocol (FTP): Internet service for uploading and downloading files.

Filter: (1) A filter blocks access to selected websites. (2) A filter will locate or display records from a table that fit a set of conditions or criteria when using programs like Excel.

Firewall: Security hardware and software. All communications into and out of an organization pass through a special security computer, called a proxy server, to protect all systems against external threats.

FireWire bus: Operates much like USB buses on the system board but at higher speeds.

FireWire port: Used to connect high-speed printers, and even video cameras, to system unit.

First-party cookie: A cookie that is generated and then read only by the website you are currently visiting.

Flash drive: *See* USB drive.

Flash memory: RAM chips that retain data even when power is disrupted. Flash memory is an example of solid-state storage and is typically used to store digitized images and record MP3 files.

Flash memory card: A solid-state storage device widely used in notebook computers. Flash memory also is used in a variety of specialized input devices to capture and transfer data to desktop computers.

Flat-panel monitor: Or liquid crystal display (LCD) monitor. These monitors are much thinner than CRTs and can be used for desktop systems as well.

Flatbed scanner: An input device similar to a copying machine.

Folder: A named area on a disk that is used to store related subfolders and files.

Foreground: The current program when multitasking or running multiple programs at once.

Fourth-generation language (4GL): Task-oriented language designed to solve a specific problem and requiring little special training on the part of the end user.

Fragmented: Storage technique that breaks up large files and stores the parts wherever space is available.

Freedom of Information Act of 1970: Law giving citizens the right to examine data about them in federal government files, except for information restricted for national security reasons.

Friend: An individual on a list of contacts for an instant messaging server.

g

Galleries: Feature of Microsoft Office 2007, 2010, and 2013 that simplifies the process of making selections from a list of alternatives by replacing dialog boxes with visual presentations of results.

Game controller: A device that provides input to computer games.

Gamepad: An input device designed to be held by two hands and provide a wide array of inputs including motion, turning, stopping, and firing.

Gaming laptop: A laptop with high-end graphics hardware and a very fast processor specifically designed to play computer games.

Gaming mice: A game controller that provides greater precision, faster response, programming buttons, and better ergonomics than a traditional mouse.

General ledger: Activity that produces income statements and balance sheets based on all transactions of a company.

General-purpose application: Application used for doing common tasks, such as browsers and word processors, spreadsheets, databases, management systems, and presentation graphics. Also known as productivity applications.

Generations (of programming languages): The five generations are machine languages, assembly languages, procedural languages, problem-oriented languages, and natural languages. *See also* Levels.

Gesture control: The ability to control operations with finger movements, such as swiping, sliding, and pinching.

Gestures: A feature of Mac OS 10.7 that allows the use of fingers to run programs and to control the content of a display screen.

Global positioning system (GPS): Devices that use location information to determine the geographic location of your car, for example.

Gloves: Interactive sensory equipment that collects data from your hand movements.

Google+: *See* Google Plus.

Google Cloud Print: A Google service that supports cloud printing.

Google Plus: A combination of some of Google's previously existing services with some new services, many of which are similar to Facebook's services.

GPU (graphics processing unit): *See* Graphics coprocessor.

Gramm-Leach-Bliley Act: A law that protects personal financial information.

Graphical user interface (GUI): Special screen that allows software commands to be issued through the use of graphic symbols (icons) or pull-down menus.

Graphics card: Device that provides high-quality 3D graphics and animation for games and simulations.

Graphics coprocessor: Designed to handle requirements related to displaying and manipulating 2D and 3D graphic images.

Grayscale: The most common black ink selection in which images are displayed using many shades of gray.

Grid chart: Chart that shows the relationship between input and output documents.

Group decision support system (GDSS): System used to support the collective work of a team addressing large problems.

Groups: In Microsoft Word, each tab is organized into groups that contain related items.

Guest operating system: Operating system that operates on virtual machines.

h

Hacker: Person who gains unauthorized access to a computer system for the fun and challenge of it.

Handwriting recognition software: Translates handwritten notes into a form that the system unit can process.

Hangouts: A service offered through Google Plus, for communicating with up to 10 people at a time.

Hard copy: Information presented on paper; also referred to as printer output.

Hard disk: Enclosed disk drive containing one or more metallic disks. Hard disks use magnetic charges to record data and have large storage capacities and fast retrieval times.

Hardware: Equipment that includes a keyboard, monitor, printer, the computer itself, and other devices that are controlled by software programming.

Head crash: When a read-write head makes contact with the hard disk's surface or particles on its surface, the disk surface becomes scratched and some or all data is destroyed.

Header: A typical e-mail has three elements: header, message, and signature. The header appears first and includes addresses, subject, and attachments.

Headgear: Interactive sensory equipment that collects data from embedded earphones and three-dimensional stereoscopic screens.

Headphones: Typically worn around the head providing audio output.

Headsets: Audio-output devices connected to a sound card in the system unit. The sound card is used to capture as well as play back recorded sound.

Health Insurance Portability and Accountability Act (HIPAA): A federal law that protects medical records.

Help: A feature in most application software providing options that typically include an index, a glossary, and a search feature to locate reference information about specific commands.

Hexadecimal system (hex): Uses 16 digits to represent binary numbers.

Hi def (high definition): The next generation of optical disc, with increased storage capacity. *See also* BD (Blu-ray disc).

Hierarchical database: Database in which fields or records are structured in nodes. Organized in the shape of a pyramid, and each node is linked directly to the nodes beneath it. Also called one-to-many relationship.

Hierarchical network: *See* Tree network.

High Definition Multimedia Interface (HDMI) port: Port that provides high-definition video and audio, making it possible to use a computer as a video jukebox or an HD video recorder.

Higher level: Programming languages that are closer to the language humans use.

History file: Created by the browser to store information on websites visited by your computer system.

Hits: The sites that a search engine returns after running a keyword search, ordered from most likely to least likely to contain the information requested.

Home network: LAN network for homes allowing different computers to share resources, including a common Internet connection.

Host: Also called a server or provider, is a large centralized computer.

Host operating system: Operating system that runs on the physical machine.

Hotspot: Wireless access points that provide Internet access and are often available in public places such as coffee shops, libraries, bookstores, colleges, and universities.

HTML: *See* Hypertext Markup Language.

HTML editor: *See* Web authoring program.

Hub: The center or central node for other nodes. This device can be a server or a connection point for cables from other nodes.

Human resources: The organizational department that focuses on the hiring, training, and promoting of people, as well as any number of human-centered activities within the organization.

Hyperlink: Connection or link to other documents or web pages that contain related information.

Hypertext Markup Language (HTML): Programming language that creates document files used to display web pages.

Hypertext transfer protocol secure (https): A widely used protocol for web traffic and to protect the transfer of sensitive information.

i

Icons: Graphic objects on the desktop used to represent programs and other files.

Identity theft: The illegal assumption of someone's identity for the purpose of economic gain.

IF-THEN-ELSE structure: Logical selection structure whereby one of two paths is followed according to IF, THEN, and ELSE statements in a program. *See also* Selection structure.

IFPS (interactive financial planning system): A 4GL language used for developing financial models.

Illusion of anonymity: The misconception that being selective about disclosing personal information on the Internet can prevent an invasion of personal privacy.

Illustration program: Also known as drawing programs; used to create digital illustrations and modify vector images and thus create line art, 3D models, and virtual reality.

Image editor: An application for modifying bitmap images.

Immersive experience: Allows the user to walk into a virtual reality room or view simulations on a virtual reality wall.

Incognito mode: A privacy mode available from the Google Chrome browser.

Income statement: A statement that shows a company's financial performance, income, expenses, and the difference between them for a specific time period.

Individual database: Collection of integrated records used mainly by just one person. Also called personal computer database.

Information: Data that has been processed by a computer system.

Information broker: *See* Information reseller.

Information reseller: Also known as information broker. It gathers personal data on people and sells it to direct marketers, fund-raisers, and others, usually for a fee.

Information system: Collection of hardware, software, people, data, and procedures that work together to provide information essential to running an organization.

Information systems manager: Oversees the work of programmers, computer specialists, systems analysts, and other computer professionals.

Information technology (IT): Computer and communication technologies, such as communication links to the Internet, that provide help and understanding to the end user.

Information utility: *See* Commercial database.

Information worker: Employee who creates, distributes, and communicates information.

Infrared: Uses infrared light waves to communicate over short distances. Sometimes referred to as line-of-sight communication because light waves can only travel in a straight line.

Inkjet printer: Printer that sprays small droplets of ink at high speed onto the surface of the paper, producing letter-quality images, and can print in color.

Input: Any data or instructions used by a computer.

Input device: Piece of equipment that translates data into a form a computer can process. The most common input devices are the keyboard and the mouse.

Instant messaging (IM): A program allowing communication and collaboration for direct, "live" connections over the Internet between two or more people.

Integrated circuit: *See* Silicon chip.

Interactive whiteboard: *See* Digital whiteboard.

Internal data: Data from within an organization consisting principally of transactions from the transaction processing system.

Internal hard disk: Storage device consisting of one or more metallic platters sealed inside a container. Internal hard disks are installed inside the system cabinet of a personal computer. It stores the operating system and major applications like Word.

Internet: A huge computer network available to everyone with a personal computer and a means to connect to it. It is the actual physical network made up of wires, cables, and satellites as opposed to the web, which is the multimedia interface to resources available on the Internet.

Internet of Things (IoT): Continuing development of the Internet that allows everyday objects embedded with electronic devices to send and receive data over the Internet.

Internet scam: Using the Internet, a fraudulent act or operation designed to trick individuals into spending their time and money for little or no return.

Internet security suite: Collection of utility programs designed to make using the Internet easier and safer.

Internet service provider (ISP): Provides access to the Internet.

Internet telephony: *See* Telephony.

Interpreter: Software that converts a procedural language one statement at a time into machine language just before the statement is executed. No object code is saved.

Intranet: Like the Internet, it typically provides e-mail, mailing lists, newsgroups, and FTP services, but it is accessible only to those within the organization. Organizations use intranets to provide information to their employees.

Intrusion detection system (IDS): Using sophisticated statistical techniques to analyze all incoming and outgoing network traffic, this system works with firewalls to protect an organization's network.

Inventory: Material or products that a company has in stock.

Inventory control system: A system that keeps records of the number of each kind of part or finished good in the warehouse.

iOS: Previously known as iPhone OS, mobile operating system developed for Apple's iPhone, iPod Touch, and iPad.

IP address (Internet Protocol address): The unique numeric address of a computer on the Internet that facilitates the delivery of e-mail.

IP telephony: *See* Telephony.

iPhone OS: *See* iOS.

IT security analyst: Person responsible for maintaining the security of a company's network, systems, and data. Employers look for candidates with a bachelor's or associate's degree in information systems or computer science and network experience.

j

JavaScript: A scripting language that adds basic interactivity to web pages.

Joystick: Popular input device for computer games. You control game actions by varying the pressure, speed, and direction of the joystick.

k

Key: Another term for encryption key.

Key field: The common field by which tables in a database are related to each other. This field uniquely identifies the record. For example, in university databases, a key field is the Social Security number. Also known as primary key.

Keyboard: Input device that looks like a typewriter keyboard but has additional keys.

Keystroke logger: Also known as computer monitoring software and sniffer programs. They can be loaded onto your computer without your knowledge.

Knowledge base: A system that uses a database containing specific facts, rules to relate these facts, and user input to formulate recommendations and decisions.

Knowledge-based systems: Programs duplicating human knowledge. A type of artificial intelligence that uses a database to provide assistance to users.

Knowledge work system (KWS): Specialized information system used to create information in a specific area of expertise.

Knowledge worker: Person involved in the creation of information, such as an engineer or a scientist.

l

Land: *See* Lands and pits.

Lands and pits: Flat and bumpy areas, respectively, that represent 1s and 0s on the optical disc surface to be read by a laser.

Language translator: Converts programming instructions into a machine language that can be processed by a computer.

Laptop: A small, portable system unit that contains electronic components, selected secondary storage devices, and input devices.

Laptop computer: Portable computer, also known as a notebook computer, weighing between 4 and 10 pounds.

Laptop keyboard: Almost all laptops have attached keyboards and screens.

Laser printer: Printer that creates dotlike images on a drum, using a laser beam light source.

Levels: Generations or levels of programming languages ranging from "low" to "high." *See also* Generations (of programming languages).

Light-emitting diode (LED): A technology for flat-panel monitors that have a more advanced backlighting technology. They produce better-quality images, are slimmer, and are more environmentally friendly as they require less power and use fewer toxic chemicals to manufacture. Most new monitors are LED.

Link: A connection to related information.

LinkedIn: The premier business-oriented social networking site.

Linux: Type of UNIX operating system initially developed by Linus Torvalds, it is one of the most popular and powerful alternatives to the Windows operating system.

Liquid crystal display (LCD): A technology used for flat-panel monitors.

Local area network (LAN): Network consisting of computers and other devices that are physically near each other, such as within the same building.

Location: For browsers to connect to resources, locations or addresses must be specified. Also known as uniform resource locators or URLs.

Logic error: Error that occurs when a programmer has used an incorrect calculation or left out a programming procedure.

Logic structure: Programming statements or structures called sequence, selection, or loop that control the logical sequence in which computer program instructions are executed.

Logical operation: Comparing two pieces of data to see whether one is equal to (=), less than (<), or greater than (>) the other.

Logical view: Focuses on the meaning and content of the data. End users and computer professionals are concerned with this view as opposed to the physical view, with which only specialized computer professionals are concerned.

Loop structure: Logic structure in which a process may be repeated as long as a certain condition remains true. This structure is called a "loop" because the program loops around or repeats again and again.

Low bandwidth: *See* Voiceband.

Lower level: Programming language closer to the language the computer itself uses. The computer understands the 0s and 1s that make up bits and bytes.

LTE (Long Term Evolution): A wireless standard, comparable to WiMax.

m

Mac OS: Operating system designed for Macintosh computers.

Mac OS X: Macintosh operating system featuring a user interface called Aqua.

Machine language: Language in which data is represented in 1s and 0s. Most languages have to be translated into machine language for the computer to process the data. Either a compiler or an interpreter performs this translation.

Magnetic card reader: A card reader that reads encoded information from a magnetic strip on the back of a card.

Magnetic-ink character recognition (MICR): Direct-entry scanning devices used in banks. This technology is used to automatically read the numbers on the bottom of checks.

Mainboard: *See* Motherboard or System board.

Mainframe computer: This computer can process several million program instructions per second. Sizable organizations rely on these room-size systems to handle large programs and a great deal of data.

Maintenance programmer: Programmer who maintains software by updating programs to protect them from errors, improve usability, standardize, and adjust to organizational changes.

Malware: Short for malicious software.

MAN: *See* Metropolitan area network.

Management information system (MIS): Computer-based information system that produces standardized reports in a summarized and structured form. Generally used to support middle managers.

Many-to-many relationship: In a network database, each child node may have more than one parent node and vice versa.

Marketing: The organizational department that plans, prices, promotes, sells, and distributes an organization's goods and services.

Mass storage: Refers to the tremendous amount of secondary storage required by large organizations.

Mass storage devices: Devices such as file servers, RAID systems, tape libraries, optical jukeboxes, and more.

MaxiCode: A code widely used by the United Parcel Service (UPS) and others to automate the process of routing packages, tracking in-transit packages, and locating lost packages.

Media: Media are the actual physical material that holds the data, such as a hard disk, which is one of the important characteristics of secondary storage. Singular of media is medium.

Medium: *See* Media.

Medium band: Bandwidth of special leased lines, used mainly with minicomputers and mainframe computers.

Megabits per second (Mbps): The transfer rate of millions of bits per second.

Memory: Memory is contained on chips connected to the system board and is a holding area for data instructions and information (processed data waiting to be output to secondary storage). RAM, ROM, and CMOS are three types of memory chips.

Menu: List of commands.

Menu bar: Menus are displayed in a menu bar at the top of the screen.

Mesh network: A topology requiring each node to have more than one connection to the other nodes so that if a path between two nodes is disrupted, data can be automatically rerouted around the failure using another path.

Message: The content portion of e-mail correspondence.

Methods: Instructions for retrieving or manipulating attribute values in an object-oriented database.

Metropolitan area network (MAN): These networks are used as links between office buildings in a city.

Microblog: Publishes short sentences that only take a few seconds to write, rather than long stories or posts like a traditional blog.

Microprocessor: The central processing unit (CPU) of a personal computer controls and manipulates data to produce information. The microprocessor is contained on a single integrated circuit chip and is the brains of the system. Also known as a processor.

Microwave: Communication using high-frequency radio waves that travel in straight lines through the air.

Middle management: Middle-level managers deal with control and planning. They implement the long-term goals of the organization.

MIDI: *See* Musical instrument digital interface.

Midrange computer: Refrigerator-sized machines falling in between personal computers and mainframes in processing speed and data-storing capacity. Medium-sized companies or departments of large companies use midrange computers.

Mini DisplayPort (MiniDP or mDP) port: A port that an audiovisual device typically uses to connect large monitors. These ports are used with many Apple Macintosh computers.

Mini notebook: A type of very portable laptop. They are lighter and thinner and have a longer battery life than other laptops. Also known as ultrabooks or ultraportables.

Mini tablets: A type of tablet with a smaller screen.

Mistaken identity: Occurs when the electronic profile of one person is switched with another.

Mobile apps (applications): Add-on features for a variety of mobile devices, including smartphones, netbooks, and tablets.

Mobile browser: Special browsers designed to run on portable devices.

Mobile operating system: Embedded operating system that controls a smartphone.

Mobile OS: *See* Mobile operating system.

Modem: Short for modulator-demodulator. It is a communication device that translates the electronic signals from a computer into electronic signals that can travel over telephone lines.

Modulation: Process of converting digital signals to analog signals.

Module: *See* Program module.

Monitor: *See* Display.

Motherboard: Also called a system board; the communications medium for the entire system.

Motion-sensing device: An input device that controls games with user movements.

Mouse: Device that typically is moved across the desktop and directs the cursor on the display screen.

Mouse pointer: Typically in the shape of an arrow.

Multicore processor: A new type of chip that provides two or more separate and independent CPUs.

Multidimensional database: Data can be viewed as a cube having three or more sides consisting of cells. Each side of the cube is considered a dimension of the data; thus, complex relationships between data can be represented and efficiently analyzed. Sometimes called a data cube and designed for analyzing large groups of records.

Multifunctional devices (MFD): Devices that typically combine the capabilities of a scanner, printer, fax, and copying machine.

Multimedia messaging service (MMS): Supports the sending of images, video, and sound using text messaging.

Multitasking: Operating system that allows a single user to run several application programs at the same time.

Multitouch screen: Can be touched with more than one finger, which allows for interactions such as rotating graphical objects on the screen with your hand or zooming in and out by pinching and stretching your fingers.

Musical instrument digital interface (MIDI): A standard that allows musical instruments to connect to the system using MIDI ports.

n

Natural language: A fifth-generation computer language (5GL) that allows a person to describe a problem and some constraints, and then request a solution using a common language like English.

Network: The arrangement in which various communications channels are connected through two or more computers. The largest network in the world is the Internet.

Network adapter card: Connects the system unit to a cable that connects to other devices on the network.

Network administrator: Also known as network manager. Computer professional who ensures that existing information and communication systems are operating effectively and that new ones are implemented as needed. Also responsible for meeting security and privacy requirements.

Network architecture: Describes how networks are configured and how the resources are shared.

Network attached storage (NAS): Similar to a file server except simpler and less expensive. Widely used for home and small business storage needs.

Network database: Database with a hierarchical arrangement of nodes, except that each child node may have more than one parent node. Also called many-to-many relationship.

Network gateway: Connection by which a local area network may be linked to other local area networks or to larger networks.

Network interface card (NIC): Also known as a network adapter card. Used to connect a computer to one or more computers forming a communication network whereby users can share data, programs, and hardware.

Network operating system (NOS): Interactive software between applications and computers coordinating and directing activities between computers on a network. This operating system is located on one of the connected computers' hard disks, making that system the network server.

Network server: This computer coordinates all communication between the other computers. Popular network operating systems include NetWare and Windows NT Server. *See also* Network operating system.

Node: Any device connected to a network. For example, a node is a computer, printer, or data storage device and each device has its own address on the network. Also, within hierarchical databases, fields or records are structured in nodes.

Notebook computer: *See* Laptop *and* Laptop computer.

O

Object: An element, such as a text box, that can be added to a workbook and can be selected, sized, and moved. For example, if a chart (object) in an Excel workbook file (source file) is linked to a Word document (destination file), the chart appears in the Word document. In this manner, the object contains both data and instructions to manipulate the data.

Object code: Machine language code converted by a compiler from source code. Object code can be saved and run later.

Object-oriented database: A more flexible type of database that stores data as well as instructions to manipulate data and is able to handle unstructured data such as photographs, audio, and video. Object-oriented databases organize data using objects, classes, entities, attributes, and methods.

Object-oriented programming (OOP): Methodology in which a program is organized into self-contained, reusable modules called objects. Each object contains both the data and processing operations necessary to perform a task.

Object-oriented software development: Software development approach that focuses less on the tasks and more on defining the relationships between previously defined procedures or objects.

Objectives: In programming, it is necessary to make clear the problems you are trying to solve to create a functional program.

Office automation system (OAS): System designed primarily to support data workers. It focuses on managing documents, communicating, and scheduling.

Office software suites: *See* Productivity suites.

Office suites: *See* Productivity suites.

One-to-many relationship: In a hierarchical database, each entry has one parent node, and a parent may have several child nodes.

Online: Being connected to the Internet is described as being online.

Online identity: The information that people voluntarily post about themselves online.

Online office suite: Office suite stored online and available anywhere the Internet can be accessed.

Online processing: *See* Real-time processing.

Online storage: Provides users with storage space that can be accessed from a website.

Open source: A free and openly distributed software program intended to allow users to improve upon and further develop the program.

Operating system (OS): Software that interacts between application software and the computer, handling such details as running programs, storing and processing data, and coordinating all computer resources, including attached peripheral devices. It is the most important program on the computer. Windows 7, Windows 8, and Mac OS X are examples of operating systems.

Operational feasibility: Making sure the design of a new system will be able to function within the existing framework of an organization.

Operational model: A decision model that helps lower-level managers accomplish the organization's day-to-day activities, such as evaluating and maintaining quality control.

Operators: Operators handle correcting operational errors in any programs. To do that, they need documentation, which lets them understand the program, thus enabling them to fix any errors.

Optical carrier (OC): Provides support for very high speed, all-digital transmission for large corporations.

Optical-character recognition (OCR): Scanning device that uses special preprinted characters, such as those printed on utility bills, that can be read by a light source and changed into machine-readable code.

Optical disc: Storage device that can hold over 17 gigabytes of data, which is the equivalent of several million typewritten pages. Lasers are used to record and read data on the disc. The three basic types of optical discs are compact discs (CDs), digital versatile or video discs (DVDs), and Blu-ray discs (BDs).

Optical disc drive: A disc is read by an optical disc drive using a laser that projects a tiny beam of light. The amount of reflected light determines whether the area represents a 1 or a 0.

Optical-mark recognition (OMR): Device that senses the presence or absence of a mark, such as a pencil mark. As an example, an OMR device is used to score multiple-choice tests.

Optical mouse: A type of mouse that emits and senses light to detect mouse movement.

Optical scanner: Device that identifies images or text on a page and automatically converts it to electronic signals that can be stored in a computer to copy or reproduce.

Optimize Drives: A Windows utility that optimizes disk performance by eliminating unnecessary fragments and rearranging files.

Organic light-emitting diode (OLED): Replaces LED monitor's backlighting technology with a thin layer of organic compound that produces light.

Organization chart: Chart showing the levels of management and formal lines of authority in an organization.

Organizational cloud storage: High-speed Internet connection to a dedicated remote organizational Internet drive site.

OS X Mavericks: Mac operating system announced in 2013 that provided better power management and enhanced workflow options for multiple monitor setups.

OS X Yosemite: Mac operating system released in 2014 that provided a new user interface similar to the iOS interface.

Output: Processed data or information.

Output device: Equipment that translates processed information from the central processing unit into a form that can be understood by humans. The most common output devices are monitors and printers.

P

Packet: Before a message is sent on the Internet, it is broken down into small parts called packets. Each packet is then sent separately over the Internet. At the receiving end, the packets are reassembled into the correct order.

Page layout program: *See* Desktop publishing program.

Parallel approach: Systems implementation in which old and new systems are operated side by side until the new one has shown it is reliable.

Parallel processing: Used by supercomputers to run large and complex programs.

Parent node: Node one level above the node being considered in a hierarchical database or network. Each entry has one parent node, although a parent may have several child nodes. Also called one-to-many relationship.

Password: Special sequence of numbers or letters that limits access to information, such as electronic mail.

Password managers: Programs that help users create, use, and recall strong passwords.

Patches: Programming modifications or corrections.

Payroll: Activity concerned with calculating employee paychecks.

PC: *See* Personal computer.

PCI Express (PCIe): New type of bus that is 30 times faster than PCI bus.

Peer-to-peer (P2P) network: Network in which nodes can act as both servers and clients. For example, one personal computer can obtain files located on another personal computer and also can provide files to other personal computers.

People: End users who use computers to make themselves more productive.

Periodic report: Reports for a specific time period as to the health of the company or a particular department of the company.

Personal area network (PAN): A type of wireless network that works within a very small area—your immediate surroundings.

Personal computer: Small, low-cost computer designed for individual users. These include desktop computers, laptops, and mobile devices.

Personal computer database: *See* Individual database.

Personal laser printer: Inexpensive laser printer widely used by single users to produce black-and-white documents.

Phased approach: Systems implementation whereby a new system is implemented gradually over a period of time.

Phishing: An attempt to trick Internet users into thinking a fake but official-looking website or e-mail is legitimate.

Photo editor: *See* Image editor.

Physical security: Activity concerned with protecting hardware from possible human and natural disasters.

Physical view: This focuses on the actual format and location of the data. *See also* Logical view.

Picture element: *See* Pixel.

Pilot approach: Systems implementation in which a new system is tried out in only one part of the organization. Later it is implemented throughout the rest of the organization.

Pit: *See* Lands and pits.

Pixel (picture element): Smallest unit on the screen that can be turned on and off or made different shades. Pixels are individual dots that form images on a monitor. The greater the resolution, the more pixels and the better the clarity.

Pixel pitch: The distance between each pixel on a monitor.

Plagiarism: Representation of some other person's work and ideas as your own without giving credit to the original source.

Plagiarist: Someone who engages in plagiarism.

Platform: The operating system. Application programs are designed to run with a specific platform. *See also* Operating system.

Platform scanner: Handheld direct-entry device used to read special characters on price tags. Also known as wand reader.

Platter: Rigid metallic disk; multiple platters are stacked one on top of another within a hard-disk drive.

Plotter: Special-purpose output device for producing bar charts, maps, architectural drawings, and three-dimensional illustrations.

Plug and Play: Set of hardware and software standards developed to create operating systems, processing units, expansion cards, and other devices that are able to configure themselves. When the computer starts up, it will search for the Plug and Play device and automatically configure it to the system.

Plug-in: Program that is automatically loaded and operates as part of a browser.

Podcast: An Internet-based medium for delivering music and movie files from the Internet to a computer.

Pointer: For a monitor, a pointer is typically displayed as an arrow and controlled by a mouse. For a database, a pointer is a connection between a parent node and a child node in a hierarchical database.

Pointers: Within a network database, pointers are additional connections between parent nodes and child nodes. Thus, a node may be reached through more than one path and can be traced down through different branches.

Pointing device: A device that provides an intuitive interface with the system unit by accepting pointing gestures and converting them into machine-readable input.

Port: Connecting socket on the outside of the system unit. Used to connect input and output devices to the system unit.

Portable language: Language that can be run on more than one type of computer.

Portable scanner: A handheld device that slides across an image to be scanned, making direct contact.

Power supply unit: Desktop computers have a power supply unit located within the system unit that plugs into a standard wall outlet, converting AC to DC, which becomes the power to drive all of the system unit components.

Preliminary investigation: First phase of the systems life cycle. It involves defining the problem, suggesting alternative systems, and preparing a short report.

Presentation file: A file created by presentation graphics programs to save presentation materials. For example, a file might contain audience handouts, speaker notes, and electronic slides.

Presentation graphics: Graphics used to combine a variety of visual objects to create attractive and interesting presentations.

Primary key: *See* Key field.

Primary storage: Holds data and program instructions for processing data. It also holds processed information before it is output. *See also* Memory.

Printer: Device that produces printed paper output.

Privacy: Computer ethics issue concerning the collection and use of data about individuals.

Privacy mode: A browser feature that eliminates history files and blocks most cookies.

Private Browsing: A privacy mode provided by Safari. *See also* Privacy mode.

Procedural language: Programming language designed to focus on procedures and how a program will accomplish a specific task. Also known as 3GL or third-generation language.

Procedures: Rules or guidelines to follow when using hardware, software, and data.

Processing rights: Refers to which people have access to what kind of data.

Processor: *See* Central processing unit.

Production: The organizational department that actually creates finished goods and services using raw materials and personnel.

Productivity suites: Also known as office suites; contain professional-grade application programs, including word processing, spreadsheets, and more. A good example is Microsoft Office.

Program: Instructions for the computer to follow to process data. *See also* Software.

Program analysis: *See* Program specification.

Program coder: *See* Application generator.

Program definition: *See* Program specification.

Program design: Creating a solution using programming techniques, such as top-down program design, pseudocode, flowcharts, logic structures, object-oriented programming, and CASE tools.

Program documentation: Written description of the purpose and process of a program. Documentation is written within the program itself and in printed documents. Programmers will find themselves frustrated without adequate documentation, especially when it comes time to update or modify the program.

Program flowchart: Flowchart graphically presents a detailed sequence of steps needed to solve a programming problem.

Program maintenance: Activity of updating software to correct errors, improve usability, standardize, and adjust to organizational changes.

Program module: Each module is made up of logically related program statements. The program must pass in sequence from one module to the next until the computer has processed all modules.

Program specification: Programming step in which objectives, output, input, and processing requirements are determined.

Programmer: Computer professional who creates new software or revises existing software.

Programming: A program is a list of instructions a computer will follow to process data. Programming, also known as software development, is a six-step procedure for creating that list of instructions. The six steps are program specification, program design, program code (or coding), program test, program documentation, and program maintenance.

Programming language: A collection of symbols, words, and phrases that instruct a computer to perform a specific task.

Project manager: Software that enables users to plan, schedule, and control the people, resources, and costs needed to complete a project on time.

Property: Computer ethics issue relating to who owns data and rights to software.

Protocol: Rules for exchanging data between computers. The protocol http:// is the most common.

Prototyping: Building a model or prototype that can be modified before the actual system is installed.

Proxy server: Computer that acts as a gateway or checkpoint in an organization's firewall. *See also* Firewall.

Pseudocode: An outline of the logic of the program to be written. It is the steps or the summary of the program before you actually write the program for the computer. Consequently, you can see beforehand what the program is to accomplish.

Purchase order: A form that shows the name of the company supplying the material or service and what is being purchased.

Purchasing: Buying of raw materials and services.

q

Query-by-example: A specific tool in database management that shows a blank record and lets you specify the information needed, like the fields and values of the topic you are looking to obtain.

Query language: Easy-to-use language and understandable to most users. It is used to search and generate reports from a database. An example is the language used on an airline reservation system.

r

RAID system: Several inexpensive hard-disk drives connected to improve performance and provide reliable storage.

RAM: *See* Random-access memory.

Random-access memory (RAM): Volatile, temporary storage that holds the program and data the CPU is presently processing. It is called temporary storage because its contents will be lost if electrical power to the computer is disrupted or the computer is turned off.

Rapid applications development (RAD): Involves the use of powerful development software and specialized teams as an alternative to the systems development life cycle approach. Time for development is shorter and quality of the completed systems development is better, although cost is greater.

Raster: *See* Bitmap image.

Read-only: Optical disc format that does not allow a disc to be written on or erased by the user.

Read-only memory (ROM): Refers to chips that have programs built into them at the factory. The user cannot change the contents of such chips. The CPU can read or retrieve the programs on the chips but cannot write or change information.

ROM stores programs that boot the computer, for example. Also called firmware.

Real-time operating system (RTOS): *See* Embedded operating system.

Real-time processing: Or online processing. Occurs when data is processed at the same time a transaction occurs.

Record: Each row of information in a database is a record. Each record contains fields of data about some specific item, like employee name, address, phone, and so forth. A record represents a collection of attributes describing an entity.

Recordable (R): Optical disc format that allows a disc to be written on once. Also known as write-once disc.

Redundant arrays of inexpensive disks (RAID): Groups of inexpensive hard-disk drives related or grouped together using networks and special software. They improve performance by expanding external storage.

Relation: A table in a relational database in which data elements are stored in rows and columns.

Relational database: A widely used database structure in which data is organized into related tables. Each table is made up of rows called records and columns called fields. Each record contains fields of data about a specific item.

Repetition structure: *See* Loop structure.

Repetitive strain injury (RSI): Any injury that is caused by fast, repetitive work that can generate neck, wrist, hand, and arm pain.

Research: The organizational department that identifies, investigates, and develops new products and services.

Resolution: A measurement reflecting the quality of an image.

Rewritable (RW): Optical disc format that allows a disc to be written to multiple times.

RFID (radio-frequency identification) reader: A device used to read radio-frequency identification information.

RFID tags: Microchips that contain electronically stored information and can be embedded in items such as consumer products, driver's licenses, passports, etc.

Ribbon GUI: An interface that uses a system of ribbons, tabs, and galleries to make it easier to find and use all the features of an application.

Ribbons: Feature of Microsoft Office 2007, 2010, and 2013 that replaces menus and toolbars by organizing commonly used commands into a set of tabs.

Ring network: Network in which each device is connected to two other devices, forming a ring. There is no host computer, and messages are passed around the ring until they reach the correct destination.

Robot network: *See* Botnet.

Robots: Typically use cameras, microphones, and other sensors as inputs. Widely used in factories and other applications involving repetitive actions.

Rogue Wi-Fi hotspot: Imitation hotspot intended to capture personal information.

Role playing game (RPG): Computer game in which players assume persona of one of the game's actors.

ROM: *See* Read-only memory.

Router: A node that forwards or routes data packets from one network to their destination in another network.

S

Sales order processing: Activity that records the demands of customers for a company's products or services.

Satellite: This type of communication uses satellites orbiting about 22,000 miles above the earth as microwave relay stations.

Satellite connection services: Connection services that use satellites and the air to download or send data to users at a rate seven times faster than dial-up connections.

Scam: A fraudulent or deceptive act or operation designed to trick individuals into spending their time and money for little or no return.

Scanner: *See* Optical scanner.

Scanning devices: Convert scanned text and images into a form that the system unit can process.

Schema: *See* Data dictionary.

SD Card: Type of expansion card designed for laptops, tablets, and smartphones.

Search engine: Specialized programs assisting in locating information on the web and the Internet.

Search services: Organizations that maintain databases relating to information provided on the Internet and also provide search engines to locate information.

Secondary storage: Permanent storage used to preserve programs and data that can be retained after the computer is turned off. These devices include hard disks, magnetic tape, CDs, DVDs, and more.

Secondary storage device: These devices are used to save, back up, and transport files from one location or computer to another. *See also* Secondary storage.

Sector: Section shaped like a pie wedge that divides the tracks on a disk.

Secure file transfer protocol (SFTP): *See* File transfer protocol.

Security: The protection of information, hardware, and software.

Security suites: A collection of utility programs designed to protect your privacy and security while you are on the web.

Selection structure: Logic structure that determines which of two paths will be followed when a program must make a decision. Also called IF-THEN-ELSE structures. IF something is true, THEN do option one, or ELSE do option two.

Semiconductor: Silicon chip through which electricity flows with some resistance.

Sequential structure: Logic structure in which one program statement follows another.

Server: A host computer with a connection to the Internet that stores document files used to display web pages. Depending on the resources shared, it may be called a file server, printer server, communication server, web server, or database server.

Shared laser printer: More expensive laser printer used by a group of users to produce black-and-white documents. These printers can produce over 30 pages a minute.

Signature: Provides additional information about a sender of an e-mail message, such as name, address, and telephone number.

Silicon chip: Tiny circuit board etched on a small square of sandlike material called silicon. Chips are mounted on carrier packages, which then plug into sockets on the system board.

Slot: Area on a system board that accepts expansion cards to expand a computer system's capabilities.

Smart card: Type of credit card that contains an embedded microchip to provide added security.

Smartphone: A type of cell phone that offers a variety of advanced functionality, including Internet and e-mail.

Smartwatch: A wearable computer that acts as a watch, fitness monitor, and communication device.

SMS (short messaging service): Texting or process of sending a short electronic message using a wireless network to another person.

Social networking: Using the Internet to connect individuals.

Socket: Sockets provide connection points on the system board for holding electronic parts.

Soft copy: Output from a monitor.

Software: Computer program consisting of step-by-step instructions, directing the computer on each task it will perform.

Software development: *See* Programming.

Software development life cycle (SDLC): A six-step procedure for software development.

Software engineer: Programming professional or programmer who analyzes users' needs and creates application software.

Software environment: Operating system, also known as software platform, consisting of a collection of programs to handle technical details depending on the type of operating system. For example, software designed to run on an Apple computer is compatible with the Mac OS environment.

Software piracy: Unauthorized copying of programs for personal gain.

Software platform: *See* Software environment.

Software suite: Individual application programs that are sold together as a group.

Software updates: Patches in which modifications to the software are typically more extensive and significant.

Solid-state drive (SSD): Designed to be connected inside a microcomputer system the same way an internal hard disk would be but contains solid-state memory instead of magnetic disks to store data.

Solid-state storage: A secondary storage device that has no moving parts. Data is stored and retrieved electronically directly from these devices, much as they would be from conventional computer memory.

Sort: Tool that rearranges a table's records numerically or alphabetically according to a selected field.

Source code: Occurs when a programmer originally writes the code for a program in a particular language. This is called source code until it is translated by a compiler for the computer to execute the program. It then becomes object code.

Spam: Unwelcome and unsolicited e-mail that can carry attached viruses.

Spam blocker: Also referred to as spam filter. Software that uses a variety of different approaches to identify and eliminate spam or junk mail.

Spam filter: *See* Spam blocker.

Speakers: Audio-output devices connected to a sound card in the system unit. The sound card is used to capture as well as play back recorded sound.

Specialized applications: Programs that are narrowly focused on specific disciplines and occupations. Some of the best known are multimedia, web authoring, graphics, virtual reality, and artificial intelligence.

Specialized search engine: Search engine that focuses on subject-specific websites.

Specialized suite: Programs that focus on specialized applications such as graphics or financial planning.

Spider: Special program that continually looks for new information and updates a search server's databases.

Spreadsheet: Computer-produced spreadsheet based on the traditional accounting worksheet that has rows and columns used to present and analyze data.

Spy removal programs: Programs such as Spybot and Spysweeper, designed to detect web bugs and monitor software.

Spyware: Wide range of programs designed to secretly record and report an individual's activities on the Internet.

Stand-alone operating system: Also called desktop operating system; a type of operating system that controls a single desktop or notebook computer.

Star network: Network of computers or peripheral devices linked to a central computer through which all communications pass. Control is maintained by polling. The configuration of the computers looks like a star surrounding and connected to the central computer in the middle.

Start screen: Offered in Windows 8 consisting of tiles to link to applications.

Storage area network (SAN): An architecture that links remote computer storage devices such as enterprise storage systems to computers so that the devices are available as locally attached drives.

Storage device: Hardware that reads data and programs from storage media. Most also write to storage media.

Strategic model: A decision model that assists top managers in long-range planning, such as stating company objectives or planning plant locations.

Strategy: A way of coordinating the sharing of information and resources. The most common network strategies are terminal, peer-to-peer, and client/server networks.

Streaming: *See* Webcast.

Structured program: Program that uses logic structures according to the program design and the language in which you have chosen to write the program. Each language follows techniques like pseudocode, flowcharts, and logic structures.

Structured programming techniques: Techniques consisting of top-down program design, pseudocode, flowcharts, and logic structures.

Structured query language (SQL): A program control language used to create sophisticated database applications for requesting information from a database.

Stylus: Penlike device used with tablets and PDAs that uses pressure to draw images on a screen. A stylus interacts with the computer through handwriting recognition software.

Subject: Located in the header of an e-mail message; a one-line description used to present the topic of the message.

Supercomputer: Fastest calculating device ever invented, processing billions of program instructions per second. Used by very large organizations like NASA.

Supervisor: Manager responsible for managing and monitoring workers. Supervisors have responsibility for operational matters.

Switch: The center or central node for other nodes. This device coordinates the flow of data by sending messages directly between sender and receiver nodes.

Syntax error: Violation of the rules of a language in which the computer program is written. For example, leaving out a semicolon would stop the entire program from working because it is not the exact form the computer expects for that language.

System: Collection of activities and elements designed to accomplish a goal.

System board: Flat board that usually contains the CPU and memory chips connecting all system components to one another.

System bus: There are two categories of buses. One is the system bus that connects the CPU to the system board. The other is the expansion bus that connects the CPU to slots on the system board.

System chassis: *See* System unit.

System flowchart: A flowchart that shows the flow of input data to processing and finally to output, or distribution of information.

System software: "Background" software that enables the application software to interact with the computer. System software consists of the operating system, utilities, device drivers, and language translators. It works with application software to handle the majority of technical details.

System unit: Part of a personal computer that contains the CPU. Also known as the system cabinet or chassis, it is the container that houses most of the electronic components that make up the computer system.

Systems analysis: This second phase of the systems life cycle determines the requirements for a new system. Data is collected about the present system and analyzed, and new requirements are determined.

Systems analysis and design: Six phases of problem-solving procedures for examining information systems and improving them.

Systems analysis report: Report prepared for higher management describing the current information system, the requirements for a new system, and a possible development schedule.

Systems analyst: Plans and designs information systems.

Systems audit: A systems audit compares the performance of a new system to the original design specifications to determine if the new procedures are actually improving productivity.

Systems design: Phase three of the systems life cycle, consisting of designing alternative systems, selecting the best system, and writing a systems design report.

Systems design report: Report prepared for higher management describing alternative designs, presenting costs versus benefits, and outlining the effects of alternative designs on the organization.

Systems development: Phase four of the systems life cycle, consisting of developing software, acquiring hardware, and testing the new system.

Systems implementation: Phase five of the systems life cycle is converting the old system to the new one and training people to use the new system. Also known as conversion.

Systems life cycle: The six phases of systems analysis and design are called the systems life cycle. The phases are preliminary investigation, systems analysis, systems design, systems development, systems implementation, and systems maintenance.

Systems maintenance: Phase six of the systems life cycle consisting of a systems audit and periodic evaluation.

t

T1: High-speed lines that support all digital communications, provide very high capacity, and are very expensive.

T3: Copper lines combined to form higher-capacity options.

Tab: Used to divide the ribbon into major activity areas, with each tab being organized into groups that contain related items.

Table (in database): The list of records in a database. Tables make up the basic structure of a database. Their columns display field data and their rows display records. *See also* Field *and* Record.

Tablet: A type of personal computer that contains a thin system unit, most of which is the monitor. The best-known tablets are Apple's iPad, Motorola's Xoom, and HP's Slate.

Tablet computer: *See* Tablet.

Tactical model: A decision model that assists middle-level managers to control the work of the organization, such as financial planning and sales promotion planning.

Task-oriented language: Programming language that is nonprocedural and focuses on specifying what the program is to accomplish. Also known as 4GL or very high level language.

Technical feasibility: Making sure hardware, software, and training will be available to facilitate the design of a new system.

Technical writer: Prepares instruction manuals, technical reports, and other scientific or technical documents.

Telephone: An input and output device for receiving and sending voice communication.

Telephone line: A transmission medium for both voice and data.

Telephony: Communication that uses the Internet rather than traditional communication lines to connect two or more people via telephone.

Temporary Internet file: File that has web page content and instructions for displaying this content.

Text messaging (texting): The process of sending a short electronic message typically less than 160 characters using a wireless network to another person who views the message on a mobile device, such as a smartphone.

Thermal printer: Printer that uses heat elements to produce images on heat-sensitive paper.

Third-generation language (3GL): *See* Procedural language.

Third-party cookie: A cookie generated by an advertising company that is affiliated with the website you are currently visiting. Often also referred to as a tracking cookie.

Thumb keyboard: Small thumb-operated keyboard for smartphones and other portable devices. Designed primarily for texting and connecting to the web.

Thunderbolt port: A specialty port for high-speed connections to up to seven separate devices connected one to another.

Tile: Part of the Windows 8 start screen that displays active content.

Toggle key: These keys turn a feature on or off, like the Caps Lock key.

Toolbar: Bar located typically below the menu bar containing icons or graphical representations for commonly used commands.

Top-down analysis method: Method used to identify top-level components of a system, then break these components down into smaller parts for analysis.

Top-down program design: Used to identify the program's processing steps, called program modules. The program must pass in sequence from one module to the next until the computer has processed all modules.

Top-level domain (TLD): Last part of an Internet address; identifies the geographic description or organizational identification. For example, using www.aol.com, the .com is the top-level domain code and indicates it is a commercial site. *See also* Domain name.

Top management: Top-level managers are concerned with long-range (strategic) planning. They supervise middle management.

Topology: The configuration of a network. The five principal network topologies are *ring, bus, star, tree,* and *mesh.*

Touch pad: Used to control the pointer by moving and tapping your finger on the surface of a pad.

Touch screen: Monitor screen allowing actions or commands to be entered by the touch of a finger.

Tower computer: A desktop system unit placed vertically.

Tower unit: *See* Tower computer.

Track: Closed, concentric ring on a disk on which data is recorded. Each track is divided into sections called sectors.

Tracking cookies: *See* Third-party cookie.

Traditional keyboard: Full-sized, rigid, rectangular keyboard that includes function, navigational, and numeric keys.

Transaction processing system (TPS): System that records day-to-day transactions, such as customer orders, bills, inventory levels, and production output. The TPS tracks operations and creates databases.

Transfer rate: Or transfer speed, is the speed at which modems transmit data, typically measured in bits per second (bps).

Transmission control protocol/Internet protocol (TCP/IP): TCP/IP is the standard protocol for the Internet. The essential features of this protocol involve (1) identifying sending and receiving devices and (2) reformatting information for transmission across the Internet.

Tree network: Also known as a hierarchical network. A topology in which each device is connected to a central node, either directly or through one or more other devices. The central node is then connected to two or more subordinate nodes that in turn are connected to other subordinate nodes, and so forth, forming a treelike structure.

Trojan horse: Program that is not a virus but is a carrier of virus(es). The most common Trojan horses appear as free computer games, screen savers, or antivirus programs. Once downloaded they locate and disable existing virus protection and then deposit the virus.

Troubleshooting program: A utility program that recognizes and corrects computer-related problems before they become serious. Also called diagnostic program.

Tweet: A twitter message.

Twisted-pair cable: Cable consisting of pairs of copper wire that are twisted together.

Twitter: The most popular microblogging site that enables you to add new content from your browser, instant messaging application, or even a mobile phone.

Two-in-one laptop: Laptop that includes a touch screen and the ability to fold flat like a tablet computer. It offers the advantages of a laptop with the convenience of a tablet.

u

Ultra-high-definition television (UHDTV): Delivers a much clearer and more detailed wide-screen picture than regular HDTV.

Ultrabook: A very portable laptop that is lighter and thinner with a longer battery life than other laptops.

Ultraportable: *See* Ultrabook.

Unicode: A 16-bit code designed to support international languages, like Chinese and Japanese.

Uniform resource locator (URL): For browsers to connect you to resources on the web, the location or address of the resources must be specified. These addresses are called URLs.

Universal Product Code (UPC): A bar code system that identifies the product to the computer, which has a description and the latest price for the product.

Universal serial bus (USB): Combines with a PCI bus on the system board to support several external devices without inserting cards for each device. USB buses are used to support high-speed scanners, printers, and video-capturing devices.

Universal serial bus (USB) port: These ports have replaced serial and parallel ports. They are faster, and one USB port can be used to connect several devices to the system unit.

UNIX: An operating system originally developed for midrange computers. It is now important because it can run on many of the more powerful personal computers.

Uplink: To send data to a satellite.

Uploading: Process of transferring information from the computer the user is operating to a remote computer.

USB drive: The size of a key chain, these hard drives connect to a computer's USB port enabling a transfer of files.

User: Any individual who uses a computer. *See also* End user.

User interface: Means by which users interact with application programs and hardware. A window is displayed with information for the user to enter or choose, and that is how users communicate with the program.

Utility: Performs specific tasks related to managing computer resources or files. Norton Utility for virus control and system maintenance is a good example of a utility. Also known as service programs.

Utility suite: A program that combines several utilities in one package to improve system performance.

V

Vector illustration: *See* Vector image.

Vector image: Graphics file made up of a collection of objects such as lines, rectangles, and ovals. Vector images are more flexible than bitmaps because they are defined by mathematical equations so they can be stretched and resized. Illustration programs create and manipulate vector graphics. Also known as vector illustrations.

Very high level languages: Task-oriented languages that require little special training on the part of the user.

VGA (Video Graphic Adapter) port: A type of port that provides a connection to an analog monitor.

Video editor: Program for editing videos to enhance their quality and appearance.

Video game design software: Program for organizing and providing guidance for the entire game design process including character development and environmental design.

Videoconferencing system: Computer system that allows people located at various geographic locations to have in-person meetings.

Virtual keyboard: Displays an image of a keyboard on a touch-screen device. The screen functions as the actual input device, which is why the keyboard is considered virtual.

Virtual machine: A software implementation of a computer that executes programs like a physical computer.

Virtual memory: Feature of an operating system that increases the amount of memory available to run programs. With large programs, parts are stored on a secondary device like your hard disk. Then each part is read in RAM only when needed.

Virtual private network (VPN): Creates a secure private connection between a remote user and an organization's internal network. Special VPN protocols create the equivalent of a dedicated line between a user's home or laptop computer and a company server.

Virtual reality (VR): Interactive sensory equipment (headgear and gloves) allowing users to experience alternative realities generated in 3D by a computer, thus imitating the physical world.

Virtualization: A process that allows a single physical computer to support multiple operating systems that operate independently.

Virtualization software: Software that creates virtual machines.

Virus: Hidden instructions that migrate through networks and operating systems and become embedded in different programs. They may be designed to destroy data or simply to display messages.

Voice over IP (VoIP): Transmission of telephone calls over networks. *See also* Telephony.

Voice recognition system: Using a microphone, sound card, and specialty software, the user can operate a computer and create documents using voice commands.

Voiceband: Bandwidth of a standard telephone line. Also known as low bandwidth.

VR: *See* Virtual reality.

W

WAN: *See* Wide area network.

Wand reader: Special-purpose handheld device used to read OCR characters.

Warm boot: Restarting your computer while the computer is already on and the power is not turned off.

Wearable device: A type of mobile computer such as Apple's Watch that contains an embedded computer chip. Also known as a wearable device.

Web: Prior to the introduction of the web in 1992, the Internet was all text. The web made it possible to provide a multimedia interface that includes graphics, animations, sound, and video.

Web 1.0: The first generation of the web, which focused on linking existing information.

Web 2.0: The second generation of the web, which evolved to support more dynamic content creation and social interaction.

Web 3.0: The third generation of the web, which focuses on computer-generated information requiring less human interaction to locate and to integrate information.

Web auction: Similar to traditional auctions except that all transactions occur over the web; buyers and sellers seldom meet face to face.

Web authoring: Creating a website.

Web authoring program: Word processing program for generating web pages. Also called HTML editor or web page editor. Widely used web authoring programs include Adobe Dreamweaver and Microsoft FrontPage.

Web-based e-mail system: An e-mail system that does not require an e-mail program to be installed on your computer.

Web-based file transfer services: A type of file transfer service that uses a web browser to upload and download files, allowing you to copy files to and from your computer across the Internet.

Web bug: Program hidden in the HTML code for a web page or e-mail message as a graphical image. Web bugs can migrate whenever a user visits a website containing a web bug or opens infected e-mail. They collect information on the users and report back to a predefined server.

Web log: A type of personal website where articles are regularly posted.

Web page: Browsers interpret HTML documents to display web pages.

Web page editor: *See* Web authoring program.

Web suffix: Identifies type of organization in a URL.

Web utilities: Specialized utility programs making the Internet and the web easier and safer. Some examples are plug-ins that operate as part of a browser and filters that block access and monitor use of selected websites.

Webcam: Specialized digital video camera for capturing images and broadcasting to the Internet.

Webcast: An Internet delivery medium that uses streaming technology, in which audio and video files are continuously downloaded to a computer while the user is listening to and/or viewing the file content.

Webmail: E-mail that uses a webmail client.

Webmail client: A special program that runs on an e-mail provider's computer that supports webmail.

Webmaster: Develops and maintains websites and web resources.

Wheel button: Some mice have a wheel button that can be rotated to scroll through information displayed on the monitor.

Wide area network (WAN): Countrywide and worldwide networks that use microwave relays and satellites to reach users over long distances.

Wi-Fi (wireless fidelity): Wireless standard also known as 802.11, used to connect computers to each other and to the Internet.

Wiki: A website that allows people to fill in missing information or correct inaccuracies on it by directly editing the pages.

Wikipedia: An online encyclopedia, written and edited by anyone who wants to contribute.

WiMax (Worldwide Interoperability for Microwave Access): Technology that extends Wi-Fi networks to operate over greater distances.

Window: A rectangular area containing a document or message.

Windows: An operating environment extending the capability of DOS.

Windows 8: OS from 2012 that is designed to better integrate Microsoft's desktop OS with its mobile OS. It provides support for gestures, cloud integration, and apps.

Windows Mobile 10: A mobile operating system introduced in 2015 to replace Windows 8. It is able to run many powerful programs designed for desktop and laptop computers.

Windows 10: OS from 2015 that merged Windows' desktop and mobile operating systems. It introduced Cortana, a digital assistant that can accept commands through text or speech.

Windows Phone 8: Introduced in 2012 by Microsoft to support a variety of mobile devices including smartphones. It has the ability to run many powerful programs designed for desktop and laptop computers.

Windows RT: A version of Windows 8 designed to run with tablets using a particular microprocessor from ARM.

Wireless access point: Or base station. The receiver interprets incoming radio frequencies from a wireless LAN and routes communications to the appropriate devices, which could be separate computers, a shared printer, or a modem.

Wireless charging platform: Recharging device for laptops, tablets, and wearable computers that does not require a connecting cable.

Wireless communication: The revolutionary way we now communicate on devices like tablets, smartphones, and wearable devices.

Wireless LAN (WLAN): Uses radio frequencies to connect computers and other devices. All communications pass through the network's centrally located wireless receiver or base station and are routed to the appropriate devices.

Wireless modem: Typically a small plug-in USB or ExpressCard device that provides very portable high-speed connectivity from virtually anywhere.

Wireless mouse: *See* Cordless mouse.

Wireless network card: Allows computers to be connected without cables.

Wireless network encryption: Restricts access to authorized users on wireless networks.

Wireless revolution: A revolution that is expected to dramatically affect the way we communicate and use computer technology.

Wireless wide area network (WWAN) modem: *See* Wireless modem.

Word: The number of bits (such as 16, 32, or 64) that can be accessed at one time by the CPU.

Word processor: The computer and the program allow you to create, edit, save, and print documents composed of text.

Worksheet file: Created by electronic spreadsheets to analyze things like budgets and to predict sales.

Worm: Virus that doesn't attach itself to programs and databases but fills a computer system with self-replicating information, clogging the system so that its operations are slowed or stopped.

WPA2 (Wi-Fi Protected Access): A secure encryption protocol.

Write-once: *See* Recordable.

WWW (World Wide Web): Provides a multimedia interface to the Internet. Also known as the web.

WYSIWYG (what you see is what you get) editors: Web authoring programs that build a page without requiring direct interaction with the HTML code and then preview the page described by the HTML code.

Z

Zombie: A computer infected by a virus, worm, or Trojan horse that allows it to be remotely controlled for malicious purposes.

Subject Index

C

d

e

f

n

o

p

q

r

s

t

U

V

W

y

z